Infancy, Childhood, & Adolescence

Development in Context

Infancy, Childhood, & Adolescence

Development in Context

Laurence Steinberg

Temple University

Jay Belsky

Pennsylvania State University

Roberta B. Meyer

McGraw-Hill, Inc.

*New York   St. Louis   San Francisco   Auckland   Bogotá
Caracas   Hamburg   Lisbon   London   Madrid   Mexico   Milan
Montreal   New Delhi   Paris   San Juan   São Paulo
Singapore   Sydney   Tokyo   Toronto*

Infancy,
&Childhood,
Adolescence

Development in Context

1 2 3 4 5 6 7 8 9 0 VNH VNH 9 5 4 3 2 1 0

ISBN 0-07-557109-9

Credits appear on page 541 and on this page by reference.

This book was set in New Baskerville by York Graphic Services, Inc.
The editors were Jane Vaicunas and Lauren G. Shafer;
the designer was Jo Jones;
the production supervisor was Friederich W. Schulte.
Cover photograph by John Pinderhughes.
Von Hoffmann Press, Inc., was printer and binder.

Library of Congress Cataloging-in-Publication Data

Steinberg, Laurence D., (date).
    Infancy, childhood, and adolescence: development in context /
    Laurence D. Steinberg, Jay Belsky, Roberta B. Meyer.
    p.   cm.
    Includes bibliographical references and indexes.
    ISBN 0-07-557109-9
    1. Child development.   2. Adolescence.   I. Belsky, Jay, (date).
II. Meyer, Roberta B.   III. Title
HQ767.9.S74   1991
305.23′1—dc20   90-6380

About the Authors

Laurence Steinberg is Professor of Psychology at Temple University. He graduated from Vassar College in 1974 and received his Ph.D. in Human Development and Family Studies from Cornell University in 1977. A Fellow of the American Psychological Association's Division of Developmental Psychology, Professor Steinberg has taught previously at the University of California, Irvine, and the University of Wisconsin, Madison. He is the author of numerous scholarly articles on child and adolescent development, as well as the books *Adolescence* (2nd edition), *When Teenagers Work: The Psychological and Social Costs of Adolescent Employment* (with Ellen Greenberger), and *You and Your Adolescent: A Parent's Guide for Ages 10 to 20* (with Ann Levine).

Jay Belsky is Professor of Human Development at Pennsylvania State University. He graduated from Vassar College in 1974 and received from Cornell University his M.S. in Child Development in 1976 and his Ph.D. in Human Development and Family Studies in 1978. A Fellow of the American Psychological Association's division of Developmental Psychology, and recipient of the Boyd McCandless Award for outstanding early career contribution in developmental psychology from the organization, Professor Belsky has taught at Penn State since earning his doctoral degree. In 1985 he was awarded a National Institute of Mental Health Research Scientist Development Award. Professor Belsky is the author of numerous scholarly articles on infant and family development, day care, and child abuse; the author of *The Child in the Family* (with Richard Lerner and Grahm Spanier); and the editor of *Clinical Implications of Attachment* (with Teresa Nezworski).

Roberta B. Meyer before co-writing *Infancy, Childhood, and Adolescence,* was an editor in the Random House college department. She has developed, written, and edited introductory text books in the fields of psychology and sociology. She is a graduate of Cornell University, where she majored in child development, and received an M.A. in English from Columbia University, Teachers College.

Contents
in Brief

vii

Contents

PART

FOUR

Middle Childhood   341

PART

FIVE

Adolescence   431

CHAPTER 15   *Physical and Cognitive Development in Adolescence*   433

CHAPTER 16   *Social and Emotional Development in Adolescence*   465

Preface

Since our own student days, a quiet revolution has changed the field of child development. It is a revolution that has taken researchers beyond the university laboratory, into living rooms, day care centers, classrooms, playgrounds, suburban backyards, and city streets—the places where growth and change occur. What we've seen in these settings has changed what we ask about development and what we think about children.

No longer do we debate which is more important, nature or nurture. Now we ask a far more intriguing question: How do the forces of biology and environment together shape the course of development? The image of the "child as clay," sculpted by environmental influences—by parents or peers, teachers or television—has changed as well. Today we see the child as an active shaper of his or her own development—as someone with an innate temperament, who is not only acted upon, but who can also influence others. Above all, our viewpoint underscores the flexibility of development and the individual's capacity for change. Each of these themes is echoed repeatedly through this book.

Finally, the revolution in our field has led researchers to new, vital areas of study, including the effects of day care and divorce, television violence and drug use, early pressure to achieve, and teenage pregnancy. This book reflects these changes and these times.

Style, Goals, and Organization: A New Book for a Changing Field

We have tried to make this book lively and practical, minimizing the lists of labels, levels, and categories that are likely to be forgotten before the final exam is graded. Instead, we emphasize basic research findings and the ways they apply to children, parents, and the adults who work with both.

A glance at the Contents will show you that our book is organized chronologically, from conception, heredity, birth, and infancy, through early childhood, middle childhood, and adolescence. For each stage, physical and cognitive development and social and emotional development are discussed in separate chapters, but always, we point to the interplay between these topics—how cognitive changes can spur social development, for example, or the ways that children's emotional growth affects their relations with parents or peers.

A third chapter in each developmental part distinguishes this text from all others. These are the chapters on the **context of development:** 8, 11, 14, and 17. These four chapters highlight the links between the major settings in a child's life—family, school, and peers—and her or his development. For example, after reading a thorough discussion of the development of attachments in Chapter 7, "Social and Emotional Development in Infancy," in Chapter 8, students learn how one infant changes the entire family system, and how, in turn, those changes may affect the infant herself. In Chapter 11 we cite the links between poverty and child abuse, and in Chapter 14 we note how schools can affect development. After reading about the adolescent's struggle for identity and autonomy in Chapter 16, students, in Chapter 17, encounter examples of real teenagers struggling to stay off drugs and stay in school in environments that are often more hostile than helpful. Throughout the text, we tie "real world" issues (parental leave, heavy television viewing, teenage pregnancy, and drug use) back to development (infant attachment, cognitive development, and autonomy). Throughout the book, our goal is to reveal the links between the whole child and all the worlds in which he lives.

Features

ISSUES & OPTIONS

In every chapter, an "Issues & Options" essay identifies an issue facing parents, teachers, and other professionals who work with children. Then we ask questions, discuss research, and offer practical suggestions. For example, in Chapter 8, "The Social Context of Infancy," we ask: How does day care affect infants? What does the research show? Some would say that depends on whom you ask. And while the experts argue, the millions of women who choose to work or who must work during their infant's first year of life ask a different question: Which day care arrangements are best? In an "Issues & Options" essay in Chapter 8 we look closely at the research on infant day care and at the debates it has spawned. We also look at the research process itself, encouraging students to think critically about the data. What are the flaws inherent in these studies, and how might those flaws affect the results? Finally, we offer practical suggestions for students who may, in a few years, be balancing babies and careers, or who may be working in or running day care centers themselves. Other issues explored in these essays include: Is breast feeding really better than bottle feeding? Does television harm children's development? How can we encourage children to achieve without unduly pressuring them? What sorts of arrangements should parents make for children who must care for themselves after school? Does working after school teach teenagers responsibility? We think that students will find these essays lively, provocative, and useful.

FOCUS ON

FOCUS ON essays present current research findings on topics that are both timely and thematically linked to the text. For example, a FOCUS ON essay comparing day care in the United States, China, and Japan clarifies the influence of culture on development. Other essays underscore the plasticity of development and the value of intervention. After reading about overly aggressive children, for example, a FOCUS ON essay describes a program that helps such children. Support programs for low-income mothers, preventing suicide, drug abuse, and teenage pregnancy—in all of these essays, students see how development can be influenced by parents, peers, and professionals. And again when research is incomplete or inconsistent, we encourage students to think critically.

APPENDIX: WORKING WITH INFANTS, CHILDREN, AND ADOLESCENTS

Students planning to work with children will find the appendix useful. For careers ranging from the obvious (a preschool teacher) to the overlooked (an adoption agency caseworker), we describe both the occupation and the requirements for an entry-level job. Again, our aim is to show students how the scientific study of development contributes to a better understanding of children in the real world.

Supplemental Materials

This text's value as a learning and teaching tool is enhanced by the availability of a variety of supplementary materials. The *Study Guide* contains information about effective studying and test taking, learning objectives, two kinds of chapter outlines, and self-tests comprised of multiple-choice, matching, and essay questions. The *Test Bank* features matching questions, 80 multiple-choice questions per chapter that are keyed to the learning objectives, essay questions with sample answers, and a complete answer key. There will also be computerized versions of the *Test Bank* available in Macintosh, Apple, and IBM. The *Instructor's Manual* provides information that will assist the instructor with course planning and instruction. It offers potential class activities and projects, chapter outlines designed for the instructor, and ideas for examinations and term papers. In addition, a complete set of four-color *Overhead Transparencies* will be available.

Acknowledgments

Our idea for this book was first nurtured by the psychology editor at Random House, Mary Falcon. In time, Mary moved on but we gained Rochelle Diogenes, and she deserves our thanks as well. We want to thank Roberta Meyer for her creativity, hard work, and belief in this book. We also thank our dedicated editing supervisor, Lauren Shafer, and Jane Vaicunas, our sponsor at McGraw-Hill. Jane came to this project late, but has given us her enthusiastic support. Suzanne Thibodeau has coordinated this complex cast from the start, and Jo Jones created a bright and lively design for all of our work.

We would also like to express our thanks for the many useful comments and suggestions provided by colleagues who reviewed this text during the course of its development, especially to Janet Burke, University of Lowell; Thomasita Chandler, Univerity of Akron; William Chase, Joliet Junior College; Donald Cusumano, St. Louis Community College; Anne Louise Dailey, Community College of Allegheny County; Mary Dellman-Jenkins, Kent State University; Marjorie Gelfond, County College of Morris; Artin Goncu, University of Illinois; Hurst Hall, Northwest State University of Louisiana; Barbara Kane, Indiana State University; Linda Olshina Levine, State University of New York at Cortland; David MacPhee, Colorado State University; Carole Martin, Rutgers University; Patricia Mather, Utica College of Syracuse University; Cathleen McGreal, Michigan State University; Karla Miley, Black Hawk College; Steve Mitchell, Ball State University; Philip Mohan, University of Idaho; Virginia Monroe, University of South Dakota; JoAnn Nelson, Southern Illinois University; Ardis Peterson, Contra Costa Community College; Dana Plude, University of Maryland; Sherrill Richarz, Washington State University; Ann Southerland, Pensacola Junior College; Alice Wakefield, College of Charleston; Joan Wyde, Houston Community College; and Pearline Yeatts, University of Georgia.

A Personal Note

One hears often of projects that have been "years in the making." It is certainly the case for this book. Its earliest origins can be traced to a conversation about the nature of development that the authors began after class one day during their undergraduate years at Vassar College. We continued this conversation as graduate students together at Cornell University, and have maintained it, and our friendship, over the past 20 years. Each of us has been fortunate to have had teachers, colleagues, and students who have fueled our mutual enthusiasm for the study of child development, and who, in a sense, have kept our conversations with each other fresh and vigorous. In the course of our own intellectual development, Anne Constantinople, Urie Bronfenbrenner, John Hill, and Henry Ricciuti have all been enormously influential. We are grateful to each of these wonderful teachers. If this book can inspire any students as much as these teachers inspired us, we will have more than achieved our goal.

Laurence Steinberg

Jay Belsky

Infancy, Childhood, & Adolescence

Development in Context

The Study of Human Development

human development
process through which we
grow, mature, and change

Michael's early life reads like a page from a social worker's case-book. A hastily wed teenage mother gives birth to a high-risk premature baby in Kauai, Hawaii. She takes the boy home to her parents while her husband is away in the army. The family is poor and stressed, and when Michael's father returns, life does not improve. Divorce follows 6 years later, and at 8 years, Michael moves in with his paternal grandparents, who are strict with the child and unhappy with each other. The boy never hears from his mother again.

Few of us would predict a bright future for Michael, yet at 18 that is exactly what he had. A high-achieving, popular student, Michael graduated among the top ten in his class and won a scholarship to college. Despite the losses and stress of his early years, he grew into a young man with high self-esteem, sound values, a genuine concern for others, and strong achievement motivation.

That Michael thrived where other children might have failed is a triumph for him and a challenge for us. While no student of human development can ever fully explain a single life, we can try to discover the forces that shaped it—the same forces that shape all our lives. Michael's story introduces you to the study of **human development**, the process by which people grow, mature, and change over time. Although this book begins with conception and ends with adolescence, development continues throughout life.

The Developmentalist's Work

Four verbs sum up the work of a developmentalist: to describe, to explain, to predict, and to advise. Developmentalists *describe* how people of different ages think, feel, and act. A toddler differs fundamentally from an 8-year-old and an adolescent because we don't just grow bigger and more knowledgeable—we *change* mentally, emotionally, and behaviorally. Michael the toddler had little ability to think abstractly, control his emotions, or follow society's rules. But Michael the college freshman did all these things. Developmentalists chart the universal changes that mark growth. The key word here is *universal*, because development unfolds through a series of norms or patterns: We all begin sitting, standing, walking, talking at about the same time; we all grow emotionally, socially, and cognitively in the same ways.

Nevertheless, we differ from each other at every stage of life, which is why developmentalists also focus on variation. You may have spoken at 10, 12, or 18 months; you may have been a calm, easygoing baby or an active, demanding one; perhaps you made friends easily or were shy or unpopular. Students of human development want to *explain* why people develop as they do. Why was Michael, for example, able to overcome the stresses of his early life? Why didn't he develop serious social and emotional problems? Did it have something to do with his inborn temperament? With supportive people in his environment? With his way of viewing the things that happened to him? All these factors and many more help explain why every person's development is unique.

This baby was born with an active temperament. She dislikes being in her crib and frequently calls to be taken out. (*Joel Gordon*)

A further goal of studying human development is *prediction*. What are the chances that Michael the adolescent will get involved with drugs, drop out of college, or have trouble keeping a job? Developmental researchers want to pinpoint the factors about Michael, or any other person, that will help us make educated guesses about the future. We can, in fact, predict which third graders will become dropouts, which 3-year-olds will benefit from Head Start-type programs, which 5-year-olds will be overly aggressive at age 8.

Finally, prediction makes it possible to *intervene*, to *advise* people about enhancing the quality of human development, to prevent developmental problems from arising, or to correct problems that have already emerged. Throughout this book, you will read about programs designed to help children or adolescents who are having difficulties, or who are at risk for developing them.

Themes in the Study of Human Development

BIOLOGY AND ENVIRONMENT: INTERACTING FORCES

To understand *why* Michael became the person he did, we first go back to a time before the 1970s, when Michael's life story would have been hotly debated: Was he a product of *nature* (his own biology) or *nurture* (his environment)? At one pole were those who argued that biology, or nature, governed development. Biological factors are all those traits that are genetically based.

These include characteristics that all or most humans share (the ability to speak, to walk upright, to think abstractly, for example), as well as traits that make each of us unique—a long or a short nose, straight or wavy hair, a fiery or a placid temperament. At the opposite pole were the environmentalists who argued that upbringing—the way we are nurtured—influences development more strongly than genes do. Whether we would grow up emotionally healthy, do well in school, and lead a successful adult life was grounded in our social environment, in elements outside of ourselves. These include the people with whom we live, the things we see and use, and the social class, culture, and time in which we live.

In Michael's case, we would have asked whether he was a high achiever because he inherited genes that made him smart or because he was encouraged to work hard in school. Did Michael avoid emotional problems because, by nature, he coped well with stress, or was it because he had gradually learned to deal with adverse situations? Today, developmentalists don't ask such either/or questions. Research has confirmed that biology and environment work *together*, that inevitably both nature and nurture influence the course of development.

A major theme of this book, *the constant interplay of biology and environment*, stands out in research findings regarding "resilient" children like Michael (Werner & Smith, 1982), children who thrive in spite of excessively harsh experiences. Even in infancy, these children shared several personality traits that are partly a product of their inborn temperaments. These traits, in turn, tend to encourage certain learning experiences that make them better able to deal with stress. For example, even as a baby, Michael was very active; he did not just sit back and let things happen to him. This inborn trait is related to a later tendency to "take charge" of adversity and try to overcome it. Taking charge of adversity, in turn, teaches a valuable lesson about one's own ability to control negative events. In this way, then, temperament and learning repeatedly interact, enhancing resilient children's ability to cope with stress. Similarly, most resilient children like Michael are cheerful, outgoing, and sociable by nature, traits that make it easier for them to form close relationships with adults. Such relationships, in turn, provide the emotional support needed to help deal successfully with stress.

DEVELOPMENT IS DYNAMIC

Like Michael, all children influence their own development. Accordingly, the second major theme of this book is that *development is a dynamic process*, a two-way street. Far from being passive recipients of environmental influences, children actively shape their world and give meaning to their experiences. By so doing, they help to create the very conditions that affect their own development.

This dynamic process involves attitudes, perceptions, and behaviors. Michael, for example, viewed the world positively, and so was able to make potentially devastating events less distressing. He came to see his mother's desertion not as his fault, but due to *her* needs and problems. As a teenager he declared the relationship "over and done with" rather than continually longing for a mother who would never return. This attitude helped to prevent the development of deep emotional scars.

From childhood on, the way we interpret experiences shapes the way others respond to us and the way we feel about ourselves. A child may isolate herself yet feel rejected by others. *(Bob Daemmrich/Stock, Boston)*

Even young children interpret their experiences in very personal ways. A 4-year-old girl, for example, invites a little boy to play, but he refuses. The girl interprets this as personal rejection and concludes that other children don't like her. She retreats to a corner and makes no further overtures of friendship. The other children respond by ignoring her. She then feels even more rejected, and spends more time in the corner. Soon, other children don't even think of playing with her. Notice that this child has isolated herself, yet she *perceives* other children's behavior in a way that reinforces her feelings of rejection. Another child, also rejected at first, shrugs it off and asks other children to play until she finds a willing partner. In this way, she positively shapes the events that affect her life. Throughout this book, we'll point to the dynamic nature of development, that mix of responding to others, eliciting reactions from others, and interpreting our own experiences.

DEVELOPMENT OCCURS IN A SOCIAL CONTEXT

Not long ago, a group of developmental psychologists spoke to a congressional committee debating the funding of day care programs for poor children. The legislators wanted the experts' opinions: How does day care affect children? What makes a good program? Do preschool programs really give deprived children a head start? Are the benefits worth the costs? Other experts have also testified in Washington about other child-related issues: Does televised violence increase aggressiveness? How does advertising affect children? Can sex education prevent teenage pregnancies and the spread of AIDS?

Although the experts don't always agree, congressional interest in these issues underscores our third major theme: No matter how much interpersonal

When children live—not just where and with whom— strongly influences development. At the turn of the century, before laws requiring schooling and prohibiting working were passed, children from poor families often spent their days in factories. *(Lewis Hine)*

social context
all the elements in one's immediate and distant environment

dynamics and individual traits shape development, another very powerful component is the **social context** in which we live. Social context includes all of the elements in your environment—your family's income, social class, neighborhood; the schools you attended, your family's values and attitudes, and society's attitudes toward you, even the time in which you live. The backdrop for every stage of development, the influence of social context is enormous. Our chances in life—even whether we are born healthy, at risk, or die during infancy—are directly related to social context (Chapter 8).

DEVELOPMENT IS FLEXIBLE

If you were to conclude from the above discussion that social context and innate traits fix the course of every child's life, you would be wrong. The fourth theme of this book, and perhaps its most important lesson, is that *development is flexible*. Undernourished, underweight babies can "catch up" to well-fed babies if their diets are improved in time; overly aggressive children can learn new ways to get what they want; teenage mothers can improve their lives and learn parenting skills; would-be dropouts can become motivated to stay in school and believe in their futures. Throughout this book, you'll see that through many kinds of intervention, or simply through changes in circumstances, children and adolescents can overcome the obstacles that their environment often presents.

Theories: How We Think about Development

During the 1940s, pediatricians typically advised mothers to "let the baby cry." Picking up babies before their scheduled feeding time would spoil them, went the thinking then. Today, we know better. Picking up a crying newborn won't spoil her; it will help her to develop feelings of trust. Pediatricians now counsel parents to pick up and comfort a young infant, advice that reflects a change in theories about child development.

Developmental psychologists, as well as parents everywhere, have theories about how children grow and change, the reasons for these transformations, and the implications for child-rearing. What makes psychologists' theories different from those of ordinary parents is that psychologists base their theories on the accumulation of scientific information, and they revise them as information changes. Psychologists always try to verify their explanations with extensive scientific research, a process we'll describe later in this chapter.

The major theories of human development fall into three categories: psychoanalytic, behavioral/learning, and cognitive. Each type of theory tends to focus on a different aspect of development. Psychoanalytic thinkers, who study human *emotions*, are particularly interested in the psychological conflicts that arise at different stages of development. Learning theorists, or behaviorists, in contrast, focus on *behavior* rather than feelings. Outside stimuli in the environment, not internal feelings, they contend, mold and shape behavior.

How-to books for parents change from generation to generation as newer research causes us to revise older theories. *(Robert Brenner/PhotoEdit)*

Finally, cognitive theorists are concerned with processes of *thought*, with how people perceive, understand, and think about their world. This school argues that we can best understand development by looking closely at how individuals reason. No one theory is complete, but together these different theoretical perspectives provide insights that help us understand the path of development from infancy through adolescence.

PSYCHOANALYTIC THEORIES

"It seems my fate," wrote Sigmund Freud, "to discover the obvious: that children have sexual feelings, which every nursemaid knows, . . . and that night dreams are just as much a wish fulfillment as day dreams" (quoted in Jones, 1963, p. 223). Freud's insight was ironic. True, many of his observations seem obvious today because we are so accustomed to them. Modern parents expect a 4-year-old boy to vow that he will marry his mommy or a preschool girl to flirt with her daddy. But in turn-of-the-century Vienna, where Sigmund Freud lived and worked, suggesting that children had sexual feelings was scandalous. So too was Freud's entire theory of human development.

Stages of psychosexual development in Freud's theory

Sigmund Freud (1856–1939) was a medical doctor who specialized in treating nervous disorders, such as sudden paralysis in some part of the body, extreme agitation and inability to sleep, or overwhelming fears. Most physicians of his time believed that these were physical problems, disorders of the brain or nervous system, but Freud suspected otherwise. He was intrigued by the fact that when he placed his patients under hypnosis and encouraged them to talk about their problems, their symptoms were often relieved. Gradually, he came to believe that many nervous disorders were psychological, not physical in origin. These ailments, he contended, were caused by unconscious drives and conflicts, often related to early childhood experiences and often sexual in nature.

Freud's thinking was influenced by the theory in physics that energy can be neither created nor destroyed; it can only be converted to different uses. Freud concluded that psychic energy—the energy that drives human behavior—must conform to this same physical law. Each of us, he held, is born with a finite amount of energy that fuels all our thoughts and actions for the rest of our lives. This psychic energy, called **libido**, is expressed in two instinctual drives—a drive toward life and procreation and a drive toward aggression and death. In most people, the life instinct is far more powerful than the death instinct and prevents self-destruction (Freud, 1953).

The part of the life instinct that fascinated Freud the most was the sexual. In fact, the term *libido* is often used as a synonym for sexual energy and impulses. Freud proposed that as children grow older, their sexual feelings center around different parts of the body: first the mouth, then the anus, and finally the genitals. In suggesting this progression of *psychosexual* stages, Freud outlined one of the first developmental theories that charted the stages individuals move through as they mature. He also was one of the first theorists to suggest that there were systematic childhood precursors of adult behavior and

libido
according to Freud, finite amount of psychic energy that fuels thought and behavior

During the oral stage, chewing gives babies pleasure, often regardless of taste. (*James H. Simon/The Picture Cube*)

personality. Specifically, Freud hypothesized that failure to gratify sexual urges appropriately during early psychosexual stages could lead to problems later on.

The oral stage   During a child's first year, erotic pleasure comes from sucking, chewing, and biting on things—the mother's breast, a rubber nipple, a thumb, a blanket, a rattle, or any other object that can fit into the mouth. Freud believed that if babies are denied enough oral gratification, or given too much, some of their libido can become fixated at the oral stage. As adults, such people may continue striving for oral stimulation by overeating or smoking, for example.

The anal stage   Freud contended that between ages 1 and 3, a child's libido is centered in the anal region. Erotic pleasure comes from using the anal muscles to expel or retain feces. In many Western countries, the anal stage coincides with toilet training, and if this training is too lax *or* too severe, the resulting frustration can make people either too loose (messy and wasteful) or too controlled (holding back everything, including their feelings).

The phallic stage   Freud believed that between ages 3 and 5, children's libido shifts to the genital region. A boy develops sexual feelings toward his mother, casting his father as a rival for his mother's affections. The boy wants to replace his father, but fears his father will punish him for his incestuous feelings. This is the famous **Oedipus complex**, a term Freud drew from the Greek myth of Oedipus, who unknowingly killed his father and married his mother. Paralleling a boy's development, a girl falls in love with her father and fears punishment from her mother. Freud called this the **Electra complex**,

Oedipus complex
according to Freud, a psychological conflict for boys, arising from their sexual feelings toward their mothers

Electra complex
according to Freud, a psychological conflict for girls, arising from their sexual feelings toward their fathers

after Electra, the tragic Greek heroine who plotted to kill her mother. The fact that both the Oedipus and the Electra complexes are depicted in Greek mythology did not surprise Freud. He believed that our literature naturally reflects our deepest psychological struggles. These struggles are not usually waged on a conscious level, Freud argued. Much of the battle occurs in the unconscious, the deep recesses of the human psyche that are outside our awareness.

How are the Oedipus and Electra complexes resolved? For Freud, the healthiest resolution is for the child to realize that he or she cannot triumph over the same-sex parent and sexually possess the parent of the opposite sex. So instead the child tries to become like the same-sex parent who enjoys the longed-for physical union. He or she adopts the same-sex parent's attitudes, behaviors, and moral values, a process called **identification**. In turn, this internalization of moral values gives rise to the **superego**, the part of the personality that serves as a conscience.

identification
process in which children adopt same-sex parent's attitudes, behaviors, values

superego
according to Freud, part of the personality that serves as a conscience

The latency stage Following the phallic stage is a period of sexual latency, during which sexual urges move to the background while children concentrate on learning how to control their impulses and find appropriate outlets for their drives. Children become increasingly able to share, wait their turn, refrain from physically striking out at others, and so forth. They also engage industriously in sports, hobbies, and projects of various kinds which teach them how to direct their psychic energy toward socially acceptable goals. This period of psychological development generally lasts until about age 12.

The genital stage At puberty, genital sexuality reawakens, but in a more mature form. Youngsters now become interested in peers as sexual partners. If healthy development has occurred in the preceding stages, adolescents are ready to enter into intimate relations that involve a *mutual* give-and-take of physical pleasure. In contrast, if previous stages have been problematic, youngsters are less able to meet the demands of adult sexual relationships.

Freud's view of personality structure

In Freud's theory of personality development competing forces struggle to influence behavior. One powerful force is the pool of psychic energy that includes the libido. This energy exists in the part of the personality Freud called the **id**. At birth, personality is all id; it consists only of inborn drives. With the development of the **ego** comes that part of the personality that regulates emotion, thought, and behavior. The superego, which represents ethical values and conscience, develops primarily during the phallic stage. From then on, it is constantly at odds with the id, for the two have very different goals. Whereas the id seeks instant satisfaction, without regard for reason or morality, the superego is a highly moralistic watchdog, trying to restrict how instinctual drives are expressed.

id
according to Freud, part of the personality that includes all inborn human drives

ego
according to Freud, part of the personality that regulates emotion, thought, and behavior

Mediating this struggle between the id and the superego is the ego. The ego tries to satisfy the demands of the id in ways that are simultaneously pleasurable, realistic, and acceptable to the superego. Frequently the ego uses

defense mechanisms to repress or redirect the id's demands, but these aren't always satisfactory. Too much repression of instinctual drives can lead to great anxiety and psychological problems.

Freudian theory has made an enormous contribution to our understanding of psychological and emotional development. Many concepts that we now take for granted, such as the existence of unconscious feelings and wishes, or the influence of early childhood experiences, originated with Freud. Over the years, other psychoanalytic theorists have extended Freud's ideas to include a wider range of developmental issues and challenges. One of the most influential of these theorists is Erik Erikson.

Erikson's theory of psychosocial development

Erik Erikson's theory of human development does not so much contradict Freud's as go beyond it. Erikson, like many other psychoanalysts who followed Freud, felt that Freud placed too much emphasis on the impulsive, pleasure-seeking id and not enough on the ego, with its ability to reason and solve problems. Erikson argued that all of us face a series of psychological and social challenges as we develop, and that the ego's job is to meet these challenges and in so doing shape personality. Whereas Freud outlined psycho*sexual* stages of development, Erikson proposed psycho*social* stages. He contended that the challenges we face as we mature have more to do with our relationships with other people and society's demands than with our libido and instinctual drives. At each stage, the important people in our lives (parents, siblings, peers, spouses, children, coworkers) and the social institutions we encounter (family, work, school, community) help to frame the challenges we face and influence our solutions to them.

As outlined in Table 1-1, Erikson (1950) proposed eight developmental stages. (In later chapters we discuss the first five of these stages.) He believed that each is paramount for only a limited time. We cannot linger indefinitely over a developmental challenge, for new ones inevitably arise as we enter new phases of life. So if we haven't successfully met a challenge by the end of a given stage, we proceed to the next stage handicapped by a set of unresolved conflicts and psychosocial shortcomings. Children who fail to acquire basic trust during infancy, for example, are handicapped as toddlers when they strive to become more independent from their parents because their feelings of anxiety interfere with their desires to explore the world. Similarly, youngsters who do not acquire some independence as toddlers are plagued by self-doubts and find it hard to take initiative during the preschool years. Thus, how children resolve the developmental challenge at each stage affects their ability to cope with future developmental tasks.

LEARNING THEORIES

While the theories of Freud and Erikson are different in many ways, they both hold that emotions and feelings are central to development. Other psychologists stress experience over emotions. They focus on the means by which we learn certain patterns of behavior from the experiences we have.

defense mechanisms mechanisms used by the ego to repress the id

TABLE 1-1   ERIKSON'S PSYCHOSOCIAL DEVELOPMENTAL STAGES

Age*	Psychosocial Stage	Psychosocial Conflict	Favorable Outcome	Unfavorable Outcome
Birth to 18 months	Infancy	Basic trust vs. mistrust	Hope; tolerates frustration, can delay gratification	Suspicion, withdrawal
18 months to 3 years	Early childhood	Autonomy vs. shame, doubt	Will; self-control; self-esteem	Compulsion, impulsivity
3 to 6 years	Play age	Initiative vs. guilt	Purpose; enjoys accomplishments	Inhibition
6 to 11 years	Middle childhood	Industry vs. inferiority	Competence	Inadequacy, inferiority
Puberty to early twenties	Adolescence	Identity vs. role confusion	Fidelity	Diffidence, defiance, socially unacceptable identity
Early twenties to 40	Young adulthood	Intimacy vs. isolation	Love	Exclusivity, avoidance of commitment
40 to 60 years	Middle adulthood	Generativity vs. stagnation	Care; concern for future generations, for society	Rejection of others, self-indulgence
From 60 years	Old age	Integrity vs. despair	Wisdom	Disdain, disgust

*Ages approximate. Erikson (Erikson & Hall, 1987) recently has suggested that the period of generativity may last much longer today, now that adults remain healthy and active until an advanced age.

behaviorism
learning theory that looks at how concrete stimuli shape human behavior

social learning theory
learning theory that looks at how people are influenced by one another

There are several different learning theories of human development. **Behaviorism** looks at how concrete stimuli in the environment can, through reinforcement and punishment, produce observable changes in people's behavior. Another, **social learning theory**, looks not just at the concrete circumstances that shape behavior, but also at the way social rewards and punishments influence our behavior and our expectations. In the following sections we will examine both these learning perspectives.

The behaviorist view

A little boy, age 2½, is being toilet trained. Every time he has an accident, his mother scolds him severely. Within a few months the accidents stop, but some unusual behavior begins. Unlike other boys his age, this child hates to get his hands or clothes dirty.

A Freudian would say that the child's id impulses were too severely punished, resulting in conflict and anxiety regarding bowel movements. The boy became fixated at the anal stage of development and now expresses this fixation symbolically by being overly fastidious. But a behaviorist would argue that concepts like conflict, anxiety and fixation are completely unnecessary in explaining the boy's responses. In fact, focusing on these internal thoughts and feelings diverts attention from the real cause of the problem—the *punishment* the boy has received. When a behavior is punished we tend to avoid repeating it in the future, so this child, as expected, has stopped soiling his pants. What's more, he has generalized what he has learned to similar situations. He now avoids getting dirty in other ways as well.

Behaviorists have searched for universal laws of behavior, laws that specify how concrete, observable stimuli in the environment cause organisms to act in particular ways. In their search for these laws they have focused on several different kinds of learning. One, called classical conditioning, was first demonstrated by the famous Russian physiologist Ivan Pavlov. Another, called operant conditioning, is closely associated with the contemporary American psychologist B. F. Skinner.

Classical conditioning Fourteen-year-old Mark walks down the corridor of his high school heading for room 127. When the door is in sight his stomach starts churning, his face becomes flushed, and his palms begin to sweat. Behind that door he must take a test in his worst subject, math.

Mark's response to the anticipation of taking a math test is an example of **classical conditioning**. Classical conditioning involves learning to make some reflex response upon encountering a stimulus that has previously been paired with another stimulus that evokes the reaction. In Mark's case, he sees a door (which would normally be a neutral stimulus) and he reacts with symptoms of anxiety because the door has been paired with taking math tests.

classical conditioning
learning through the repeated pairing of a stimulus and a response

Pavlov discovered classical conditioning when working with dogs in his laboratory. He rang a bell just before feeding time when the dogs were given meat. After several pairings of the bell and the meat, the dogs began salivating at the sound of the bell alone, even when meat *wasn't* given. The bell (which had previously been a neutral stimulus) now elicited salivation because of its repeated association with food.

One of the first experiments applying classical conditioning to human beings involved an 11-month-old child named Albert and a harmless white laboratory rat. Albert showed no fear of the rat when he first saw it. In fact, he seemed to like watching it and even tried to play with it. But then behaviorist John B. Watson and his assistant Rosalie Raynor began pairing the rat with a stimulus that *did* arouse fear. Every time they presented the rat to Albert, they struck an iron bar with a hammer right behind the child's ear. This sudden loud noise made Albert jump, cry, and bury his face in the mattress. Soon the sight of the rat alone was enough to evoke the fear reaction. And Albert's fear generalized to similar-looking objects—a rabbit, a dog, a sealskin coat, even a bearded Santa Claus mask.

Children learn through classical conditioning outside the laboratory too. For instance, babies often begin reflexively sucking at the sight of the mother's breast, even before the nipple is in their mouth. The sight of the breast has been repeatedly paired with a stimulus which elicits sucking, until that sight alone is enough to evoke the sucking response.

Operant conditioning It is 7:30 and 3-year-old Joshua is being tucked into bed. "Now here's Teddy and here's Opus and here's Mickey Mouse," his mother tells him as she places the stuffed animals under the covers beside her son. "They're all tired and ready to sleep. You close your eyes and go to sleep

In a "Skinner box," this rat learns through operant conditioning to perform and avoid specific behaviors. *(Ken R. Buck/The Picture Cube)*

too." Joshua smiles sweetly and closes his eyes, but 10 minutes later he is calling out: "Mom! Mom! Mommy!" His mother arrives. Joshua wants some water; she gets it. "Good night," she says again. Five minutes later, "Mom! Mom!" Mother returns. "You didn't kiss Teddy good-night." She complies, kissing Teddy's bedmates as well. Ten minutes later Joshua wants and gets a new bandage for the minor scratch on his hand. On it goes until finally, around 10:30, he falls asleep.

Joshua's parents describe their son as a real "night owl," but people who understand operant conditioning might reach a different conclusion. They know that the *consequences* of behavior influence future actions. Joshua's parents are inadvertently creating positive consequences for staying up late by giving their son lots of loving attention whenever he calls out. As a result, Joshua keeps calling and calling, and takes hours to fall asleep.

Operant conditioning is the process whereby an organism learns either to make or withhold a voluntary response because of the consequences it brings. A consequence that produces *repetition* of the response is called **reinforcement** or reward. Joshua's parents are providing ***positive* reinforcement**—they are introducing stimuli (hugs, kisses, words, attention) that their son finds pleasant. Behavior can also be rewarded with ***negative* reinforcement**—that is, the removal or avoidance of some *un*pleasant stimulus. If a child forces himself to stay awake to avoid a recurring nightmare, staying awake is being negatively reinforced. But whether negative or positive, reinforcement always has the same result: It *increases* the frequency of the response that precedes it.

Of course, some consequences *decrease* the frequency of the behaviors that precede them because those consequences are aversive. Such consequences are called **punishment**. If one of the stuffed dolls in Joshua's bed were removed every time he called out to his parents, this staying-awake tactic would be systematically punished and would probably decrease in frequency. Punishment, whether it involves the removal of some pleasant stimulus or the introduction of some unpleasant one (hitting, scolding, criticizing), always results in

reinforcement
consequence that produces repetition of behavior

positive reinforcement
reinforcement through addition of stimulus

negative reinforcement
reinforcement through removal of stimulus

punishment
consequence that decreases the frequency of a behavior

TABLE 1-2   REINFORCEMENT VERSUS PUNISHMENT

Positive Reinforcement	**Negative Reinforcement**
Increases behavior through addition of a pleasant stimulus (e.g., giving a child a present)	Increases behavior through withdrawal of an aversive stimulus (e.g., when a parent stops yelling)
Positive Punishment	**Negative Punishment**
Decreases behavior through addition of an aversive stimulus (e.g., severely scolding a child)	Decreases behavior through withdrawal of a pleasant stimulus (e.g., taking away a child's toy)

suppression of the response that precedes it. Table 1-2 summarizes the differences between reinforcement and punishment.

Punishment works best under certain conditions. When a mother slaps her 2-year-old's hand as he reaches toward the stove, and then says: "Don't touch that! It's very hot and will burn you!" her efforts to discourage this behavior are apt to be effective. The reason is that the punishment *immediately* follows the unwanted behavior and is accompanied by an *explanation* appropriate to the child's age (Aronfreed, 1968). Punishment tends to be effective also when it is given by someone with whom the child has a warm relationship, when it is meted out in a consistent fashion, and when the punisher suggests alternatives to the undesired behavior (Parke, 1977; Sears, Maccoby, & Levin, 1957). Thus, a loving father who consistently scolds his daughter when she misses the school bus, but who also suggests that she get up earlier in order to have more time, is using punishment in a way that is likely to work.

Some psychologists believe that everything we do can be best understood by examining the rewards and punishments for the behavior. Chief among this group is B. F. Skinner. In Skinner's view, and the view of others who are considered "radical" behaviorists, actions can be explained solely in terms of the environmental conditions that shape them (Skinner, 1938). We needn't talk about internal motives, feelings, or thoughts in order to understand the "why" of behavior, Skinner says. All we need to do is analyze the observable consequences that a certain action brings. A mouse, which lacks the higher reasoning powers of a human, is just as affected by rewards and punishments as a person is, claims Skinner. According to him, all animals, including humans, learn from rewards and punishments in much the same way.

Social Learning Theory

Andrew, age 5, catches a frog and picks it up by the legs. Dangling it, he approaches his 3-year-old sister Laura and waves it in front of her face. Laura is fascinated by the frog and gently strokes its body. Apparently disappointed by Laura's response, Andrew moves on to his older sister, Kim. Kim screams

Skinner contends that the emotional rewards this child receives for his good report card will motivate him to excel in school. *(Elizabeth Zuckerman/PhotoEdit)*

when she sees the frog and runs away from it, with Andrew in gleeful pursuit. Laura watches, and when Andrew approaches her again she too screams and runs.

Laura has begun to acquire a new set of behaviors—screaming, running, and acting fearful at the sight of a frog. Yet there seems to be no reward shaping her response. How, then, can we explain the process by which Laura learned? **Social learning theorists**, psychologists who study the way people learn from one another, would say that Laura learned by watching her older sister, and that concrete rewards or punishments are *not* needed for this kind of learning to occur. We all acquire a wide range of thoughts, feelings, and actions just by observing how other people behave. Such **observational learning** helps to explain how even very young children can acquire the habits, outlooks, and mannerisms of those close to them.

A classic study by psychologist Albert Bandura and his colleagues (Bandura, Ross, & Ross, 1961) demonstrated just how powerful observational learning is. Nursery school children watched one of two adults: either an adult who ignored a large, inflated "Bobo" doll while playing quietly with another toy, or an adult who fiercely attacked the doll, pinning it to the floor and punching it in the nose, tossing it in the air, beating it with a hammer, and kicking it around the room. Later, the children were placed in a mildly frustrating situation and given access to the doll. Those who had observed the adult's "Bobo abuse" behaved more aggressively than the other children did, and they tended to imitate what they had seen. They, too, punched, beat, kicked, and threw the doll, just as the adult model had done.

In a later study Bandura (1965) showed that watching a model being rewarded or punished can also influence an observer's behavior. Again nursery school children watched an adult attacking a Bobo doll, but this time some

social learning theorists psychologists who study how people learn from one another

observational learning learning through imitation of others

In Bandura's experiment, preschool children who watched an adult attack an inflated doll later abused the doll themselves. Social learning theorists contend that much learning occurs through observation. (*Courtesy of Albert Bandura*)

of the youngsters also saw consequences of the adult's behavior. One group saw the aggressive adult being praised and rewarded with candy; the other group saw the adult being punished with a scolding. Later, when mildly frustrated and given access to the doll, the children who had seen the aggressive adult rewarded were more likely to imitate abuse of the toy than were those who had seen the adult punished. Apparently, the *expectation* of being rewarded or punished (even when we have not experienced that consequence ourselves) can influence whether we decide to imitate someone else's behavior.

For Bandura (1977) and other social learning theorists, the trouble with Skinner's behaviorism is that it ignores the qualities that set people apart from rats and pigeons. Unlike laboratory animals, Bandura argues, humans have expectations and motives. We do not just respond to rewards and punishments automatically; we analyze situations and think about how to behave. Sometimes we don't understand our own motives. Humans can be conflicted, impulsive, even self-destructuve. Often we act without the promise of concrete rewards or punishments. Laura decided to imitate her sister Kim even though she did not see Kim praised for showing fear of frogs. Apparently, for Laura, being like her older sister is its own reward.

COGNITIVE THEORIES

Much of modern social learning theory emphasizes cognition, or thought. Social learning theorists want to know how people interpret the stimuli around them, for these interpretations affect how the stimuli will shape their behavior. Applied to the study of children, social learning theorists stress the perceptions that youngsters have of other people, themselves, and their prospects for rewards or punishments. For example, in deciding when, whether, or how much to study for a test, a child might weigh the costs and benefits—if she studies in the afternoon, she won't miss her favorite TV show at night; if she doesn't study at all or enough, she might fail or do poorly on the test. How much do those things matter to her?

Some cognitive psychologists focus less on perceptions and more on the development of thinking itself. Specifically, they study the way thought patterns change as children mature. For example, if you asked a 3-year-old and a 12-year-old why it gets dark at night, the 3-year-old might say that it gets dark "so I can sleep," whereas the 12-year-old can tell you about the rotating earth. The 3-year-old has noticed the setting sun, but at this age children interpret everything from their own perspective. It is natural for them to think of darkness in terms of its benefits for them.

Cognitive theorists try to understand changes in children's behavior and feelings in terms of such changes in thought. For example, young children who tend to see things only from their own perspective would understandably have trouble sharing toys or understanding that their actions can sometimes hurt others. One researcher who was highly insightful at identifying differences in how children think and the implications for behavior was the Swiss psychologist Jean Piaget (1896–1980). We will be discussing Piaget's research at many points in this book. Here we provide a broad outline of his theory of cognitive development.

Piaget's theory

Even as a child Piaget was a careful observer of living things. An article he wrote about an albino sparrow he saw in the park was published when he as only 11. As a teenager, Piaget conducted studies on sea organisms, and by age 21 he had earned a doctorate in natural sciences. But Piaget was also fascinated by philosophy, especially the question of how people perceive and understand reality. With this question in mind he went to Paris to study psychology. There he had a chance to work with Theodore Simon, one of the psychologists who had helped develop the first IQ test. Piaget was hired to translate tests from English to French. As he tried out French versions of the questions on children, Piaget grew curious about the *wrong* answers children gave. Youngsters the same age tended to give the *same* wrong answers, as if they shared a way of thinking which differed from that of younger or older children. Piaget hypothesized that as children mature, they pass through stages of cognitive development, and in each stage, from birth to adolescence, their ways of thinking are qualitatively distinct (Piaget, 1959). Describing these progressive changes in thinking became Piaget's life's work (see Table 1-3). We will discuss each stage in more detail in later chapters.

Piaget believed that human thought is always organized, even in the youngest children. Youngsters automatically construct a view of reality, a way of mentally representing the world and acting upon it. These mental representations and patterns of action that structure a person's knowledge are called **schemes** in Piaget's theory. For instance, a young baby's knowledge of the world is tied to sensing and doing. He or she does not "know" things in the abstract, as older children do. A ball is known only as something that can be squeezed and rolled, a teddy bear only as something that can be hugged and chewed. Thus, a young baby's knowledge of the world is structured by simple actions that can be performed on objects—shaking, mouthing, smelling, sucking, biting, and so forth. These recurring patterns of action organize the infant's reality. They are schemes that give the world some order and structure. Piaget's aim was to identify the kinds of schemes that characterize each major

schemes

according to Piaget, mental representations of action that structure a person's knowledge

---

TABLE 1-3 STAGES IN PIAGET'S COGNITIVE-DEVELOPMENTAL THEORY

Stage	Age*	Major Characteristic
Sensorimotor	Infancy (birth to age 2)	Thought confined to action schemes
Preoperational	Early childhood (ages 2 to 6)	Representational thought; thought intuitive, not logical
Concrete operational	Middle childhood (ages 6 to 12)	Systematic, logical thought, but only in regard to concrete objects
Formal operational	Adolescence and adulthood (from age 12)	Abstract, logical thought

*Ages approximate.

stage of development. He did not see children at one level of development as "more intelligent" than children at another. As children mature, however, they do become capable of using increasingly complex and abstract schemes.

Important, too, in Piaget's theory was his belief that we actively participate in our own development: Children are constantly absorbing information and actively trying to make sense of it. Two important processes play a vital role in this task. One is **assimilation**, the process by which people incorporate new information into their current ways of thinking or acting—that is, into their existing schemes. The other is **accommodation**, by which people fundamentally alter their old ways of thinking or acting to adapt to new information that doesn't "fit" an existing scheme.

To understand the difference between assimilation and accommodation, consider a 15-month-old boy who has learned that radiators are hot and should not be touched. He toddles around the house, pointing at radiators, bringing his hand near them without actually touching, and saying "hot." Apparently, he has developed a scheme of certain things as both hot and not to be handled. Soon thereafter, he reaches for a pot of boiling water on the stove and again is told "Hot! Don't touch!" The same thing happens when he reaches for a lighted candle and a burning electric bulb. The child *assimilates* all this new information into his scheme that a certain group of objects are forbidden and also hot.

But then one day he spots his father's briefcase, with papers sticking out. Hurrying over to it, he begins to touch and crumple the pages. "No!" shouts his father. "Don't touch!" The little boy points to the briefcase and solemnly proclaims it: "Hot." "No," says his father. "It's not hot. But you mustn't touch it anyway." Now the child looks puzzled. How could this be a "no touch" thing and not be hot? He is forced to *accommodate* his existing scheme of "no touch"

assimilation
according to Piaget, process by which people incorporate new information into existing schemes

accommodation
according to Piaget, process by which people alter existing schemes to fit new information

If his mother tells him often enough, this toddler will learn not to touch electrical cords. Piaget called the process of incorporating new information into one's behavior "assimilation." *(Mary Kate Denny/ PhotoEdit)*

equilibration
process through which balance is restored to the cognitive structure

objects to suit this new information. Gradually, he comes to realize that there are many reasons why certain things should not be touched. This new, more sophisticated view of reality constitutes a new scheme. Note how this change in thinking restores the child to a cognitive state of equilibrium, or balance, in which all the various pieces of his knowledge again fit together. Piaget called this process **equilibration**. It is through the processes of accommodation and equilibration, Piaget said, that children progress from one stage of cognitive development to another.

Contemporary cognitive views

Piaget conducted much of his research from the 1930s through the 1950s. By the 1960s, his ideas had gained a prominent place in developmental psychology. But just as Freud's and Skinner's conclusions have been criticized, debated, and refined, Piaget's theory also has been tested and questioned. To it, the "neo-Piagetians" have added a number of important modifications. For instance, most neo-Piagetians believe that cognitive development is more gradual and more differentiated than Piaget proposed. Children do not move to a higher level of development in one giant step. Moreover, they seem to acquire a more advanced way of thinking in some areas before others. For instance, a 12-year-old might be able to reason quite abstractly about numbers and math, but not about moral issues. Why this unevenness in cognitive development? If the child has moved to a higher cognitive stage, as her math skills imply, why isn't this change reflected in all areas of her thinking? Some neo-Piagetians believe that explaining such inconsistencies should be a central part of any cognitive developmental theory.

Other cognitive psychologists are far more critical of Piaget's views. For instance, some argue that we indeed see improvements in cognitive abilities as children grow older. Especially prominent are the cognitive "leaps" that occur around ages 2, 6, and 12. But these, they say, are not due to fundamental changes in how children reason about the world, as Piaget maintained. Instead, they result from differences in how youngsters "process" information. According to this perspective, humans are information-processing systems, much like highly complex computers. As they develop, their processing skills improve due to both a gradual increase in their memory capacities and their acquisition of more sophisticated strategies for dealing with cognitive tasks. We will say more about information-processing theory later in this book. The point here is that it has become an important alternative to Piaget's theory.

Research Methods: How We Study Development

How do psychologists know that their theories of human development have validity? They cannot just assume that what "seems right" is valid, for sometimes what seems right turns out to be wrong. Consider again pediatricians' changing attitudes on "spoiling" young infants. The early view, against picking up a crying baby in the middle of the night, was based on a strict behaviorist perspective. Rewarding an unwanted behavior would only increase its frequency. On the surface, this argument seems reasonable enough, but is it accurate? To find out, psychologists would need to apply the scientific method.

USING THE SCIENTIFIC METHOD

The **scientific method** is a procedure to collect reliable, objective information that can be used to support or refute a theory. The first step in the scientific method is to define the question to be studied. In our example, the question is: Do babies cry more or less often when they are picked up promptly and comforted right after they start to cry? Next comes a review of the scientific literature on the topic to see what conclusions others have reached. This knowledge may help in formulating an hypothesis, which is the third step in the scientific method. An **hypothesis** is an educated proposition about how the factors being studied are related to each other. In this case, the hypothesis might be: If a crying baby is picked up promptly and comforted, it will cry more often. The fourth step is to choose a research design and a method for gathering data that can be used to test the hypothesis. Finally, researchers analyze their data and draw objective conclusions as to whether their hypothesis is correct.

scientific method
procedure to collect reliable information, used to support or refute a theory

hypothesis
educated proposition about how factors studied relate to each other

When developmental psychologists tested the hypothesis used in our example, they found it to be wrong. Young babies generally cry *less* often when parents pick them up promptly after crying begins. Apparently, a behavioral explanation is wrong in this situation. The reason probably is that babies have little control over their crying; they cry *automatically* whenever they are distressed. So a better approach to reducing the frequency of crying is to eliminate the discomfort that causes infants' distress. This can be done by promptly picking up the baby whenever he cries. Over the long run, the child will feel less distressed; more secure in his relationship with the caregiver, he'll have less reason to cry.

Psychologists could never have discovered this link between comforting and crying without the scientific method. Through the use of this procedure, they have gathered a wealth of information about human development. The scientific method enables us to examine how development unfolds, what factors cause it to proceed as it does, and what interventions will be most effective when development goes awry.

CHOOSING A RESEARCH DESIGN

Our brief summary of the scientific method made step four sound easy: Investigators simply choose a research design and a method for gathering data that can be used to test their hypotheses. In practice, though, this step is far more complicated, and researchers often choose from among several designs, each appropriate in its own way.

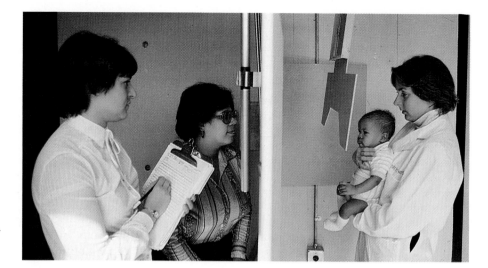

In experiments that recorded infants' reactions, researchers discovered that the infants prefer striped patterns to solid grey. *(Hank Morgan/Rainbow)*

The experiment

experiment
scientific tool designed to investigate causes

The **experiment** is a scientific tool specifically designed to investigate causes. An experimenter systematically manipulates some factor suspected of causing a certain result and then objectively measures the actual consequences. She or he tries to ensure that all subjects in the experimental group experience exactly the same conditions so that no unintended influences bias the results. Experiments also have a control group to provide a source of comparison. The control group experiences all the conditions that the experimental group does *except* the key factor that the researcher is studying. This procedure enables the researcher to conclude that any significant difference in how experimental and control groups respond is due to the factor that has been manipulated.

For example, an experimental study was designed to test the hypothesis that young children who frequently witness angry confrontations between adults will become both distressed and more aggressive toward their own peers (Cummings, Iannotti, & Zahn-Waxler, 1985). In their experiment, a team of researchers brought pairs of 2-year-olds to play together in the living room of a small apartment. The control subjects played without interruptions, but while the experimental subjects played, two adults interacted in a room nearby. At first the adults talked to each other in a warm, friendly way, but then one got annoyed with the other, and an angry exchange followed. Finally, the two reconciled and were friendly once again.

The researchers watched the children's reactions through a one-way mirror. They found that the youngsters typically reacted to the angry exchange with signs of emotional distress. Some became more aggressive toward their playmate, just as the researchers had predicted. These responses intensified a month later when the experimental subjects were exposed to the same situation again. In contrast, control subjects, who merely played together with no adults interacting in the background, showed none of these negative effects. Apparently, hearing the arguing adults caused the experimental subjects to behave as they did.

Experiments like this one help us test whether the factor being manipulated *causes* a change in behavior. By standardizing the conditions to which subjects are exposed, the researcher makes it very unlikely that some extraneous factor produced the results. An experiment has one important drawback, however. Sometimes the situation created is so artificial that one wonders whether the results can be generalized to behavior in the real world.

One way around this problem is to conduct a **natural experiment**. Here, the investigator takes advantage of an "experiment" that occurs naturally outside the laboratory. For instance, a developmental psychologist might hear that a local factory will be laying off workers after the first of the year, a situation that is bound to cause tension and conflict within families. So the psychologist might contact people at the plant who have kindergarten children and ask them if they and their families would participate in a study. Those who agreed would be asked to monitor the number and intensity of arguments between husband and wife that occurred in front of their children during a given period. The youngsters could then be observed in their kindergarten classrooms and assessed for their emotional adjustment and levels of aggression toward peers. This would give the researchers valuable baseline data. Later, when the layoffs at the factory occurred, those who were out of work would form the experimental group, while those who kept their jobs would be the control group. Again the number and intensity of family quarrels would be measured, and again the children would be evaluated. Suppose that parents in the experimental group (but not in the control group) experienced a significant increase in marital conflict, coupled with poorer emotional adjustment and more peer aggression among their children. In this case, the researchers would have evidence to suggest that the worsening marital quarrels were a *cause* of the children's negative behavior.

Natural experiments are clearly less artificial than experiments conducted in a laboratory, but they have one big disadvantage. In minimizing artificiality, investigators lose some of the control that they have in their own research settings. How do we know, for instance, that the children in the experimental group weren't experiencing other factors that made their behavior deteriorate? If so, their problem behavior could be causing their parents' increased conflict, rather than the other way around. Of course, the researcher could try to rule out such other influences by thoroughly investigating the subjects' lives. This process would be very time-consuming, however, and there is always the chance that something important would be overlooked. With natural experiments, in other words, you cannot be so certain that your cause-and-effect hypotheses are right.

natural experiment experiment that takes advantage of a naturally occurring event

The correlational study

Correlational studies yield even less certainty about causes. Here, a researcher assesses the extent to which two or more factors tend to be related— that is, to occur together. Such related factors are said to be *correlated* with each other. A correlational study can suggest *possible* causes, but it does not demonstrate them. Correlational studies merely tell us that certain factors go together, not that one necessarily causes another.

The relationships found in correlational studies are nevertheless intrigu-

correlational studies assessment of extent to which two or more factors are related

ing. In one such study researchers examined the relationship between high school students' grades and the parenting styles they experienced (Dornbusch et al., 1987). They found that the children of parents with an "authoritative" style (expecting mature behavior and clearly setting rules, but also recognizing youngsters' rights and encouraging communication) received much better grades than did children whose parents displayed either a "permissive" (anything goes) style or an "authoritarian" (domineering) one. This is an interesting finding, for it suggests that parenting style might be one factor causing academic success. This study, however, does not allow us to say that this hypothesis is right. It shows only that good grades among teenagers *are related* to certain behaviors in their parents. It says nothing about the reason for this relationship. Perhaps youngsters who work hard in school and get good grades encourage the respectful style of parenting labeled "authoritative." Other types of studies would have to be done to determine cause and effect.

Correlational studies are very common in the field of child development where researchers want to know what behaviors are related to increases in age. Language skills, abstract thinking, intimacy in peer relations, and the ability to exert self-control are just a few of the things that tend to "go with" children growing up. But just knowing that these correlations exist does not explain them. Correlational studies are simply starting points for further investigations into causes.

The case study

One benefit of a correlational study is that researchers can examine many different people. For instance, the study of parenting styles and high school grades that we just described solicited information from nearly 8000 U.S. teenagers. With such a large number of subjects, researchers are more likely to find that the correlations they discover are reliable. Sometimes, however, investigators are willing to forgo the benefits of studying large numbers in order to obtain in-depth, detailed information about one, or at most a few, people. Such an in-depth investigation is called a **case study**.

case study
study that amasses detailed information about one or a few people

In one interesting case study a developmental psychologist explored dominance relationships among six boys who shared a cabin at a summer camp (Savin-Williams, 1976). The psychologist served as the cabin counselor and so had a chance to observe the boys closely for many hours each day. During certain times of the day he kept written records of all the dominance interactions that occurred (one boy ordering, threatening, ridiculing, or shoving another, and so forth). He found that a stable dominance hierarchy had emerged by the third day of camp. Each boy had a "place" in the pecking order, which rarely changed much. The higher-status boys organized and led activities; the lower-status boys followed orders and carried out tasks. Interestingly, the number of dominance interactions between high- and low-status youngsters dropped significantly after the first 2 weeks of camp. It was as if the hierarchy was now accepted and the boys no longer had to vie for position.

Because case studies focus on a relatively small number of people, they usually yield more detailed information than we can get from studies with a large number of subjects. And when a particularly insightful researcher is involved, a case study may also suggest some important principles of human

From earlier case studies, we know that if this group of children plays together over time, a hierarchy will develop, with each child having a place in the pecking order. (*Michal Heron/ Woodfin Camp & Associates*)

behavior and development. But a case study by itself, no matter how brilliantly conducted, cannot *prove* that certain principles operate. There is also a risk that case study results are specific to the people examined. The findings, in short, may not generalize to others.

Approaches to studying change over time

Methods for studying how people change over time are essential to developmentalists, for such change is the very core of their subject matter. One approach to studying developmental change is the longitudinal study. In a **longitudinal study**, researchers follow the same group of people over a period and gather information about them at various points along the way. They then compare data collected at one time with data collected at another in order to draw conclusions about the nature and extent of change.

longitudinal study
study following same group of people over extended period of time

Consider, for example, a correlational study that also employed a longitudinal design (Vandell, Hendersen, & Wilson, 1988; Vandell & Powers, 1983). In this study, the researchers twice observed middle-class children who as preschoolers attended day care centers of different qualities. The first observations were made in the day care setting when the youngsters were 4 years old. The second observations were made when the children played together in groups of three at the age of 8. The researchers found that at age 4 the youngsters in poorer-quality day care spent more time in solitary play, while their peers in better-quality day care had more positive interactions with teachers. Would these patterns have any long-term effects? The follow-up study suggested they did. At age 8, the children who had previously experienced poor-quality day care had more developmental problems than their peers who had experienced high-quality care. In play groups they were relatively unfriendly, shy, and poor at social give-and-take. Of course, since this is a correlational study, we cannot be certain that poor-quality day care *caused* these negative effects. Perhaps there was something about the mothers and fathers of these children that caused them to select poor-quality day care. Perhaps the parents' own behavior encouraged developmental problems. The results of the study, however, are suggestive enough to warrant further research.

A longitudinal design like this one is the most straightforward way to study change over time, for it follows the same group of people from one age to another. But longitudinal studies may take years to complete and are costly. There is also the danger that when people are repeatedly observed, interviewed, and assessed, they may respond differently than they would under normal circumstances.

cross-sectional study
study using subjects of different ages and assessing them simultaneously

An alternative to the longitudinal study is the cross-sectional design. In a **cross-sectional study**, researchers select subjects of different ages and assess them simultaneously in terms of the key factors under investigation. For instance, researchers interested in studying the long-term effects of day care could select a group of 4-year-olds and a group of 8-year-olds. Each group would have a similar profile regarding socioeconomic background, age of the parents, parents' child-rearing methods, and so forth. But in each group, some of the children would have attended poor-quality day care centers, while others would have gone to good-quality ones. The researchers would then evaluate all of the children's social and emotional adjustment. If they found more social and emotional problems among the 4- and 8-year-old children with a history of inadequate day care, they would have evidence suggesting that a negative day care experience could have long-term ill effects on social and emotional development.

Cross-sectional studies are faster and less expensive than longitudinal ones, and since the subjects are examined only once, there is less chance that the observations themselves will affect behavior. The disadvantage of cross-sectional designs, however, is that they do not really study change over time; they merely estimate it. So the results of a cross-sectional study must be viewed cautiously. Subjects in the various age groups might differ in some significant way that biases the results. This problem is magnified the farther apart the different age groups are, for people born in different eras—during the Depression or the 1950s, for example—will have had different experiences that shape their development in ways that researchers can't control for.

cross-sequential study
study using subjects of different ages studied over time

A compromise between the long and costly longitudinal study and the more risky cross-sectional design is the cross-sequential approach. In a **cross-sequential study**, researchers start with groups of different ages, but also study them over a period of time. Because they have a range of ages to begin with, they usually don't have to study their subjects for as long as they would with a longitudinal design. Psychologists interested in the long-term effects of day care, for example, might select some 4-year-olds, some 6-year-olds, and some 8-year-olds with different day care histories and assess their social and emotional development. Two years later they could assess the same children again, thus obtaining data on youngsters between the ages of 4 and 10. This is one-third of the time required for a comparable longitudinal study.

GATHERING DATA

The research designs you've just read about are frameworks for studying questions about human development, but they don't explain how developmentalists actually gather their data. Collecting information about how people think, feel, act, and change over time can be done in a number of ways.

Structured observation

Structured observations are observations of people in structured or controlled environments. The experimenters discussed earlier, who deliberately exposed children to a fight between adults, used structured observation to collect their data. The children's reactions to the quarrel were videotaped from behind one-way mirrors. Later, trained observers viewed the tapes and used predetermined scoring procedures to rate each youngster for the emotions he or she displayed as well as for the amount and intensity of the child's aggression. Such structured observations are useful because they permit researchers to standardize the conditions under which data are gathered. But a highly structured setting can also be artificial, and so might prompt people to behave in ways they otherwise would not.

structured observations
observations of people in controlled environments

Naturalistic observation

Artificiality can be largely eliminated by conducting **naturalistic observations**. Here subjects are observed in their own "natural" environments. In the study of how a dominance hierarchy emerged among a group of campers, for example, the researcher did not interfere with the boys in any way. He simply kept a careful record of what they said and did as they interacted with each other. Naturalistic observations are clearly less contrived than structured ones, but by allowing the situation to be completely uncontrolled, researchers can leave key questions unanswered. How, for instance, might the dominance hierarchy among these young campers be affected if they were asked to perform tasks at which different boys excelled? Would the same children continue to dominate the activities, or would new leaders emerge? Would increased conflict be created, or would adjustments be made smoothly? The researcher involved had no chance to address these issues because he recorded only what was happening naturally.

naturalistic observations
observations of people in their own environments

Questionnaires

In the correlational study we described earlier, where researchers looked for a relationship between parenting style and high school grades, the main tool for gathering data was the **questionnaire**, a written set of carefully prepared questions which subjects answer (Figure 1-1). The questions may have a set of possible responses to choose from (a multiple-choice format), or they may be open-ended, allowing people to answer however they wish. Questionnaires are often used when studying a large number of people. One important drawback to the questionnaire is its impersonality and superficiality. Respondents

questionnaire
written set of questions given to subjects to answer

33. These are some of the things that parents (stepparents and guardians) say to their children. Please think about your family conversations. Indicate for each of the following items how frequently your parents say things like: (Darken one choice for each line.)

	Never	Rarely	Some-times	Often	Very Often
Tell you that their ideas are correct and that you should not question them	☐	☐	☐	☐	☐
Say that you should always look at both sides of the issue	☐	☐	☐	☐	☐
Answer your arguments by saying something like "You'll know better when you grow up."	☐	☐	☐	☐	☐
Say that you should give in on arguments rather than make people angry	☐	☐	☐	☐	☐
Admit that you know more about some things than adults do	☐	☐	☐	☐	☐
Talk at home about things like politics or religion, where one takes a different side from others	☐	☐	☐	☐	☐

FIGURE 1-1
SAMPLE ITEM FROM A QUESTIONNAIRE
(*Source:* Based on Dornbusch et al. [1987]. The relation of parenting style to adolescent school performance. *Child Development,* 58, 1244–1257. © The Society for Research in Child Development, Inc.)

simply fill in their answers and return the survey. Researchers don't get an in-depth look at their subjects, and they never know if respondents have answered the questionnaire honestly.

Interviews

interview
research technique in which researchers personally question people

The **interview** overcomes the superficiality of the questionnaire by allowing researchers to personally ask people how they think, feel, or act (Figure 1-2). Some interviews are very tightly structured; subjects are asked specific questions in a specific order. Other interviews are loosely structured; the conversation takes many twists and turns depending on the respondent's answers. Piaget made excellent use of loosely structured interviews to find out exactly how children think at different ages. This topic lends itself nicely to the interview technique, for it is often hard to probe cognitive processes without asking people to explain their thinking. Interviews are also useful when observing behavior might cause people to act unnaturally. For instance, a mother who is a severe disciplinarian might treat her children less harshly than she normally does when she knows a researcher is watching. Yet in an interview, if the researcher is not critical, the same woman might discuss her usual child-rearing tactics. Of course, there is no guarantee that an interviewee will be completely truthful. This is one drawback to all self-report methods of gathering information. It is especially problematical, however, in the face-to-face interview, where people are often reluctant to divulge attitudes, actions, or feelings that they think others might disapprove of.

Supermarket checker: Some people are rude sometimes. I just ignore it and say "thank you" and they walk away. Some people are really rude. I just figure it's their problem, if they want to be rude. They bought about $500 worth of groceries, that's what I'm here for, you know, they pay my salary . . . but whatever, I'll put up with them . . .

Interviewer: How about learning to deal with people, do you think you've learned anything about that?

Worker: Yeah, probably . . . You know it pays to kinda ignore them, if they get really ornery . . . but I try to keep them happy. Like if I don't know where something is I try to find out. Sometimes if you don't, they get really mad and they bitch . . . you can get in trouble if they really want to get you in trouble . . . you learn how to deal with them, kinda just keep them off to the side, but then keep them happy, too.

Salesperson: I know how to handle people better. When they come up and they're obnoxious, just turn around on them and try to be as nice as you can be, then they can't get mad at you . . . I've gotten to where I'm a little bit stronger when people start cutting you down and things like that. I know what to say back to them now, which is great because I love being able to stand up for myself.

FIGURE 1-2
EXCERPT FROM A RESEARCH INTERVIEW
The research study from which this interview is taken investigated the effect of adolescent work experiences on the development of social understanding. (*Source:* Steinberg, L., Greenberger, E., Jacobi, M., & Garduque, L. [1981]. Early work experience: A partial antidote for adolescent egocentrism. *Journal of Youth and Adolescence, 10,* 141–157. Reprinted with permission of Plenum Publishing Corporation.)

Standardized tests

Sometimes the best way to collect information about human development is to administer a **standardized test**. There are standardized tests for measuring many facets of human life, from intelligence quotient (or IQ) to self-esteem. Most standardized tests have been carefully developed, tried out on a great many people, and proven both reliable and valid. These tests have the benefit of allowing subjects' scores to be compared with previously established norms. But there might not always be a standardized test suited to a particular researcher's needs. In such cases, researchers must develop their own test questions.

standardized test
carefully developed test that allows individual scores to be compared with established norms

ETHICS AND RESEARCH

Over 30 years ago, in a film, *The Conscience of a Child,* kindergarteners confessed their misdeeds to a psychologist. While the researchers gained insight into their consciences, the children showed obvious distress. Conflicts between researchers' goals and subjects' rights have a long history. Ever since John Watson conditioned little Albert to fear furry white creatures, psychologists have been criticized for putting their own interests ahead of their subjects' feelings. Today, in the ethics code of the Society for Research in Child Development (SRCD), subjects come first. The code's principal guidelines are as follows:

1. *The child's interest always comes first, not the researcher's.* No matter how important the study seems to be, it should not be conducted if the children involved will be harmed in any way, either physically or psychologically. For instance, it would be useful to know the effects on growth and development of depriving children of certain nutrients. But we cannot deliberately withhold these nutrients from youngsters to find out. Doing so would clearly endanger their welfare.

2. *Children (if old enough) and usually their parents, too, must give informed consent before participating in a study.* This means that youngsters and their parents must be told in advance what the study is about and what the subjects will be asked to do. They then must be given the chance to refuse participation without coercion of any kind. And even when they agree to be involved in a study, subjects must be told that they still have a right to say no and withdraw from the study at any time.

3. *Researchers should not deliberately deceive the subjects in their studies unless that deception causes no psychological harm and there is no other way to collect the information wanted.* Suppose, for instance, that researchers want to identify successful and unsuccessful ways of coping with failure. They could wait for each child in a group of selected students to experience failure in the classroom and then try to assess each child's reactions to it. This approach would be time-consuming as well as hard to carry out. Another tactic would be to give children tasks, such as arithmetic problems, and tell them that they did poorly even though they did not. The youngsters could then be given additional tasks to work on, in order to see if and how their behavior is affected by the previous failure. This deliberate deception could injure a child's self-esteem, so the researchers would have to be careful to "undo" any harm done. At the end of the study, they would have to inform the youngsters that their earlier failure was not due to them, but due to the experimenters. Without procedures for ensuring no lasting ill effects, this study would be unethical and should not be conducted.

4. *Finally, researchers should protect the privacy of all participants in their studies.* The data they collect should be treated with the utmost confidentiality. They should not divulge the identities of their subjects when they report their findings. In fact, the records that they keep should have all such identifying information removed. The only time that data on a particular youngster should be released is if that child appears to have serious problems, in which case the parents should be informed.

Several groups assess current developmental studies to make sure that the researchers involved are adhering to these ethical standards. Most colleges and universities have ethics review boards that must approve any research on human subjects conducted at their institutions. Similarly, the U.S. government appoints qualified people to evaluate the ethics of all research paid for by its grants. Such screening procedures help to ensure that anyone who participates in a scientific study will not be harmed in the search for knowledge about human beings.

Even when the guidelines are followed, problems may still arise. Recently, a graduate student planned her research around a group of teenagers who were visiting a family planning clinic. Because the subjects were minors, their parents' permission was necessary for their participation in the study, but the teenagers were attending the clinic without their parents' knowledge. Getting permission would have respected the SRCD code, but not the students' right to confidentiality. Faced with the such sensitive situations, researchers must always balance their own needs against the needs of their subjects, always putting the children's interest first.

Summary

1. Human development is the process by which people grow, mature, and change over time. Development continues throughout life.

2. Developmentalists *describe* how people of different ages think, feel, and act. As we grow, we change mentally, emotionally, and behaviorally; developmentalists chart these changes. They also *explain* why people develop as they do, how each person's unique traits and environment shape development. A further goal is *prediction*: identifying the factors that can help us make educated guesses about an individual's future. Finally, developmentalists want to *design interventions*, in order to enhance the quality of human development.

3. A major theme of this book is that development is a product of both nature and nurture, of biology and environment. Development is also a dynamic process in which children actively shape their world and give meaning to their experiences. By so doing, they help to create the very factors that affect their development. How we behave toward others, for example, influences how they behave toward us, and how we *perceive* others' behavior shapes our own perception of ourselves as well as our behavior.

4. Another powerful component of development is social context, the total environment in which we live. Social context includes social class, neighborhood, schools, values, the historical time in which we live, and more. Our development is shaped by the social context in which we live.

5. Development is flexible. Through many kinds of intervention, or through changes in circumstances, children and adolescents can overcome the obstacles that their environments often present.

6. The major theories of human development fall into three categories: psychoanalytic, behavioral/learning, and cognitive. Psychoanalytic theory focuses on emotions, particularly the psychological conflicts that arise at different stages of development. Freud, the founder of psychoanalysis, charted psychosexual development through five stages: the oral stage, the anal stage, the phallic stage, the latency stage, and the genital stage. He also identified three components of the psyche which, he argued, influence all behavior: the id, ego, and superego.

7. Erik Erikson, another psychoanalytic thinker, has proposed a psychosocial theory of development. He has contended that the challenges we face as we mature have more to do with our relationships with other people and with society's demands than with our libido and instinctual drives.

8. Learning theories stress experience over emotions. These theories focus on the means by which we learn certain patterns of behavior from the experi-

ences we have. Behaviorism focuses on how concrete stimuli in the environment can, through reinforcement and punishment, produce observable
changes in behavior. Social learning theory looks not just at the concrete circumstances that shape behavior but also at the social rewards and punishments that influence our behavior and expectations.

9. Cognitive theorists focus on the development of thinking, on how thought
patterns change as children mature. In turn, these changes affect behavior
and feelings. The foremost cognitive theorist was Jean Piaget. Piaget hypothesized that as children mature they pass through stages of cognitive development and that in each stage children's modes of thinking are qualitatively
distinct.

10. To test the accuracy of their theories, developmentalists use the scientific
method. The steps in this process include defining the question to be studied,
reviewing the literature to learn what is already known, formulating an hypothesis, and choosing a research design and a method for gathering data that
can test the hypothesis. Finally, researchers analyze their data and draw objective conclusions as to whether their hypothesis is correct.

11. The major research designs include the experiment, the correlational
study, the case study, the longitudinal study, the cross-sectional study, and the
cross-sequential study. Data can be gathered through structured observation,
naturalistic observation, questionnaires, interviews, or standardized tests.

12. The code of ethics outlined by the Society for Research in Child Development prohibits research that may harm subjects, either psychologically or
physically. The code calls for subjects' consent, prohibits deception, and protects the privacy of participants.

Key Terms

accommodation	id
assimilation	identification
behaviorism	interview
case study	libido
classical conditioning	longitudinal study
correlational studies	natural experiment
cross-sectional study	naturalistic observations
cross-sequential study	negative reinforcement
defense mechanisms	observational learning
ego	Oedipus complex
Electra complex	positive reinforcement
equilibration	punishment
experiment	questionnaire
human development	reinforcement
hypothesis	schemes

scientific method   standardized test
social context   structured observations
social learning theorists   superego
social learning theory

Suggested Readings

Bandura, A. (1977). *Social learning theory.* Englewood Cliffs, NJ: Prentice-Hall. A good overview of the basic principles of the social learning viewpoint, written by one of its most important proponents.

Bronfenbrenner, U. (1979). *The ecology of human development: Experiments by nature and design.* Cambridge, MA: Harvard University Press. A prominent developmental psychologist explains why we need to study development in context and suggests a number of ways to do it.

Erikson, E. (1958). *Childhood and society.* New York: Norton. This classic work summarizes Erikson's stage theory of psychosocial development and focuses especially on the developing child.

Kidder, L., and Judd, C. (1986). *Research methods in social relations* (5th ed.). New York: Holt, Rinehart and Winston. A solid introduction to the methods and procedures used in the social sciences.

Piaget, J. (1974). *The language and thought of the child.* New York: New American Library. This is one of Piaget's more accessible books, and it is filled with conversations with children that illustrate his stage theory of development.

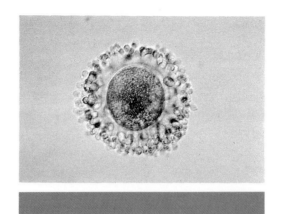

After talking about it forever, my husband and I decided over a year ago to start trying to have a baby. In anticipation, I looked at child development texts around my office, skimmed pregnancy books in bookstores, and, when conception didn't happen immediately, poured over fertility guidebooks. I acquired a precise understanding of the role of the ovum and the role of the sperm; of genes and chromosomes; of changing hormonal levels; and of each stage of prenatal development. I thought I knew everything. Now, nearly 5 months pregnant, I've just started feeling the flutter of fetal movement. And I find that all the science, all the knowledge and reading, can't explain this process after all: We've created a brand new person, and it's a miracle.

A New Life
Begins

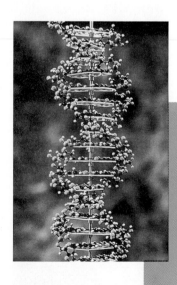

Conception and Heredity

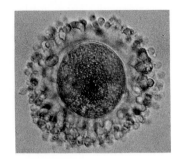

All normal, healthy babies are born with the capacity to develop skills: to walk upright, to speak, to smile and laugh, to use their hands to make tools and their heads to imagine a better world. In these and countless other ways, we are all alike. Moreover, the basic story of human development is much the same, whether the plot unfolds in a thatched village in New Guinea or on Manhattan's Park Avenue. We all babble before we talk and stand before we run; we take our first steps and speak our first words at about the same ages. The similarities among human beings are the result of a genetic "program" that is thousands, perhaps millions, of years old. This program is what makes each of us human—it is what makes each of us like other members of our species.

At the same time, each human being is unique. No one else looks, acts, or thinks exactly as you do; no one else has your voice or your smile. Individuality also has it roots in heredity. With the exception of identical twins, each person inherits a unique combination of genes. Even brothers and sisters are set apart by heredity, and the environment compounds genetic differences. Siblings grow up in the same family, live in the same community, and often attend the same schools, but each experiences and responds to these shared environments in his or her own way.

Chapter 2 shows how heredity establishes both similarities and differences among people. We begin with conception, a more complicated process than most people imagine. Then we'll look at genes and how these basic units of heredity shape the development of each new life. We will also consider genetic abnormalities, and we'll discuss how counseling and medical technology can help would-be parents learn whether their children will be at risk for developing these abnormalities. Finally, in "Issues & Options," we'll consider the impact of the new technologies on couples facing difficult choices.

Human Conception

During sexual intercourse, a man can ejaculate hundreds of millions of sperm into a woman's body. To reach a mature egg, or ovum, the sperm must swim about a foot upstream—a distance that is thousands of times its own length. Only a few hundred sperm make this journey, and only *one* of these can fertilize the ovum. The chance that a sperm will find a mature ovum at the end of its journey is also small. An ovum is only available for fertilization for a very limited period each month. The odds of a *particular* sperm fertilizing a *particular* ovum are infinitesimal, but for most couples who are engaging in regular intercourse without using birth control, conception generally occurs within 3 to 6 months.

THE FEMALE REPRODUCTIVE CYCLE

ovaries
the pair of almond-shaped female organs that store ova

Human females are born with millions of immature ova, which are stored until maturity in two small, almond-shaped organs called the **ovaries**. A wom-

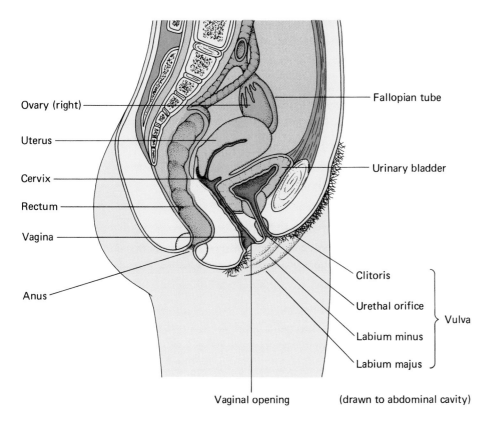

Ovary (right)

Uterus

Cervix

Rectum

Vagina

Anus

Fallopian tube

Urinary bladder

Clitoris

Urethal orifice

Labium minus

Labium majus

Vulva

Vaginal opening   (drawn to abdominal cavity)

FIGURE 2-1
THE FEMALE REPRODUCTIVE SYSTEM
This cross section of the female pelvic region shows the organs of reproduction.

an's reproductive system also contains two **fallopian tubes**, one of which transports an ovum each month from an ovary to the uterus, and the **uterus** (or womb), which holds and nurtures the developing fetus if the woman conceives. (See Figure 2-1.) Only a very small proportion of the female's immature ova present at birth ever reach maturity (Hofer, 1981). From puberty on, one ovum matures about every 28 days. The ovum then leaves the ovary, enters the fallopian tube, and drifts toward the uterus. A normal, healthy woman is fertile from puberty (which occurs between ages 11 and 15) to menopause (which usually begins between ages 45 and 53), but she can only conceive on 1 or 2 days—from 24 to 36 hours—each month. This fertile period varies from woman to woman, and even for the same woman from month to month, so the calendar can never tell a woman with certainty when she can become pregnant.

In the first phase of the female reproductive cycle, **preparation**, a projection that resembles a blister forms on one ovary. This "blister" contains a maturing ovum. Several days after it appears, it begins to produce the hormone estrogen, a biochemical messenger that stimulates the lining of the uterus to thicken and secrete a rich nutritive substance.

The second phase, **ovulation**, occurs about 14 days into the cycle. In this phase, the woman's body prepares for fertilization and pregnancy. The blister bursts, releasing the ovum. It drifts down one of the fallopian tubes toward the

fallopian tubes
tubes that transport mature ova to the uterus and in which fertilization occurs

uterus
female organ in which the fetus grows

preparation
first phase of female reproductive cycle

ovulation
release of a mature ovum from one of the ovaries into one of the fallopian tubes

uterus, a journey that takes several days. At the same time, progesterone, a hormone that promotes *gestation* (the growth of the embryo and fetus), is produced.

The third phase begins when and if the ovum reaches the uterus *without* being fertilized. If the ovum does not meet a sperm and is not fertilized, the ovum disintegrates, and the levels of estrogen and progesterone in the woman's body drop, causing **menstruation**. The uterus discharges the lining and the blood it has collected in preparation for a pregnancy, and the cycle begins again. If the woman has conceived, her hormones act to retain the fertilized ovum, now called the zygote. In Chapter 3 we follow the zygote as it develops from a single cell to a fully formed infant.

THE MALE REPRODUCTIVE SYSTEM

The male's reproductive system, illustrated in Figure 2-2, includes the **testes**, which produce sperm; the **epididymis**, coiled tubes in the testes in which sperm mature and are stored until ejaculation occurs; the *penis*, which deposits the sperm in the woman's vagina; and the **prostate gland**, which, just before ejaculation, produces a milky substance to help sperm on their journey.

Male fertility differs from female fertility in two basic ways: First, unlike the female, who is only fertile 1 or 2 days a month, a healthy male can father a child at any time. Men's testes produce sperm more or less continually, at a

menstruation
third phase of female reproductive cycle, in which uterine lining is discharged

testes
male sperm-producing organ

epididymis
coiled tubes in the testes in which sperm are stored until ejaculation

prostate gland
male organ that produces semen, a substance released with sperm

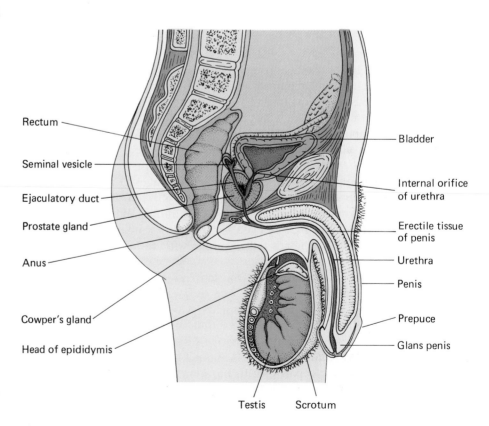

FIGURE 2-2
THE MALE REPRODUCTIVE SYSTEM
This cross section of the male pelvic region shows the organs of reproduction.

Rectum

Seminal vesicle

Ejaculatory duct

Prostate gland

Anus

Cowper's gland

Head of epididymis

Bladder

Internal orifice of urethra

Erectile tissue of penis

Urethra

Penis

Prepuce

Glans penis

Testis   Scrotum

very high rate (if the man is healthy). Second, men do not experience a genetically programmed end to fertility, comparable to female menopause. A man may father a child at any age, but health problems (such as diabetes), medications (for high blood pressure, for example), or high alcohol consumption often cause a decline in fertility in a man's later years.

FERTILIZATION

A couple has sexual intercourse, and the timing is right: Ovulation has just occurred or is imminent, and the odds for fertilization are at their highest. Even so, conception is not guaranteed.

Once ejaculation has taken place, 300 to 400 million sperm enter the woman's vagina. They now make their own way through the **cervix** (the narrow passage connecting the vagina to the uterus), into the uterus, and up one of the fallopian tubes where the ovum awaits. Sperm "swim" toward the egg by vibrating tiny hairlike cilia along their length and whipping their tails. The average sperm moves at a speed of about 5 millimeters per minute—the equivalent of a person running a 10-minute mile. As if in a race, two sperm swimming together move faster than does one by itself, and the closer they come to an ovum, the harder they work. But all sperm are not alike: Some are Olympic material, and others are sluggish. The speed and stamina of sperm (and whether they complete their journey) seem to depend on the exact location in the testes where they were manufactured (Hofer, 1981). But even the fastest sperm may not reach the ovum if the conditions in the woman's reproductive system are not right.

cervix
narrow passage connecting uterus and vagina

During most of the month, a woman's cervix is blocked by a thick, opaque mucus plug. (This plug helps to prevent infections in the uterus and fallopian tubes, a major cause of sterility in women.) At ovulation, however, the mucus is clear and thin. In this state, the mucus is no longer a barrier, and sperm can easily pass through the cervix. This is one reason that the timing of intercourse is critical (Hofer, 1981). The environment in the woman's body must be ready for the sperm.

After passing through the cervix, the sperm must go through the uterus to the fallopian tubes. The rhythmic uterine contractions that occur during female orgasm assist in transporting the sperm toward the fallopian tubes (Rossi, 1978). In some ways, then, the female reproductive system can assist the sperm on its journey toward conception.

In other ways, though, the female body creates *obstacles* to conception. When the sperm are in the uterus, the woman's immune system reacts to them as if they were foreign matter, coating them with antibodies. Many sperm are disabled at this point, and only some of the original millions can continue on their journey. (In some cases a couple cannot conceive because her antibodies kill his sperm.)

The next stage presents another challenge. The cilia in the woman's fallopian tubes gently push the ovum toward the uterus, creating a downstream current. Thus to reach the ovum, sperm must travel upstream. Why would the female body actively fight sperm, reducing the chances of conception? One possibility is that the female reproductive system "selects" or "chooses" the strongest, hardiest sperm among the contenders.

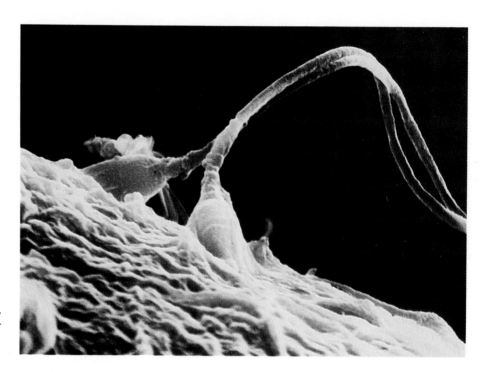

Of the 300 to 400 million sperm that approach the ovum, only one will penetrate and fertilize it. *(Sundstrum/Gamma Liaison)*

Suppose that 200 sperm come within reach of the ovum. Only one can penetrate and fertilize it. We don't fully understand why one particular sperm is successful, but the sperm and ovum probably engage in a "biochemical dialogue" that enables them to assess their compatibility. This assessment system isn't perfect, however. Spontaneous abortions, or miscarriages, and birth defects suggest that mismatches do occur. No one knows, of course, how many mistakes are avoided. During the dialogue process, one sperm releases a digestive enzyme and "eats" its way into the ovum. The surface of the ovum then hardens, so that other sperm cannot enter. At this point, the development of a new person begins.

One interesting footnote to this story concerns the sex of the baby. Sperm genetically coded to create male offspring are more likely to penetrate the ovum than are sperm coded to produce females. Apparently, male-producing sperm have smaller, rounder heads and longer tails than do female-producing sperm (Rosenfeld, 1974). As a result, for every 100 females conceived, approximately 160 males are conceived. Yet at birth, only 105 boys are born for every 100 girls. The fact that so many more males than females are conceived but only a few more are born highlights the fact that males, not females, are the "weaker sex." Throughout pregnancy, birth, childhood, and even into adolescence, males succumb to stress more readily than do females. In fact, by the end of the first year of life, the numbers of boys and girls are about equal.

Ten years ago, our discussion of conception could have ended here. Today, however, intercourse is only one of several ways to conceive a baby.

FERTILITY PROBLEMS AND TREATMENTS

Approximately one out of every six American couples tries to conceive a child for a year or more and fails (Blakeslee, 1987), and the incidence of infertility has tripled in the last two decades. Physicians blame the rise in infertility on changes in lifestyle. Women are more sexually active today than they were in the past and therefore are more likely to contract infections that leave their fallopian tubes blocked. Scar tissue from an intrauterine device may also block the tubes. Furthermore, more couples postpone parenthood until their middle or late thirties, and research evidence indicates that after age 35, time for conception increases from an average of 6 months for younger women to 2 years or more. Women in high-stress occupations and women who follow a demanding exercise program (long-distance runners and dancers, for example) often experience temporary infertility.

Just as often, inability to conceive a child can be traced to the man. The most common causes of male infertility are insufficient production of sperm, the production of misshapen or inactive sperm, or obstruction of the ducts that permit sperm to pass from the testes to the penis. These problems may be caused by infections of or injury to the testes, by prostate disease, or by hormonal insufficiencies.

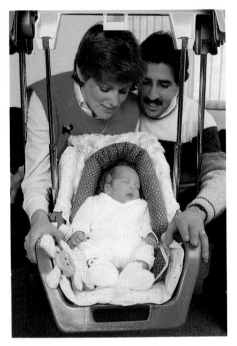

This couple's baby was fertilized *in vitro*. A test tube holding an egg and sperm is placed in an incubator allowing fertilization to occur. (both: *Hank Morgan/Rainbow*)

TABLE 2-1   CAUSES AND CURES FOR INFERTILITY

Male		Female	
Problem	**Treatment**	**Problem**	**Treatment**
Low sperm count	Change of environment Antibiotics Surgery Hormone therapy Artificial insemination	Vaginal structural problem	Surgery
		Abnormal cervical mucus	Hormone therapy
		Abnormal or absence of ovulation	Hormone therapy Antibiotics for infection
Physical defect affecting transport of sperm	Microsurgery	Blocked or scarred fallopian tubes	Surgery *In vitro* fertilization
Genetic disorder	Artificial insemination	Uterine lining unfavorable to implantation	Hormone therapy Antibiotics Surgery

Source: Compiled from Milunsky, A. (1987). *How to have the healthiest baby you can.* New York: Simon & Schuster.

In about 20 percent of cases, both partners have problems. The woman's fallopian tubes may be blocked by scar tissue, and the male's sperm count may be too far below the number required for conception under ordinary conditions.

The good news is that nearly 95 percent of infertility cases can be diagnosed, and about half of these problems can be corrected. (Major causes and cures for infertility are shown in Table 2-1.) Women who do not ovulate regularly can be treated with hormones, and microsurgery can open blocked fallopian tubes. Similarly, microsurgery can open sperm ducts or remove varicose veins in the scrotum that are interfering with sperm production in men. If the male has a low sperm count, the couple can try **artificial insemination**—with a high concentration of either his sperm or a donor's sperm. Between 10,000 and 20,000 American babies are conceived this way each year. (See "Issues & Options" at the end of this chapter for further discussion.)

artificial insemination fertilization by placement of husband's or a donor's sperm directly into the cervix

Heredity: The Genetics of Life

At the moment of conception, you were a single cell, invisible to the naked eye. As an adult, you consist of a thousand million million cells, organized into a head, trunk, limbs, organs, and a nervous system, capable of action and thought, love and hate, building families and nations, and appreciating (if not producing) science and art. Without your knowing or willing it, your body maintains a stable temperature, fights off many diseases, and prepares you to cope with stress. Human consciousness enables you to contemplate the past, make sense of the present, and imagine the future. How did this extraordinary transformation occur? You inherited a complete set of "blueprints" for human development from your parents, via their genes.

GENES AND CHROMOSOMES

In the late twentieth century, the word "genes" is part of our common language. We automatically attribute many of a person's traits to heredity: "It's in his genes." In the nineteenth century, however, an intelligent, well-read person, even one who was interested in science, would not have known what we were talking about. Charles Darwin himself, the creator of the theory of evolution, never used the term *gene*.

Genes were discovered by a nineteenth-century Austrian monk named Gregor Mendel, whose work was not recognized until many years after his death. Virtually all Mendel's contemporaries believed that human heredity resulted from a mixture of body fluids during the act of conception. Offspring were thought to inherit a blend of their parents' characteristics. Mendel's experiments with pea plants in his monastery garden ultimately disproved that theory. He found that when he crossed plants bearing smooth, green peas with plants bearing wrinkled, yellow peas, he did not get semismooth yellow-green peas, as one might expect. The different traits (smooth and wrinkled, green and yellow) did not blend but maintained their integrity across many generations. Mendel did not know why this happened, but after many breeding experiments he concluded that there was some mechanism within the plants that carried instructions for specific traits to each new generation. It remained for future scientists to discover what that mechanism was. Today we know that the messages of heredity are carried by the discrete particles we call **genes**.

These genes that are passed along from parent to offspring are strung like beads on threadlike structures called **chromosomes**, which reside in the nucleus of every cell in the body. A *single* human chromosome contains about 20,000 genes, with each gene occupying a specific place—its own **locus**—on a particular chromosome. (We can also define a gene as a segment of a chromosome.) The number of chromosomes in the cell nucleus varies from species to species. Each of us has 46 chromosomes that carry all the information necessary for human development—the master blueprint we alluded to earlier.

Every cell in the body contains a complete set of chromosomes. The body, then, is like a giant building in which every room contains a bookcase with a full 46-volume set of blueprints for the entire building. The "rooms" of this building are the cells of the body; the "bookcase" is the cell nucleus; and the 46 "volumes" of architect's plans are the chromosomes. The "pages" in these volumes are the genes.

All human beings have the same basic genetic library in their cells. The design for *Homo sapiens* evolved over millions of years. We inherited this plan from our parents, their parents, and theirs, all the way back to our remotest

genes
the basic units of heredity; each gene consists of a segment of a chromosome that controls some aspect of development

chromosomes
twisted strands of DNA that carry genetic instructions from generation to generation

locus
specific location of a gene on a chromosome

Gregor Mendel's experiments with pea plants revealed that genetic traits were transmitted across generations. (*The Bettmann Archive*)

ancestors. Some elements of the design are found in every edition, but each printing of the plan differs in many details. For example, all human beings have the same basic facial features: two eyes, a nose, and a mouth. But some of us have brown eyes, others blue or green eyes; some of us have 20/20 vision, while others are near-sighted. All normal children begin to walk and talk at about the same ages; as human beings, we all inherit the capacity for bipedal (two-legged) locomotion and language. But some of us have the potential to become Olympic athletes, while others are slow and clumsy. Some of us are eloquent, and others are frequently tongue-tied. The capacity for complex thought is also part of our human heritage, but some of us are quicker, more intelligent, more creative than others, and some of us are extraordinary. All these variations stem from both genetic and environmental factors—an interaction that we will point to again and again.

THE GENETIC CODE

Mendel published his theory of genetics in 1865, and chromosomes were first observed under the microscope in the 1870s. But almost a hundred years would pass before scientists could explain the chemistry of genetic inheritance. The credit goes to James Watson and Francis Crick, who shared the Nobel prize for this discovery in 1958.

Watson and Crick demonstrated that chromosomes are long strands of a chemical substance known as **deoxyribonucleic acid (DNA)**, shaped in a double helix. If you took a ladder and twisted it like a spiral staircase, you would have a double helix. In the case of DNA, the two sides or railings of the ladder are made up of sugar and phosphate molecules; the rungs are made up of four amino acids: adenine, thymine, cytosine, and guanine, commonly referred to as "A," "T," "C," and "G." These four letters are the alphabet of heredity.

All the instructions needed for the making and maintenance of a living, breathing, thinking human being are written in this four-chemical code. Genes are distinguished from one another by the *order* in which these chemicals are strung together on the chromosomes. This is where the analogy between the genetic code and the alphabet comes in. The letters of the Roman alphabet can be used to produce many different languages (English, French, Swahili). The order in which these letters are strung together creates differences among languages ("*Hello*," "*Bonjour*," "*Jambo*"). The order of letters also determines the meaning of words within a language (end, den, Ned). And words can be put together in a variety of ways to communicate different messages ("Jonah ate the whale," or "The whale ate Jonah"). So it is with the genetic code. A four-letter alphabet provides the instructions for creating and maintaining life. The way those letters are arranged on the chromosomes will distinguish one individual's genes—and one individual—from all others.

Chromosomes perform two crucial functions. They supervise the *production of proteins* within cells. Some proteins are the physical building blocks of the body; others are worker proteins—the enzymes and hormones that keep things running inside you. When, for example, it is necessary to produce a new blood, liver, or other cell, the part of the chromosome that contains instructions about that type of cell opens up. A ribonucleic acid (RNA) molecule

deoxyribonucleic acid (DNA)
carrier of genetic information in chromosomes

As this model shows, the DNA molecule is shaped like a double helix with amino acid "rungs" connecting sugar and phosphate sides. *(CNRI/Science Photo Library/Photo Researchers)*

then carries the instructions out of the nucleus into the cell body, where other molecules then produce the new cell. A similar process leads to the production of enzymes and hormones.

Chromosomes also make copies of themselves, enabling new cells to be created and ensuring that each new cell has the right set of instructions for protein production. This process is called **mitosis**. The DNA ladder "unzips" down the middle, and the two sides of the molecule separate, migrating to opposite ends of the cell. Then, each of the old strands uses raw materials in the cell to create a second strand that is a mirror image of itself. Next, a new cell wall forms down the middle, converting the original cell into two daughter cells. These two cells divide into four, the four into eight, and so on up to the thousand million million that make up your body. This copying process is nearly flawless. In the words of one biologist, mitosis "is as precise and well ordered as the drill of a regiment of soldiers in a parade ground" (Stebbings, 1982, p. 32).

THE PRODUCTION OF SPERM AND OVA

One chapter in the chromosome library concerns the production of sex cells (sperm and ova) through **meiosis**. This form of cell reproduction only occurs in the female's ovaries and the male's testes. Meiosis makes possible the conception of new life. It also guarantees genetic differences between children and their parents, making each new life different from all others.

The first stage of meiosis is similar to mitosis—but not identical. As shown in Figure 2-3, the chromosomes unzip into chromatids, migrate to opposite sides of the cell, and form mirror images of themselves called "homologues." But meiosis is not as neat and orderly as mitosis. In the process of dividing, bits and pieces of the chromosomes change places—a phenomenon known as **crossing-over**. A gene for blue eyes may change places with the gene for green eyes, for example. In addition, copying errors—called **mutations**—may occur. The "letters" of one segment of DNA may be out of order; a "word" may be dropped or duplicated. Most mutations are either so insignificant as to go unnoticed or so lethal that the cell does not survive. Others fall in between

mitosis
process of cell duplication in which chromosomes make exact copies of themselves

meiosis
multistage production of sperm and ova, which contain only half of the number of chromosomes in all other cells

crossing-over
the exchange of chromosomal segments during meiosis

mutations
alterations in genes; the cause of many birth defects

**FIGURE 2-3
SUMMARY OF MAJOR EVENTS IN MEIOSIS**
(*Source*: Adapted from J. Postlethwait and J. L. Hopson. [1989]. *The nature of life.* New York: Random House.)

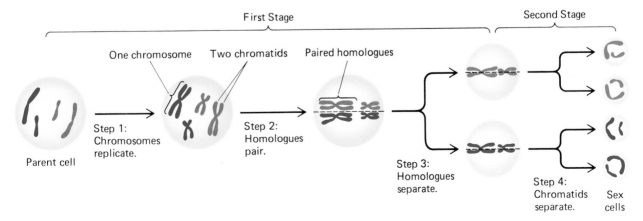

First Stage

Second Stage

One chromosome   Two chromatids   Paired homologues

Parent cell

Step 1: Chromosomes replicate.

Step 2: Homologues pair.

Step 3: Homologues separate.

Step 4: Chromatids separate.

Sex cells

these extremes, causing abnormalities that we call birth defects. (We will discuss these later in the chapter.) The key point to keep in mind is that meiosis produces two daughter cells that are not quite the same as the mother cell. As a result, meiosis guarantees the development of offspring that differ from both parents.

In the second stage of meiosis, the two cells divide into four. Once again, the chromosomes unzip, migrate to opposite ends of the cells, and the cells divide. But this time the chromosomes do not duplicate themselves: Instead of having 46 chromosomes apiece, the four granddaughter cells each have only 23 chromosomes. This halving guarantees that when the sperm and ovum unite, the fertilized ovum will have 23 *pairs* of chromosomes, or 46 single strands. One half of these chromosomes (23) are contributed by the mother's ovum and one half (23) are contributed by the father's sperm.

Meiosis is the beginning of individuality. No two sperm or ova are exactly alike, which explains, in part, why brothers and sisters are all unique. Although they have the same parents, each child in a family inherits a different combination of genes from their parents. Identical (or *monozygotic*) twins are the exception to this rule, and we'll discuss the way in which they are formed later in the chapter.

THE GENETICS OF CONCEPTION

When a sperm fertilizes an ovum, the child-to-be inherits one set of chromosomes from the mother and another from the father. Our cells contain not 46 individual chromosomes but 23 *pairs* of chromosomes. These pairs of chromosomes are like different editions of the same encyclopedia. Each contains a volume on body build, with chapters on height, weight, and proportions; each includes a volume on building a nervous system, with chapters on sense organs, muscle connections, memory, emotional reactions; and so on through 23 volumes. But although the outlines of each volume are the same, the details within sections often differ. The chapter on eye color from the mother's chromosome may contain directions for brown eyes; and the chapter on height, instructions for making a short person. The chapters from the father may contain alternative sets of directions; for example, they may contain directions for blue eyes and a tall person.

Alternative genes for the same trait (such as eye color) are known as **alleles**. A child who inherits the same alleles for a trait (alleles for brown eyes, for example) from both parents is **homozygous** for that trait (from the Greek *homo*, meaning "same"). A child who inherits different alleles for a single trait is **heterozygous** for that trait (from the Greek *hetero*, for "different").

What happens when a child inherits contradictory genetic directions for a trait depends on the genes in question. In some cases, the allele from one parent overrides the gene from the other parent. A child who inherits a gene for brown eyes from her mother and a gene for blue eyes from her father will have brown eyes, not brownish-blue eyes. This happens because the gene for brown eyes overrides the gene for blue eyes. The brown-eyes gene is called a **dominant gene**. The gene that is not expressed—the blue-eyes gene—is a **recessive gene**. In order to have blue eyes, then, a child must inherit two recessive genes—one gene for blue eyes from *each* parent. When that hap-

alleles
alternative genes for the same trait.

homozygous
inheriting the same alleles for a given trait from both parents

heterozygous
inheriting different alleles for a given trait from each parent

dominant gene
a gene that is expressed whether paired with an identical or a recessive allele

recessive gene
gene that is not expressed if paired with its dominant allele

Dark-haired parents may have a blonde child if they carry recessive genes for light hair. *(W. Rosin Malecki/PhotoEdit)*

pens, a dominant brown-eyes gene does not mask the blue-eyes gene. Anyone who has blue eyes, then, is *homozygous* for eye color; both genes for that trait carry instructions to make blue eyes.

When the gene for a recessive trait, such as blue eyes, is masked by a dominant gene, such as that for brown eyes, the blue-eyes gene doesn't necessarily disappear from the family. If a brown-eyed woman with a recessive gene for blue eyes marries a man who also has a recessive gene for blue eyes (another blue/brown heterozygote), the chances are 1 in 4 that a child of theirs will have blue eyes. (See Figure 2-4.)

Some of the traits controlled by recessive genes include gray, green, blue, and hazel eyes; baldness; blonde hair; thin lips; and color blindness. Traits

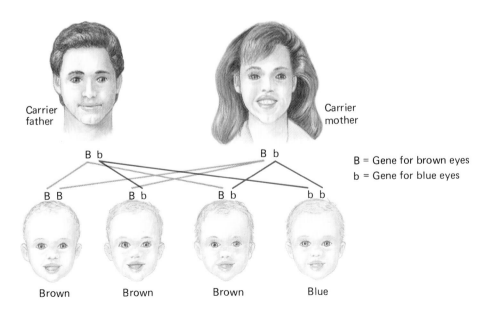

Carrier father

Carrier mother

B = Gene for brown eyes
b = Gene for blue eyes

B B — Brown
B b — Brown
B b — Brown
b b — Blue

FIGURE 2-4
RECESSIVE INHERITANCE FOR BLUE EYES
Both parents have brown eyes, but each carries a recessive gene for blue eyes. The odds for eye color for each child are: (1) 25% chance of receiving two dominant genes, thus having brown eyes; (2) 50% chance of receiving one dominant and one recessive gene, thus being brown-eyed but carrying the recessive gene for blue eyes; and (3) 25% chance of receiving two recessive genes, thus having blue eyes. This same principle applies to the risks of inheriting a recessive genetic defect from parents who are both carriers.

governed by dominant genes include brown eyes, brunette hair, curly hair, thick lips, normal color vision, and far-sightedness.

Many diseases and defects are carried on recessive genes, including sickle-cell anemia, Tay-Sachs disease, hemophilia (all of which we'll look at later in the chapter), congenital deafness, and some 700 others. A child who inherits a recessive gene for a disorder from each parent will develop the disorder. That is why the taboo in most cultures against people marrying close relatives makes good biological sense: Their children have a higher risk of inheriting a harmful recessive gene for a single trait from *each* parent than do the children of unrelated parents. Now that you understand the dominant-recessive mechanism, we should note that most characteristics of human beings are *not* determined by single pairs of dominant and recessive genes but rather by the combined effects of many genes. Characteristics such as height, skin color, and intelligence are **polygenic**.

polygenic
caused by the interaction of a number of genes

Sex determination

In every baby, sex is determined by the twenty-third pair of chromosomes; the chromosomes in this pair are called, appropriately, the **sex chromosomes**. There are two types of sex chromosomes: X-shaped and Y-shaped. In females, the twenty-third pair of chromosomes is a double X, and in males, it is an X and a Y.

sex chromosomes
the twenty-third pair of chromosomes, which determine the sex of the child; there are two types, X and Y

Recall that during meiosis, when the ovum and sperm are produced, each cell contains only half of the full set of chromosomes and genes. Each ovum carries one X chromosome, and each sperm carries *either* an X or a Y chromosome, half of the twenty-third pair. At conception, if an X-bearing sperm fertilizes the ovum, the twenty-third pair of chromosomes in the fetus becomes XX, female. If a Y-bearing sperm reaches the ovum first, an XY combination produces a male. It is the sperm, then, that "decides" the child's sex. The kings and tribal chieftains of history who have divorced or even killed the women who bore them only daughters were wrong, biologically as well as morally.

In this karyotype, a picture of a full set of human chromosomes, a Y chromosome in the twenty-third pair denotes maleness. *(Dr. J. H. Tjio)*

FROM GENOTYPE TO PHENOTYPE

While biologists study the molecular structure and behavior of genes, developmental scientists want to identify the aspects of human traits and behaviors that are influenced by genes. We say *influenced* because the environment plays an active role from the beginning. For this reason, scientists distinguish between a person's **genotype**—the set of genes the person inherits—and her or his **phenotype**—those observable physical and behavioral traits that emerge during development. A phenotype is not a direct reflection of a person's genotype but rather the expression of genetic *potential* in a particular *environmental context*.

Some aspects of development are under such tight genetic control that the environment has little if any influence on their expression. **Canalization** is the term used to describe the extent to which a trait is susceptible to modification by the environment or experience (Waddington, 1966). Highly canalized traits are relatively difficult to modify. For example, the major motor developments of the first year (turning over, sitting up, crawling) are highly canalized. Babies sit up when they are biologically ready to sit; parents can do little to speed things up. Moreover, individual differences are slight. Virtually all normal babies follow similar timetables of motor development, even when they grow up in very different environments—unless, of course, those environments are extremely depriving.

But many other aspects of development we will consider in this book— indeed, most—are not highly canalized, so there is considerable room for variation in phenotype. Each child's genotype establishes a *potential*; what actually happens during development depends on the interaction of that potential with the environment. Height, a trait that most of us think of as genetically "determined," illustrates this. Height is hereditary; generally, tall parents have tall children, and short parents have short children. But nutrition and health clearly affect how tall a person will grow. A boy with "tall genes" who grows up in a poor rural village, or who is sickly as a child, may be only 5 feet 7 inches as an adult. If he is healthy and well-fed as a child, he might be 6 feet as an adult.

Height is one of many instances in which genes do not determine a trait but establish a **reaction range**, or upper and lower limits on development. Intelligence is another. Like height, intelligence runs in families. Bright parents tend to have bright children, and slow parents generally have not-so-bright children. Suppose, though, that a child's parents both have IQs in the below-average range of 80 to 90. (An IQ of 100 is average.) The parents were not very good students, but they are able to hold jobs and function adequately. If the child grows up with his parents, his IQ will probably be about the same as theirs. But if he is adopted by parents with above-average IQs (about 130), parents who read to him, answer his questions, take him on trips to museums, and otherwise provide a stimulating environment, there is a very good chance that he will develop an average or even above-average IQ, say, 110. However, if he is placed in an institution at an early age and given only minimal care, he may only develop an IQ of 70, which is in the mildly retarded range. For IQ, this child's reaction range is 70 to 110. He will never be a genius, but he should always be capable of learning basic skills. Where he falls within this range—his phenotype—depends on his environment.

genotype
an individual's genetic makeup, consisting of all inherited genes

phenotype
an individual's observable physical and behavioral traits, the result of the interaction of genotype and environment

canalization
genetic restriction of a trait to a narrow range of timetables and outcomes

reaction range
genetically established upper and lower limits to development of a given trait; a trait's potential for expression

A child's environment includes experiences as well as things. When adults stimulate a child's curiosity they influence intellectual development and create an emotional bond as well. *(Eastcott/Momatiuk/The Image Works)*

Genes and the environment

In the not-too-distant past, scientists thought of heredity and the environment as opposing forces: Either one or the other prevailed. Today, however, most recognize that genetic and environmental factors usually work in the same direction (see Chapter 1). In technical language, genotype and environment are often correlated (they co-relate, or go together). Robert Plomin, an expert in the area of behavioral genetics (the inheritance of behavior), and his colleagues have identified three types of gene-environment correlations (Plomin, DeFries, & Loehlin, 1977). Each can be illustrated by considering the development of intelligence and sociability. A child who inherits a high genetic potential for intelligence usually has highly intelligent parents. Intelligent parents are likely to do things with the child that stimulate her intellectual growth. Similarly, a child who inherits a predisposition to sociability is likely to have outgoing parents who chat with people they meet on the street, invite guests to their house, and generally provide their child with many opportunities to interact with others, thus encouraging her to be outgoing. These are called *passive* gene-environment correlations. The child is the passive recipient of genetic and environmental influences that work in the same direction—in these examples, to make the child more intelligent or more sociable.

Children who have the genetic potential for high intelligence are also likely to act in ways that evoke intellectual stimulation from the people around them. For example, they ask questions, beg to be taken to the library, and volunteer answers in school more often than children with less intellectual potential. Responding to their intellectual curiosity, adults and older children treat them differently. Similarly, inherently sociable children are more likely to smile and seek attention than are shy children; as a result, others are more likely to respond to them, thereby reinforcing their tendency to be friendly.

These are *evocative* gene-environment correlations: Because of their genetic predispositions, the children evoke certain types of reactions from their environment.

Children who inherit high intellectual potential also actively seek environments that encourage or reward intelligent behavior. The intelligent child selects playthings that are cognitively challenging, chooses books that are a little beyond her current reading level, picks friends who are as advanced as she is. The child who is genetically sociable chooses play activities involving other children rather than solitary pastimes. These choices—which psychologists refer to as "niche-picking" (Scarr & McCartney, 1983)—tend to strengthen the phenotypic display of genotypic predispositions. The choices are called *active* gene-environment correlations: The child actively seeks and shapes an environment that fits her genetic predisposition.

Separating genetic and environmental contributions

Given the overlap between genetic and environmental influences, how do psychologists know how much any one characteristic in any person is shaped by heredity? One approach is to study children who were adopted at an early age. Similarities in a given trait between these children and their adoptive parents (with whom they live but with whom they share no genetic history) reflect environmental influences; similarities between children and their biological parents (with whom they share a genetic background but no experience) reflect genetic influences. A second approach is to compare identical and fraternal twins. **Identical twins** develop when a single fertilized ovum divides in two, leading to the birth of children with completely identical genes. They are the same sex, look strikingly alike, and are very similar in other ways

identical twins
twins born from a single fertilized ovum that divides in two

When sociable babies smile, adults smile back and act warmly toward them, reinforcing the infants' tendency to be friendly. *(Joel Gordon)*

fraternal twins
twins born from two different ova fertilized at the same time by two different sperm

as well. **Fraternal** (meaning, literally, "brotherly") **twins** are born when two ova are fertilized at the same time by two different sperm. Like identical twins, fraternal twins share the same prenatal and postnatal environment. Genetically, however, fraternal twins are no more alike than brothers and sisters. Differences between identical and fraternal twins in degrees of similarity for a given trait are used to estimate the degree of genetic influence on that trait.

Studies of intelligence with twins and adopted children as subjects illustrate the interplay of genetic and environmental factors in development. The correlation in IQ scores for identical twins is .85 (on a scale where 0 indicates no relationship and 1.00 signifies total similarity); the correlation for fraternal twins, about .55 (Plomin & DeFries, 1983). As these correlations show, heredity is a major factor in intelligence. A study of adoption and IQ (Scarr & Weinberg, 1983) confirmed this conclusion. The researchers found that the correlation in IQ scores between children and their biological parents (who had given them up for adoption) was higher than that between children and their adoptive parents (who raised them). But the same study showed that the environment also has a significant impact. The adopted children in this study were born to poor parents with below-average IQs but raised in middle-class homes by parents with above-average IQs. Apparently as a result of this stimulating environment, the children's IQ scores were significantly higher than their biological parents' (an average of 110 compared to an average of 80). But the adopted children's IQs were not as high as their adoptive siblings, who had the double advantage of their parents' genes *and* a stimulating environment.

What conclusions can we draw? Children inherit from their parents a set of genetic potentials. Within their genetic program, some traits are strongly canalized, and others have a wide reaction range. How children actually develop depends on the interplay between what they bring to the environment and the sorts of experiences they have in that environment. The question is not *how much*? How much of intelligence, sociability, and so forth, is hereditary, and how much results from experience? Rather, the question is *how*? How do genes and the environment *work together* to influence development? And ultimately, how can we shape environments so that all children come closer to their full potential? In the next section we examine several abnormalities in development that have genetic bases. But even among these genetic abnormalities, we will find that the environment still plays an important role.

Genetic Abnormalities

In the normal course of fetal development cells multiply and migrate to their appropriate destinations so that organs and limbs form where they should. Usually, the genes perform flawlessly, but mistakes can and do occur. Half of all conceptions are never implanted, and 25 percent of implanted embryos are spontaneously aborted in the first month or two of pregnancy. Many of these miscarriages result from genetic defects. In other cases, development continues and the baby is born with defects that may cause serious or even life-threatening problems. We'll look first at two genetic abnormalities carried on the X chromosome: color blindness and hemophilia.

COLOR BLINDNESS AND HEMOPHILIA

Biologically, males are the weaker sex. One reason has to do with the nature of the X and Y chromosomes. X chromosomes carry more genes than Y chromosomes, making females less vulnerable to some inherited disorders than males. A disadvantageous gene on one X chromosome may be dominated by an advantageous gene on the other X chromosome, and the negative trait will not appear. We call these traits **sex-linked** because the genes for them are carried on the X chromosome.

Color blindness is one such trait, occurring far more often in males than in females because it is controlled by a gene or genes on the X chromosome. The Y chromosome does not carry the allele for color vision. A female may have one gene for color blindness on one X chromosome and another gene for normal vision on her other X chromosome. This normal gene is dominant, so the woman has color vision, but she *carries* the gene for color blindness. If, at fertilization, her X chromosome bearing the color-blind gene unites with a Y chromosome, her son (recall that XY makes a boy) will be color-blind. The boy will have nothing on the Y chromosome to mask the gene for color blindness on the X chromosome: Color blindness results.

Hemophilia is a far more serious sex-linked disorder, also carried on the X chromosome. A girl who inherits this gene can lead a normal healthy life; a boy may not. A recessive gene on the X chromosome blocks production of a necessary blood-clotting substance, so that even a minor injury can cause a hemophiliac to bleed to death. Women *carry* the disorder (the genotype) but are less likely to suffer the effects (the phenotype) than men are because, as with color blindness, females have two X chromosomes and stand at least a 50/50 chance of inheriting a dominant, "healthy" allele that overrides the defective gene. Males, who inherit only one X chromosome, are unprotected. So if a male's X chromosome carries the hemophilia gene, he will have the disease.

sex-linked traits
traits determined by genes on the X chromosome

hemophilia
a sex-linked hereditary disorder in which production of a necessary blood-clotting substance is blocked

DOWN SYNDROME

Probably the best-known genetic disorder is **Down syndrome** (named for the physician who first described its symptoms). Down syndrome children have a distinctive appearance coupled with marked mental and physical handicaps. Typically, their eyes are almond-shaped, with a downward-sloping skin fold at the inner corners. Their heads tend to be small and rounder than other children's, and their noses flatter. Limbs are short, and the children walk with an awkward and flat-footed gait. The mental development of Down children is much slower than normal, never reaching average adult levels. These children show a high rate of heart defects, and they are also more susceptible to a variety of physical diseases and disorders, including leukemia, respiratory infection, and eye and ear problems. As a result, they run a high risk of early death. This risk decreases if they survive the first years of life.

Down syndrome
a hereditary disorder caused by an extra twenty-first chromosome

Home life can foster the development of Down syndrome children in ways that institutional living rarely does. This girl enjoys a game of scrabble with her siblings at home. *(Mario Ruiz/ Picture Group)*

The cause of Down syndrome has been traced to the twenty-first pair of chromosomes. The Down child has an extra twenty-first chromosome, or a piece of one. (The technical term for this is *trisomy 21*, or three twenty-first chromosomes.) In rarer cases, the third twenty-first chromosome, or part of it, is attached to another chromosome. Down syndrome has been linked to the age of the mother (see Table 2-2 for age-related statistics). Why should the incidence of the defect increase so sharply with maternal age? Recall that a female is born with all the ova she will ever have, so the ova of a woman who bears a child at age 45 have been around a lot longer than those of a woman who conceives at age 25. The older ova also have been exposed to more diseases and more environmental pollutants, so it may be only partly correct to

TABLE 2-2 INCIDENCE OF DOWN SYNDROME ACCORDING TO MATERNAL AGE	
Maternal Age	**Incidence of Down**
Under 30 yrs.	1 in 1500 live births
30	1 in 885
35	1 in 365
40	1 in 109
45	1 in 32
50	1 in 12

Note: These data are from Sweden, where prenatal care is excellent.
Source: From E. Hook and A. Lindsjo. Down syndrome in live births by single-year maternal age in a Swedish study. *American Journal of Human Genetics*, Volume 30, No. 19, 1978. Reprinted by permission of the American Society of Human Genetics.

say that Down syndrome is a genetic disorder. Genetic and environmental influences may both be at work here.

Down children face very different prospects today than they once did. Not too long ago, most Down children were placed in institutions, but now parents are advised to keep the child in their home as long as possible. Despite their slow motor and mental development, time spent teaching these children is time well spent. Many Down children can learn simple skills that will enable them to contribute to their own support and lead semi-independent lives as adults. When encouraged by responsive mothers to play and explore actively as infants, Down children do become more competent (Crawley & Spiker, 1983). Special education programs have shown too that these children have more learning potential than anyone suspected 15 or 20 years ago (Sroufe & Cooper, 1988). Thus, it is clear from recent evidence that the environment can powerfully affect the expression of this genetically determined disorder; the reaction range is much larger than was once thought. Taking this to heart, plastic surgeons are experimenting with techniques to change the appearance of Down children, in the hopes of evoking more positive responses from others, which might in turn positively influence these children's development.

PKU

Phenylketonuria (PKU) is a metabolic disorder caused by a double dose of a recessive gene. If a child inherits this gene from *both* parents, his or her body will not produce the enzyme that breaks down the amino acid phenylalanine. High levels of this amino acid circulating through the bloodstream kill nerve cells, causing irreversible brain damage. However, if the disorder is diagnosed shortly after birth and the child is put on a phenylalanine-free diet (this eliminates milk and other high-protein foods), little or no damage occurs. The genes are still there, but their effects are barely noticeable. Here, then, is another example of gene-environment interaction: Only under certain environmental conditions—that is, when there are no dietary restrictions—does the potential of the gene express itself phenotypically.

phenylketonuria (PKU) hereditary metabolic disorder caused by a double dose of a recessive gene that blocks amino acid breakdown

ABNORMALITIES IN THE SEX CHROMOSOMES

Some abnormalities of the X and Y chromosomes have a direct effect on sexual development. A problem can occur when the chromosomes do not separate completely during meiosis (as in many cases of Down syndrome). Some of these disturbances afflict females; others affect males.

In **Klinefelter's syndrome**, a male has an extra X chromosome (resulting in an XXY genotype, rather than the normal male XY genotype). In childhood, these youngsters are phenotypically normal; that is, they look like normal boys, but during adolescence they do not go through the routine changes of male puberty. They do not develop facial hair; their voices do not become lower, their penises and testicles do not grow. Often they develop female curves (breast enlargement and rounded, broad hips). They may be taller than average, but they do not appear masculine. Moreover, they are sterile. Hormone treatments can make these men appear more typically male but cannot make them fertile. The incidence of Klinefelter's syndrome is about 1 in 1800

Klinefelter's syndrome hereditary disorder caused by an extra X chromosome in males

live births, and like Down syndrome, it is more common in the sons of older women (Kennedy, 1971).

Turner's syndrome
hereditary disorder caused by a missing X chromosome in females

Turner's syndrome is a genetic disorder of females. Girls with this syndrome have only one X chromosome; they are usually small and often have extra folds of skin on the neck, making it appear webbed. At adolescence, these girls do not develop breasts or begin to ovulate and menstruate. Hormonal treatment can stimulate the development of secondary sex characteristics and a more normal female appearance but cannot cure these women's sterility.

SICKLE-CELL ANEMIA

sickle-cell anemia
hereditary disorder that affects the ability of red blood cells to carry oxygen

Some genetic disorders affect certain populations more than others. **Sickle-cell anemia** is an example. About 1 in every 100 Americans carries the recessive sickle-cell gene, but among Hispanic Americans, the ratio is 1 in 20, and among black Americans, it is 1 in 10. Why does this disorder affect these groups more than others? Sickle cells (red blood cells bent in the shape of a sickle) provide protection from malaria, so in the tropical regions of Africa, Central America, and the Caribbean, where malaria is common, the trait is adaptive. People who inherited the sickle-cell gene from only one parent stood a better than average chance of avoiding malaria, surviving childhood, and bearing children. Some of their children inherited the trait, passed it on to *their* children, and so on down many generations. As a result, the sickle-cell gene is more common in groups that live or once lived in the tropics.

Heterozygotes, who have inherited the sickle-cell gene from only one parent, have some normal and some sickled red blood cells. The sickled cells provide protection from malaria, and the normal cells ensure that sufficient oxygen is carried through the system to various organs. But for homozygotes, who have inherited the gene from both parents, the gene is not adaptive at all. (See Figure 2-5.) A double dose causes painful disabilities. All the red blood cells are bent in the sickle shape, move slowly, and carry very little oxygen.

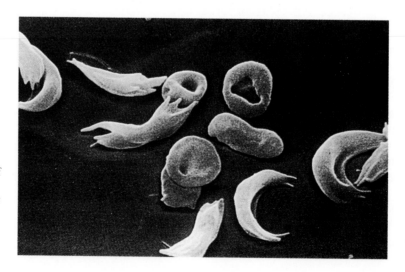

The crescent-shaped red blood cell signaling sickle-cell anemia appears in a high proportion of Hispanic and black Americans. In tropical regions, where those populations once lived, the sickle-cell gene confers immunity to malaria. *(Omikron/Photo Researchers)*

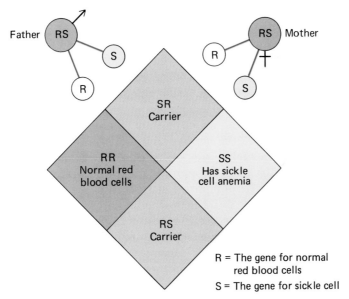

FIGURE 2-5
INHERITANCE OF SICKLE-CELL ANEMIA
This chart indicates the *probability* that a husband and wife who both carry the sickle-cell gene will have a child who has the disease, carries the trait, or has normal red blood cells. But it is only a probability chart. In actuality, their children's genotypes depend on which sperm chances to meet which egg.

The effects of a double dose of sickle-cell genes vary from individual to individual. In severe cases, sickle cells cause frequent crises, during which the individual's joints are painfully swollen, heart and kidneys fail, and early death results. In milder cases, the person experiences frequent shortness of breath and fatigue. Those afflicted can lead relatively normal lives, although certain situations (especially pregnancy and surgery) create special complications for them.

TAY-SACHS DISEASE

Tay-Sachs disease is another selective genetic disorder, found mostly among Jewish people of Eastern European descent. Tay-Sachs resulted from a mutation that remained within a small segment of that population, because for many generations Jews and Gentiles rarely intermarried.

A child who inherits the Tay-Sachs gene from both parents seems normal and healthy at birth. Then, gradually, development slows. The baby who was initially happy and responsive becomes lethargic; the child who was active becomes helpless, unable to move or even eat. A normally harmless chemical in the brain has built up to poisonous levels, destroying nerve cells. There is no known cure for this disease, and afflicted children rarely survive beyond their third birthdays. Fortunately, a simple test can determine whether prospective parents carry the Tay-Sachs gene, as you'll see shortly.

Tay-Sachs disease
hereditary disorder that destroys nerve cells, leading to mental retardation, loss of muscle control, and death

OTHER GENETIC DISORDERS

For the disorders we have described so far, a single gene, or a specific pattern of gene-environment interaction, has been identified. In the majority of cases, however, scientists do not know why a baby is born with handicaps. The trait may be polygenic—caused by the interaction of a number of genes from the mother and/or father. Cleft palates and cleft lips, childhood diabetes, and spina bifida (an open spine) are probably polygenic. An abnormality may be caused by a combination of genetic traits and environmental factors.

If scientists have not been able to identify the gene or genes responsible for a disorder, how do they know it is hereditary? Sometimes they look at identical twins, who have the same genotype. But remember, identical twins also experienced the same prenatal environment (they developed in the same uterus) and usually grow up in the same home. In some cases, researchers have been able to locate identical twins who were separated at birth and reared in different environments, but such cases are rare.

More often, researchers who are interested in heredity study the *distribution* of a trait in families. Suppose a mother has problem Z. If this disorder is hereditary, her children will be more likely to suffer from the Z disorder than her first cousins, her first cousins will more likely be afflicted with Z than her third cousins, and so on. In other words, the distribution of Z will be more or less the same as the distribution of blue eyes in a family—or that of wrinkles in Mendel's peas.

Research based on the family distribution model shows that many disorders, from stuttering to diabetes to schizophrenia, run in families. This is not to say that these disorders are "genetically determined," as in the case of Down syndrome. Rather, they are genetically *influenced*. The child inherits a vulnerability to the disorder, but whether the problem develops depends on environmental factors. In the words of one physician, "The genetic factor may be the loaded gun, but it takes an environmental element to pull the trigger" (in Andrews, 1982, p. 99).

Genetic Counseling and Prenatal Diagnosis

What can prospective parents do to avoid the often tragic consequences of a child's genetic defect? First and foremost, they can find out what risks they run of having children with such problems. Thanks to modern science, there are tests for many difficult disorders that can determine whether one or both partners carry a defective gene *before* they attempt to conceive a child. (If only one carries the sickle-cell gene, for example, the parents have nothing to fear because it is a recessive trait.) If there is a risk, they can learn through prenatal testing whether a particular fetus is afflicted and either decide on an abortion in the hope that another pregnancy will be problem-free or prepare to care for a handicapped child. These are not easy choices, to be sure. But new genetic knowledge and technology have allowed thousands of couples to become parents who would not have risked giving birth to an afflicted child in the past. Both genetic counseling and prenatal diagnosis of genetic problems are available to prospective parents. What are the procedures, and who should seek them?

GENETIC COUNSELING

Genetic counselors are physicians (usually obstetrician/gynecologists) who advise couples on the likelihood that they will conceive a child with a genetic defect. Couples who already have a child with a genetic disorder, whose relatives have a genetic disorder, who come from an ethnic group known to be at risk, or who have suffered spontaneous abortions are advised to seek genetic counseling.

The counselor begins by taking the couple's family histories, including causes of death of close family members. If there is reason to suspect that a genetic defect runs in one or both families, the counselor will recommend tests to determine whether these individuals are carriers. Tissue samples from the would-be parents are used to produce a profile of each spouse's chromosomes, called a **karyotype**. (Remember, all body cells contain a full set of chromosomes.) Carriers of sickle-cell anemia, Tay-Sachs, hemophilia, and other disorders can be identified this way.

karyotype
profile of an individual's chromosomes created from a tissue sample

Genetic counselors can inform a couple of their risk of bearing a child with a genetic disorder. They can let the couple know what options may be available. But they *cannot* tell the couple whether a particular conception will produce a disabled child. If both parents carry a harmful recessive gene, the risk is 1 in 4, just as the "risk" of having a child with blue eyes is 1 in 4 if both parents carry the recessive blue-eyes gene. Most important, genetic counselors cannot tell the couple whether to take the risk. If the couple decide to try to conceive and do, they can to some extent rely on prenatal testing to reveal the presence of certain (not all) genetic defects in the fetus. However, these tests are not foolproof, and they have raised controversial issues, as you'll see in "Issues & Options."

PRENATAL DIAGNOSIS

A generation ago, there was no way of knowing whether a baby would be genetically normal until the child was born (or in some cases, as with Tay-Sachs disease, until even later). Today there are a number of tests for identify-

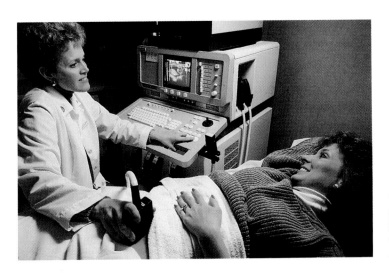

Ultrasound uses sound waves to produce a picture of a fetus, helping doctors monitor development. *(Charles Gupton/Stock, Boston)*

Issues & OPTIONS

Medical Advances, Human Dilemmas

Twenty-five years ago infertility was for life. Couples who could not conceive adopted or went childless. And if a baby had Down syndrome, Tay-Sachs disease, or a malformed neural tube, no one knew it until the baby was born. Medical advances have altered both of these situations. Infertility can often be corrected, and if genetic defects cannot yet be corrected during gestation, some can be diagnosed before birth. But the benefits of these advances carry costs as well, in the form of painful choices, ethically questionable practices, and unforeseen human reactions.

Couples having difficulty conceiving a child may be candidates for a number of options—artificial insemination, surgical corrections, fertility drugs, in vitro fertilization, and mother surrogacy. Infertility can be overcome in many cases. But treatment usually takes months and can even take years.

During this time the couple must keep meticulous temperature charts (a reflection of the woman's hormone levels), have intercourse by the calendar, and undergo innumerable tests to determine when conception is likely. Procedures can be embarrassing—recording each instance of sex, rushing to the doctor after intercourse, masturbating into a bottle to produce a sperm sample. Some tests are uncomfortable or even painful. But for most couples, the most painful part is waiting each month to see if they have succeeded.

Earlier, we discussed the use of amniocentesis as a means of detecting Down syndrome. For most women over 35 the results are negative, but what if tests show that the fetus *has* Down syndrome? The question of abortion presents a very difficult choice for many couples. Down syndrome children are mentally and physi-

cally handicapped, to be sure, but many can lead reasonably content (if not entirely normal) lives. Children with hemophilia or sickle-cell anemia are not retarded but usually experience bouts of intense pain and require frequent, expensive medical treatment. Can the couple afford to care for a severely handicapped child, emotionally as well as financially? Is it fair to their other children? Fair to the child? Some argue that it is morally wrong to deny a child life because he or she is not perfect. Others maintain that it is wrong for a couple to burden society with a child who will require lifelong support when they might have a healthy child from another pregnancy. These questions are being debated by scientists, clergy, and philosophers—and by anyone interested in the ethical dilemmas posed by the advances of technology.

Another unanticipated conse-

amniocentesis
a medical technique for diagnosing genetic abnormalities *in utero* by analysis of amniotic fluid.

ultrasonography
technique that produces a picture from sound waves bounced off the fetus; used for diagnosing developmental problems *in utero*

ing genetic disorders while the child is still unborn, or *in utero*. Couples who are known to carry genetic defects and women who are over 35 (and thus have a higher risk of bearing a child with Down syndrome or other disorders) are advised to take these tests.

The most widely used procedure for prenatal diagnosis is **amniocentesis**, which became available in the 1970s. A doctor inserts a syringe into the pregnant woman's uterus and draws out some of the amniotic fluid that surrounds the fetus. This fluid contains some of the fetus's own cells. These cells are then analyzed in the laboratory for possible genetic defects. Because a complete set of chromosomes is analyzed, this test also tells parents the sex of the fetus.

Amniocentesis is usually accompanied by **ultrasonography** (ultrasound),

Issues & OPTIONS

quence of the new technology is the illusion that physicians can guarantee parents a healthy child. They cannot. Prenatal tests identify only a small number of disorders, and no test is perfect. Couples of Eastern European descent, for example, can be screened for the defective gene responsible for Tay-Sachs disease, but the test isn't foolproof. When couples carrying the gene receive negative test results instead of being positively identified as carriers, they may still conceive a child with Tay-Sachs. Does the couple have the right to sue the doctor and the laboratory involved in the testing? Should doctors be held responsible for the birth of an imperfect child? Even those who believe they should be recognize that the costs of medical insurance for obstetricians, and hence the costs of prenatal care, have risen sharply because of the rise in malpractice suits.

Legal and moral dilemmas also surround the practice of mother surrogacy, when one woman agrees to bear a child for another who cannot become pregnant herself. In this procedure, the surrogate mother is artificially inseminated with sperm from the infertile woman's husband. The pregnant woman agrees—often in a contract—to relinquish the baby shortly after birth, usually in exchange for a fee.

A highly publicized example of the problems that can result from this solution to infertility was the Baby M case. Baby M was born because one woman agreed to have a child for another for whom pregnancy posed a health risk. Although doctors could artificially inseminate the surrogate mother with the husband's sperm, they could not keep her from changing her mind after the baby was born. When she decided that she could not give the baby up, a prolonged court battle ensued, and the surrogate mother ulti-

mately lost the right to custody of the child.

Everyone involved in this tragic case suffered greatly, and the whole issue of mother surrogacy as a solution to infertility has been debated anew. Who in fact is the surrogate mother—the woman who is the child's biological mother, or the woman who will later raise the child? Is it ethical for one woman to pay another to become pregnant because she cannot? Is this a form of baby bartering? It can be argued that the very painful emotional consequences that can result from mother surrogacy should remove it from the choices available to childless couples. In this view, just because we *can* do something doesn't necessarily mean that we *should*. But it can also be argued that human variables are inherent in many technical procedures, and mother surrogacy can still be a choice available to people willing to take the risks.

in which sound waves bounce off the fetus, producing a picture, or *sonogram*, on a screen. Ultrasound by itself has become a very common prenatal diagnostic technique. The sonogram enables physicians to look for visible defects, which may or may not be genetic in origin. These procedures are highly accurate, relatively painless, and almost risk-free. Complications develop in fewer than 1 in 1000 cases (Globus et al., 1979). The main drawback is that amniocentesis cannot be performed until the fourth month of pregnancy, and results take 3 to 4 weeks. By this time the fetus is nearly 20 weeks old; deciding whether to have an abortion at this point becomes a very painful choice.

Scientists are working on a new technique for extracting a sample of fetal tissue that can be performed earlier in a pregnancy than amniocentesis. This

chorionic villus biopsy (CVB)
prenatal diagnostic technique that analyzes cells taken from hairlike villi on the embryonic sac for genetic problems

new technique, called **chorionic villus biopsy (CVB)**, can be performed 9 to 11 weeks after conception. In this test, cells are taken from the hairlike projections, or villi, attached to the sac that surrounds the fetus. Within a few days, results can indicate the presence of Down syndrome, Tay-Sachs disease, and other disorders. In a series of studies, doctors have been comparing the rate of miscarriages following amniocentesis and the chorionic test. In the meantime, many obstetricians are offering the newer test to pregnant women, advising them that it is about as risky as amniocentesis. (See "Issues & Options" for a discussion of the ethical problems raised by this and other types of prenatal medical technology.)

Another technique for diagnosing defects prenatally is a maternal blood test, performed between the fourteenth and twentieth weeks of pregnancy. This test is used when there is a risk that the child may be born with spinal or brain abnormalities. The fetus's liver produces a protein known as alpha fetoprotein (AFP), some of which leaks into the mother's bloodstream. Low levels of AFP are normal at this point in pregnancy; high levels indicate that something may be wrong. We emphasize "may" because this test is not as reliable as the others we have described. Levels of AFP in the mother's bloodstream may be elevated for a number of reasons. According to the American College of Obstetricians and Gynecologists, if 1000 women are tested, about 50 will have abnormal AFP levels. Further testing will reveal only 1 or 2 carry a fetus with a neural tube defect.

In the near future, techniques similar to those now used for diagnosis may be used to actually correct defects before the fetus is born. Physicians have already used ultrasonography to aid in performing life-saving surgery on a fetus. Researchers are working on techniques to correct enzyme and vitamin deficiencies *in utero*. Someday it may even be possible to correct the genetic defects that cause Down syndrome and other disorders (Lerner, 1986).

Summary

1. Only one of hundreds of millions of sperm that are ejaculated can fertilize an ovum. Whether fertilization occurs depends partly on timing. The male reproductive system produces sperm continuously, but a woman's reproductive cycle is divided into three phases: preparation, ovulation, and menstruation. The egg (ovum) released during ovulation can be fertilized only during a brief period.

2. Although more couples are experiencing infertility, more can now be done to alleviate these problems. Successful techniques include hormone treatments, surgery, and artificial insemination.

3. Human heredity is directed by the genes which appear on threadlike chromosomes in every body cell.

4. Every human cell (except sex cells) contains 23 pairs of chromosomes, made up of twisted strands of DNA. The order of amino acids on these double strands comprises the genetic code. Chromosomes govern essential protein production in each cell; they also make the production of new cells possible through mitosis, in which the chromosomes make exact copies of themselves and two daughter cells result from one original.

5. Sex cells are produced by meiosis. The chromosome strands unwind, producing sperm and ova with only 23 single chromosomes each. At conception, the mother's and father's chromosomes are joined, passing on a complete set to their child. Males and females both have one pair of sex chromosomes, XX in females and XY in males. If a sperm bearing a Y chromosome fertilizes the ovum, the child will be a boy. An X-carrying sperm and an ovum produce a girl.

6. Some traits are controlled by a dominant/recessive genetic mechanism. Most traits are polygenic—determined by the combined effects of a number of rather than a single pair of genes.

7. A person's genotype (genetic makeup) does not "determine" her or his phenotype (observable, or expressed, characteristics). Some traits and developmental schedules are strongly determined, or canalized. More often, genes establish a wide reaction range, that is, upper and lower limits on potential development. Who we become is the result of interplay between our genes and the environment.

8. Pregnancies with genetic abnormalities usually end in spontaneous abortions. In some cases, however, the baby survives and is born with mild to serious problems. Scientists have identified the genetic origins of some disorders, including hemophilia (one of a number of sex-linked disorders), Down syndrome, PKU, sickle-cell anemia, and Tay-Sachs disease; scientists suspect that many other developmental disorders result from an inherited vulnerability.

9. Couples learn through genetic counseling what risks they run of having children with genetic defects. Prenatal tests (amniocentesis, ultrasonography, chorionic villus biopsy, and maternal blood tests) can detect a number of fetal genetic defects in time for the couple to prevent or prepare for the birth of a handicapped child.

Key Terms

alleles	Down syndrome
amniocentesis	epididymis
artificial insemination	fallopian tubes
canalization	fraternal twins
cervix	genes
chorionic villus biopsy (CVB)	genotype
chromosomes	hemophilia
crossing-over	heterozygous
deoxyribonucleic acid (DNA)	homozygous
dominant gene	identical twins

karyotype

Klinefelter's syndrome

locus

meiosis

menstruation

mitosis

mutations

ovaries

ovulation

phenotype

phenylketonuria (PKU)

polygenic

preparation

prostate gland

reaction range

recessive gene

sex chromosomes

sex-linked traits

sickle-cell anemia

Tay-Sachs disease

testes

Turner's syndrome

ultrasonography

uterus

Suggested Readings

Jiminez, S. (1982). *The other side of pregnancy.* Englewood Cliffs, NJ: Prentice-Hall. What happens when a baby is lost during pregnancy? In this sensitively written book by a woman who has worked with many expectant parents, both the causes of miscarriage and the emotional consequences are discussed.

Lewontin, R. (1982). *Human diversity.* New York: Freeman. One of the world's leading biologists examines the evolutionary basis of human diversity, including consideration of mechanisms of genetic influence.

Plomin, R. (1986). *Development, genetics, and psychology.* Hillsdale, NJ: Erlbaum. A leader in the study of the inheritance of behavior details the foundations of developmental behavior genetics, including the interrelation of heredity and environment across the lifespan.

Walters W., and Singer, P. (Eds.) (1982). *Test-tube babies.* New York: Oxford University Press. In a series of chapters, the ethics of *in vitro* fertilization are examined. Other issues pertaining to infertility, such as surrogate mothering, are also considered.

Prenatal Development

Environmental Influences

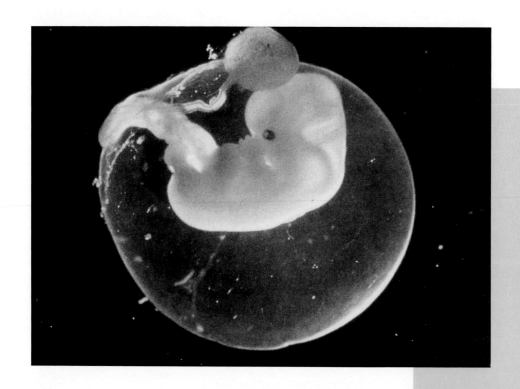

Prenatal Development

*I*n a mere 9 months, a single cell is transformed into a living, breathing human being. A head and limbs take shape, organs form, nerve cells connect, blood begins to circulate, movement begins—all in sequence. The stages and timing of prenatal development are universal. All normal babies develop according to a common human pattern, carved by evolution. In the human design, babies emerge from the uterus 9 months after conception, equipped for life and ready to grow and learn.

Students often assume that genes govern development in the prenatal period but that, once the baby is born, the environment takes over. This is wrong. As you read in Chapter 2, *genetic and environmental factors interact from the beginning.* The mother's diet during pregnancy plays a major role in determining how healthy and alert a baby is at birth. The physical surroundings, and even the time in which she lives, have an effect. Wars, famines, and environmental pollution hurt the unborn as much as or more than they harm the living.

In the first half of this chapter we will trace the universal program of human development from conception to birth, showing how the different aspects and phases of development are synchronized. In the second half we look at environmental factors that may disrupt this plan. Fortunately, we know far more about these hazards today than we did in the past, and many unnecessary risks can now be avoided. "Issues & Options," later in this chapter, offers guidelines for parents-to-be.

Prenatal Development

precocial
describes pattern of prenatal development marked by brief gestation and large litter of helpless young

gestation
period of prenatal development

altricial
describes pattern of prenatal development marked by long gestation and small number of well-developed young

Biologists teach us that there are two basic patterns of prenatal development. One pattern, **precocial** maturity, is seen in rodents, for example. These animals have a relatively brief **gestation** period (the time before birth), and they bear large litters of poorly developed young—tiny, hairless, uncoordinated, helpless babies whose eyes are still sealed shut. Typically, such animals possess small brains, do not develop complex social behavior, and have short lifespans. The second pattern, **altricial** maturity, is seen in larger mammals, and is characterized by a long gestation period and the birth of a small number of well-developed offspring capable, at least in part, of fending for themselves at birth. Within hours, a baby zebra can run with the herd and kick attackers. Typically, these animals have large brains, develop complex social behavior, and live relatively long lives.

There is one glaring exception to this pattern—humans (and other primates). We have small "litters," large brains, long lifespans, and complex social behavior (the second pattern). Yet, compared to other large mammals, we are relatively helpless and undeveloped at birth (as in the first pattern). As the evolutionary biologist Stephen Jay Gould (1976) has expressed it, human babies are "embryos" at birth and remain embryos for much of the first year of life. Developments that occur *in utero* in many other species occur after birth in humans.

The immaturity of human babies has a number of important implications. Many human characteristics and skills develop after we are born, not before. Whereas members of other species mature in the relative quiet and calm of the uterus, we are exposed to all kinds of physical, social, and cultural influences while maturing. No other animal is as good at learning or as dependent on learning—throughout the lifespan—as we are. Moreover, because of our long period of immaturity outside the uterus, it is possible for each individual (even members of the same family) to be exposed to somewhat different environmental influences during maturation, contributing to variations among individuals.

Although we are still immature at birth, we become more "human" in anatomy, physiology, and behavior much earlier than most people realize. The human heart begins beating 3 to 4 weeks after conception, and thumb sucking is an activity most fetuses begin long before birth. Prenatal development proceeds in a predictable sequence and can be divided into three basic stages: the germinal period, the embryonic period, and the fetal period.

THE GERMINAL PERIOD

The **germinal period** includes the first 2 weeks of fetal development. The 4 days immediately following conception are the fastest period of growth in the entire human lifespan. Within hours after their contact in a fallopian tube, the ovum and sperm fuse to become a unique new cell, the **zygote**. The zygote travels down the fallopian tube to the uterus. As it moves along, cell division by mitosis takes place, beginning sometime during the first day after conception. The single, fertilized cell divides into two; these cells divide to produce four; those four divide into eight; and so on—each with an identical set of chromosomes. By day 4 the new organism consists of 60 to 70 cells, arranged in the form of a hollow ball called a **blastula**.

Even before the blastula reaches the uterus, development has begun; cells on the outer edge of the blastula join on one side and become the **embryonic disk**, out of which the baby will develop. The other cells will develop into the

germinal period
the first 2 weeks of prenatal development

zygote
fertilized cell resulting from fusion of ovum and sperm

blastula
from about 4 days to 2 weeks following conception, the hollow-ball form the new organism takes

embryonic disk
the cells on the outer edge of the blastula that will develop into the embryo

Four days after fertilization, the human zygote has grown to a blastula, 60 to 70 cells shaped in a hollow ball. At this point it is ready to begin implantation into the uterine wall. *(Petit Format/Nestle/Photo Researchers)*

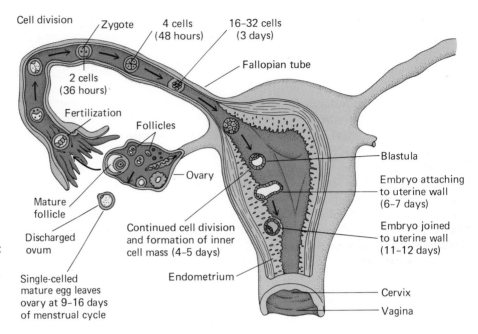

**FIGURE 3-1
EARLY HUMAN DEVELOPMENT:
THE GERMINAL PERIOD**
The drawing depicts the female
reproductive system, the fertilization of the ovum, and the
early growth of the embryo.

structures that will protect and nourish the baby (the placenta, the umbilical cord, and the amniotic sac, described below).

When it reaches the uterus, the blastula floats freely for a day or two. Then it begins to develop microscopic, threadlike **villi**, whose job is to burrow into the blood-rich lining of the uterus. (These are the villi that are sampled in the prenatal diagnostic technique chorionic villus biopsy, discussed in Chapter 2.) When the villi make contact, blood vessels in the uterine lining burst, pro-viding the zygote with its first nourishment. It is the villi that attach the blas-tula to the mother, a process known as **implantation**. Full implantation occurs by the twelfth day after fertilization. At this point, the mother seldom knows she is pregnant. Yet the new organism is already "seeking" contact and nour-ishment. Figure 3-1 illustrates the events that take place during the germinal period, from conception through implantation. Implantation initiates the sec-ond phase of prenatal development, the embryonic period.

Of course, things are a little different in the case of twins. As you saw in the last chapter, identical twins are also known as *monozygotic* twins—because they are formed when a *single* zygote (a single ovum, fertilized by a single sperm) divides into identical halves, which each then develop independently but identically. It is not known why a zygote divides in this way. Fraternal, or *dizygotic*, twins result when *two* ova are fertilized by *two* sperm, yielding two zygotes that are not genetically identical.

THE EMBRYONIC PERIOD

At the beginning of the **embryonic period** (weeks 2 through 8), the baby-to-be is a cluster of cells. By the end of the period, it looks like a tiny baby with all the essential pieces in place. This is the period of structural development, when

villi
hairlike projections from the
blastula that burrow into the
uterine lining

implantation
process by which the blastula attaches to the uterus

embryonic period
the second stage of prenatal
development, from 2 to 8
weeks after conception

different parts of the body (the brain, the digestive system, arms and legs, eyes and nose, and so forth) are formed.

Support systems

Throughout gestation, the embryo and later the fetus are kept alive by three organs that form a vital support system: the placenta, umbilical cord, and amniotic sac. Present in rudimentary form at implantation, these structures will mature during the embryonic period.

Almost as remarkable as the embryo itself is the **placenta**. This disk-shaped organ that forms along the wall of the uterus between the mother and the baby is a highly sophisticated organ of exchange. In the mature placenta, blood vessels from the mother and baby meet but do not actually merge. The placenta membranes that separate them prevent the mother's blood cells from entering the fetus's bloodstream and thus keep many harmful substances in the mother's system from reaching the developing baby. The embryo is attached to the placenta through its **umbilical cord**—the lifeline that brings the embryo oxygen, water, and nutrients gathered from the mother's bloodstream in the placenta. Through the umbilical cord, too, carbon monoxide and other wastes from the embryo's bloodstream are carried back to the placenta and then pass into the mother's system for disposal (see Figure 3-2). Nourishment is not all the placenta provides. It maintains sufficient hormone levels so that menstruation does not occur during pregnancy. It also helps protect the embryo from the risk of infection. As the pregnancy continues, the mother's breasts prepare to produce milk, and eventually contractions that will deliver

placenta
organ along the uterine wall where nutrients and oxygen from the mother and wastes from the baby are exchanged

umbilical cord
the lifeline attaching the embryo (and fetus) to the placenta; it transports maternal nutrients from, and wastes to, the placenta

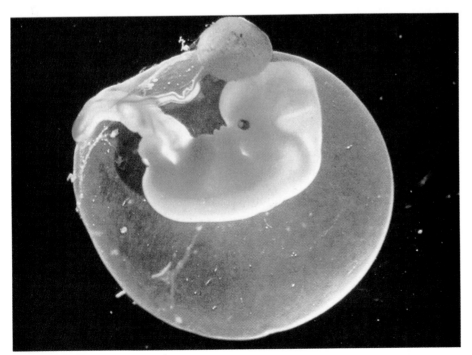

A 6-week-old human embryo floating in amniotic fluid. The dark spot is the retina of the eye; the arms and legs have budded; the heart is beating. The brain is in three parts, with a large space at the base which will be filled by later growth. Above the embryo is the placenta, attached to the baby by the umbilical cord. *(Petit Format/Nestle/Photo Researchers)*

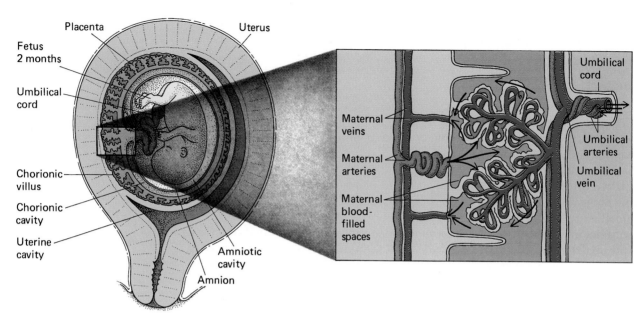

FIGURE 3-2
THE PLACENTA AT WORK
The chorionic villi attached to the amniotic sac each house a blood vessel. Maternal blood fills
the spaces around the villi, and exchange of materials takes place across the layer separating the
maternal and fetal blood supplies. Thus the bloods never merge. (*Source*: Adapted from J.
Postlethwait and J. L. Hopson. [1989]. *The nature of life*. New York: Random House.)

amniotic sac
protective, fluid-filled membrane surrounding the embryo and fetus

endoderm
innermost layer of the embryo which will become the internal organs

mesoderm
middle layer of the embryo; will become the skeleton and muscles

ectoderm
outer layer of the embryo; eventually becomes the skin and nervous system

differentiation
process by which groups of cells descended from the same zygote become specialized for the various tissues and organs

the baby begin, all as a result of the placenta's hormones. It is a remarkable, multipurpose organ.

The **amniotic sac** is a protective membrane that surrounds the embryo and grows with it. Filled with fluid, the amniotic sac cushions the baby from shocks caused by the mother's movements. Suspension in fluid also facilitates the fetus's own movements at a later stage of prenatal development.

In the first weeks of the embryonic period, the implanted blastula develops three distinct layers of cells. The innermost layer, the **endoderm**, will develop into the gut and related organs; the middle layer, the **mesoderm**, will become the skeleton and muscles; and the outer layer, the **ectoderm**, will give rise to the nervous system and the skin. At first the cells in each layer are indistinguishable from each other, yet invisible chemical changes are already taking place. Although all the embryo's cells are descended from the same fertilized egg and contain the same genes, some will develop into kidney cells and others into heart cells; some become blood cells and others branching nerve cells. This process, called **differentiation**, seems to be regulated by the chemical environment in and around the cells. As the embryo matures, some genes are activated by chemical messages to switch "on" while others remain "off."

The development of the blastula's three layers of cells into specialized tissues and organs follows a universal timetable. During the third week of gestation (the first week of the embryonic period), the heart takes shape, and the neural tube starts to develop. (The neural tube is the beginning of the nervous system; it develops into the spinal column.) By the end of week 4, the neural tube has closed—if it does not, the embryo has the defect called spina bifida—and the brain is forming. In week 5, limb buds are putting out dimpled shoots that will become hands and feet, and stalked eye cups have grown from the brain. The ears and teeth appear in week 6. In the seventh and eighth weeks, the embryo's face looks human; its limbs are hinged on joints; rudimentary hands and feet have appeared; and a primitive genital bud has formed. By the end of week 8, the internal organs are in place, and some have begun to function. Although the embryo *is barely an inch long*, it has all (or most) of the makings of a human being.

If a serious error occurs during the embryonic period—say, something is wrong in the basic design of the heart or lungs—development usually stops. Spontaneous abortions are nature's way of reducing the frequency of birth defects. Examination of miscarried embryos suggests that most would have had an extremely small chance of survival if they had endured long enough to be born.

Sex differentiation

One major development of the embryonic stage is sex differentiation. Sex is controlled by the X and Y sex chromosomes, as explained in Chapter 2. For the first 6 to 8 weeks of gestation, boys and girls are indistinguishable. At 5 to 6 weeks both develop primitive gonads (or sex glands). Unless one examines the fetus's chromosomes, it is impossible to tell whether it will become male or female at this stage. Then at about 6 to 8 weeks, the Y chromosome in males triggers the production of testosterone, which causes the primitive gonads to develop male sex organs. A female embryo, whose chromosomes are XX, does not receive the Y chromosome signal, and so the fetus develops female sex organs. The male and female reproductive systems have a common origin and follow parallel developmental paths. Genes direct the early stages of sex differentiation, but then hormones take over. Sexual development is not complete until puberty (see Chapter 15).

THE FETAL PERIOD

Once the basic structure of a human being has been established in the embryonic period, prenatal development moves into its final and longest stage—the **fetal period** (8 weeks on, or the third through the ninth months). Whereas the major theme of the embryonic period was differentiation, the major themes of the fetal period are growth and maturation.

At the end of the third month, the fetus is about 3 inches long and weighs about ¾ of an ounce. The fourth and fifth months are times of rapid change. The fetus's weight increases tenfold. Many finishing touches—eyelids, fingernails, taste buds, sweat glands, and hair—appear. By the fourth month, the expectant mother has probably felt the "fluttering" or "quickening" of fetal movement. In the fifth month, activity is even more pronounced.

The seventh month is transitional for the fetus. It is about 16 inches long (nearly 80 percent of its final length) and weighs about 4 pounds (roughly 50

fetal period
the third and final stage of prenatal development, from 8 weeks to birth

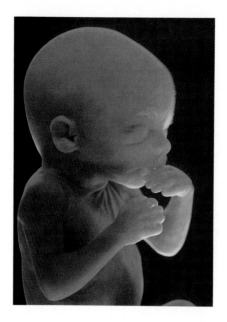

During the fourth and fifth month, the fetus's weight increases tenfold. Eyelids and fingernails have formed. *(J. Stevenson/Photo Researchers)*

percent of its final weight). If it is born in the seventh month, it can survive with medical intervention. During the eighth and ninth months the fetus gains another 3 to 4 pounds, partly in the form of an insulating layer of fat under the skin. Its respiratory system matures, so that it will be able to breathe without help after birth. During the ninth month, the fetus's quarters are cramped, and the mother can feel it squirming to get into a comfortable position. Toward the end of this month, the fetus usually settles in a head down position. The top of its head moves down toward the mother's cervix, and its face turns toward her back. When this happens, the fetus is said to be *engaged*. Birth is imminent. Table 3-1 summarizes the principal stages of prenatal development.

BEHAVIORAL DEVELOPMENT

The fetus is not a clay statue that springs into action when it emerges from the birth canal and issues that famous first cry. It responds to stimuli at a very early stage in prenatal development and acts on its own initiative months before birth.

Behavioral development can be divided into three stages (Hofer, 1981). The first stage runs from about 6 to 16 weeks. At the beginning of this stage, the fetus reacts to stimulation with muscle contractions. This behavior is not spontaneous but is a direct response to stimulation. Then (between 9 and 11 weeks) signs of reflex behavior can be seen. For example, studies of very prematurely born fetuses have revealed that if the fetus's palm is touched, its fingers close—a forerunner of the grasping reflex seen in newborns. Between 11 and 17 weeks, fetal movements become more graceful and flowing, less mechanical in appearance. Spontaneous, whole-body movements become

TABLE 3-1   THE SEQUENCE OF PRENATAL DEVELOPMENT

Period	Time	Developments
		First Trimester
Germinal	0–4 days	Cell division; zygote travels to uterus.
	4–8 days	Beginning of implantation.
	12–13 days	Implantation is completed.
Embryonic	14 days	Placenta begins to develop.
	15–20 days	Rapid development of placenta.
	21–28 days	Eyes start to develop; heart begins to beat; system of blood vessels develops.
	5 weeks	Arm and leg buds form.
	7 weeks	Facial structures connect.
	8 weeks	Major organ development completed.
Fetal	8–12 weeks	Arm and leg movement; emergence of startle and sucking reflex; appearance of genitals; facial expressions occur.
		Second Trimester
	13–16 weeks	Development of skin and hair; skeleton hardens.
	17–20 weeks	Quickening—noticeable movement; heartbeat can be heard.
		Third Trimester
	25–28 weeks	Fat is laid down; can survive (28 weeks) if born prematurely.
	38 weeks	Fetus is plump; testes descend in males.

more frequent, varied, and detectable. (This is when many mothers feel a quickening.)

Then, rather suddenly, activity drops. In the second stage, about 17 to 24 weeks, the fetus is still. Often, women who felt the quickening worry that something is wrong with their baby, but this slowdown in movement is a normal part of prenatal development. In the first stage, behavioral responses and activity were controlled by the spinal cord. At about 17 weeks, the brain begins to take over. However, it takes time for the neural pathways from the brain to different parts of the body to make their connections. Activity declines during this transitional period. Not all behavioral systems disappear at once; rather, they fade one by one in a predictable order. At the end of this stage they reappear in the same order. Now whole-body movements are replaced by isolated, controlled movements of the trunk, legs, or some other body part.

The most significant development in the third stage, 24 to 36 weeks, is the origin of behavioral rhythms, which will persist throughout the individual's life. Like the seasons in a year, our bodies have their own rhythms and cycles. Sleep and waking are timed to a biological clock. (Think how often you wake up 5 minutes before your alarm sounds.) During our waking hours we also experience more or less regular 90-minute peaks and troughs in energy and activity levels. The first signs of these behavioral cycles appear between 24 and

32 weeks of gestation. In fetuses, peaks in activity occur about every 40 minutes—a pattern that continues through the second year of life. (Children attain the adult 90-minute cycle when about 10 years old.) As the time of birth approaches (32 to 36 weeks), episodes of quiet or "rest" are apparent, and transitions to activity are well-defined. The fetus's activity is more vigorous and lasts longer. It has begun to cry, yawn, suck its thumb, and grunt.

Environmental Influences

No relationship is closer than that between a mother and her unborn child. Each stage in prenatal development causes changes in her shape, her body chemistry, and her feelings about herself. At the same time, her body is the unborn baby's first environment. Her health, diet, lifestyle, and moods provide that baby's first "experiences." Prenatal development may be genetically programmed, but as we have stressed, genes depend on the environment both for building materials and for signals about when to turn "on" or "off." Because so much of what happens to the mother affects the fetus, the impact of *her* environment is anything but trivial.

NUTRITION

Studies of European women who gave birth during World War II made the effects of nutrition on prenatal development painfully clear. During the German siege of Leningrad in 1942, when thousands starved to death, 40 percent of pregnant women delivered prematurely, and 30 percent of their babies died shortly after birth (Antonov, 1947). In Holland, where the Nazis severely restricted food supplies, most babies were born small for their age. This was especially true if the mother had gone hungry during the last trimester of pregnancy, when the fetus was developing from a miniature human into a full-sized newborn.

The association of malnutrition during pregnancy with higher rates of stillbirths and premature deliveries is incontestable (Burke et al., 1943; Read et al., 1973), but this is only part of the story. What a mother eats or fails to eat during pregnancy affects both prenatal and *postnatal* development. And it's not just what she eats after she becomes pregnant that has an impact. Women with poor nutritional *histories*—that is, women whose diets have been poor *before* pregnancy—stand a greater risk of delivering low-birth-weight babies. Early births and low birth weights are associated with a host of medical and behavioral problems (as we will explain in Chapters 4 and 5). The biological preparedness of a woman's body, determined by a lifetime of nutritional experience, shapes the prenatal environment of the developing child.

Malnutrition and the brain

Both anatomical and behavioral evidence indicate that nutrition affects brain development. During the first 6 months of pregnancy, the most important aspect of brain development is cell *division*—the multiplication of brain cells. We are born with all the brain cells we'll ever have, and the mature human brain has about 100 billion cells! During the last 3 months of pregnancy (and the first 2 years of life) brain development consists of cell *growth* (Winick, 1970). In several studies, autopsies of malnourished children revealed that their brain cells were both small in number and small in size (Brown, 1966; Naeye, Diener, & Dellinger, 1969). In addition, fetal malnutrition may disrupt **myelinization**, the process by which nerves become insulated by a layer of myelin, which forms a fatty sheath. Myelinization increases the speed and efficiency of neural transmission, the passage of nerve impulses from nerve to nerve throughout the body. Lack of such insulation is one reason that fetal malnutrition is associated with subsequent mental retardation (Davison & Dobbing, 1966). (Nutrition after birth is also important to the continuing myelinization process, as we'll see in Chapter 5.)

myelinization
process by which nerves become insulated with myelin, which forms a fatty sheath

Obviously, researchers would not deliberately deprive mothers of food to study the effects of hunger on their unborn children. But researchers have compared the babies of poor women in third-world countries who have been given food supplements to the babies of other poor women who were not (Habicht et al., 1974; Read et al., 1973). In one study in Bogota, Colombia, mothers in the experimental group were given medical care plus food supplements (cooking oil, dry skim milk, and protein-enriched bread). Mothers in the control group were given the same medical care but no food supplements. At 15 days, the babies of mothers in the experimental group were more alert visually and responded to visual stimuli in a more sophisticated way than did babies of mothers in the control group (Vuori et al., 1979).

A related study (Barrett, Radke-Yarrow, & Klein, 1982) found that early nutrition can have long-term consequences for social development as well. In this research, prenatal supplements for the mothers were followed by supplements for the babies from birth to age 2. At ages 6 to 8, these children were interested in their environment, able to express anger and happiness, and actively involved with their agemates. In contrast, children from similar villages where supplements were not available tended to be passive, dependent on adults, and anxious with their peers. The researchers hypothesized that babies who are alert, energetic, and responsive elicit more attention from their mothers than do apathetic babies. As a result, they have more opportunities to learn basic skills for relating to other people, skills that carry over into friendships with peers when they begin to move beyond their family. Malnourished babies are less energetic, less demanding, and less rewarding to a parent. As a result, they receive less attention and have fewer opportunities to learn basic social skills.

Food supplements and prenatal medical care enhance fetal and postnatal development in third-world nations. This healthy mother and baby live in Ghana. *(Christina Dintiman/Rainbow)*

Fortunately, many children can recover from the effects of early malnutrition. In one observational study, Korean children who were early victims of malnutrition were adopted by U.S. families, who provided three nutritious meals a day. Most of these children performed about as well on intelligence tests as did their U.S. agemates, whose families had never experienced hunger. However, those Korean children who had been severely deprived did not do as well on these tests as did their Korean agemates whose poverty had been less severe (Winick, Meyer, & Harris, 1975).

Most children who suffer from prenatal malnutrition are not magically transported to a life of plenty after they are born. As we will see in Chapter 5, for all too many children, here and abroad, the effects of prenatal malnutrition are compounded by the effects of postnatal poverty.

Issues & OPTIONS

Choices for Pregnant Women

How can a pregnant woman maintain her own health and provide a sound growing environment for her developing baby? How much will she have to change her lifestyle while she is pregnant? Is it better to bear children while she is young, or can she safely wait until her thirties?

Advice on diet has changed over the generations. In the early part of this century, pregnant women were admonished to eat heartily: "You're eating for two." Then, in the 1940s and 1950s, women were told to watch the scale, on the theory that small babies made for easier deliveries. Both views have turned out to be wrong (Hillard, 1983).

A woman who is significantly overweight before pregnancy, or who gains a great deal of weight during pregnancy, has a greater risk of problems associated with obesity in general. But pregnancy is not a time to diet. Doctors now know that low birth weights are harmful, not helpful. Further, women who do not eat enough during pregnancy "give up" to their developing child calcium and fat they need for their own health. Current standards call for a pregnant woman to consume about 2300 calories a day—300 to 500 more than a healthy woman who is not pregnant—and gain about 25 pounds during pregnancy.

TABLE 3-2	DAILY DIET GUIDELINES FOR PREGNANT WOMEN

Protein
    Meats
    Nuts
    Legumes
    Eggs
	2–3 3-oz. servings

Calcium
    Milk
    Cheese
    Yogurt
    Cottage cheese
	4 1-cup servings

Fruits and vegetables with vitamin C e.g., 1 orange, ½ grapefruit, broccoli, potato, etc.	1 serving
Leafy green vegetables with vitamin A and folic acid e.g., spinach, kale, romaine lettuce, etc.	2 servings
Other fruits and vegetables, including some with vitamin A e.g., carrots, winter squash, apple, etc.	1 serving

Breads and cereals
    1 slice whole grain bread
    ½ cup cooked cereal
    ¾ cup ready-to-eat cereal
    ½ to ¾ cup rice or pasta
	2–3 servings

Fats and oils
    Butter
    Margarine
    Mayonnaise
    Salad dressing
    Vegetable oil (not palm or coconut)
	2 1-tablespoon servings

Source: Adapted from Shapiro, H. I. (1984). *The pregnancy book for today's woman.* Mt. Vernon, NY: Consumers Union; and Olkin, S. K. (1987). *Positive pregnancy fitness.* Garden City Park, NY: Avery Publishing Group.

Equally important are the kinds of food a pregnant woman eats. The building of new tissues requires extra protein and folic acid (found in liver, legumes, and leafy green vegetables). Iron and calcium (found in milk products) are important for making blood

Issues & OPTIONS

cells and building bones. Vitamins are also important. Pregnant women should get the nutrition they need if they follow the guidelines shown in Table 3-2.

Should a woman exercise during pregnancy? Fifteen years ago it was unheard of for a pregnant woman to swim laps in a pool, play tennis, or engage in any form of exercise beyond daily chores. Today, however, as part of the general fitness trend, women are signing up for "pregnancy workouts" in increasing numbers. Physicians advise caution. Women who have a history of miscarriages, high blood pressure, diabetes, anemia, or other serious health problems should avoid exercise, as should women who did not exercise before they became pregnant. Given the trend, of course, more women *are* exercising before pregnancy, and they are often encouraged to continue—with warnings and qualifi-

ers. Exercises that involve jumping or bouncing (jogging, aerobic dancing) subject the fetus to too many jolts and are taboo for all pregnant women. Taboo also are exercises performed lying on one's back, which may press the fetus against the placenta, cutting off its supply of oxygen and nutrients. All women should watch for such danger signals as pain, palpitations, shortness of breath, and vaginal bleeding. On the positive side, exercises designed to improve breathing and posture, to stretch thigh muscles, and to strengthen pelvic muscles are generally a good idea and will help prepare the woman for childbirth.

Another decision most women face today is when to stop working. The right time depends in part on the job, in part on the woman. In the later stages of pregnancy, long periods of standing or sitting may be uncomfortable. But in most cases, a woman

can do whatever makes her happy. Some women work right up to the day of delivery; others feel they need time off from work to give their bodies and their minds time to prepare for the new arrival.

Is it safe for a woman to travel while she is pregnant? Travel does pose risks. If problems develop, a new doctor will not have quick access to her medical records. Air travel, jostling of the body, or prolonged sitting may bring on early delivery in a plane or a train, where no medical assistance is available. The risks are greatest during the period closest to delivery, so it is best to avoid travel during that time if possible.

What is the best age to bear children? Women who become pregnant while still in their teens are high-risk mothers-to-be. Babies born to mothers under age 15 are 2.5 times more likely to die

(continued)

Workouts that strengthen muscles help to prepare pregnant women for childbirth. *(Kathy Sloane)*

Issues & OPTIONS

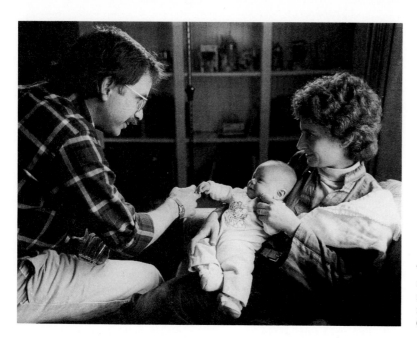

Today, many women are having their first child after age 30. With proper medical care, most have normal pregnancies and healthy babies. *(Elizabeth Crews/Stock, Boston)*

in their first year and more likely to have birth defects than are the babies of first-time mothers in their early twenties (U.S. Bureau of the Census, 1980). Poor outcomes for these births are likely because teenage mothers tend to be poor, single, undereducated, and otherwise socially handicapped. A teenage mother's ability to care for a child may also be limited.

At the other end of the female reproductive range are the increasing numbers of women who bear their first child when they are over age 30. Reports on delayed motherhood are mixed. Simply because they have lived longer, older women may be in poorer general health than are younger women. Older women are also more likely to have contracted infections that cause infertility and may have difficulty conceiving, especially after age 35. However, if a women in her thirties has a good health history, shows normal weight gain during pregnancy, and receives good prenatal care, the chances are that she will have a healthy, normal baby.

In short, there are only a few hard and fast rules for pregnant women. Women who are overwhelmed by sometimes conflicting advice from their physician, family, and friends, not to mention the mass media, might do well to follow a guideline posed by the ancient Greeks: Act in moderation.

TERATOGENS

In 1979, when the governor of Pennsylvania was told that something had gone wrong at the Three Mile Island nuclear power plant, his first act was to order the evacuation of all pregnant women and preschool children within a 5-mile radius. He did not yet know what had happened at the plant, but he was not taking any chances. Unborn children are exceptionally vulnerable, and they may suffer irreversible damage from exposure to substances that cause little or no damage to older children and adults.

The term **teratogen** (from the Greek, "monster-creating") refers to any substance, agent, or influence that causes malformation in the developing fetus. Many drugs, disease-causing viruses, and environmental agents such as chemicals and radiation fall into this category. Sometimes a teratogen causes physical or behavioral problems later in life.

A particularly tragic example of a teratogen is the drug **thalidomide**. In the late 1950s and early 1960s, physicians in 28 countries prescribed thalidomide for women who had problems with sleeplessness and nausea during the early months of pregnancy. The drug had been carefully tested on animals, with no side effects. The physicians and the drug company were confident that the drug was safe. Too late they discovered that thalidomide caused phocomelia, a physical malformation in which the arms and/or legs do not develop and the hands or feet grow directly from the body. Because their mothers had taken this drug, 8000 babies were born with serious malformations (Schardein, 1976).

In general, the effect of a teratogen depends on *timing*, on when during gestation the embryo or fetus is exposed. There are **critical periods** for the development of the various physical structures and organs—times when these structures are most vulnerable to teratogens. The structures or organs that are in the process of developing are most vulnerable; those that are already established are least likely to be harmed. Teratogens are generally most dangerous in the embryonic period, when the basic structure of the baby is developing. During this period, teratogens will often lead to spontaneous abortions. After this point, the effects may vary. Babies whose mothers had taken thalidomide between the 38th and 46th days of pregnancy were born with deformed arms or no arms; those whose mothers had taken the prescription between the 40th and 46th days of pregnancy had deformed legs or no legs; and those whose mothers had taken thalidomide after the 50th day of pregnancy displayed no effects whatsoever. Most of the infants with severe thalidomide defects did not survive for long.

Sometimes very serious effects of exposure to a teratogen during a critical period do not show up at all at birth. Fetuses who were between 8 and 15 weeks old when the atomic bomb fell on Hiroshima became mentally retarded. At the time of exposure, the fetuses were at a critical period for brain development. Older fetuses who had passed that critical period were at a much lower risk of developing retardation (Otake & Schull, 1984). The critical periods for the formation and development of different structures and organs are shown in Figure 3-3.

teratogen
any substance, influence, or agent that causes birth defects

thalidomide
a drug given to pregnant women in the late 1950s and early 1960s that caused serious birth defects

critical periods
periods during which particular developing organs and structures are most vulnerable to environmental influences

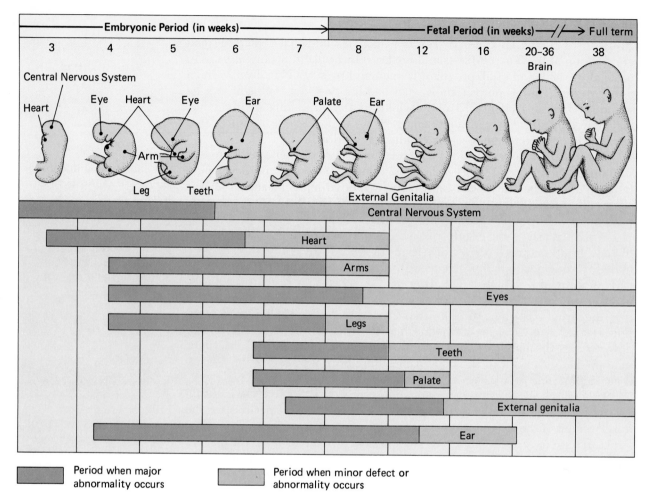

FIGURE 3-3
CRITICAL PERIODS IN THE DEVELOPMENT OF VARIOUS ORGANS, SYSTEMS, AND BODY PARTS
Each organ, system, and part has its own critical timetable in its development, and is most susceptible to disruption during that time. (*Source*: Adapted from Moore, K. L. [1982]. *The developing human* [3rd ed.]. Philadelphia: Saunders.)

Prescription and over-the-counter drugs

Even after the thalidomide tragedy, many prescription drugs still do not carry a warning to women who think they may be pregnant. Any drug the mother takes may pass through the placenta into the fetus's bloodstream. Drugs that may be good for the mother—such as the antibiotics streptomycin and tetracycline, or megadoses of certain vitamins—can be harmful to the fetus.

In some cases, a woman who is taking a drug has not discovered that she is pregnant. For example, a woman who is taking oral contraceptives may assume she cannot get pregnant. (She is wrong; no contraceptive is 100 percent effective.) Although not all studies find the same effects, there is some evidence that oral contraceptives increase the risk of spontaneous abortions and heart defects, especially if the woman also smokes (Carr, 1970; Grant, 1985).

In other cases, teratogenic drugs have delayed, or "sleeper," effects. **Diethylstilbestrol (DES)**, a synthetic hormone once given to pregnant women, is an example. Between 1945 and 1955 DES was frequently prescribed to prevent miscarriages. The drug worked, but it was later discovered that the daughters of mothers who took DES during pregnancy stood a high risk of developing vaginal problems and cervical cancer when they reached adolescence. Furthermore, when they sought to have children themselves, they were more likely than other women to have spontaneous abortions or premature deliveries (Sandberg, Riffle, Higdon, & Getman, 1981). These premature deliveries, in turn, increased the risks of a variety of developmental disorders in the *grandchildren* of the women who originally took DES.

In general, women should avoid all drugs when they suspect or know that they are pregnant, unless the drug is essential to their health. And they should be sure to inform a physician that they may be pregnant before taking any prescription or undergoing any medical procedures, including x-rays. Even aspirin, a drug many people use regularly, can be harmful to fetuses. Frequent use during pregnancy can result in lowered birth weight and increase risk of fetal or infant death both before and shortly after birth (Corby, 1978; Turner & Collins, 1975). Aspirin can also lower the IQs of children whose mothers used it often during their pregnancies. In one study, women who avoided aspirin but used its substitute, acetaminophen, did not put their children at risk (Streissguth et al., 1987). Acetaminophen, an easily available pain reliever, seems to pose no risk to fetuses, but even it should be used cautiously during pregnancy.

diethylstilbestrol (DES) a synthetic hormone given in the late 1940s and early 1950s to prevent miscarriages; found to affect daughters of women who took it

Illegal drugs and addicted babies

Even stronger cautions apply to illegal drugs, such as marijuana, heroin, and cocaine. It is often difficult to isolate the effects of a single drug, since women who use illegal drugs often use more than one, but a fair amount of evidence indicates that these drugs are very dangerous. Women should view marijuana use during pregnancy as hazardous; the drug may impair the fetus's central nervous system (Osofsky, 1987). Babies of mothers who use heroin are themselves addicted to the drug at birth. Heroin can be lethal for newborns: Their chances of surviving their first days or weeks are not good (Ostrea & Chavez, 1979). Those who live must be cured of addiction by gradually lowering their dosage. These babies go through withdrawal symptoms similar to those seen in adults: restlessness, sleeplessness, irritability, tremors, and convulsions (Fricker & Segal, 1978; Strauss et al., 1975). These symptoms make the infants "problem babies" who are difficult to feed, bathe, calm, or cuddle. The mother, finding interaction with her baby so unrewarding, may neglect or even abuse the child, and the child is likely to respond by becoming more difficult. A vicious cycle has been set in motion.

There is some evidence that cocaine endangers the pregnancy itself. Ira Chasnoff and his colleagues at the Northwestern University Medical School (1985) compared 23 women who were using cocaine regularly at the time they became pregnant to drug-free women and to women who had used heroin in the past and took methadone during their pregnancy. More than half of the women in the study group continued to take cocaine during their pregnancy.

The medical histories of the cocaine users revealed a much higher than average rate of spontaneous abortion. During the study, four of the women went into premature labor immediately after they had injected cocaine. Miscarriages were averted, but when tested shortly after birth, the cocaine babies had weak reflexes, did not focus their eyes for more than a split second, and were difficult to comfort. These findings suggest neurological problems. Two of the babies died in early infancy, and one was completely paralyzed on one side at birth. Women who consider themselves merely "recreational" users of cocaine may unknowingly risk their baby's health if they take cocaine before they realize they are pregnant.

Social drugs

The fetus does not distinguish between legal and illegal drugs, medications and libations. Scientists now know that alcohol and nicotine are teratogens, and, like heroin, they affect a child's *behavior* as well as physical development. Caffeine may also pose some risks.

Alcohol is the most widely used and easily obtainable drug in the United States. In recent years, evidence has mounted that both heavy and moderate drinking on the part of a mother may affect her child. Alcoholic mothers put their children at considerable risk for a range of problems. Alcohol crosses the placental membrane almost immediately, enters the fetal bloodstream, and remains there for a considerable period, depressing central nervous system activity (Landesman-Dwyer, 1981). In fact, babies of alcoholic mothers often suffer from **fetal alcohol syndrome** (**FAS**), a collection of troubling problems that includes

> Mental retardation, poor motor development, hyperactivity, and limited attention span
>
> Retarded growth, both before birth and throughout childhood, even with an adequate appetite
>
> Atypical facial appearance, including short eye slits, low nasal bridge, short nose, indistinct ridges between nose and mouth, narrow upper lip, small chin, flat midface, and drooping eyelids (Streissguth, Landesman-Dwyer, Martin, & Smith, 1980).

No one knows how common FAS is. Estimates range from 1 per 1000 live births in France, to 1 per 750 in the United States, to 1 per 600 in Sweden (Landesman-Dwyer, 1981).

Alcoholic mothers are not the only ones who are risking their babies' futures. New studies show that even "social drinking" has long-term effects on physical and behavioral development. Researchers have found that pregnant women who "only" drink a little wine or an occasional cocktail still have a higher-than-average risk of spontaneous abortion (Harlap et al., 1979; Warburton et al., 1979), stillbirths (birth of a dead fetus) (Kaminski, Rumeau, &

fetal alcohol syndrome (FAS)
group of symptoms, including cognitive, motor, and growth retardation, suffered by some children of alcoholic mothers

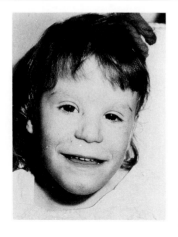

This child, with fetal alcohol syndrome, was born to an alcoholic mother. (*James W. Hanson, M.D., Professor of Pediatrics, Division of Medical Genetics, University of Iowa*)

Schwartz, 1978), and both major and minor birth defects (Oyellette et al., 1977).

One team of researchers observed newborns on their first day of life (Landesman-Dwyer, Keller, & Streissguth, 1978). Even after accounting for such factors as maternal smoking, infant birth weight, and the child's sex, they found that the amount of alcohol the mother had drunk during her pregnancy was related to increased body tremors, decreased alert periods, and less vigorous body activities in the infant. Other investigations indicate that these types of effects of prenatal exposure to alcohol continue at least through the early elementary school years. The developmental progress of infants, measured by standardized tests of mental and motor abilities, was somewhat related to the mother's consumption of alcohol (Streissguth, Barr, Martin, & Herman, 1980). When these children were 4 years old, those whose mothers had had one or more drinks a day during pregnancy had poorer attention spans, appeared more fidgety, and were less likely to comply with parental demands than were children of nondrinking mothers (Landesman-Dwyer, Ragozin, & Little, 1982; Streissguth et al., 1984). And at 7 years of age these children showed a shortened attention span (what psychologists call an *attention deficit*) which might compromise their ability to concentrate on class work and succeed in school (Streissguth et al., 1986). Because of these known effects of alcohol, the state of New York now requires bars to post a notice: "Warning: Drinking Alcoholic Beverages During Pregnancy Can Cause Birth Defects."

Evidence that *smoking* has harmful effects on the embryo and fetus began to build in the 1940s and 1950s. Today this evidence is overwhelming. Women who smoke increase their risk of spontaneous abortion or stillbirth by 30 to 50 percent, and even full-term babies of smokers typically have lower than average birth weights (Landesman-Dwyer & Emmanuel, 1979). These newborns may also be higher risks for what is known as **sudden infant death syndrome (SIDS)** (death for no apparent reason in early infancy—see the box on SIDS in Chapter 4).

sudden infant death syndrome (SIDS)
death in early infancy for no apparent reason

Like alcohol, nicotine has long-term effects on children's behavior. A longitudinal study of 12,000 British youngsters born in 1958 found that maternal smoking was associated with poor intellectual and social development at age 7 years (Davie et al., 1972), effects that increased with age (Butler & Goldstein, 1973). The Collaborative Perinatal Project, which followed 28,000 U.S. children from birth to age 7, confirmed these results and added that the *amount* the mother smoked during pregnancy was related to levels of hyperactivity at age 7 (Nichols, 1977). Over the long term, prenatal exposure to nicotine seems generally to undermine attention (Streissguth et al., 1984) and, indirectly, achievement (Kirchner & Knopf, 1974).

Many people who disapprove of alcohol and cigarettes think nothing of having a cup of coffee to increase energy, but the *caffeine* in coffee (as well as in tea, chocolate, and colas) is just as much a drug as the nicotine in cigarettes. Although caffeine does cross the placenta (Julien, 1981) and is found in the plasma and urine of newborns (Morris & Weinstein, 1981), there is no evidence at present that caffeine causes birth defects in human babies. New evidence suggests that the amount of coffee a woman consumes *before* she becomes pregnant can affect her child. Jacobson (1983) found that the more coffee a mother had consumed, the more likely that her newborn would be

Smoking during pregnancy increases the risk of spontaneous abortion and stillbirth. Low birth weight and long-term effects on behavior have also been observed. *(The American Heart Association)*

low in birth weight and alertness and high in arousal and irritability. Because of the lack of consensus among experts, the U.S. Food and Drug Administration now simply recommends that the safest thing for mothers-to-be is to reduce their caffeine consumption (FDA, 1980).

At this point some readers may balk. Perhaps you know women who have smoked occasionally, drunk socially, and never skipped their morning cup of coffee during pregnancy, yet nevertheless have had normal, healthy babies. But think for a moment. Would you blow smoke into an infant's face or add a little alcohol to his formula to make him giggly? Of course not. In effect, this is what a mother who uses these social drugs is doing to her fetus. Individual babies react differently to teratogens. Some are hearty by nature; others vulnerable. But perhaps the baby whose mother had wine every night before dinner, or just a few cigarettes each day, might have been less fussy, more cuddly, and more curious if the mother had abstained.

Diseases

Diseases contracted during or even before pregnancy can also act as teratogens. The placenta protects the fetus from most bacteria, but it cannot protect the developing baby from viruses.

Twenty-five years ago, the disease pregnant women feared most was **rubella**, or German measles. A mild disease for an adult, rubella has devastating effects on the fetus. If the mother gets this virus early in her pregnancy, her baby may suffer from mental retardation, heart defects, deafness, and blindness. Advances in immunology have all but eliminated this risk. A woman who has had German measles at any time before becoming pregnant has antibodies to the disease that prevent her from contracting it again. A simple medical test reveals the presence of rubella antibodies. Women who haven't had the disease can be vaccinated to stimulate the production of these antibodies, preferably at least 6 months *before* becoming pregnant. (The vaccine contains small amounts of the virus that will not make the mother sick but can harm a fetus.)

Some of the most serious risks to the fetus are posed by venereal, or sexually transmitted, diseases. The most common among these in the United States today is also the least well-known: **chlamydia**. Infecting between 3 million and 10 million Americans annually, this bacteria-caused disease can leave women sterile. If a pregnant woman contracts chlamydia, her fetus can become infected while moving through the birth canal. Conjunctivitis (an eye inflammation) or pneumonia can result. Chlamydia also increases the risk of prematurity and stillbirths. All these consequences can be avoided by diagnosis followed by treatment of chlamydia with specific antibiotics (Wallis, 1985).

Gonorrhea and **syphilis** respond to antibiotics as well, but with syphilis in particular, early detection is crucial. That is because, unlike other bacteria, the syphilis bacteria can cross the placenta and infect the fetus. But penicillin crosses the placenta too, killing the bacteria in the fetus. However, many people do not develop or recognize the symptoms of syphilis. If the disease is not detected, or if the pregnant woman contracts syphilis in the fourth month of pregnancy, the fetus may die. If it lives, the baby may suffer blindness, deafness, and/or other deformities. All these consequences are preventable if a man and woman are both tested for syphilis before conceiving a child. (Most states require a syphilis test before issuing a marriage license.)

Genital herpes, a sexually transmitted disease that infects up to 500,000 people each year, is caused by a virus and therefore cannot be treated with antibiotics. The disease may lie dormant for months, then suddenly erupt. Herpes does not affect a baby unless the infection is active at the time of delivery, when the baby may become infected as it passes through the birth

rubella
German measles

chlamydia
bacterial sexually transmitted disease that can harm fetus during birth

gonorrhea
sexually transmitted disease caused by a bacterium

syphilis
bacterial sexually transmitted disease that can cross the placenta

genital herpes
sexually transmitted viral disease that can infect infants during birth

canal. In some cases infection at delivery may cause a localized skin infection in the baby; in others, it may cause a more generalized infection, neurological damage, and even death (Nahmias et al., 1975; Peacock & Sarubbi, 1983). These problems can be prevented by delivering the baby by Caesarean section. Mothers who know or suspect they have herpes should inform their obstetrician so that he or she can check for active infections as birth approaches.

The gravest threat to unborn children is the lethal disease **acquired immune deficiency syndrome** (**AIDS**). AIDS in the United States is not confined to the homosexual community, as it once seemed to be. A woman who has intercourse with an infected man may contract AIDS. Moreover, the AIDS virus may lie dormant for years, producing no symptoms. The birth of children who have AIDS suggests that the virus crosses the placenta. In Chapter 15 we will discuss AIDS and protecting against its transmission in more detail.

Toxemia, or preeclampsia, is an illness that affects only pregnant women. The symptoms, which appear in the last trimester, include sudden weight gain due to water retention, protein in the urine, and high blood pressure. If untreated, the mother and fetus may die, or the baby may be severely brain damaged. This treatable disease underscores the importance of regular medical checkups for pregnant women.

acquired immune deficiency syndrome (AIDS)
a deadly viral disease that attacks the immune system; transmitted through body fluids

toxemia
illness affecting pregnant women, causing water retention, high blood pressure, and, if untreated, death

The Rh factor

A serious but treatable problem that may occur during pregnancy results not from a disease but from the mother's immune system treating the fetus's blood cells as if they were foreign bodies. The **Rh factor** is a protein produced by a dominant gene and found on the surface of red blood cells. Most people have the Rh factor—they are "Rh positive." Problems arise if the father is Rh positive but the mother is Rh negative (she does not have the Rh factor). This incompatibility does not affect a first child but may affect a second child. If the first child inherits the dominant gene, some of its Rh-positive blood cells cross the placenta into the mother's bloodstream just before or during birth, when the infant's blood normally mixes with its mother's. Her body reacts by producing antibodies to the Rh-positive cells. If a second child is also Rh-positive, the mother's antibodies, which remain in her bloodstream, cross the placenta and attack the fetal blood cells. If they are "successful," the baby may be born deaf or with cerebral palsy or may die. In the past, there was no way to avert this tragedy. Today, an Rh-negative mother can receive a vaccine 3 days after the birth of her first child; the vaccine prevents the formation of Rh antibodies in her blood and frees future pregnancies from the risks of Rh incompatibility.

Rh factor
protein found on red blood cells

Environmental hazards

Some hazards pregnant women and their physicians cannot control. Exposure to high levels of *radiation*, for example, causes lethal chromosome damage and cancer in unborn children. Studies conducted after atomic bombs were dropped on Hiroshima and Nagasaki in 1945 provide the horrible proof. Not one of the pregnant survivors who was within a mile of the blast gave birth to a live infant. Seventy-five percent of those within 4 miles of the explosion had miscarriages or stillborn babies, and many surviving infants suffered serious deformities and leukemia (Apgar & Beck, 1973). The effects on fetuses of the Soviet nuclear accident at Chernobyl in 1986 are still unknown. We do know that even low levels of radiation, such as dental x-rays, are risky, and pregnant women should avoid them.

Harder to avoid are the environmental teratogens that come from *industrial pollutants*. A tragic example of pollution hazards occurred in Japan in the 1950s. An industrial plant discharged mercury-laden waste into Minamata Bay, and the mercury rose in the food chain until it appeared in the large fish eaten by local residents, including pregnant women. Their infants suffered from extreme deformation and mental retardation along with other neurological impairments (Milunsky, 1977). Because of these dangers, the United States has set limits on the amount of mercury permitted in the U.S. food supply (Osofsky, 1987).

We have also begun to study the effects of another group of pollutants, PCBs. Researchers found subtle behavioral deficits in the babies of women who were exposed to low but chronic doses of PCBs (Jacobson, Jacobson, Fein, & Schwartz, 1984). The mothers had eaten salmon or trout from Lake Michigan two or three times a month. When tested at birth, their babies

Industrial pollutants can affect fetal development in ways that are still being discovered. *(Bruce Davidson/Magnum)*

showed poor muscle control and depressed responsiveness; at 7 months they scored below their age level on tests of visual recognition and interest in novel stimuli. As with other environmental hazards, how long these effects will last is not yet known.

Lead has long been known to be toxic to children and adults. We now know that it can damage an infant *in utero*. Infants whose umbilical cord blood showed higher than normal levels of lead consistently showed some slowing of mental development through age 2 (Bellinger et al., 1987). This finding is particularly disturbing because these children had been exposed to levels of lead previously considered safe. It may be that fetuses are particularly vulnerable to this teratogen.

THE MOTHER'S EMOTIONAL STATE

For many if not most mothers, pregnancy evokes mixed emotions. Periods of joyful anticipation alternate with periods of worry and doubt, and even dread is not uncommon. According to one survey, 87 percent of pregnant women worry about the health of their unborn child, 74 percent are scared about childbirth, and 52 percent fear losing their physical attractiveness (Light & Fenster, 1974). Even women who planned the pregnancy and eagerly awaited a positive test may be caught off guard by spells of depression and irritability.

Sontag (1941) was one of the first to warn that a woman's emotions could affect her pregnancy. Since that warning, other researchers have documented the causes and consequences of maternal anxiety (Carlson & Labarba, 1979). Anxious women are more likely to have pregnancies marked by pronounced vomiting, toxemia, and other problems. They have a higher risk of premature deliveries, and their newborns may be as nervous as they are—fidgety, irritable, and difficult to soothe (Carlson & Labarba, 1979). And the newborn's crying, squirming, and general resistance to mothering may reinforce the notion the mother fears most—that she is not competent to be a parent.

How can emotions influence the baby's development and postnatal behavior? How is the mother's anxiety transmitted to the fetus? One possibility is that anxiety may cause chemical changes in her body (increased adrenaline flow, for example) and that these chemicals may pass through the placenta to the fetus. Another possibility is that the same genetic factors that predisposed the mother to be anxious during pregnancy may also cause her baby to be irritable at birth. (The baby inherits nervousness from her.) A third explanation is that the environmental stresses that made her anxious (poverty, a poor marriage, no marriage, or other conflicts) may affect the baby as well. All three processes may be operating at once.

The best antidotes to maternal anxiety are support and information. An understanding and supportive mate, relatives and friends the woman (and man) can turn to for advice and humor, and a good relationship with her obstetrician or nurse-midwife can all ease anxiety. Similarly, concrete information about pregnancy, birth, and babies can allay many fears, especially for first-time mothers. We begin with these topics in the next chapter.

Summary

1. After a long period of gestation, humans are relatively immature at birth. Dependent on the care of others for many years after birth, we learn from and are influenced by our environment as we develop.

2. Prenatal development is divided into three stages or periods: germinal, embryonic, and fetal. In the germinal period (conception to 2 weeks), the zygote divides, becoming a hollow ball called a blastula in a matter of days. The blastula continues down the fallopian tube to the uterus, where it becomes implanted.

3. In the embryonic period (2 to 8 weeks), the life-supporting placenta, umbilical cord, and protective amniotic sac mature. The umbilical cord carries oxygen, water, and nutrients from the mother to the embryo and carbon dioxide and other wastes from the embryo. The placenta also protects against infection and produces hormones important to the childbearing process.

4. Also in the embryonic period, three distinct layers of cells differentiate and develop into the major organs, tissues, and structures of the body. Sex differentiation begins at about 6 to 8 weeks, under hormonal direction.

5. Differentiation completed, growth and maturation are the major tasks of the fetal period (8 weeks to birth). Behavior follows a predictable sequence, starting with reflexes and spontaneous movements; finally, rhythmic cycles—well-defined, alternating periods of rest and activity—develop.

6. The prenatal environment strongly affects fetal development. Maternal nutrition, for example, affects birth weight, prematurity, the development of the nervous system, and even social development.

7. Teratogens are substances that can cause malformation during fetal development or physical or behavioral problems later in life. Teratogens include certain prescription and over-the-counter drugs, addictive drugs, and social drugs; viruses and bacteria; and environmental toxins. A teratogen's effects depend mainly on when the fetus is exposed to it.

8. To prevent tragedies like those caused by thalidomide and DES, pregnant women should avoid all unnecessary drugs—whether legal or illegal. Heroin-addicted mothers can pass on their addiction to their babies, and maternal use of cocaine has been connected with miscarriages and neurological problems. Social drinking and smoking also pose risks to the fetus, and pregnant alcoholics expose their babies to the risk of fetal alcohol syndrome.

9. The consequences to the fetus of rubella can be prevented if the mother is vaccinated *at least* 6 months before conception. Sexually transmitted diseases can have severe effects on a fetus, but early treatment with antibiotics and precautions during birth can help to ensure fetal health. AIDS poses the gravest threat, as a woman who has this fatal disease can transmit it to her fetus.

10. Radiation and industrial pollutants such as mercury, PCBs, and lead, especially in large amounts, can cause severe birth defects.

11. A woman's emotional state may affect her pregnancy and her child. Highly anxious women can suffer from difficult pregnancies, and babies born to these women may be highly irritable. Body chemistry, genes, and environmental factors may all be contributing factors.

Key Terms

acquired immune deficiency
   syndrome (AIDS)

altricial

amniotic sac

blastula

critical periods

diethylstilbestrol (DES)

differentiation

ectoderm

embryonic disk

embryonic period

endoderm

fetal alcohol syndrome (FAS)

fetal period

germinal period

gestation

herpes

implantation

mesoderm

myelinization

placenta

precocial

Rh factor

rubella

sudden infant death
   syndrome (SIDS)

teratogen

thalidomide

toxemia

umbilical cord

villi

zygote

Suggested Readings

Hotchner, T. (1984). *Pregnancy and childbirth: The complete guide for new life.* New York: Avon. A talented and informative communicator comprehensively examines all aspects and options of pregnancy and birth, while providing a balanced presentation of the alternatives available.

Kitzinger, S. (1985). *Birth over thirty.* New York: Penguin. With more and more women bearing a child, even their first child, well into their thirties, this book fills a void by addressing the unique needs and concerns of older mothers. Risks associated with such pregnancies are discussed, and related conditions that lighten or reduce these risks are considered.

Nilsson, L. (1977). *A child is born.* New York: Delacorte Press. An outstanding photographer shares remarkable pictures of life in the making and life in the womb, along with clear descriptions of the genetics and biology of life.

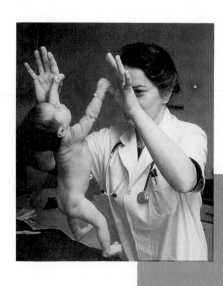

Birth and the Newborn

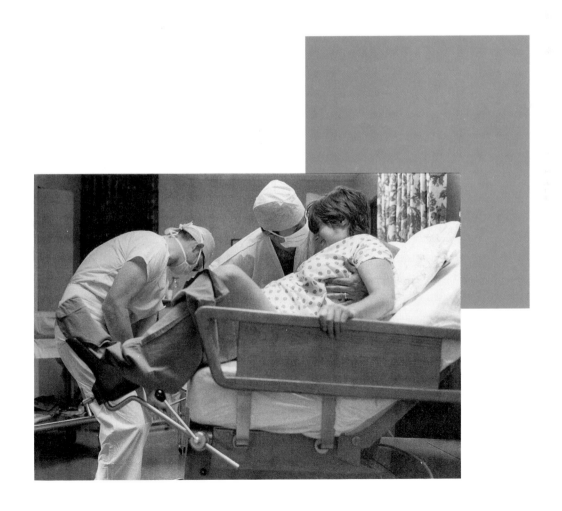

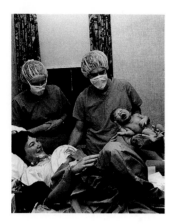

The moment of birth is like no other. Elated, amazed, and relieved, parents finally see the baby they could only imagine for 9 months. For newborns, the experience is wholly different, as they leave the protection of the uterus for the outside world. How this happens—how the fetus begins that journey with the first signs of labor, moving down the narrow passage of the birth canal, pushed along by the contractions of the uterus until a head and body emerge—is the subject of this chapter.

We will begin with the parents as they prepare for their infant's birth. Then we'll review the process of birth, from the earliest signs of labor to delivery. Next, we'll look at what newborns themselves bring to their first days to life. Infants' physical characteristics, behaviors, and capacities influence not only their own adjustment to life but how others respond to them as well. All babies adjust to life outside the uterus in ways that are both the same and different, and each infant's style marks the beginning of the "fit" between child and parents, as parents learn to "read" and react to their infant's personal signals. High-risk babies, born before their bodies are ready to support life outside the uterus, need their own kind of special care. We'll discuss some of the causes of premature births as well as the medical technology that can reduce the risks for many preterm infants.

Preparing for Childbirth

During the 1940s and 1950s, hospital childbirth was often a blur of pain and fear. When not left alone to labor in a featureless room with an impersonal hospital staff, women were placed with other laboring women whose anxieties and insecurities intensified their own. During the delivery itself many women felt like machines responding to the demands of doctors and nurses who seemed more interested in technology than in the baby or its mother. Four decades ago a woman might not even remember this much, as general anesthesia was thought preferable to the pain of giving birth. (The effects of ether on the baby were unknown at the time. See "Issues & Options" on choices for birth.) Many women awoke with a feeling, not of joy, but of loss, as if "their treasure had been stolen" (Simone de Beauvoir, cited by Kitzinger, 1972, p. 216).

prepared (natural) childbirth
childbirth without medication or anesthetics, based on relaxation techniques and psychological and physical preparation

But then came **prepared (or natural) childbirth**. This revolution changed not just hospitals, doctors, and deliveries but the whole experience of pregnancy for mothers as well as fathers. As one modern mother expressed it: "Giving birth was the greatest experience of my life! It was thrilling and fantastic to see our baby coming out of my body" (Marzollo, 1976, p. 97).

For many couples, information, preparation, and confidence have replaced fear and ignorance. Being prepared for childbirth means making knowledgeable choices that influence the pregnancy, the delivery, and even the relationship between mother and father.

CHILDBIRTH CLASSES

A booklet for prospective parents issued by a major New York City hospital begins this way:

> We believe that fear-reducing knowledge of what to expect in labor and delivery, in addition to breathing and relaxation techniques, are [sic] the greatest tools that a couple can have in labor. However, there may be a need for medication in labor or delivery, as no doctor can tell you . . . how long your labor will last or how it will feel. . . . Training and knowledge should enable you to have a more comfortable labor and delivery with less medication, but *do not set rigid goals for yourself*. . . . We hope that you will acquire the ability to be flexible, to enable you to apply what you have learned to your own childbirth experience. (New York Hospital, Cornell University Medical Center).

Childbirth classes prepare parents-to-be for the predictable and unpredictable in labor and delivery. Even though deliveries follow certain patterns, each, like the baby being born, is unique. Almost all obstetricians encourage childbirth preparation now, and women from widespread ethnic origins, socioeconomic levels, and geographic areas choose it (Wideman & Singer, 1984). Hospitals and medical personnel have become part of the team, with 99 percent of the hospitals in one survey allowing fathers to accompany mothers into the labor and delivery rooms (Wideman & Singer, 1984). In many hospitals, those rooms have become cheerful, pleasant places, featuring rocking chairs, sofas, and pastel colors. All these changes, in a relatively short time, stem from the work of two European doctors.

It was in 1933 that the father of prepared childbirth, an English obstetrician named Grantly Dick-Read, published *Natural Childbirth*, his method of relieving what he called the fear-tension-pain cycle. Dick-Read believed that

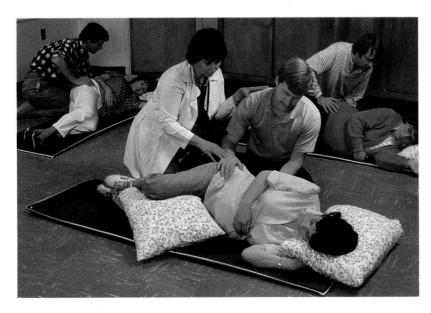

During Lamaze childbirth classes women learn relaxation techniques and men practice their roles as coaches. (*Joseph Nettis/ Photo Researchers*)

Issues & OPTIONS

Choices for Birth

With the advent of Lamaze classes and the philosophical shift to a family-centered birth experience, couples began to have many choices to make about their infant's birth. Some couples choose to deliver at home and avoid hospitals altogether. But since most modern hospitals are now more attuned to the medical and emotional needs of both infants and parents, the risks of home deliveries may outweigh the benefits. A hospital birth need not be a sterile, impersonal experience if couples choose an obstetrician or midwife compatible with their own needs. Many hospitals now offer homey birthing rooms, and rooming-in for newborns and mothers is a common practice. Women need no longer deliver on an operating table with their legs in stirrups; they can choose to use a birthing chair or a birthing position they find comfortable. But long before birth, a couple begins the decision process by selecting the people who will deliver their infant.

Obstetrician versus Midwife

Choosing between an obstetrician and a midwife for prenatal care and delivery is a relatively new phenomenon in the United States. Certified nurse-midwives are trained in prenatal care and delivery. They are usually affiliated with doctors, birthing centers, or hospitals so that they have access to more technical help if it is needed. Midwives can deliver babies either at home or in a hospital. Some couples feel that a midwife is more caring and supportive than an obstetrician, because a midwife is often more available throughout the pregnancy and for all of labor and delivery. An obstetrician may not have as much time to spend with each woman and, if in a group practice, might not be the one to deliver the baby. Obstetricians are trained to deliver babies through all types of medical emergencies, but not all possess the social and emotional skills that can elevate childbirth from a medical procedure into a joyous and fulfilling experience. Naturally, some physicians are more personable than others, and some midwives are less so. What is important for the expectant couple is to choose the person who can be most sensitive to their needs for both medical and personal attention.

Obstetrical Medication: Uses and Effects

Until the middle of the nineteenth century, there was no serious threat to the enforcement of the biblical edict: "In sorrow thou shall bring forth children" (*Genesis*, III:16). But on January 19, 1847, a Scottish obstetrician, James Young Simpson, used ether on a patient to relieve her pain during childbirth. Within 5 months of this successful experiment, ether was being used in

the fear of pain produced more pain. He reasoned that with the proper outlook and training, fear and tension could be avoided, pain reduced, and the need for medication—an unnatural requirement, he thought—eliminated. He educated his patients about what was to happen and was himself the support person he felt every woman should have to foster relaxation. His work was published in this country in 1944 as *Childbirth without Fear*, but this was only the beginning of the revolution.

Issues & OPTIONS

England, France, Ireland, Germany, and the United States (Brackbill, 1979).

Pain relief during childbirth has come a long way since then. Although few women having vaginal deliveries are put to sleep with ether, recent studies of newborns have found that many other forms of anesthesia have potentially harmful effects on the unborn, just delivered, and developing child. Infants whose mothers had received heavy and prolonged doses of a variety of anesthetics were found to have limitations in their motor abilities during their first year (Brackbill, 1979; Conway & Brackbill, 1970; Standley et al., 1974). Highly medicated mothers have to stimulate their infants more to nurse than do those exposed to minimal medication (Brown et al., 1975; Parke, O'Leary, & West, 1972). One English investigation found that babies born to medicated mothers were less involved in social inter-

action, and even at 1 year old these babies were picked up less frequently (Richards & Bernal, 1972).

Drugs can be problematical to an infant because they rapidly cross the placenta and enter the baby's system. The baby's liver and kidneys are still too immature to break down the drugs easily and eliminate them. Harmful effects of medication are related to the kind used, the size of the dose, and the duration of exposure. Risks to the infant are minimized if drugs are administered in small doses close to the time of delivery.

It is wise to discuss the matter of medication with an obstetrician before labor begins, but it is generally agreed that the smallest effective dose, or no anesthesia at all, is best for both the baby and the mother when circumstances permit (Yarrow, 1984). But all births are different, and labor can become lengthy, intense, and un-

expectedly complicated. When needed, medication should be regarded as an appropriate aid.

Rooming-in

Most hospitals offer daytime "rooming-in" privileges to the mother during her stay. This means that she can choose either to keep the baby with her in her room or to let the nursery staff take care of the baby in the nursery. Some women want their infants with them all the time. Other women need time to recover physically and mentally from labor and make the transition from pregnancy to parenthood. They can choose to let the staff take care of their baby for part of or all their hospital stay. Some hospitals have flexible policies so that a mother can be with her baby when she wishes and at feeding times and at other times let the staff care for the infant in the nursery.

In the early 1950s, Fernand Lamaze, a French obstetrician, made a trip to the Soviet Union where he saw that the Russians had developed a childbirth technique based on conditioning (see Chapter 1). Through conditioning, women were taught to relax instead of tensing up when they had a contraction. This allowed blood to continue flowing freely to the muscles, thereby reducing pain. Lamaze brought the method home. He modified it for his French patients, added *effluerage* (a light abdominal massage), and called the

Lamaze method
natural or prepared childbirth

package *accouchement sans douleur*, or childbirth without pain. The **Lamaze method** does not discourage the use of drugs when needed, but women who have prepared childbirth tend to report less pain than women in general (Rosenblith, 1985).

An American living in Paris, Marjorie Karmel, attended one of Dr. Lamaze's classes out of curiosity. Her own child was delivered by the Lamaze method, and in 1959 she published *Thank You, Dr. Lamaze*, which became a best-seller here. Karmel, through her book, is largely responsible for the popularity of prepared childbirth in the United States. The book found a receptive audience among women who wanted to have more control over their bodies than their mothers had had. And Lamaze's method attracted men who wanted to be more involved with their children than many felt their own fathers had been.

The now-commonplace Lamaze classes concentrate on five essential elements: information about anatomy and physiology; breathing techniques to match the contractions; conditioned relaxation; visual distraction (a picture from home, for example); and support from both the "coach" and the medical staff. The father's involvement as the mother's "coach" has in fact become one of the major appeals of Lamaze childbirth (Rosenblith, 1985). As the mother's coach, the father attends classes with her and helps during labor by timing her contractions, massaging her legs and back, and providing emotional support.

These techniques taught in the Lamaze classes have psychological as well as physiological benefits. So do the classes themselves. Being in a preparation class is a public expression of belief in the training, which reinforces that belief. Similarly, believing that it is possible to control the delivery process helps to make it so. Not to be underestimated either are the psychological pluses of sharing classes with other parents-to-be (Wideman & Singer, 1984).

FATHERS AND BIRTH

The father's role in childbirth is so accepted now that we forget how isolated men were from the process just 15 or 20 years ago. Today, men too are discovering the joy of childbirth.

> Then the glorious moment when the being was wholly released from the vagina. "It's a girl," I shouted, "It's a girl, honey." I was beside myself with joy. I had given birth along with my wife. It was glorious, just glorious. We are so very happy. This experience has made a bond between us that no [other] experience could have done. (Kitzinger, 1972, p. 212)

Another father recalled:

> I felt an overwhelming and thoroughly unique sensation that the moment of birth marked a new era in my life: fatherhood. I also felt an intense responsibility to the very small, defenseless person I had just met. (Marzollo, 1976, p. 97)

New fathers report that they enjoy just looking at and holding their babies. Many say that they can recognize their own babies in the nursery, and others talk of being drawn to the baby as to a magnet (Greenberg & Morris, 1974).

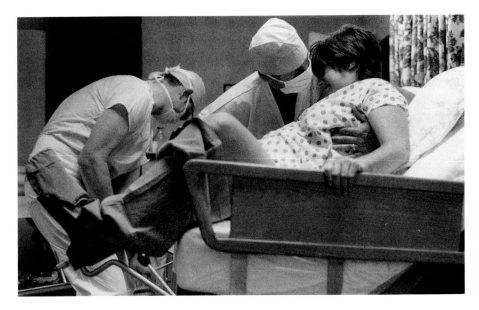

Not too long ago, fathers were excluded from the delivery room, but now, more family-centered hospital policies enable many to be with their wives during birth. (*Mimi Forsyth/Monkmeyer*)

Fathers' involvement with their newborns is sometimes called **engrossment**, a term denoting absorption, preoccupation, and interest in the infant (Greenberg & Morris, 1974). Engrossment may exist as an innate potential among all fathers, but it can be blocked by reservations about what it is manly to feel, by hospital procedures that close fathers out, and by mothers who are threatened by the father's interest.

engrossment
parental absorption in infant

Giving Birth

Few women give birth Hollywood-style—a sudden onset of intense labor pains, a reckless drive to the hospital, a just-in-time delivery. Usually, especially for first-time mothers, the term "labor" is very apt. Giving birth is a slow process, proceeding in definite stages. During each part of labor, a woman feels specific sensations and emotions as she and her baby work together toward birth.

Before the earliest signs of labor, the woman's cervix, the opening through which the baby will move from the uterus to the vagina, is closed. But at birth the opening in the cervix is 10 centimeters (over 4 inches) wide, big enough to allow a 6- to 8-pound baby to pass through. Labor is a process of dilation, or expansion, of the cervix. This slow, sometimes painful, process has but one goal: to allow the baby to move through the cervix, into the vagina, and out into the world.

THE SIGNS OF LABOR

For most women, the end of pregnancy is a mixture of expectation, excitement, and anxiety. Weekly visits to the obstetrician are full of questions: How much weight have I gained? How big is my baby? Is its heartbeat normal? What is its position? And finally, When will the baby be born? This last question can never be answered precisely, but there are signs indicating that birth is near.

One of the most significant signs is **engagement**, or **lightening**: The fetus moves into position for birth, low in the abdomen with its head very close to the mother's cervix. Some women experience engagement as long as 4 weeks before their baby's birth; others, especially those who have given birth before, may not feel it until labor actually begins. And for some, it doesn't happen at all. Not all fetuses get into position for a "classic" birth, and later in the chapter, we will discuss the exceptions. Let's look now at the way labor most often begins.

After engagement, increased discharges of vaginal mucus may occur, and pressure builds in the woman's pelvic region. Often the earliest sure sign of impending labor is the **bloody show**, the appearance of blood-tinged mucus on underwear or in the toilet. This mucus, which during pregnancy has formed a seal at the opening of the cervix, is dislodged as the cervix begins to *efface* (grow thinner) and dilate (open). The mucus is mixed with blood because when the cervix expels the mucus plug, small blood vessels around it break.

A few days before labor begins, the mother-to-be may find that her weight has dropped a few pounds and that she has pains similar to menstrual cramps. These early contractions, also called "false labor," may occur on and off until true labor begins. About this same time, she may notice that her baby is less active than usual. Full-term babies outgrow the uterus, leaving no room for kicking and wriggling. As the baby becomes less active, the woman may become more so. For some, lethargy gives way to a spurt of energy 1 to 2 days before labor begins.

Another sign of labor is the *breaking of the amniotic membranes*, known familiarly as "the breaking of the water." Inside the uterus, the fetus is surrounded by amniotic fluid, encased by the membranes of the amniotic sac. This fluid, which serves as a shock absorber for the baby throughout pregnancy, is commonly called "the water." As labor begins, the membranes may rupture, releasing the amniotic fluid. Without the protective seal of the amniotic membranes, the baby risks illness. A common virus or bacteria entering the vagina can now infect the unprotected fetus. To prevent this, the baby is generally delivered within 24 hours after the membranes break. (Occasionally, the amniotic membranes do not rupture spontaneously, even though labor is under way. The obstetrician or nurse-midwife will then rupture them mechanically.)

The clearest sign that labor is beginning—one that may occur *before* either the bloody show or the breaking of the amniotic membranes—is the onset of rhythmic contractions. **Contractions** are movements of the muscular walls of the uterus that push the baby down through the birth canal and ultimately out of the mother's body. The first contractions may feel like menstrual cramps, gas pains, backache, pelvic pressure, or other aches and pains. But as these pains begin to recur in a regular rhythm, and then become more and more frequent, the woman, with growing excitement and perhaps not a little dread, realizes that her baby is on the way. Figure 4-1 illustrates the stages of birth.

engagement (lightening)
movement of the fetus into position for birth

bloody show
blood-tinged mucus in a pregnant woman's urine or discharge, a sign of impending labor

contractions
movements of the muscular walls of the uterus that push the baby out of the mother's body

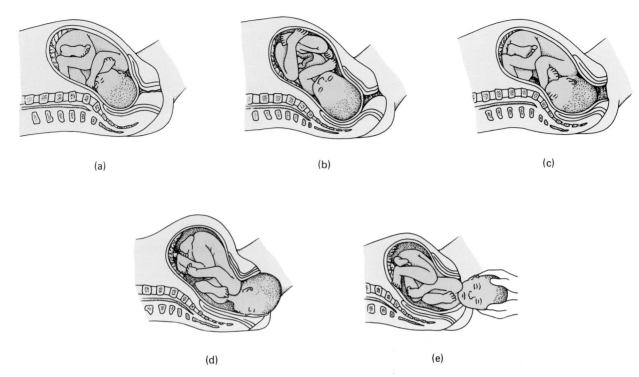

(a)　　　　　　　　　　(b)　　　　　　　　　　(c)

(d)　　　　　　　　　　(e)

FIGURE 4-1
THE STAGES OF A NORMAL BIRTH
(*a*) Engagement: The fetus's head is very close to the mother's cervix before labor begins; not all babies assume this position.
(*b*) Labor, first stage: Contractions increase and the cervix dilates.
(*c*) Transition: Contractions intensify and the cervix becomes fully dilated. The baby is positioned to enter the birth canal.
(*d*) Labor, second stage: The mother pushes and the baby moves through the birth canal, until the head emerges through the vagina.
(*e*) The baby is turned, easing the shoulders and the rest of the body out.

LABOR: FIRST STAGE

The first stage of labor is the longest, averaging 10 to 14 hours for first pregnancies. Several substages have been identified. In *early first-stage labor*, contractions occur at regular intervals. The cervix dilates to about 4 centimeters (approximately 1½ inches), and the amniotic membranes usually rupture. Although contractions may cause some pain in the back or abdomen, between contractions women may be quite alert and eager to sit up, walk, talk, or read.

During the middle of first-stage labor, contractions become stronger, longer, and closer together. The pain is more severe, and some women are given pain-killing medication. At the end of this substage, the cervix has opened to about 8 centimeters (over 3 inches).

The last part of the first stage of labor is **transition**. It is the shortest, most intense phase of the entire process, usually lasting for no more than an hour or two. But transition is also the most painful part of labor; it does not seem short to the woman experiencing it. During this phase the cervix opens to about 10 centimeters; contractions are frequent and strong. The urge to push

transition
end of the first stage of labor, with cervix fully dilated

the baby out begins, but if this urge comes too soon—before the cervix is fully dilated—pushing must be delayed. Premature pushing will only swell the cervix, narrowing the opening and delaying birth.

Because of the pain and the need to counteract the natural urge to push, a woman in the transition stage is usually very uncomfortable. The ordeal her body is going through may show itself in several ways: She may feel nauseated and need to vomit, she may belch or get the hiccups, she may sweat or feel cold, her legs may tremble or cramp. A woman in transition can become physically exhausted and irritable. It is a relief when the doctor says to begin pushing. Now the second stage of labor begins.

LABOR: SECOND STAGE

The second stage of labor begins when the cervix is fully dilated. Contractions can become less frequent now or even stop temporarily. Now the mother is told to push, and as she does, the baby moves through the birth canal. Soon the baby's head "crowns"—appears at the vaginal opening—and most obstetricians will perform an **episiotomy**. This is a surgical incision made below the vaginal opening (in the perineum) that allows the baby to emerge without tearing the mother's vaginal tissues. (The incision is stitched up following delivery.) Once the baby's head has passed through the birth canal, the baby is turned to ease out the shoulders. The rest of the body usually slips out easily. With the cutting of the umbilical cord, birth is complete.

For all those present at the delivery, the first cry of the newborn is a thrilling sound. Most mothers, exhausted though they may be from the long process of labor, find that cry and the first glimpse of their infant an exquisite moment of joy, amazement, and relief, unlike any other in life. Fathers, too, with their new place in the delivery room, can share this incredible moment.

LABOR: THIRD STAGE

The birth of the baby, though certainly the dramatic climax of the labor process, is not the end. The final stage is the delivery of the placenta, the all-important nourishing organ that has connected the baby to its mother during the months of pregnancy. The uterine contractions continue until the placenta, now detached from the uterine wall, is delivered. After this, the mother's uterus, which has expanded greatly to accommodate the growing child, begins shrinking back to its normal size. The doctor now sews up the episiotomy, if one was performed, and the mother is soon given her baby to hold and to nurse if she plans to breast-feed.

Gentle birth

Some have objected to the abrupt transition from the safety and quiet of the uterus to the bright, noisy world of the delivery room. Frederic LeBoyer (1975), a French obstetrician, suggested a softer way to come into the world.

For the LeBoyer method of gentle birth, the delivery room is kept quiet, quite warm, and semidark. The infant is laid on top of its mother's belly and gently massaged after birth. This massaging continues until the umbilical cord

episiotomy
incision made below vaginal opening during childbirth

As Carl Sandburg has written in his prologue to the classic photo essay, *The Family of Man* (1955), "The first cry of a newborn baby in Chicago or Zambowango, in Amsterdam or Rangoon, has the same pitch and key, each saying, 'I am! I have come through! I am a member of the Family!'" (*M. Richards/PhotoEdit*)

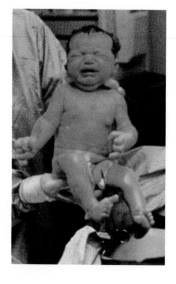

stops pulsating and the baby is breathing independently. At this point the cord is cut and the infant is bathed in warm water, a simulation of life in the uterus where the amniotic fluid cushions movement and muffles sounds.

LeBoyer believed this gentle entrance into the world would enhance the psychological and physiological future of the baby. Many physicians object to the LeBoyer method because a careful examination of the newborn is difficult to do in the dark. They also feel that the hospital works best with its own procedures. Many argue too that the very shock of the infant's arrival helps establish regular breathing. The one careful study comparing babies born by the LeBoyer method with babies born by conventional childbirth revealed no real differences in their birth experiences (Nelson et al., 1980).

PROBLEMS AND INTERVENTION

The labor and delivery we have described took place under ideal conditions. The fetus moved headfirst down the birth canal and through the vagina, emerging as a healthy newborn. Often, though, labor does not go so smoothly, and birth can be more complicated. Sometimes the fetus's own position causes the problem. In about 4 percent of vaginal deliveries the fetus is in the *breech* position, with the feet or buttocks pointing toward the cervix. Because **breech births** can be difficult, many obstetricians elect to deliver the baby by Caesarean section, as discussed below (Kitzinger, 1985). A fetus lying in a horizontal or crossways position in the uterus—this is called a **transverse presentation**—is blocking the cervical opening. The obstetrician will try to move the fetus into the head-down or the breech position, but if this fails, delivery will be by a Caesarean section.

Even when the baby is in the best position for birth, there can be complications. Labor may be delayed, if the baby is overdue, or too slow, if the mother's cervix doesn't dilate properly, or if contractions are too weak or too far apart. In either case, to prevent damage to the mother and/or baby, the physician may induce or attempt to speed up labor.

Inducing labor involves rupturing the mother's amniotic membranes, giving her medication, or both. To rupture the membranes, the doctor places a long, thin plastic instrument up the birth canal and gently pricks the membranes, a procedure that is quick and usually painless. Often **oxytocin** is used to speed a prolonged or delayed labor. This hormone produces uterine contractions or strengthens them if they are too weak or far apart.

A major source of concern during all deliveries is the prevention of **anoxia** or lack of oxygen in the fetus, a condition that can cause brain damage. Damaging anoxia may occur during an overly long or stressful labor if contractions repeatedly reduce the flow of blood to the fetus. With the help of a fetal monitor, doctors can anticipate the likelihood of anoxia and can act to prevent it. The **fetal monitor** is an electronic device that tracks both the fetal heartbeat and the pressure of the uterus during contractions. By fitting a beltlike device around the mother's abdomen, doctors can receive continuous data that sometimes signals trouble. If the heartbeat is weak, or if labor is progressing too slowly, doctors will often decide to intervene.

One method of intervention is the forceps delivery. Forceps are two pieces of metal, shaped like two large interlocking spoons, which the doctor

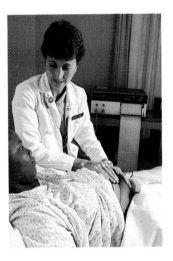

The fetal monitor tracks the rate of the baby's heartbeat and the strength of uterine contractions during labor. (*Charles Gupton/Stock, Boston*)

breech birth
birth in which the baby emerges feet or buttocks first

transverse presentation
condition in which fetus lies horizontally in the uterus

oxytocin
hormone given to induce or strengthen contractions

anoxia
lack of oxygen

fetal monitor
electronic device that keeps track of the fetal heartbeat and uterine pressure during childbirth

fits around the baby's head. Then, as the obstetrician pulls, the mother pushes, and the baby moves down the birth canal. Forceps deliveries entail their own risks, though. They may cause head injuries, resulting in permanent brain damage to the baby. For this reason, they are used less often than they once were. Now physicians are more likely to use a vacuum extraction tube which pulls or "sucks" the baby out. Most often this happens when the monitor indicates true fetal distress or when the fetus's head is too large to pass through the mother's pelvis. Under certain conditions, physicians will perform a Caesarean delivery.

Caesarean deliveries

Caesarean section
surgery in which the uterus
is opened and the baby
lifted out

In the **Caesarean section** (or C-section), the surgeon makes an incision in the mother's abdomen through to the uterus, suctions out the amniotic fluid, and lifts the baby from the uterus. Although this procedure has been known since ancient times, until fairly recently it was considered a last resort—a desperate attempt to save the life of the baby, the mother, or both. But the development of antibiotics (to fight infection), safer anesthesias, and fetal monitoring have made C-sections much more common. While the rate in 1968 was 5 percent (Donovan, 1977), in 1985 C-sections accounted for 10 to 15 percent of all births, and in the United States, some hospitals have been reporting a rate of 25 percent or more Caesarean deliveries (Kitzinger, 1985).

In part, this steep rise has resulted from more frequent use of fetal monitoring, and no doubt many Caesarean deliveries have prevented brain damage or even infant deaths. But a good many Caesareans may also be performed for other reasons. With advanced technology has come an expectation for perfection; and in recent years, malpractice suits have become much more common. This means that if an infant is born defective, parents are more likely to sue the obstetrician. In such a climate, many doctors are performing Caesareans sooner than they might have in the past, to protect not just the infant, but themselves.

The First Hours

vernix
slippery substance that coats
the newborn

"I was surprised how ugly newborn babies are!" (Marzollo, 1976, p. 97). The newborn's "ugliness" comes from the rigors of birth itself. Passing through the narrow birth canal can flatten and elongate the baby's head, and pressure on the face can bruise and distort the nose, cheeks, and eyes. And the **vernix**, which protected the skin from becoming waterlogged in the uterus, now appears as a sticky-whitish coating. Some babies have hair on their body as well as on their head, and many are completely bald. After a few days, the baby's head becomes more rounded and the marks of passage begin to fade. With vernix gone, skin is smooth, and the hair, or lack of it, begins to seem more natural. What matters far more than appearance at birth, of course, is the baby's ability to survive outside the uterus.

SURVIVAL: THE FIRST CHALLENGE

At the moment of birth the infant's physiological systems undergo a series of radical changes. Before birth the fetus received oxygen, along with all other necessary nutrients, from the placenta. Now the lungs and circulatory system must function independently, and the mother's 98.6-degree body temperature is abruptly replaced by an environment of about 72 degrees. Space changes too: Suddenly freed from the confinement of the uterus, the baby can move freely.

The Apgar score

The baby's transition to life outside the uterus is evaluated almost immediately after birth by the **Apgar test**, a series of observations made by delivery room nurses or doctors. Named for Dr. Virginia Apgar, who developed it, this test evaluates the baby's transition to a biologically separate existence in five crucial areas: heart rate, breathing, muscle tone, reflex irritability, and color. Each of these functions is rated (0, 1, or 2), and the five-figure total gives the *Apgar score* (see Table 4-1). An Apgar of 10 denotes excellent condition in all five areas. The test is given twice: first when the baby is 1 minute old, and again 5 minutes after birth.

    The Apgar score was designated to identify newborns who need special assistance, either immediately or during the first few days of life. A total score in the 7- to 10-point range is considered normal; the 4- to 6-point range is poor, and the 0- to 3-point range is considered dangerous. Because the newborn's condition is evaluated at both 1 and 5 minutes after birth, the *change* in score may also be very meaningful. One of the authors of this book, for example, had a son born quite pale and not breathing. His first score was 6, but within seconds, after being massaged by a doctor, he began breathing and "pinked up." His second score was 9. This kind of change signals the medical staff that the baby's own internal systems have taken hold. A second low Apgar would have called for immediate medical intervention.

Apgar test

test that measures a baby's heart rate, breathing, muscle tone, reflexes, and color immediately after birth

---

TABLE 4-1   CRITERIA AND SCORING OF THE APGAR TEST

Score	A Appearance (Color)	P Pulse (Heart Rate)	G Grimace (Reflex Irritability)	A Activity (Muscle Tone)	R Respiration (Respiratory Effort)
0	Blue, pale	Absent	No response	Limp	Absent
1	Body pink, extremities blue	Slow (below 100)	Grimace	Some flexion of extremities	Slow, irregular
2	Completely pink	Rapid (over 100)	Cry	Active motion	Good, strong cry

Source: V. Apgar. (1953). A proposal for a new method of evaluation of the newborn infant. *Current Research in Anaesthesia and Analgesia, 104,* 419–428.

While the Apgar is a good index of immediate postnatal risk, this test is much less useful in predicting individual differences in later infancy or childhood. Many babies come through difficult deliveries, have poor Apgar scores, seem dangerously feeble in their first days, and then develop into normal babies and children.

FIRST CONTACTS WITH PARENTS

In some species the mother and her offspring *must* be together immediately after birth or a bond ensuring proper maternal care does not form. Do humans have the same need? Is early contact between human mothers and their babies essential for forming a strong mother-infant bond? This question seemed particularly important in the days when many hospitals were separating mother and baby minutes after birth, keeping them apart for most of their hospital stay.

To gain insight into the effects of this practice, Kennell and Klaus (1976) identified two groups of mothers. The control group followed the usual routine—"a glance at their baby shortly after birth; a short visit six to twelve hours after birth for identification purposes, and then 20- to 30-minute visits for feeding every four hours during the day" (Kennell et al., 1974). The other group had their babies with them for approximately an hour shortly after delivery and for several hours each day thereafter. When the researchers observed the two groups, both in the hospital and in several follow-up sessions, they concluded that the mothers who had more contact with their babies

Whether or not babies need to bond with their parents right after birth is controversial, but spending time with their newborn is undeniably a joyous time for parents. (*Beringer/ Dratch/The Image Works*)

seemed more "motherly" as long as a year later. These mothers looked at, fondled, and picked up their babies more often than those in the control group (Klaus et al., 1972).

These initial findings have been disputed. Several researchers tried to reproduce the results of Klaus and Kennell's early experiment and failed (Gewirtz, 1979; Grossman, Huber, & Wartner, 1981; Svejda, Campos, & Emde, 1980). And critics have noted that many people studying bonding are strongly biased in favor of immediate and sustained contact between mother and newborn, perhaps making their research unreliable (Belsky & Benn, 1982; Lamb & Hwang, 1982). Probably the best way to sum up the conflicting research is to say that early contact between *some* mothers and infants may *sometimes* enhance the bond between them (Lamb & Hwang, 1982).

The debate over bonding has had several consequences. On the positive side, hospitals and medical staff have become more sensitive to the needs of mothers—and fathers—to spend time with their new babies. Many mothers now opt for rooming-in arrangements (see "Issues & Options"), and fathers now participate in the birth process.

On the negative side, the emphasis on early mother-infant contact has made many mothers and fathers of high-risk babies (those with medical problems, who must be taken to the intensive-care nursery) wonder whether their babies will suffer from the isolation. These parents fear that their children's emotional health may be damaged without the immediate experience of loving physical contact. Psychologists now believe that a warm and loving family environment when the baby comes home from the hospital is more important than a few hours or even days of close contact between mother and baby in the hospital. There are indications that premature infants in incubators get a developmental boost from extra stimulation and physical contact, but close early contact between a mother and a full-term baby does not seem to be crucial to the child's normal development or to the establishment of a maternal bond.

Behavior Patterns in Newborns: The First Days

A newborn's first days are usually marked by physiological instability: There can be random changes in skin color and body temperature, rounds of hiccuping and vomiting, intervals of irregular breathing. All these are adjustments to life outside the uterus, and they normally disappear within a few days.

Crying, however, continues. The average newborn sleeps about two-thirds of every day and cries from 4 to 15 minutes out of every hour (Korner et al., 1985). Crying may be unpleasant for parents, but it is very valuable to infants. Able to do so little for themselves, infants' very lives depend on getting help. And crying, the distress signal that the long course of evolution has built into the human repertoire, ensures that they can seek the help they need.

FOCUS ON   *Soothing a Colicky Baby*

Usually, satisfying an infant's need for food, sleep, comfort, or stimulation will stop her crying, but when a baby has colic (intestinal spasms), nothing seems to work. Actually, there are several techniques to try. A parent or caregiver should stay with each technique long enough to give it a chance before trying another.

Pick up a crying baby quickly. This won't "spoil" an infant; in fact, babies who are picked up quickly tend to cry less at 1 year.

Carry or rock the baby. Continuous rocking in a back-and-forth pattern works best.

Soothing sounds. Despite advertisers' claims, teddy bears with built-in tapes of human heartbeats or sounds from the womb are not as effective as an old-fashioned lullaby sung by a parent or another loving adult. Soft music works too; let the baby's preference decide which to use.

Use a pacifier. Babies like to suck, and a pacifier is often very soothing. Infants send their own signals when they want extra sucking, including hand biting and yawning, and a pacifier can be tried at those times. The best time to offer a pacifier is after feeding, before crying begins.

Swaddling. During the first month, swaddling, or snugly wrapping an infant in a soft, thin blanket can help infants cry less and sleep more.

Massage. A relaxed baby doesn't cry, so massaging babies before their usual crying time can prevent crying. Specific techniques can be found in infant-care books.

Finally, if even these methods don't work, distressed parents should seek relief for themselves. Babysitters or relatives can provide necessary time away from the stress of a colicky infant. It is much easier to care for a difficult baby if parents are relaxed themselves.

INTERPRETING CRIES

A baby's cry is a distress call, signaling the need to be held, turned over, changed, or soothed. For some newborns, the pitch of the cry itself signals trouble.

Seriously brain-damaged infants and babies suffering from nervous system disorders have cries that sound different from those of healthy infants (Wasz-Hockert et al., 1968). Down syndrome infants, for example, have a low-pitched, hoarse, gutteral cry. Newborns sick from oxygen deprivation (asphyxia), meningitis, or hypoglycemia have an extremely high-pitched cry (Zeskind & Lester, 1978). Now researchers have found that the cries of infants whose biological risk is less obvious *also* differ, in duration and pitch, from otherwise healthy infants (Lester & Zeskind, 1982; Zeskind, 1983). The unusual cry seems to be a subtle index of an underlying central nervous system problem and may be a signal for early medical intervention.

Once a baby goes home from the hospital, a high-pitched or unusual cry will affect the way parents respond. In the best case, such a cry brings special care from parents, care that can promote normal development. But some parents may find their baby's cry so unpleasant that they avoid, or even abuse, the infant. Ultimately, the effect of the unusual cry depends on the way parents respond. Cries, in fact, form one part of the first communications system between parent and child, and when a parent learns to read an infant's cry, both are gratified. Failing to quiet a crying baby can be discouraging, especially when the baby has colic. Colicky babies are not ill, but they cry for long stretches of time, sometimes for hours. Parents who have "tried everything" to comfort their infant can begin to feel resentful and angry. Some may even stop properly caring for their baby, and in extreme cases, they may become abusive. How can parents or other caregivers soothe a baby who won't stop crying? In "Focus On," we offer several strategies.

REFLEXES

A **reflex** is a motor behavior that is not under voluntary control. Stroke a newborn's cheek with your finger or a nipple, and she will turn her head toward the stroke, open her mouth, and begin sucking. This is the *rooting* reflex. Put your finger on her palm, and the baby will clutch your finger tightly, a reflex called the *Palmar grasp*. These responses are two of the reflexes with which all healthy babies are born. (See Table 4-2.)

Some of the reflexes we are born with, such as blinking and sneezing, remain throughout life, but others are present only during infancy and disappear at predictable times. (Many of these reflex actions reappear later, under

reflex
motor behavior not under conscious control

TABLE 4-2   SELECT LIST OF NEWBORN REFLEXES

Reflex Name	Stimulus	Description of Reflex	Age of Disappearance
Rooting	Stroke cheek with nipple or finger	Head turns toward stroke; mouth opens; sucking begins	2 to 3 months
Moro	Sudden loud noise; head is dropped a few inches	Arms extend outward from body; then brought toward each other; back arches	6 to 7 months
Palmar	Rod or finger pressed against infant's palm	Infant's fingers close around and grasp object	3 to 4 months
Babinski	Sole of foot, on the side, is gently stroked from heel to toe	Toes fan outward and foot twists inward	By end of 1st year
Sucking	Finger inserted into mouth	Sucking	(Persists)
Stepping	Baby held under arms to support in upright position; bare feet flatly touch surface	Rhythmical stepping movements	3 to 4 months
Placing	Top of foot rubbed	Foot withdrawn	3 to 4 months

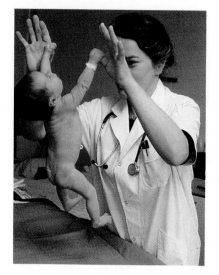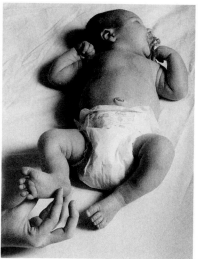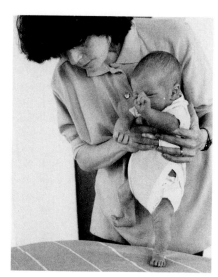

The Palmer, or grasping, reflex allows a newborn to hold on tightly. Toes fan out in the Babinski reflex when an infant's foot is stroked, and a 9-day-old baby demonstrates the walking reflex. (left to right: *Petit Format/J. da Cunha/Photo Researchers; Spencer Grant; Elizabeth Crews/The Image Works*)

conscious, higher-brain control.) Physicians look for reflexes at birth and during routine office visits to assess neurological development. If the reflexes are missing at birth, or present for longer than they should be, a neurological problem may exist.

The newborn reflexes that most often surprise new parents are the *stepping* and *placing* reflexes that make the infant appear to walk. Although these reflexes seem to disappear at 3 months, immersing the lower part of the infant's body in water elicits them again (Thelen, 1984). The legs, though heavier by 3 months, are light enough in water to "walk" reflexively once more.

The function of many reflexes seems to be protective: A blinking eye is less easily hit or poked, gagging prevents choking, and sneezing clears the nose and throat. And both the *sucking* and *rooting* reflexes may be built-in aids for survival, enabling infants to nurse soon after birth.

The Palmar grasp and the *Moro*, or startle, reflex enable infants to cling for support. These behaviors may have originated in our primate ancestors, and we can still see them among young monkeys and apes, who cling tightly to their mothers.

STATES OF AROUSAL

states of arousal
varying levels of energy, attention, and activity

Most of us are aware that our moods and energy levels vary from time to time. We feel energetic, lethargic, anxious, or excited depending on our physical or emotional state. Newborns, too, experience different levels of activity and mood. We call these **states of arousal**. Some newborns sleep through much of the night, take long naps, and perhaps even doze off while nursing. Others sleep less and cry for much of the time they are awake. The six states of arousal, from sleep to crying, are listed in Table 4-3. How much time babies spend in one state or another is so individual that parents cannot predict, until they know their infant well, what state to expect next.

TABLE 4-3 INFANT STATES OF AROUSAL

State	Description
Regular sleep	Eyes remain closed and the body shows no movement. Breathing tends to be slow and regular, and the face remains relaxed (no grimaces or eyelid movements).
Irregular sleep	Eyes remain closed, yet rapid eye movements can be noted periodically. Respiration tends to be irregular, grimaces and other facial expressions can be seen, and gentle limb movements are observed.
Drowsiness	Relatively inactive state, with eyes opening and closing intermittently. Breathing is faster than during sleep, but regular. Eyes are dull or glazed when they do open.
Alert inactivity	This is the state for testing newborns. Eyes are open, bright, and shiny. Activity is limited, face relaxed.
Waking activity	Movements are uncoordinated and usually involve the whole body. Breathing is highly irregular. Eyes are open, though not alert.
Crying (distress)	Vigorous activity and grimacing occurs along with crying.

Source: Wolff, P. (1966). The causes, controls, and organization of behavior in the neonate. *Psychological Issues*, *5*, (1, Whole No. 17).

States of arousal influence not just infant behavior and responsivity but parent behavior as well. When infants are in the "alert inactive" state, they are most able to interact with others, and this is also when parents find them most engaging. In the first few days of life, however, infants spend very little time in this quiet, alert state. Sleeping occupies almost two-thirds of their time, and parents who try to play with a drowsy baby may soon have a crying one. The quiet, alert state is usually only a brief transitional zone between sleep, fussing, and feeding (Hofer, 1981). Parents who pay close attention to their infant's level of arousal eventually learn what kinds of stimulation cause distress, what kinds are welcome, and when.

How parents respond to their baby's dominant state of arousal is influenced by their own needs and temperaments. A quiet, sleepy baby may be ideal for the mother tired from a long labor, but a disappointment to an energetic, eager mother who wants a more active infant. And the parent who considers noise a form of healthy self-assertion may take pride in a baby who frequently fusses and screams. When the "fit" between baby and parents is right, both will thrive. In Chapter 7 we'll look closely at the mother-infant fit, what influences it, how it can change, and how important it is for the growing baby.

During the "alert inactive" state, newborns are relaxed, wide-eyed, and at their most engaging. (*Kasz Maciag/The Stock Market*)

Brazelton Newborn Behavioral Assessment Scale test evaluating newborn's state control, sensory capacities, reflexes, and motor abilities

THE BRAZELTON SCALE: ASSESSING INDIVIDUAL DIFFERENCES

A week to 10 days after birth, many babies are tested on the **Brazelton Newborn Behavioral Assessment Scale**. Devised by the prominent pediatrician T. Berry Brazelton, the scale assesses the baby's states of arousal and respon-

state control
tendency of newborns to shift from one state of arousal to another

sivity, as well as reflexes. Test results can help a physician, psychologist, or nurse assess the baby's capacity for interaction (Brazelton, 1978).

These insights can help parents respond appropriately to their infant's individual needs. One aspect of behavior the Brazelton scale evaluates is **state control**. State control, for example, is the ability of newborns to shift from one state of arousal to another in response to either internal or external stimulation. Some newborns can make the transition on their own—they can soothe themselves if they start crying. Others require intervention through touching, talking, or rocking. Some babies are visually responsive—they attend to a brightly colored ball moved across their line of vision—while others are more attentive to a voice. Some babies are prone to startle, while others simply pay attention to a bell rung near their ear.

Besides testing responsiveness, the scale also assesses the baby's motor abilities. Her legs and arms are gently moved away from her body and then released to see if they spring back or remain extended. The baby may also be raised to a sitting position to see how she holds up her head. Finally, some 20 reflexive behaviors are assessed, including sucking, rooting, walking, and crawling.

Although the Brazelton examination helps to discern differences among babies and gives parents clues to their baby's needs, it is *not* a good predictor of future development. One reason is that an infant's behavior changes dramatically during the early days of life. Scientists are now trying to understand if the pattern of change could itself be predictive of later development.

The Competent Infant

Human babies, unlike the young of most species, are relatively helpless at birth. They cannot forage for food, crawl into a burrow for shelter, or run from their enemies.

Being born "early," human babies do much more of their developing outside the uterus, in a world rich in sights, sounds, smells, textures, and tastes. A hard-headed, better-developed baby could not fit through the human birth canal. It is advantageous or adaptive, then, for human infants to be born small and immature, with a still-pliable skull. It is also intellectually advantageous. During the early years of life, while their bodies are developing, babies' brains are being stimulated by other people; by objects; by interesting sights, sounds, and smells. Babies can benefit from this unique early exposure to the outside world, if they begin life with some capacity to sense, to perceive, and to act. How well developed are the newborn's senses? How does the newborn-adult interaction help ensure the infant's survival? And what kinds of learning are infants capable of?

THE NEWBORN'S SENSES

Newborns' senses function far better than we once thought. Indeed, research data of the past two decades has led psychologists to speak of "the competent infant" (Stone, Smith, & Murphy, 1973).

Vision

A newborn baby looks out at the world through a blur. With eyes that test 20/600, a baby's vision is about 30 times worse than that of most adults. But by the age of 6 to 12 months, **visual acuity**, or clarity, has improved to 20/20 (Cohen, DeLoache, & Strauss, 1979). Even with only 20/600 vision, however, the newborn can see a good deal, especially at about 1 foot away from the face.

When a newborn looks at you, one eye may seem aimed at you, while the other seems to stare fixedly at the baby's own nose. At times the eyes will rove in different directions, only to roll back into a cross-eyed gaze. The capacity to focus both eyes on the same object, known as **binocular convergence**, will emerge later, but even from birth, infants can distinguish light from dark and respond to brightness and movement. They can follow a slowly moving object that is between 6 and 13 inches away, although their tracking is jerky and they often lose the object. By about 2 months their eyes can smoothly follow moving objects (Aslin, 1981).

Newborns like to look at some things much more than others: They seem to prefer objects with fairly complex shapes, contours, and details to objects that are flat and plain, and patterns attract them more than solid colors do (Fantz, 1963; Milewski, 1976). Parents can enrich a baby's environment with colorful shapes and interesting patterns, but they need not overdo it. No one wants to be stimulated all the time; in fact, too much stimulation can upset the infant.

Researchers have found that infants' visual behavior is predictable (Haith, 1978):

1. Awake and alert infants will open their eyes.
2. Even in the dark, infants seek something to focus on.

visual acuity
clarity of vision

binocular convergence
ability to focus both eyes on the same object

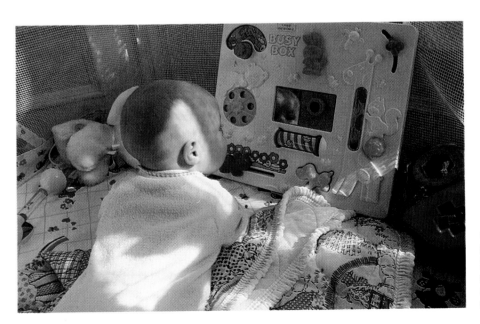

When they aren't sleeping, eating, or crying, infants like to look at patterns and complex shapes. This toy stimulates without overdoing it. (*George Goodwin/Monkmeyer*)

3. When they find something light enough to see, infants will look for outlines distinguishing that shape from its background.
4. Once infants see an outline, they will focus on it but also look around it—thus "holding their place" while exploring new sights.

These "rules" are interesting to psychologists because they suggest that infants are motivated to learn about their world and that they have inborn strategies for seeking out information.

Hearing

Human fetuses can hear even before they are born. By the gestational age of 32 weeks, fetuses respond differently to different sounds. A loud crash or boom on a movie sound track may startle both the expectant mother and the fetus as the mother sits in the darkened theater. Immediately after birth, infants may not hear well because their ears are often filled with fluid. But within hours they can react to all major aspects of sound, including pitch, loudness, and rhythm (Eisenberg, 1970).

Hearing, like vision, gets sharper in the first months of life. Although newborns don't hear very soft sounds, this ability increases over the first year (Schneider, 1986; Weier, 1974). A newborn's ability to orient or locate the source of a sound is also better than we once thought. If conditions are right, a newborn can turn and look in the direction of the sound. Short blasts from the stereo won't do it. What turns a newborn's head is a prolonged sound—a *voice*, not a tone. The baby's position is also important: If, at the same time the voice can be heard, the infant is held upright, she'll turn toward the sound (Chun, Pewsat, & Forster, 1960; Muir et al., 1979). Interestingly, babies often seem to "lose" this skill of **sound localization** during their first 2 or 3 months, only to regain it again at 4 months. Why this ability declines only to recover later remains a mystery (Aslin et al., 1983), although it may well have to do with neurological reorganization and a shift in control from lower to higher brain areas.

Infants prefer some sounds to others. Low-frequency sounds get more attention than high-frequency sounds (Eisenberg, 1970), and sounds pitched within the range of the human voice are especially favored (Webster, Steinhardt, & Senter, 1972). This, together with the evidence that newborns are likely to turn toward a voice, suggests that humans may be born with the ability to pay attention to the human voice and human speech. With such sensitivity to speech sound, babies soon learn to tell one voice from another. Even 3-day-old infants who listened to recordings of two voices discerned and preferred their own mothers' (DeCasper & Fifer, 1980). Right from birth, infants' senses help them learn.

Smell and taste

The newborn's sense of smell is sharp. An infant's ability to distinguish different odors begins to develop during the first 3 days of life (Self, Horowitz, & Paden, 1972). Once fully functional, the sense of smell remains relatively constant throughout life, unlike vision and hearing, which tend to decline more

sound localization
ability to locate the source of a sound

markedly in old age (Rovee, Cohen, & Schlapack, 1975). But like vision and hearing, smell is a built-in tool for learning, and even a newborn can use it effectively. In experiments, 6- to 10-day-old infants were exposed to breast pads worn by their own mothers and to pads worn by other mothers. These newborns spent more time turned toward the pads of their own mothers, presumably because they were able to recognize her distinctive smell (Mac-Farlane, 1975). Further research indicates that the ability to recognize the mother's smell is particularly acute in breast-fed (as opposed to bottle-fed) babies, probably because of the extra time spent close to mother's naked breast (Cernoch & Porter, 1985).

If a sense of smell helps newborns find their mothers, taste too seems adapted for survival. A baby's first food, breast milk, is a very sweet liquid. Babies seem to prefer sweet liquids; generally, the sweeter, the better (Desor, Maller, & Greene, 1977). In one study, infants actually smiled after tasting sweet liquids but pursed their lips in response to sour tastes (Steiner, 1977). Considered together, these discoveries suggest that from very early in life, humans prefer sweets. This preference probably stems from our evolutionary past. In an environment where many sour-tasting foods were poisonous or unwholesome and many sweet-tasting foods, such as fruits, were healthful, a preference for sweets would have aided survival.

NEWBORNS AND ADULTS: A NATURAL MATCH

Without a willing adult, an infant would never survive. Although newborns are "competent"—their senses function, and they have the capacity to develop and learn—they need help from adults who can provide opportunities for learning and support for their development. Even more immediately, they need food, shelter, and affection. Parents and babies are like the interlocking pieces of a puzzle. A baby's hunger cry, for example, is a genetically programmed call for food—a built-in signal for survival (Wolf, 1960). Like an alarm, it goes off every few hours, often loud enough to awaken even the soundest sleeper. Only food will stop this noise. When babies cry, and parents feed them, the pieces fit. And when hunger or fatigue is not causing the cry, an adult's built-in response to lift the infant to a shoulder tends to quiet the baby and bring it to a state of eye-open alertness, heightening its ability to be stimulated (Korner & Grohstein, 1967; Korner & Thoman, 1972). Once again, infant and adult have formed a complementary pair, a natural match enhancing the baby's ability to survive.

Now consider sight. With 20/600 vision, newborns focus most clearly on things that are 6 to 13 inches away. Interestingly, this is the distance most adults tend to hold their faces from babies, probably because of clues they pick up from the infant. The distance between mothers' eyes and breasts is also about 12 inches; when the baby is nursing, eye-to-eye contact between mother and baby is natural. Adults also tend to move their heads and exaggerate their facial expressions (with big smiles or frowns, for example) when talking to babies, and such movements fit nicely with what infants can see.

With hearing, too, the same pattern of infant-adult compatibility appears. Recall that newborns prefer some sounds over others. Most adults, whether males or females, tend to raise the pitch of their voice when they talk to babies.

They also exaggerate articulation in the same way they articulate facial expression: Speech is slowed down, and words and sounds are frequently repeated (Stern, 1974). All these seemingly automatic adjustments that adults make in their behavior when they are with an infant fit perfectly with the skills, the capacities, and the preferences of the infant. And people tend to behave in this way even if they have never read a book like this and learned what infants like to look at and listen to.

LEARNING IN THE NEWBORN

learning
more or less permanent change in behavior that occurs as a consequence of experience

Learning is a more or less permanent change in behavior that occurs as a consequence of experience. We've already noted that babies only a few days old can distinguish between their mother's voice and a stranger's, and that almost as quickly, they can pick out their mother's smell. How do newborns learn?

Psychologists have identified several ways in which we learn, including classical conditioning and operant conditioning (see Chapter 1). Although some researchers have questioned newborns' capacity to be classically conditioned (Sameroff & Cavanaugh, 1979), one set of investigators recently demonstrated that if the mouths of 2- to 48-hour-old newborns were gently stroked immediately before giving them a sweet-tasting substance, the babies would eventually suck in response to the stroking alone (Blass, Ganchrow, & Steiner, 1984). Other researchers have found that newborns could be conditioned to show the sucking response by applying pressure to the palms (Cantor, Fischel, & Kaye, 1983). Operant conditioning has also been demonstrated in newborns. When offered a sweet substance to suck (the reward) each time they turned their heads in a specified direction (the behavior), head turns in the "right" direction increased (Siqueland, 1968). This means that even a newborn can learn that a specific behavior can bring a specific reward.

observational learning
learning through observation and imitation

And even a newborn can learn by observing and imitating the behavior of others, a process we call **observational learning**. Babies as young as 12 to 24 days old can mimic several adult facial gestures—pushing out their lips, opening the mouth, and sticking out the tongue (Meltzoff & Moore, 1977). Later experiments have found that newborns as young as 0.7 to 71 *hours* could also imitate mouth opening and tongue protrusion (Meltzoff & Moore, 1983). In another study, infants averaging 1½ days old could imitate an examiner's "happy," "sad," and "surprised" expressions (Field, Woodson, Greenberg, & Cohen, 1982). There has been, and is still, considerable controversy over findings like these; some critics have questioned whether infant imitation is really that or merely reflexive. But the research *does* suggest that the capabilities of newborns are only beginning to be uncovered.

High-Risk Infants

Fewer than 10 percent of U.S. newborns have any abnormalities, and many of the problems that *are* present disappear as the baby grows. The small percentage of newborns whose physical and psychological well-being may be in jeopardy are known as **high-risk infants**. Two conditions that place an infant at risk are prematurity and low birth weight. Either or both of these complications, which commonly occur together, can lead to developmental difficulties. A **premature**, or **preterm**, **baby** is born at least 3 weeks before the normal 38-week term of pregnancy is over. A baby with **low birth weight** weighs less than 5½ pounds, sharply under the 7½-pound average.

We do not always know why an infant was born too soon or too small. But we do know that many of the conditions that affect fetal development can also lead to prematurity and/or low birth weight. These conditions, which we discussed in the last chapter, include:

1. Insufficient prenatal care
2. Poor nutrition
3. The mother's age (over 35 or under 19)
4. The mother's reproductive condition (too many pregnancies too close together)
5. The mother's drinking and smoking habits

These characteristics have a cumulative effect. One alone may not cause serious problems, but babies of mothers with several of these conditions are likely to be born at risk.

Before 1967, not a single infant who weighed less than 1000 grams (about 2¼ pounds) and needed help breathing survived. Survival rates have since jumped to 73 percent, and more than 70 percent of these survivors have childhoods free of major handicaps (Cohen et al., 1982). This dramatic change reflects great advances in **neonatology**, the branch of medicine that focuses on newborns (Lee et al., 1980).

Despite these advances, statistics on the number of low-birth-weight infants are disturbing, as shown in Table 4-4. According to the Children's Defense Fund, one-quarter of a million low-birth-weight babies are born in the United States annually, and they have a 1-in-10 chance of dying during their first year (Children's Defense Fund, 1987). The total number of U.S. babies who do not survive the first year is estimated at 40,000 (Johnson, 1989). Poverty and lack of prenatal care are the major culprits. The highest infant mortality rates occur in the poorest neighborhoods of large cities: In some poor urban areas, 30 or more infants in 1000 die during their first year—an astoundingly high rate (National Center for Clinical Infant Programs, 1986).

Many of these babies' mothers are teenagers, single, poorly educated, unemployed, unable to afford prenatal care, or unaware of the need for it; they may not want the child they carry, and they may drink or smoke heavily through pregnancy. High infant mortality rates are also attributable to increasing numbers of pregnant women who are drug abusers (Johnson, 1989). Attempting to reduce the infant death rate, several cities offer outreach programs and free or low-cost prenatal care. Congress has also passed legislation to provide funding for such programs at a national level.

PHYSICAL CHARACTERISTICS OF HIGH-RISK INFANTS

High-risk infants look different from normal babies. They have smaller eyes, narrower, almost pointy, heads, and a relatively long distance between their

high-risk infants
infants whose physical and psychological well-being may be in jeopardy due to premature birth and/or low birth weight

premature (preterm) baby
baby born before 35 weeks of gestation

low birth weight
weight of less than 5½ pounds at birth

neonatology
the branch of medicine focusing on newborns

TABLE 4-4 RECENT U.S. BIRTHS AND MORTALITY STATISTICS				
	White	**Nonwhite**		**Total: All Races**
		Black	**Total**	
Births	2,970,439	621,221	786,108	3,756,547
Low birth weights: percentage of births (per 100 live births)	5.6	12.5	11.2	6.8
Mothers 19 and younger: percentages of all low birth weights	14.4	24.1	22.6	17.3
Mortality percentages, (per 1000 live births)	8.9	18.0	15.7	10.4

Source: National Center for Health Statistics. Calculations by Children's Defense Fund. Published in *The Health of America's Children: Maternal and Child Health Data Book*, 1989, Children's Defense Fund, Washington, D.C. Reprinted with permission.

respiratory distress syndrome (RDS)
breathing disorder in premature babies, caused by immaturity of the lungs and lack of pulmonary surfactant

pulmonary surfactant
essential lubricating substance in the lungs

incubator (isolette)
glass or Plexiglas life-support box with controlled temperature and airflow for high-risk infants

noses and mouths. A high-risk baby may be perceived as less attractive than a normal infant, and this perception may affect the way a baby is treated within the family. Parents, for example, may be less likely to interact with a baby whose looks disappoint them.

Probably the greatest threat to the health of the high-risk infant stems from an immature respiratory system. Such babies are prone to **respiratory distress syndrome (RDS)**, also known as hyaline membrane disease. This disorder, the leading killer of premature infants, is usually treated by giving the baby oxygen through a tube placed in the nose. But even this may not save the very premature baby, since RDS infants lack an essential chemical, **pulmonary surfactant**, in their lungs. Before birth, pulmonary surfactant is found in the amniotic sac; after birth, it lubricates the lungs, helping them to inflate on inhalation and preventing surfaces from sticking together on exhalation. Surfactant does not develop until the fetus is about 35 weeks old, so infants born before this time are especially prone to RDS. A promising new treatment for RDS involves dripping surfactant into the lungs of premature infants. Evidence suggests that this procedure may cut the rate of death among preterm infants by more than 50 percent (Merritt et al., 1986).

In addition to their respiratory problems, high-risk infants also have trouble maintaining normal body temperature and are usually placed in an **incubator**, or **isolette**, a glass or plexiglass box in which temperature and air flow can be controlled. The incubator also protects the baby from germs, which in so vulnerable an infant might lead to life-threatening infection.

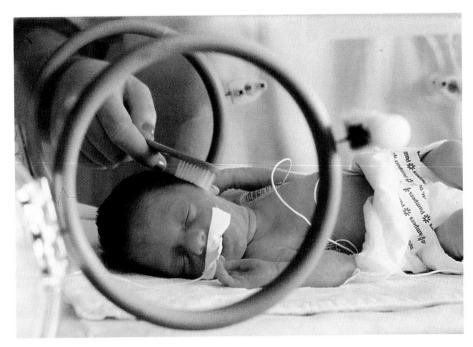

In the controlled environment of the incubator, high-risk premature infants can continue to develop while protected from infection. (*Joseph Nettis/Stock, Boston*)

Weak reflexes, especially the sucking reflex, put the high-risk infant in danger as well (Bakeman & Brown, 1980). Low-birth-weight babies who have trouble sucking are at special risk, because they may not be able to take in enough food to gain weight. Such infants are usually fed intravenously until they can suck on their own. Weak reflexes may also be a factor in sudden infant death syndrome, which is discussed in "Focus On."

BEHAVIORAL CHARACTERISTICS OF HIGH-RISK INFANTS

Even when they fall asleep, high-risk infants are different. Normal newborns usually fall into a fairly predictable wake-sleep pattern, but high-risks may sleep according to almost no pattern at all. The high-risk infant's irregular waking and sleeping, which can last throughout the first year of life, often puts great stress on parents, who can rarely count on a few hours of uninterrupted sleep. High-risk infants also cry more, and their cries sound more distressed than those of full-term babies (Friedman, Zahn-Waxler, & Radke-Yarrow, 1982; Frodi et al., 1978). Such babies are particularly hard to quiet (Friedman, Jacobs, & Wertmann, 1981), and this prolonged, highly distressed crying may make infants more vulnerable to neglect or abuse.

High-risk infants have a narrower band of arousal than normal babies (Field, 1982); they slip from an alert state to a fussy state more quickly or from a drowsy state to an alert state more slowly. They tend to smile less than other babies and are less responsive to their parents' efforts to play with them. Finding the right kind of playful stimulation can make a difference. In one experiment, when parents calmly imitated their baby's own behavior—gurgling or

FOCUS ON   *Sudden Infant Death Syndrome*

Each year 6500 infants go to sleep apparently healthy but do not wake up again. These babies, whose parents find them suffocated, are the victims of sudden infant death syndrome (SIDS), or crib death. More guesses than facts surround this tragic syndrome; babies who die of SIDS typically show no symptoms that might alert parents or doctors to any danger. All we really know about SIDS is that it is more likely to strike preterm infants; it most often occurs between ages 1 and 6 months, but it is most common around the age of 3 months; it strikes more frequently during the winter; and it occurs more often in nonwhite and poor families (Lewak, Zebal, & Friedman, 1984). Babies of mothers who smoke, later-borns (babies who are not first-born children), and bottle-fed infants are also at risk.

One theory relates SIDS to a faulty reflex. Most infants automatically clear their respiratory passages of mucus or saliva, but SIDS victims may be unable to do so. A congenital defect, this theory suggests, impedes the reflex, and infants choke to death (Lipsitt, 1979).

Another theory claims that SIDS is a lethal form of *apnea*, the brief periods during sleep when all infants stop breathing. Most babies automatically breathe again after a few seconds, but, according to the apnea theory, some infants who die of SIDS do not start breathing again and thus suffocate.

Why breathing stops, however, remains a mystery.

While causation is still uncertain, prevention is moving ahead, particularly with babies who seem at greatest risk: those who were born prematurely, those who have had a sibling die of SIDS, or those born with a neurological impairment making them more prone to apnea. These babies are attached to an electronic monitor during sleep. Whenever breathing stops during a period of apnea, an alarm sounds, signaling parents to pick up the baby and pat her rapidly on the back. This is usually enough to start the baby breathing again.

Although potentially life-saving, the apnea monitor is not perfect. Technical difficulties can cause false alarms, and living in a continuous state of emergency is often stressful for parents. In one study, two out of three mothers reported that the monitors had "drastic effects" on family life (Black, Hersher, & Steinschneider, 1978). Infants attached to apnea monitors were not only more closely watched and more frequently held than other infants, but the monitor's loud alarm signals also caused quarrels between parents. The inconveniences pale next to the tragedy of crib death, and until the reasons for SIDS are better understood, many infants at risk may be saved by an early warning system.

yawning when the baby did, for example—the baby quieted down and became more alert (Field, 1982). Still, premature babies in general are less responsive to their parent's efforts to play with them (Goldberg, 1978).

Just as with normal babies, there are individual differences among high-risk infants. Not all of them look so different from other babies, not all have extremely piercing cries, and some are more active and responsive than others. All these differences can have consequences, for the infants and for their parents. For example, unusually alert premature babies tend to be more responsive to their parents. These active babies are more likely to gaze at their parents during feedings, and, perhaps as a result, they receive more cuddling than less alert preterm infants do (DiVitto and Goldberg, 1983). This is another example of how babies actively contribute to their own development. Those who are more responsive *to* their parents often get more *from* their parents.

PROSPECTS FOR PREMATURE INFANTS

In the lives of many children, intervention will alleviate stresses, facilitate learning, promote growth. For high-risk newborns, intervention promotes life itself. Supported in the controlled environment of the incubator, high-risk infants continue to develop until their own bodies are mature enough to sustain life.

In most progressive hospitals, psychological health is promoted too. Preterm infants in incubators can hear recordings of a heartbeat or of their own mother's voice (Katz, 1971; Segal, 1972). They get extra chances to suck and are stroked and rocked, stimulation which helps to prevent developmental delays (Field, 1982; Powell, 1974; Rose, Schmidt, & Bridger, 1976). High-risk infants who receive such attention during their first year are more responsive and have stronger motor skills than those who do not receive extra stimulation (Cornell & Gottfried, 1976; Field, 1980; Sostek, Quinn, & Davitt, 1979).

Stimulation can even be in the form of an evaluation. In one study, for example, mothers were taught to stimulate their babies by administering a neonatal exam at birth and then weekly during the babies' first month of life. The testing encouraged interaction and closer mother-infant relationships (Field, 1982a; Field, Dempsey, Hallock, & Shuman, 1978).

Intervention in the form of greater support for parents can also benefit their high-risk infants. Groups in which parents share their experiences and feelings can foster confidence in their ability to care for their babies. Parents who join such groups tend to stimulate their babies more than parents who lack this kind of support (Minde et al., 1980). Since the family is the crucial environment in which babies—and parents—develop, intervention that helps parents helps children as well.

If this crucial environment is itself beset by difficulties and deprivations, chances for the premature child to catch up are limited. In fact, premature babies born into highly stressed families, especially poor families, are at the greatest risk for developmental problems (Birch & Gussow, 1970; Davie, Butler, & Goldstein, 1972; Drillien, 1964; Sameroff & Chandler, 1975). (See Figure 4-2.) Parents for whom everyday life is already a struggle are not likely to have the extra time, attention, energy, and affection to lavish on a difficult baby. Of course, preemies born into more comfortable households may not get the extra care they need, either. Nevertheless, a child born prematurely into a well-functioning family and community is generally better off than a healthy child born into a high-risk environment.

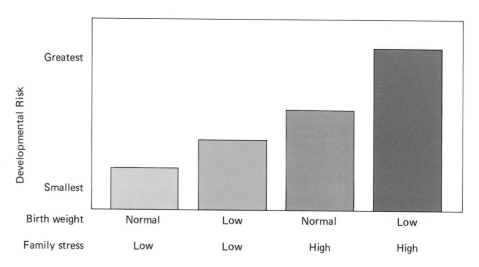

FIGURE 4-2
BIRTH WEIGHT AND FAMILY ENVIRONMENT: INTERACTIVE EFFECTS ON DEVELOPMENTAL RISKS
Family stress refers to such factors as level of poverty and emotional problems. A low-birth-weight baby is usually considered to be at high risk at birth. Notice, though, that family stress appears to be a more significant factor in predicting developmental risks than is birth weight.

Summary

1. Prepared childbirth has revolutionized labor and delivery in the last 20 years. Childbirth classes based on Lamaze techniques teach *both* parents-to-be how to minimize pain and maximize the experience of birth. Modern parents can make many choices about how they want their baby to be born.

2. Signs that birth is near include lightening (movement of the fetus into position for birth), the bloody show (appearance of blood-tinged mucus), rupture of the amniotic sac, and the beginning of uterine contractions.

3. The first stage of labor—the longest—has three substages: early first stage, during which contractions become regular; middle first stage, when contractions become stronger and the cervix begins to dilate; and transition, the shortest and most painful stage, in which the cervix dilates completely. Birth occurs during the second stage of labor, and the placenta is delivered during the third stage.

4. Most babies are born vaginally, emerging head first. Babies in the breech or transverse position are likely to be delivered by Caesarean section, surgically removed from the uterus. Complications during labor may also lead to a Caesarean delivery, especially if the fetal monitor shows a too-slow heartbeat. In such cases, doctors act to prevent anoxia, a lack of oxygen to the brain.

5. At birth, the baby's lungs and circulatory system must begin functioning independently. The 10-point Apgar test, given after 1 and 5 minutes of life, evaluates the baby's heart rate, breathing, muscle tone, reflexes, and color. Low scores signal the need for emergency medical intervention.

6. Early mother-infant contact does not seem essential for mother-infant bonding or later infant development. Close early contact *may* enhance the bond between mothers and infants, but a loving family at home is probably more important for both the relationship and the child's development.

7. Crying is an inborn response enabling a baby to seek help. Cries of babies with an abnormality or illness are distinct from those of healthy babies. The way a baby cries affects parents' responses, which in turn affect the child.

8. Reflexes are motor behaviors that are not under voluntary control. Some of the reflexes we are born with disappear at predictable times. Most newborn reflexes seem to be adaptive.

9. Babies have six natural states of arousal: regular sleep, irregular sleep, drowsiness, alert activity, waking activity, and crying (or distress). States of arousal influence the way babies respond to stimulation as well as the way parents respond to babies.

10. The Brazelton Newborn Behavioral Assessment Scale is used to assess babies' reflexes, state control, vision and hearing, and motor abilities.

11. Human infants are relatively helpless at birth, but a prolonged period of learning is intellectually adaptive.

12. The competent newborn has sensory capacities much greater than were once thought. Visual "rules" newborns follow suggest that they actively seek to learn about the world. Newborns have definite preferences for certain types of visual stimuli, sounds, smells, and tastes.

13. The capacities of the newborn mesh well with the way adults tend to respond to babies. The complementary pairing ensures the baby's survival and fosters learning.

14. Babies seem to begin learning shortly after birth. Recent research shows that newborns probably learn in at least three ways—by classical conditioning, operant conditioning, and observation.

15. Premature and low-birth-weight babies are high-risk infants. Insufficient prenatal care, poor nutrition, exposure to teratogens such as nicotine and alcohol, and maternal age can all affect prematurity and birth weight.

16. Respiratory distress syndrome is one of the greatest threats to the health of high-risk infants, who must usually be placed in protective incubators or isolettes. Stimulation for infants in incubators can help prevent developmental delays, and support for parents of high-risk infants helps them feel confident about caring for their babies.

17. Premature babies raised in highly stressed families, especially poor ones, are at the greatest risk for developmental problems.

Key Terms

anoxia

Apgar test

binocular convergence

bloody show

Brazelton Newborn Behavioral
   Assessment Scale

breech birth

Caesarean section

contractions

engagement (lightening)

engrossment

episiotomy

fetal monitor

high-risk infants

incubator

Lamaze method

learning

low birth weight

neonatology

observational learning

oxytocin

premature (preterm) baby

prepared (natural) childbirth

pulmonary surfactant

reflex

respiratory distress syndrome (RDS)

sound localization

state control

states of arousal

transition

transverse presentation

vernix

visual acuity

Suggested Readings

Goldberg, S., and Devitto, B. (1983). *Born too soon: Preterm birth and early development*. New York: Freeman. Research on the development of premature babies is reviewed by two developmental psychologists who have conducted their own longitudinal study of premature infants.

Leboyer, F. (1975). *Birth without violence*. New York: Knopf. In this volume a radical obstetrician shares his approach to delivery that has contributed to the revolution in childbirth that has occurred in America over the past two decades.

MacFarlane, A. (1977). *The psychology of childbirth*. Cambridge, MA: Harvard University Press. Emotional aspects of childbirth, including morning sickness, hospital versus home delivery, and mother-infant bonding are examined by a well-known pediatrician.

The discovery of independent locomotion and the discovery of a new self usher in a new phase in personality development. The toddler is quite giddy with his new achievements. He behaves as if he had invented this new mode of locomotion (which in a restricted sense is true) and he is quite in love with himself for being so clever. From dawn to dusk he marches around in an ecstatic, drunken dance, which ends only when he collapses with fatigue. He can no longer be contained within the four walls of his house and the fenced-in yard is like a prison to him. Given practically unlimited space he staggers joyfully with open arms toward the end of the horizon. Given half a chance he might make it.

—Selma Fraiberg, *The Magic Years*

Infancy

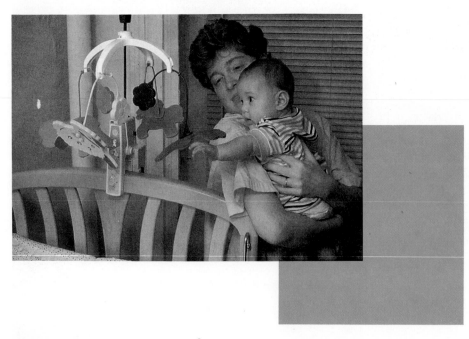

Physical Development in Infancy

The newborn we described in the last chapter could neither turn her head nor lift her body. Hold her, and her head rests on your shoulder; her knees bend and her bottom is up. Lay her down, and her body assumes the same curled-up position. Unsupported, her head flops down, and her back slumps forward. In 6 months, the same baby is sitting up in a high chair feeding herself. A few months later she's crawling, and by 15 months she's walking. By the end of infancy, she'll be up and running.

As we look at this sequence of motor development, we will ask some questions that are particularly interesting to developmentalists: How does the environment influence physical growth and development? Do practice and training encourage motor skills? Can (and should) infants be "taught" to sit or stand or walk earlier than their genetic timetables dictate? We'll also consider the ways in which motor development affects an infant's relationships with the rest of the family and with other adults. We'll focus, too, on the brain and the nervous system and on an extremely important element for all of development, nutrition.

Growth

An average newborn weighs about 7½ pounds, *3 billion* times more than the fertilized ovum from which he or she began. Although we will never grow at this rate again, growth during infancy is still very rapid. In fact, if you had continued growing at the rate of your first year of life, by age 3 you would have weighed 200 pounds and measured over 5 feet tall! Not until puberty will we grow nearly so quickly again. In part, these physical changes are genetically determined: We all show the same patterns of growth, but some of us will grow taller and faster than others. From infancy on, how genetic instructions are carried out will be influenced by each infant's environment—by nutrition, care, and experience.

CHANGES IN WEIGHT, HEIGHT, AND SHAPE

During the first year alone, a baby's weight triples to about 20 to 24 pounds. Until about 9 months, this gain is mostly fat; after that, it is mainly bone and muscle. Fat quickly disappears once the child begins walking, so even chubby babies usually become lean toddlers. During the second year, weight gain slows down to about half a pound a month. So a baby who weighed 7 or 8 pounds at birth quadruples in weight to about 30 pounds by age 2.

Even more startling than infants' weight gain is the way they grow. The newborn, whose whole arm fits comfortably in the palm of his parent's hand, has by the end of 1 year grown from about 20 inches to 30 inches, a 50 percent increase. By the end of the second year, height has reached another 25 percent—to about 35 inches. In just 2 years, infants grow to half (or even more) of their adult height. Growth slows down from the age of 2 on, speeding up again at puberty.

Predicting adult height from length at birth is a bit tricky, because like weight, length is strongly influenced by the environment in the uterus. Either teratogens or poor fetal nutrition (or both) can affect growth *in utero*. But by the second year, after the infant has has sufficient time to grow outside the uterine environment, predictions become more reliable. Tall 2-year-olds do tend to become tall adults.

CHANGES IN PROPORTION

Growth involves more than a simple increase in height and weight. The parts of an infant's body grow at different rates, and their relative proportions change as well. This is called the **proportional phenomenon**, and it follows the same pattern we saw during fetal development, from the head down. (We'll look at this pattern again shortly.)

A newborn's head is unusually large relative to the rest of her body. At birth, the head accounts for about one-fourth of body height; by childhood, it makes up only one-tenth of total height. One reason for the infant's large head is that the skull must accommodate the growing brain. At birth, an infant's brain already weighs one-quarter of its adult total weight, and by age 2, the brain has already grown to three-quarters of its adult weight. But a 2-year-old's whole body is only about one-fourth of her full adult weight (Tanner, 1970).

proportional phenomenon that different parts of the infant's body grow at different rates, resulting in alterations in their relative proportions

A large head and short legs create a high center of gravity, so to keep their balance, babies walk with legs apart. *(Hella Hammid/Photo Researchers)*

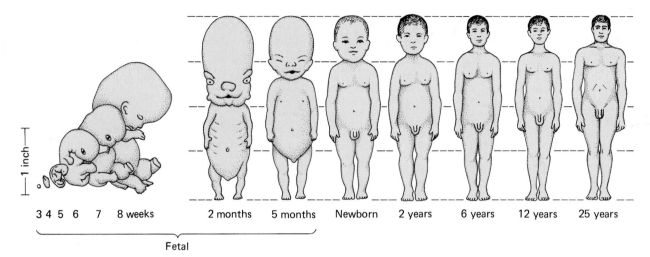

3 4 5 6   7   8 weeks   2 months   5 months   Newborn   2 years   6 years   12 years   25 years

Fetal

FIGURE 5-1
CHANGES IN THE FORM AND PROPORTION OF THE HUMAN BODY
The drawing depicts the growth of a male's body during the embryonic, fetal, and postnatal stages. Note the developmental changes in the size of the head and limbs in relation to the size of the body. (*Source: From Conception to Birth: The Drama of Life's Beginnings* by Roberts Rugh and Landrum B. Shettles. Copyright © 1971 by Roberts Rugh and Landrum B. Shettles. Reprinted by permission of Harper & Row Publishers, Inc. From *Growth* by W. J. Robbins et al., Yale University Press, 1928. Reprinted by permission.)

motor development
the increasing ability to control the body in purposeful motion

cephalocaudal development
pattern of growth proceeding from head downward

In contrast to the head, which gradually decreases in its proportion to overall body length, the legs *increase* their relative proportion. At birth, they make up about one-third of an infant's length, but by adulthood, legs account for about half of height. Figure 5-1 illustrates these changes in proportional development from the prenatal period through adulthood.

As body proportions change, so does the center of gravity. During infancy, a large head and short legs create a high center of gravity, so when babies walk, they keep their legs far apart to stay balanced. By age 4, longer legs shift the center of gravity downward, and posture straightens up (Sinclair, 1973).

Motor Development

Motor refers to motion, and **motor development** is the infant's growing ability to use his or her body for purposeful, voluntary motion. *Purposeful* is the key word here, because newborns have little conscious control over their bodies. Many of their movements are reflexive, as we saw in Chapter 4, and even though they can lift a foot or move a hand, they lack willful control over their muscles, and their movements appear jerky and random (Leach, 1980).

We'll look at the way control emerges, first from a general perspective and then in more specific terms. The newborn's reflexive kicks and squirms may indeed seem random, but perhaps you won't be surprised to find that they fit into an overall logical sequence of development that is not random at all.

DEVELOPMENTAL TRENDS AND PRINCIPLES

Notice in Figure 5-2 (the *order* of development) that motor skills develop from head to foot. This is called **cephalocaudal development**, and it explains why infants gain control of their neck muscles before their chest muscles and why

FIGURE 5-2
THE SEQUENCE OF MOTOR DEVELOPMENT
The ages at which the average infant achieves a given behavior. (*Source:* M. M. Shirley, *The First Two Years: A Study of Twenty-Five Babies*, Vol. 2. Copyright © 1933 by the University of Minnesota, renewed 1960. Reprinted by permission of the University of Minnesota Press.)

proximodistal development
pattern of growth from center of the body outward

mass-to-specific development
pattern of growth from large to small muscles

differentiation
ability to make specific, goal-directed movements

they sit before they stand. This cephalocaudal trend is apparent in fetal development as well—recall the newborn's relatively large head and small legs.

Growth and control also proceed from the center of the body outward; this is known as **proximodistal development**. Infants can control their arms at the shoulders before they can direct their hands and fingers. At 3 months they may reach for and miss an object, but by 5 months their fingers can grab and hold objects within reach.

Yet another growth trend is **mass-to-specific development**—large to small muscle control. At first, infants reach with both arms, but by 7 months, most can reach out with just one arm at a time. Actions, then, become more specific and directed. A 6-month-old sees an object, wants it, reaches for and takes it in a smoothly controlled movement. This ability to make specific moves toward specific goals is **differentiation**. It develops along with the infant's maturing nervous and muscular systems. (Sometimes these systems are considered together and called the neuromuscular system.)

GAINING BODY CONTROL

Unless seriously handicapped or otherwise uncoordinated, adults perform most simple motor acts in a skilled and graceful manner, whether the act is drinking from a cup or putting on gloves. These supposedly simple, basic movements are actually complex motor behaviors, performed with a high degree of temporal (time-related) and spatial coordination among limb and body segments. When you drink from a glass, you straighten your arm at the elbow to extend your hand toward the glass; your fingers open on the way and close just as they come into contact with the glass; then the elbow bends so that the glass can be brought to the edge of the lips just as the mouth opens to take that drink.

Because large muscle control precedes small muscle coordination, babies can reach for things before they can easily grasp them. *(Robert Brenner/PhotoEdit)*

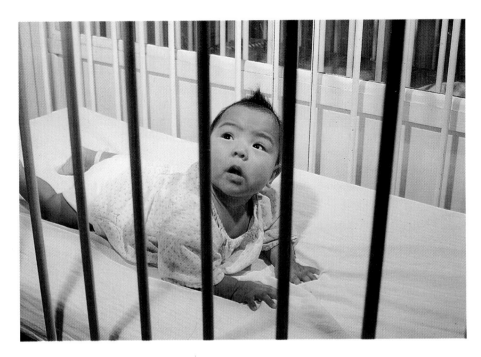

Motor development follows the same basic pattern in all infants. By 2 months, most can lift their chest off the mattress. *(Fujihira/ Monkmeyer)*

By comparison, of course, the young infant's movements seem jerky and uncoordinated. But a recent series of simple, yet elegant experiments on simple motor movements have revealed that even these limb movements of young infants are coordinated to a surprising degree. When 6-week-old babies lying on their backs had a weight attached to one leg, the kicking of the unweighted leg sped up, to compensate for the drag on the other leg. This means that even by the second month of life, the two legs are not separate kicking instruments but are coordinated—in a way that resembles walking (Thelen, Skala, & Kelso, 1987).

With maturity such simple coordination is refined, and new motor skills emerge. For several days or even weeks before a new motor skill appears, many babies go through a kind of practice. Turning over may be preceded by rocking from side to side; crawling, by rocking back and forth on their hands and knees. These repetitive movements of the head, chest, and limbs are called **rhythmical stereotypies**. The name makes sense. These movements are both rhythmical and stereotyped: They are repeated almost exactly for a certain period, and they do not seem to be under voluntary control. They seem to represent a transition from random movements to deliberate, coordinated motor control (Thelen, 1981). When the stereotypy appears unusually early, so does the related voluntary activity. These relationships suggest that once the "wiring" in the nervous system is in place, the "circuits" are tested by the repeated practice of the stereotypy (Thelen, 1979). A little later in the chapter, we'll look in more detail at how the maturation of the nervous system influences the appearance and efficiency of motor skills.

So, although newborns cannot sit, stand, walk, or even hold up their heads very well, by a few weeks after birth they can lift their heads up when lying face down to look around for a few moments; and by 2 months they can lift their chests off the mattress. By 6 months they are sitting up; by 9 months

rhythmical stereotypies apparently reflexive, repeated rhythmic movements that serve as transition from random to controlled movement

they may be crawling. Within another 3 to 6 months they will be walking—or at least toddling (refer back to Figure 5-2) (Burnside, 1927). All infants follow this general sequence of motor development; but skills may appear considerably earlier or later than charts predict. Some babies walk at 10 months or earlier and others not until 15 months. Similarly, some babies skip a step to their first step—and some children develop their own idiosyncratic adaptations: Instead of crawling, for instance, they may "scoot" on their bottoms. Others may "walk" upright on their knees before getting to their feet in the second year. Unless there is a series of delays or irregularities in motor development, there is no need to be concerned about somewhat advanced or delayed motor abilities. Variation is normal and does not predict future athletic ability.

HEREDITY AND ENVIRONMENT

If motor skills develop in the same sequence and at roughly the same age, does that mean the genes determine motor development? The traditional answer was yes (Gesell & Ames, 1937). Even when children from different backgrounds are compared, the motor schedule seems fairly fixed.

In a now classic study, Wayne Dennis compared two groups of Hopi Indians (Dennis, 1940). The groups were genetically similar, so any notable differences in development would have to be due to environmental differences. One group cared for their infants as the tribe had always done: Babies, tightly swaddled to "cradle boards," were carried on their mother's backs. The infants could move almost nothing except their heads. The second group used contemporary U.S. childcare practices, allowing their infants free movement. In *both* groups, infants walked by 15 months. They all achieved the same degree of neuromuscular skills at the same time whether or not they had been attached to cradle boards. This study suggests that genes, rather than specific childcare practices, strongly influence motor development.

But Dennis still wondered about environmental influences, and two decades later he published another report demonstrating that experience does influence the process of motor development (Dennis, 1960). Like the Hopi study, the research also involved infants who shared similar hereditary background but were cared for in different ways. This time, his subjects were Iranian orphans raised in three different institutions. In two of these, the babies were simply left lying in their cribs, with feeding administered via a bottle propped against pillows. Sheets covered the sides of their cribs, restricting their views. Except when they were picked up to be bathed, they could neither touch nor see other people. In the third orphanage, infants were encouraged to sit up, to play, and to interact with others.

Dennis found that in the first two orphanages, the major milestones of motor achievement were markedly delayed. Most of the children were not even sitting up by the age of 1 year, and many were still not sitting by 21 months. Even by the age of 3 years, the majority of the children from these two institutions were still not walking. This study illustrates that genes alone do not direct motor development. Normal growth requires both physical and social stimulation.

But what if a child gets *more* than a normal amount of stimulation—can some child-rearing practices speed up or enhance motor development? And even if development can be accelerated, *should* it be? The answer to the first question is a cautious "yes." In an experiment done in the United States, for

Although Hopi Indian babies can move only their head when laced onto a cradle board, their motor skills mature at the same rate as those of babies who are not confined. *(Lionel Delevingne/ Stock, Boston)*

example, walking was advanced by several months when parents stimulated the stepping reflex in infants during the first 2 months of life (Zelazo, Zelazo, & Kolb, 1972). And among the Kipsigi tribe of Kenya, whose infants spend more than 60 percent of their waking time sitting in someone's lap, infants *are* able to sit alone earlier than would be expected. In many African tribes, babies are traditionally carried (unswaddled) on someone's back; such infants do seem to develop stronger trunk, buttock, and thigh muscles. On the other hand, crawling and creeping rarely appear precociously among African infants, possibly because babies in Africa are rarely placed on the ground on their stomachs (Kilbride, 1977; Super, 1981).

There is also evidence that early experience of self-produced locomotion, like crawling or using an infant walker, may speed up development of certain emotional and cognitive abilities by about a month or so. In one series of experiments, infants who crawled sooner than others were found to be more afraid of falling off an edge (as on a bed), and noncrawlers who could move themselves around in an infant walker developed fear of heights before noncrawlers with no experience with walkers (Bertenthal, Campos, & Barnett, 1984; Campos, Svejda, Campos, & Bertenthal, 1982.) The fear of falling and of heights seems to indicate some increased understanding of location in space. In other research, out of a group of 10- and 11-month-olds who all watched while an object was hidden, those who had the chance to crawl across the room located the hidden object more easily than did their agemates who were carried across the room (Benson & Uzigiris, 1985).

However, even though such research tells us that motor development and related emotional and cognitive abilities *can* be accelerated at least in the short term, this does not mean that they *should* be. In fact, efforts to speed motor development can actually backfire, as one researcher discovered when he tried to influence infants' ability to reach for objects. Offering too many kinds of objects at the same time confused and agitated the babies (White, 1967). When infants are not neurologically ready for further development, too much stimulation achieves nothing and may even be counterproductive.

We can conclude once again that heredity sets the *sequence* of motor development, but its *expression* in each infant is influenced by experience. The culture infants live in, their families, and others in their lives will affect the outcome of every baby's genetic plan for growth and development. It can be delayed by emotional and sensory deprivation, or it can be speeded up—within limits—by extra physical stimulation. And whatever physical changes that take place, we can be sure that these will interact with and influence other areas of the baby's development.

CONSEQUENCES OF MOTOR DEVELOPMENT

A baby who can barely lift his head up has a very limited view of his surroundings, but each new motor skill expands his world, allowing him to see, reach, manipulate, and finally move toward anything that interests him. Sitting, for example, enables him to look around in any direction, gathering information. Upright, he can also manipulate objects with his hands, practicing and developing hand-eye coordination. And as you just read, emotional and cognitive capacities develop alongside motor skills.

New motor skills not only change the baby's relationship with and understanding of the environment; they alter her relationship with her parents and siblings as well. The baby who cannot even turn over presents a very different challenge from the baby who can crawl around the house. When babies begin creeping, parents should begin "childproofing." The goal is to strike a balance among various needs: the need to protect the baby from physical harm; the needs of family members to protect their possessions from the baby; and the baby's need to exercise new skills and to satisfy normal curiosity.

Once this baby begins crawling, her parents will have to balance her need to explore against their need to keep her—and their possessions—safe. *(Alan Carey/The Image Works)*

The way this challenge is met is influenced by the whole family, including the baby herself. A not-too-active first child at home with a relaxed mother may run up against very few restrictions. But suppose a relentlessly curious 10-month-old second child has a tense mother and a 3-year-old brother, and they live in a small apartment. Before the baby could crawl, her mother enjoyed taking care of her, but now the mother worries whenever the baby is out of sight; sometimes the playpen seems the only way to limit the child's exploring. Soon the mother begins scolding: "Stop that!" "Behave yourself!" A similarly active first-born baby, or one with a more relaxed mother and a larger home, could have a very different experience.

What we want to stress is that motor skills also affect relationships, which, in turn, affect the child's development. This is a process we will observe again and again. The child's own development—whether it is motor, cognitive, or emotional—affects the way others respond to him, which in turn affects development. In Chapter 7, for example, we will look at infant temperament and at how infants and parents mesh or "fit" with each other.

To sum up, then, we can make the following points about motor development:

1. Our common human heredity ensures a similar sequence of motor development for all infants.
2. At the same time, experience influences the expression of every infant's unique motor "timetable."
3. A serious lack of stimulation can retard motor development.
4. But most infants receive enough stimulation to ensure normal motor development.
5. Extra stimulation can speed development, but this is not necessarily good for infants, and too much stimulation offered at the wrong time can be stressful.
6. All infants influence their own development, since new motor skills affect the way others respond to them.

Brain and Nervous System Development

All the motor or cognitive skills that appear during infancy are influenced by the maturing *nervous system*, which includes the brain, the spinal cord, and the nerves. The nervous system controls the actions of all the bones, muscles, glands, and organs of the body. This control is exercised through electochemical impulses which pass through bundles of long, thin cells called **neurons**. The brain is composed of at least 10 billion such cells. As an impulse passes from one neuron to another, it jumps across a tiny space called a *synapse*. To pass from your brain to your hand, for example, an impulse jumps thousands of synapses—all in a fraction of a second.

The last part of the brain to develop and the least mature at birth is the

neurons
nerve cells; primary functional units of the nervous system

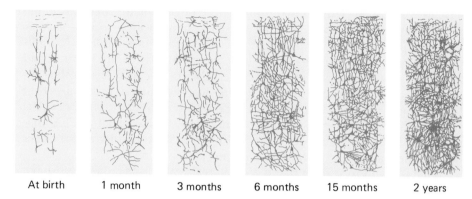

At birth	1 month	3 months	6 months	15 months	2 years

FIGURE 5-3

In humans, the brain tissues mature rapidly after birth. These drawings of sections of brain tissue from the cerebral cortex illustrate the increasing complexity of the neural networks in the maturing human brain. (*Source:* Reprinted by permission of the publishers from *The post-natal development of the human cerebral cortex* by J. L. Conel. Cambridge, Mass.: Harvard University Press. Copyright © 1959 by the President and Fellows of Harvard College.

cerebral cortex
the wrinkled outer layer of the brain; the most highly evolved part of the brain, responsible for perception, muscle control, thought, and memory

arborization
proliferation of connections among neurons by branching

myelin
insulating fatty sheath on nerve fibers

outermost area, the **cerebral cortex**. In fact, not until adolescence is the cortex fully developed (Tanner, 1978). This part of the brain contains areas which control motor development, sensory skills, and higher-order cognitive skills. As you read this, for example, your cortex controls your ability to see and understand the words and to turn the page. Between 6 months and 2 years, considerable development occurs in the areas of the cortex responsible for complex cognitive activities, such as anticipation and reasoning.

From birth on, two kinds of changes are occurring: First, the number of connections between neurons increases (*not* the number of neurons). This process, **arborization,** increases the brain's size and complexity (see Figure 5-3). Second, the neurons become insulated by a fatty sheath of **myelin**, which speeds up and improves the efficiency of message transfers (Morell & Norton, 1980). These changes seem to come in periods of rapid growth and development, or growth spurts, and we can see their effects during the first 3 months of an infant's life.

The kind of movements infants can make after birth, inborn reflexes rather than controlled movements, reflects the fact that the cortex is undeveloped. But by 3 months, the cortex is at least partially controlling the movements of the upper body and arms. By this age, too, the cortex plays a greater role in the functioning of the senses, including hearing and vision. We know these changes have occurred because 3-month-olds have far more control over their movements than they had at birth. Voluntary actions have begun to replace reflexes.

BIOLOGY AND EXPERIENCE

Both biology and experience influence brain development. Although genes determine the timing of changes within the brain, normal development depends both on *adequate* sensory experience and on nutrition. For example, when researchers reared cats so that they only saw vertical lines and not horizontal ones, their ability to respond to horizontal lines at a later time was impaired (Hirsh & Spinelli, 1970). Similarly, if one of an animal's eyes is covered at birth, its ability to evaluate depth (binocular vision) will suffer later on (Buisseret et al., 1978).

As you saw in the classic Dennis study of orphanages, deprivation of stimulation has marked negative consequences for development. In Chapter 8, we will see how intervention programs can help prevent the harmful effects of environmental deprivation during the early years. However, most infants get the basic stimulation they need for normal development of the sensory areas of the cerebral cortex through ordinary daily life (Greenough, Black, & Wallace, 1987). Parents do not have to give their infants any special "brain training." Although there is a trend among middle-class parents today to provide all kinds of special toys, games, and training in an attempt to produce a smarter, "better" baby, moderation, adequate stimulation, sensitive care, and balance are the things to keep in mind and in practice.

Physical Development and Nutrition

All along in this text, we have been emphasizing the interaction of genetic potential with the environment. There is no clearer example of this interaction than infant nutrition and its impact on physical development. If your parents are tall, chances are you will be too, but whether you reach your genetically programmed height is strongly influenced by diet. Enough food, and the right kind of food, are essential for normal growth.

Nutrition can work either toward the upper or the lower level of your potential for height. After World War II, for example, children who had lived under near-famine conditions in Germany lagged 10 to 20 months behind their expected rates of growth (Sinclair, 1973). If proper nutrition begins, growth can speed up. If the period of malnutrition has been brief, *catch-up* growth can restore children to their genetically predicted height. But when serious malnutrition is prolonged, the lost potential for growth becomes permanent.

Even with all the other kinds of stimulation present, if an infant is not adequately nourished, the genetic plan for physical development will be compromised, sometimes so severely that serious disease or even death results. Infant growth involves the creation of new cells at a very rapid rate. Recall that during the first year alone, infants triple their weight and increase their length by one-half. Like adults, they are also maintaining the cells and tissues that they already have. To meet these demands, each day an infant needs more than twice the calories and three times the protein per pound of body weight that an adult needs.

BREAST VERSUS BOTTLE FEEDING

Probably the most passionately argued controversy surrounding the nurturing of infants has been the breast-versus-bottle debate (see "Issues & Op-

Issues & OPTIONS

The Breast or the Bottle?

For many women, deciding to nurse is based as much on emotional issues as it is on nutritional ones. Proponents claim that the act of breast feeding itself creates a special mother-infant bond that bottle feeding cannot equal. Does it follow then that bottle feeding, with its less intimate connection between baby and mother, means more psychological distance? Does it interfere with the mother-child bond?

Not necessarily. In fact, there is really *no evidence* suggesting that breast-fed babies as a group have better relationships with their mothers than bottle-fed babies do. What matters are the feelings surrounding feeding. If either the breast or bottle is offered warmly, attentively, and with pleasure, the baby will thrive.

Nevertheless, pediatricians do encourage mothers to nurse their infants, if only for the first few months, because of the nutritional and immunological benefits of breast milk. Whether a woman continues to breast-feed, or even whether she chooses to nurse for just a few months, depends on her own needs and lifestyle. A baby breast-fed by a mother who resents or dislikes the experience is not going to profit from it.

Psychologist Penelope Leach (1980) advises women to choose the method that is right for them; that choice will be best for their infants as well. Leach suggests two basic questions that each woman should ask and answer for herself:

1. Do you welcome physical contact? A woman who feels comfortable with physical contact and wants to have a close physical relationship with her baby will probably like breast feeding. If nursing is embarrassing or distasteful to a woman, she might feel happier bottle feeding.

2. What kind of a life do you want to lead? A woman who is planning to stay home with her infant will find nursing more convenient than a working mother. But there are ways to make nursing possible for working mothers as well. Breast milk can be expressed into a bottle for a later feeding by a sitter. Fathers can also participate in feeding their infants in this way.

Finally, women who are undecided about breast feeding can choose to try it. The women who expected to be uncomfortable with such close physical contact might actually find nursing pleasurable; the mother who foresaw embarrassment may discover pride and satisfaction.

Feeding an infant can be a close, rewarding experience for mother—or father—and baby regardless of the method. If a bottle is used, don't prop it against the baby—this is bad for teeth and gums. Always hold the infant, and offer the nipple for as long as the baby wants it. Don't try to force a baby to suck when she has lost interest. By tuning in to their baby's signals, sensitive parents foster feelings of trust, an important emotional issue that we'll turn to again in Chapter 7.

tions"). For most of human history, mother's milk was all there was, but the advent of infant formula early in this century offered a choice. The first formulas were time-consuming to prepare and were used mainly as an occasional substitute for breast milk. But as they became more convenient, their use spread, and by 1971, 75 percent of U.S. babies were formula-fed (Martinez, 1984).

Why did U.S. mothers switch to the baby bottle? Mostly because it was convenient and dependable. For example, a bottle may be given by either

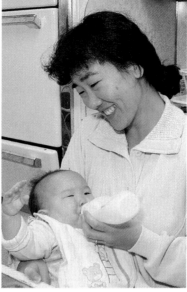

Although breast feeding offers some nutritional and immunological benefits to infants, there is no evidence that it enhances the mother-infant bond. What matters most—whether breast or bottle is used—are the feelings offered with the feedings. (*Joel Gordon; Robert Brenner/ PhotoEdit*)

parent or by another caregiver, giving the mother some relief from the demands of infant care. Formula is also dependably nutritious, regardless of the mother's health, and it is free of any medication she may be taking. Finally, a bottle can be easily offered almost anywhere, if the mother feels embarrassed about nursing in public.

What about nutrition? Formula, which is generally based on cow's milk, or soy protein with added vitamins, minerals, and lactose, is certainly adequate. It provides sufficient calories plus other elements required for growth and development. But following manufacturer's directions is essential for using any infant formula safely. Misuse is extremely dangerous, since it can cause severe malnutritional problems, as you will see shortly.

Despite early enthusiasm for formula, American opinion and practice have swung back to favoring breast feeding. During the late 1970s and the 1980s, the move toward natural childbirth among middle-class, educated American women was accompanied by a rising interest in all things natural—including nursing. Childbirth classes often promoted the nutritional and emotional benefits of nursing, and many new mothers decided to try. In 1984, Surgeon General Everett Koop declared that "breast feeding gives babies complete nutrition plus immunology benefits to launch them on a healthy life" (Koop, 1984). American mothers listened; breast feeding has been steadily gaining in popularity, and estimates are that in 1990, 75 percent of all mothers were nursing their babies (New York State Department of Health, 1987).

Why do most pediatricians consider breast milk the ideal first food?

1. Breast milk is always sterile and at a comfortable temperature.
2. Breast milk is easier to digest than cow's milk, and far fewer babies develop allergies to breast milk than to formula.
3. The iron in breast milk is more readily absorbed, as are certain other nutrients.

4. Breast milk has a somewhat higher sugar content and also produces a softer curd, which helps to prevent constipation.

5. Breast milk contains antibodies that help babies resist minor infections. (Temporary resistance to major infections was conveyed in the uterus and is subsequently boosted by routine immunizations.)

6. Nutrients in breast milk are balanced to promote rapid brain growth and myelinization, whereas those in cow's milk are geared primarily for muscle growth.

MALNUTRITION: CAUSES AND EFFECTS

In the United States today, about one-quarter of all children under 4 grow up in poverty. For black children, the rate is nearly *one in two* (National Center for Clinical Infant Programs, 1987). With poverty goes malnutrition, so poor babies are very likely to be small and underweight babies. For example, among poor families in Chicago, nearly one-third of the children under 2 fell below the tenth percentile for height and weight and were therefore likely to be malnourished (National Center for Clinical Infant Programs, 1987).

Infants are particularly vulnerable to the consequences of malnutrition because protein is essential for normal physical development. Because neurons in the brain's cortex grow very rapidly during infancy and continue to mature until adolescence, you would expect malnutrition during infancy to have consequences for brain development, and it does. Too few calories toward the end of pregnancy and during infancy can slow the rate of brain cell growth and can actually *lower* the number of brain cells in malnourished infants (Winick & Rosso, 1969). Such children also show both reduced growth of individual cells and delayed neural maturation (Dobbing, 1964; Dyson & Jones, 1976).

Trying to prevent these consequences, Congress enacted the Women, Infants, and Children (WIC) program in 1972, authorizing funds of $20 million. The program has thrived since and today serves over 1 million children at a cost of over $1.5 billion annually (American Academy of Pediatrics, 1985). The funds provide supplemental nutritious foods to pregnant women, breast-feeding mothers, infants, and children up to age 5 who are considered at risk. Results of the program are promising. Improved prenatal care has helped to increase birth weights, possibly because the boost in nutrition has fostered longer pregnancies. To get these benefits, mothers must be enrolled in the program for at least 6 months of their pregnancy (General Accounting Office, 1984; Kotelchuck, Schwartz, Anderka, & Finison, 1984; Stockbauer, 1986). Infants who receive WIC benefits tend to be healthier children. It is believed that for every $1 spent on WIC benefits, $3 are saved in future medical costs (National Public Radio, 1989). WIC is a clear example of how social policy can help developmental problems. It is estimated, though, that only about half of all eligible infants and children are receiving this benefit (National Public Radio, 1989).

In general, however, the incidence of infant malnutrition today is startling. It is a worldwide problem, though it is more pronounced in third-world countries, especially in sub-Saharan Africa. Malnutrition usually starts when infants are weaned from the breast to the bottle. Traditionally, infants in un-

About one-quarter of all children in the United States grow up in poverty. A government-funded program provides food and medical care to poor women and their children, but only half of those eligible are receiving this benefit. *(Paul Conklin/Monkmeyer)*

derdeveloped nations were breast-fed until age 2, but recently, particularly during the 1970s, mothers in these countries were encouraged to switch to formula during their infant's first year. Many of these mothers, inadequately instructed by distributors, unable to read manufacturers' instructions, and anxious to stretch food as far as possible because of poverty, diluted the formula—often with contaminated water—with tragic consequences. Many of their babies died. The contamination caused disease, and the dilution deprived infants of essential protein calories. Lack of proper refrigeration, another common problem among poorer populations, can also spoil formula and lead to illness. Considerable public pressure in the industrialized nations has been put on manufacturers to halt advertising ploys like free distribution of formula samples in underdeveloped countries.

The physical conditions most often associated with severe malnutrition are marasmus and kwashiorkor. **Marasmus**, linked with an overall insufficient amount of food, usually affects infants less than a year old. They stop gaining weight and eventually begin to lose weight. They appear more and more emaciated, with wasted muscles, wrinkled skin, wizened faces, and swollen bellies (Vaughn, McKay, & Nelson, 1975). They also suffer from diarrhea and anemia. Often, their food supply is contaminated, so intestinal infections

marasmus
disease affecting infants under 1 year, caused by insufficient and often contaminated food supply

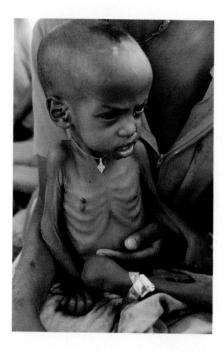

Infant malnutrition, a major world health problem, has been devastating in sub-Saharan Africa. This Ethiopian infant is suffering from marasmus. The disease, caused by severe malnutrition, affects physical, emotional, and social development. If not treated, it may lead to death. *(Chris Steele Perkins/ Magnum Photos)*

kwashiorkor
disease affecting children ages 2 to 3, caused by severe protein deficiency, usually after weaning

worsen their condition (Galler, 1984). **Kwashiorkor** tends to affect children who are weaned at age 2 or 3 without being provided with a nutritionally adequate breast milk substitute. Stomachs swell, muscles waste, and growth is seriously retarded. Hair may discolor, skin grows pale and may develop irritations (Vaughn, McKay, & Nelson, 1975). Diarrhea, anemia, apathy, and irritability also mark this life-threatening condition (Galler, 1984).

Severe malnutrition affects both cognitive and social development. In a number of separate studies, malnourished infants have shown a range of difficulties, including lowered attention and responsiveness to other people (Brazelton, Tronick, Lechtig, Lasky, & Klein, 1977; Lester, 1975), heightened irritability, and lowered tolerance for frustration (Mora et al., 1979). Moreover, these effects continue. Guatemalan children who had been malnourished as infants were examined as 6- to 8-year-olds. Compared to children who had received food supplements during their first 2 years, the malnourished group was less socially involved, less active, more dependent on adults, and more anxious (Barrett, Radke-Yarrow, & Klein, 1982).

More recently, a group of 129 Barbadian children aged 5 through 11, who had suffered from marasmus as infants, were compared with their properly nourished classmates. Not surprisingly, the malnourished children were smaller and scored lower on intelligence tests. They also had more trouble with schoolwork and had more behavior problems as well: They were easily distracted, had poor attention spans, and were uncooperative. Malnourished boys also had more frequent temper tantrums and crying spells (Galler, Ramsey, & Solimano, 1984).

Adequate nutrition in infancy is essential for later development, but malnourished children don't just have inadequate food, they have inadequate *care* as well. They are undernourished emotionally, socially, and cognitively. A

Mexican study found, for example, that malnourished boys and girls had received less social, emotional, and cognitive stimulation from their mothers *even before* they became malnourished (Cravioto & DeLicardie, 1976). And in studies done in Jamaica and Barbados, families with malnourished children were different from others—even when their social class was the same (Galler et al., 1984; Kerr et al., 1978). The Barbadian mothers arranged fewer social contacts for their children, told them fewer stories, and were more depressed than the mothers of adequately nourished children living in the same social and economic conditions (Galler et al., 1984).

Finally, malnourished infants may be treated differently by people who care for them because of the way they look. This can be a continuing cycle, with a mother who is malnourished herself responding poorly to her own malnourished child. The child, in turn, develops poor social skills, compromising his development still further (Lester, 1979; Rosetti-Ferreira, 1978). The point we want to stress is that, like the rest of development, even malnourishment occurs in a social context.

THE INFANT'S LATER NUTRITIONAL NEEDS

When infants weigh about 12 pounds, breast milk or formula alone doesn't supply enough calories or iron, so a small amount of solid food is usually added to the daily diet (Leach, 1980). Most American pediatricians recommend introducing solid foods by adding new categories one at a time. Cereal, which supplies iron and B vitamins, comes first, often accompanied by strained fruits. Yellow and green vegetables follow, and finally, meat, fish, and eggs are added.

Although all infants need an adequate number of calories and nutrients for healthy growth, the actual amount of food each needs will differ. Highly active and fast-growing infants will need more calories than more placid or slower-growing babies. Overfeeding an infant may satisfy some psychological need in a parent, but it may be at the baby's expense.

Infant obesity

There is good evidence that bottle feeding is more likely than breast feeding to promote overeating. Whether overfeeding definitely leads to obesity either in infancy or in later life is currently being debated, as is the connection between infant obesity and obesity in adolescence or adulthood. Some studies have found that bottle-fed babies who eat solid foods at an early age are more likely to be obese than breast-fed infants who eat solids later (Kramer et al., 1985). But other studies have indicated that such feeding practices are unrelated to infant obesity (Wolman, 1984). It had also been widely believed that overfeeding increases the number of fat cells and that the number of fat cells developed during infancy determines whether a baby will grow up to be an obese adult (since the number of fat cells developed in infancy and in adolescence stays about the same throughout life). However, scientific evidence for this view is very weak (Edelman & Maller, 1982). About all that is certain is that genetic factors play a critical role in determining which *infants* will grow up to be overweight *children*, which may also mean obesity later on (Borjeson, 1979).

Summary

1. Growth during infancy is very rapid, especially during the first year, when a baby's weight triples and length increases 50 percent.

2. Parts of infants' bodies grow at different rates, and their relative proportions alter (the proportional phenomenon). Legs grow relatively longer, the head decreases in relative size, and the center of gravity shifts downward toward the center of the body.

3. Motor development follows a pattern. In cephalocaudal development, motor skills appear first in the head region and then proceed downward. Proximodistal development refers to motor skills that appear first near the center of the body and proceed gradually to the extremities. Also important to the order in which skills appear is mass-to-specific development, meaning that control proceeds from the larger muscles to the smaller. This is related to differentiation, the process by which movement becomes increasingly specific and goal-directed.

4. Rhythmical stereotypies, repeated movements that precede the appearance of motor skills, appear to be a kind of reflexive practice for those skills.

5. Although the general sequence of motor development is similar from infant to infant, there is a wide range of individual variations in timing and sometimes even in sequence.

6. Deprivation can cause developmental delays, and stimulation can accelerate the appearance of motor skills; early opportunities to move around also appear to speed up certain emotional and cognitive abilities in the short term. Overstimulation, however, is counterproductive.

7. As new motor skills appear and become more coordinated and refined, the infant's relation with the environment and the family also changes.

8. Continuing maturation of the nervous system, especially the cerebral cortex, the most complex part of the brain, explains the infant's growing ability to control and coordinate movements. There are two very significant processes: the proliferation of connections among nerve cells and the insulation of some nerve fibers with myelin for efficient message transmission. Brain development is affected by both genes and experience, including nutrition.

9. Nutrition plays a major role in infant development. Severe, prolonged malnutrition can stop growth permanently.

10. Breast milk is the ideal food for infants, since it is sterile, easy to digest, full of important nutrients and it contains antibodies to guard against infection. Formula is still considered an acceptable substitute if used properly.

11. Malnutrition often accompanies poverty in the United States and in underdeveloped nations.

12. Two conditions associated with severe malnutrition are marasmus and kwashiorkor, both life-threatening.

13. Malnutrition affects cognitive and social development. Effects include lowered attention and responsiveness, irritability, poor social skills, and difficulties with schoolwork.

14. Bottle feeding can lead to overfeeding. But whether overfeeding leads to obesity in infancy or in later life is not clear.

Key Terms

arborization

cephalocaudal development

cerebral cortex

differentiation

kwashiorkor

marasmus

mass-to-specific development

motor development

myelin

neurons

proportional phenomenon

proximodistal development

rhythmical stereotypies

Suggested Readings

Sinclair, D. (1980). *Human growth after birth.* Oxford: Oxford University Press. The nature and course of physical growth and development is examined in detail by one of the world's experts.

Spock, B. (1985). *Dr. Spock's baby and child care.* New York: Pocket Books. America's most famous pediatrician provides important information about infant health in an easily accessible way that has proven handy to millions of parents in the United States and around the world.

Stratton, P. (Ed.) (1982). *The psychobiology of the human newborn.* New York: Wiley. In a series of well-written chapters, phenomena related to early growth and development are discussed by outstanding researchers.

Cognitive and Language Development in Infancy

Alittle before his second birthday, Benjamin developed a keen interest in the story of *Snow White and the Seven Dwarfs*. He was especially fascinated by the witch (which he pronounced "vitch") and would plead with his parents to read and reread the story daily. One morning, he climbed into bed with his parents and pulled the blankets off his mother's feet. "This is Snow White," he said, grabbing one foot, "and this is the vitch," pointing to the other. "They are fighting." The next morning, he appeared again. His mother pointed to one of her feet and said, "Here's Snow White." "No!" Benjamin shouted. "That's the vitch!"

Benjamin's ability to substitute his mother's feet for Snow White and the "vitch" signals a cognitive milestone that marks the end of infancy—*representational thinking*. He was using one object (his mother's foot) to stand for, or *symbolize*, another (Snow White). Representational thinking, which develops along with the growth of language, is a major turning point in the development of cognitive abilities, for it allows children to use symbols to stand for things that they have experienced through sight, sound, touch, taste, or smell.

As a newborn, Benjamin couldn't understand what a foot was, no less pretend that it was Snow White. He knew the world only through his senses and reflexes. By the end of infancy, children can experience the world by *thinking* about it, in much the same way that adults do. Moreover, they are beginning to use the most important symbols available to humans—words—to communicate their experiences to others.

In this chapter, we trace the growth of cognitive and linguistic skills, first charted by Jean Piaget. We'll find that there are several key turning points, or transitions, along the way. These transitions, at about 3 months, 8 months, 12 months, and 18 months, correspond roughly to changes in the maturing brain and nervous system that we noted in Chapter 5. Recently, scientists have begun to link specific biological changes to the emergence of specific cognitive skills. As yet we can only speculate that major reorganizations in the way infants think originate from major reorganizations in the brain and nervous system.

Cognitive Development: Piaget and Beyond

Jean Piaget, the Swiss psychologist who studied cognitive development, theorized that an infant's way of knowing the world is different from a child's, an adolescent's, or an adult's. He argued that cognitive development progresses through a series of stages, and at each succeeding stage we understand the world in more complex, more sophisticated ways. What we couldn't understand at 3, or what we "understood" incorrectly or partially, is easily grasped at 8, not just because we know more, but because the *way* in which we understand and think about the world has become more advanced.

Do these stages unfold naturally, without any help from parents, or do infants need some kind of special stimulation along the way? Piaget would have taken exception to the word "special." He believed that biology and experience work together in cognitive development, and that the ordinary experiences of life ensure the unfolding of each stage at about the same time in every infant. Unless a child is severely deprived of contact with humans and objects, each cognitive stage emerges naturally. The first 2 years form the first phase in Piaget's scheme, the sensorimotor stage. And at its start, infants explore the world not with their minds, but with their mouths.

SENSORIMOTOR INTELLIGENCE

To understand the kind of intelligence young infants have, it helps to know first what they lack. If you show a 1-month-old baby girl a picture of the mobile that hangs above her crib, it means nothing to her; she won't recognize it as the dangling object she looks at every day. If you give her the picture, she might try to suck it, because she explores the world with her mouth. Unlike an adult, or even a 2-year-old, she can't remember what the mobile does; she can't predict what will happen if someone shakes it; she can't connect the word "mobile" to the thing she looks at. Not only do infants lack words; they don't even know that things *exist* when they are out of sight. Infants comprehend the world only in the present time. Notions of past and future do not exist; nor does the concept that symbols represent concrete things (that the word "mobile" or a picture of a mobile stands for a real mobile). Absent too is the understanding that actions have consequences, that one thing leads to another: Drop a rattle on the floor and a noise occurs.

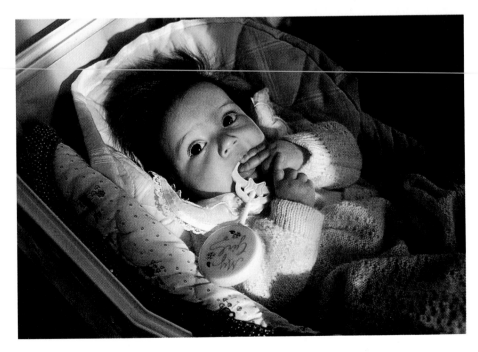

During the sensorimotor period of intelligence, infants learn about things through their senses and motor actions. For this 3-month-old, rattles are best explored by shaking and tasting. (*Joel Gordon*)

sensorimotor
describes Piaget's first stage of cognitive development, in which infants explore their world with senses and motor actions

decentration
focusing on more than the self; extension of activity and awareness beyond one's own physical boundaries

intentionality
purposeful coordination of activity toward a goal

object permanence
slowly developing under-standing that objects exist separate from one's percep-tion of them

Piaget documented the gradual emergence of the basic elements of intel-ligence during the first 2 years of life. A baby begins to understand an object by tasting, touching, seeing, hearing, and smelling it; by bumping into it, grasping it, lifting it, and dropping it. Because it is based on the senses and on motor actions, Piaget used the term **sensorimotor** to describe this first period of cognitive development.

As they move through the sensorimotor period, infants gain three basic cognitive abilities: First, they gradually understand that they are separate from the other things and people in their world. There is self, and there are others. Infants gradually extend their activity and awareness beyond the boundaries of their own body. Piaget called this process **decentration**—literally, moving away from *centering*, or focusing, on their physical selves. The second basic skill babies gain during the sensorimotor period is the ability to plan and coordinate their actions. Not until 8 months will most infants know that kicking their legs will make a mobile attached to the crib move. The new and very rudimentary skill is called **intentionality**. Finally, infants begin to understand that even when they can't see, hear, or feel something, it still exists. Piaget called this concept **object permanence**. Tracing its development during the sensorimotor period was one of his greatest contributions toward our understanding of cognitive development.

Piaget initially proposed six substages within the sensorimotor period. Although he identified specific periods for the emergence of each stage of sensorimotor development, we now know that the timing varies from infant to infant—some babies will spend more time in some stages than others. The *sequence* of cognitive development, however, is always the same, and each ac-complishment lays the foundation for the next (Flavell, 1977). In Piaget's view, the skills gained in one period lead to the unfolding of the next. The early skills do not disappear, however. Even as an adult, you could still learn through sensorimotor experience if you needed to, although you would prob-ably find it cumbersome. Sensorimotor intelligence is simply incorporated into more sophisticated ways of knowing and learning.

A NEW LOOK AT PIAGET

Over five decades have passed since Piaget first published his insights into the minds of infants in the 1930s. As with any theory, later research by others has called for a number of changes in Piaget's framework. An important new proposal is that infants progress through four cognitive substages instead of Piaget's six, with important transition points at 3, 8, 12, and 18 months (Fischer, 1987; Fischer & Silvern, 1985). Figure 6-1 summarizes the tradi-tional and new theories. At each transition a new aspect of sensorimotor intel-ligence begins to unfold. What is most interesting is that this new timetable coincides with changes occurring in the brain: New research shows that brain waves, sleep cycles, and perceptual abilities are all changing *at the same time* that the new cognitive skills appear (Fischer & Silvern, 1985). We turn now to these transitions, paying special attention to the major accomplishments in decen-tration, intentionality, and object permanence that occur at each point.

Substages (Piaget)	Transition points (Fischer and others)
0 to 1 month: Reflexes	
1 to 4 months: Adapting reflexes; primary circular reactions	
4 to 8 months: Secondary circular reactions	3 months: Primary circular reactions
8 to 12 months: Beginnings of object permanence and intentional behavior; anticipation of events	8 months: Beginnings of intentional behavior and decentration; secondary circular reactions; beginnings of object permanence (in moving objects)
12 to 18 months: "Little scientist" exploration (tertiary circular reactions)	12 months: Purposeful trial-and-error "little scientist" exploration; broadened object permanence
18 to 24 months: Representational thinking; deferred imitation; complete object permanence	18 months: Emergence of representational thinking; deferred imitation; complete object permanence

FIGURE 6-1
ACHIEVEMENTS OF THE SENSORIMOTOR PERIOD: OVERLAPPING VIEWS
The concept of four major transition points within the sensorimotor period incorporates the achievements proposed by Piaget, but it allows for greater "timetable" flexibility. This flexibility accounts for individual variation in timing and provides a simpler, more clear-cut framework. Also, there is evidence that the four-transition scheme corresponds closely to the way the brain is developing during the first 2 years.

The 3-month transition: From reflex to accidental discovery

A pacifier placed in a newborn's mouth will cause her to suck—not because she "wants" to suck, but because the sensation in her mouth triggers a sucking reflex. For the first month, infants have no control over their actions; they are "reflexive" beings. Some of the reflexes we are born with disappear, but others change, marking the beginning of cognitive development. For example, all newborns suck the same way whether on a breast or bottle nipple. Gradually, the nursing infant notices that the breast nipple differs from the bottle nipple, and both differ from the pacifier. She begins sucking one way on the breast nipple and another way on the bottle nipple. This kind of change—a shift in response keyed to differences between objects—marks the beginning of sensorimotor intelligence.

The next step occurs at about 3 months when infants make another discovery. Picture a 3-month-old boy lying in his crib, staring at a mobile hanging above him. Excited, he waves his arms. They catch his attention, and then disappear. Again he looks at the mobile; again he waves his arms, and again, he is intrigued. Now, he starts to move around, trying to see his arm again. Eventually, the arm reappears. He pauses and gurgles, then repeats the movements again and again. Piaget called the repetition of action and response a

The Progress of Play: Playing Is Learning

Give a 4-month-old a toy, and she may put it in her mouth, shake it, turn it over, bang it, drop it, or simply look at it. Whether it is a rattle or a doll, a teddy bear or a ball, she'll do the same things. This universal way of dealing with objects is called "undifferentiated exploration" (McCall, Eichorn, & Hogarty, 1977).

At around the time of the 8-month transition an important change occurs. Although undifferentiated exploration does not disappear (indeed, it remains the most important way of exploring *new* objects for some time), the baby can now explore the unique, as opposed to bangable or suckable, properties of objects. If you give her a ball, she discovers that it rolls, and she will repeatedly make it do that. If you give her a toy telephone, she examines it, and when she finds the dial, she'll spin it over and over again. This new kind of exploration, linked to the special properties or functions of the individual object, is called "functional activity."

At about 8 months, infants are fascinated by the special properties of objects. Rolling out toilet paper or lifting the toilet seat over and over can be very intriguing. *(Elizabeth Crews/Stock, Boston)*

Another kind of activity begins now as well. Babies start combining things that do not "go" together. By trying to balance a peg on a toy telephone or placing a toy car on a ball, babies are beginning to explore the ways objects can relate to each other. In "relational play," objects are paired without any apparent logic.

Around the 12-month transition, something changes again. Now if you give a baby a peg and a pegboard, or a toy telephone, he'll put the peg in the board and the receiver on the phone. He has reached the "functional-relational" level of play—he can figure out the obvious way in which two things relate to each other. He may raise the receiver of his toy telephone—not to his ear, but over his head. Or he might hold a plastic cup next to his cheek instead of his mouth. He knows that *some* sort of relationship exists between two things, but he still hasn't figured it out.

By their first birthday, most infants also begin to show true "pretense play." Now, a baby will "drink" from an empty cup and talk into a toy telephone, even if he doesn't get the telephone receiver positioned just right. And soon he'll bring others into his game, offering his mother or a teddy bear a pretend drink, or putting a doll to sleep on the floor. Sometime around the 18-month transition, toddlers begin to substitute some objects for others, putting a doll to bed on a block and then covering it with a newspaper blanket, for example. Symbolic thinking opens up a whole new world of play and, in so doing, affects the way in which the child learns about the world.

primary circular reaction
an infant's repetition of a chance action involving a part of the infant's body

circular reaction. The early form of it is a **primary circular reaction**, because the infant's actions center around his own body. Remember that during this stage, the movements that lead to the infant's "discoveries" always happen first

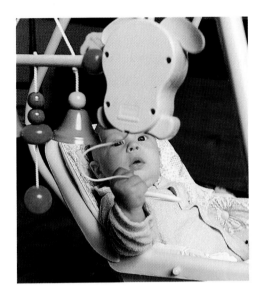

If this 4-month-old pulls the cord, he'll discover that his toy will move. If he likes the sight, he'll try to grab the rope to see it again. (*Joel Gordon*)

by *accident*. They are repeated as the baby tries to make the event happen again and again. As neuromuscular control increases, infants' skill at performing circular reactions improves. These primary circular reactions signal the earliest awareness of cause and effect. They also form the foundation for the development of intentionality, decentration, and object permanence, all of which begin to emerge during the next 5 months.

The 8-month transition: From accidental discovery to intentional behavior (8 to 12 months)

From 6 to 12 months, infants are still exploring their environment through circular reactions, but now the patterns of repetition include *objects* as well as parts of their own body. Piaget called these patterns **secondary circular reactions**. When a 5-month-old girl looks up at her mobile and moves her arms and legs with pleasure, the crib's vibrations shake the mobile. But now something new happens. She stops moving and stares at the mobile; she kicks her leg again—the mobile moves again. Another kick, the mobile quivers again. Now, she makes the connection, and squeals with delight as she repeatedly makes the mobile move. Her interest has shifted from her own movements to the mobile's; something in the "nonbaby" world has become more interesting than her own body. The emergence of secondary circular reactions marks the start of true decentration, one of the key achievements of sensorimotor development.

Whereas the 7-month-old discovers how to see his arm, the 8-month-old discovers what the arm can *do*: Shake a rattle, it makes a noise; bat a mobile, it moves. Infants' learning that their own actions cause *separate* results is the hallmark of this phase and signals the start of true **intentional behavior**.

Toward the end of the first year, infants make great strides in the development of intentional behavior. When his son Laurent was about 10 months

secondary circular reactions repetitions of actions that trigger responses in the external environment (squeeze toy—it squeaks)

intentional behavior goal-directed activity, which begins to appear from 8 to 12 months

By 8 months, a baby can intentionally grab a ring and make his mobile swing. *(Sonya Jacobs/ The Stock Market)*

old, Piaget placed a small pillow between the baby and a familiar toy. Laurent paused, batted the pillow out of the way, and reached for the toy. Laurent wanted something, and he got it. Sometime between 8 and 12 months, all infants can do what Laurent did: No longer are they merely responding to accidental events. Now they can deliberately act toward getting what they want. By this time, babies also can coordinate physical skills, as Laurent coordinated batting and reaching, to achieve a goal. They can also recall the way that two actions can be coordinated, a sign of increased memory.

The development of object permanence

During this phase, the baby also begins to perceive something new about the permanence of objects: What leaves may return. Until about 6 months, out of sight seems to be out of mind: If a ball rolls out of his crib, an infant won't look for it, even if he was just touching it. But by 8 months something changes. Now if any object drops out of sight, a baby will look toward the spot where it disappeared, as if expecting it to reappear. You can demonstrate this easily with a toy train and a tunnel. Show an 8-month-old a train moving into and out of the tunnel. Repeat this several times, and very soon the baby will look toward the end of the tunnel, waiting for the train to appear (Nelson, 1971). You can do the same thing with a ball that rolls behind a cushion and appears at the other side. Soon the baby looks for the emerging ball.

Although infants can now anticipate the reappearance of moving objects, at the beginning of this stage they are still uncertain about the permanence of stationary objects. If you cover a bottle with a towel so that an identifying part, such as the nipple, is still visible, the baby will reach for it. But if the bottle is entirely covered by the towel—even if you cover it while she is watching, *and even if she was already reaching for the bottle*—she will stop reaching when she can't see it anymore. For the 8-month-old, the object still seems to disappear, but within a few months, she'll pull the towel off the bottle.

Although babies of this age will search for an object that has been moved, they do not always look in the right place. If a ball on the left side of a table is covered by a cloth, then uncovered and moved to the right side and covered with another cloth *while the infant is watching*, the baby will still search for it on the left side—where it was *first* hidden.

Why does a second move or second disappearance of an object confuse these babies—or does it confuse them at all? Piaget held that infants stop searching for an object because they think it no longer exists. But many psychologists today think otherwise. It may be that the child can focus on only one aspect of the object's existence, in this case, one location; they get "stuck" on the first place they discovered the object (Flavell, 1985). Or perhaps the infant's memory is not yet developed enough or adaptable enough to process and hold onto two locations in a sequence (Harris, 1983). It is also possible that infants simply do not know what to do when their initial attempts to find an object fail; they have no established routines for this sort of thing (Harris, 1983). But whether the problem is one of concept, memory, or learned routines, the main point is that the child cannot yet handle more than one dislocation or disappearance of an object. And psychologists agree that whatever the reasons, object permanence develops only gradually during the second half of an infant's first year.

The 12-month transition: From intentional behavior to systematic exploration (12 to 18 months)

As babies begin their second year, another important transition begins as well: active, purposeful, trial-and-error exploration. The infant who at 6 months *accidentally* discovered that her mobile moved when she kicked now *searches* for discoveries with relentless abandon, moving from room to room emptying drawers, wastebaskets, bookcases, then examining her finds for their hidden potential. Pots can be drums, containers, or stools. A wooden spoon can be a drumstick, a hammer, or a tool for exploring the toilet.

Selma Fraiberg, an astute observer of children, describes the "little scientist" this way:

Hiding this 10-month-old's toy didn't fool her. She pushes away the cloth and finds it. Just a few months before she wouldn't have looked for it once the toy was hidden from sight. *(Hazel Hankin)*

The study of a cup will occupy him for weeks, for countless mealtimes, while the function of the cup as perceived by his mother will hardly interest him at all. To drink milk from the cup will be the least absorbing activity in connection with the cup while he is conducting his research on the nature of a cup. He examines the outer surface of the cup, explores the inner surface, discovers its hollowness, bangs it on the tray for its sound effects. Rivers of milk, orange juice, and water cascade from cup to tray to kitchen floor, adding joy to the experiment. His mother, engaged in unceasing labor with sponges and mops, can hardly be blamed if she does not encourage these experiments, but she is never consulted. . . . Before he concludes these experiments he has discovered every property of a cup that can be extracted through his study and experimentation (including breakage) and then settles down to a utilitarian view of a cup which gratifies his mother. We can multiply such studies in the nature of objects to include nearly everything accessible to him. (Fraiberg, 1959, p. 53)

And, with a more mature understanding of object permanence, more things *are* accessible. Now, when a ball is hidden first under one cloth and then under another—if he *sees* the ball being moved—the child can find it. He picks up the second cloth and makes his discovery. Now children know the ball is separate from the actions associated with it: it still exists, even in a new place (Flavell, 1985).

The 18-month transition: From sensorimotor functioning to representational thinking

The transition that occurs around 18 months is the shift from the intelligence of infancy to the kind of symbolic thinking we use throughout life. It is a transition to true symbolic thinking: the ability to represent things mentally, to

Wearing a bowl as a hat delights this 18-month-old girl who can now pretend that one thing can be another. *(Hank Morgan/Rainbow)*

At about 1 year old, babies can imitate behaviors they've seen before. *(Michal Heron/Woodfin Camp & Associates)*

imagine *what if*. This **representational thinking** involves the mental manipulation of images, or symbols. One real object can "stand for" another. A child can now *pretend* that a block is a car or a building or that a foot is Snow White. Symbolic thinking also makes mental experiments and **mental combinations** possible. That is, several actions can be coordinated and "acted out" mentally in a sequence. A 2-year-old girl, for example, goes to a cabinet, pulls out a pot, pauses, gets a spoon, throws a block into the pot, and stirs. She has performed a series of activities because she was able to imagine: "What do I want to do?" "What do I need?" "Where do I get it?" And finally, "How do I do it?"

Finally, thinking symbolically allows children to apply their growing memory skills. The past becomes related to the present, and **deferred imitation** becomes possible. Because they can now duplicate behavior they have seen before, a child may take her toy dog for a walk, offer her teddy bear a drink, or imitate her mother reading a book.

No longer limited to the trial-and-error experiments of earlier periods, toddlers can solve problems mentally. Piaget's daughter Lucienne provided his classic illustration of this achievement. Lucienne wanted to get something that was inside of a matchbox, the kind that slides open and shut. Her father, the experimenter, refused to slide it open. She sat holding the box and, while looking at it, began to open and close her mouth, *representing to herself* the solution to the problem. Finally, having thought the problem through, she pushed open the box and claimed her prize.

Complete object permanence

Children who can think symbolically can solve the most advanced object permanence problem, the one involving "invisible displacement." Pick up a ping-pong ball and then move your hand and the ball under a cloth. Then, remove

representational thinking thinking that involves manipulation of mental images (symbols)

mental combinations mental coordinations of several actions in sequence

deferred imitation duplication of behavior seen or experienced earlier

your hand, leaving the ball under the cloth, where it makes an obvious lump. In earlier stages, infants would look for the ball under your hand, but by 24 months, children can find the ball even if you pass your hand under several cloths before or after actually placing the ball under one of them. If the child doesn't find it where she thinks it ought to be, she searches where she thinks it might be, and if she still cannot find it, she looks surprised. What has happened is that she now can represent the object mentally: She can imagine it and she knows it exists *somewhere*. Only now, said Piaget, does the child fully possess the concept of object permanence.

Attending and Perceiving

An infant girl lies in her crib looking up at a mobile dangling above her. Patterned bumpers line her crib, and her sheets have a colorful design. What will attract her to those stimuli, and how will she begin to make sense out of them?

We know that infants are born with the sensory capacities to receive information which permits learning (Chapter 4). How those capacities develop has long interested students of child development. Specifically, we want to know what captures infants' *attention* and how that changes as they mature. What do infants *perceive*, and what can they *understand*?

ATTENTION

During the first 2 months, newborns like familiarity; they want to see today what they saw yesterday (Hunt, 1979; Weizman, Cohen, & Pratt, 1971). But by 2 months, infants can process more information, and novelty begins to interest them. As they grow older, infants look longer at pictures of unfamiliar toys than familiar ones. They also start to prefer real toys that look and sound different from the ones they've been used to (Eckerman & Whatley, 1975; McCall, 1974). But too much novelty may overwhelm immature nervous systems, and interest wanes. In short, infants seem to seek an optimal level of novelty—a balance between the familiar and the unfamiliar (McCall, 1974) (see "Issues & Options").

complexity
number and intricacy of traits like color or pattern in a stimulus

More complex images become interesting too. (**Complexity** refers to characteristics such as number of colors and contrasts, pattern, organization, and intricacy of design.) A pentagon is more complex and captures more attention than a triangle, for example, simply because it has more sides. And infants look longer at a realistic drawing of a human face than at a circle with dots for the eyes and nose and a curved line for a mouth (Fantz, 1965; Greenberg, 1971). But as with novelty, complex figures or objects attract attention as long as they are not *too* complex; infants need to process information without being overwhelmed by it.

How do scientists know what infants prefer? Researchers show them designs and shapes of varying complexities. Then they note what the babies *choose* to look at and how long they look. For example, infants might see a complex geometric design, like a hexagon, and a simple design, like a triangle, at the same time. If they look longer at the hexagon, researchers conclude that infants prefer complex designs to simple ones.

PERCEPTION

Attention alone doesn't lead to understanding. A baby could look at a mobile all day and still not know that two of the figures are alike or that the clown's nose is the same color as a tomato. Interpreting what the senses can only transmit is a cognitive skill that develops along with the ability to **perceive**, to assign meaning to sensations. That ability, researchers say, takes a leap forward at 3 or 4 months, a time of significant changes in the brain and nervous system.

perceive
to interpret sensations

Color perception

Infants like color almost at first glance. Newborns look longer at color pictures than at black-and-white images, and by 3 months, red, yellow, blue, and green get the longest stares. Finer distinctions occur after 3 months, when babies can tell blue from green (Adams, 1987; Bornstein, 1981). When two colors are presented sequentially, say, a blue picture followed by a green picture of the same object, researchers measure the baby's heart rate and time spent looking at the pictures. When interest flags, eyes turn away and heart rate increases. This loss of interest to a constant stimulus is called **habituation**. Its opposite, **dishabituation**, occurs when a new image or color excites a baby's attention. Then she focuses on the new stimulus, and heart rate slows.

habituation
adaptation to (loss of interest in) an unchanging stimulus

dishabituation
reaction to (recovery of interest in) a novel stimulus

By 4 months, infants can perceive both similarities and differences between colors. They understand that colors can be slightly different yet still belong to the same category (Bornstein, 1981). In short, they know that shades of blue are still blue. This ability reflects one of the most important concepts in the study of perception—**equivalence**. Like is grouped with like in spite of differences.

equivalence
recognition that similar stimuli, or the same stimuli under changed conditions, belong to the same basic category

Equivalence permits infants to make sense out of the welter of stimuli they face each day. As their cognitive skills develop, equivalence will be a basic tool for understanding the physical world. Even though two balls may be different colors and sizes, they're still balls. A spoon is still a spoon even when it has a slightly different shape or design; a pear and a peach are both "fruit." Without notions of equivalence, the world would remain a confusing, ever-multiplying mass of images.

Face perception

When an infant stares at her mother's face, how does it look? Can the infant perceive all its features or only a few? Can she tell this special face from a stranger's? from her father's or sister's? The answers to these questions depend on when you ask them, because perceiving faces improves with age. During their first 3 months, infants look mostly at the borders of a face, (Maurer & Salapatek, 1976). At 3 months, infants become interested in a single feature, the eyes (Haith, Bergman, & Moore, 1977). This physical change

Issues & OPTIONS

Raising Smart Babies:
More Is Not Always Better

Not long ago, a major newspaper reported that black and white were the "in" colors for infants. Researchers had learned that babies liked these hues: They were stimulating. Soon, trendy shops were stocking black-and-white patterned crib mobiles, stretchies, sheets, and bumpers. And parents, eager to follow the experts' advice in the raise-your-baby's-IQ sweepstakes, were buying.

Black-and-white patterns *do* attract infants' attention, but babies don't need a special curriculum and special outfits for optimal cognitive development. What they do need is loving, playful attention. Simply stated, babies who receive a lot of attention from their parents function better intellectually as children than those who received less parental attention. *Parental attentiveness* includes many kinds of behaviors; even just looking at an infant can make a difference. In fact, the amount of time parents spend just watching their babies is a strong predictor of cognitive functioning (Clarke-Stewart, 1973; Rubenstein, 1967). *Physical contact* between parent and child is also related to intellectual competence in infancy and beyond (Lewis & Goldberg, 1969; Tulkin & Covitz, 1975; Yarrow, 1961). Actually, it may not be the parents' attentiveness *in itself* but what they do while holding their infants that is the key factor. Parents who *talk* to their babies, for example, engage the infant's attention and encourage a response such as a smile or vocalization. Over time, infants who have gotten a lot of *verbal stimulation* become more skilled at using language themselves and show higher levels of general cognitive functioning (Beckwith, 1971; Clarke-Stewart, 1973; Engel & Keane, 1975; Nelson, 1973).

Parents also influence cognitive development by giving their infants toys and other objects to look at, touch, and manipulate (Bell, 1971; Bradley & Caldwell, 1976, 1984; Clarke-Stewart, 1973; Engel & Keane, 1975). Such *material stimulation* is best when it is geared to the child's level of development and interest—a

has a social consequence: Now when parents look at their babies, their babies can look directly back.

At about 4 months, a major transition occurs. Infants begin to prefer pictures of whole faces to those of isolated features (Gibson, 1969). They also prefer normal-looking, attractive faces to pictures of scrambled features and unattractive faces (Langlois et al., 1987). They know how a face is supposed to look, how the features should be arranged, that certain arrangements are more attractive than others—and that is what they want to see. This shift illustrates a major principle in perceptual development: *Perception has moved from the part to the whole* (Kagan, 1967; Thomas, 1973). Within the next 2

Issues & OPTIONS

2-month-old is stimulated by mobiles hanging over her crib, for example, while an 8-month-old likes to explore a box full of soft blocks. Playthings need not be elaborate; often the best "toys" are ordinary household items. Pots and pans, wooden spoons, and plastic cups make excellent playthings, and toddlers love to "cook" beside their parents.

Another dimension of cognitive stimulation is the parent's *responsiveness*. Watch a sensitive mother interacting with her 4-month-old baby: She talks, he babbles back; she laughs and coos, so does he. He drops a toy and fusses, she picks it up. Children whose parents respond to them in this way are more competent intellectually—both in infancy and later on—than children the same age with less responsive parents (Carew, 1980; Clarke-Stewart, 1973; Hardy-Brown et al., 1981; Martin, 1981; Yarrow et al.,

1973). Parental responsiveness may help children feel that they have control over their world, and that feeling encourages them to go on to further activity and learning (Lewis & Goldberg, 1969).

So far, it sounds as if the more attention a baby gets the better, but in fact, too much interaction and involvement can be overstimulating (Wachs et al., 1971). A parent who has been separated from a baby all day may try, in the evening, to engage the infant in "meaningful" activities, but soon the baby becomes irritable and fussy. It's disappointing when your own child won't play with you, but parents need to be sensitive to their baby's need for stimulation. Sometimes just holding an infant is enough.

Like too much stimulation, too much restriction can also work against a baby. In fact, frequent restrictions, whether verbal or physical, can undermine cognitive

development (Clarke-Stewart, 1973; Engel & Keane, 1975; Tulkin & Kagan, 1972). Infants are naturally curious, and overly restrictive supervision can squelch their interest in the world or at least limit the time they have for exploring. When babies spend long periods in a high chair or playpen—or if they frequently hear "No. Don't. Stop that!"—the basic information-gathering activities that foster intellectual development are limited. Of course, giving a toddler the freedom to explore an unprotected stairway or a medicine cabinet is hardly in the child's best interests. The most effective infant care provides intellectual stimulation which promotes cognitive development *and* protects the child from overstimulation and dangerous activities. And no special outfits are required.

months, infants will be able to discriminate between different faces, and they'll recognize familiar faces even when they appear in unfamiliar expressions, angles, or contexts (Cohen, 1972; Fagan, 1976), another instance of equivalence.

New perceptual abilities foster social and emotional growth as well, as infants begin learning the language of facial expressions. Raised eyebrows are now part of a whole face that may be expressing delighted surprise or wariness. An upturned mouth signals happiness. Until they can talk, perceiving and understanding facial expressions provides answers to unasked questions. In new situations, for example, 7-month-olds will read a familiar person's facial expression before reacting themselves (Campos & Stenberg, 1981). Babies look to their mothers when strangers approach; if mothers smile, infants usually do too. If mothers look wary, so do babies (Boccia & Campos, 1983).

Looking to someone else to find an emotional response for yourself is **social referencing**. If you have ever "read" other students' faces as they read a test paper, seeking to know if the questions were easy or hard, that was social referencing. Your ability to read expressions of worry, danger, comfort, or happiness dates back to infancy. And it now seems that this sensory ability, long believed to develop only with time and experience, appears very early as well.

social referencing
looking to someone else for guidance in emotional response to new stimuli or situations

CROSS-MODAL TRANSFER

In an experiment, a 6-month-old girl is given a paper towel tube to hold and manipulate for 30 seconds, but she can't see it. Then she looks at a picture of the tube. Does she recognize it? Does information gained by her sense of touch "cross over" to sight? Piaget said no. He held that each of our senses works independently at birth, and only after much experience does information from one sense transfer to another—from touch to sight, for example (Piaget, 1952; Piaget & Inhelder, 1956).

But newer research data suggest otherwise. It seems that the senses work *together* almost from birth. Information gained by one sense, by touch, taste, or smell, for example, can be processed by vision, without much experience at all. (Walker-Andrews & Gibson, 1987). Proof of these early **cross-modal abilities** (abilities that cut across sensory modes) comes from studies in the laboratory.

cross-modal abilities
abilities that cut across sensory modes; abilities to transfer data from one sensory system to another

Researchers gave 6-month-olds two kinds of cylinders that they could hold but not see. One type was smooth-sided; the other had indentations. One group of babies had 30 seconds to manipulate the objects; the other had 1 full minute. When shown pictures of the cylinders, the 1-minute group looked longer at the object they had held. The other group, with only 30 seconds of touching experience, did not seem to recognize their type of cylinder, but when given a full minute of holding and manipulation, they did as well as the other babies (Gottfried, Rose, & Bridger, 1977; Rose, Gottfried, & Bridger, 1981). The researchers concluded that, after only 1 minute of experience, information was transfered from touch to sight.

In another experiment 4-month-olds watched a film of blocks hitting against each other and another film of water-filled sponges being squeezed. When the films were accompanied by sounds, the infants looked longer at the blocks when they *heard* the sounds of the blocks, and longer at the sponges while listening to squishing sounds (Bahrick, 1983). Even more surprising, 5-month-olds can match films of an approaching or retreating car with motor sounds that grow louder or softer (Walker-Andrews & Lennon, 1985).

Are infants making these connections between sight and sound because they have had enough experience to do so, even by 4 or 5 months? Perhaps, but other studies show that even 1-month-olds have cross-modal abilities (Gibson & Walker, 1984; Rose & Ruff, 1987). Babies that young look longer at something they've held in their mouth than at something they haven't. So, while experience is needed, infants seem to begin life with some cross-modal abilities already in place.

Language Development

"Ba-ba-ba-ba-ba. Pa-pa-pa-pa-pa." These are not the lyrics of a fifties do-wop group, but the babblings of a 5-month-old. By 1 year, some of these sounds will have meanings, and even if they are just one syllable long, they will carry the child into the world of words.

How do the babbling sounds change into one-syllable words, which are then combined into two-word sentences, and finally into sentences of growing complexity? Since infants everywhere usually progress through the same stages at about the same time, biology is clearly at work. Human genes allow us to create human speech; but genes are not enough. Without experiencing the speech of other humans, no child, despite genetic potential, would learn to talk.

The process of language development begins long before words appear, as infants and adults communicate during the first year. In this period of prelinguistic communication, gestures, social games, and a lot of adult intuition prepare infants for the use of real language.

PRELINGUISTIC COMMUNICATION

Watch a mother as she changes her infant's diaper. She looks at the baby, talking to him gently as she slips off the wet diaper and slides a new one in place. Whenever she can, she watches the infant's face. Then she plays for a minute, tickling his tummy and making up a funny song.

Long before babies have any inkling of language, parents in all societies communicate with them in playful ways. These first games, because they involve gestures, sounds, facial expression, and imitation, are considered **prelinguistic communication**. They often have a teaching component as well. The familiar patty-cake and peek-a-boo, along with variations invented by parents, are important preparations for language acquisition. Since parents are gratified when their infants seem pleased or interested, the games that please are repeated over and over again. Many of these exchanges resemble conversation because they require a certain amount of give-and-take, or **turn-taking**. The parents will make a sound or movement, then pause for a response, make

prelinguistic communication
literally, before-language communication; communication between parents and infants through games, gestures, sounds, facial expressions

turn-taking
conversational give-and-take

Playfulness between adults and infants, besides being fun for both, is a kind of prelinguistic communication, the give-and-take of conversation. (left, *Hazel Hankin/Stock, Boston;* right, *Suzanne Szasz/Photo Researchers)*

another sound or movement in response, with another pause for the baby to react, and so on (Bruner, 1975).

This kind of interaction takes time to develop. In a primitive version of "catch," for example, a 5-month-old boy's mother may offer him a small toy. He doesn't actually catch the toy; rather, she places it in his hands or lap, from which it is likely to fall. She takes it back and repeats the action, with the same result. All this is very one-sided, but by about 10 months, the baby begins to play a more active role, actually grasping the toy and, still later, returning it to his mother. At some point, *he* initiates this "behavioral dialogue," waving the toy, later offering it to her, and subsequently tossing it to (or, more likely, *at*) her (Schaffer, 1979). By the baby's first birthday, he is skilled at this game. In a game like catch, a baby learns to take turns—a skill that will be essential for later conversations.

Essential too for effective communication is the capacity to use language *intentionally* to say what you mean. Recall that one of the major aspects of the infant's cognitive development is the gradual emergence of goal-directed activity, or intentionality. As with other sensorimotor accomplishments, infants grow in their ability to use language intentionally. This ability develops during the first year and is nurtured by adults who respond to infants' sounds *as if* they had meaning (Bates, Camaioni, & Volterra, 1975). Consider the following "conversation" between a mother and her 3-month-old (Snow, 1977):

Mother	Baby
	[Smiles]
Oh, what a nice little smile!	
Yes, isn't that pretty?	
There now.	
There's a nice little smile.	
	[Burps]
What a nice wind as well!	
Yes, that's better, isn't it?	
Yes.	
Yes.	
	[Vocalizes]
Yes!	
There's a nice noise.	

Although all the meaning comes from the mother here, early dialogues like this are an important foundation for language development. By 12 months, many babies will be communicating intentionally, beginning to use their first words.

Paralleling this progress toward real language is the baby's decreasing reliance on physical effort to get what she wants. If a 5-month-old girl wants her teddy bear, which is just out of reach, she will reach for it, fail, and utter a despairing cry. Mother or father may deduce the problem and hand her the toy. By 9 or 10 months, the child, though physically more capable of getting the toy, may simply stretch an arm toward the teddy bear, at the same time looking toward mother. Again, she gets the message—but notice how the baby's communicative skills have improved. Soon, the child actually points to the toy, and mother gets it. Typically, she talks as she responds to the request, saying something like, "Oh, your teddy bear? Do you want your teddy bear? Okay, here's the teddy bear." And one day, stretching, reaching, or even pointing will no longer be necessary. The baby will say "Teddy," and mother will get the bear. How do infants reach this next milestone in communication?

EARLY SOUNDS

No matter what language their parents speak, all babies begin to make the same sounds at about the same time. By 2 or 3 months, infants begin cooing—they repeat the same vowel sound, varying the pitch from high to low. By 5 months, they add consonants to the vowels and string the sounds together ("ba-ba-ba-ba," "do-do-do-do"). These sound combinations are called **babbling**, and the sequence of sounds that infants make when they babble appears to be universal.

babbling
infant's repetitive sound combinations, before first words are spoken

In general, the first sounds are the easiest for babies to say (Menyuk, 1985). For infants everywhere, sounds made with the lips ("p" or "b") precede sounds made with the tip of the tongue ("d" or "n"). Similarly, "stop sounds" (made with "b," for instance) appear after "nasal" sounds, such as those made with "m" (Irwin, 1947).

Even children with deaf parents show the same babbling patterns (Lenneberg, 1967). When they begin speaking, U.S. children will say "tut" before "cut"; Swedish children will say "tata" before "kata"; and Japanese children will say "ta" before "ka" (Lamb & Bornstein, 1987). This is further evidence for the universality and biological basis of early sound production. In many languages the earliest sounds infants make are incorporated into terms used to refer to parents—in English, for example, "mama" or "papa." Table 6-1 summarizes the stages of language development that all infants seem to go through.

THE FIRST WORDS

"Mama" says a baby, and a mother is thrilled, but "mama" may also be the baby's greeting for Daddy and older sister—or even the family pet. When the first real word arrives, between 10 and 14 months, it may not be used again for weeks or months (Nelson, 1973).

TABLE 6-1   MILESTONES IN LANGUAGE DEVELOPMENT

Milestone	Approximate Age
Cooing	2 to 3 months
Babbling	By 5 months
First words	10 to 14 months
Ten words in usable vocabulary; comprehends about 50	12 months
Two-word sentences	21 to 24 months
Two hundred words in vocabulary	24 months

At first, most infants acquire words one at a time, mastering about 10 words by 15 months, and about 200 by 2 years. But babies understand much more than they can say. In fact, understanding is about 6 months ahead of speech—in other words, language *comprehension* precedes language *production* (Benedict, 1976). At 12 or 13 months, a baby who can use only about 10 words meaningfully can *understand* five times that number. Children may not be able to identify a teddy bear in so many words, but if someone says, "Where's your teddy bear?" they will probably be able to get it or point to it.

Infants' first words typically share the following characteristics:

1. The words babies say first are not necessarily those they hear most. They tend to name things that are important to them, or that they have experienced often. "Mama," "dada," "baba" (bottle) are apt to be early words, along with "baw" (ball), "bre" (bread), or whatever toys or foods may be most significant. All these are people or things they have frequently seen or heard in action or manipulated themselves.

2. English-speaking babies usually say nouns, verbs, and pronouns before adjectives, adverbs, and other modifiers. They say the names of familiar things, along with "have" and "want," before, "big," "fast," or "more" (Bowerman, 1976; Nelson, 1973).

3. At first, babies use words very narrowly. Later, meanings become overly broad. In the following interchange (all too familiar to most parents), the child is after one very particular toy vehicle, which she has labeled "truck." The father attempts to give his daughter what *he* calls a "truck"—and they both end up frustrated:

18-month-old:	Truck.
Father:	Here's your truck.
18-month-old:	No. *Truck.*
Father:	Yes. Here's your truck.
18-month-old, loudly:	*Truck!*

underextension
using words too restrictively

This is an example of **underextension**, too restrictive a use of words. Toddlers make this mistake when they use a word label to refer only to one type of thing actually included in the concept—*truck* means only red trucks, or real trucks, or dump trucks—or to one specific truck, as in the dialogue above.

overextension
using words too broadly; using the same word to stand for a number of similar things

Later, just the opposite happens. A word may be used too broadly, so that *truck* may mean all vehicles or all things with wheels, even a wheelbarrow; any four-legged animal may be a *kitty*. This **overextension** shows that the baby is forming mental categories, an important cognitive advance.

4. Single words often stand for whole sentences or phrases. The **holophrase** "dog" can mean, "There's a dog." "I want my dog." "The dog is barking." "I'm afraid of this dog." "I like this dog."

holophrases
single words that stand for whole thoughts

TWO-WORD SENTENCES

By 24 months, most children begin using two-word sentences: "More car." "More milk." "Open it." "Shut it." "Hold it." Though brief, these sentences represent a major step. Language is now a **symbolic system**, where words not only name things, but express the relations between them (Nelson, 1977). We saw similar accomplishments around this age when we looked at the development of representational thinking and of functional-relational play. (See "Focus On" earlier in the chapter.) These symbols also express the child's wishes about things (Nelson, 1974). What was only implied by a single word, such as "car," now becomes explicit. "More car" means "Daddy, wind it up again" in one context or "I want to keep riding" in another.

Interestingly, the kinds of two-word sentences that children create fall into standard categories. This probably reflects the level of cognitive development reached by most children toward the end of their second year (Slobin, 1970). These include:

Recurrence:	More juice.
	Play again.
Attribution:	Big dog.
	Red ball.
Possessive:	Dada hat.
	Baby milk.
Agent action:	Barbara cry.
	Mama eat.
Action object:	Throw rattle.
	Hit dog.

Notice that most of these early sentences are neither requests nor urgent reports—they are observations about the world, maybe even attempts to understand it through language (Halliday, 1975). Early sentences also describe the obvious things that older children take for granted. Finally, the order of the words follows the patterns of adult syntax. Toddlers say "more milk," not "milk more"; "want that," not "that want."

INDIVIDUAL DIFFERENCES IN LANGUAGE DEVELOPMENT

Although most infants have a 50-word vocabulary by 24 months, many reach that level earlier or later. And a small minority of children even begin talking in phrases at the age of a year or so, learning single words at a later time. These phrases, known as **compressed sentences**, are usually slurred, so that they may sound more like one long complicated word ("I-no-know") than like a multiword phrase ("I don't know") (Brown, 1977; Nelson, 1973).

The role of experience

Seeking to understand more about the way children learn language, Katherine Nelson studied a group of 18 toddlers (1973). She found that early talkers, children with large vocabularies by age 2, had mothers who accepted their early speech as meaningful. Later talkers had mothers who were more rejecting of their early attempts at talking. Nelson provides the following examples:

symbolic system
system, like language, that represents and labels elements of the world and their interrelations

compressed sentences
phrases made up of several words slurred into one long sound

Accepting Mother

Mother: Jane. Here's a bottle. Where's the bottle? Here's a bottle.
Jane: *Wah wah.*
Mother: Bottle
Jane: *Bah bah.*
Mother: Oh, bah bah. Here's a ball.
Jane: *Baw.*
Mother: Ball. Yes.
Jane: *Uh. Uh boo?*
Mother: Ball.

Rejecting Mother

Paul: *Go.*
Mother: What? Feel.
Paul: *Fe.*
Mother: What's that? A dog. What does the dog say? One page at a time. Oh, that one over there. What's that one there?
Paul: *Boah.*
Mother: What? You know that.
Paul: *Bah.*
Mother: What?
Paul: *Ah wah.*
Mother: What?
Paul: *Caw.*
Mother: Car?
Paul: *Caw, awh.*
Mother: Little kitty, you know that.

It is not hard to imagine why the first child's acquisition of language is likely to be swifter than the second's.

Nelson's data also showed something else. She found that there are two styles of vocabulary learning and language use in young children (Nelson, 1973, 1981). The early vocabulary of some children consisted mostly of nouns ("dog," "hat," "house"), proper nouns ("Steve"), and adjectives ("big," "red"): words all related to labels, objects, and descriptions. Other children used more words related to social routines and "formulas" ("stop," "want," "don't," "don't do," "bye-bye," "now")—words involved in actions and social feelings (Lamb & Bornstein, 1987). Nelson called the first group of children *referential*, since their words referred primarily to objects rather than people. She called the second group *expressive*, because their vocabularies expressed something about their involvement with people. The two types of vocabularies are not mutually exclusive; but they show, from a very early age, individual differences in the way we use language.

Although both referential and expressive children will acquire their first 50 words by about the same age, expressive children acquire language at a slow and steady rate, whereas referential children start slowly and then speed up. By 2½ years, referential children have larger vocabularies, but expressive children have more facility in forming two-word combinations (Nelson, 1973).

Where do these different language styles come from? Partly, says Nelson

It is possible that mothers speak less to later-born children because their attention is spread among several children. (*James Holland/Stock, Boston*)

(1981), from the different language styles of mothers. Referential children have mothers who frequently label things and events, whereas expressive children have mothers who speak to them conversationally. Nelson (1973) also noticed family and social differences. Referential children were most often first-borns in middle-class homes; expressive children were more likely to be later-born children with less-educated parents. Why? Possibly because middle-class first-borns get the benefit of their educated mothers' full attention, which often includes reading aloud and direct vocabulary teaching. Later-borns may get less direct teaching, either because the mother's time is more divided or because with more than one child, she becomes more focused on controlling their behavior than on their vocabulary. Less-educated parents, who may be under financial and other pressures, may tend to concentrate less on reading or building vocabulary.

The role of genetics

Other evidence of environmental influences on language development comes from a study of 1-year-olds, their biological mothers, and their adoptive parents (Hardy-Brown, Plomin, & DeFries, 1981). The adoptive mothers who were more responsive to their infants' vocalizations raised the more linguistically skilled babies. But the study also showed that genetic factors play a role as well. In language development, as in every other aspect of human growth, biology and experience work together.

TALKING TO INFANTS EFFECTIVELY: MOTHERESE AND EXPANSION

"Does baby see the doggie?" "Look at the doggie!" No matter whether their speech is referential or expressive, most mothers speak to their infants in **motherese**, a style of speaking that is slow and high-pitched, with exaggerated

motherese
form of slow, high-pitched, simplified, well-enunciated language used by mothers and others in speaking to infants

intonation. Sentences are short, well-formed, and grammatically simple, usually referring to things that the baby can see (Newport, 1976). Actually, "motherese" is a misnomer, since it is used by fathers, other caregivers, and even other children as well (Jacobson, 1983; Phillips & Parke, 1981). Whatever it is called, though, speech that has these characteristics is more likely to capture and hold infants' attention (Benedict, 1976). Infants seem to prefer motherese to other forms of speech (Fernald, 1985). And motherese appears to be nearly universal: It can be found in languages such as Mandarin Chinese and German as well as English (Fernald & Simon, 1984; Grieser & Kuhl, 1988).

One of the ways motherese reinforces language learning is by exaggerating the differences between sounds so the child can clearly distinguish one sound from another (Karzon, 1985). In addition, parents and other sensitive adults tend to *elaborate* (fill out by adding details to) a child's speech in a technique called *expansion*:

Baby: "Doggie."
Parent: "Yes, the doggie just went out the door."
Baby: "Where blankie."
Parent: "Where is your blanket? Let's look in your crib."

Parents' responses are typically a little more complex grammatically than their child's level of speaking, which gives the child a kind of linguistic foundation for further progress (Schaffer, 1979).

Assessing Infant Development

So far, we have focused mainly on universal aspects of infant cognitive development. But what about differences *between* individual babies? In the assessment of an infant's development, a particular baby's physical and cognitive skills are compared to established norms or averages. In later chapters, we will examine intelligence tests and their use in predicting school achievement. Here, we'll look briefly at the most commonly used infant tests.

GESELL DEVELOPMENT SCHEDULES

Gesell Development Schedules
one of the first sets of tests for assessing children 1 month to 6 years old on physical, cognitive, language, and social skills according to average developmental rates

Devised in the 1940s by a Yale University pediatrician, Arnold Gesell, the **Gesell Development Schedules** provided standardized procedures for observing and evaluating a child's development from 1 month through 6 years. These scales originated out of a need for "normative" information about "average" rates of growth and development in four different areas: *motor* (e.g., balance, sitting, locomotion), *adaptation* (e.g., alertness, intelligence, exploration), *language* (e.g., vocalization, gestures, facial expression), and *personal-social behavior* (e.g., feeding, dressing, toilet training). Although no longer as widely used as they once were, the Gesell Development Schedules formed the foundation upon which many other infant tests were built. The best known and most widely used of these other tests are called the *Bayley Scales of Mental and Motor Development*.

THE BAYLEY SCALES

The Bayley Scales focus on two areas of development. The mental scale assesses perceptions, senses, memory, learning, problem solving, and language. The motor scale assesses gross motor and fine motor capacities and coordination. On the basis of their performance, infants are given two scores: the *Mental Development Index (MDI)* and the *Psychomotor Development Index (PDI)*. These scores are then compared to the scores received by most other children of the same age (a 6-month-old would be compared with other 6-month-olds, and so on). A child who performs at about the same level as her agemates receives a score called a **developmental quotient**, or **DQ**, of 100. A child who performs at a level that is less advanced than expected for her age would score lower than 100, and a child who outscores her age norms would be rated higher than 100. The lower or higher the score, the more delayed or advanced the child is presumed to be, relative to babies of the same age. Table 6-2 lists several items from both the mental and the motor scales with their standard age of achievement.

Bayley Scales
tests for assessing infant's mental and motor skills by comparison with age-related norms

developmental quotient (DQ)
score on Bayley Scales relative to agemates' scores

THE VALUE OF INFANT TESTS

Infant tests such as the Bayley Scales are used for two general purposes: assessing development at the time of the test (is the baby developing normally?) and predicting the infant's future functioning (will a relatively slow 12-month-old be a relatively slow 3-year-old?) In general, the tests are far better at evaluating a child's present development than they are at predicting that child's future. The exception is in cases of severe retardation or other neurological or sensory difficulties, when the tests *are* useful for identifying children who will need special attention and intervention.

TABLE 6-2 SAMPLE ITEMS FROM THE BAYLEY SCALES OF INFANT DEVELOPMENT

Mental Scale		Motor Scale	
Age (in months)	Item	Age (in months)	Item
0.1	Responds to sound of rattle	0.1	Lifts head when held at shoulder
1.5	Social smile	1.8	Turns: side to back
2.0	Visually recognizes mother	2.3	Sits with support
3.8	Turns head to sound of cube	3.2	Turns: back to side
4.1	Reaches for cube	5.3	Pulls to sitting
4.8	Discriminates stranger	6.4	Rolls: back to stomach
6.0	Looks for fallen spoon	6.6	Sits alone steadily
7.0	Vocalizes 4 different syllables	8.1	Pulls to standing
9.1	Responds to verbal request	9.6	Walks with help
13.4	Removes pellet from bottle	11.7	Walks alone
14.2	Says two words	14.6	Walks backward
18.8	Uses words to make wants known	16.1	Walks upstairs with help
19.3	Names one picture (e.g., dog)	23.4	Jumps off floor

Infant tests and beyond: Predicting later development

During childhood most tests of intellectual development measure verbal skills and representational thinking. Testing these abilities in infancy is difficult, since first words appear only toward the end of the first year and representational thought doesn't emerge until about 18 months. Until recently, predicting young infants' future intellectual capacities during the sensorimotor stage seemed impossible.

However, some new tests, given in the first year of life, *can* have predictive value. This discovery has altered developmentalists' views, not only about the value of infant testing, but also around the issue of continuity from infancy through childhood (Bornstein & Sigman, 1986). Researchers found that tests of infants' **visual recognition memory** (how they remember things they've already seen), given as early as 5 months, are strongly predictive of intelligence test scores later in childhood (Fagan & McGrath, 1981). Visual recognition tests assess an infant's ability to discriminate between two visual stimuli— one seen before and one never seen. Tests of visual recognition measure the infant's heart rate while the baby looks at a series of pictures or objects. Some object or picture that the infant has already seen is inserted into the series; if the heart rate changes when the already-viewed picture is shown, researchers conclude that the infant is actually *recalling* the picture or object.

Other infant tests that measure discrimination abilities—distinguishing strange from familiar people (Rose & Ruff, 1982) or familiar and unfamiliar sounds (O'Connor, Cohen, & Parmelee, 1984)—are also highly correlated with later intelligence. Why should this be? Are discrimination abilities so important, and so constant? The answer appears to be yes. Discrimination tasks may tap very basic cognitive processing abilities, such as perceiving and remembering, that underlie intelligence at all ages (Bornstein & Sigman, 1986).

One of the values of a test that predicts later development more reliably is its ability to alert parents, teachers, and others to potential problems *before* they become severe. *Early identification* of problems makes *early intervention* possible to the extent that experience can positively influence cognitive development (Fagan, 1984). The broad aim of evaluative testing is to foster every child's intellectual abilities.

visual recognition memory memory for stimuli seen before

Summary

1. Jean Piaget theorized that cognitive development progresses through a series of stages. In the sensorimotor stage, spanning the first 2 years of life, infants understand the world through their senses and physical actions. The major accomplishments of the sensorimotor period are decentration, intentionality, and object permanence.

2. Piaget proposed six substages in the sensorimotor period. Later theorists describe four substages, marked by transitions at 3, 8, 12, and 18 months.

3. For the first month infants have no control over their actions; they are reflexive beings. Gradually, changes in objects (a breast nipple versus a bottle nipple, for example) begin to elicit changes in responses. This subtle shift marks the beginning of sensorimotor intelligence.

4. The 3-month transition signals the appearance of primary circular reactions, repetitive actions and responses centering around the infant's own body. A movement which gives a baby pleasure, such as seeing her own arm, is repeated again and again.

5. Intentional behavior begins to emerge during the 8-month transition. Now, infants begin to see that their own actions cause separate results. They can act purposefully to get what they want. Secondary circular reactions emerge now, as infants repeat actions involving *objects*. This interest in the nonbaby world marks the appearance of decentration. Awareness of object permanence continues to develop, but it is not yet complete.

6. During the 12-month transition, active, purposeful, trial-and-error exploration begins. Babies become "little scientists," avidly studying everything around them.

7. True symbolic thinking begins with the 18-month transition. This is the ability to represent things mentally, to imagine *what if*. It is the kind of thinking we use throughout life. Now, children can solve problems mentally without first performing trial-and-error experiments, and object permanence is now fully understood. Two-year-olds know that even when they can't see something, it exists somewhere.

8. Newborns like familiarity, but by 2 months, infants begin paying attention to more novel and complex images and objects.

9. At 3 or 4 months, perception, assigning meaning to sensations, improves markedly. This is also a time of significant changes in the brain and nervous system.

10. Infants like color from birth on and can distinguish blue from green after 3 months. By 4 months, they demonstrate the principle of equivalence: They perceive that colors can vary slightly, yet still belong to the same category. This permits infants to make sense out of the welter of stimuli around them.

11. For the first 3 months, infants look at the borders of faces. Then they prefer eyes, followed by whole, normal-looking faces. Perception has moved from the part to the whole. Improved perception means improved social understanding, as infants begin to read the language of faces, a form of social referencing.

12. Information gained by one sense, say, touch, can be processed by another, say, vision, with almost no experience. This ability, called cross-modal transfer, appears in infancy much earlier than was previously believed.

13. Universally, infants go through the same linguistic stages at around the same age. This tells us that language development is at least partly determined by genes. Language acquisition begins with prelinguistic communication between parents and infants, involving gestures, sounds, and facial expressions.

14. All babies begin to make the same sounds at about the same age, progressing from cooing to babbling. First words appear from 10 to 14 months, naming people or things infants most commonly experience.

15. Meanings of words are first too narrow (underextension) and then too broad (overextension). Babies also use holophrases, single words that stand for entire thoughts or sentences.

16. By 24 months, two-word sentences generally appear. Language is now a symbolic system, where words not only name things, but express the relations between them.

17. Both biology and experience influence individual differences in language development. Parents of early talkers generally encourage their infants' early language attempts. Some children tend to be referential—their vocabularies have more labels and description. Others may be more expressive—their vocabularies have more words associated with actions or social routines.

18. Motherese is a speech style that is slow, simple, high-pitched, and exaggerated. Virtually all people communicating with infants use it, and babies seem to prefer it.

19. Infant tests like the Gesell Schedules and the Bayley Scales compare infants' motor and cognitive abilities to age-related norms. To predict *later* intellectual development, however, researchers have turned to tests of sensory recognition memory. These tests, given to infants as young as 5 months, have been found to correlate well with later intelligence scores.

Key Terms

babbling

Bayley Scales

complexity

compressed sentences

cross-modal abilities

decentration

deferred imitation

developmental quotient (DQ)

dishabituation

equivalence

Gesell Development Schedules

habituation

holophrases

intentional behavior

intentionality

mental combinations

motherese

object permanence

overextension

perceive

prelinguistic communication

primary circular reaction

representational thinking

secondary circular reactions

sensorimotor

social referencing

symbolic system

turn-taking

underextension

visual recognition memory

Suggested Readings

deVilliers, P., and deVilliers, J. (1979). *Early language.* Cambridge, MA: Harvard University Press. The authors are married, parents, and world-renowned scientists in the study of language development. In this volume they outline the magic of language mastery, from birth to the beginning of formal schooling, providing insightful examples to illustrate their points.

Gottfried, A., and Brown, C. (Eds.). (1986). *Play interactions.* Lexington, MA: Lexington Books. Leading experts in child development explain what play is, what it reveals about children's perceptions, and how it affects their development.

Kaye, K. (1984). *The mental and social life of babies: How parents create persons.* Chicago: University of Chicago Press. A careful observer of infant-mother interaction wisely describes both the capabilities and limits of young infants and how they shape the way others relate to them.

Leach, P. (1983). *Babyhood* (2nd ed.). New York: Knopf. A remarkably sensitive author writes clearly and knowledgeably about major developments in the infant's life. Her common-sense approach provides insight into coping with the inquisitive and demanding child as well as guidance promoting competent development.

White, B. (1985). *The first three years of life* (rev. ed.). New York: Simon & Schuster. One of America's best-known parent educators outlines the major cognitive accomplishments in the early years and shows what parents can do to give their children a head start.

Social and Emotional Development in Infancy

Two couples, each with a 7-month-old infant, are traveling on a plane from New York to California. Danny continually fidgets and cries while his parents walk up and down the aisles, offering milk, toys, anything they can think of to calm him. Linda sleeps for 2 hours, nurses when she wakes, and contentedly rests on her father's lap for most of the trip. On land, these babies are as different as they are in the air. When a family friend gently greets Danny, he screams and clings tightly to his father. Meeting a new adult, Linda clings to her mother, but she doesn't cry.

In this scenario, and in these two babies, we can see several important truths about infants' social and emotional development. Like Danny and Linda, many 7-month-olds become anxious when meeting new people, but some are more anxious than others. Babies share many aspects of social and emotional development, but the expression and intensity of those emotions differ from baby to baby. These inborn differences, which we call temperament, can make the same experiences very different for different babies.

In this chapter we will look at temperament and at the landmarks that chart the emotional development of all infants. We examine mother-infant attachment, a relationship that is both universal and highly individual. Infants' early relationships with their peers interest us too. Finally, we will see the infant begin to form a sense of herself as a person separate from all others, as a growing child learning to say "I."

Temperament

A mother of two sons recalled the difference between them as infants: "My first son ate and slept. Sometimes his naps were so long I would check to see if he was still breathing. At 6 weeks, he slept through the night. When he was awake, he played with me or watched his mobile. He could also be content just looking around. He babbled a lot and only cried when he was tired or hungry. My younger son was very different. It seemed as though he never slept and never stopped crying. When I put him in his crib, he'd scream if I left the room. His mobile interested him briefly; then he began crying again. I don't think he slept through the night until he was 2."

Research has confirmed what mothers have always observed: Babies are born as individuals, each with his own body rhythms and his own style of responding. This unique set of characteristics, present in each of us from birth, is **temperament**. Temperament includes how susceptible babies are to emotional stimulation, how quickly and intensely they respond, their general mood and strength of mood, and how much their mood changes.

Temperament should not be confused with **personality**—the combination of behavior and reaction patterns each of us develops as we grow and learn. Personality is shaped and molded by experience and can continue to develop throughout life. Newborns, who have lived only a short time, cannot have much personality, but they do have a group of inborn behavior tendencies—the raw materials out of which personality is shaped.

Until recently, the mother quoted above, like many parents, probably

temperament
unique, inborn pattern of responsiveness and mood

personality
behaviors and response patterns developed through experience

would have blamed herself for her second baby's irritability. Influenced by theories which held that infants are the products solely of their experiences, generations of parents have wondered what they were doing wrong, especially if their first-born was a difficult baby. A new view, though, emphasizes the role of heredity in temperament; infants are seen from this perspective as shapers of their own development. Far from being a blank slate, every infant is born with a personal signature, which we call temperament.

DIMENSIONS OF TEMPERAMENT

Since the 1960s, doctors Stella Chess and Alexander Thomas have been studying patterns of infant temperament. In their early work, Chess and Thomas periodically observed 140 children from infancy through adolescence and described their findings in the widely respected **New York Longitudinal Study (NYLS)** (Thomas & Chess, 1977, 1980; Thomas, Chess, & Birch, 1968). These early observations identified nine dimensions of infant temperament, but later research has narrowed these down to three central traits: negative emotionality, activity level, and sociability.

All babies have more or less of these three core traits, and how these traits are combined marks each infant's personal style or temperament. Negative emotionality is at the core of the **difficult child**'s temperament. The baby boy in the introduction to this chapter who cried his way through a plane ride was born with a heavy dose of negative emotionality. Difficult babies cry a lot, are easily distracted, and tend to be fearful of new things and experiences. Like all babies, they set their own timetables for eating and sleeping, but unlike other babies, the difficult child's schedule is subject to frequent shifts: Irregularity is his benchmark. When this baby wakes from a nap, he lets you know it in no uncertain terms, with cries, not gurgles. Difficult children may also have a high activity level, another component of temperament. Highly active babies can show this trait very early in infancy (Buss & Plomin, 1984). Even in their cribs, they are the movers, and when they begin to crawl, action itself propels them on. Finally, difficult children may be low in sociability, the third central trait defining temperament. Perhaps because they are somewhat fearful of anything new, they react less positively to people than do other babies.

Parents of a difficult baby who later have an **easy child** are astounded at the differences between the two. Easy babies eat and sleep "on schedule." Usually calm and predictable, with little negative emotionality, they approach rather than shun new objects and experiences. Adaptability defines them. After napping, for example, if they're not too hungry, they may lie contentedly in their cribs, amusing themselves till someone comes in to check on them. Even when they crawl, these babies will sit for long periods. Easy-going babies also tend to be high in sociability.

In Chess and Thomas's original study, easy-going babies made up 40 percent of the sample, while only 10 percent were difficult. Between these two extremes is the **slow-to-warm-up child**. These infants are distressed by new things and experiences initially but, as the label implies, will "warm up" if given time. Their reactions and behaviors tend not to be intense or extreme. Fifteen percent of babies in Chess and Thomas's sample were slow to warm up.

Meal time can be fun for parents and babies, but with a difficult infant, crying is more typical than gurgling. *(Michael Edrington/The Image Works)*

New York Longitudinal Study (NYLS)
pioneering study of infant temperament

difficult child
baby with high negative emotionality and an undependable schedule

easy child
adaptable, calm baby with a predictable schedule

slow-to-warm-up child
child characterized by mild emotions and initial fear of new experiences

The whole concept of infant temperament presents a challenge to parents and other caregivers. Learning to live compatibly with an infant whose nature is very different from your own can be trying, but it is also likely to be intriguing. An understanding of temperament can also be reassuring. After all, knowing that your infant is the way she is because she was born that way, that she cries or is irritable or fearful because of her own internal chemistry, can prevent a lot of guilt and insecurity. In other words, parents need not—and cannot—shoulder the responsibility (or guilt) for, say, turning a difficult infant into an easy one. Instead, mothers and fathers must to some degree adapt themselves and learn, for example, what sort of play suits their easily distracted infant best.

TEMPERAMENT AND HEREDITY

Thomas and Chess linked temperament to heredity, and more recent research has confirmed that link. The temperaments of identical twins (100 percent alike genetically) are more alike than those of fraternal twins, who are not identical genetically (Campos et al., 1983). Specifically, inherited traits of temperament include activity level, sociability, attention span, fearfulness, and fussiness (Goldsmith & Campos, 1982; Goldsmith & Gottesman, 1981; Matheny, 1980; Plomin & Rowe, 1977). Among the traits that last through childhood (Matheny, Wilson, & Nuss, 1984), activity level is especially enduring. In one study of 50 children, those who were most active at *4 days* of age were also most active *8 years* later (Korner et al., 1985).

Does this mean that temperament is fixed from birth, that a shy 3-year-old becomes a timid adult, that a difficult baby never loosens up? Not necessarily. When temperament meets environment almost anything can happen. Heredity may create temperament, but experience shapes it. The slow-to-warm-up baby, for example, may end up adapting *more* rapidly to new experience than other children if her individual style is acknowledged, appreciated, and responded to sensitively. Similarly, an easy baby whose needs are not met when he cries may eventually become cranky and difficult. Experience can also reinforce temperament. In studies of adoptive families, for example, parents who are socially outgoing tend to have sociable infants, and those who are more retiring tend to have shy babies (Daniels & Plomin, 1985). And as we would expect, when environment and heredity work together, their joint influence is stronger than either alone would be. At 2 years, the biological children of sociable parents were the most sociable, and the biological children of shy parents were the most shy (Daniels & Plomin, 1985).

TEMPERAMENT AND DEVELOPMENT

Temperament affects development in two ways: It influences the responses babies *evoke* from others, as well as the activities and experiences that infants *choose for themselves.* To illustrate the *evocative* effects of temperament, the way it influences behavior toward the infant, let's consider a difficult infant. At 2 months old, Susan still wakes several times every night, is difficult to comfort, and cries as soon as she's back in her crib. During the day, she fusses during feedings, baths, and diaper changes. Exhausted, Susan's mother finds little

Easy babies easily amuse themselves and adapt well to new situations. Because of their sweet natures, their parents enjoy being with them. (*Joel Gordon*)

pleasure in caring for her. During the brief periods when Susan is quiet or calm, her mother avoids her, welcoming a few precious minutes of peace.

The story of Susan and her mother reflects the real experiences of some mothers and babies. In two research studies, mothers who rated their infants' temperaments as difficult spent less time with them and were less responsive to their needs (Campbell, 1979; Milliones, 1978). Another study found that mothers who had described their sons as difficult at a year old spent less time teaching their children 6 months later (Maccoby, Snow, & Jacklin, 1984). Difficult infants do not always receive poor quality care, of course, nor do easy infants always receive the best care. A particular infant lives with particular parents who respond to their infant according to *their* own temperament and needs.

The second way in which temperament affects development—through activities infants choose for themselves—is complex as well. At 4 or 5 months, a difficult baby girl, very sensitive to new experiences, may be spitting rice cereal at her mother. When she is a year old, she quickly crawls from one activity to the next, first banging some blocks around, then rolling a ball across the floor, then pulling pillows off the sofa. An easy baby will taste the rice cereal eagerly and easily add it to her diet. At 1 year, she sits with a book and turns the pages; she fingers the dial of a play telephone trying to make the bell ring. Her attention span is longer than the irritable girl's, and this will serve her well.

On standardized tests of infant development, babies who have longer attention spans and are more persistent perform better than babies with very high activity levels. In this way, persistent babies with a high attention span can enhance their own development through the learning they generate for themselves (Campos et al., 1983; Goldsmith & Gottesman, 1981; Seegmiller & King, 1975). Similarly, high-activity babies who score lower on IQ tests may be less focused and persistent, perhaps impeding their early cognitive development (Goldsmith, 1978). However, these babies may be gaining physical skills earlier. Generally, for both kinds of babies, interaction with the environment is shaped by their individual temperaments, with very real consequences for development (Scarr & McCartney, 1983).

Goodness of fit

goodness of fit
the way the personalities and expectations of parents mesh with their child's temperament

As we have noted, neither easy nor difficult temperaments evoke only one kind of response from parents, and no one temperament is ideal for every set of parents. An easy baby whose needs are not met when she cries can become withdrawn and socially unresponsive. A slow-to-warm-up baby who is rarely offered a second chance may develop a resistance to anything new. The key is *interaction*: Both infant temperament and parental characteristics influence each baby's development. Psychologists use the term **goodness of fit** to stress that the outcome of these first social encounters depends on *both* sides, on how well the personalities and expectations of the parents mesh with the child's basic temperament (Thomas & Chess, 1977).

The baby boy who accepts new things easily, for example, is a perfect match for an anxious, perfectionistic, first-time mother. As they go through their first year together, his calm manner reassures her again and again. She enjoys spending time with him, reading and playing quietly. A highly active, assertive baby would probably be a poor fit for this mother but would mesh well with another mother, who might admire her spunky, strong-willed spirit. This mother, eager to allow her baby to be herself, tries to stay a step ahead of her, responding to her needs before the baby loses control. This style of parenting is rewarding to this mother and extremely helpful to her baby.

The important point is that temperament strongly *influences* development; it does not determine it. Development is a dynamic process in which the raw material of temperament is shaped by experience—experience that infants generate for themselves as well as the reactions they help to evoke from others. In Chapter 8 we will see how the social contexts of parents, family, class, community, and culture influence individual development as well. Now, we turn from the ways infants differ to the patterns of social and emotional development that all babies share.

Landmarks in Social and Emotional Development

Seeking to understand human emotional development, researchers have asked people around the world, "What is the person in this picture feeling?" When the face is smiling, the answer is always the same: happiness, joy, de-

Joy: Mouth forms smile, cheeks lifted, twinkle in eyes

Anger: Brows drawn together and downward, eyes fixed, mouth squarish

Surprise: Brows raised, eyes widened, mouth rounded in oval shape

Distress: Eyes tightly closed, mouth, as in anger, squared and angular

Interest: Brows raised or knit, mouth may be softly rounded, lips may be pursed

Disgust: Nose wrinkled, upper lip raised, tongue pushed outward

Sadness: Inner corners of brows raised, mouth corners drawn down

Fear: Brows level, drawn in and up, eyelids lifted, mouth retracted

**FIGURE 7-1
INFANT FACIAL ARCHETYPES
OF EMOTION**
The photos depict the facial expressions that Carroll Izard believes are associated with the basic emotions. (*Source*: Carroll Izard)

light. The same is true for facial expressions conveying sadness, surprise, fear, anger, and disgust. Americans and Aborigines, Germans and Nigerians, Filipinos, Peruvians, and Cambodians all find the same feelings in the same faces: Human emotions are universally recognizable (Ekman, 1972; Izard, 1971).

For some psychologists, this means that emotions, their expressions, and the ability to recognize them are inborn. Researchers have found distress, disgust, and interest in newborns' faces, and by 3 months, joy, sadness, and anger appear (Malatesta & Haviland, 1982). Figure 7-1 shows the various facial expressions associated with different emotions in infants.

Some psychologists hold that we can experience all basic emotions from birth, but as we mature, as our experiences become more complex, so do our emotions. Whereas a hungry infant may feel pure happiness when he is fed, an older child, perhaps with a few pounds to lose, will eat an ice cream sundae with a more complicated mix of emotions (Campos et al., 1983; Lamb & Bornstein, 1987).

How babies, especially newborns, actually experience emotions is difficult to know. (See "Issues & Options.") Most researchers concur that infants *express* discrete (separate and specific) emotions from a very early age, possibly from birth. What remains unclear is whether the actual internal emotional states accompany these expressions. But perhaps the similarity between the infants' expressions and those of adults is so great that we must assume the infant to be

Issues & OPTIONS

Early Lessons in Emotional Expressions: Do Parents Know Best?

What do babies really feel? Psychologists may argue about this, but parents seem to *know* (Johnson et al., 1982). The mother who holds her sobbing infant close to her in the middle of the night is convinced that the baby is lonely and fearful in her crib. The father changing his squirming infant's diaper is positive that she's unhappy about it. And when their baby smiles, parents know the smile's for them.

Some psychologists claim this cannot be. They say that parents are *projecting*—confusing their own complex feelings, wishes, and needs with their babies. Where the objective scientist sees only a reflex, the loving mother sees an adoring smile on her newborn's face. The father who wants to be proud of his daughter's achievements believes that at 3 weeks she is trying to count the number of plastic keys on her toy. The psychologist believes she won't even be able to distinguish between herself and the object until later in her first year. What matters for infants is not what researchers think or even know, but what parents think and feel, for these are the things that influence parents' responses to babies, and in turn, the way babies and children respond to the world.

In fact, how parents interpret their babies' emotions may help to explain why men and women, boys and girls, tend to express emotions differently. Many psychologists trace these differences to the different ways that parents respond to boys and to girls. The 10-year-old boy who strikes out at the plate and walks back to the bench dry-eyed may have learned his lesson in the crib: Boys don't show they're upset. The girl who cries when her doll gets lost may have learned the opposite: If you're upset, you cry (there may be another part of the rule that says, but girls don't get angry). Parents may actually respond less frequently to a baby boy's distress than to a girl's! In one study, when baby girls expressed pain, their mothers went to them and comforted them; but when baby boys cried and showed distress, their mothers ignored them (Malatesta & Haviland, 1982). In time, a boy might learn to hide his vulnerability. So learning may have a great deal to do with what emotions we show and how we show them.

Suppose you were a parent who did not want your boy to grow up believing he had to hide his feelings or your girl to grow up believing she must never get angry and tears are a girl's best friend? How could you work toward your goal? Babies of both sexes may be best served by parents' simply acknowledging and responding sensitively to all their emotions. A smile can get a smile back, a sad look can be answered with empathy and a gentle touch. Distress usually calls for soothing and comforting. When parents respond to their infant's full range of expression, they may be fostering a personality that will be able to handle and express a full emotional range.

feeling what she seems to be feeling. In other words, does a baby's smile or frown or wide-eyed look really mean that the baby *feels* joy or sadness or surprise? Research suggests that the answer depends on age. There seems to be an inborn schedule governing the appearance of emotions and how often, how intensely, and how responsively they are expressed.

SMILING AND LAUGHING

That wonderful, mysterious neonatal smile is not considered a true **social smile**. The earliest smiles usually appear when the baby is resting comfortably or in a sleep state accompanied by rapid eye movements (Emde, Gaensbauer, & Harmon, 1976). But there is no evidence that these early smiles reflect feelings of pleasure.

By 6 to 9 weeks, something new happens: Babies smile just as adults do—in reaction to pleasure. Soon they will smile at anything that delights—not just people, but nonsocial stimuli such as lights, bells, and toys. Even so, the emerging smile serves a useful social function: It rewards the caregiver for paying attention to the baby. Parents often say that they feel their infant is a real person once a reliable social smile sets in. By about 4 months babies smile more selectively and begin to laugh as well.

Where do smiling and laughter come from?

Social smiling emerges when the baby is biologically "ready to smile." The onset of social smiling is so predictable that it must be a biologically timed event, keyed to the baby's developing central nervous system. Premature infants begin to smile socially at the same *gestational age* (see Chapter 4) as full-term babies, evidence that biological maturation, not the baby's experience in the world, governs the appearance of the smile (Dittrichova, 1969). Even babies blind since birth tend to start smiling around the same time as sighted infants—further evidence for the role of maturation (Fraiberg, 1977).

But if smiling begins from within, it is influenced from without. Social reinforcement, such as picking up the baby, vocalizing, and smiling back, can

social smile
infant smile for pleasure in response to familiar people

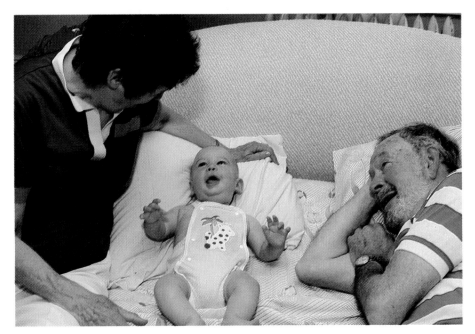

When baby develops a social smile adults begin to feel he is a "real person." Few things please relatives more than the give-and-take of smiles with a baby. *(Robert Brenner/PhotoEdit)*

increase the frequency of smiling (Brackbill, 1958), and negative experience can disturb the timetable: Infants living in very unstimulating institutional environments smile later than babies raised at home (Ambrose, 1961; Gewirtz, 1965).

Psychologist Jerome Kagan believes that cognitive maturation influences the onset of smiling. Babies smile first at faces and things they have seen before, the *smile of recognition* (Kagan, Kearsley, & Zelazo, 1978). Laughter too is influenced by cognitive maturation and by increasing muscle tone and muscle control (Cicchetti & Sroufe, 1976).

STRANGER WARINESS

The 3-month-old boy who flashed his smile at parent and stranger alike is very different some 3 to 5 months later. At 7 months he greets strangers with cries and grimaces, even if they are among his closest relatives. That friendly baby has not turned antisocial. He has simply matured to the point where he knows whom he knows. As babies become able to differentiate one person from another and to remember the familiar faces, most also become more wary of strangers. Recognizing the familiar also means recognizing the *un*familiar. Like social smiling, **stranger wariness** (or fear of strangers) occurs on such a predictable schedule that we consider it another major landmark of emotional development (Ainsworth, 1973; Dennis, 1940).

stranger wariness
fear of unfamiliar people; sets in at about 6 to 8 months

As with smiling, Kagan and his colleagues link the predictable onset of stranger wariness to maturing cognitive processes (Kagan, Kearsley, & Zelazo, 1978). According to their hypothesis, infants between 6 and 9 months old are slowly beginning to make sense out of their world. From then on, when they cannot figure out why something is happening, they become afraid. They are less afraid if they have some idea of who strangers are, why they are present,

Stranger wariness, which begins sometime after 6 months, signals children's ability to wonder about the people in their world. Adults in costume—even a baby's own father—can be very threatening because they are so atypical. *(David Krathwohl/Stock, Boston)*

and what they are likely to do. In Kagan's view, fear develops when a baby has the ability to raise questions about the unfamiliar person but is unable to answer them.

Still, personal temperament influences the way each baby shows stranger wariness. Some babies cry and get very upset while others retreat into quiet or clinging behavior. And though wary, infants can also be very *curious* about the unfamiliar, including unfamiliar people. Given the right conditions, an infant will smile at and even approach a new person. But it depends on the situation and on the approach of the stranger. Babies tend to be more fearful when exposed to an unfamiliar person in an unfamiliar setting (an observation room in a university, for example) than when they meet an equally strange person in a familiar setting such as their own home (Sroufe, Waters, & Matas, 1974). And from 6 to 12 months, babies in one study were less fearful of strangers when their mothers were holding them. When their mothers were only 4 feet away, many of the same babies fussed and cried (Morgan & Ricciuti, 1969).

Experience with strangers and strangers' behavior makes a difference, too (Sroufe, 1977). Infants who are accustomed to meeting strangers are less afraid than those who rarely meet new people. New people who approach slowly, who are friendly and smiling, and who talk to the baby or offer a toy, evoke far less fear. Indeed, such a considerate approach may elicit a curious and positive response from the infant or toddler (Bretherton, 1978; Bretherton, Stolberg, & Kreye, 1981).

Finally, the stranger's age and sex make a difference. Babies seem to react less fearfully to females than to males, probably because most infants have more experience with women (Brooks and Lewis, 1976; Greenberg, et al., 1973; Morgan & Ricciuti, 1969). Infants are also less wary of other children than they are of adults (Lenssen, 1973), possibly because of size, or because of the differences infants are beginning to perceive between themselves and others—the greater the difference, the greater the fear (Lewis & Brooks, 1974).

SEPARATION PROTEST

Parents of infants across the globe struggle with it: that tearful, clinging, frantic leave-taking psychologists label **separation protest**. Figure 7-2 shows that the onset of separation protest is universal across many cultures. Even when babies know the person who will substitute while a parent is gone, from about 9 to 12 months goodbyes are wrenching. Why?

separation protest
infant's reaction, based on fear, to separation from mother or other caregiver

Kagan's explanation echoes his view of stranger anxiety: The child is confronted with a situation he cannot figure out—Why is Mommy leaving? Where is she going? When will she return? He responds with distress. In an attempt to test this notion, Littenberg, Tulkin, and Kagan (1971) observed babies' reactions to their mothers leaving a room in their own homes. When the mothers left by going into another room in the house and closing the door behind them, the babies did not protest, presumably because they could answer their own questions about this familiar exit. But when mothers stepped into a closet and closed the door, the behavior was too unusual for the infants to process, and they became distressed.

If Kagan is right about the reason for separation protest, it makes sense to

FIGURE 7-2

Separation protest seems to reach its peak at about the same age in a variety of cultures. (*Source:* Reprinted from *Infancy: Its Place in Human Development* by Jerome Kagan, Richard B. Kearsley, and Philip R. Zelazo. Cambridge, Mass.: Harvard University Press. Copyright © 1978 by the President and Fellows of Harvard College. All rights reserved.

Where are you going? Across the world, from about 9 to 12 months, babies hate to say goodbye. *(Mary Kate Denny/ PhotoEdit)*

provide children with information to relieve their uncertainty and reduce their distress. Weinraub and Lewis (1977) tested this notion with toddlers and observed less separation protest if mothers told their children when they would be back than if the mothers simply left without explanation. There was even less separation protest when mothers suggested an activity to take up the time until they returned. The least effective technique for handling separation protest was an extended leave-taking. Parents who hesitated, doubled back, or delayed their departure only prolonged the anguish. A swift exit was far less upsetting to everyone concerned.

The themes we have touched on here reappear in the next section on attachment. Just as infants' fears about strangers and separation are balanced by their curiosity and their knowledge about the world, so are their needs for security, safety, and trust offset by desires to explore and to be independent.

Attachment Relationships

Watch a sensitive, loving mother feeding her infant son. He sucks, then turns his head away. She waits. They touch each other tenderly and gently. Gazing into each other's eyes they seem like lovers, in a world of their own. Is this just our own romantic fantasy, or is it really a relationship? While not all mothers are as sensitive as this one, what happens between a mother and her baby is indeed part of a developing relationship, and it is one of the most important interactions in a person's life.

What exactly is it that happens between these two? First, there are *behaviors*: The baby cries, the mother comes and feeds her; the baby snuggles, the mother hugs her. In time, the mother tickles, the baby smiles. Out of these

Ties of love between mother and baby can grow from the simplest things they do together. *(Ellis Herwig/Stock, Boston)*

interactions, day after day and night after night, something happens: Feelings and expectations grow. The baby feels distressed and hungry, then relieved of distress and full of milk; the mother feels tenderness, joy, annoyance, exhaustion, pleasure. As the baby grows older, after many interactions with the mother, the baby begins to expect that the mother will come and care for her when she cries. For her part, the mother will respond to and even anticipate her baby's needs. All these elements together form the prototype for a developing *relationship*, a combination of behaviors, interactions, feelings, and expectations that are unique to these two people.

One of the major events in the infant's social development is the emergence of this first relationship. By the end of the first year, most babies who are cared for in families develop what psychologists call an *attachment relationship*, usually with their mother. (Although others, including fathers, form attachments with the infant, the most research has been done on mother-infant attachments.) This relationship is central to the child's developing sense of self, to how he relates to others, and to how he is likely to develop as he moves away from his mother to become an autonomous and curious toddler and preschooler.

DEFINING THE ATTACHMENT RELATIONSHIP

attachment
close, significant emotional bond between mother (or father) and infant

Mary Ainsworth (1973), a developmental psychologist who has studied infants around the world, explains **attachment** as "an affectional tie that one person forms to another specific person, binding them together in space and enduring over time." Freud argued that the infant-mother relationship is, for the infant, "without parallel, laid down unalterably for a whole lifetime, as the first and strongest love-object and as the prototype for all later love relations (1938, p. 66). Freud's work led him to conclude that an infant's tie to his mother influences all his future relationships—in childhood, in adolescence, and even in adulthood.

Freud may have been overstating the case for the life-long effects of the attachment relationship; its significance is now hotly debated. Some psychologists still maintain that this first attachment is very important to a lifetime of relationships; others consider the first relationship less crucial in its influence on overall development. In their view, and ours, later experience can influence the effects of early attachment. Later in this section we will look at research findings that measure the influence of the first attachment relationship on the developing child.

THEORIES OF ATTACHMENT

Freud traced the origins of the attachment relationship back to the hunger drive. When a mother feeds an infant, at the breast or bottle, the baby's hunger drive is satisfied. Gradually, the baby comes to associate the pleasure of having her hunger satisfied with her mother's presence.

Learning theorists have applied general principles of conditioning (see Chapter 1) to explain why mothers acquire such positive value for their infants (Sears, Maccoby, & Levin, 1957). When hungry infants nurse, milk reduces their hunger. Milk—which satisfies the need—is a primary reinforcer. Because mother is present at the same time that a biological drive, such as hunger or cold, is being satisfied by milk or warmth, she takes on a value as a **secondary reinforcer**. She becomes associated with the milk and warmth. In time, the mere presence of the mother is pleasing, even when she is not satisfying a primary drive.

Over the years, researchers testing Freudian and learning theories of attachment found that it isn't actually the feeding of the infant that accounts for the strength of the mother-infant bond (Schaffer & Emerson, 1964). A classic study of Rhesus monkeys in fact revealed that the monkeys would choose the "creature comfort" of a terry-cloth monkey-doll over the wire-mesh "mother" that provided milk (Harlow & Zimmerman, 1959). Today, many social scientists believe that love between a baby and her mother exists not simply because of the infant's association of mother with food but for one very crucial reason: to ensure the survival of the human species. This point of view, known as **ethological theory**, looks back to the early stages of human evolution (Bowlby, 1969, 1973).

John Bowlby, the first to articulate this theory, argues that attachment behaviors such as smiling, clinging, crying, stranger wariness, and separation protest all served at one time in our human history to protect infants by increasing their chances for survival. In the physically dangerous environment in which humans are believed to have evolved, an environment filled with hungry, prowling animals, behaviors like crying would have brought caregivers to the baby's side. Similarly, stranger wariness would have helped to keep a baby away from danger, and both separation protest and following made babies more likely to stay with their caregivers. In Bowlby's theory, then, mother-infant attachment is a biologically based relationship that protected infants from the real dangers that once threatened our early ancestors. Although Bowlby's theory is not universally accepted, it has sparked much thinking and research concerning the emotional development of infants.

secondary reinforcer anything (or anyone) associated with the satisfaction of a need, so chances of a given response recurring are increased by its presence

ethological theory analysis of human and animal behavior patterns in evolutionary terms

In his now famous experiments, Harry Harlow concluded that baby monkeys went to their mothers for comfort as well as for food. Deprived of their real mothers, baby monkeys clung to terry cloth, even when wire "mothers" provided milk. (*Martin Rogers/Stock, Boston*)

Attachment and exploration: The "secure base"

By 1 year, a child's need to stay near her "attachment object," usually her mother, is balanced by another need—to explore the world. These two behavior systems are in balance. In a familiar setting, such as her home, or wherever the baby feels comfortable, the exploratory system will be activated. The child leaves her mother, her **secure base**, to do some exploring. When she feels she's gone too far, or is frightened by something strange, the attachment system is activated, and the infant moves closer to visually "check in" with her mother. She may even hurry back to be at her side. Once "refueled" with emotional security, the child again moves away from her secure base. As they move about their environment, most 1-year-olds will regulate their own activity, meeting both the need for attachment and the need to explore. Even if no threat arises, an infant will routinely check back with her mother, almost as if she is "fueling up" with security. She stops exploring for a moment to make contact either to touch, see, or hear her mother. Once reassured, she goes off again to explore. In Bowlby's view, both the *attachment and the exploring behaviors* were necessary for the survival of the human species.

DIFFERENCES IN ATTACHMENT

Virtually all infants form attachment relationships with their mothers, but not all these relationships are of the same quality. The most important way in which attachment relationships differ is in the strength of their security. *Security of attachment* is the extent to which a child can count on his mother's availability to meet his needs, on her being there when he needs her. Because infant-mother attachment seems to have important developmental consequences, social scientists have been very interested in assessing individual differences in the quality of attachment.

The strange situation

Mary Ainsworth devised an ingenious procedure to observe and assess differences in mother-infant attachment (Ainsworth & Wittig, 1969). Her thesis was that security of attachment would be revealed if the child was put under stress. Two things that stress babies a great deal are separation from their mothers and approaches by strangers.

Ainsworth's procedure, known as the **strange situation**, allows psychologists to observe children under both kinds of stress. A mother and her child, a 1- to 2-year-old, are brought to an unfamiliar room. A stranger enters the room, and the mother leaves after a few minutes, leaving the infant alone with the stranger. Soon, the mother returns and the stranger exits. The mother leaves again, and the infant is left alone briefly. The stranger then reenters, leaves, and finally, the mother rejoins her child. During all the comings and goings, the infant's reactions are carefully observed.

The strange situation shines a spotlight on the attachment relationship, revealing distinct patterns in the way children and mothers relate to each other. Children who use their mother as a secure base for exploration may or may not become distressed when their mother leaves. But they greet her in an

secure base
attachment object (usually the mother) who provides a foundation for curious exploration

strange situation
experimental procedure for observing attachment patterns

The strange situation. At left, a mother holds her infant in an unfamiliar room. After leaving the baby with a stranger *(right)* she will return. Babies' reactions during these separations and reunions reveal attachment patterns with their mothers that affect development in many ways. *(Courtesy of Mary Ainsworth)*

unambiguous way, by either approaching her and seeking to be picked up (if distressed), or by smiling at and perhaps vocalizing to her and showing her a toy (if not distressed). These children, says Ainsworth, have developed a **secure attachment**. If distressed, they seek their mothers for comfort. By contrast, children who have an **insecure attachment** may show their distress in either of two ways. Unwilling to explore, they may want their mother close by, show much distress when she leaves, and, after seeking to be picked up once she returns, kick or push away from her (this is particularly significant). These children have formed an **anxious-resistant attachment**. A child who has formed an **anxious-avoidant attachment** seems indifferent to the mother's presence, shows little distress at her absence, and ignores or refuses to look at her when she returns (Ainsworth, 1979). Toddlers at home show the same patterns of attachment that they do in the laboratory, suggesting that the results are not skewed by the laboratory setting (Ainsworth et al., 1978).

EXPLAINING DIFFERENCES IN ATTACHMENT

Knowing that such differences exist, psychologists want to understand their causes. Why do some infants form close, secure relationships with their mothers while others don't? One theory focuses on the way mothers behave toward their infants. Another emphasizes the behavior and temperament of the infants themselves.

For Ainsworth (1979), the attachment relationship grows out of infants' experiences with their mothers during the first year of life. And the key element in that experience is the mother's sensitivity in responding to her infant's signals. Does she go to the infant soon after he begins to cry? Does she understand the baby's different cries? Does she know when he is hungry or tired? Does she sense when he wants to play? Does the mother pick up her baby with pleasure and warmth, or is she tense and uncomfortable with physical contact? A sensitive mother who can read her infant's cues and respond appropriately to the baby's needs is fostering trust. In turn, this trust forms the foundation for a secure attachment to the mother.

secure attachment
positive, healthy relationship of infant to mother (or father), based on infant's trust in the parent's love and availability

insecure attachment
relation of infant to mother (or father) based on lack of trust

anxious-resistant attachment
insecure attachment in which infant shows much distress at separation and anger at reunion

anxious-avoidant attachment
insecure attachment in which infant shows indifference to parents and avoids interaction with them

Sensitive Mothering and Affect Attunement

A 9-month-old boy sits facing his mother. He has a rattle in his hand and is shaking it up and down with a display of interest and mild amusement. As the mother watches, she begins to nod her head up and down, keeping a tight beat with her son's arm motions.

A 9-month-old girl becomes very excited about a toy and reaches for it. As she grabs it, she lets out an exuberant "Aaaah!" and looks at her mother. Her mother looks back, scrunches up her shoulders, and does a shimmy with her upper body, like a go-go dancer. The shimmy lasts only about as long as her daughter's "Aaaah!" but is equally excited, joyful, and intense.

What is happening in these scenes? Notice that the mothers aren't just copying their babies' actions; they are expressing the same *feelings*. They are matching their infant's joy or excitement with their own. Psychiatrist Daniel Stern, who videotaped these scenes and others like them, calls this kind of emotional matching "affect attunement" (1985). As Stern explained to an interviewer: "If you just imitate a baby, that only shows you know what he did, not how he felt. To let him know you sense how he feels, you have to play back his inner feelings in another way. Then the baby knows he is understood" (Daniel Stern in Goleman, 1986). Mothers who can do that are communicating something very special to their babies: I accept and share your feelings; I am in tune with you. According to Stern, the mother's emotional "reflection" helps infants to develop their sense of self, what Stern calls their "subjective" self—that part of us that connects with and shares with others. Infants are reassured by the attuned parent's response that they are not alone but are connected deeply to another person.

Stern has theorized that small moments of attunement or nonattunement deliver specific messages of "understood" or "not understood" to the infant. The moments add up over time, forming a pattern that can have a large impact on a child's life. Stern and others have challenged the notion that our personalities are formed in stages. Rather, they say, it is the *cumulative* effect of daily interchanges between parent and baby that is important: What infants learn through these early, moment-by-moment interactions colors their views of future relationships. But, Stern cautions, early experience is not all-determining: It can be reversed, and possibly reversed again.

Ainsworth's theory has been supported by several research studies. Sensitivity *does* seem to promote secure attachment. When mothers were sensitive to infant feeding signals, when they were responsive to crying, when they offered a balanced amount of interaction, and when they were comfortable in close body contact with their babies, their infants were securely attached by 1 year (Ainsworth et al., 1978). A German study of the development of mother-infant relations also supports the sensitivity-security link, as does another U.S. study suggesting that just the right amount of stimulation from the mother (neither too much nor too little) promotes secure attachment (Grossman & Grossman, 1982; Belsky, Rovine, & Taylor, 1984). (See "Focus On" for examples of sensitive mothering.)

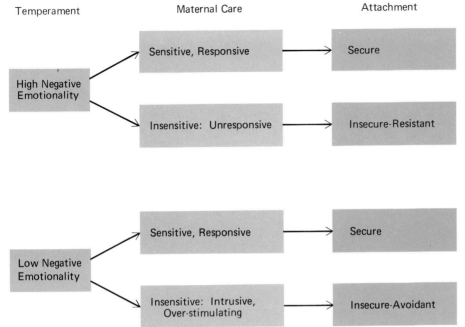

FIGURE 7-3
INFANT TEMPERAMENT, MATERNAL CARE, AND ATTACHMENT SECURITY
"Negative emotionality" refers to distress an infant may be prone to. As the figure indicates, maternal care is a more significant factor in determining a baby's level of attachment than is the baby's temperament. A baby not prone to distress (low negative emotionality) will nevertheless develop an insecure attachment if maternal care is insensitive.

While the quality of care that mothers provide appears to determine whether or not a secure of insecure attachment develops, the baby's temperament shapes the way in which security and insecurity are expressed (Belsky & Rovine, 1987). Infants prone to distress who receive insensitive, often unresponsive care tend to develop insecure-*resistant* attachments, while those who are *not* prone to distress and receive insensitive, often intrusive overstimulating care tend to develop insecure-*avoidant* attachments. Infants prone to distress who receive sensitive, responsive care are the secure babies who, while upset by the strange situation, express their security by seeking and finding comfort in their mothers' arms. Infants who are not prone to distress who receive sensitive, responsive care express their security by smiling at and vocalizing to their mothers across a distance (Belsky, Rovine, & Taylor, 1984; Isabella, Belsky, & vonEye, 1989). This interrelation of temperament, maternal care, and attachment security is outlined in Figure 7-3.

Events, experiences, and occurrences in the social world also influence the developing attachment relationship. What, for example, are the effects of marital happiness and child-care arrangements on infant development? With so many mothers working outside the home, other adults are sharing the care of their infants in day care centers and at home. How do such arrangements affect infants' attachments to their mothers? In Chapter 8 we will suggest some answers to this very important question.

CONSEQUENCES OF INFANT-MOTHER ATTACHMENT

Knowing that some infants are securely attached to their mothers while others are not raises some very important questions. Will differences in attachment

Securely attached toddlers tend to be curious and undaunted by physical boundaries *(left)*. These children are also often industrious problem solvers *(right)*. (left, *Junebug Clark/Photo Researchers;* right, *Robert Brenner/PhotoEdit*)

affect social and emotional development? Will a secure attachment ease the way in new situations, with new playmates and adults? Will independence be fostered? And will insecurely attached infants have more trouble relating to others and functioning independently? Considerable evidence suggests that the answer to all these questions is yes.

In one long-term study that followed infants through age 3, securely attached infants and their mothers continued to have strong positive feelings for each other. Anxiously attached infants and their mothers continued to show more negative feelings. By the age of 22 months, securely attached infants had become cooperative toddlers who worked well with their mothers and with unfamiliar adult researchers as well (Londerville & Main, 1981; Main, 1973).

The security that fosters good social skills benefits infants in another way— it enhances curiosity. An infant explorer moving from place to place without fear will have many opportunities for problem solving. Instead of crying when her ball rolls behind a chair, she goes after it. Not burdened by undue anxiety, this child takes things apart, turns switches on and off, empties drawers. And she'll learn in the process. If she pulls a drawer out too far, it falls on her feet. Eventually she learns to pull the drawer out just far enough before it falls. Over time, her curiosity and motivation to explore will be strengthened by similar problem-solving experiences that she has generated for herself. In studies that followed children first observed at 18 months, those who had been securely attached sought their mother's help in solving a difficult problem at age 2. During free play, they were both more enthusiastic and more cognitively advanced than the less secure group. And by age 5, now in preschool or kindergarten, the securely attached children were more competent and resourceful than the others. They were not only able to solve easy problems on their own (such as retrieving a toy from behind a barrier), but they also knew how to get help in more difficult situations (such as opening a locked toy box). When faced with the same problems, the children who had insecure attachments were frustrated, whiny, and negative (Matas, Arend, & Sroufe, 1978).

Kindergarteners who had been securely attached as infants spent more time exploring a "curiosity box" of interesting gadgets (doors, bells, locks) and manipulated more objects more carefully than children who had been insecure as infants (Arend, Gove, & Sroufe, 1979). When preschool teachers rated their children for positive or negative feelings (happiness and pleasure versus sadness and anger), the children who showed more positive feelings were also the ones who had been securely attached as infants (Sroufe, Waters, & Matas, 1974).

A foundation of trust

Overall, then, infants with secure attachments to their mothers grow into secure, autonomous, industrious, interpersonally skilled, and achievement-striving preschoolers. These findings provide support for certain elements of Erik Erikson's (1950) theory of psychosocial development. For Erikson (see Chapter 1), the basic developmental task of infancy involves the establishment of a sense of **basic trust** (Erikson, 1963). Those infants who have a strong foundation of trust will have a developmental advantage going into the toddler and preschool stages. During those stages, the basic psychosocial issues are the development of autonomy and initiative, or the ability to be independent, resourceful, and self-motivated. (We'll return to Erikson's view of these issues at the end of the chapter.) Preschoolers who, during infancy, have developed a strong sense of basic trust will see their world as dependable and safe. Free to relate to other people without too much anxiety or anger, they will learn how to give and take, how to perceive the needs of others. These trusting children will probably welcome social experiences more than their less securely attached agemates will. Peer relationships by the age of 4 or 5 for children with secure attachments in infancy will differ significantly from those formed by children with insecure early attachments. We will look more closely at these differences in Chapter 10.

basic trust
infant's strong sense that its needs will be met and the world is not a threatening place; according to Erikson, establishment of trust is the major task of infancy

A foundation of insecurity

What do we know about the way *insecurely* attached infants develop? We would expect that, without a strong sense of basic trust, they would be both more anxious and less socially skilled than more secure children. And that is exactly what research studies have found: Insecurely attached infants do have more behavior problems as preschoolers. Some are more hostile and tend to be socially isolated. Others are more tense, helpless, and fearful (Erickson, Sroufe, & Egeland, 1985; Sroufe, 1983). And in one study, 40 percent of the boys who had been classified as insecurely attached at 1 year showed signs of psychopathology when they were 6 (Lewis et al., 1984). These boys were also more aggressive in first, second, and third grade than were boys with secure attachment histories (Renken et al., 1989).

A LONG VIEW: ATTACHMENT RELATIONSHIPS OVER THE LIFE SPAN

It looks as if the quality of infant-mother attachment does indeed lay the foundation for the child's emotional future. In study after study, secure infant-mother attachment has been linked to many kinds of favorable outcomes in later years. The studies show, too, that insecure attachment not only undermines competence but also can point to actual problems in development.

These findings might tempt us to think that there is a direct, inevitable link between infant-mother attachment and later development. But in reality, that link is only as strong as the child's experience. In other words, *securely attached infants who continue to have good experiences continue to develop well. But insecurely attached infants whose experience improves can also improve emotionally.*

Given equal degrees of stress, the secure child is likely to manage better than the insecure child. But infants whose first attachment was insecure may still develop competence if they have new experiences that encourage competence. Again, development is strongly linked to environment, or context. Experiences beyond infancy can either support the developmental patterns laid down in infancy or they can go in new directions—either positive or negative. There is no direct, simple line from past to future.

In fact, recent research tells us that security does not *necessarily* prevent behavior problems in preschoolers, and insecurity is not *necessarily* related to later behavior problems. Some anxiously attached infants have developed into well-functioning preschoolers. How? The care they received after infancy became more responsive to their needs (Erickson et al., 1985). The reverse situation can occur, too: Securely attached infants may show behavior problems as preschoolers. Again, conditions in the children's environment may have changed. Perhaps maternal care that had been high quality during infancy changed at some point, and the children's needs were no longer met as effectively (Erickson et al., 1985). However, these children may be well-equipped to handle stress because of their early secure attachment. They can bounce back. An insecurely attached child, with fewer resources to begin with, might experience more lasting difficulties if conditions worsen or are not improved.

THE INFANT-FATHER RELATIONSHIP

By now, it is reasonable to ask the same question that researchers posed about the infant-mother attachment relationship: What about fathers? Do infants become as attached to fathers as they do to their mothers? The earliest studies of infant-father attachment sought to answer that question. Reports by mothers in one English study revealed that by 18 months, 71 percent of the babies appeared to be attached to their fathers, as shown by their protesting separation from him (Schaffer & Emerson, 1964).

Rather than relying on mothers' reports, other researchers observed babies and fathers in the strange situation, the experimental procedure used to learn about infant-mother attachment. This work also revealed that most infants who live with both their parents have developed focused attachment relationships with their fathers by 18 months (Lamb, 1981). One-year-olds who become wary when a stranger approaches use their fathers as a secure base, especially if their mothers are absent.

Babies form separate relationships with each parent, so it is possible to be securely attached to mother and insecurely attached to father, for example (Belsky, Garduque, & Hrncir, 1984; Grossman, Grossman, Huber, & Wartner, 1981; Lamb, Hwang, Frodi, & Frodi, 1982; Main & Weston, 1981). Infants who are securely attached to *both* parents appear more competent than those securely attached to only one, and infants securely attached only to mother seem more competent than those securely attached only to father (Belsky, Garduque, & Hrncir, 1984; Main & Weston, 1981).

Actually, fathers can be just as involved and sensitive caregivers as mothers; they just do it less often (Parke, 1978; Parke & Sawin, 1975). Mothers and fathers can be equally good at interpreting subtle signals from their newborn: When the babies in one study turned their heads away from the bottle, mothers *and* fathers responded appropriately by pausing. Fathers adjusted their speech for the newborn, just as mothers did; both parents spoke in shorter phrases and repeated sounds more often for their baby than when they were talking to an adult (Phillips & Parke, 1981).

Fathers can talk like mothers, give bottles like mothers, and be sensitive like mothers. But when they play, fathers are fathers. In general, fathers' play is vigorous and physically stimulating (Lamb, 1981; Parke, 1978), while mothers' play is more likely to involve words, toys, and games (Clarke-Stewart, 1977, 1980; Power & Parke, 1981; Yogman, Dixon, & Tronick, 1977). Although mothers—even those who work outside the home—spend more time with the baby overall (Belsky & Volling, 1989), infants seem to prefer their fathers' play (Clarke-Stewart, 1977; Lamb, 1976), perhaps because it is usually more physically and emotionally stimulating.

Outside the laboratory, in their own homes, mothers were more involved than fathers in every type of behavior researchers observed, including holding, talking, showing affection, and stimulating with a toy (Belsky, Gilstrap, & Rovine, 1984; Belsky & Volling, 1989; Greenbaum & Landau, 1982; Lamb, Frodi, Hwang, Frodi, & Steinberg, 1982a). But when men *do* become the primary parent for their infant, they adopt a more motherly style. This gap between fathers' abilities and their performance raises a fundamental question: If fathers *can* become as sensitively and competently involved with their infants as mothers do, why don't more fathers do it? The answer has to do with custom. In our society, men have been expected to support babies, while women take care of them. And even with both parents working, baby care is still defined primarily as woman's work. Fathers who become more involved in

Middle-of-the-night feedings do not have to be for mothers only. Fathers can be as "motherly" as mothers when they care for their children. When it comes to play, though, fathers' style is their own—vigorous and active. (left, *David Woods/The Stock Market;* right, *Bob Daemmrich/Stock, Boston*)

infant care usually are breaking some very strong social norms. They are behaving very differently from the way their fathers and grandfathers probably did. Such basic social change takes more than a generation to occur, no matter how just and desirable it may be. And just as women vary in their ability to be sensitive and responsive to their infants, so do men. Every parent fills the role of mother or father in her—or his—own way.

Relations with Peers

Even just crawling toward another baby to get a better look is a way of making social contact. Simple give-and-take responses aid social development during infancy. *(Barbara Alper)*

A child's social relationships with other children begin very early. Even 3-month-olds will stare intensely at each other, sometimes jerking their arms and legs excitedly and straining forward as if to get a better look (Fogel, 1979). But true social behavior begins at about 6 months, when babies begin interacting verbally and physically. Then, infants will smile and coo at each other, and once crawling begins, they will approach, follow, and reach for each other (Bridges, 1932; Durfee & Lee, 1973).

Between 9 and 12 months, infants become increasingly social. They offer and accept toys from each other, especially when they already know the other child (Durfee & Lee, 1973; Vincze, 1971). This sort of exchange is important for social development because it involves seeking and receiving a response from another person (Bronson, 1986). Nine- to twelve-month-old infants also play social games, such as crawl-and-chase and peek-a-boo. By 14 months, infant "friends" will imitate each other's behavior (Mueller & Vandell, 1979). Finally, between the ages of 1 and 2 years, these early social behaviors such as smiling, approaching, offering toys, and vocal exchanges begin to occur together. Toddlers will smile while offering a toy, for example, and turn-taking exchanges become longer (Brownell, 1986; Howes, 1987).

DIFFERENCES IN SOCIABILITY

As in all other areas of development, in social development we see both a universal pattern and individual differences. Although all normal infants and toddlers show the same *sequence* of early social behaviors, the ability to begin and maintain social exchanges varies from baby to baby and is probably related to temperament. Some infants appear to be more extroverted than others (Vandell, 1980). These differences in sociability and then in social behavior seem to persist as children grow older. Toddlers who frequently approached their peers at 16 months were just as sociable 6 months later. And individual children had the same frequency of unsuccessful approaches to their playmates at the ages of 16 and 22 months (Vandell, 1980).

In a study of five children in day care, from infancy through age 2, a girl named Jenny was the child others wanted to play with most often (Lee, 1973). The least popular child was Patrick. How were they different? Jenny was friendly and cooperative. She tended to begin an exchange by looking at or moving toward another child, and she was usually willing to take turns. In contrast, Patrick was intrusive and unsociable. Of the five, he was the most likely to approach others by grabbing their toys, and he tended to communicate only when he began the exchanges.

Explaining the differences

Every group of 2-year-olds has its Jennys and Patricks. How can we explain these pronounced differences at such an early age? Temperament is part of the answer, but sociability may also stem from a close infant-mother attachment. This theory is supported by studies which have found that securely attached infants *do* have more successful interactions with their peers during the preschool years (Lieberman, 1977; Sroufe, 1979). (See Chapter 10.)

Other psychologists believe that the mother-infant relationship has little to do with peer relationships, because the social skills necessary to deal with a powerful adult are very different from the skills required to play with another infant (Lewis & Schaeffer, 1979). Both arguments may be partly correct. The two kinds of social interaction may actually influence each other: The relationship between mother and baby may affect the baby's relationship with other infants, and at the same time the relationship between the infant and her peers may affect the relationship between mother and baby (Easterbrooks & Lamb, 1979; Vandell, 1980).

Learning to Say "I": The Emerging Self

If you dab red rouge on a baby's nose and then show the baby a mirror, the baby may look at her nose, but she won't reach for it unless she is older than 12 months (Lewis & Brooks, 1978). Until then, she doesn't know that the face in the mirror is hers. In fact, she won't know that she exists as a person, separate from all others, until she is 18 months old.

Psychologist Margaret Mahler argues that a young infant feels completely merged with his mother. While nursing he doesn't know where he begins and his mother ends. In fact, the breast that he suckles during his first few months may seem to be a part of himself. This inability to distinguish the self from another is called **symbiosis**. Mahler (1975), who has studied the infant-mother relationship in great depth, theorizes that the baby is so completely helpless that fusion with the mother is essential for survival.

As babies begin to realize that they are separate people, they are also preparing emotionally to move away from near-total dependence toward greater independence. Mahler called this gradual process of discovering a separate sense of self **individuation and separation**. (Erikson also has been concerned with this movement toward independence, as we discuss below.) The process progresses from about halfway through the first year until age 3. Mahler was particularly interested in the way mothers can affect this dual process. Some mothers are more comfortable with a passive, dependent baby; others take pleasure in their child's growing capacity for communication, because this enriches parent-child contact. Mothers who are overly attached to the symbiotic relationship they share with their babies can feel a keen sense of loss when their children start testing their powers of independence. Such mothers may have difficulty letting their children grow toward autonomy (Mahler et al., 1970).

The 2-year-old dragging a blanket around is trying to cope with the process of individuation. Young children often form attachments to **transitional objects** such as a blanket or a teddy bear (Winnicott, 1971). Children clutch these comforters when they are tired or upset, often insisting on taking them everywhere. The child's feelings of attachment to another person, usually her mother, have been partly transferred to the "security blanket." Parents and other caregivers should accept a child's need for a transitional object, even when it is inconvenient. By the age of 4 or 5, even the most fervently attached child will have begun the journey toward independence, leaving transitional objects behind.

GROWING TOWARD INDEPENDENCE: COPING WITH THE "TERRIBLE TWOS"

"Play in the sandbox," a toddler says, but as you approach, he shouts "No come here!" He'll call to a friend but won't share his toys. (See "Focus On.") "Me do. Me do," he says, but then he wants to be cuddled and fussed over. Ask

symbiosis
merging of self with another, as infant with mother

individuation and separation
according to Mahler, the striving toward independence and a sense of separate self during infancy and toddlerhood

transitional object
object like a blanket or teddy, to which an infant transfers attachment feeling as he moves toward independence

A favorite blanket can help a young child feel secure when he is tired or unhappy. As children become more independent, their *transitional objects* will be left behind. (*Jerry Berndt/Stock, Boston*)

him if he wants an ice cream cone, and he nods "yes" while saying "no!" If the 2-year-old's message is mixed, so is his motive: He wants to break away while staying close, to be secure and independent at the same time. By saying "no," in defiant self-assertion, both when he is cooperating and when he isn't, a child is communicating, to himself and to others, his newfound sense of himself as an "I," a separate person.

Erikson describes this conflict as the stage of **autonomy versus shame and doubt** (Erikson, 1963). The child who is moving away from dependency feels guilty about severing the symbiotic relationship with his mother. He doubts his ability to go it alone, but he is nevertheless ready to say "I," "me," and "mine." If his need for independence is denied and his "I" behavior punished, guilt and doubt may plague him, keeping him from moving forward. The challenge for parents and other adults is to gain the toddler's cooperation almost without his knowledge. If you want some toys picked up, a game works better than an order: "Can you clean up your toys before I finish straightening up my room?" "Can everyone put the blocks away before we have a snack?" It is possible to get a toddler to want to do what must be done (Leach, 1980). The same attitude can reduce conflict around toilet training, the classic arena in which toddlers express their desire to let go (eliminating) while holding on (retention). Linking his theory to Freud's ideas about the anal stage of development (see Chapter 1), Erikson argued that children who gain a sense of self-control without loss of self-esteem have a lasting sense of autonomy and pride. But children who are subject to toilet training too early or parental overcontrol may experience feelings of impotence and a lasting sense of doubt and shame (Erikson, 1959/1980). Toilet training, then, calls for sensitivity to the child's still maturing physical and emotional systems. Patience and support, rather than rigid demands for quick control, will help children feel good about their success and about themselves.

autonomy versus shame and doubt
according to Erikson, the toddler's major "crisis" as the sense of self emerges

Why Sharing Isn't Always the Best Policy

"Mine!" Sarah screams, grabbing the toy phone from her friend Kathy.

"Sarah," says her mother, "you need to share your toys. Let Kathy play with the phone."

Once toddlers begin playing together, this scenario becomes all too familiar. The children shout "Mine!" and their parents say "no," trying to discourage such "selfish" behavior. In fact, though, Sarah's possessive cries are a necessary and healthy part of her development. Such behavior does not mean that the child will become selfish. Instead, a child who can use words like "mine," "my," and "your" is developing a healthy sense of self. By allowing this sense of self to blossom, parents and other caregivers pave the way for children to interact in a more mature way later on, when they will be ready and able to share.

Levine (1983) tested this theory with 78 children between 2½ and 3 years old. To determine the children's sense of self, researchers noted the child's ability to distinguish between "my" and "your" and between "me/I" and "you." Then the children were observed for 20-minute periods in a room amply stocked with toys. Children who could distinguish between words like "my" and "your" were more apt to claim toys as their own when playing with peers. They were more likely to try to take toys that other children showed an interest in. After boundaries had been staked out, though, these "selfish" children played on friendlier terms. And in the second half of their play period, these children stopped claiming toys. It seems that those shrill shouts of "Mine!" are not always aggressive behavior to be discouraged. Rather, they represent an important part of a children's development, showing that they can define their social world.

When toddlers play "It's mine," it signals not selfishness, but a healthy sense of self. Before they are ready to share, children need to feel in control. *(Andrew Brilliant/The Picture Cube)*

Summary

1. Babies are born with unique body rhythms and styles of responding. This set of characteristics is temperament. Temperament includes susceptibility to emotional stimulation, speed and intensity of response, general mood, and the frequency of mood changes.

2. The three central traits of temperament are negative emotionality, activity level, and sociability. These traits combine to form several basic patterns of temperament: the difficult child, the easy child, and the slow-to-warm-up child.

3. Studies of twins have shown that heredity strongly influences temperament, but environment helps to shape it as well.

4. An infant's temperament influences the responses babies evoke from others as well as the activities and experiences that infants choose for themselves.

5. How the personalities of parents and infants mesh is called goodness of fit. The quality of this fit affects development.

6. One of the first social-emotional landmarks, smiling, appears from 6 to 9 weeks as a reaction to pleasure.

7. Stranger wariness, which begins at 7 months, signals an infant's ability to distinguish familiar from unfamiliar people. Temperament and experience with strangers influence the discomfort each infant feels with strangers.

8. From about 9 to 12 months infants protest when their parents leave. Kagan explains separation protest as the babies' response to an ambiguous situation: They don't know if their mothers are coming back.

9. By the end of their first year, most infants have formed an attachment relationship, usually with their mother. This relationship strongly affects children's sense of self, how they relate to others, and how they are likely to develop as toddlers and preschoolers.

10. Freud and learning theorists linked attachment to the hunger drive. Ethological theorists, such as Bowlby, argue that attachment behaviors such as smiling, clinging, crying, stranger wariness, and separation protest increased infants' chances for survival in the early stages of human evolution.

11. All infants form attachment relationships with their mothers, but the attachments differ in security, that is, in the extent to which children can count on their mothers' availability to meet their needs.

12. Mary Ainsworth believed that putting a child under stress would reveal the security of attachment. To test her theory, she devised the strange situation procedure to assess infant attachment.

13. For Ainsworth, the attachment relationship reflects the infant's experience with his mother during the first year of life. Sensitive mothering fosters trust and a secure attachment. Infants affect the relationship too: Whether or not they are prone to distress affects not so much whether or not they will be secure, but how they express their security or insecurity.

14. Securely attached infants tend to become secure, autonomous, socially skilled preschoolers. Insecurely attached infants, with a weaker feeling of basic trust, are more anxious and less socially skilled preschoolers.

15. Although the quality of an infant's attachment relationship with her mother strongly influences development, *experience* can sharply modify development. Insecurely attached infants whose emotional needs are met later can become well-functioning preschoolers. The reverse can happen as well.

16. Most infants who live with both parents also form focused attachment relationships with their fathers by 18 months. When men become the primary parent, many can be just as sensitive caregivers as mothers. Ultimately, every parent fills the role of mother or father in her or his own way.

17. Social relationships among children begin very early. During their first year, social exchanges progress from smiling, to offering toys, to playing social games, such as peek-a-boo. By 2 years, all these behaviors occur together.

18. All babies show the same sequence of social development, but the degree of sociability varies from infant to infant. It is probably related to temperament. The quality of mother-infant attachment may be a factor as well.

19. Margaret Mahler argues that until about 18 months, infants cannot distinguish themselves from their mothers (symbiosis). From 18 months on, individuation and separation—the baby's gradual move toward independence—begin.

20. Wanting to break away yet remain secure is a conflict for 2-year-olds. Erikson described it as the stage of autonomy versus shame and doubt. Parents and other adults need to be sensitive to the child's needs for both independence and security.

Key Terms

anxious-avoidant attachment

anxious-resistant attachment

attachment

autonomy versus shame and doubt

basic trust

difficult child

easy child

ethological theory

goodness of fit

individuation and separation

insecure attachment

New York Longitudinal Study (NYLS)

personality

secondary reinforcer

secure attachment

secure base

separation protest

slow-to-warm-up child

social smile

stranger wariness

strange situation

symbiosis

temperament

transitional object

Suggested Readings

Brazelton, T. (1983). *Infants and mothers: Differences in development* (rev. ed.). New York: Dell. A world-renowned pediatrician brings individual differences in infants to life by describing the way three different—and healthy—babies develop from birth through their first year.

Greenspan, S., and Greenspan, N. (1985). *First feelings.* New York: Penguin. A clinically astute and sensitive child psychiatrist and his wife chart the stages of a child's emotional growth during infancy with an eye toward enabling parents to enhance early psychological development.

Parke, R. (1981). *Fathers.* Cambridge, MA: Harvard University Press. A developmental psychologist who has spent years studying fatherhood, as well as being a father, provides a highly readable, authoritative account of the characteristics, consequences, and determinants of fathering.

Thoman, E., and Browder, S. (1988). *Born dancing: How intuitive parents understand their baby's unspoken language and natural rhythms.* New York: Harper & Row. A developmental psychologist who has spent thousands of hours observing and recording the interactions which take place between mothers and their young infants shares her knowledge about the wisdom that parents and infants so often express in their communication with one another.

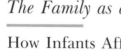

The Social Context of Infancy

On the same day, in very different places, three infants are born. One, the son of two teachers, will live in a suburban neighborhood, where his mother will stay home with him until he is ready to begin school. His father is eager to share experiences with his wife and son. Another baby born that day is the daughter of an unmarried, poor, teenage mother. She will take her baby home to her mother's already crowded inner-city apartment and return to school. A third baby is born in a rural Chinese village to parents who work in the fields for much of each day.

We know nothing about the inborn temperaments and abilities of these infants and nothing about the quality of care they will receive from their parents and other adults. Nor do we know anything about the attachment relationship these babies will form. But we do know that each of these infants will start life in a very different environment. That environment, which we call *social context* (introduced in Chapter 1), refers to all the interpersonal, community, and cultural influences that surround each person. Social context begins at home: Every infant is born into some kind of family—whether an extended family of several generations living together, a nuclear family of parents and children, or a single-parent family. Whatever its size and makeup, every family influences children in complex and powerful ways. And that influence flows in many directions, with each family member affecting all others.

But the social context surrounding each child extends far beyond the family. Every family lives in a neighborhood, and is part of a larger culture. A baby in the United States will be brought up differently from a baby born into another society, no matter where it is. And the suburb, inner city, and village that the infants we described above will call home represent only a fraction of the places in which babies live: an ethnic neighborhood of a larger city; a farm miles away from the nearest neighbor; an apartment house in a wealthy urban neighborhood; a poor rural town. In each of these settings children enter a

Children growing up in San Francisco's Chinatown and in Lake Worth, Florida, will be shaped by the values and norms of two different subcultures. But they will also share the larger context of American culture. (left, *Vicki Silbert/PhotoEdit*; right, *Alan Carey/The Image Works*)

way of life influenced by culture, class, geography, and ethnicity. All these elements of social context will forcefully shape children's lives, often even before birth. The prenatal care of a middle-class or wealthy woman differs significantly from an inner-city teenager's, and that difference affects each of their babies' health and chances for survival. Even *when* children live is a part of social context. Styles of child-rearing, theories of education, war, peace, a booming or depressed economy are all shifting social conditions that help to shape our lives.

As we look at the ways in which family, community, and culture influence development during infancy, we will see that this influence moves in two directions: The social context both influences and is influenced by the child. This reciprocal influence is most obvious when we consider the social context at the level closest to the baby—the family.

The Family as a System

For all their dependency, infants have enormous power. Their birth changes every relationship in a family because the family is a **system**, an interacting and interdependent group that functions as a whole. Each member of the family influences and is influenced by the others. Even the smallest traditional family includes a variety of people (man, woman, child) and a variety of roles (wife, mother, husband, father). Additional children add one more role (sibling) but considerably more complexity to the family system. The relationship between husband and wife affects the developing child and is itself affected by the birth of the child.

system
an organized, interacting, interdependent group, functioning as a whole

HOW INFANTS AFFECT MARRIAGES

When a couple's first baby is born many things in their lives change—the way they spend their time, the friends they see, the things that seem important, and certainly the way they relate to each other.

Couples confront four kinds of problems in adjusting to parenthood (Sollie & Miller, 1980). The first involves the *physical demands* of caring for an infant who needs to be fed and changed at least every 3 to 4 hours. New parents report feeling stressed and fatigued by lack of sleep. Mothers seem to be more susceptible, as they are more likely to feel the strain associated with adding primary caregiver to the role of wife, homemaker, and often employee as well.

Strains in the husband-wife relationship create the second problem. New parents complain that they have no time together as a couple anymore and no time for or interest in their sexual relationship. Fathers often feel that their wives pay more attention to their infants' needs than their own (Glenn & McLanahan, 1981). But for their wives, waking several times each night can easily create a need for sleep stronger than any need for sex or conversation. One mother expressed this difficulty well:

Taking care of an infant can be exhausting, especially if middle-of-the-night feedings persist for months. (*Judy Gelles/ Stock, Boston*)

In the early weeks things were fine. It was settled that we had to fix our attention on the baby, developing some kind of routine for dealing with waking, feeding, and sleeping for all three of us. It was the next month or so that was terrible. The baby still woke twice between ten and five. Rob was past the early nervous stage when he woke and helped. He was feeling pushed outside the charmed circle of those intense minutes in the dark and quiet. I would feed the baby, soothe her, lay her down to sleep—then go to bed with Rob where we would make love, or at least talk—then what seemed like only minutes later, I would hear the baby cry. I would go to her, feed and soothe her, lay her down to sleep, return to bed—and it would be morning all over again. I began to feel like an orange slowly being pulled into separate sections—one for the baby, one for Rob, one for me, one for the baby . . . (Boston Women's Health Book Collective, Inc., *Ourselves and Our Children*, 1978, p. 51).

Becoming parents has direct *emotional costs*, the third class of problems in the transition to parenthood. The responsibility of caring for an infant can seem overwhelming, and as parents come to realize that being a parent is a lifetime job, doubts about competence can also cause stress. The fourth problem area involves *loss of freedom and opportunities*. Parents frequently complain about the restrictions on their social lives. Freedom to travel is limited, and doing anything on very short notice is almost impossible. Most new parents discover that life with an infant is far more complicated than they had imagined. They want to go to a movie, but they can't find a babysitter; they take the baby to a restaurant, and he cries through dinner. Some new parents give up and just stay home. In addition to restrictions on mobility, having a child is expensive, and not just in money spent. If one parent stays home, there may be a significant loss of potential earnings as well.

All these strains on new parents can also strain their marriages (Cowan & Cowan, 1983; Miller & Sollie, 1980). Two longitudinal studies of working and middle-class families found that overall marital satisfaction drops from the last

3 months of pregnancy through the ninth month after the baby's birth, as shown in Figure 8-1 (Belsky, Lang, & Rovine, 1985; Belsky, Spanier, & Rovine, 1983). Wives' satisfaction declines more sharply because women are responsible for child care in most families. But the same studies also found that the ranking of couples, from most satisfied to least satisfied, hardly changed. Although husbands and wives generally become less happy with their marriages after the birth of their child, the marriages that were most happy or least happy before the arrival of the baby stayed that way after the baby was born. So, while having a baby does affect marriages, it does not generally ruin good ones or improve bad ones.

One of the greatest challenges to new parents is coping with the added work that accompanies parenthood. Division of labor often becomes more traditional after a baby arrives, with women doing more household chores, including laundry, cooking, and cleaning (Cowan, 1983; Lamb, 1978a). Interestingly, when household division of labor becomes more traditional, wives become more dissatisfied. But the extent of dissatisfaction a new mother feels depends on who she is. Women who view themselves as nontraditional, that is, women who are more independent and career-oriented, are the most unhappy with the changes a baby brings (Belsky, Lang, & Huston, 1985). Their daily activities are inconsistent with their views of themselves, breeding conflict and dissatisfaction.

Another difference among couples that affects their transition to parenthood is whether they have been realistic in their expectations about the baby.

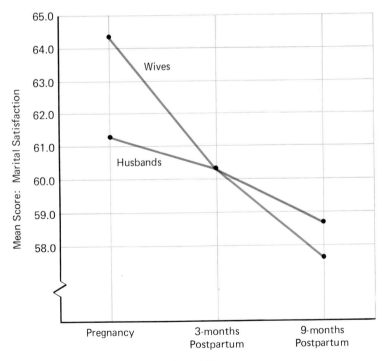

FIGURE 8-1
MARITAL SATISFACTION: THE EFFECTS OF PARENTHOOD
Changes in the marital satisfaction of husbands and wives during the transition to parenthood. (*Source*: Belsky, J., Lang, M., & Rovine, M. [1985]. Stability and change across the transition to parenthood: A second study. *Journal of Marriage and the Family, 47*, 855–866. Copyrighted 1985 by the National Council on Family Relations, 3939 Central Ave., N.E., Suite #550, Minneapolis, MN 55421. Reprinted by permission.)

Cooperation between parents helps to reduce the stress all family members feel when a new baby arrives. *(Michal Heron/Woodfin Camp & Associates)*

Couples often romanticize parenthood, imagining a blissful family unit instead of the combination of joy and stress that being a parent really is. When stresses such as the disruption of sleep and sexual relations are not anticipated, they can have a particularly strong impact on the couple. New parents are also subject to too much advice from well-meaning parents, in-laws, friends, and neighbors. When the advice differs from their own views, it can add to the parents' stress (Belsky, Ward, & Rovine, 1986; Garrett, 1983; Kach & McGhee, 1982).

A couple's age and the number of years they've been married also affect their adjustment. Newly married couples or those who are very young have the most trouble adjusting to parenthood. Older couples and those who have been married longer report fewer problems (Dyer, 1963; Hobbs & Wimbish, 1977; Russell, 1974; Tooke, 1974). How a baby affects a marriage also depends on the baby. Infants with more difficult temperaments, who are fussier, or who experience more illness generate more stress for their parents, and this stress can harm a marriage (Hobbs, 1965; Russell, 1974).

Before you decide that babies bring nothing but stress to their parents, we will add that they also bring great pleasure. Babies add work, but they also add fun. The feelings of love, joy, and happiness that commonly accompany parenthood can be a deep source of emotional richness. A sense of family cohesiveness also emerges as a positive theme. Many parents see their children as a link, binding them sometimes even more strongly than their marriage vows (Miller & Sollie, 1980). These pleasures, most strongly associated with the first child, help to balance some of the stress experienced by many parents.

Becoming a parent can also have positive effects on the psychological development of both the mother and the father as individuals. The experience

Sharing a pleasant moment with one's baby is deeply satisfying and offsets the stresses and demands of parenting. (*John Eastcott/Yva Momatiuk/The Image Works*)

of parenthood can bring greater maturity; caring for an infant can lead to feelings of accomplishment and self-enrichment. Parents often report that they feel more like adults, less self-centered, less selfish, and more thoughtful about the future (Gutman, 1975).

Adoption

The transition to parenthood can become even more complicated when couples adopt. Infertility, the main reason for adopting, can itself cause problems for both individuals and couples (Shapiro, 1982), including a decreased self-image, anxiety, depression, and disruptions in both marital communication and sexual relations. If left unresolved, all these problems can undermine family relations that foster trust, security, and unity (Brodzinsky & Huffman, 1988).

Stress comes, too, from an uncertain timetable. Biological parents know when to expect their baby's birth, but adopting couples live in limbo, waiting a few months or several years to become parents. Waiting is bad for babies as well. Attachment theorists favor adoption during an infant's first 4 to 6 months, before the child has formed a secure attachment to a caregiver, an attachment which will then be broken (Bowlby, 1980). And in fact, children who are adopted within the first few months of life are as likely to form secure attachments with their mothers as are nonadopted infants (Singer et al., 1985); the emotional difficulties associated with adoption are more likely when placement occurs after 6 to 7 months of age (Yarrow et al., 1973).

In light of these special challenges, it is particularly noteworthy that few studies show that the transition to adoptive parenthood exerts a more negative influence on marriage than transition to biological parenthood. In fact, the trend appears to be in the opposite direction, with adopted parents reporting more marital satisfaction (Humphrey & Kirkwood, 1982) and being less intrusive, less controlling, and less authoritarian as parents than nonadoptive parents (Hoopes, 1982). Such differences could result from the careful screening of prospective adoptive parents by adoption agencies or from the fact that adoptive parents are often older and thus more psychologically mature than other parents. Adoptive parents are likely to have been married longer and so may have experienced as a couple more stressful experiences that help prepare them for parenthood (Brodzinsky & Huffman, 1988).

Husbands and wives with handicapped infants

Caring for any infant is stressful, as parents cope with fatigue, loss of freedom, and changes in their own relationship. Usually, the joy of loving their babies and watching them develop balances the stress, but parents of handicapped infants often have additional burdens. Because a handicapped infant typically violates parents' expectations and can be so demanding, caring for such an infant is often very stressful for the entire family. Many parents feel guilty and ashamed about "causing" the handicap in the first place. This may be why some fathers of handicapped children are less involved with their disabled child than are fathers with normal children (Bristol, Gallagher, & Schopler, 1988). Mother-infant relations can be affected as well. In one study, not only did handicapped infants smile and vocalize less than healthy infants, but their mothers were less responsive, smiling and talking to them less than mothers of normal infants (Brooks-Gunn & Lewis, 1982). And the more severely handicapped infants are, the less responsive mothers tend to be toward them.

Affected too by the stresses of coping with a handicapped infant is a couple's relationship. Marriages that are already troubled can deteriorate further (Howard, 1978), but the opposite can happen as well. If a marriage is very strong, the birth of a handicapped child can actually bring a couple closer together (Gath, 1978). Ultimately, the effect of a child's handicap on the family depends on the severity of the handicap and on the family and community context. Are there other children to care for? Can the family afford extra

A family with a handicapped child can be as loving and close as any other. Some couples are drawn even closer together by caring for a disabled son or daughter. *(Zabala/Monkmeyer Press)*

medical expenses? Are there relatives and friends nearby to give relief? Can parents cope with their complex feelings toward the child? Availability of services with the community can make a big difference. When special home-visiting programs offer support to parents, or when relatives offer aid in a sensitive way, the family is often protected from some of the negative effects of rearing a handicapped infant (Parke & Beitel, 1988).

HOW MARRIAGES AFFECT INFANTS

Consider the workday of an at-home mother of a 1-year-old boy. By 4:30 on a typical weekday afternoon this woman has changed six diapers, prepared and helped her child eat two meals and three snacks, mopped up innumerable spills, spoken thousands of words to him, praised his own efforts to talk, read three stories, piled blocks into towers, bruised her foot on a block, washed the teddy bear her son spit up on the night before, scolded, endured tantrums, pushed the baby on the swing at the park, and tried to get him to take a nap. Now she is facing what is often the most terrible hour of her day. Mother and baby are both exhausted, and father won't be home until 6:00.

As soon as her husband comes home, she hands him the baby and heads for the bedroom, where she relishes a few minutes of privacy and relaxation. How does her husband respond? He has just come home from his own difficult day. Before the baby was born, he could relax after work. Now there is another job waiting for him at home.

The unfolding of this family drama can have strong implications for the child's development, because for fathers and mothers the quality of their marriage affects the quality of their parenting (Feldman, Nash, & Aschenbrenner, 1985; Pedersen, Anderson, & Cain, 1979; Price, 1977). A close husband-wife relationship apparently encourages a father's interest in his infant's development. Fathers who rank high in marital communication also show high involvement with their infants (Belsky, 1979; Belsky, Gilstrap, & Rovine, 1984; Belsky & Volling, 1985). For wives, marital satisfaction during the transition to parenthood influences the security of the infant-mother attachment (Isabella & Belsky, 1985). In one study, women who experienced the most dramatic and continuous decline in marital happiness during the last trimester of pregnancy through the infant's ninth month had babies who developed insecure attachments by 12 months (Isabella & Belsky, 1985). These findings strongly suggest that marital stress can interfere with a mother's ability to respond sensitively to her infant, which affects the child's emotional tie to his mother. Since insecurely attached infants often do not develop as competently as securely attached infants do, the quality of the mother's marital relationship can influence both her parenting and her infant's development.

If we pull together all these strands of influences on development, we can make several points: Babies with secure attachments to both parents have a developmental advantage. Infants, by their own temperaments, affect the way their parents feel about and relate to them. Babies affect the way their parents feel about and relate to *each other*. How mothers and fathers feel about each other also affects the relationship they form with their baby. And this, in turn, affects the way the baby develops. The key point here is **reciprocal feedback**:

reciprocal feedback
pattern of mutual, interdependent influences in which each member of a system affects and is affected by the others

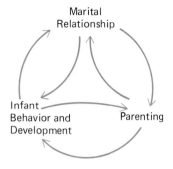

FIGURE 8-2

The interaction of marriage, parenting, and infant development in the family system. (*Source*: Belsky, J. [1981]. Early human experience: A family perspective. *Developmental Psychology*, *17*, 3–23. Copyright 1981 by the American Psychological Association. Reprinted by permission of the publisher.)

Babies and parents form a system of mutually affecting relationships. Parenting affects and is affected by the child, who both influences and is influenced by the marriage—which both affects and is affected by parenting. Figure 8-2 shows how marriage, parenting, and infant development are interrelated.

INFANTS AND SIBLINGS

Figure 8-2 focuses on only three family members: Mother/wife, father/husband, and infant. When siblings enter the system, it becomes even more complex. Research on sibling relations during infancy is not extensive, but two basic observations stand out: Infants tend to be more interested in their older siblings than the other way around. Infants love to spend time watching, following, and imitating their preschool siblings, while their siblings show less interest in them (Dunn & Kendrick, 1981; Lamb, 1978b; Pepler, Abramovitch, & Corter, 1978).

Nevertheless, older siblings invariably teach the infant a great deal, and they can even function as sources of security. By 14 months, half of the infants in one study were reported to miss their brothers and sisters if the siblings were away, and over one-third sought their older siblings for comforting (Dunn & Kendrick, 1982). Mothers in another study left their infants with the infants' siblings in an unfamiliar lab. The siblings' attempts to comfort their baby brothers and sisters were so successful that many of the babies returned to their play without anxiety (Stewart, 1983).

Exactly what happens between siblings seems related to the attention older children get from their mothers. Children whose mothers deliberately spend extra time with them *before* the baby is born may have the hardest time adjusting. When their mothers then become absorbed with the new infant, the older child is likely to feel the loss, and sibling interactions can become negative (Dunn & Kendrick, 1981). The older sibling apparently resents the infant as a competitor for the mother's attention. In Chapter 11, we will discuss the

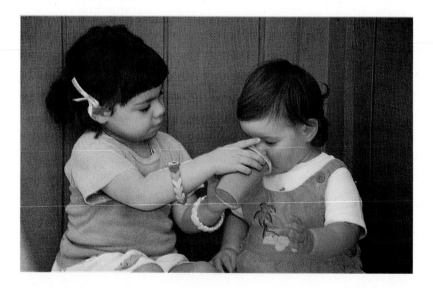

Even a small child can comfort a younger sibling. (*Lew Merrim/ Monkmeyer Press*)

ways that parents can help siblings deal with their negative feelings toward a new baby.

As you might predict from our discussion of the family as a system, the entire family structure—not just the relationship between the first-born child and mother—is deeply affected when new members are added. *Stage one* in the family's development spans the first year of a new infant's life: Parents redistribute work and attention. They may share the same chores, cleaning the house and bathing the children, for example, or they may each do different tasks. On weekends, a father might do the shopping and spend more time with the older child, while the mother does the cooking and takes care of the baby.

When the younger child begins to crawl and then to walk, family dynamics shift into *stage two*. Now parents must settle disputes between their children. The territory in question is not just parents' attention but actual space and belongings, especially those of the older child. "Get out of my room!" screams a 4-year-old as her 13-month-old brother blithely topples her block tower. She knocks him down in return, and when a parent rushes in, both children are crying. In settling such squabbles, coalitions tend to form, most often between older children and fathers and younger children and mothers. After the younger child learns to talk, new alliances of adults and of children form, creating a separate system of sibling relationships within the family (Kreppner, Paulsen, & Schuetze, 1981).

The Community and Social Class

Toss a stone into a pond and you'll see it splash, making ripples that move out across the water in a series of concentric rings. Now think of the nuclear family as the first ripple. Surrounding each individual in every family are everwidening rings of social context, including the local community, the family's **social class**, and their culture. These are all parts of the baby's social ecology. In this section, we'll see how the immediate community of neighbors and friends affects child care, both by offering support and by creating stress. We will also consider the profound influence of social class on development.

social class
measure of an individual's or family's standing in society, based primarily on income, education, and occupation

PARENTS AND INFANTS IN SOCIAL NETWORKS

A couple walking down a street may go unnoticed, but add a baby in a carriage, and even strangers stop to talk. Babies are social magnets, especially attractive to other couples with babies. Infants affect their family's social relationships by bringing their parents into contact with other young families (Belsky & Tolan, 1981). Such contact, and the support it can bring, have a generally positive impact on both psychological and physical health (Caplan, 1974). In fact, the degree of support parents receive, whether from friends or relatives, can influence the way they care for their infant.

Infants bring their parents into contact with other parents, socializing that benefits adults and children alike. *(Lester Sloan/ Woodfin Camp & Associates)*

Social networks function in three general ways to support parents: They provide *emotional support*; they provide *instrumental assistance*, including information, advice, and help with routine tasks; and they provide *social expectations*, or guidelines for child-rearing (Caplan, 1974; Cochran & Brassard, 1979).

Not all networks necessarily provide support, however. For some families, socializing with neighbors can do more harm than good, especially if their values are very different. Neighbors who advise you to let your newborn baby cry are not helpful if you feel babies should be comforted immediately. In fact, such advice often causes new parents to doubt themselves, leaving them feeling more insecure than before.

Suppose a woman who has put a high-power career on hold to have a baby and plans to return to work in 6 months is criticized by more traditional mothers. She may begin to feel less satisfied with herself as a parent. But if most of her friends also plan to combine a career and motherhood, she'll probably feel better about her own decision to do the same (Power & Parke, 1983). What's needed is a good match between the values of the community and the parents (Lamb & Easterbrooks, 1980; Minturn & Lambert, 1964; Powell, 1979).

Mothers who see their friends often and get support from them are also the most effective parents (Crnic et al., 1983). In fact, mothers receiving high levels of emotional support, material aid, and overall assistance reported the fewest symptoms of depression (Colletta, 1983). Mothers who have weekly or more frequent contact with friends are more verbally and emotionally responsive to their babies (Powell, 1980). Again, these are the very qualities of mothering that affect infant competence.

Community support

As the importance of social support for new parents becomes more widely understood, new community services have arisen to help parents through their transition. Mother-infant drop-in centers, parent discussion groups, various kinds of parent education, and other grass-roots resources are becoming more common. Some parents prefer to discuss their concerns with "experts," such as their family doctor or pediatrician. Others benefit most from informal contact among their friends. However they get it, more and more parents are coming to appreciate their own need for some kind of social support for their child-rearing efforts. Growing numbers of mothers who work outside the home seek that support in infant day care centers. "Issues & Options" explores the issue of day care and its effects on infants.

For women at home with their babies, a mothers' group can lift spirits by reducing isolation. Babies, too, can benefit from the chance to socialize. *(Carol Palmer/The Picture Cube)*

Issues & OPTIONS

Infant Day Care and Infant Development

When a woman in Finland has a baby, she can stay home with her infant for 35 weeks, receiving full salary from her employer. Italy guarantees its mothers 22 to 48 weeks of paid maternity leave, and Chilean women get full pay for 18 weeks. Of all the industrialized countries in the world, only two lack a national policy for maternity leave: South Africa and the United States. In this country, each family must make some hard choices after a baby is born. For half of all U.S. mothers with babies under a year old, the choice is to work either full- or part-time (U.S. Bureau of the Census, 1987). They go out every workday to offices, shops, and factories, leaving their infants in some kind of day care (see Table 8-1).

If ever there were a case of psychological theory hitting against social reality, the day care issue is it. If theorists are right about the importance of infant-mother attachment, and if separations are stressful, then how are thousands of infants being affected by their mothers' absences? Is infant-mother attachment affected? Are babies in day care more anxious than babies whose mothers are at home? The best way to answer these questions would be to compare children who are in day care with those who are not, but this is more complicated than it seems.

Until 1980, the research about the consequences of infant day care generally showed *no* differences between children cared for at home by their mothers and children reared in a variety of other settings during their first year of life (Belsky & Steinberg, 1978). But these were mostly studies of children cared for in

TABLE 8-1   WHO'S WATCHING THE BABY?

Day Care Arrangements Used by Working Mothers		
Type of Care	**Age of Child**	
	Under 1 year	**1 to 2 years**
Care in own home (by father, relative, or nonrelative)	37.3%	32.8%
Care in another home (by relative or nonrelative)	40.7%	41.8%
Group care (day care centers and nursery schools)	14.1%	17.3%
Care by mother while working	8.1%	8.2%
Total	1,796,000	Not reported

Source: U.S. Bureau of the Census. (1987). *Who's minding the kids? Childcare arrangements: 1984–85*. Current Population Reports, Series P-70, No 9. Washington, D.C.: U.S. Government Printing Office, p. 5.; Hofferth, S., & Phillips, D. (1987). Child care in the United States, 1970–1995. *Journal of Marriage and the Family, 49*, 559–571.

Issues & OPTIONS

centers set up by universities for research purposes, which provided care of the highest quality. Since 1980, however, evidence gathered from work using the strange situation (see Chapter 7) on children growing up in more typical community child-care arrangements has indicated that the quality of infant-mother relationships among day care-reared infants may indeed differ from those of infants who spend most of their day at home with their mothers. The studies suggest that infants who spend 20 or more hours of each week in day care are more likely to appear insecurely attached to their mothers (Barglow, Vaughn, & Molitor, 1987; Belsky 1988; Belsky & Rovine, 1988; Jacobsen & Willie, 1984; Schwartz, 1983; Vaughn et al., 1980). And boys in day care for 35 or more hours each week are more likely to show insecure attachments to their fathers as well (Belsky & Rovine, 1988; Chase-Lansdale & Owen, 1987). This does *not* mean that all day care children will feel insecure, but it does mean that children reared in some kind of nonparental care for an extensive period during their first year of life *may* be more likely to show this pattern of development—at least in the kind of day care arrangements that are typically available to American families.

As we saw in Chapter 7, insecure attachments during infancy are linked to difficulties in future development. Recent research indicates that in some cases, pre-

school and school-age children who experience extensive nonparental care in their first year of life are more aggressive and disobedient and have more difficulty coping with frustration than children whose mothers were home with them during their first year (Barton & Schwarz, 1981; Haskins, 1985; Rubenstein & Howes, 1981; Schwarz et al., 1974; Vandell, 1980). These consequences of infant day care are not found in every study, nor do they apply to every child in nonparental care. They suggest, though, that full-time day care during the first year, at least as currently available and routinely used in the United States, *may* promote aggression, disobedience, and low tolerance for frustration.

Not all psychologists agree. First, ask the critics of studies of day care and attachment, are the children's responses being interpreted correctly? When infants who spend 20 hours or more each week away from their mothers are reunited with them at the end of the day, they may not greet their mothers as warmly as children do who rarely experience long separations. But are they showing "avoidance," a behavior to be concerned about, or "independence," a healthy adaptation to separation (Clarke-Stewart & Fein, 1983)? Different researchers observing the same behaviors can reach very different conclusions.

A second problem concerns the real source of the behaviors we are observing in infants with

extensive day care experience. Is day care itself causing trouble for these children, or is the problem in the kinds of families that use extended day care for their infant? If you think back to Chapter 1 and the difference between causation and correlation, you will get a sense of the kind of problem we face in day care research. Because we are observing children after separations from their mothers, we assume that the separation and the experience of day care cause the behaviors we see. But perhaps the root of these behaviors lies not in day care but within the child's family. It may be that the stresses on parents caused by money worries, cramped living conditions, and raising children alone create more problems for infants than the day care experience.

We also need more information about parents who choose to use extensive day care during their infant's first year. Are mothers who opt to return to work shortly after their baby's birth different from those who stay home during the first year? If they are, how do those differences affect their children? In short, the causes of the behaviors we see in day care children may be far more complex than the day care experience itself. When we draw conclusions about infants in day care, then we must guard against mistaking correlations for causation. Continued research can only expand our insights into the day care experience.

(continued on next page)

Issues & OPTIONS

In the meantime, what should working parents do to meet their infants' needs as well as their own? If possible, one parent might decide to work part-time during the baby's first year. But not every parent can choose to stay at home. Single parents and couples who need both incomes may *have* to use day care; working part-time may simply be impossible. If, for whatever reason, parents choose day care for their infant, what should they look for? Parents and those who counsel them should keep the following criteria in mind:

• *A nurturant caregiver is the top priority.* The single most important factor for infant development at home or away from home is the quality of the caregiver. Someone warm, responsive, and affectionate, a person who has experience with infants and genuinely likes them, is best.

• *A caregiver should be trustworthy, easy to talk to, and generous with time and information.* Parents need a full report at the end of the day, not just a few mumbled words. Information they get from the caregiver can help parents

themselves provide more sensitive care. Feeling comfortable with the person who is caring for their infant can do a lot to relieve anxieties. By interviewing sitters before the baby is born, parents can avoid having to settle for someone who doesn't feel right.

• *Stability and consistency are important.* Frequent changes in day care arrangements are stressful for infants and make it difficult for them to form secure attachments. Such changes also can wreak havoc in parents' lives. Parents should choose a day care arrangement with a reputation for constancy.

• *The number of children per adult should be small.* Infants demand a lot of attention and need a lot of care. No more than three infants to one adult is best. Since day care centers typically enroll larger numbers of children and tend to turn over staff more often, a babysitter or family day care is often better for the baby's first year.

• *The setting is the least important consideration.* Don't be too influenced by fancy physical facilities. Infants don't need designer interiors or elaborate toys, but

they do need a safe, sanitary setting. A warm, responsive caregiver and a limited number of other children are much more important than expensive toys.

• *Goodbyes shouldn't be too long or drawn out.* To make the separation as easy as possible each morning, parents should say goodbye and *then leave*. Lingering in the doorway only makes the separation harder, as separation-protest studies (discussed in Chapter 7) have shown.

• *Infants need time for adjustment.* At both drop-off and pick-up, a baby or toddler needs time to make the transition to a new setting, time to say goodbye and hello. Don't cut goodbyes off *too* abruptly. And at the end of the day, parents should give their babies time to warm up and should stay alert to their cues. This sensitivity to the baby, as we saw in our discussion of attachment, is central to the development of trust, confidence, and well-being.

• *Infants can thrive in the care of others.* Parents need not despair. Finding the right situation for parent and infant can take a lot of effort but can add immeasurably to the well-being of both.

SOCIAL CLASS, PARENTING, AND INFANT DEVELOPMENT

In Greene County, Alabama, the sixty-sixth poorest of Alabama's 67 counties, a baby is seven times more likely to die during the first year of life than is a Japanese baby (Children's Defense Fund, 1987; Wilkerson, 1987). U.S. infant mortality rates are worse than those of many other developed countries (see

Figure 8-3), largely because of high rates in poor urban and certain rural areas (Children's Defense Fund, 1987). American infants born to lower-income parents have up to a two to three times greater chance of dying before their first birthday than middle-class infants (National Center for Clinical Infant Programs, 1987). These figures reflect a high rate of teenage pregnancies, insufficient diets, and almost no prenatal care among the poor. In underdeveloped countries, where poverty, malnutrition, and often famine are widespread and the "middle class" is tiny, infant death rates are even higher.

Social class also has important effects beyond survival. A family's level of affluence affects how well its children are fed, clothed, housed, educated, and otherwise provided for. But beyond the material things that social class determines, it is reflected in a family's values. If we know a person's social class, we can make some fairly accurate predictions about what he or she is likely to value, do, and think.

Research suggests that parents in different social classes actually behave differently with their children. For example, middle-class mothers tend to talk

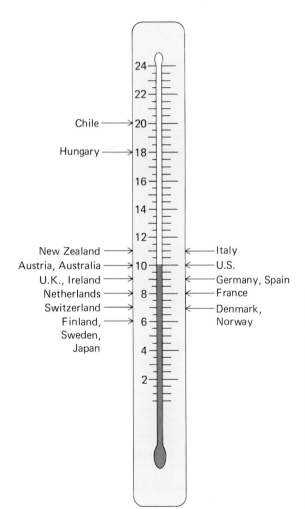

FIGURE 8-3

INFANT MORTALITY THERMOMETER: DEATHS OF INFANTS YOUNGER THAN 1 YEAR, PER 1000 BIRTHS

In 1986, among selected industrialized countries, the United States ranked thirteenth in infant mortality rates, behind Spain, Ireland, Japan, Germany, and France. Overall, the U.S. infant mortality rate ranked eighteenth worldwide. (*Source: A Children's Defense Budget, FY 1988.* © 1987, Children's Defense Fund, Washington, D.C.)

Support Programs for Low-Income Families: Intervention and Infant Development

Aware that middle-class children seem to get a head start in cognitive development, psychologists wondered whether the same boost could be given to lower-class children. Would middle-class-style support and encouragement enhance lower-class children's development?

The answer appears to be yes. Support programs designed to help lower-class mothers have enhanced their relationships with their children and their children's development as well. (We'll look at other programs for older children, such as Head Start, in Chapter 11).

In a New Haven, Connecticut, study, a group of poor families (most were headed by single mothers) received a variety of services from the time of a child's birth up to the age of 30 months. Services included a home-visitor program, pediatrician care, developmental evaluations, and day care. Ten years after the mothers had been enrolled in this program, they seem more involved with and sensitive to their children than mothers in similar circumstances who had not been enrolled. The women in the program had gotten more education in the 10-year period; they had had fewer children, at more widely spaced intervals, and their families were more likely to be self-supporting. The children of these mothers were rated as better-adjusted by their teachers; the children missed fewer days of school and were less likely to have been enrolled in remedial programs. The effects of this experimental program were broad: Mothers as well as children were helped, and the benefits were lasting (Rescorla, Provence, & Naylor, 1982; Seitz, Rosenbaum, & Apfel, 1985).

In Houston, Texas, another enrichment program enrolled a large group of low-income Mexican-American parents (Johnson & McGowan, 1984). This program served children for two years, from age 1 to age 3. A control group of other families with similar incomes and background did not receive any special services. In the first year, a home educator visited each family in the experimental group twice each week. To promote interaction between mothers and their babies, the visitor emphasized the

to and stimulate their infants more than lower-class mothers do (Lewis & Wilson, 1972; Tulkin & Kagan, 1972). Middle-class mothers are also more likely to give babies freedom to explore their environment, "child-proofing" an entire house, for example, rather than confining the baby to a crib or playpen (Ramey, Mills, Campbell, & O'Brien, 1975). Lower-class parents as a group may be less likely than others to encourage independent, curious, "achieving" behavior in their infants. In a recent study, lower-class mothers of babies aged 9 to 23 months held more conformist and fewer self-directed values. More than middle-class mothers, these mothers believed that babies could be spoiled and that they shouldn't be allowed to explore and play on the floor. For these mothers, controlling and disciplining their infants were extremely important (Luster et al., 1989). These attitudes may be linked to a fatalistic view of life (Kohn, 1977). If you believe that outside social forces

mother's role as a teacher and the value of being sensitive to her infant's emotional states and newly developing abilities. Entire families attended several weekend sessions, where family communication and decision making were discussed. During the second year of the program, four mornings each week, children attended nursery school while mothers met in small groups to discuss topics related to parenting.

The results? Mothers in the program were more affectionate, used less restrictive controls, encouraged their children's speech more, provided a more stimulating home environment, and held less traditional values than mothers in the control group. When measured at 2 and 3 years of age, the children scored higher than controls on IQ tests. Between the ages of 4 and 7, boys who had not participated in the program were more destructive, overactive, and negative and less emotionally sensitive than boys who had participated (Johnson & Breckenridge, 1982). And the benefits lasted. When teachers evaluated the children's behavior in the second, third, and fourth grades, the same results appeared (Johnson & Walker, 1987).

Infant cognitive development was the focus of another enrichment program, this one aimed at low-income black teenage mothers (Field, Widmayer, Stringer, & Ignatoff, 1980). Again, when mothers learned specific techniques for stimulating their infants—even by playing peek-a-boo— and when they became more sensitive to their infants' emotional needs, the babies scored higher on a test of mental development than did control-group babies.

What these and similar studies show is that helping mothers helps babies. And programs that include the whole family benefit babies the most. As in the first study described above, a multifaceted family support program not only encourages more sensitive and stimulating mother-infant interaction; it also aids the mother's own development by supporting her efforts to get more schooling, for example. And when a parent's own life improves, so do the family's environment, the parent-child relationship, and the developing child.

---

determine your future, then encouraging independence and initiative may seem futile. But if, as middle-class parents characteristically do, you believe that personal abilities and hard work will bring success, you will be more likely to encourage your baby's efforts with a confident, "You can do it!" Children from lower-class families need not fall behind, though. Intervention programs, such as those described in "Focus On," can make a difference.

These differences in parenting may be linked to later differences in children's cognitive development (Levine, Fishman, & Kagan, 1967; Wachs, Uzgiris, & Hunt, 1971). Social class differences in cognitive functioning start to show up around the end of the second year, when tests of intellectual development begin to rely heavily on language. It may be that the extra verbal stimulation that middle-class parents typically give to their children encourages and reinforce understanding and use of language.

Studies may consistently show that in households with greater economic, educational, and occupational resources, parents provide more cognitively stimulating care, but the studies do *not* imply that parents from lower-class environments love their children less. Many lower-class parents provide their children with sensitive, stimulating care. When caregiving is compromised, it is usually because the stress that accompanies poverty saps the emotional resources needed to provide quality care (Tulkin & Kagan, 1972).

The Culture

A Japanese mother is awakened at 3 A.M. by her crying infant. She immediately reaches out to soothe the baby nestled in bed beside her and holds him until he falls asleep. An American mother, waking to the same distressed cry, lies in her own bed for a few minutes waiting to see if her baby, sleeping in a crib in a separate bedroom, will continue to cry or go back to sleep. Like many American mothers, she does not believe in immediately rushing to comfort her baby every time he cries. And like her own mother, who believed that infants could be "spoiled," she wants to give her son an early lesson in self-reliance.

The differences between Japanese and American mothers have more to do with culture than with kindness. Psychologist Jerome Kagan argues that we treat our infants in accord with the values of our culture (Kagan, Kearsley, & Zelazo, 1978). In Japan, where cooperation and community life are strongly valued, parents feel that their infants need to be brought into the group. Babies are considered too *independent*, so dependency is fostered. Until their fifth birthday, children are indulged by parents and other family members. Making a child sleep alone is considered a punishment. Japanese mothers spend much more time with their babies than American mothers do, rarely leaving them with babysitters (Vogel, 1963; Miyake et al., 1985). Besides breast feeding and sleeping with their babies, Japanese mothers also bathe with them and carry them on their backs (Lebra, 1976).

In our own culture, relatives, pediatricians, and child-care books promote the American message: Infants shouldn't become too dependent on their parents. Dr. Benjamin Spock, whose book *Baby and Child Care* has guided millions of American parents, writes: "It is good . . . for babies to get used to falling asleep in their own bed, without company, at least by the time any 3-month colic is over" (1989, p. 199).

As in Japan, Chinese mothers would find Dr. Spock's instructions odd. Chinese babies sleep cuddled against their mothers, who breast-feed on demand. Soon after the baby is a month old, the mother returns to her work outside the home, leaving the baby with a grandmother or another older female relative or family friend. As in other traditional cultures, older siblings also attend to the baby. In fact, the entire extended family and the other villagers as well are concerned about the infant's upbringing. The government provides a village day care nursery, but most families think home care is best, at least until the child can talk (Chance, 1984).

A. Japanese mothers rarely use babysitters and encourage close ties between children and family members. B. While all parents feel proud of their toddlers' first steps, for Americans, walking is a sign of growing independence, a trait highly valued in their culture. C. In many traditional cultures, older siblings care for younger ones while their parents are working in the village. (A, *Bruno Barbey/ Magnum;* B, *Elizabeth Crews/ Stock, Boston;* C, *Chester Higgins, Jr./Photo Researchers*)

Among the Rajput of northern India, parenting practices differ sharply with our own. And again, cultural values set the style. Middle-class U.S. parents, believing they can strongly influence their children's development, actively try to shape it. Rajput parents think the opposite and behave accordingly. A child's fate, they maintain, is determined by forces beyond human control; even the infants' future careers are predetermined by their caste. Rajputs do not try to shape their children's early experiences (Kagan, Kearsley, & Zelazo, 1978). For the first 2 years of life Rajput children observe their world passively (Minturn & Hitchcock, 1963), while many American babies are being stimulated and encouraged to explore.

Sibling relations also vary across cultures. In traditional tribal societies, siblings are like substitute parents: When the mother cannot be right at the baby's side, older brothers or sisters will take over. In one village in the Philippines, for example, child "nurses" are trained at age 3 to care for infants under adult supervision. And among the Gusii in Kenya, 5- to 8-year-olds are responsible for total care of infants when the babies are 2 months old.

This sampling of family, class, and cultural influences raises an intriguing question: Would any of us develop into the people we are had we been raised in another culture? Probably not. Certainly, we reflect what we are born with—genes and temperament strongly influence development—but we are also shaped by where we are born and to whom.

Summary

1. Development is strongly influenced by social context: the family, community, social class, and culture in which an infant lives.

2. Families are systems, with parents and children influencing and being influenced by all the others.

3. Couples confront four kinds of problems in adjusting to parenthood: (*a*) the physical demands of caring for an infant; (*b*) strains on the relationship caused by decreased desire for sex and conversation; (*c*) fears about the life-long commitment of parenthood; (*d*) loss of freedom and opportunities.

4. Both how a couple adjusts to being parents and the quality of their marriage affects the quality of their parenting, which in turn affects their child's development. Marital stress is associated with insecure infant attachment.

5. Infants tend to be more interested in their siblings than their siblings are in them, but older siblings teach infants a great deal. When a new baby enters the family, dynamics shift in several ways. Parents have to redistribute their work and attention; they must learn to settle disputes between their children for attention, space, and belongings.

6. Support from social networks—from family, friends, and community groups—can affect new parents' psychological and physical health positively. The social contacts can provide emotional support, help with ordinary tasks, and information about child-rearing. Mothers who feel supported by friends are the most effective at parenting.

7. Children's development is strongly influenced by their family's social class. Infant mortality rates, for example, are much higher for poor than for middle-class families. Social class affects values and parenting styles, with middle-class parents tending to offer more cognitive stimulation and freedom to infants than lower-class parents do. Often the stress in poor families that is related to poverty compromises the quality of care parents would otherwise provide.

8. Support programs for poor families, many headed by young unmarried mothers, have helped both parents and infants over an extended time. In several research studies, mothers learned to become more sensitive to their infants and improved their own lives as well.

9. Cultural values strongly influence how parents treat their infants. Asian parents foster dependency and family closeness, while Americans encourage independence.

Key Terms

reciprocal feedback
social class
system

Suggested Readings

Brazelton, T. (1985). *Working and caring*. Reading, MA: Addison-Wesley. One of America's foremost pediatricians discusses in his characteristic sensitive and understanding manner the needs and desires of young children and their working parents.

Fraiberg, S. (1977). *Every child's birthright*. New York: Basic Books. A sensitive child psychologist outlines her beliefs on why babies need their mothers' care—rather than someone else's—in their first years of life.

Michaels, G., and Goldberg, W. (Eds.) (1989). *The transition to parenthood: Current theory and research*. Cambridge, England: Cambridge University Press. In a series of excellent chapters, the state of research on the transition to parenthood is examined, including research on prematurity, marital relations, adult development, and intervention programs.

Scarr, S. (1985). *Mother care, other care*. New York: Basic Books. An eminent developmental psychologist with a strong feminist orientation argues for the benefits of maternal employment—for mother and child alike.

"Hey, Stuart, you wanna be a witch in my spaceship?"

"Can I be Darth?"

"That's your blanket, Stuart," Mollie says. "Fix it like mine is."

"First I have to bang my gun."

"This isn't a gun. It's for the baby to hold."

"No, Mollie. I made it for a gun. Bang! Bang! . . ."

"Don't shoot it, Stuart. You'll bother the baby. . . ."

"Aren't we witches? You said we're witches in the spaceship, Mollie."

"Right. This *is* the witch's house. You be the daddy witch, okay, Stuart? Let's take the baby to the witch's place."

"No, to the Star Wars place. . . . Don't forget. I'm Darth."

. . .

"Who am I, Mollie?" Christopher asks from the window seat.

"Do you want to be a boy thing or a girl thing?"

"A boy thing."

"Then you're the Dukes. Put your bed here and be very quietly. The baby is sick. No noise."

Vivian G. Paley, *Mollie Is Three*

Early
Childhood

Physical, Cognitive, and Language Development in Early Childhood

*O*ne of the truest things we can say about preschoolers is that they always seem to be in motion. The inquisitive 2-year-old who explores everything in sight becomes the 3-year-old who never tires of climbing, jumping, and running. By age 4, children have developed enough motor coordination to hit a baseball, kick a soccer ball, and hop on one foot. Five-year-olds channel their energy into games, both competitive and cooperative, that reveal higher levels of social interaction, communication, and understanding, as well as greater physical coordination.

One of the best places to see these developmental gains is on a playground. Watching children play is enjoyable, and you can also identify prominent characteristics of preschoolers' play and ask critical questions about their development. The little girl struggling to climb the jungle gym reveals her motivation to master a challenge. How can parents and other adults promote such motivation? The 5-year-old boys arguing about who won a game show us how hard it is for a young child to negotiate rules and social contracts. Why do they stubbornly stick to rigid rules? The 3-year-olds in the sandbox playing with toys chatter away but seem to be talking to no one in particular. Is this playful language or poor communication? You may see groups of 4- and 5-year-olds pretending to be cowboys, superheroes, or tigers as they chase each other. Does role playing depend on cognitive development? How have preschoolers' cognitive skills progressed since infancy? If you listen to children pretending to prepare and eat lunch, you may hear an exchange like this:

A: "Do you want a sand-ish?"
B: "Uhhuh."
A: "What kind?"
B: "Peanut butter and jelly."
A: "There it is. Now I'm going to cut it into pieces."
B: "No, no! I'm not that hungry. I can only eat one sand-ish."

Although most preschoolers have similar physical abilities, they play according to their own interests, social skills, and temperament. *(Gerald Fritz/ Monkmeyer Press)*

In this chapter we discuss children's physical, cognitive, and linguistic growth from ages 2 to 6 years—growth that sets the foundation for childhood.

Physical Development

The rapid growth of infancy slows down during the preschool years. In fact, between their second and third birthdays, children gain fewer pounds and grow fewer inches than at any age until after puberty.

The other most visible difference from infancy is the change in body shape and proportion. Two-year-olds still have the short-limbed, large-headed, pot-bellied look of infants, but over the next 3 to 4 years, arms, legs, and torso grow quickly, becoming longer in proportion to the head. By age 5 or 6, children's body proportions are nearly the same as young adults'. Throughout the preschool years, boys are slightly taller and heavier than girls, a difference that continues until adolescence, when girls, who mature earlier physically, shoot ahead of boys.

SIZE AND GROWTH RATES

Among young children, size and rate of development vary greatly, but 2-year-olds generally weigh 20 to 25 pounds. Over the next 3 years, most children gain about 6 to 7 pounds per year, so by age 5 or 6, an average child in the United States weighs approximately 40 pounds. Preschoolers also grow an

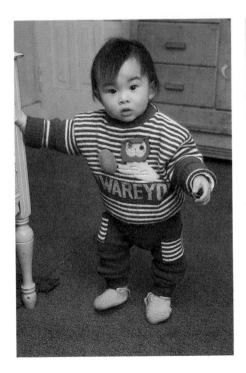

The top-heavy, short-limbed toddler whose wide-apart legs help him balance will have very different body proportions by age 5 or 6. Now, limbs are longer in proportion to the head, and pot bellies have slimmed down. (left, *Sybil Shackman/Monkmeyer Press;* right, *Bob Daemmrich/The Image Works*)

average of 2 to 4 inches per year; the average 5-year-old is about 43 inches tall. Doubling a child's height on the second birthday is a rough estimate of adult height. Predictions improve as the child gets older: Height during childhood is correlated highly with adult height.

The factors influencing size and growth of children are the same two that influence all development—heredity and environment. In this case, heredity is so powerful that from the age of 2 on, parents' height can be used to predict children's height. This prediction is moderately accurate but increases as children get older. Linked to heredity is race. Children from North America, Africa, and northern Europe are among the tallest in the world whereas those from southern Asia are among the smallest. Within the United States, the tallest preschoolers tend to be those of African descent; Caucasians are a bit shorter, and children of Asian descent shorter still. Racial differences reflect hereditary influences and will vary widely depending on the stature and growth of children's parents.

The environmental factor that influences growth most strongly is nutrition. When children do not get enough calories to maintain growth, they become listless and apathetic, and when the calorie level drops further during temporary starvation, famine, or malnourishment, growth stops. Short periods of malnutrition can be overcome with catch-up growth if children are returned to a normal diet (Acheson, 1960). As in infancy, the causes of malnutrition are social, or environmental. Researchers in a number of countries have found that children in upper socioeconomic groups are taller and heavier than their peers in lower socioeconomic groups (Meredith, 1984; Tanner, 1978), who often have irregular sleep and exercise habits, inadequate diets, and irregular health care (Butler, Starfield, & Stenmark, 1984). Many other environmental factors can affect children's growth and development as well. For example, western European children grow faster in the spring and summer than in autumn and winter. In tropical countries, seasonal variations in rainy and dry periods influence the food supply and frequency of infections, and this has direct effects on children's growth. Children growing up in densely populated urban areas are usually larger than children from rural areas. This may be a function of the availability of food as well as health, sanitation, and recreational services.

Growth abnormalities

Delayed growth is associated sometimes with family characteristics and sometimes with environmental conditions. Recall from Chapter 5, for example, that in some cultures, particularly in Central America, infants are often swaddled on a board during the first year of life. This restricted movement impedes physical and motor development during early childhood, but by age 5 or 6 considerable catch-up growth compensates for early restricted movement (Dennis, 1960). We saw, too, that specific dietary deficiencies can also disrupt physical growth. Kwashiorkor, for example, is a common ailment among infants in developing countries, caused by prolonged protein deficiency. When deprivation is severe, irreversible physical and mental retardation can result (Cravioto & Delicardie, 1970). At the other end of the scale, obesity is *increas-*

ing among U.S. children, partly because of increased availability of junk food, more television watching, and less physical exercise.

Short stature can result from two types of endocrine disorders, **growth hormone deficiency** and **thyroxine deficiency**. Too little growth hormone slows growth from birth on. This is a rare condition occurring only in about 1 in 10,000 births, afflicting boys four times more often than girls. Growth hormone deficiency is sometimes linked to problems in the pituitary gland and, when diagnosed promptly, can be treated effectively, sometimes by injections of growth hormone during childhood and adolescence. Shortness can also result from an insufficient amount of thyroxine, a hormone produced by the thyroid gland. An underactive thyroid can cause cretinism, a condition characterized by stunted growth and mental retardation.

growth hormone deficiency
an endocrine disorder causing short stature

a thyroid disorder that may cause short stature, stunted growth, and mental retardation

BRAIN GROWTH

By age 2, the brain has grown to about 75 percent of its adult weight and size, and by age 5, it totals 90 percent of its adult weight (Schuster & Ashburn, 1986). In contrast, an infant's birth weight is only about 5 percent of his future adult weight, and by age 10, a child weighs only half of what he'll weigh as a young adult. Although the brain grows most quickly during infancy, it develops continuously throughout childhood. Myelin, the fatty sheath that surrounds neurons and promotes the rapid transmission of information, continues to grow until puberty. The same is true for **cerebral lateralization**, the process by which some functions are located in one hemisphere or the other. For example, lateralization of hand dominance and speech continues until early adolescence. Brain waves, too, develop throughout childhood, taking on an adult form at adolescence. Throughout early childhood the speed of transmission improves. Babies respond slowly to new sights and sounds, but by age 4 children respond as quickly as adults do (Parmalee & Sigman, 1983). Because the brain and nervous system grow continuously during childhood, there is a **plasticity**, or flexibility, in response to early damage caused by malnutrition, tumors, deprived environments, or closed head injuries. There is a strong possibility that the brain can recover or show catch-up growth later on.

cerebral lateralization
process by which certain brain functions are located in one hemisphere

The brain develops fastest while children are beginning to speak, becoming physically coordinated, and experiencing rapid cognitive and social development. These are reciprocal developments—the stimulation provided by physical activity, language, and thinking promote brain growth as much as neurological changes influence the way young children respond to the environment. The key point here is that environment strongly affects a child's cognitive and social development, a topic we focus on in Chapter 11, when we discuss early education programs and the effects of poverty.

plasticity
flexibility

MOTOR DEVELOPMENT

Gradually, preschoolers leave the clumsiness of toddlerhood behind as coordination and agility continue to increase. Maturing **gross motor skills** improve children's ability to jump, climb, and pedal. By age 3, children can run in a straight line and leap off the floor with both feet. Four-year-olds can throw objects and catch a large ball with both hands. They can skip, hop, and pedal a

gross motor skills
physical abilities involving large-muscle groups

tricycle on their own. Five-year-olds resemble adults more than toddlers because their bodies have lengthened and become less top-heavy. A 5-year-old's balance has improved, her muscles have grown stronger, and she can ride a bicycle, swim, and do acrobatics. Many of these changes reflect stronger muscles, greater physical coordination, and improved balance stemming from better body proportions. (Table 9-1.)

fine motor skills
physical abilities involving small-muscle groups

Fine motor skills, which include smaller, more precise and delicate movements, improve markedly as well. Three-year-olds struggle with buttons, zippers, and shoelaces, but by age 5, children can usually dress themselves and manipulate a variety of tools as well. For example, most 5-year-olds can cut out shapes with scissors, use rulers, play video games with joysticks, and easily copy letters and numbers with crayons and pencils. The increased coordination of small muscles and manual dexterity also allows children to play simple musical instruments, draw more precisely, and begin to write.

hand dominance
strong preference for using the left or right hand

One clear developmental change for preschoolers is **hand dominance**. Most toddlers tend to use one hand more often than the other when throwing a ball, drawing, and so forth, but strong preference for handedness may not appear until age 5 (Goodall, 1980). Although some people believe that left-handed children are more awkward than right-handers, children who prefer *either* hand consistently are more coordinated than children with inconsistent hand preferences (Gottfried & Bathhurst, 1983; Tan, 1985).

Although gender influences the development of motor skills, differences between boys and girls are not exclusively due to innate characteristics. Boys, for example, tend to have more muscle and are somewhat stronger than girls (Garai & Scheinfeld, 1968). They may have better gross motor skills, but girls usually excel at fine motor skills. One explanation for these differences is environmental: From toddlerhood on, boys are encouraged to run, jump, and play in a rough-and-tumble way, whereas girls are encouraged to use their hands at drawing, sewing, or playing musical instruments. In Chapter 10 we'll

What children do influences what they *can* do. Boy-girl differences in motor skills may have more to do with children's activities than with their gender. (left, *Stephen McBrady/PhotoEdit;* right, *Coco McCoy/Rainbow*)

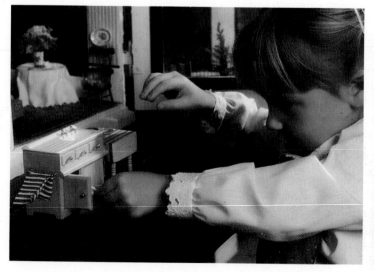

TABLE 9-1 GROSS AND FINE MOTOR SKILL ACCOMPLISHMENTS

2	2½	3	3½	4	4½	5
Gross Motor Skills by Age						
Walks up and down stairs alone, one step per tread Can walk backward Can throw a ball overhand Kicks large ball forward on request May pedal tricycle	Can walk on tiptoe Balances for 1 second on one foot Jumps with both feet "in place" Helps dress and undress self	Runs well but will stumble or fall occasionally Can use hands and feet simultaneously, e.g., stamping foot while clapping hands Can throw a ball without losing balance Jumps from bottom step (12 inches) Alternates forward foot going up stairs Rides tricycle with no difficulty Handles most of dressing; puts on own shoes	Runs smoothly with acceleration and deceleration Skillful in balancing on toes, can run on tiptoes Briefly hops on one foot Catches bounced ball (hands held in viselike position, elbows extended)	Balances on one foot for 4–8 seconds Skips "lame duck" on one foot Descends stairway with alternating feet (may need some help)	Hops on non-dominant foot Leaps over objects 10 inches high Hops forward three hops, maintains balance (knees should flex slightly) Can turn somersault Dresses self except for tying shoes	Two-hand catch (often fails to catch ball) May bounce ball in place, catch each bounce May be able to hit a swinging ball Skips rope
Fine Motor Skills by Age						
Can deal with some mechanical devices: screw-type toys, door knobs, faucets	Copies a crude circle Can imitate vertical and horizontal strokes on paper	May be able to unbutton some front buttons; side buttons with difficulty Can copy a circle reasonably well May be able to use scissors Completes simple puzzles	May be able to copy a crude square (square will be lopsided with rounded corners)	Copies square (vertical lines usually longer) May button front buttons	May copy a recognizable triangle (sides will not be equal, nor will base be parallel to edge of paper)	Can manipulate buttons well

Source: Compiled from L. Skinner (1979), *Motor development in the preschool years.* Courtesy of Charles C Thomas, Publisher, Springfield, Illinois.

consider how biology and society influence the ways that girls and boys choose to play.

CHILDREN'S ARTWORK: A SILENT LANGUAGE

Preschoolers happily cover sheets of paper with crayon, paint, and pencil marks, and their artwork reveals much about their development. First, progressive physical coordination allows children to move from scribbles to designs to representational art. Second, children learn to express their emotions through their art and symbolic play. Third, as children learn number sequences, the alphabet, and common words, they begin to draw and write to express their increasingly complex thoughts. Although 3-year-olds produce repetitive scribbles that may not have a theme or an apparent message, 4- and 5-year-olds invent elaborate stories for their artwork. Because drawing involves the manipulation of symbols, it can be a silent language, a nonverbal "window" on the young child's mind.

For example, in one research study, after children transferred to a new preschool program, some of them drew pictures with no mouths, with distorted facial features, misplaced limbs, and dark colors, revealing the sadness and stress they were feeling after their move (Field, 1984). In another study, the drawings of 5-year-olds were related to the security of their attachments to their mothers (Assor, 1988). Researchers concluded that insecurely attached children were more likely to create drawings showing either too much or too little attention to their mothers. Sometimes the mother was much larger or much smaller than other figures; sometimes there were too many or too few details used to depict her (that is, with or without hair, ears, shoes, jewelry), and sometimes children drew themselves either very close or very far from the mothers.

Artwork, then, is a means of exploring children's thoughts and feelings about important people and events. Developing drawing skills, and possibly drawing styles as well, also reflect growing cognitive capacities. Just as in the development of language, where words come to stand for objects, people, and events, pictures also have a symbolic purpose: A picture of a horse is a symbol of the horse and proves that the child has some mental image of a horse. Being able to represent the world around us within our own minds, visually as well as verbally, and then to communicate these images in words or pictures is central to our intellectual growth, and like all development, these skills grow in stages.

From Scribbles to Pictures

Ask a 2- or 3-year-old "What are you drawing?" and the answer you're likely to get is "I'm just *drawing!*" That is because the youngest preschoolers are much more interested in the drawing *process* than in the finished product. Until about age 3, drawing consists primarily of simple, random marks—scribbles, basically. Rhoda Kellogg (1970), who has studied children's art extensively and identified four stages in its development, calls this scribbling phase the *placement stage.* In the next stage, the *shapes stage* (ages 3 to 3½), children combine

marks to create crosses, squares, and closed curves. Recognizable geometric figures, such as rectangles and circles, combined and attached to one another—circles within circles or cross marks inside or radiating from a rectangle—emerge in the next stage, the *design stage* (from about 3½ to 4 or so). Finally, at about age 4 or 5, drawing becomes *representational*: Children begin to depict people, animals, buildings, flowers, and trees. This is called the *pictorial stage*. From this point on, children add increasing levels of detail to their drawing. Eventually, they will be able to combine images of single objects or people in one drawing or painting and so depict an entire scene or story: "Mommy on a business trip" or "Daddy and Mommy at home" (Fischer, 1983). Figure 9-1 provides some examples of the various stages of children's drawing.

Overall, children move logically from random marks to mastering simple components such as circles and rectangles, to more and more complex combinations of these things. This "logical" movement reflects the course of most development (Bruner, 1973; Fischer, 1983). Similarly too, there is considerable variation from child to child, as each pursues his own developmental way with pencil or crayon in hand. By 4 or 5, some children have even developed their own *style* of drawing, using favorite colors and shapes and even personal themes or subjects (Gardner, 1980).

FIGURE 9-1
CHILDREN'S ARTWORK: FROM SCRIBBLES TO PICTURES
(*a*) Placement stage: scribbles (age 32 months); (*b*) basic shapes: circle (42 months); (*c*) design stage: combination designs (40 and 47 months); (*d*) pictorial stage: sun (45 months); (*e*) pictorial: humans (48 to 60 months). (*Source:* Rhoda Kellogg, *Analyzing children's art*, 1970. Reprinted by permission of Mayfield Publishing Company.)

Cognitive Development

Children's artwork creatively expresses their language, emotions, and thoughts. The key to their drawing is the *manipulation of symbols*, the hallmark of preschoolers' development. This growing ability shows up in many other accomplishments, for example, the development of language and in pre-schooler's symbolic play or fantasy. Four- and five-year-olds can use language in playful, humorous, and creative ways. For example, a little girl points to a boat sailing in the middle of a lake and says, "Mommy, Mommy, the boat is taking a bath" or a little boy stripped of his swimsuit after a dip says, "I am barefoot all over." Or the child who asks "Mother, who gave birth to me? You? I knew it. If it was Daddy, I'd have a mustache" (Chukovsky, 1963).

symbolic thought
mental representation of the world

Symbolic thought is the ability to represent the world mentally. Children learn to use images, art, symbols, and language to stand for objects, events, and concepts. Because they can think abstractly, preschoolers are not tied as closely to their actions. They can manipulate symbols in complex ways. Symbolic thought appears in preschoolers' dreams, imagery, and play, as preschoolers slowly break the bonds of the here and now and begin to fantasize and create novel images. Symbolic thinking is evident in children's abilities to imitate behavior that they've seen. Children can also search for hidden objects because they know that the objects exist and can imagine possible hiding places. The earliest instances of symbolic thinking occur at about 2 years of age, marking the beginning of the preoperational period in Piaget's theory of cognitive development. Because Piaget's theory was one of the first to describe the child's thinking at different ages, we shall examine the preoperational period and Piaget's theory itself in some detail.

When preschoolers begin to think symbolically, imagination makes anything possible. A boy can be a ballerina, a block can be a bird, a tower can be 10 feet tall. *(Sybil Shackman/Monkmeyer Press)*

PIAGET'S APPROACH

Recall from Chapter 1 that Jean Piaget pioneered in charting the major stages of cognitive development. He wanted to understand how children solve problems and how our thinking changes as we mature. Piaget's research showed that the origins of intelligence lie in the coordination of sensory and motor responses during the first 2 years of life. But a dramatic shift to symbolic thinking occurs by age 2 and continues to develop until a rapid change in logical thinking occurs at around 7. We will consider these more sophisticated forms of reasoning in Chapters 12 and 15.

It is important to place Piaget's theory and methods in historical perspective. Most of Piaget's observations were ground-breaking at the time they were published. He collected information from his own children and Swiss children in the community, developed a theoretical interpretation of his observations, and wrote his findings in a series of books that span more than 50 years. Piaget himself changed his methods, his terms, and his interpretations during those 50 years.

As we noted in Chapter 6, new methods and theories have challenged many of Piaget's conclusions. Today, Piaget's theory is regarded as an extraordinary first step in charting cognitive development that must be modified and tempered with new data. For example, in the following section we discuss some of Piaget's claims about the limitations in the reasoning of young children. Piaget believed that from ages 2 to 5 years, children had a very limited ability to understand concepts and relationships. However, recent research has shown that when tasks and instructions are simplified, young children show more sophisticated reasoning than Piaget thought possible. Cultural differences or changed experimental methods may explain some of these results. New test procedures, for example, may elicit more mature thinking from young children. Below, we describe some of Piaget's claims about the limits of young children's reasoning as well as the recent research that shows them to be more sophisticated problem solvers than he thought possible.

THE PREOPERATIONAL PERIOD: REASONING BASED ON APPEARANCES

Preschoolers tend to believe "what you see is what you get." For example, when researchers placed a mask of a dog's face on a cat's head, 3- and 4-year-olds thought that the cat had become a dog (DeVries, 1969). They thought the cat would bark and prefer dog food because the cat *looked* like a dog. These children are thinking as Piaget thought they would. That is, they are focusing, or centering, their attention on only one aspect of the stimulus (the mask). Piaget called this **centration**. Because preschoolers do not process all the available information, they are often fooled by appearances. Six-year-olds were not as easily fooled. They predicted that the cat would remain a cat, but when the mask was placed on the cat's head they were not so sure. The same thing happens when preschoolers see people dressed up as Santa Claus or the Easter Bunny, or wearing Halloween costumes. Preschoolers react as if the costume changes the person within it. Why? Piaget believed that because thought is centered, children do not perceive that one person can be two

centration
focusing on one aspect of a stimulus

These young children would be amazed if Mickey Mouse removed his head and "became" a person. In the preoperational period, children are still fooled by appearances. *(Eve Arnold/ Magnum)*

preoperational period
Piaget's period of transition from sensorimotor intelligence to rule-governed thought

different things simultaneously. At this stage, appearance overpowers any other possibilities.

Piaget also identified the time period from 2 to 7 years as a transition from the sensory motor intelligence of infants to the rule-governed thought of school-aged children. He named this time as the **preoperational period**, because preschoolers were thought to lack the sophisticated cognitive operations he saw in school-aged children. According to Piaget, younger children thought intuitively and conceptually but not logically. Not only are they fooled by the appearances of objects, but when they try to explain *why* things happen, their limited understanding of causality becomes clear. Piaget's research also suggested that children see the world from their own point of view, without considering other people's perspectives.

Although the limits in young children's reasoning that Piaget identified are often clear, research during the past 15 years suggests that Piaget underestimated the cognitive abilities of preschoolers. In a series of studies, John Flavell and his colleagues have shown that 3-year-olds often do confuse appearance and reality. When a 3-year-old is shown a glass of milk behind a green filter, the child says that the milk *looks* green and actually *is* green. When given a sponge that is gray and looks like a rock, a 3-year-old says that it *is* a rock and *looks* like a rock. When 3-year-olds watched a familiar woman put on a Miss Piggy costume, they insisted that she had turned into Miss Piggy. Because they have trouble distinguishing between the way things look and the way they really are, reasoning is difficult for young children. But this confusion may be briefer and more selective than Piaget had imagined. By age 5, children can often distinguish between appearance and reality. Even 3-year-olds can do this if those appearances concern the way things *feel* rather than the way they look. In one experiment, a group of 3-year-olds was asked to touch an ice cube barehanded and with a gloved finger. Even after they touched the cube with the covered finger, about 80 percent of the children confirmed that the ice cube was "really and truly" cold, even though it no longer felt icy (Flavell, Green, & Flavell, 1986). Based on such experiments, Flavell and other cognitive researchers suggest that between the ages of 3 and 6, preschoolers develop a theory of the mental world in which they begin to distinguish between appearance and reality. In short, they may not be as "realistic" in their thinking—as ruled by their perceptions—as Piaget believed (Flavell, 1988; Wellman, 1988).

perception bound

Reversible Thinking and Conservation of Number

"Do you have a brother?" "Yes," says a 4-year-old boy who has a new baby brother. But when asked "Does your brother have a brother?" he might answer "No."

Typical for his age, this little boy doesn't perceive that the relationship of brother points two ways. As Piaget discovered, young children tend to think in one direction only. Consequently, they have trouble with the concept of **reversibility**, that objects can be arranged and then rearranged to return to the same starting point. For example, if you make two equally long rows of five cookies and ask 4-year-olds if the rows have the same number of cookies, most will say yes. But if you spread out one row so that it *looks* longer than the other row, even though they still both have five cookies, a 4-year-old is likely to say that the longer row now has more cookies. According to Piaget, part of the problem is that 4-year-olds lack the concept of reversibility, so they don't understand that you can push the cookies back into a row of the same length. In other words, they do not recognize that an action can be done and undone, that the number of cookies stays the same no matter how the appearance of the rows may change. Part of the reason for this, Piaget believed, is that preschoolers are most likely to pay attention to the state of something in its present form, a limitation in thinking about **states and transformations**. For example, when looking at a row of cookies that was spread out, children tend to think of it only as a long row and not as a short row that was lengthened. They do not seem to understand that it can be transformed to the original row or indeed rearranged into any shape.

When children do understand that the numbers of cookies in the rows stays the same despite rearranging the length of rows, Piaget would say that they had learned to *conserve* number. **Conservation** is the term that Piaget used to describe the knowledge that basic physical dimensions, such as number, mass, distance, volume, and area, remain the same despite superficial changes in the appearance of objects. Conservation of quantities despite changing appearances is a fundamental accomplishment of the concrete operational period that Piaget thought appeared at about 7 years of age. Piaget thought that preschoolers couldn't understand transformations of objects, couldn't understand that rearrangements could be reversed, and couldn't understand that a quantity can be conserved despite changes in appearances. But again, research counters some of his conclusions. Studies suggest that young children *can* attend to transformations, and reversibility can be taught to preschoolers (Gelman & Baillargeon, 1983). In one study, for example, children learned that given a certain number of dolls and the same number of

reversibility
concept representing that an action can be done and undone

states and transformations
concepts involved in understanding that objects and states can be transformed and rearranged

conservation
knowledge that basic physical dimensions remain the same despite superficial changes in appearance

More or the same? Without special training, preschoolers think that the shape of a container affects the amount of the water within it. Once they grasp the concept of conservation, children know that a quantity doesn't change just because its appearance does. *(Steve McCarroll)*

doll beds, any rearrangement of either the dolls or the beds would maintain the one-to-one fit of dolls to beds (Wallach & Sprott, 1964). In another study, 3- and 4-year-olds looked at picture sequences where changes had been made. Children were then given a selection of possible answer cards that would complete the sequences and were quite able to put the cards in the proper order. Thus they understood that objects can be reordered into different sequences and were not always fooled by attending only to the present states (Gelman, Bullock, & Meck, 1980).

Hundreds of studies have attempted to teach conservation to preschoolers. Dorothy Field (1987) reviewed 25 of these conservation training studies and concluded that there is evidence that, with training, 4- and 5-year-olds can do better than Piaget originally proposed.

YOUNG CHILDREN'S UNDERSTANDING OF NUMBER: AN UPDATE

Contemporary researchers are learning that children's thinking is less limited by centration, appearances, and nonreversible thinking than Piaget had thought. In fact, not only can preschool children conserve number, they can also count spontaneously and *systemically* (in a consistent way). This has been revolutionary news for researchers studying cognitive development. One of the leaders in this area, Rochel Gelman, argues that like the ability to learn language, number abilities may also be inborn and universal (Flavell, 1985; Gelman, 1982). Even young children, 3- to 6½-year-olds, for example, were consistently able to distinguish between rows of two and three toy animals, no matter how much space appeared between the animals (the experimenter changed the amount of space in various ways). Piaget would have expected children to explain their answers in terms of the density or length of the row, but that is not what happened. Even the 3- and 4-year-olds in Gelman's study were counting (Gelman, 1982).

Based on her extensive work, Gelman has suggested that young children can not only count but count according to five discoverable principles (Flavell, 1985; Gelman, 1979; Gelman & Gallistel, 1978). First, preschoolers tend to assign only one number to each item and count each item only once. Children don't always follow this rule, especially when confronted with large groups of items, which they find daunting. But they do tend to correct their own mistakes and notice others' mistakes of this type. Second, preschoolers use names for numbers—though not necessarily the correct names—in a consistent way. For example, a 2½-year-old who counts "2, 6, 10" will consistently count items as 2, 6, 10 and will often say there are "ten" items in the set (Gelman & Gallistel, 1978). Gelman compares the use of incorrect but consistent number names to the kind of consistent, rule-oriented language mistakes children make at a certain age (Gelman & Baillargeon, 1983). (We'll come back to this pattern when we look at preschoolers' language later in the chapter.) Again, the youngest preschoolers may not always follow the principle that the last number name in a counting list is the correct number of items. Nevertheless, they will often correct others' incorrect answers, and they can often answer correctly themselves if someone else does the actual counting for them and then asks them, "How many?" Third, young children also seem to consider anything countable—people, animals, events, ideas, toys. Fourth, children as young as three seem to understand that unlike number *names*, the counted items themselves can be rearranged without altering the amount: Count them backward or forward, it's all the same. (This could also be considered an aspect of number conservation.) Finally, preschoolers have a basic understanding of adding and subtracting items, and many can solve simple arithmetic problems with small sets of items—by counting (Gelman, 1982; Gelman & Baillargeon, 1983; Siegler & Robinson, 1982).

By age 3 or 4, many children have acquired the five principles of early number knowledge. They use this knowledge in many ways. For example, most 4-year-olds can answer questions such as "Which is bigger, 6 or 2?" These children can add and subtract numbers from 1 to 10 and may be able to count up to 100. These skills are refined by 5- and 6-year-olds when they enter school. From research on children's early counting and number knowledge, we know that 3- and 4-year-olds can judge numerosity, compare quantities, and infer numerical correspondence to a greater extent than Piaget thought (Sophian, 1988). Preschoolers understand a great deal about numbers and quantities that helps prepare them for schooling and more complex problem solving.

What do all these updates on Piaget, children, and numbers tell us? First, no one is proposing that preschoolers are mathematical whizzes—only that they have some grasp of numbers from fairly early on and are generally much more competent and resorceful in using numbers than was once thought. According to Gelman, Piaget and others did not see this competence before for a simple reason: They were neither looking for it nor designing tests with it in mind (Gelman, 1979). Gelman has urged psychologists to concentrate less on what preschoolers can't do and more on what they can. ("Issues & Options" discusses early academics for preschoolers.)

Issues & OPTIONS

Superbaby, Superkid: A Head Start or a Misstart?

Give Your Child a Superior Mind reads the title of a parents' manual. Can you? Should you? Also on the shelves are *Supertot, Superkids, Smart Toys*. These books are being gobbled up by parents eager to spur their children's intellectual development by starting formal kinds of training earlier and earlier. But do you need to begin academic training at 3 or 4? Do French lessons at 5 and 6 do more for the parents or the child?

The 1980s saw the start of a "superkid boom," as a generation of educated, competitive parents began the "search for excellence" for their preschoolers. The children, however, are showing signs of wear. Just as infants can be overstimulated by overeager parents, so can preschoolers be overwhelmed with inappropriate cognitive and physical demands. Psychologists and counselors are reporting increased incidence of stress symptoms such as stomachaches, headaches, and sleeping problems in preschoolers and depression in school-age children. Many think these are the results of what noted child psychologist David Elkind (1981) calls the "miseducation" of the young. Like many other child development experts, Elkind finds the whole trend to involve preschoolers in formal training disturbing and potentially quite dangerous.

While they increase stress, early academics also decrease the child's freedom to find her own fun, to learn through play. Young children learn by discovering, spurred along by their innate curiosity. And curiosity is reinforced by the very pleasure of gaining understanding. The 3-year-old who pulls all the pots and pans off the kitchen shelves may look like she's into mischief—but her mischief is often educational. Not only may she be learning about size and shape—which is bigger, which fit inside which—but the fantasy play that she can engage in encourages intellectual growth. Practicing sums or drilling vocabulary drains pleasure from the experience of learning, which is one of young childhood's greatest gifts. When school starts, will that pleasure be recoverable? Very often it is not.

Paradoxically, educators and parents who stress early lessons are ignoring one of Piaget's most important ones: Children are not and do not think like little adults. The drive to find out how things work, the desire to know why things are the way they are, the hunger to explore—processes that come naturally to preschool children—are being threatened by formal lessons and overly competitive experiences. Psychological research has also been misapplied. Look at Head Start programs, say some well-meaning legislators and parents. Don't they raise the intellectual capacities of children from impoverished homes? Yes, they do (see Chapter 11), but this does *not* mean that more and more educational experiences will benefit preschoolers whose days are already filled with interesting things to play with and caring people to

CAUSAL REASONING

If you ask a 5-year-old why she fell off her bicycle, she might answer, "Because I skinned my elbow." Confusing cause and effect is one of the twists of logic typical of preschoolers' explanations. Preschoolers also tend to look for direct causes for things; they reject accidental or random causes, as in the following exchange:

Issues & OPTIONS

For whose benefit are these girls performing? Formal lessons for young children can backfire later, causing stress and fear of failure. (*Jacques Chenet/Woodfin Camp & Associates*)

share discoveries with. And yes, it is also true that preschoolers are more competent than was once thought. Nevertheless, simply because 3- and 4-year-olds do have rudimentary concepts of number and numerical principles, it does not follow that these children should be *taught* addition and subtraction before they reach first grade.

Academic gains, warns Elkind, may lead to personal losses. Needing to know the right answers at too early an age can enhance conformity as it stifles curiosity. When demands for right answers are made too soon, fear of failure replaces the fun of discovery. Feelings of inadequacy, inferiority, and shame may grow while lifelong potential may be undercut.

Many parents who feel pressed to sign their preschoolers up for academic lessons or structured physical activities need reassurance. There is so much for young children to learn and so much for them to do—life itself, in these early years, provides more than enough of a curriculum. Sharing discoveries, reinforcing curiosity, and participating in the joy of knowledge are probably what count most.

A: "Why do birds fly?"
B: "'Cause God made them that way."
A: "Why don't dogs fly?"
B: "Because they're not birds."

This final-sounding, single-cause explanation for everything is not usually logical, but it is satisfying to preschoolers nonetheless. Preschoolers also believe that God, or someone who is like a human, created everything and that human actions can explain all events. For example, children often told Piaget that mountains arose where someone planted stones a long time ago and that the sun and the moon were created by someone lighting a match in the sky. Piaget called this kind of thinking **animism**, giving nonliving things the capacities and qualities of living things—sometimes including the thoughts and feelings of humans. Children often assign animistic qualities to the sun, the moon, and the mountains. A 4-year-old might worry that a tree could get lonely or that a stone would feel pain if someone kicked it.

animism
crediting nonliving things with human qualities

Although young children's conclusions are often wrong, their reasoning is consistent: It follows principles of looking for simple, direct causes that can be traced to a humanlike agent. Sometimes the causes and effects are jumbled, and sometimes things are placed out of sequence, but note that children are constructing order and imposing explanations on the world around them. Preschoolers do not seem to reason from general instances to particulars (i.e., deduction) or from single instances to generalizations (i.e., induction); rather, they seem to reason from one instance to another. Sometimes isolated events are linked in a causal explanation when in fact there is no relation. For example, if there is a violent thunderstorm while a preschooler is riding in a car to grandma's house, the child may think that the next time he rides to grandma's house there will be another storm. Piaget called this reasoning **transduction** because it connects isolated events as if there were a cause-effect relationship.

transduction
reasoning that connects isolated events

EGOCENTRISM

In one of his experiments, Piaget showed children a scene of three mountains and a group of pictures showing the scene from different directions. He asked children to select pictures that showed what other children seated around the table would see from their position (Piaget & Inhelder, 1956). Most of the preoperational children chose pictures identical to their own perspective: They thought that other children saw what they saw. We know that preschoolers tend to focus their attention on the salient features of an object or a situation. They do not know that what you see depends on where you look (Shantz, 1983). Piaget regarded this inability to consider other people's perspectives as a self-centered outlook on the world, and he labeled it **egocentrism**. It doesn't mean egotistical or selfish; egocentrism means that people tend to see things from their own points of view.

egocentrism
inability to consider others' perspectives

But is the three-mountain task a fair demonstration of children's egocentrism? Like many of Piaget's tasks, it is complicated. It requires children to use mental imagery and to rotate objects in a spatial arrangement. Perhaps these tasks are too difficult. More recently, another researcher simplified the experiment by letting children turn the table to find the view that other children would see. In this form of the experiment, preschoolers were not egocentric as Piaget had claimed (Borke, 1975).

A 3-year-old's perspective is limited, in the sense that it stays close to home. At that age, children are not used to considering the "big picture," either literally or figuratively. Nevertheless, this limitation does not seem to be based, as Piaget described, on consistent egocentrism.

MEMORY DEVELOPMENT: RECOGNITION AND RECALL

Show a group of preschoolers some toys, mix them up with some unfamiliar ones, and then ask them to identify the ones you showed them. Even the 2-year-olds will choose right almost all of the time. But if you ask the same children to just *name* the toys you have shown them, without looking at them, accuracy drops to 20 percent for 3-year-olds and 40 percent for 4-year-olds (Myers & Perlmutter, 1978). Why the difference? Because two types of memory are required, and preschoolers are much better at one than the other. The first task, such as a multiple-choice test where you are asked to pick the right answer, relies on **recognition memory**. The second task is more like an essay exam—you have to retrieve information at request (either yours or someone else's) *without strong cues*. This type of task relies on **recall memory**. Both kinds of memory improve as preschoolers gain more knowledge and experience, but recognition continues to be stronger than recall (Myers & Perlmutter, 1978).

Recognition memory is stronger than recall throughout development. Sometimes children's recognition memory is astounding. Even preschoolers can remember whether they have seen long lists of pictures (Kail, 1984). For example, 4-year-olds can recognize which pictures they have seen before when given a long series of pictures that are not too different (Brown & Campione, 1972). Recognition memory is aided by parents' repetitive reading of books and stories. Even 2-year-olds will quickly fill in missing words from their favorite picture books. Young children also remember sequences of day-to-day activities, sometimes referred to as **scripts**, quite well. Ask a typical 4- or 5-year-old what goes on at preschool each morning, and she will be happy to tell you: First there's a play period downstairs, then the group goes upstairs for circle time, then everyone works at the tables, and then they have a snack. Children this age know, too, when a script has been changed, and they respond to the humor of an illogical script. If you tell a preschooler that you woke up this morning, got out of bed, got dressed, took a bath, and ate your dinner, he will find this very funny because he knows that's not the way things are (Nelson, 1981; Nelson & Gruendel, 1981). Recent research suggests that young children remember familiar events by incorporating them into scripts, or schemes, based on experience. Then recurring events such as meals and errands or birthday parties may be collections of many specific episodes, which may make it difficult to remember what happened on a specific errand or who attended a particular birthday party. Novelty helps children distinguish specific episodes from these more general scripts (Nelson & Hudson, 1988).

Some of the first and most salient memories of young children involve familiar routines established around eating, play, bedtime rituals, and other familiar activities. Two- and three-year-olds easily recalled familiar household routines such as taking a bath, brushing teeth, and saying prayers at night (Wellman & Somerville, 1980), and for 3- and 4-year-olds, remembering advertising jingles, nursery rhymes, and TV characters is a simple task. In one study of intentional memory in 2- to 4-year-olds, children were asked to remind their parents to do something in the future; 4-year-olds were much better than 2-year-olds when reminding parents to do some dull tasks such as taking the laundry out, but both ages were equally good, correct about 80 percent of the time, at reminding their parents to buy them candy.

recognition memory
memory based on recognition of a previously seen object

recall memory
memory based on information retrieved without strong clues

scripts
sequences of day-to-day activities

Young children easily memorize their favorite books if they hear them often enough. (*Jon Feingersh/Stock, Boston*)

memory strategies
plans that aid recall

Memory strategies are tricks or plans that aid recall. For example, the simple statement "Every good boy does fine" helps music students remember the treble clef lines, E, G, B, D, F. Memory strategies organize information for us and repackage it economically. Even preschoolers can use memory strategies effectively. For example, 3- and 4-year-olds can remember which cup is covering a hidden object if they stare at it, point at it, and touch it (Wellman, Ritter, & Flavell, 1975).

rehearsal
labeling and repeating of names to aid memory

When you look up a phone number and then walk to the phone repeating it to yourself over and over again, you are using the powerful memory strategy called **rehearsal**. By 4 to 5 years of age, many preschoolers spontaneously label and rehearse the names of objects they are asked to remember (Weissberg & Paris, 1986). Early efforts to remember are gradually reinforced with effective strategies as children learn to devote time and effort to the goal of remembering. Strategies such as rehearsal then become deliberate ways to repackage and practice items for later recall (Ornstein, Baker-Ward, & Naus, 1988).

Children under 5 or 6 don't usually organize or rehearse information on their own, but if strategies are *specifically suggested* to them, they will use them. In one study, preschoolers were shown pictures of two normally unrelated objects (sheep, pillow) in some relation (sheep stands on pillow). The children who were instructed to "think back to the pictures" had much better recall later than children who did not receive the thinking back instruction (a strategy known as **interactive imagery** or **elaboration**) (Pressley & MacFayden, 1983).

interactive imagery (elaboration)
strategy for recall based on imagining the object

It may be that young children do not think of using strategies on their own because they don't feel the need to remember things. They don't say to themselves, "Ah, I should remember this," unless an adult asks them to try (Flavell, 1977; Pressley, 1982). Their increasing awareness of the usefulness of strategies and the need to apply them is part of the development of **metacognition**, that is, learning to understand and control one's own thinking skills (Flavell, 1985).

metacognition
thinking about thinking

In research studies, preschoolers learn how to remember word pairs, and in their daily lives, without trying hard, they are remembering more, more, and still more words and how to combine them. Increasingly, their world is becoming a place made meaningful through language.

THOUGHT AND LANGUAGE

The relation between thought and language is an old, old question, debated over centuries, and still not answered. No one questions whether language and thought *are* related, but as to which "comes first," theories differ.

For Piaget (Chapter 6), language develops as a form of representational or symbolic thought (Piaget, 1959). Others, particularly the Russian psychologist A. R. Luria (1961), think that language directs thinking and organizes what we do. In this view, children's thinking is shaped and directed by their increasing language abilities.

For another Russian psychologist, Lev Vygotsky, and for Jerome Bruner, a noted U.S. psychologist, language skills and cognitive growth interact and influence each other; separating thought from language is almost impossible. Language transforms experience and development influences language. For example, preschoolers gradually internalize language and use "inner speech" to help them plan their actions or control their thinking. They literally talk to themselves, saying "don't touch" as they near a stove, for example. Older children automatically keep their hands off without having to say the words. The concept of inner speech describes how speech *becomes* thought. But under some circumstances, language and cognition may be more independent than Bruner and Vygotsky suggested. Studies of deaf children, for example, have shown that even without speech and in some cases without good language skills, deaf children's cognitive processes are not hampered (Furth, 1971).

But for most children, thought and language are interrelated. The relationship between cognitive and language development will become clearer as we discuss how children acquire vocabulary, grammar, and communication skills.

Language Development

Josie is playing with her truck. "Vroom, vroom! I'll make it go so it rides to the couch. Then to the hall. No! Don't play in the hall. Come back, truck. Don't touch that!"

Several children are building with blocks. "I'm the best builder," says Nancy. "No, I'm the best, I know," says Bernardo.
"Uh-uh, I'm better than the best," says Jan, "because my building will be as big as the sky!"
"I'm better than anybody, even the president," Lee says.

In Chapter 6, we traced the development of language from prelinguistic parent-baby exchanges through babbling, first words, and finally, at the end of the second year, rudimentary two-word sentences. Now, in the preschool years, children's vocabularies are growing rapidly, they are learning and applying the rules of their language, and they are becoming increasingly skilled at using language to communicate. Just as infants repeat physical actions over and over, exercising new abilities, preschoolers flex their growing verbal skills. At night, for example, many children chatter away in bed, repeating the names of everyone they saw that day. As we'll see when we discuss language's role in "inner speech," language can also help children guide their own actions as they talk themselves through activities ("No, not that way, this way!") and even scold themselves ("No! Don't go near there!")

BUILDING VOCABULARY

During the preschool years children learn as many as two to four new words daily (Pease & Gleason, 1985), and by age 6, vocabulary totals between 8000 and 14,000 words (Carey, 1978). These words fill many grammatical categories—they are not just nouns—but the words children seem to use the most are the "five Ws": As they search for causal explanations, "what," "where," "who," "when," and "why" loom large (Bloom, Merkin, & Wooten, 1982; Brown, 1968; Ervin-Tripp, 1970). "Why does the sun shine? Why is it raining? Why isn't *Sesame Street* on now?" And when children answer "when" questions themselves, we find that they are not as limited to one-directional thinking as Piaget thought. When an appropriate context is provided, 3- to 5-year-olds can reason about antecedents or consequences as they answer "when" questions (French, 1989).

Two- and three-year-olds often fill gaps in their vocabulary by inventing compound words. A team of researchers tested young children's understanding of compound words by showing them four pictures (a hat, a mouse, a hat on a mouse, and a hat on a fish). When the researchers pointed to the hat on the mouse and said "Show me the mousehat," most 4-year-olds readily picked out the hat on the mouse. Two-year-olds were often wrong. In fact, 2-year-olds had difficulty generating compound words to describe the pictured objects, but 3- and 4-year-olds used compound words almost as often as adults did (Clark, Gellman, & Lane, 1985).

As children begin to understand more complex relations among objects, people, situations, and time periods, they also learn to use the words that help express these relationships: prepositions such as "in," "on," "under," "before," "after," and comparative adjectives such as "more," "less," "bigger," "smaller," "older," "younger." These words emerge in a predictable order, and even within each category, a sequence is followed. "In," for example, usually appears before "on," which appears before "under" (Halpern, Corrigan, & Aviezer, 1983). Earlier in the chapter, we noted that preschoolers are using words such as "yesterday," "tomorrow," "next week," "last year"—words that express time relations—but sometimes their grasp of the real meaning of the concept is fuzzy. "Tomorrow" may mean any time in the future, and "yesterday" may mean any time in the past, including the hour just gone by.

Even children's acquisition of prepositions and adjectives reveals the interplay between the development of cognition and language. Children's use of words such as "in front of," "behind," "next to," "beneath," and "over" suggests that they are beginning to understand spatial relations. Although some 3-year-olds confuse "more-less," "big-small," and "tall-short," most 5-year-olds understand these dimensions.

GRASPING THE RULES OF GRAMMAR

"We runned from the playground and seed the mouses in the cage," Ronnie tells the teacher. By the time he is 5 to 6 years old, Ronnie will be saying "ran" and "saw," applying the rules of English grammar.

Grammar is simply the set of rules that governs the use of words—how they are combined or altered—in a language. Formal schooling teaches us technical terms such as the parts of speech, participles, subjects, and objects, but young children figure out and apply many rules automatically simply by hearing other people speak.

For example, very young children catch on quickly to the basic structure of English sentences: subject-verb-object ("Dog chases ball"), and they learn to build on it. "*The big* dog chases *the red* ball," includes two articles and two modifiers. Soon, simple sentence structure gets expanded by joining two sentences with *and*: "The big dog chases the red ball, and he catches it," or "The big dog chases the red ball, and I chase the big dog."

Preschoolers also learn to modify statements in other ways—to negate, for example. At first they will simply add "no," as in "No dog chase ball"—which may mean anything from "The dog didn't chase the ball" to "I don't want the dog to chase the ball." Later they begin inserting negatives within a sentence: "Dog not chase ball." Still later, children start using the syntax that makes their meaning clear. "The dog didn't chase the ball," or "I don't want the dog to chase the ball."

Paradoxically, the kinds of errors children make reveal how much grammar they actually know. When Ronnie said, "We runned from the playground and seed the mouses in the cage," he used two rules of English grammar: He formed the past tense by adding *-ed* to the verb ("runned"), and he formed the plural by adding *-s* ("mouses"). But because the English language has many irregularities—"run/ran," "see/saw," "mouse/mice"—when children follow a rule too consistently, they make mistakes. Errors like these, applying the rules of grammar too regularly, are called **overregularization**.

Interestingly, 2- to 3-year-olds will use the correct past tense of irregular verbs, saying "ran" and "saw," but later when they induce the *-ed* rule, they begin saying "ranned," "sawed," and even using a double past tense, saying "ated" and "wented" (Kuczaj, 1978). Typically, preschoolers continue to overregularize, even in the face of multiple, insistent corrections:

> *Child:* "My teacher holded the baby rabbits and we patted them."
> *Mother:* "Did you say that your teacher held the baby rabbits?"
> *Child:* "Yes."
> *Mother:* "What did you say she did?"
> *Child:* "She holded the baby rabbits and we patted them."
> *Mother:* "Did you say she held them tightly?"
> *Child:* "No, she holded them loosely." (Cazden, 1968)

Preschoolers tend to be confused by complex sentences, especially when time relations are involved. Some of this confusion may stem from the child's

overregularization
applying grammatical rules too regularly

still hazy sense of past, present, and future. If a parent says to a 4-year-old, "Before you turn on the TV, you must finish your dinner," the child assumes that the first thing in the sentence is the first thing to be done, so she slides away from the table and turns on the television. It's as if she had heard, "You turn on the TV, and then you finish your dinner"—two simple sentences joined together.

Finally, sentences that depart from the basic rule of simple sentence structure—subject-verb-object—may also confuse preschoolers. In a sentence such as "The dog was chased by the girl," the verb ("was chased") is passive, and the grammatical subject of the sentence ("dog") is actually the object of the action described. But most children under 5 would interpret the sentence to mean that the dog chased the girl (Bever, 1970). Even so, preschoolers do understand passive constructions that make sense only in one direction: They would not hear "The pool was filled by Daddy" as "The pool filled Daddy."

COMMUNICATING: COMPETENCE AND LIMITATIONS

By ages 3 and 4, vocabulary is increasing rapidly, and most children have grasped the basic rules of grammar. But how skilled are they at communicating?

In many ways, children of 3 and 4 are quite accomplished: They can say what they want; they can bargain; they can hurl insults; they can lie; they can manipulate. A 4-year-old can delay his bedtime for a long time with announcements and pleas ("I want a drink of water." "I have to go pee-pee." "Sing me just one more song." "There's a tiger behind the door.") (Garvey & Hogan, 1973).

But still, communication is far from mature, especially when preschoolers are describing something for someone else to identify (Krauss & Glucksberg, 1977). (This is called **referential communication**, because it is communication that refers to something specific). For example, a 3½-year-old tells her

referential communication communication that refers to a specific

Communication preschool-style often resembles a monologue more than a conversation.
(Susan Lapides/Design Conceptions)

friend to go and get "Jenny doll" from her bedroom. The bed is covered with dolls. How will he know which one is Jenny? Typically, preschoolers fail to mention the relevant features of whatever it is they're describing. They also may describe something only in terms of their own experience—which may be meaningless to the listener.

If this reminds you of the egocentrism we discussed earlier, Piaget would have agreed. When children play, he noted, much of their talking resembles a monologue more than a conversation. They seem to talk to themselves without any regard for the listener. Thus Piaget considered the speech of preoperational children as egocentric. Consequently, he felt that the problems preschoolers have in communicating stem from their limited perspective-taking abilities and their egocentric cognitive viewpoint (Piaget, 1952). Communication does improve when we can see things from another's perspective. Preschoolers who are more advanced in perspective-taking are also better at describing things—at what we call referential communication (Roberts & Patterson, 1983). But Piaget seems to have overstated the relationship between egocentrism and preschoolers' speech. Newer research shows that preschoolers are better at communicating with language than Piaget assumed, and that it is not so much egocentrism that limits communication at this age but difficulty with processing information and coordinating communication skills (Shatz, 1983).

Preschoolers can take another's perspective and communicate effectively when speaking to younger children. Just as adults do (recall "motherese" from Chapter 6), 4-year-olds speak differently to 2-year-olds than to adults, altering their language to suit the younger child's cognitive level. For example, in one important study, 4-year-olds showed a new toy to adults and to toddlers (Shatz & Gelman, 1973). Speaking to the toddlers, they used simple, short sentences and attention-grabbing language ("Watch this!" "Look here!"), but with adults, they were more polite, asked for more information, and referred to the adults' thoughts. Young children playing with mentally retarded peers will

When talking to a young child, an older child will simplify speech to be understood more easily. *(Renate Hiller/Monkmeyer Press)*

also simplify their language to be better understood (Guralnick & Paul-Brown, 1977).

Clearly, preschoolers' speech is more sensitive to others and less egocentric than Piaget thought. Preschoolers are also aware of what confuses them in a conversation, and, at times, they know how to clear up their confusion (Schmidt & Paris, 1984). In one study, 3-, 4-, and 5-year-olds had to listen to a description of an object and then identify it (Lempers & Elrad, 1983). Some descriptions were clear; others were deliberately confusing. On the whole, the children *did* recognize the need for more, or more logical, information in two circumstances: when a red-haired doll was described but not shown, and when the description was not specific enough. When there were several red-haired dolls, the children didn't know which to pick. However, the children did not realize that they needed more information, nor did they know how to ask for it when the description was interrupted by a fit of coughing or when the descriptions contained a mispronounced or nonsense word.

We come now to the second major point about Piaget's claims of egocentrism and language. The preschoolers' problems with language may actually have more to do with information processing than with egocentrism (Menyuk, 1977). A speaker or a listener must figure out things such as—Is my partner (Am I) listening carefully? Does she (Do I) know what's really being talked about? Is she (Am I) familiar with the topic generally and/or specifically? Does she (Do I) care about it? As adults, we make these judgments almost automatically, but we didn't always. At 3 or 4 we could not have handled so much at once.

Preschoolers cannot easily *coordinate* all the skills we use in conversations—skills like gaining and keeping a listener's attention, paying attention to someone else, giving (or asking for) information, considering another person's point of view, and adjusting language accordingly. Preschoolers have these skills, but they don't use them automatically yet (Schmidt & Paris, 1984).

SELF-COMMUNICATION: INNER SPEECH

"Put this piece here and this one here," says a 4-year-old doing a puzzle. When they think aloud, preschoolers are communicating with themselves, guiding their own actions (Vygotsky, 1962). Children frequently regulate their impulses by cautioning themselves the way a parent would. "Wait till company comes!" says a 4-year-old to herself, trying to stay away from a plate of cookies.

inner speech
verbal self-communication

Gradually this kind of self-communication, or **inner speech**, becomes silent, moving "inside" the head. Transitional steps include whispering or muttering to oneself and then silently mouthing the words.

The course of inner speech is well illustrated by recent studies (Berk & Garvin, 1984; Frauenglass & Diaz, 1985). Children aged 3½ to 6 solved complex problems like assembling puzzles and sorting pictures into categories (people, pets, furniture, foods—all things they were familiar with). As they worked, they talked aloud, whispered, muttered, or mouthed: "That piece won't fit here, it goes there"; "Cat goes with dog"; "That's ice cream, that's to eat." The youngest children spoke out loud far more than the older ones, who did much more whispering and muttering. The investigators concluded that inner speech does indeed go "underground" and helps direct children's thinking as the child matures.

Inner speech never disappears altogether. We've all heard ourselves and others say things like "1 cup of flour, 2 tablespoons of sugar" or "O.K., insert cassette, right . . . set input signal selector, right . . . push selector button." Psychologists and educators have found that teaching preschoolers as well as school-age children to "talk through" the steps of a troublesome process or repeat important instructions or reminders helps memory, increases patience, and improves schoolwork. Here, then, as at so many points, language, memory, and cognitive competence intersect.

BILINGUALISM AND LANGUAGE-LEARNING

For many thousands of preschoolers in the United States today, mostly in Miami, the Southwest, and New York City, learning English is more complicated than it is for millions of others. The children of recent immigrants, they are learning two languages simultaneously. Researchers who wondered about the effects of bilingualism found that young children tend to mix the two linguistic systems, thus developing an "interlanguage" system. In time, though, the two languages become distinct and develop independently (Garcia, Maez, & Gonzalez, 1981). Usually, at about age 3 or 4, children become aware of speaking two different languages (McLaughlin, 1984).

Problems are most likely to occur when children speak one language at home and learn a second through contacts with acquaintances and playmates. In many Mexican-American households in the Southwest, for example, parents and children speak Spanish to each other, but at school, children speak mostly in English (Garcia, 1983). Conditions like these can upset the language-learning process as interference between the two languages increases. But even when learning a second language proceeds slowly among bilingual preschoolers, they usually catch up by the early elementary school years (McLaughlin, 1984).

Beyond language development, researchers are also interested in knowing how bilingualism affects intellectual development overall. Among Spanish-speaking kindergarteners and first-graders who were learning English as a second language, studying English actually enhanced their general cognitive development (Diaz, 1985). For these children, researchers speculated that "the positive effects of bilingualism are probably related to the initial efforts required to understand and produce a second language" (Diaz, 1985, p. 1387).

Summary

1. During the preschool years, children gain less weight and grow fewer inches than at any time until after puberty. By age 5 or 6, they have lost their baby look, as body proportions have become more adultlike.

2. Both heredity and environment influence children's growth rates. Nutrition is the most important environmental factor, because if children lack sufficient calories they will become ill and even stop growing. Excessive shortness can also result from physical abnormalities, including growth hormone and thyroxine deficiency.

3. Brain growth during early childhood promotes cognitive and social growth and is in turn promoted by those developments.

4. Maturing gross motor skills and improved coordination and agility mean that preschoolers can ride bikes, throw and catch balls, swim, and do other athletic activities. Fine motor skills improve as well, and a preference for one hand over the other appears by about age 5.

5. Children's artwork reflects developing motor skills as well as cognitive abilities. It can also reveal a great deal about feelings and relationships. Technically, artwork moves from random marks to simple shapes such as circles and rectangles to complex combinations of figures. By age 4 or 5, many children have developed their own style of drawing, reflected in favorite shapes, colors, or subjects.

6. The ability to use symbols, evident in preschooler's artwork, language, and play is the key feature of cognitive development at this age. Although many of Piaget's conclusions about preschoolers' cognitive abilities have been supplanted by more modern research, his findings still have much to tell us about the development of children's thinking. Young preschoolers, for example, are limited by centration: They focus on a single detail of a stimulus instead of considering the whole. By age 6, however, newer research reveals that children can consider more information and that they are less easily fooled by appearances.

7. Piaget described the thinking of 2- to 7-year-olds as preoperational, meaning that it was based on intuition, not on the rules of logic. He believed too, that at this age children could not see things from another's perspective. Later research has attributed more sophisticated reasoning to children than Piaget believed possible.

8. Piaget observed that young children do not perceive that actions can be done and undone, that appearance doesn't necessarily change quantity. In short, they lack the concept of reversibility. He contended that they are limited in thinking about states and transformations, and pay attention primarily to the state of things in their present form. New research indicates that preschoolers can attend to transformations, and reversibility can be taught to them.

9. Children's understanding of numbers appears to be more sophisticated than Piaget believed.

10. Preschoolers' reasoning does not follow the rules of cause and effect. Rather, they focus on isolated events, connecting them as if there were a cause and effect relationship. Piaget believed that their perspective was bound by egocentrism, by the inability to see another perspective besides their own. But again, more recent research suggests that children are less egocentric than Piaget had claimed.

11. Throughout development, recognition memory is stronger than recall. Preschoolers can learn to use simple memory strategies that aid recall.

12. Language development during the preschool years includes an expanding vocabulary, learning and applying the rules of language, and using language to communicate. Young children use question words frequently, as they try to learn about their worlds.

13. Typically, preschoolers apply grammatical rules too rigidly, making errors of overregularization. They also tend to be confused by complex sentences, especially when time relations are involved. Preschoolers have no trouble making their desires known, but when they are describing something for someone else to identify—referential communication—they are less accurate. While Piaget would have attributed this problem to egocentrism, newer research suggests that the problem has more to do with the limits of information processing abilities and difficulties in coordinating communication skills at this age.

14. Inner speech describes a form of self-communication. When children speak aloud to themselves, they are guiding their own actions and regulating their impulses as a parent would. Gradually, their words become silent, what we call inner speech. We use inner speech even as adults, as an aid to memory and to assist us in solving problems.

15. Children born to non–English-speaking parents tend to mix their parents' language and English until they are about 3 or 4. By that time they are aware of speaking two different languages. Problems occur most often when children speak one language at home and another with friends. But even in such situations, bilingual children usually do well with their second language by the time they reach the early elementary school years.

Key Terms

animism

centration

cerebral lateralization

conservation

egocentrism

fine motor skills

gross motor skills

growth hormone deficiency

hand dominance

inner speech

interactive imagery (elaboration)

memory strategies

metacognition

overregularization

plasticity

preoperational period

recall memory

recognition memory

referential communication

rehearsal

reversibility

scripts

states and transformations

symbolic thought

thyroxine deficiency

transduction

Suggested Readings

Chukovsky, K. (1963). *From two to five.* Berkeley, CA: University of California Press. The cognitive skills of young children, particularly as revealed through their language and imagination, are discussed by a renowned author of children's tales in Russia.

de Villiers, P., and de Villiers, J. (1979). *Early language.* Cambridge, MA: Harvard University Press. A husband-wife team of researchers clearly present the process of language acquisition during the infancy, toddler, and preschool years. The many examples provided richly illuminate the phenomena under consideration.

Fraiberg, S. (1959). *The magic years.* New York: Scribner's. A classic by a renowned child psychologist who reveals the meaning of a child's behavior in terms of his own developing capabilities and limitations.

Gardner, H. (1980). *Artful scribbles.* New York: Basic Books. A developmental psychologist with expertise in neurological development provides an illuminating analysis of the drawings of children.

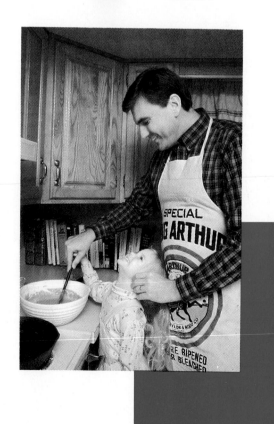

Social and Emotional Development in Early Childhood

Mollie, Stuart, and Margaret are absorbed in their latest version of "Are you my friend?" in which one child answers no, then repeats the question to the next person.

"Are you my friend, Stuart?"

"No. Are you my friend, Mollie?"

"No. Are you my friend, Margaret? Now say yes. Now we all have to say yes, okay?"

Libby rushes into the doll corner, breathless. "Watch out, Mollie. Move! Samantha, hurry! Scream when you see John!"

"Can I do it?" Mollie asks.

"Hide, Amelia. Under there. Boys can't come in. No boys in here."

"No you don't, Libby," John shouts. "I'm Tri-Klops. Dump it out. I broke my leg."

"Well, I'm Trap Jaw," Erik says, "I'm eating this chair. Get off Stuart."

"No, you don't," Libby warns. "No chair-eating in houses."

"Only girls live in houses," Maria calls from the crib. "Except if they're fathers."

"I'm a girl," Margaret says happily.

"Are you a girl, Erik?" Mollie asks.

"No, he ain't a girl, *girl!*" Maria screams.

"Can't you see he ain't a girl? Are you crazy?" (Paley, 1986, pp. 41–42)*

Mollie isn't crazy at all. She's a curious 3-year-old asking the questions all young children ask: Who are my friends? What sex am I? What can I do? Who will I become? Children puzzle over these questions throughout the preschool years, acting out their answers in fantasy after fantasy.

One of the most fascinating puzzles preschoolers are piecing together concerns sex roles. Young children think about boys and girls, men and women in ways that surprise many adults. What they think interests us, as does *why* they think what they think: Where do messages about gender come from? We'll look at these questions, and we'll focus too on the social skills that preschoolers are struggling with—learning to share, to help, to wait, to know when and how to be aggressive and when not to be. We'll also explore why these skills come more easily to some children than to others. Friendships are becoming increasingly important, so we'll look at this aspect of the preschool years as well. But we turn first to an area of development that we introduced in Chapter 7—an area that will concern us throughout this book: the child's growing sense of autonomy.

The Growing Self

The toddlers of Chapter 7, taking their first shaky steps toward independence, were conflicted about remaining safe while moving away. This struggle, expressed in the temper tantrums and negativism of the "terrible twos," centered around becoming separate *from* one's mother (Erikson's crisis of *auton-*

---

*Several excerpts in this chapter appear from V. G. Paley, *Mollie Is Three: Growing Up in School*, 1986. Reprinted by permission of the University of Chicago Press.

omy versus shame and doubt). Now the main issue is growing up in relation *to* mother, father, and the adult society. Secure enough to be independent from parents for part of the day, preschoolers want to be *like* Mom and Dad. By age 3, most children would rather imitate adults than defy them.

Fantasies about adulthood fill their play. For example, when 3-year-old Alice gives herself a "make-over" with her mother's lipstick, eyeliner, powder, and blusher, she explains that she is trying to be a mommy and that when she is a "grown-up," she will wear mommy's lipstick and live with daddy. Proud of their growing physical and mental skills, preschoolers like Alice don't always understand that they can't do everything adults can. But society's agents, parents and other adults, reveal the truth: Children may not do many of the things they think they can do or would like to do. From this conflict, says Erikson, comes the crisis of **initiative versus guilt**, a crisis balanced on one side by the wish to do and, on the other side, by prohibitions against doing.

The child who emerges from this developmental period with a sense of initiative feels confident that what he is inclined to do, as well as what he is inclined not to do, is consistent with the expectations of others. Not only does such a sense enable him to function free of worry—to take the initiative—but it also bolsters his positive feelings about growing up. In contrast, the child who emerges from this period with a strong sense of guilt is inhibited and remains unsure of the appropriateness of his actions. Rather than experiencing the pleasure of "having done good," he repeatedly experiences the anxiety of "not doing right."

For parents and other caregivers, the challenge in fostering initiative rather than guilt involves striking a sensitive balance between the "mays" and the "may nots." Alice's mother, for example, can tell her that she may not wear mommy's makeup, but she can have some cosmetics of her own to play with. And when 4-year-old Mitchell drops eggs all over the floor while trying to

initiative versus guilt
in Erikson's theory, the conflict for preschoolers between the wish to do and prohibitions against doing

Playing doctor, or dressing up like one, is a way of trying adult roles children may someday play. *(Lester Sloan/Woodfin Camp & Associates)*

imitate his father making pancakes, a sensitive parent can show him how to clean up the mess without belittling his attempt to cook like an adult.

Erikson subtitled this stage the "anticipation of roles." While pretending to be superheroes or mere adults, boys and girls are doing the emotional work of this stage: imagining themselves as competent adults, learning the rules of adult society. Among the most interesting and mysterious rules are those about gender—what it means to be male and female.

Sex-Role Development

A 1950s picture book chronicles a Saturday afternoon in the lives of Bobby and Jane. Bobby helps his father build a bird house while Jane and her mother cheerfully clean house. When the children help their father hang a picture, Bobby wields the hammer, while Jane holds the nails. In the kitchen, Mom is busy cooking. Between the lines of this innocent little book about middle-class family life is a powerful message about **sex roles**, the tasks and traits that society assigns to males and females: who does what work, who cares for the children, who can show which emotions. How children grow into these roles, how they come to behave in the ways we call masculine and feminine, is the process of **sex-role development**. How this process unfolds has been hotly debated by Freudians, Skinnerians, and Piagetians. And fueling the debate today is the issue of the roles themselves. How did traditional sex roles affect children and the men and women they became? Are today's boys and girls getting a different message about masculinity and femininity than Jane and Bobby got? If they are, then why do preschool teachers still find more boys in the building corner than at the doll house (Paley, 1984)? The answers are multifaceted, as are the ways we think about masculinity and femininity in the 1990s.

sex roles
the tasks and traits that society assigns to females and males

sex-role development
how children learn to behave in the ways we call feminine and masculine

MASCULINITY AND FEMININITY

Traditionally in Western society, masculinity and femininity were considered opposites. Independence, competitiveness, self-confidence, strength, and dominance were masculine traits. Gentleness, helpfulness, kindness, empathy, appreciativeness, and sentimentality were feminine traits. A person was *either* masculine or feminine. If you were strong, you could not also be sensitive: Real men didn't cry.

Psychologists now emphasize that the qualities we call masculine and feminine exist to some extent in *both* sexes (Hall & Halberstadt, 1980; Huston, 1983). People who are helpful, gentle, and supportive, for example, can also be self-confident, independent, assertive, and competitive—whether they are men *or* women. To describe this new approach to masculinity and femininity, social scientists use two new terms: agency and communion. **Agency** refers to active, assertive, and self-confident behavior that we do independently. **Communion** refers to supportive, helpful, empathic behavior that we do with or for others (Chodorow, 1978; Gilligan, 1982).

agency
active, assertive, and self-confident behavior

communion
supportive, helpful, and empathic behavior

People with many *communal* traits are considered strongly feminine, while those with strongly *agentic* traits are considered masculine. Men and women strong in both communal and agentic behaviors are *androgynous*.

While social scientists are coining new terms, children are busy trying to figure out what it means to be male or female. And because of their cognitive limitations, most cling to more rigid views of what men and boys, girls and women, are really like. As we look at the way sex-role development unfolds, we'll try to answer three basic questions:

1. When does the knowledge of being either male or female develop?
2. What are the differences in boys' and girls' behavior in early childhood?
3. Where do the differences come from, and do they have to exist at all?

GENDER IDENTITY

> Could you be a boy . . . if you wanted to be?
> When you are grown up, will you be a woman or a man?
> Have you ever been or can you ever be a boy?
> Will you still be a girl if you wear boys' pants and cut your hair? If you play with trucks and soldiers?

When researchers asked preschoolers these questions they got some surprising answers (DeVries, 1969; Marcus & Overton, 1978; Slaby & Frey, 1975). Three-year-old girls said they could become boys if they acted like them. And boys of this age report that a change of clothes or hairstyle can turn a Sam into a Samantha. The reason for this uncertainty about gender lies in the cognitive limitations of this age. Preschoolers are easily fooled by appearances; they focus on states, not transformations.

Children don't reliably know their **gender identity**, that they are boys or girls, until age 2 to 3. And even after that, they aren't certain that gender is for life.

gender identity
the knowledge that one is female or male

At about 4 or 5, children begin to understand that their sex will never change (**gender constancy**) (Huston, 1983). First, preschoolers begin to realize that wishing will not change their sex. Then, slowly, they comprehend that they *cannot* change their sex no matter what they do.

gender constancy
the understanding that one's sex will never change

SEX STEREOTYPES

By age 3, girls and boys "know" that blocks, hammers, trucks, and rough-and-tumble are for males, while pots and pans, dolls, and aprons are for females (Connor & Seabin, 1977; Huston, 1983). Three-year-olds will actually avoid playing with toys associated with the other gender even when there are few alternatives (Hartup, Moore, & Sage, 1963). By age 5, boys often tell you that all the television commercials selling girls' toys are "yucky." This host of social expectations about how boys and girls are to behave are **sex stereotypes**. By age 4 or 5 children even have stereotypes for careers: In their play, nurses, teachers, and secretaries are girls; doctors, police officers, fire fighters, truck drivers, and superheroes are boys (Huston, 1983).

sex stereotypes
social expectations about how males and females behave

Sexism at a young age? Pre-schoolers cling to sex-role stereo-types, often more fiercely than adults. Typically, boys shovel the dirt and girls pour the tea. (left, *Harriet Newman-Brown/Monkmeyer Press;* right, *Jerry Howard/Stock, Boston*)

Young children stereotype personalities as well as professions. Women are soft and gentle, men are brave and strong. In one study, when 5-year-olds from the United States, England, and Ireland listened to a story about a very gentle adult, nearly 80 percent of them said the person was a woman. Similarly, almost all the children identified a strong and robust character in another story as a man (Best et al., 1977).

Have the children of the 1980s learned a different lesson? With over half of all mothers today working at least part-time, and many at professional jobs, do today's preschoolers hold fewer sex stereotypes? No. Even recent studies show that sexual stereotypes are alive and well among preschool girls and boys (Liben & Bigler, 1987) and may even be a necessary step in the gender-identification process (Stangor & Ruble, 1987). That is, just as crawling usually precedes walking, stereotyped thinking may be the foundation for nonstereo-typed thinking.

DIFFERENCES IN BOYS' AND GIRLS' BEHAVIOR

A 3-year-old girl described the difference between the sexes this way: "They don't want to be fancy because girls *do*. They just like not to be the same as us" (Paley, 1984, p. 10).

In her vividly detailed book, *Boys and Girls: Superheroes in the Doll Corner,* Vivian G. Paley records the ways in which preschool boys and girls act "not the same." In scene after scene, boys play more physically and aggressively than girls: While the boys chase Darth Vader to the "death star," the girls play mother and baby in the doll corner. In the "tumbling room" boys run and climb, resting only when they "fall down dead." The girls do somersaults and then "stretch out on the mats and watch the boys." When the boys leave, the girls indulge, at least temporarily, in more characteristic "boy" behavior. "The change is dramatic. With the boys gone, the girls run, climb, and tumble with a new vitality" (Paley, 1984, p. 66). But soon they return to their doll play.

Throughout this discussion, remember that statements about sex differences are statements about *averages*. Many boys and girls are more or less aggressive than the norm, an example of the overlapping distributions commonly found in scientific research. We are talking about consistent *patterns* of behavior. The main pattern Paley observed is the basic difference between young boys and girls everywhere: Most boys are *more active and aggressive* than most girls (Block, 1983; Parke & Slaby, 1983). Their play is rougher; they try more often to dominate their peers, and their behavior is more antisocial. Boys are far more likely than girls, even during the preschool years, to respond to a physical assault with physical force (Duvall & Cheyne, 1981). Even children themselves notice the difference.

Karen:	Girls are nicer than boys.
Janie:	Boys are bad. Some boys are.
Paul:	Not bad. Pretend bad, like bad guys.
Karen:	My brother is really bad.
Teacher:	Aren't girls ever bad?
Paul:	I don't think so. Not very much.
Teacher:	Why not?
Paul:	Because they like to color so much. That's one thing I know. Boys have to practice running.
Karen:	And they practice being silly. (Paley, 1984, pp. 25–26)

Boys also tend to be more curious and to do more exploring. For example, they will work harder to get around barriers blocking them from things they want (Block, 1983). Preschool girls handle frustration and control their impulses better than boys do, but they are also anxious and timid more often than boys. Three- and four-year-old girls also tend to be both more nurturant and more compliant (Best et al., 1983).

These behavior differences show up once children are firmly aware of their gender identity. At 2 and 3, boys will still join the girls in the doll corner, but by age 4 or so most boys keep out, or enter only on brief forays. Superheroes have taken over. However, while they may not like to admit it, boys too are playing with dolls. Their "action figures"—cartoon characters, soldiers, robots—are just dolls in tough-guy clothes. The real difference is in the way they think about and use them. Again, the boys focus on action fighting and physical strength, while the girls play at mothering and dressing up.

By the time children reach kindergarten, the division between the sexes is firmly set, and as they play, children seek separate social distinctions for "boy" and "girl." In one kindergarten class, for example,

you hop to get your milk if you are a boy and skip to the paper shelf if you are a girl. Boys clap out the rhythm of certain songs; girls sing louder. Boys draw furniture inside four-story haunted houses; girls put flowers in the doorways of cottages. Boys get tired of drawing pictures and begin to poke and shove; girls continue to draw. (Paley, 1984, p. xi)

Clearly, then, sex-typed behavior begins early in children's development and matches, in many ways, the adult sex stereotypes of our culture. Why?

WHERE DO SEX-TYPED DIFFERENCES COME FROM?

In the classic nature-nurture debate, the "nature" side claimed that inborn, biological differences shaped behavior as well as bodies, while the environmentalists said boys and girls are *taught* to be different. Today, we would argue that both sides are right; as with all other aspects of development, biology and experience are both at work.

The influence of biology

androgens
the class of hormones, including testosterone, that occur in higher levels in males

Animal behavior studies reveal that in every mammalian species, males are more aggressive than females, beginning early in life. Among our own species too, in preschools and playgrounds, boys tend to hit, push, and shove more than girls do. Such universals always *suggest* (even if they do not prove) at least a partially biological basis for behavior. It may be that the hormone testosterone, at higher levels in boys' blood at birth, accounts for greater aggression in males (Maccoby, Doering, Jacklin, & Kraemer, 1979; Sussman et al., 1987). In fact, girls who have been prenatally exposed to especially high levels of **androgens** (the class of hormones, including testosterone, that males have more of) develop more traditionally masculine and fewer traditionally feminine interests. They are more likely than other girls to be described as tomboys, and they tend not to play with dolls (Money & Ehrhardt, 1972). In one study, both girls and boys who had been exposed before birth to synthetic androgens scored higher in physical aggression than their unexposed siblings (Reinisch, 1981).

This kind of evidence underscores the influence of biological factors on aggression. None of the other sex-typed behaviors have been so clearly linked to biochemistry, but research is continuing. One complication is that biochemistry and behavior affect one another. Not only do hormones influence behavior, but experience and behavior can affect hormone levels. Being aggressive, for example, can stimulate the production of androgens, leaving researchers wondering which comes first.

Psychoanalytic explanations

Recall from Chapter 1 that Freud saw infant and child development as a series of stages in which children gain control of basic biological urges. Emotionally healthy children can resolve the conflicts between their biological drives and the demands of society at each stage of development. For Freud, the conflict of the preschool years centers around the biological urges of genital sexuality. (See the discussion of the *phallic stage* in Chapter 1.) During this stage, children wish to "possess" the opposite-sex parent: "I'm going to marry daddy," says a little girl, while a little boy imagines himself as mommy's husband.

castration anxiety
Freud's label for a little boy's fear that he will be punished for being his father's rival

In these wishes, said Freud, are the seeds of conflict. A little boy needs his father but fears he will be punished for being his father's rival, a fear Freud labeled **castration anxiety**. Freud termed this struggle the *Oedipus complex* (Chapter 1) because of its similarity to the classic Greek story of Oedipus, who unknowingly killed his father and then married his mother. The Oedipal conflict is resolved when the boy *represses* (removes or rejects from consciousness) his desire for his mother and identifies with his father. In this process of *identification* the boy works to become just like his father—to incorporate the father's behaviors, attitudes, beliefs, and values into himself. That is how he learns what it means to be a male.

In the same way, a girl, said Freud, wants her father for herself and fantasizes about her mother going away or dying. He called this internal strug-

Where are the boys? Whether the reasons are biological or learned, or both, by age 4, when girls set up house, boys keep out. *(Elizabeth Crews/The Image Works)*

gle the *Electra complex* (see Chapter 1) after the Greek legend in which Electra plots to kill her mother. The little girl becomes aware of her father's love for his wife and feels jealous but also fears the mother. Gradually, she represses her desire for her father and identifies with her mother. Through this identification the little girl learns what it means to be female. Freud also believed that girls were jealous of the male's penis and felt diminished by its absence, a condition he called "penis envy." Many psychologists disagree, suggesting that what girls want is the independence and power that boys are traditionally raised to expect.

Along with the attitudes and behaviors that come with gender identification, children also internalize their parents' moral standards. These standards form the *superego*, or conscience, and they mark the beginning of moral development (see Chapter 1). Freud believed that with the resolution of the Oedipal/Electra complex, children would become increasingly able to regulate their moral behavior from within, via the superego.

Several research studies support Freud's view that sex-role development hinges on the child's identification with the same-sex parent. When same-sex parents are accepting, warm, and nurturing, children generally show "appropriate" sex typing and are apt to imitate that parent (Biller & Borstelmann, 1967; Mussen, 1969). And when the opposite-sex parent encourages sex-typed behavior, a child is even more likely to behave in traditionally masculine or feminine ways. So a little girl with an affectionate, supportive mother and a father who gives her dolls and praise for acting like a "little lady" is most likely to behave in a typically feminine way (Hetherington, Cox, & Cox, 1978).

What happens when the same-sex parent is absent? Some research on boys without fathers seems to support Freud's ideas. In a number of studies, boys with absent fathers did score lower on sex-role orientation scales and were less interested in masculine-typed activities than boys whose fathers lived at home (Beere, 1979; Drake & McDougall, 1977; Hetherington, 1966). Boys who showed the most lasting effects had been separated from their fathers before age 5—before gender identity was set. The point here is not that boys must have fathers at home for healthy sex-role development. Rather, according to Freudian theory, a boy needs to identify with some involved male figure—stepfather, uncle, older brother, or family friend (Chapman, 1977; Shinn, 1978). Even without a father or father substitute, however, masculinity can still be encouraged by a mother who helps her son to be assertive and independent (Biller, 1970; Biller & Bahm, 1971).

Cognitive explanations

Biological explanations for sex-role development stress biochemical and genetic factors. Psychoanalytic explanations stress emotion and the process of identification with the same-sex parent. For cognitive theorists, the child's developing intellectual abilities and limitations are critical. According to cognitive developmental theorists, such as Lawrence Kohlberg (1966), sex-role development begins by age 3, when children first label themselves boys or girls. Recall that children slowly come to understand that gender never changes during the Piagetian period of preoperational thinking (see Chapter 9). We can think of gender constancy, then, as conservation of gender, another conservation task to be mastered: Like liquids, number, and mass, gender stays the same despite changes in appearance. In fact, children in research studies achieved conservation of gender only after they understood basic conservation of physical quantities (Marcus & Overton, 1978). Just as they need to decenter before they know that Miss Piggy is a costume, by the end of the preoperational stage children understand that a boy is a boy is a boy even if he's wearing a dress and a girl is a girl is a girl even if her hair is short and she climbs trees.

Cognitive theorists contend that once children have finally identified their sex, new information gets sorted by gender. Boys do this, girls do that. Children learn what *is* appropriate and what is *not* appropriate for their own sex by watching adults and processing the information they gather. Then they act according to the way they've divided the world. But, say cognitive theorists, children are active processors of whatever behavior they see. So active, in fact, they they recast what they see into what they think they know. For example, if you show young children girls playing with trucks and boys playing with dolls and then ask them, several days later, what they saw, they are likely to tell you that boys were playing with the trucks and girls were playing with dolls! In effect, preschoolers transform what they saw into what they think they *should* have seen (Martin & Halverson, 1981).

Because of the way children process information, we can't count on them to abandon stereotypes from a few exposures to nontraditional situations: Seeing a female doctor on television or looking at a book about a father who stays home with the baby won't revamp their thinking. What parents and teachers think young children are seeing and learning may be far different from what they are actually comprehending (Liben & Bigler, 1987). Sex-stereotyped behavior becomes rewarding in its own right, say cognitive theorists, because it is consistent with the child's ideas about being male or female, and because imitating mom or dad reaffirms this belief.

Social learning explanations

"Mommy," says 4-year-old Alicia, "Will you help me with this puzzle?" "Sure," says Mommy and quickly sorts the pieces. When Charlie, also 4, asks his mother for help, Mommy says, "Keep trying." He perseveres and she rewards him with "Good work, dear." "I want this doll, Daddy," says 3-year-old Adam in the toy store. "Wouldn't you like this truck instead?" says Dad. Over and over, boys and girls hear, see, and experience different messages about what it means to be male or female, and, say the social learning theorists, they learn these lessons well, through both *direct reinforcement* (rewards for specific behaviors) and *modeling* (imitation).

Sex-based messages begin even before babies leave the hospital. In a number of studies, parents perceived their own newborn girls as smaller, finer featured, softer, and less alert than boys. Neutral observers looking at the same newborns saw none of these differences, and indeed, they did not exist. Both men and women offer a doll more often to the baby dressed in pink and give a stereotypical masculine toy more often to the baby in blue (Frisch, 1977; Smith & Lloyd, 1978; Will, Self, & Datan, 1976). Fathers "see" greater sex differences than mothers, judging newborn sons as hardier and stronger than daughters (Rubin, Provenzano, & Lurai, 1974).

As they grow up, boys and girls aren't just perceived differently, they are reinforced (see Chapter 1) for *behaving* differently, according to sexual stereotypes (Block, 1983). Both mothers and fathers reward their sons (by approval, encouragement, and other positive reinforcements) for being competitive, achieving, independent, and responsible. Parents also encourage boys to control their feelings: "Boys don't cry." Fathers say that they are stricter with their sons and more likely to punish sons physically. Daughters are more closely supervised and more restricted than sons, but their parents are also warmer toward them, more confident of their trustworthiness and truthfulness, and more likely to encourage them to reflect on life. Mothers and fathers still expect girls to be "ladylike," and praise their daughters for compliance, cooperation, and understanding (Huston, 1983).

Parents expect different levels of academic achievement for their sons and daughters as well. Many mothers and fathers believe that finishing college and having a successful career are more important for their sons (Barnett, 1979; Hoffman, 1977; Maccoby & Jacklin, 1974), and starting with preschool, parents expect greater achievement and more independence from boys (Block, 1983; Rothbart & Rothbart, 1976).

Even among children themselves, sex-typed behavior is expected and reinforced, sometimes cruelly (Langlois & Downs, 1980). When lines are crossed, boys are criticized or teased more than girls are. A girl who prefers building to Barbies may be considered odd, but a boy who routinely opts for the doll corner can be harshly teased by other boys (Fagot, 1977; Roopnarine, 1984).

In the wake of the women's liberation movement and the push for greater equality between the sexes, are young children still getting the same messages

Showing children that most things in life can be done by either sex will help them avoid stereotypic thinking about sex roles. (left, *Spencer Grant/Stock, Boston;* right, *Carol Lee/The Picture Cube*)

modeling
a component of social learning that involves imitation

about sex roles? Are parents still perceiving and treating little boys and girls differently? The answer seems to be, for the most part, yes. In a recent series of interviews, mothers of kindergarteners were asked first about differences between girls and boys and then whether they treated girls and boys differently. The same question had been asked more than 30 years earlier in a classic study by Sears, Maccoby, and Levin. In 1987, just as in 1951, 80 percent of the mothers agreed there were qualitative differences in raising boys and girls. How did they see boys? As masculine, independent, immature, and involved in sports. Girls were described as feminine, nurturing, emotional, helpful with household chores, verbal, and involved in noncontact sports (Pinto, Moriarty, Hackenson, & Ricks, 1988). There was, however, one shift in mothers' attitudes and behavior. In 1951, mothers said they taught boys to treat girls differently than other little boys: They warned their sons not to be rough with girls, because girls were helpless. In 1987, mothers said they tended to teach their children to treat both girls and boys in the same way, equally and with respect.

Theorists would argue that real change will come only when what children hear matches what they see. The second component of social learning, **modeling**, or imitation, is a powerful teacher. When only mothers do housework, for example, children can grow up thinking that vacuums and mops are for women only. Mother may indeed work outside the home, but she is still very likely to make dinner and clean the house. Dad may help with the laundry now, but mom is more often the one who changes the diapers. Only when parents share these chores will children learn that cleaning is an equal opportunity activity. And even parents who believe that boys and girls should be treated alike often continue to treat them differently. Nevertheless, research on the effects of maternal employment shows that children's ideas are changing. Specifically, daughters whose mothers are employed show less traditional and stereotypical thinking about family roles (who does the laundry), careers (who can arrest bad guys), and even toy play (who can play with superheroes) (Katz, 1987).

Television, books, and sex roles

A major source of both sex-role models and reinforcement of traditional sex-role stereotypes is television (Calvert & Huston, 1987). Although she is a mother who is out working, Claire Huxtable on *The Cosby Show*, despite her career as a lawyer, miraculously is always home and available to her children. And Carol Brady is there for her bunch on television reruns. Even new programs with up-to-the-minute technology are often saturated with sex-role stereotypes. Both *Voltron* and *He-Man*, for example, include a token female warrior among the male characters, but in each of these cartoon series guess which sex is most often captured or caged or tied up by the villain. It's the woman almost every time who plays the victim's role.

Women characters are greatly underrepresented in all television programming, and especially in programs for children. Wonder Woman and She-Ra stand alone next to Superman, Batman, Robin, the Flash, and a legion of other male heroes in the Superfriends cartoon series. And even during commercial breaks, sex-stereotyping is the rule: Little boys play with building sets, robots, and cars while little girls play with dolls, stuffed animals, and jewelry. In adult commercials, too, the message continues. For the most part, the men still clinch the deals, drive the cars, and have the fun, while the women do the laundry and shine the floors.

Exceptions to this bleak picture of sex typing in the media certainly exist. On *Sesame Street*, *The Electric Company*, *3-2-1 Contact*, and *Mathnet*, women can be leaders, men can talk about feelings, and both sexes perform nontraditional activities. And in many new children's books, girls and women are strong central characters. Nevertheless, the media are still more likely to reinforce traditional sex roles than to be a force for change.

We began this explanation of sex-role development by noting that no one theory is sufficient: There is quite a lot of overlap. Freudians and social learning theorists both acknowledge the role of models, for example. Since each theory represents a different emphasis—feeling, thinking, and behaving—all three help us to understand how children acquire sex-typed behavior. Unconscious emotional development (psychoanalytic theory) blends with cognitive development and is reinforced by social learning. And all these processes are influenced by the unique inborn characteristics of every child. So, given the fact that, through a variety of processes, young girls and boys do show sex-typed behaviors, primarily around aggression, this raises another question: How do these differences matter?

HOW DO SEX DIFFERENCES MATTER?

Until the women's movement began in the 1970s, few people cared very much about the different ways in which boys and girls were raised, about the different messages they received, about the different opportunities that were open to them just because they were boys or girls. But the writings of feminists made us think about the implications of sex differences for boys and girls and for society as a whole.

If we lived in a nonindustrial culture, where men hunted for food and women tended to the children and did the agricultural tasks, it would make sense to encourage aggression in boys and nurturance in girls. But in industrial societies, where we buy food instead of hunting for it, what do we gain by fostering traditional sex-related differences? In the workplace and at home some assertiveness *and* nurturance are needed by *both* sexes. In such a society, it would make more sense to deemphasize the differences between the sexes.

The women's movement has made many of us aware of the potential both sexes have for the full range of human behavior and emotions. Not all men are good at sports; not all can be as assertive as others. Not all women are comfortable being full-time nurturers. Where girls are encouraged to be too passive, society is also the loser. But in a society where all children are encouraged to be fully themselves, boys and girls may then grow up to be more complete men and women.

Developing Social Skills

"Use words, don't hit!" "Wait your turn." "Share the crayons." "Don't throw the sand." "We don't spit." The timeless litany of parents and teachers. Learning to control aggression, to talk rather than fight, to cooperate, to share, and to wait one's turn are social skills that children struggle to learn all through the early years and beyond. Maturing as social beings can take a lifetime, but from 2 to 6, children begin to learn the patterns of social life and the way adults expect them to behave.

THE DEVELOPMENT OF PROSOCIAL BEHAVIOR

Five-year-old Candace is trying to comfort a younger friend, Elihu:

> "Want some pizza?" Candace asks.
> "No, I don't want pizza," Elihu says through his tears.
> "Want to ride on my bicycle?" Candace offers.
> "No, I don't wanna ride on a bicycle," Elihu says, tears still streaming down.
> "Want to see a dragon?" Candace asks in a conspiratorial tone, putting her arm around him.
> "Yeah," Elihu replies, his expression shifting almost instantly from a sorrowful frown to an eager smile (Rubin, 1980, p. 20).

empathize
to know what another person is feeling

Candace's ability to **empathize**—to know what another person is feeling—may have begun in the crib. Infants and 1-year-olds cry when they hear other babies crying, and while some claim that this is just emotional copying, sharing feelings may actually be the first step toward mature empathy (Radke-Yarrow et al., 1983; Sagi & Hoffman, 1976; Simner, 1971). One toddler will pat an-

Comforting another begins early. Even young children show concern and tenderness when another child feels sad. *(Michael Weisbrot/Stock, Boston)*

other who is crying, and 2-year-olds offer more elaborate help. They may bring a teddy bear to the distressed child, and if that doesn't help, they'll try something else. They sympathize, bring someone to help, and try to change the other's sad feelings (Radke-Yarrow et al., 1983; Zahn-Waxler & Radke-Yarrow, 1982).

Two- and three-year-olds will spontaneously give gifts and share their toys with other children and with unfamiliar adults. At these ages, gift giving is a way to begin and maintain social contact, and the gifts may be everyday objects such as pieces of wood or stone (Stanjek, 1978). Helping, too, begins early. Children will stop what they are doing to clear an obstacle from another's path. They'll also help each other clean up spilled puzzles and the like (Iannotti, 1984, p. 53).

Empathy for other children in distress, cooperation with others to achieve common goals, and helping all increase during the preschool years (Bar-Tal et al., 1982; Marcus et al., 1979; Rheingold, 1982; Savin, 1980). Some children show more of these positive behaviors than others (Murphy, 1937), and the *tendency* for some children to be more benevolent than others seems to be stable over time: Four-year-olds who were generous, cooperative, empathic, considerate, and helpful were also generous at 5. And children who are socially responsible in nursery school are still behaving more responsibly than their peers 5 to 6 years later (Mussen & Eisenberg-Berg, 1977).

Developmentalists call these positive, helping acts **prosocial behavior**. The origin of prosocial behavior has been debated since ancient times. Today, there are three important theoretical explanations for the growth of prosocial behavior in early childhood, parallel to the three we looked at in sex-role development: attachment theory (related to psychoanalytic theory), cognitive views, and the social learning perspective.

prosocial behavior
positive, helping acts

Attachment explanations

Recall from Chapter 7 that securely attached infants are also more secure as preschoolers, and that a sense of security fosters positive social skills. Research has shown that social skills are indeed better developed in children who had secure attachments. In one study, 3½-year-olds who had been securely attached were the ones other children wanted to play with. They were less withdrawn, more likely to be leaders, and more sympathetic to their peers' distress than preschoolers who had been judged insecure as infants (Waters, Wippman, & Sroufe, 1979).

Thus, preschoolers who developed a strong sense of basic trust during infancy tend to see the world as dependable and safe. Free to relate to others without too much anxiety and anger, they learn more readily how to give and take, how to perceive the needs of others. These children, then, will probably welcome social experiences, and by the time they are 4 to 5 years old, they'll have a well-developed set of social skills. Relating to their peers in a friendly, positive way will come naturally.

Cognitive explanations

"Why were you nice to Scott?" "Why did you give him a cookie?" When researchers ask these kinds of questions, boys and girls explain their behavior by talking about the needs of the other ("He's hungry") or about their own needs ("I wanted to"). Other reasons include friendship ("He's my friend") and the wish for approval (Eisenberg-Berg & Neal, 1979).

Sometimes children comfort one another in ways that suggest certain cognitive limitations. Responses to another's distress can sound very much like egocentrism, which Piaget claimed restricted preschoolers' abilities to take another's perspective. "Suck your thumb!" one child may say to a friend (or an adult) who is crying. A young child will even bring his own mother to comfort another child, even if the crying child's mother is already present. For cognitive theorists, then, empathy and prosocial behavior are linked to perspective-taking. As their egocentrism lessens and perspective-taking capacities grow, young children's prosocial behaviors increase. But whether or not young children can fully empathize and offer effective comfort, responses like "Suck your thumb" and "Wanna cookie?" show they can be very caring toward others.

Social learning explanations

For social learning theorists, kindness is a matter of imitation. In one study, preschoolers who had observed an adult model sharing, helping, and being sympathetic acted more like that themselves 2 weeks later than children who had not seen such a model (Yarrow et al., 1973). And the effects of more extensive modeling seem to endure beyond several days and sometimes even several months (Radke-Yarrow et al., 1983). Children also get reinforced for being sympathetic and for sharing, helping, and cooperating: "That's a good girl." "You're a nice boy." "Thank you for helping." Finally, there is evidence that the act of giving can itself make a child feel good and thus becomes intrinsically rewarding (Hay & Rheingold, 1974).

CONTROLLING AGGRESSION

Christopher pushes Barney down in the playground and then again in the hall-way. I [teacher, Vivian Paley] stand between the boys, glaring down at Christopher.

"No, Christopher. You can't push people."

"I'm pushing Barney," he says without emotion.

"No, you must not do it. We won't let you."

"I'm pushing Barney."

"He saw someone doing it on the playground," Mrs. Alter explains. "Some boy in the other class. Now he keeps saying that he's pushing Barney."

Mollie screws up her face. "Don't push Barney!"

"Don't say it," Christopher tells her.

"Mollie can say it, Christopher. Everyone can tell you not to push Barney." [author's italics] (Paley, 1986, p. 22)

Later that morning, Christopher pushes Barney off a step and Ms. Paley intervenes again. "Christopher, you'll have to stay next to me all morning. You can sit in my lap or in a chair or hold my hand." "Why?" "So I can be sure you won't push Barney. You have that idea in your mind and it keeps coming out" (p. 25). Sensitively, patiently, Vivian Paley helps Christopher control his aggression, but it is a lesson he will have to keep learning throughout the pre-school years. Many preschoolers become physically aggressive until they gradually learn to use words instead of fists.

This is possible because language skills and emotional control are both maturing. While children are getting better at saying what they want, they're also better at controlling what they do. At the same time, adults expect more control from them, so what's happening within the child is encouraged from

Keep out! Until preschoolers gain emotional control, pushing often takes the place of talking. *(Michael Weisbrot/Stock, Boston)*

without as well. Preschoolers begin to follow their teachers' instructions to "use words" to handle disputes, and they may be punished for fighting. The older a child is, the more likely that she or he will react to an insult with some choice words rather than with a slap or a kick. Even though boys tend to be more aggressive than girls at all ages, both sexes show these developmental trends.

Boys and girls also show the same two types of aggression: **Instrumental aggression** arises out of conflicts over ownership, territory, and perceived rights. Mary, for instance, might slap Paul for playing with her stuffed dog. Annie's older brother may kick her if her foot gets too close to his sand castle. This type of aggression decreases first. The second type, hostile aggression, abates more slowly. **Hostile aggression** can be both physical and verbal and is directed against another person. In short, it is deliberately harmful.

A child's level of aggression tends to be stable, so a highly aggressive preschooler is likely to be a more aggressive school-age child as well (Olweus, 1979, 1982; Parke & Slaby, 1983). But researchers have found that tendency need not lead to inevitability. If the forces that encourage a child to be highly aggressive change, we can expect the child's tendencies to change too. If conditions remain the same, aggressive children are very likely to become troubled adolescents. In fact, after a recent update of the New York Longitudinal Study, Alexander Thomas concluded that *"aggression in childhood is the emotional trait that is the strongest predictor of later maladjustment"* (quoted in Goleman, 1988b) [authors' italics]. Why some children have trouble controlling their aggression is a question with many answers. (See "Issues & Options" discussion of toy guns.) Cognitive and social learning theories offer explanations that may actually work together.

Cognitive explanations of aggression

Two children standing in line waiting for a drink are each bumped from behind. One turns and pushes the child who bumped him who then pushes back. Fighting begins. The other child casts a questioning look and says, "Be careful." The child who did the bumping then apologizes, explaining that another child pushed *him*.

Two bumps, two reactions. Why? For cognitive theorists, interpretation is extremely important. How you respond to people depends in large measure on how you *think* they treated you. In the bumping incident, the first child instantly assumes that the child who bumped him wanted to harm him, and he strikes back. The second child is either unsure why he got bumped or even assumes it was an accident (Dodge, 1982; Dodge, Pettit, McClaskey, & Brown, 1986). Besides misperceiving situations, overly aggressive children don't think of other possible ways to react. They push back, which ends up turning an accident into a fight. In view of such an explanation of aggression, efforts to lower children's aggressive tendencies need to focus not only on how children act, but on how they *think* other people act toward them.

Social learning and aggression

How does aggressiveness become a child's main way of dealing with others? A social learning theorist looks at the bumping incident and concludes that the

---

instrumental aggression aggression arising out of conflicts over ownership, territory, perceived rights

hostile aggression physical and/or verbal aggression that is deliberately harmful

Issues & OPTIONS

Guns in
the Toy Chest

Just a few generations ago, every American boy had a stash of toy guns for playing cowboys and Indians, cops and robbers, good guys and bad guys. But today, many parents, especially those who want their sons to appreciate the more tender, nurturant aspects of life, are uneasy about buying toy guns. Are they worrying needlessly? Do toy guns numb children to the effects of real violence, or is playing with them a normal part of growing up?

Opinions differ: In the latest edition of *Baby and Childcare*, Dr. Benjamin Spock writes, "If I had a three- or four-year-old son who asked me to buy him a gun, I'd tell him . . . that I don't want to give him a gun . . . because there is too much meanness and killing in the world, that we must all learn how to get along in a friendly way together."

But another advisor counsels: "The issue is really simple. There are things that make children angry, and playing battle games is one safe, healthy outlet for anger and aggression. Some people say that playing with guns teaches kids to be violent. That's nonsense. Children have violent fantasies with or without a toy gun or knife; they'll just use sticks instead. . . . If you try to stop

Even the experts don't agree on whether parents should buy war toys, but when children do play killing games, parents can set limits. *(Alan Carey/The Image Works)*

them, their aggressive feelings will just be channeled elsewhere, probably into less acceptable behavior. But give them their arsenal of guns at age three or four, and they'll be bored with them by the time they're six or seven, and that will be the end of it" (Siegel, 1988).

Which advice should parents follow? Many refuse to buy toy guns, hoping to teach their children that weapons can hurt people and that aggression is bad. But they soon discover a rude fact of child development: Children are so fascinated by guns and other implements of power that what they aren't given, their imaginations will create. Deny a child a

gun, and his baseball bat becomes a rifle. On any street, sticks can double as swords and lasers, and even a cardboard tube can be a pretend weapon. Then what? Should parents try to tell their children not to pretend? That would be a foolish struggle.

Parents and children will both benefit instead from talking about weapons as instruments of destruction. Whether or not parents decide to buy toy weapons, they can still discuss weapons and violence with their children. One reason parents and teachers dislike weapons is because they hurt people, so talking about what guns do and how they are used by police, hunters, soldiers, and criminals can help to educate children. And whether children play with imaginary or store-bought toy weapons, parents and teachers can still limit their use. In many homes, nursery schools, and day care centers, "killing" can only be done outside. Adults can also forbid real battles with baseball bats, and they can tell children not to touch others with their "swords."

In the end, the weapons of childhood may be something that adults have to live with, but mastering the limits of their use can help children to express and control their aggression at the same time.

aggressive child *learned* to behave that way through observation, modeling, and operant conditioning (being rewarded for one's behavior—see Chapter 1). If a child's models—her parents and older siblings—frequently hit and yell at each other, she'll learn those behaviors too. The reward for aggression is attention, along with getting your own way by overpowering others. Peers who make a fuss about overly aggressive children or laugh at the victims are actually reinforcing the behaviors they dislike. And the child who pushes ahead of another child in line, or who snatches a toy and gets away with it, is encouraged by success to try it again.

But while social learning processes can generate, maintain, and even increase behavior, they can also be used intentionally to change it. Preschool teachers can help to reduce inappropriate aggression by ignoring it, while attending to and rewarding cooperative and pleasant behavior instead (Brown & Elliot, 1965). This requires the teacher's self-control, as the worst behavior often gets the most attention, only reinforcing it. But sometimes ignoring a minor scuffle or incident is useful. Children can learn to resolve their own conflicts so long as no one is threatening to spill blood. When a child consistently abuses others, physically or verbally, the teacher should intervene. An adult must be able to judge the *degree* of aggressiveness, given the age of the child.

Social learning explanations, which emphasize the reinforcement and modeling of aggression, and cognitive explanations, which stress thought processes, are by no means mutually exclusive. The kind of experiences (especially in the family) that social learning theory emphasizes seems to foster the thinking processes that cognitive theorists stress (Pettit, Dodge, & Brown, 1988): Children who frequently witness aggression or whose parents treat them harshly grow to expect the world to be a nasty place. They begin treating others as they have been treated themselves. Attachment theory adds to our understanding as well, because it stresses the link between children's experiences in the family and the way they expect others to treat them. Such expectations guide not only what they do but how they interpret what others do (Belsky & Nezworski, 1988). (In Chapter 14 we discuss intervention programs for overly aggressive school-aged children.)

PEER RELATIONS: MAKING FRIENDS

Interviewer:	Why is Caleb your friend?
Tony:	Because I like him.
Interviewer:	And why do you like him?
Tony:	Because he's my friend.
Interviewer:	And why is he your friend?
Tony: (With mild disgust)	Because . . . I . . . choosed him . . . for my friend. (Rubin, 1980)

Preschoolers choose their friends because of physical qualities ("He is tall," "She has a pretty face"), common activities ("We like trucks"), possession of interesting things ("He has lots of army men"), and physical closeness ("He sits near me") (Berndt, 1981; Hayes, 1978). By the end of the preschool years, they begin valuing social support (sharing, helping, giving, comforting) and affection (loving, liking, caring for) in their friends.

One of the strongest criteria for choosing friends is gender. From age 2 until about 11, children everywhere usually choose friends of their own sex (Edwards & Whiting, 1988; LaFreniere, Strayer, & Gauthier, 1984; Maccoby & Jacklin, 1987). By age 5, while both sexes prefer playing with their own kind, boys are determined to keep their friendships female-free (LaFreniere et al., 1984). Why this sex segregation? It may be because boys and girls play differently, and each sex finds its own style more compatible (Maccoby, 1988). Regardless of gender, both sexes begin practicing the fine art of negotiating, a social skill that depends on understanding another's feelings:

> "Margaret, this time I want to be the mother."
> "No, I am."
> "You were the other day."
> "But Mollie, don't you know? I can't be the mother at home because my sister always is."
> "Then when I get to your house I can be?"
> "Yes. Tell my sister she could see your Pac-Man eyeglasses." (Paley, 1986, p. 84)

A year ago, at age 2, Margaret and Mollie's conversation would probably have gone like this: "I am the mother." "No. I am." "No. I am (louder)." Tears. Now, at 3 years, socially more mature, they can consider each other's feelings, as can Erik and John in the excerpt below:

> "I'm a bad Superman."
> "I'm a good Superman."
> "But, John, I'm going to be a bad Superman. Aren't you?"
> "Okay, I'm bad, too. No, I mean, I'm still good."
> "Look, John, what if you say you want to be a good guy? Say you were still my friend and I say I want to be a bad guy Superman and you say, you can say, 'I want to be a good guy Superman,' 'cause the other person could tell you when you're not your friend."
> "Well, Erik, I'm going to be a good Superman but I'm still going to be your friend."
> "But just be a bad Superman, can't you? Because I'm going to be one. C'mon, can't you, John? See, good really means bad. See, if I say good it really means *bad*."
> "Okay, we're bad, but we still could kill the bad guys, okay?" (Paley, 1986, pp. 77–78)

If "good" and "bad" are sometimes ambiguous, so is the meaning of "friend." It is often used to exclude others, as in, "I'm not playing with Bill, *just* with you, because *you* are my friend." And while threats to end friendships occur almost minute to minute, they are quickly forgotten.

> "Margaret's not my friend, Mrs. Paley."
> "Why do you think that?"
> "She said she's not my friend. She even told me. . . . "
> Mollie informs Christopher the moment he arrives.
> "Margaret is not my friend."
> "Oh," he says, not asking for reasons. "Am I your friend?"
> "Yes, if you help me make a restaurant. Bring those big blocks before Margaret gets them."

"Hi, Margaret. Are you going to be my friend today?"

"Yes."

"Then do you want Chinese noodles?"

"Cheese regular."

"Margaret, you're coming to my birthday." (Paley, 1986, p. 113)

Individual differences in peer relationships

Not every child knows the intimacy of Mollie and Margaret. Some lack a special friend, while others have several. Why are some children better at making friends than others? What determines whether children are accepted, rejected, or ignored by their peers? Several factors come into play. Physically attractive children benefit from the social stereotype that beautiful is good: Attractive children are often rated as friendly and nonaggressive, while the physically handicapped and learning disabled are more likely to be avoided and rejected by their peers (Adams & Crane, 1980; Hartup, 1983; Vaughn and Langlois, 1983).

The most important factor determining how children are regarded by their agemates is their own behavior. Popular preschoolers are more friendly and socially skilled than other children. Disliked and rejected children engage in more disruptive, antisocial behavior such as hitting, pushing, and taking things. And rather than waiting to be invited they tend to intrude into others' play (Coie, Dodge, & Kupersmidt, 1989). Not surprisingly, liked and disliked children fall into self-perpetuating cycles of social behavior, thereby maintaining their reputations as popular or disliked (Hartup, 1983).

The process works something like this: Suppose that an unpopular and a popular child each want a toy phone that a third child has been playing with. The unpopular child grabs the phone. The popular child starts talking about how much fun the phone is and then asks to play with it. Usually, the friendly request is granted while the aggression of the child who grabs the toy meets with anger. Thus, the popular child's behavior is reinforced and the unpopular child's rejection is reaffirmed. In short, because popular children are socially skilled, they enjoy the acceptance of their peers, which further encourages friendly behavior and reinforces their popularity.

But what makes some children more socially skilled than others to begin with? Recall from Chapter 7 that sociability is a trait that varies from infant to infant right from the start. While a child's family life can certainly affect the development of this trait, children who are born with an inclination to interact with others may have an advantage. In addition, children who had secure attachments as infants often have better social skills as preschoolers (Waters, Wippman, & Sroufe, 1979). As we will see in Chapter 11, how parents treat their children affects sociability as well (Parke et al., 1988). Fathers of neglected preschoolers, one recent study revealed, were least likely to engage their sons in emotionally arousing, physical play, whereas fathers of rejected boys tended to be overstimulating in their physical play (MacDonald, 1987). When parents use and endorse physical aggression to settle disputes at home, children tend to misunderstand the behavior of their peers at school and to be rejected by them (Pettit, Dodge, & Brown, 1988). In the same study, the more supportive the family was, the less likely the child was to think that peers intended to take advantage of him and the more likely he was to get along well with his classmates.

We shouldn't conclude from this evidence, though, that socially inept children are doomed to have trouble with their peers. When concerted efforts are made in classrooms to improve children's behavior, friendly interpersonal relationships can be promoted. Two things seem to be important: *decreasing* the frequency with which children engage in aversive behavior such as taking objects from others, calling them names, and hitting or pushing, and *increasing* the frequency with which children engage in sharing and other cooperative activity. These goals can be achieved in several ways. A teacher can model the appropriate behavior for the child, or show him another child's successful behavior. It helps, too, to explain why some interpersonal strategies, such as requesting or offering to trade when you want something, are more effective in the long run than taking. Finally, teachers can praise children whose behavior with peers improves (Bierman, Miller, & Stabb, 1987; Ladd & Asher, 1985).

The Work of Play

"Play is the work of childhood," says a preschool director to parents who would trade free play for a reading lesson. When children play, they produce, whether it's a fantasy or a product. A pile of blocks becomes a fort one day, a road or a train the next. When children slather paint across a piece of paper, not only are they producing something, they are learning to complete a sequence of events—wait for a turn at the easel, get a smock, paint, wash hands, hang up smock.

Play is an arena for many kinds of social and emotional as well as cognitive growth. Children create new worlds, act out their fantasies, and cope with their fears. They learn to share and to take, to follow and to lead. When the fighting starts, they learn about bullies and self-protection. Also through play, they begin to learn about themselves: what they like to do and who they like to do it with; what's fun to do with another; when it's time to be alone. Play is a training ground for expressing emotions and building relationships.

What makes the more complex types of play possible are the cognitive changes of the preschool years. Symbolic thinking permits the fantasy play through which children can safely express their emotional needs and conflicts. And the complicated plans of superhero games require children to juggle and remember a great deal of information. Similarly, the cognitive skills that enable a 5-year-old to follow the instructions for building a Lego village were only rudimentary at age 3.

FROM SOLITARY TO SOCIAL PLAY

While day care gives many children an early start at playing with others, even by age 3, when children *seem* to be playing together, each child is still focused on his or her own activity. During this play stage, which Parten (1932) labeled

parallel play
children apparently playing together but actually focused on their own activities

collective monologue
discussion between children who take turns talking but whose topics may be unrelated

parallel play, children often talk *at* but not *with* each other. In this kind of pattern, called the **collective monologue**, children take turns talking, but what each one has to say is not necessarily related at all to her partner's. Consider the following preschoolers' "conversation":

J: They wiggle sideways when they kiss.
C: (Vaguely) What?
J: My bunny slippers. They are brown and red and sort of yellow and white.
C: I have a piece of sugar in a red piece of paper. I'm gonna eat it but maybe it's for a horse.
J: We bought them. My mommy did. We couldn't find the old ones.
C: Do you like sugar? I do and so do horses.
J: I play with my bunnies. They are real. We play in the woods.
C: I guess I'll eat my sugar at lunch time. I can get more for the horses. Besides, I don't have no horses now. (Stone & Church, 1969, p. 282)

Each child keeps up a running monologue, with unheeded but accepted interruptions.

associative play
play that includes sharing of materials but not extensive interaction

group or cooperative play
play among children who are working together and sharing a theme or topic in conversation

In **associative play**, 3-year-olds begin to share toys, crayons, paper, and other materials, but they do not really interact extensively. Each child has his own task or slot. Sallie, Carlos, and Gina may play "make dinner in the kitchen," with pots and pans and one large wad of clay at the center of the table. But each child is concentrating only on her or his own "dish."

Among 4-year-olds, **group**, or **cooperative**, **play** emerges. Children actually work together now, building a house of blocks, passing materials back and forth and sharing a theme or topic in their conversations. Here, preschoolers share an imaginary train ride to New York.

Four-year-old Alfred . . . started to build what looked like a train. He set five blocks in a long row on the floor. At one end he put two blocks on top of each other and sat on them. Danny had just come in and walked over to Alfred:

Danny: "Is that a bridge?"
Alfred: "No, it's a train."
"Where's it going?" Danny asked.
"To New York," replied Alfred. "I'm the engineer. I build trains."
"I'm conductor. I drive the train," boasted Danny.
Alfred (impatiently): "No, no. I'm the engineer. I made it."
Danny: "What can I do?"
Alfred: "You collect the tickets."
Danny: "What tickets?"
Alfred: "The ones the passengers give you . . . (out loud):
"Who wants to ride on the train? . . . All ab-o-ard . . . All ab-o-ard. Train going. Woo . . . woo . . . It goes so fast."
Harry came into the room and ran over to the train.
Harry: "I want to get on." Using a small block as a telephone, he yelled, "Hello, hello. What's wrong with you? We're leaving and we gotta have food. Bring hundreds of boxes. . . . Right away, you hear?" He slammed the telephone down.
Alfred: "We got a flat. I'll fix it. Got to fix it now."

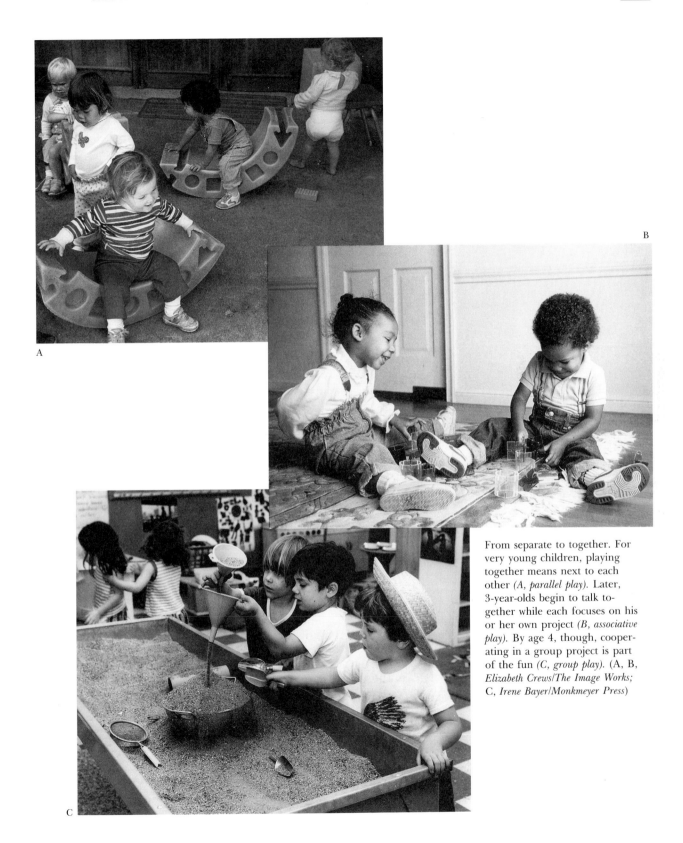

From separate to together. For very young children, playing together means next to each other *(A, parallel play)*. Later, 3-year-olds begin to talk together while each focuses on his or her own project *(B, associative play)*. By age 4, though, cooperating in a group project is part of the fun *(C, group play)*. (A, B, *Elizabeth Crews/The Image Works;* C, *Irene Bayer/Monkmeyer Press)*

With swaggering pretentiousness he removed one of the blocks from the line and turned it upside down and replaced it. Then he got back on the two blocks. (Cohen, Stern, & Balaban, 1983, pp. 74–75)*

All three children have accepted the blocks as a train and with little conflict have accepted one another's roles in the whole scheme as well. They are sharing fantasies, rules, *and* materials and improvising incidents, accidents, and conversations as they go. Note again how the capacity for symbolic thought fuels their play and propels their "train" forward.

The shift from playing alone to playing with others happens gradually (Parten, 1932), and children continue to play in all three ways throughout the preschool years (Barnes, 1971; Hartup, 1983; Smith, 1975). Four- and five-year-olds in a group, for example, may at different intervals pull out to play by themselves for a while alongside the rest of the children; then they rejoin the others, resuming group play again. Preschoolers may return to solitary or parallel kinds of play to get a break from the demands of true interaction, which they are only just learning to initiate and to maintain.

THE FORM AND CONTENT OF PLAY

functional play
play that involves simple, repetitive muscular activities

A 2½-year-old runs around the room while two others each roll their own toy car back and forth. A 3-year-old kneads a ball of clay without making anything. These activities are examples of **functional play**—simple, repetitive muscular activities that children do with or without objects. It is the least mature kind of play and declines as children develop (Rubin et al., 1983).

constructive play
play that manipulates objects to construct or create

By 4, 5, and 6 years, children spend about half of their playtime at **constructive play**, manipulating objects to construct or create something (Hetherington et al., 1979; Rubin et al., 1978, 1983). Playing with Legos, doing puzzles, and building with blocks enhance new physical and cognitive skills. As they work at and complete their projects, preschoolers gain a sense of achievement and mastery. And when they work together, building a castle or painting a mural, for example, children develop their social skills as well.

In Chapter 6 we saw that, by age 2, children begin to pretend. A block becomes a building tool, a telephone, a doll's bed. Now, the ability to pretend explodes, and preschoolers spend more and more of their playtime play-acting. In **dramatic** or **pretense play**, fantasy reigns, as they act out the parts of real people and imaginary characters. Typically, the roles they assume reflect their growing interest in society's roles, including sex roles, as well as their personal needs and concerns.

dramatic or pretense play
play in which children act out roles

Dramatic play often involves standard plots that children learn from daily life—cooking in the kitchen, going to the doctor, grocery shopping, attending a birthday party. Preschoolers' scenarios also draw heavily on the TV shows and movies they see. Usually these scenarios are stereotyped as well, involving heroes and villains, cars, trains, space stations, mommies and daddies and babies. Children take the parts of Flash and Superman; Lassie, Tim, and

---

*Reprinted by permission of the publisher from Cohen, Dorothy; Stern, Virginia; Balaban, Nancy, *Observing and Recording the Behavior of Young Children* (New York: Teachers College Press, © 1958, 1978, 1983 by Teachers College, Columbia University. All rights reserved.), pp. 74–75.

As they build and create, children are also strengthening their cognitive skills and feelings of mastery. *(Wayne Miller/ Magnum Photos)*

Tim's parents; Big Bird and Cookie Monster; Darth Vader and Luke Skywalker; and they enact fights, rescues, chases, flights, tracking down the bad guys, and rescuing the good.

From age 4 on, planning usually precedes the action, as parts and props are assigned and defined: "You be the prisoner and I'll be Superman." "This box is the space station" (Fein, 1979; Matthews, 1978; Rubin et al., 1983). Sometimes, as in the imaginary train ride, they perform as they plan; improvising their way through and changing plots and characters as the mood strikes them:

> "I'm the vampire. You're Batman. You're the monster. I'm the Green Slime. I'm the Hulk. Pretend I killed you. No, you be the Green Slime. Pretend you killed my brother." (Paley, 1984, pp. 80–81)

Adults sometimes miss the point of such a conversation, which can go on for some time. They can't understand why their kids take so long planning—it seems like "talking but not doing." But play planning is a very significant cognitive activity, a way of directing and monitoring oneself in relation to others. The talking and planning can be as important as the action itself.

Pretend play is not just an arena for safely acting out fantasies; it lets children express their developing sense of self as well. In the doll corner, it's all right to be the baby *and* the grown-up, cared for *and* autonomous. You can see how much such role playing can help a child work through conflicts between the need for protection and safety and the need for separation and independence. Solidifying their identity is another very important function of dramatic play. As seen earlier, preschoolers' play is also typically gender-bound. Boys play the superheroes, girls are the nurturers at the home front. It may sound paradoxical, but it seems to be true that acting out male and female stereotypes helps young children know who they are, providing a firm basis for growth, not necessarily as carbon copies of Mom and Dad, but as unique individuals.

Individual differences in style

In play, as in every other aspect of development, group patterns don't describe every child. At play, children cope with their fears and express their wishes, but they also seem to be expressing their own basic styles (Shotwell, Wolf, & Gardner, 1979; Wolf & Grollman, 1982). Some are *patterners*: Their play is tied to the properties of the materials they are using. In the sandbox, they dig and mound; at the clay table, they pound and shape. Other children prefer stories and social interaction, using play materials as props. These are the *dramatists*. In the sandbox, trucks can sprout wings and fly over roads, clay is shaped into cookies and fed to a doll. (See Figure 10-1.)

By age 2, children show their preference for one style or the other, and by 3 years, most will show both styles, although they continue to prefer one or the other. Neither style is better; they are just different. The distinction may even persist into adulthood, although we don't know this yet. Do children with different play styles have different personality styles as well? Future research may have some answers.

Playfulness

Besides having different play styles, some children are also just more playful than others. Every day care center or preschool has its "live wires"—the children who are everywhere, do everything, and make everybody else feel happy because of their own positive outlook (Singer & Singer, 1978; Singer, Singer, & Sherrod, 1980). Playful children are more verbal than others and more likely to engage in social and imaginative play.

Parents, teachers, and others who care for children can foster playfulness by acknowledging its importance and providing enough time, space, and materials. "Materials" is not a code word for expensive toys. With empty boxes, paper bags, cartons, and paper, children can travel to the moon or to the supermarket; they can play office or build a skyscraper. Unusual materials also delight: litter and glue, food coloring and water or a plain dough made from flour and salt, wood scraps, an old dryer or vacuum cleaner hose can spark hours of inventive play. Add to any of these an adult who is interested in what the child wants to do, who will listen and watch and admire—helping when needed—and you've created an environment in which a playful spirit can flourish.

(a) Patterner's Solution

(b) Dramatist's Solution

FIGURE 10-1
PATTERNERS' AND DRAMATISTS' SOLUTIONS TO THE CLASSIFICATION TASK: "PUT THINGS TOGETHER THAT GO TOGETHER."
(*Source:* From J. M. Shotwell, D. Wolf, & H. Gardner, "Exploring Early Symbolism: Style of Achievement," in B. Sutton-Smith, *Play and Learning*, 1979. Reprinted by permission of Johnson & Johnson Inc.

Summary

1. Children now are concerned with growing up in relation to their parents and adult society. By age 3, most children have grown past the defiance of the terrible twos and would rather be like their parents and other adults. While children want to do what adults do, often their parents must tell them that they cannot. From this conflict comes the crisis of *initiative versus guilt.*

2. During these years, children are learning their society's rules for male and female behavior, a process we call sex-role development. Until age 2 or 3, children are uncertain of their gender identity, that they are boys or girls. At about 4 or 5, they accept gender constancy, the fact that their sex will never change. Preschoolers are very bound, in their play and in their attitudes, to traditional sex stereotypes, the social expectations about how boys and girls should behave.

3. In the development of these differences, biology and experience are both at work. In psychoanalytic theory, sex-role development is linked to the child's identification with the same-sex parent. For cognitive theorists, sex-role development unfolds once gender constancy has been established. Children then sort the world into male and female categories: This is appropriate for my sex; this is *in*appropriate for my sex. Social learning theorists connect sex-role development to rewards and punishments for what adults consider sex-appropriate and sex-inappropriate behaviors.

4. From 2 to 6, children begin to develop the social skills that adults expect them to have. Both empathy and helping behaviors begin very early. Explanations for these prosocial behaviors come from attachment theory, cognitive theory, and the social learning perspective.

5. A child's level of aggression tends to be stable over time, and excessive aggression during childhood is the best predictor of emotional problems later in life. Cognitive theorists explain inappropriate aggression as a failure in interpretation: Children perceive hostility from someone when none was intended. Social learning theorists say that overly aggressive children model their behavior on overly aggressive adults, usually their parents. Attachment theory stresses the link between children's experiences in their families and the way they expect others to treat them.

6. Preschoolers choose their friends because of physical qualities and physical closeness. By age 5, children generally choose only same-sex friends. Popular children are more friendly and socially skilled than others, and disliked and rejected children engage in more disruptive, antisocial behaviors. Sociability seems to develop from a combination of inborn traits, secureness of attachment, and the degree of warmth or hostility in the child's family.

7. Play is an arena for social, emotional, and cognitive growth. Cognitive advances, such as growth in symbolic thinking, permit the fantasy play through which children express their emotional needs and conflicts.

8. Among 4-year-olds, group or cooperative play emerges. Children can share both conversations and projects now, even though they will still play alone or next to one another from time to time.

Key Terms

agency

androgens

associative play

castration anxiety

collective monologue

communion

constructive play

dramatic or pretense play

empathize

functional play

gender constancy

gender identity

group or cooperative play

hostile aggression

initiative versus guilt

instrumental aggression

modeling

parallel play

prosocial behavior

sex-role development

sex roles

sex stereotypes

Suggested Readings

Belsky, J., and Nezworski, T. (Eds.) (1988). *Clinical implications of attachment.* Hillsdale, NJ: Erlbaum. Understanding of emotional ties between young children and their parents is considered in a series of papers in terms of the psychological well-being of the young child and the development of behavioral disorders.

Boehm, A., and Weinberg, R. (1987). *The classroom observer: Developing observation skills in early childhood settings* (2nd ed.). New York: Columbia University Press. Two keen observers of children's behavior provide insight into how to systematically observe the behavior of young children.

Elkind, D. (1987). *Miseducation: Preschoolers at risk.* New York: Knopf. Are we pushing our children too hard to excel during the preschool years? An insightful observer of American childhood argues that we have lost sight of the process of developing by focusing too much on the products of development.

Winn, M. (1985). *The plug-in drug: Television, children, and the family.* New York: Penguin. What happens when children spend their mornings, afternoons, and evenings in front of the "idiot box"? In this book a journalist with particular interest in childhood and contemporary culture examines the extent to which children watch TV and what happens to them as a result.

The Social Context of Early Childhood

*I*n the doll corner of a preschool classroom, Rachel grabs a baby bottle and blanket and curls up on a mat. "I'm the baby taking my nap. You be the daddy," she tells Danny. At storytime, Rachel sits next to the teacher, as she has for the past month. We notice Richard playing with wooden figures of a man and a woman. "This is the mommy. She lives over here. This is the daddy. He lives over there," he says, moving the figures to separate places on the table. At another table, children are cutting "C" pictures from magazines to add to their alphabet books.

The teachers in this ethnically mixed, middle-class preschool are trained and licensed and the ratio of children to staff is 15 to 2. Lining the walls are shelves stocked with puzzles, books, pegboards, figures of animals, adults, and children, large and small wooden cars and trucks, and arts and crafts supplies. Children can pretend with blocks, dolls, or dress-up clothes. Daily, children hear a story, sing a song, share experiences.

Across town, in a poorer neighborhood, two untrained adults loosely supervise thirty 3-year-olds. The class seems to be run by the children themselves, and the feeling is chaotic. Toys and books are scant, and magazines are not for cutting.

While the first setting is the better one for children's emotional and cognitive development, any day care setting is only one of the contexts in a young child's life. Rachel is adjusting to a new baby in her family, and Richard's parents recently separated. Children in both classes go home to mothers and fathers with different parenting styles, with marriages, jobs, and lives that are more and less satisfying. Some of the children in each preschool will spend 4 hours at home watching television. Some will be greeted warmly by their mothers or another caring adult, and some will be rejected or even abused.

How do the contexts of family life, parenting styles, siblings, divorce, day care programs, and television affect young children's development? Does televised aggression lead to real aggression? Do *Sesame Street* and *Mister Rogers' Neighborhood* enhance development? How do parents' values and attitudes, economic status and marital happiness affect how they treat their children? We begin our study of the preschool child's social world with the most significant context in any child's life—the family.

The Family

What child hasn't watched *The Cosby Show* or *Family Ties*, or a host of other sitcoms dating back to *Father Knows Best*, and wished to live in such a family, where parents are always wise and understanding, where conflicts are easily solved, where good humor reigns? In real families, happy or not, life is far more complex, and although many parents would like to emulate the Huxtables, life doesn't always work out that way. How family life does work out for each child depends on many interacting factors: Are the parents well-off, poor, alcoholic, emotionally healthy, depressed, happily or unhappily married, divorced? How does the child's own temperament mesh with his or her parents and siblings? All these factors affect the essence of family life. As we

Explaining the rules and coping with the consequences of breaking them is the hallmark of parenting on television's *The Cosby Show. (NBC/Photofest)*

discuss the family's impact on young children, we'll consider a range of parenting styles, how children themselves influence the way they are treated, relations between siblings, and what can happen to the emotional lives of children when their parents divorce.

PARENTING STYLES

When Ruth finds her 3-year-old daughter trying to dress herself, but getting things a little bit backward, she praises the child's efforts and offers to help: "Let's see if we can just make this fit a little better, Maggie," and she helps her daughter finish dressing. Linda scolds her child for taking a long time to dress and for doing it "wrong": "What is taking you so long, Andy? I have been calling you for 5 minutes. What have you got on? You can't wear those clothes in October. Stop crying. We'll have to start all over and be late."

Developmentalists think of parenting styles in terms of two continuums, or pairs of opposite traits: accepting/rejecting and demanding/lenient (see Figure 11-1). At the accepting end of the first continuum are the parents, like Ruth, who tend to be warm and responsive toward their children, enjoying

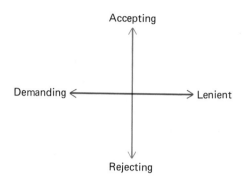

FIGURE 11-1
CONTINUUMS OF PARENTING
TRAITS

them and trying to see things from their perspective. At the other end of the continuum are those parents, like Linda, whose style tends to be both rejecting and critical. They show little pleasure in their children and are often insensitive to their emotional needs.

At one end of the second continuum—demanding/lenient—we find highly controlling parents who expect strict obedience to whatever decisions or rules they make. Such a parent might refuse her child's request for candy because "candy is bad for you." A more flexible parent with the same general attitude would make exceptions for occasional treats. At the other end of this continuum are the lenient parents who exercise little control, provide little guidance, and often yield to their child's demands. Based on these two major dimensions, Diana Baumrind, one of the leading researchers in the field of parenting styles, has identified three main patterns, or types of parents (Baumrind, 1967, 1971, 1980): authoritative, authoritarian, and permissive. How children feel about themselves and how they relate to other people is often strongly linked to the way their parents treat them at home. In the following scenario three types of parents are reacting to the same situation: It is time for their child to turn off the television and come to the table for dinner.

Authoritarian parents

Mother: Come to the table, John.
John: (No response.)
Mother: (Walks into the television room, switches off the TV, and announces in a loud voice.) Get to that table and sit down!
John: (Whining.) Turn it back on!
Mother: (Glaring at her son.) Get to that table now!

authoritarian parents
parents who have an absolute set of standards and expect unquestioning obedience

John's mother is behaving like an **authoritarian parent**. She values unquestioned obedience to her authority and does not allow discussion of the specific issue or situation. She sees no need to explain why she does what she does. Authoritarian parents have an absolute set of standards in mind with which they try to shape, control, and assess their child's behavior and attitudes. The child is expected to obey a request instantly, and if he resists, punishment usually follows. Because authoritarian parents anger easily and often, their children tend to worry about when the next "storm" will strike.

Authoritarian parents tend to assert their power through discipline, which can include physical punishment, threats of punishment, and physical handling such as grabbing the child by the arm. These parents may also punish by temporarily withdrawing affection. They may walk away from the child or refuse to talk (Hoffman, 1970). One of the real difficulties with this type of discipline is that if a child feels rejected in the first place, then any withdrawal of love will only reinforce that sense of rejection.

Children who are routinely treated in an authoritarian way tend to be moody, unhappy, fearful, withdrawn, unspontaneous, irritable, and indifferent to new experiences (Baumrind, 1967; Baumrind & Black, 1967). As they grow older, they show low self-esteem (Coopersmith, 1967). Recent work also suggests that children exposed to hostile and inconsistent parenting are more likely to be rejected by their preschool peers (Pettit, Dodge, & Brown, 1988).

Permissive parents

Mother: Dinner time, Laura. Turn off the TV.
Laura: (No response.)
Mother: (Pleading.) Come on, Laura; it's time to eat.
Laura: (No response.)
Mother: (Walks into the TV room.) Please, Laura; come sit down and have dinner.
Laura: I don't want to. I'm watching this show.
Mother: Oh, Laura! (Walks back to the table.)
Laura: (After 5 minutes, walks over to the dinner table, takes several bites of food.)
Mother: Sit down and eat with us.
Laura: Can't I take it into the other room?
Mother: (Sighing.) Oh, all right.

Permissive parents such as Laura's mother are generally noncontrolling and nonthreatening. They make few demands on their children and impose little discipline. Instead, children are allowed to regulate their own behavior and to make their own decisions, consulting with their parents only if they choose to. Permissive parents are often warm, but many are cool and detached, if not downright uninvolved. Their children tend to interpret this behavior to mean that parents don't really care what they do.

Permissive rearing that is warm and uncontrolling may sound attractive, but it poses some problems for preschoolers. How can young children regulate their own behavior in a world that demands some degree of self-control if limits are rarely set for them? Too much "freedom to be" is inappropriate at this developmental level, and, in fact, Baumrind has found that permissively reared children tend to be impulsive and aggressive, lacking both self-reliance and self-control. In nursery school, children of permissive parents are low in both social responsibility and independence. But they are usually more cheerful than the conflicted and irritable children of authoritarian parents.

permissive parents
parents who are generally noncontrolling and nonthreatening, allowing children to regulate their own behavior

Authoritative parents

Mother: Gerry, it's dinner time. Turn off the TV please and come and sit down.

Gerry: (No response.)

Mother: (Enters TV room.) Gerry! What did I just ask you?

Gerry: To turn off the TV.

Mother: That's right. Do it now, please. We all want to eat together. You can tell us what you've been watching. Come on now. If we wait any longer the food will be cold.

Gerry: (Sits down at the table.)

authoritative parents
parents who set clear standards but legitimate their authority through warmth and explanation

Gerry's mother is behaving like an **authoritative parent** (Baumrind, 1967). She sets clear standards for her child and expects cooperation, but she is also willing to explain the reasons for her actions and requests: It's dinner time; we want to eat together; the food will get cold. Authoritative parents are also willing to listen to their child's feelings and opinions, as long as they are expressed appropriately. For example, a child who becomes angry when he has to stop what he's doing might be told, "I'll listen, but first you have to calm down. You can do it. I'm here; I'll wait." Authoritative parents will usually listen to reasonable requests and are open to some degree of negotiation. Had Gerry explained that she was watching a special show, her parents might have delayed dinner. The important distinction is that authori*tarian* parents expect complete obedience to their authority, whereas authori*tative* parents have authority because they explain their demands and treat their children warmly.

To discipline their children, authoritative parents rely primarily on reasoning, trying to make the child understand *why* they expect one kind of be-

Cleaning up isn't fun, but it's necessary. That's the message an authoritative parent gives to his child. An authoritarian parent might be angered by the mess, and a permissive parent might do or say nothing about it. (*Michal Heron/Woodfin Camp & Associates*)

havior and reject another. This kind of discipline, called **induction** (it *induces*, or brings about, understanding in the child), is especially effective over the long term. Consider this: Randy's mother scolds him angrily for grabbing Gina's train engine, leaving Randy feeling demeaned, defensive, and probably angry. Melinda's father, on the other hand, using an inductive approach, tries to determine *why* Melinda yanked the doll out of Julio's hands. He asks Melinda to imagine how *she* might feel if *her* doll were yanked away. If repeated consistently, the inductive approach can help to guide Melinda's future behavior. (See "Focus On" for a discussion of authoritative parenting with difficult children.)

induction
discipline involving use of reasoning to explain expectations of parent

Authoritative parents are both demanding *and* nurturing, and their children are socially competent, energetic, and friendly. Preschoolers with authoritative parents tend to approach new, even stressful situations with curiosity and interest. They show high levels of self-reliance, self-control, and cheerfulness (Baumrind, 1967). They also get along well with agemates (MacDonald & Parke, 1984; Pettit, Dodge, & Brown, 1988). Among older children, authoritative parenting fosters high self-esteem (Coopersmith, 1967).

Of course, even authoritative parents cannot always be at their best. Any parent can sometimes sound authoritarian or permissive, particularly when stressed. And there are times when an assertive, more authoritarian approach *is* called for—when children dart out into a busy street after a ball, for example, or in any way court danger (Kuczynski, 1984). These styles are *general types*, providing *guidelines* for both professionals and parents. These concepts can help psychologists in their work with children who are having emotional problems, and the guidelines can help parents understand the potential consequences of their own behavior.

Furthermore, the advantages of particular parenting styles may be linked to the larger community and cultural context in which the family lives. Authoritarian parenting, for example, offers some advantages to families living in a dangerous and threatening environment (Baumrind, 1972; Grusec & Lytton, 1988). In inner cities, where drugs and violence are part of daily life, the risks associated with encouraging children to explore and expect that the world is accepting may well be great. Indeed, it seems that the more unstructured and precarious the world outside the family is, the more advantageous is what might otherwise be regarded as excessive levels of parental control and structuring.

WHY DO PARENTS BEHAVE AS THEY DO?

If all parents had to do was to read about the consequences of different parenting styles, most would probably choose to be authoritative. Indeed, many how-to books have been written on the subject, and many parents have gained insights and techniques from them. But how parents behave doesn't always match the way they want to or ought to be. Instead, parenting styles come from *multiple determinants*, from a pattern of forces affecting every mother and father (Belsky, 1984) (see Figure 11-2). These forces include the parents' personalities and their satisfaction with marriage and work, each child's own temperament and behavior, and the social forces of class and culture.

FOCUS ON *Being Authoritative with a Difficult Child*

What happens when a parent takes an authoritative approach with a child, and the child still gives the parent a hard time? Even easygoing children can sometimes be trying; a child with a difficult temperament challenges parents to be even more creative in avoiding a battle of the wills.

Three-year-old Steven, after a day at the beach, has decided that he is *not* taking a bath. He refuses to undress or go near the tub. Instead of demanding that he comply, his father begins telling stories about bathtime when Steven was a baby: "Did you know that you always got the cat soaking wet when you splashed in the bath?" Or he might take a doll and begin washing it in the tub. After diverting Steven's attention, he quietly begins to help his son undress. Chances are that soon Steven is in the tub, his defiance forgotten.

But suppose Steven is not persuaded by these attempts at diversion and continues to kick and scream? His father gets him ready for the bath anyway, still accompanying the undressing with playful dialogue. "You didn't tell me a crocodile lived in your shoe!" Tickling is also a good bet. It's very hard for a child to cry while he's laughing. The point is not to escalate conflict but to diffuse it. It helps too to be practical. Is the child being difficult because it's late and he's tired? Wash the child and next time start the bath earlier. Wise parents try to be sensitive to their child's needs as well as to their own requirements as parents.

The key to handling the difficult child is staying calm and avoiding battles of the will. Reducing tension through humor and play helps the child to cooperate without "losing face." The beauty of this approach is that the child comes away feeling good about himself. Yelling at the child, saying he is "spoiled" or "bad" or "impossible" only makes matters worse. The child's behavior does not improve, and he ends up feeling bad about himself and angry at his mother or father. Using the authoritative approach, however, a parent can feel pleased that the job got done without a battle.

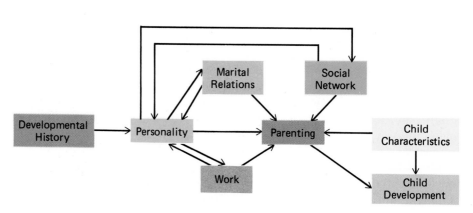

FIGURE 11-2
WHAT AFFECTS PARENTAL BEHAVIOR?
Parenting is the result of a complex system of interrelated influences. (*Source:* J. Belsky. [1984]. The determinants of parenting: A process model. *Child Development, 55*, 83–96. © The Society for Research in Child Development, Inc.)

Personal traits of parents

Many parents don't treat their children in the best Cliff Huxtable–authoritative way because they can't. Their personalities simply don't fit the role. Parents who are irritable, anxious, depressed, or low in self-esteem tend to be authoritarian with their children. Those with more positive self-images are more likely to be authoritative (Conger et al., 1984; Engfer & Schneewind, 1982; Stevens, 1988). Why is this so? One explanation for the link between personality and child-rearing has to do with the capacity to manage emotions and cope with stress. People struggling with their own problems may have little patience for a young child's behavior. Other parents actually *misinterpret* what their children do. Parents who think their children are willfully "out to get them" will react more hostilely to the same behavior than will parents who can separate themselves from their child's actions (Dix & Grusec, 1983).

Of course, how parents were treated as children influences their adult personalities and thus how they care for their own children (Ricks, 1985). We'll see later in this chapter that abused children often become abusing parents, but there are no absolutes about what kind of parents any of us may turn out to be. How we were raised will be one key factor. Another is the nature of our children.

The nature of the child

As we saw in Chapter 7, from birth on, children themselves influence the way their parents treat them. Easygoing, compliant children generally evoke warmth and build a comfortable relationship with most parents. They learn quickly that negotiating for what they want gets them further than demanding. In contrast, difficult children make many demands and often resist their parents' wishes. If parents respond harshly, the child becomes even more difficult (Grusec & Kuczynski, 1980; Mulhern & Passman, 1971, 1981). With both types of children, self-perpetuating cycles of the child's behavior and the

No parent can be playful all the time, but some find it easier than others. Satisfaction with one's marriage and career and personal traits of both parent and child strongly influence a parent's behavior. *(Dada Lynn/ Photo 20-20)*

parent's reaction can develop (see Figure 11-2). The goodness of fit between parent and child (see Chapter 7) influences the child's behavior and developing personality, which continues to affect parental response, and so on.

Parental relationships and work lives

We saw in Chapter 8 how the quality of a marriage, the birth of a baby, and the quality of parenting all affect one another. A good marital relationship encourages warm, affectionate, sensitive parenting. When marriages are emotionally supportive and harmonious, *both* mothers and fathers tend to be more nurturing and supportive toward their young children and to feel more competent as parents (Barber, 1987; Engfer, 1988). This works in reverse too: Parents in conflict—with themselves and with each other—are more likely to nag and scold their preschoolers (Brody, Pillegrini, & Sigel, 1986; Meyer, 1988). And just as in infancy, relationships outside the marriage affect parenting as well. Mothers who feel supported by friends and relatives use fewer authoritarian punishments, such as yelling and spanking. Mothers who are part of tightly knit social networks feel more competent and self-assured as parents. More isolated mothers, lacking strong support networks, are more apt to feel trapped and become irritable (Pascoe et al., 1981; Stevens, 1988).

Finally, life at work affects life at home (Bronfenbrenner & Crouter, 1982; Cotterell, 1986). For both mothers and fathers, satisfaction at work increases the possibility for harmony at home. Fathers who are deeply gratified by their work can carry that sense of well-being into their homes. These parents tend to reason with their children, relying less on severe punishment (Kemper & Reichler, 1976; McKinley, 1964). But when tension and unhappiness build at work, authoritarian discipline often increases at home. When mothers are satisfied with *their* work—and their husbands do not resent their working—mothers are more attentive to their children and, again, use more authoritative kinds of discipline than dissatisfied working mothers or those who work despite a husband's resentment (Hoffman, 1963; Stucky, McGhee, & Bell, 1982).

Interesting, too, is that values and disciplinary styles at home tend to reflect the values at the workplace. Working-class men whose jobs typically require compliance to authority tend to stress obedience at home, while parents who make their own decisions at work are more likely to encourage initiative and independence in their children (Bronfenbrenner & Crouter, 1982).

What we want to stress is that parenting is shaped by many factors: the parent's developmental history and personality, the child's behavior, and the social context of the parent's adult life. Positive factors, such as a satisfying marriage, can help to offset difficult ones, but the more weaknesses there are—a depressive personality, for example, a difficult child, little help from friends or relatives—the more likely it is that parenting will become authoritarian or even abusive (Belsky, 1984).

CHILD ABUSE AND NEGLECT

One of the horrible truths about life in the United States is that every year nearly 2 million children are abused or neglected (Children's Defense Fund, 1987). (See Figure 11-3.) Because they reflect only reported cases, these fig-

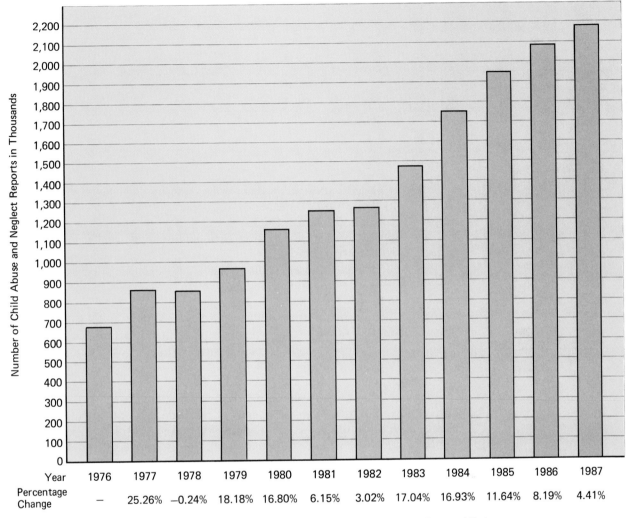

Year	1976	1977	1978	1979	1980	1981	1982	1983	1984	1985	1986	1987
Percentage Change	—	25.26%	−0.24%	18.18%	16.80%	6.15%	3.02%	17.04%	16.93%	11.64%	8.19%	4.41%

Child totals include the 50 states, District of Columbia, Puerto Rico, U.S. Virgin Islands, Guam and Marianas

ures are probably low. Like all family violence, abuse occurs behind locked doors, and many cases go unreported.

Abused children have been beaten, burned, wounded, sexually assaulted, and emotionally maltreated. Others have been neglected or abandoned, starved for emotional and/or physical attention, nurturance, or protection. Many accidents that injure or kill children stem from neglect, and parents can maltreat their children *whether or not they intend to*. In fact, most abusers have never intended any harm and are often shocked and frightened to realize what they have done.

The effects of abuse and neglect are deep and enduring, with the potential to damage every aspect of a young child's social and emotional development (Youngblade & Belsky, 1984). Abuse compromises children's feelings about their own worth as well as their ability to trust others. Abused infants

FIGURE 11-3
NATIONAL ESTIMATES OF CHILD ABUSE AND NEGLECT REPORTS
The number of actual child abuse *incidents* may not be increasing as rapidly as the graph indicates. *Reports* may have increased due to more consciousness in the general public as well as new laws that require certain professions (social workers, teachers, health care workers) to report suspected abuse. (*Source:* American Humane Association. [1989]. *Highlights of official aggregate child neglect and abuse reporting, 1987.* Reprinted with permission.)

and toddlers often have very insecure attachments to their parents (Critten-den, 1988; Lyons-Ruth et al., 1987). As older children they have trouble form-ing close ties with others; they tend to find new experiences threatening; and they are less curious and less ready to learn than other children (Aber & Allen, 1987; Hoffman-Plotkin & Twentyman, 1984). Other signs of abuse are over-aggressiveness, impulsivity, frequent temper tantrums, self-destructive behav-ior, and low self-esteem (Herrenkohl & Herrenkohl, 1981; Kaufman & Cic-chetti, 1989; Oates, Forrest, & Peacock, 1985; Reidy, 1977).

Causes of abuse

The horror of child abuse grows out of a web of factors: the parent's history and personality, the child's influence on the destructive relationship, and the impact of social and cultural forces on the parents.

A powerful force in an abusing parent's life is having grown up as an abused child (Brown & Daniels, 1968; Spinetta & Rigler, 1972; Steele & Pol-lack, 1968). Because abused children have insecure, fearful relations with their own parents, emotional and social growth suffers. Abusive parents have not learned how to form warm, secure relationships. Consequently, relations with other people, including friends, spouse, and eventually children suffer. If their only models of parenting were their own abusive parents, abusers have little to go on when it comes to being parents themselves. They often have unreasonably high expectations of their children, and when the expectations are not met, frustration and a sense of their own failure may lead to abuse.

But a history of child abuse does not *inevitably* lead parents to abuse their own children. In fact, one recent analysis indicated that only about one out of three abused children grows up to be a child abuser (Kaufman & Zigler, 1987). When parents who were poorly treated as children experience nurturing, car-ing relationships later on, they are much more likely to nurture rather than mistreat their own children (Crockenberg, 1987; Rutter & Quinton, 1984).

The child

Abusive parents often single out only one child for maltreatment, usually the one who needs the most support (Brown & Daniels, 1968; Milowe & Laurie, 1964). A high proportion of abused children were both premature and low-weight babies, those at great risk for physical and/or behavior problems (see Chapter 4) (Martin et al., 1974). Indeed, many were ill and had behavior problems before abuse began (Birrell & Birrell, 1969; Johnson and Morse, 1968; Sherrod et al., 1984). This suggests that premature, ill, or difficult chil-dren are at risk for abuse with certain kinds of parents. When other problems arise, the added stress of a sickly or irritable child can turn a vulnerable parent into an abuser.

Social and cultural factors

Chief among these external stresses is poverty. For people with little or no money saved, what frequently separates abusers from nonabusers is a job

(Light, 1973; Steinberg et al., 1981). People with too little money usually have too little space as well, and cramped living conditions only add to stress. Data from a recent national study of child abuse and neglect reveals that in 1986 children from families with incomes below $15,000 were much more likely to be maltreated than those above this level. Among these low-income children, the overall rate of maltreatment was more than five times greater than for those in households with incomes greater than $15,000 (Sedlack, 1989).

Poverty also increases the risk of drug and alcohol dependency, and substance abusers often become child abusers. Poverty is associated too with a low level of education and with teenage parents—two more elements in the abuser profile. And recall from Chapter 4 that teenage mothers are also at high risk for bearing low-birth-weight babies, the kind of babies that add stress to an already stressful situation.

Another pressure increases the stress on potential abusers: social isolation. Raising a child is both physically and emotionally demanding, and when a parent who is already at risk for becoming an abuser lacks the support of friends or relatives, the danger increases (Garbarino & Sherman, 1980). And if abuse begins, no one really knows what is going on in a "loner" family, so intervention is unlikely.

Finally, some contend that U.S. culture itself tacitly contributes to child abuse. Not only are we a violent society, but we revere both privacy and personal freedom, regarding as sacred a family's right to rear their children as they wish. Child-rearing practices in the United States contrast sharply with those of other nations. In China, for example, children are rarely punished physically (Kessen, 1979). And in Sweden, it is *illegal* to spank, hit, or otherwise physically punish children. But in this country, where disputes are often settled with violence, where children are regarded as solely their parents' responsibility or property, where many still believe that "sparing the rod spoils the child," where spanking is an accepted means of discipline, child abuse can grow in silence.

Clearly, there is no single cause of child abuse. It is a tragedy spawned by causes that are intertwined and cumulative: the parents' experiences and personality, social factors, and the abused child's own characteristics. Consider the case of a parent named Robert. Abused as a child, he may be predisposed toward maltreating his own children. But if he has a strong marriage, a secure and satisfying job, and relatively easy-to-raise children, then he will probably not be an abusing parent. But if Robert were to lose his job and have difficulty in his marriage, he might also begin to vent his frustration and irritability on his children. A spanking could become a beating. In other words, abuse stems from a mosaic of so-called risk factors. The more risk factors there are in a family, the greater the likelihood of abuse.

Intervention: Prevention and treatment

Preventing child abuse is the best kind of intervention. One successful program focused on the needs of parents at highest risk for abusing their children—poor, single, teenage mothers (Olds, 1985). During visits to a group of teenage mothers both before and after pregnancy, a nurse taught the women about infant development, helped them to develop stronger ties to their friends and relatives, and provided a link between the family and social service agencies. Most important, the nurse emphasized the women's strengths, thus enhancing their self-esteem. After 2 years, only 4 percent of the mothers had maltreated their children, compared to almost 20 percent for a control group that had not received such help. Other research suggests that when parents can turn to other parents and counselors for support with child-rearing and for their own emotional problems, abuse decreases (Powell, 1980).

SIBLING RELATIONSHIPS

> Six-year-old Sally is talking about her sister Annie. "She's nice . . . sometimes nice. It's good to have a sister, because you can play with her. . . . I do have lots of friends but my best friend is Annie." Another child, Rachel, began her "autobiography" with a list of dislikes: "Violence, eggplant and my brother." (Dunn, 1985, p. 1)

Between these extremes lies the emotion that may best describe the way brothers and sisters feel toward each other: *ambivalence*. Siblings are rivals and opponents, pals and helpmates (Dunn, 1983). Older children, despite their complaints, often offer comfort and security to their younger siblings. Many even act as teachers (Dunn, 1985; Stewart, 1983). In fact, explaining things to younger brothers and sisters is a form of cognitive stimulation for older siblings that may advance the intellectual development of some first-born children (Zajonc & Markus, 1975). Preschoolers who are close in age tend to spend a lot of time in fantasy play, a stimulus for each child's social and cognitive development (Dale, 1982).

How siblings feel about each other, at first, has a lot to do with their parents, specifically with how the older sibling has been prepared for the younger one's arrival, and how he or she is treated after the baby's birth. A

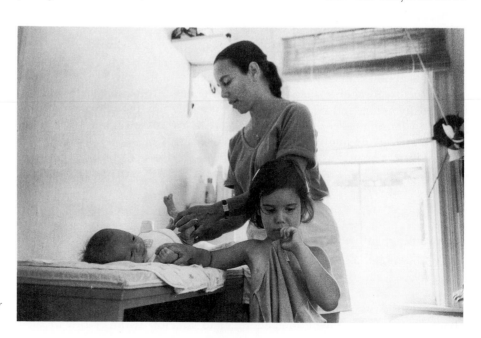

Helping with the baby doesn't always spell togetherness. A first-born preschooler typically feels both affection and resentment toward a new brother or sister. *(Randy Matusow/Monkmeyer Press)*

new baby usually means that an older preschooler gets less attention from mother (Dunn & Kendrick, 1980). And typically, as attention drops resentment grows. Many children begin to misbehave, like the little boy who, on finding his mother absorbed in his little sister, ran outside and dropped a full line of drying laundry onto the mud (Dunn, 1985). Deliberate "naughtiness" often leads to confrontations between mother and child, increasing tension even more. Given the circumstances, the older child's anger and resentment are natural, even logical, and do not mean the child is "bad." Regression is natural too, and preschool siblings are likely to cry more, want more help, and seek greater closeness to mother and father (Feiring & Lewis, 1981).

As we saw in Chapter 7, parents can help older children (and ultimately themselves) by talking about and accepting the full range of the child's emotions. Children need to know that they cannot hurt the baby, but they also need reassurance that they are still loved and accepted. Helping an older child to understand the advantages of being a big sister or brother and to see that being older can mean special privileges—conversation, later bedtimes, special outings—can make a difference too. So will reinforcement of the older child's sensitivity and empathic feelings toward the baby—making sure, in other words, that the older child sees the baby as a person with similar feelings and needs. Parents can also find ways for the older child to share in taking care of the baby. Efforts like these can foster a positive sibling relationship, and family cohesiveness is likely to be strengthened as well (Dunn & Kendrick, 1982; Stilwell, 1983).

DIVORCE AND PRESCHOOLERS

As Figure 11-4 shows, over a million children are involved in a divorce each year. Many of them are under age 5. All children whose parents divorce are affected in some way, but preschoolers show the greatest signs of stress (Wallerstein & Kelly, 1980), probably because of their cognitive and emotional limitations. At this age, children cannot grasp the reasons behind a divorce, and like the child described below, they often blame themselves.

> Ginny is being very, very, good. She sits quietly at the nursery school book table "reading" the same book she read yesterday. And the day before. Anybody can see how good Ginny is, how quiet, how cooperative. If only her mommy and daddy could see her now, they might forgive her for drawing on the wall with her crayon and pouring Daddy's aftershave down the toilet. Then Daddy would come home. And Mommy wouldn't leave her here forever every morning. . . . No one will ever know how bad, how *very* bad, she really is.

> There is no way to convince Ginny that her parents' separation had nothing to do with her. She knows she caused it. It is her terrible secret, and she knows that the only way she can make everything come out all right again is to be relentlessly good. (Francke, 1983, p. 75)

Young children often feel responsible for causing the separation, and at the same time they fantasize about a reconciliation, usually exaggerating the chances of this happening (Hetherington, 1979; Wallerstein & Kelly, 1975). Not only do preschool children believe they did something "bad" to make a

FIGURE 11-4
NUMBER OF DIVORCES AND CHILDREN INVOLVED IN DIVORCES: 1950 TO 1985
The annual number of divorces rose 15 percent between 1975 and 1985, following a large increase of 116 percent between 1965 and 1975. In recent years, about 1.1 million children have been involved annually in divorces. (*Source:* U.S. Department of Commerce, Bureau of the Census, *Statistical Abstract of the United States; Historical Statistics of the United States to 1975;* Current Population Reports, Series P-25, no. 311, 519, 917, and 1000. U.S. Department of Health and Human Services, National Center for Health Statistics, *Monthly Vital Statistics Report,* various years; *Vital Statistics of the United States,* various years.)

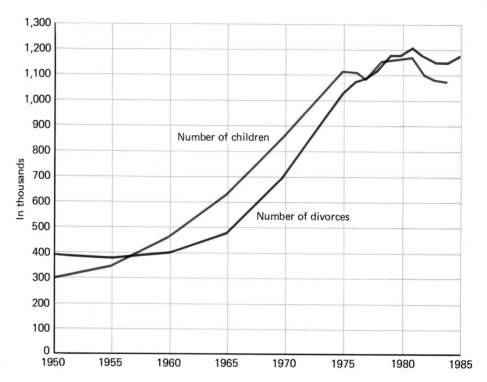

parent go away; they also assume that the parent who moves away no longer likes or loves them (Neal, 1983). Having been told that "Mommy and Daddy have stopped loving each other," it's easy for young children to assume that their parents can stop loving them too.

Preschool boys and girls show different reactions to divorce. A boy's reaction tends to be much "louder" and more visible than a girl's, though both may feel equally angry, guilty, and rejected. Young boys tend to react in one of two extreme ways. They may act out their anger, becoming impulsive, rebellious, demanding, and generally less self-controlled (Hetherington, Cox, & Cox, 1982; Santrock, 1977; Zill, 1985). These angry boys often seem to be taking on the very emotions and behavior they have been witnessing at home around the time of a separation or divorce—hostility, rage, aggressiveness. It has been found, incidentally, that angry parents are more likely to fight openly before a son than before a daughter (Hetherington, Cox, & Cox, 1982).

At the other extreme, young boys whose parents divorce may become much more dependent and seem less "masculine"—the "Mama's boy" syndrome (Hetherington, Cox, & Cox, 1978). The risk for this is greatest among boys younger than 5. After that time, sex-role identification with the father is usually established. But if a mother encourages independent behavior in her young son and expresses positive attitudes toward her ex-husband and toward males in general, her son will not be likely to show any major sex-role differences from his peers (Hetherington, Cox, & Cox, 1978). Preschool girls seem to adjust better and more quickly to the changes and stresses following divorce. We'll see in Chapter 14 that, among girls, developmental effects often show up much later, during adolescence.

Interestingly, the negative effects of divorce may result not from the parents' separation itself but from the breakdown in effective parenting that generally accompanies the separation (Hess & Camera, 1979; Hetherington, 1979; Long & Forehand, 1987). Generally, the greater the hostility involved in the breakup of a marriage, the poorer the parenting (Raschke & Raschke, 1979; Wallerstein & Kelly, 1980). If relations between parents improve after the divorce, children will benefit (Hetherington, 1979). Living with warring parents and a high level of tension is very difficult for young children, and a mother or father who feels relieved and freed by the end of any unhappy marriage may be more able to be a loving, effective parent.

THE SINGLE PARENT

In discussing the effects of divorce, we are talking about the prospects of a young child's life with a single parent. There has been a steady rise in the number of single-parent families, and as Table 11-1 shows, in 1986 one-fifth of white families, over half of all black families, and close to one-third of all Hispanic families were headed by single parents. How do single parents fare, and how does this family arrangement affect their sons and daughters? The answers are extremely complex. The degree of anger about the divorce and toward the ex-spouse will affect postdivorce parenting, as will depression, guilt, and a sense of being overwhelmed and overburdened. Financial pressures will make a big difference. A single parent struggling to make ends meet will have a harder time than one who is financially secure. The availability and quality of support from friends and relatives play roles as well (Hetherington, 1979; Bane, 1976). Many single parents have found that support groups can help them regain their footing and their self-esteem and thus help them to be more responsive to their preschoolers (Cochram & Henderson, 1985).

The sex of the child and single parent may also make a difference. Some research indicates that boys may do better with fathers and girls with mothers (Santrock, Warshak, & Elliot, 1982; Warshak & Santrock, 1983), although this is not always the case. In about 90 percent of all divorces, the mother is given **custody** (care or guardianship) of the child (Spanier & Glick, 1981). Although early research suggested that **joint custody** (both parents share equal respon-

custody
legal care or guardianship of children

joint custody
both parents sharing legal guardianship of their children equally

---

TABLE 11-1   TWO PARENTS, ONE PARENT: HOW MANY PARENTS ARE CHILDREN LIVING WITH?

	White			Black			Hispanic		
	1960	**1970**	**1986**	**1960**	**1970**	**1986**	**1960**	**1970**	**1986**
Two parents	91%	89%	80%	67%	58%	41%	(na)*	78%	66%
One parent	7	9	18	21	32	53	(na)	(na)	30

*(na) = not available

Source: U.S. Bureau of the Census (1987, December). Marital status and living arrangements: March 1986. *Current Population Reports: Population Characteristics*. Series P-20, No. 418. Washington, DC: U.S. Government Printing Office.

sibility) may be better for children than single-parent custody (Elmen, DeFrain, & Fricke, 1987), newer and better studies indicate that, to the extent that ex-spouses have difficulty resolving issues of how the child should be reared, joint custody may result in more costs than benefits (Kolata, 1988).

Day Care and Early Childhood Programs

In the television sitcoms of the 1950s and 1960s, Mom cheerfully vacuumed the rugs, baked the pies, folded the laundry, and ironed the shirts. In the days of *Leave It to Beaver*, only 12 percent of women with preschool children worked outside the home. By 1975, the figure was nearly 40 percent, and in 1987, in the wake of rising divorce rates, a growing need for two incomes, and women's desires for careers, 57 percent of mothers with children under age 6 were employed (see Figure 11-5). Their children—millions of them—are in day care.

DAY CARE: OPTIONS AND LIMITATIONS

Any child-care arrangement that parents use when they are away from their children is day care. In 1985, almost half the preschoolers in day care were

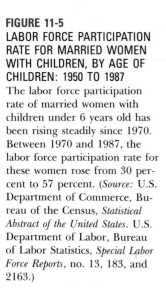

FIGURE 11-5
LABOR FORCE PARTICIPATION RATE FOR MARRIED WOMEN WITH CHILDREN, BY AGE OF CHILDREN: 1950 TO 1987
The labor force participation rate of married women with children under 6 years old has been rising steadily since 1970. Between 1970 and 1987, the labor force participation rate for these women rose from 30 percent to 57 percent. (*Source:* U.S. Department of Commerce, Bureau of the Census, *Statistical Abstract of the United States*. U.S. Department of Labor, Bureau of Labor Statistics, *Special Labor Force Reports*, no. 13, 183, and 2163.)

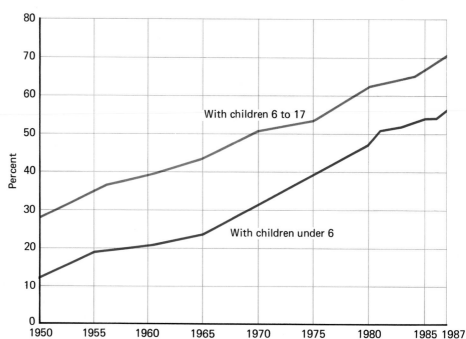

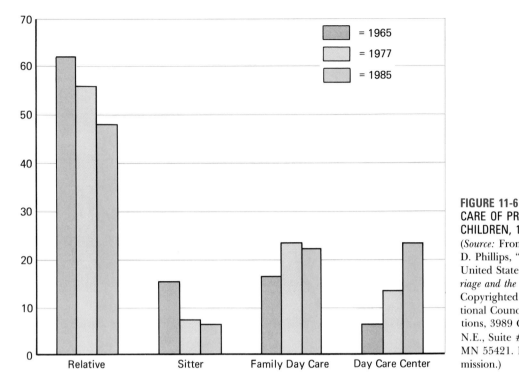

**FIGURE 11-6
CARE OF PRESCHOOL
CHILDREN, 1965–1985**
(*Source:* From S. Hofferth and D. Phillips, "Child Care in the United States," *Journal of Marriage and the Family, 49,* 1987. Copyrighted 1987 by the National Council on Family Relations, 3989 Central Avenue, N.E., Suite #550, Minneapolis, MN 55421. Reprinted by permission.)

supervised by relatives; 45 percent attended group care programs outside their own homes (see Fig. 11-6) (Hofferth & Phillips, 1987). These programs fall into two general types: family day care and center-based day care.

Family day care is provided in a private home or apartment, usually by a woman who is caring for her own young children at the same time. This kind of care has the advantage of flexible hours but the drawback of instability. If the caregiver decides to stop taking children in, parents must make new arrangements on very short notice. Most family day care homes in this country are unlicensed by the state, and most family caregivers have little or no training in child development. In many unlicensed day care homes, children spend considerable time wandering around aimlessly, feeling unhappy, and behaving aggressively (Carew, 1979). Of course, some family caregivers are very skilled, sensitive parents who enjoy young children and provide a stimulating, loving atmosphere. In that case, children are usually in good hands. Furthermore, in some communities family day care homes are administered by a social service agency which offers child care training, emotional support, and play materials to the caregivers. Children fare better in such supervised family day care homes than in unlicensed arrangements (Belsky, Steinberg, & Walker, 1982).

Center-based day care programs, located in church basements, community centers, and school classrooms, are licensed and regulated by the local government in some way. Two or more adults, some with child-care training, care for 13 or more children. While not as flexible in hours as family day care homes and certainly not "homelike," centers usually offer more stable care.

family day care
child care provided in a private home

center-based day care
child care licensed and regulated by local authority and located in a central facility

Almost half of all preschoolers in day care attend group care programs outside their homes. A small adult-to-child ratio and a variety of play materials can help children develop both social and cognitive skills. (*Joseph Schuyler/Stock, Boston*)

nursery schools
child care that offers planned social and cognitive experiences

compensatory education programs
community-based programs designed to meet needs of children at high risk of school failure

Head Start
federal program combining educational and social opportunities for 3- and 4-year-olds with social services for their low-income families

Caregivers who leave can be replaced, and most centers offer a variety of stimulating activities for at least part of the day. Over the last 20 years, the number of children in day care centers has increased steadily, surpassing family day care (see Fig. 11-6).

Nursery schools offer early social and cognitive experiences, mostly to middle- or upper-income children under 5, usually for 3 to 5 hours per day, 2 to 5 days a week. Actually, many nursery schools serve as day care centers as well, with some children attending for only part of the day and others staying all day. Nursery schools can be on college campuses, in churches, in homes, or in shopping centers. They are funded publicly and privately; routinely licensed; staffed by professionals or by parent volunteers. But most nursery schools share a common goal: helping children adjust to being away from their families as they develop both social and cognitive skills.

Compensatory education programs, often offered in church basements and community centers, are designed to serve the intellectual, emotional, and nutritional needs of children from poor families—children at high risk for failing in school. Best known among such programs is the federally mandated **Head Start** program, combining educational and social opportunities for 3- and 4-year-olds with social services for their low-income families.

Evaluating Head Start

Head Start was born as part of President Lyndon Johnson's "war on poverty," in the hope that early educational experiences could short-circuit the dire consequences of poverty on the lives of young children. Knowing how strongly home life impacts on development, Head Start planners encourage parents to continue their educations and train for better-paying jobs. The program offers classes too, where parents not only gain family skills but grow to feel more in control of their own lives. Even participating in their children's Head Start programs can help: Mothers who attended parents' night or volunteered in the classroom reported fewer psychological problems, greater feelings of mastery, and greater satisfaction with their lives at the end of a year's Head Start program than did mothers who participated less (Parker, Piotrkowski, & Peay, 1987).

While supporting Head Start, child developmentalists have been concerned that society is expecting too much from a program that began by offering disadvantaged preschoolers a few weeks of special experience in the summer. Developmental researchers warned that even programs that were extended to an entire year should not be expected to work educational miracles. As one expert observed, "We cannot inoculate children in one year against the ravages of a life of deprivation" (Zigler, 1987, p. 258). True enough, but even the gains made in just 1 year have been significant. In fact, the earliest experiments in compensatory preschool education for the economically disadvantaged have had the most long-lasting consequences. In particular, children who had been in these programs with specially trained, reasonably paid, and highly motivated teachers were, while in public school, less likely to require special education services, less likely to have to repeat a grade, and more likely as high school students to express pride in their accomplishments than agemates who did not attend these early compensatory education programs (Lazar & Darlington, 1982). Furthermore, children in these pioneer programs were less likely to become delinquent teenagers (Schweinhart & Weikart, 1980).

Troubling to developmentalists, though, is that children who attended Head Start after the "first wave" of programs have shown short-term intellectual gains which fall off over the long term (Brooks-Gunn & Schnur, 1988; McKey et al., 1985). Instead of using these findings as an excuse for criticizing Head Start, however, we should note the differences between current programs and the early models. Significantly, today's Head Start teachers are trained less, paid less, and given less for their classrooms than were teachers in the original program (Woodhead, 1988). "Closing the gap" in the cognitive development of economically advantaged and disadvantaged children requires much more than a year or two of educationally enriched preschool experience. Where Head Start excels is in supporting families, enabling parents to work, providing children with nutritious meals, and ensuring that children have periodic health checks. Benefits such as these suggest to many that Head Start should not be evaluated on the basis of intelligence scores alone. Particularly worrisome is that, because of budget limitations, the program reaches less than one-quarter of all eligible children (National Public Radio, 1989).

DAY CARE AND DEVELOPMENT

While Head Start children have been studied for almost two decades now, we are just beginning to examine the effects of other kinds of day care on the general population. The question at its simplest is "What is all this nonparental child care doing to the children?" Answering this question is difficult, for reasons similar to those relating to infant day care. Children are not randomly assigned by an experimenter to day care; they attend a family day care home or day care center or nursery school because of their parents' decisions. And parents who use day care and those who do not differ from one another in many ways, as do families that choose one kind of child care arrangement over another (Phillips & Howes, 1987). As we saw in Chapter 8, it is difficult to know whether differences in the behavioral development of day care children and those reared entirely at home result from their day care experiences or from the differences between their families. Nevertheless, a comprehensive review of research on early childhood programming has led to some general observations about the behavior patterns of children in day care (Clarke-Stewart & Fein, 1983).

Social development

When a reasonably high quality of care is provided, early childhood programs seem to enhance social development. Children attending these programs are more self-confident, outgoing, independent, assertive, and knowledgeable about the social world than are non-day care children (Clarke-Stewart & Fein, 1983). But day care children also tend to be less polite, less agreeable, less respectful, and, according to some research, louder, more aggressive, and bossier (Belsky, Steinberg, & Walker, 1982).

While family differences may influence these patterns, day care itself must also play a part. One hypothesis suggests that experience with peers leads to social competence because peers offer models for imitation as well as partners for competition and cooperation (Abramovitch & Grusec, 1978; Moely, Skarin, & Weil, 1979). In group care, children can become Darth Vader or Luke Skywalker; mother, father, or baby. They can nurture friendships and learn about fighting. When emotions run high, a teacher or other adult can offer guidance. And this guidance, say some researchers, partly explains some of the differences between children in group care and those who are not.

Teachers and other adults in early child care programs tend to be less authoritarian than mothers or other home caregivers (Hess, Price, Dickson, & Conroy, 1981). Teachers studied have been more moderate and flexible, valuing self-direction and independence. Mothers were more restrictive and demanding, valuing politeness more than personal initiative. In short, teachers' more relaxed supportive authoritative style may foster social competence in ways that mothers may not.

Cognitive development

Although there has been some evidence that children who have attended early childhood programs are likely to score higher on intelligence tests than agemates without that experience, at least up to age 5, there is actually very little cognitive difference between children with and without day care experience (Belsky, Steinberg, & Walker, 1982). When cognitive gains do appear, children have been directly stimulated by teachers and caregivers both through lessons and "guided play." Children in such programs often have advanced language abilities and know more about the physical world and social roles (Clarke-Stewart & Fein, 1983).

Health

Compared to young children reared at home, preschoolers in day care run a higher risk of sickness because they are exposed to so many other children (Haskins & Kotch, 1985). Specifically, day care children have more gastrointestinal illnesses, colds, other minor respiratory infections, and ear infections. Over the years, though, day care children may get *fewer* respiratory infections than those who stay at home. Getting sick when young may immunize them against such illnesses later on (Shannon, 1987).

QUALITY CARE

The quality of day care is marked by many of the same characteristics that define quality parenting: sensitivity, emotional support, and adequate physical and mental stimulation. Quality can be enhanced when caregivers have had some training in child development. In group care, whether in a family home or a center, both group size and the child:caregiver ratio are crucial. When groups exceed 15 to 18, and the child:caregiver ratio is more than 6 to 1 for very young children, or 10 to 1 for older preschoolers, caregivers may spend more time managing the children than instructing, nurturing, and stimulating them. For the children, this means more time spent in aimless activities and in waiting. The situation is even worse if caregivers also lack training. Quality is undermined, and a child's development is not likely to be enhanced. But, when caregivers are well trained and group sizes are small, children's development *does* tend to be positively influenced, because their day-to-day experiences are emotionally adequate and intellectually engaging (Belsky, 1984; Phillips, McCartney, & Scarr, 1988; Travers & Ruopp, 1978).

Quality care, then, is the main factor in enhancing and reinforcing cognitive and social development. It seems to matter less *where* children are cared for or what type of care they're in than *how* they are cared for day to day. And this applies to the home and to parenting styles as much as to any out-of-home day care situations.

Finally, the way day care teachers treat children, the activities that fill a day, even the way children eat their lunch and go to the bathroom are all influenced by something that is all around us but often overlooked—culture. Seeking to learn how a society's values shape its day care and, in turn, its children, three researchers visited preschools and spoke with parents and educators in China, Japan, and the United States (Tobin, Wu, & Davidson, 1989). Some of what they found appears in "Focus On."

Preschool and Culture in the United States, Japan, and China

In the typical American preschool, the teacher structures the day, and group time includes stories and songs, but otherwise, children rarely do the same thing at the same time. Teachers usually prefer variety and choice to regimentation. Lunch is noisy, and free play occupies a good part of the day. When asked in a questionnaire, "What is the most important reason for a society to have preschools?" American respondents gave as their top answer, "to make young children more independent and self-reliant." Indeed, in the preschool observed by Joseph Tobin and his colleagues, children do what appeals to them, using a variety of materials (Tobin, Wu, & Davidson, 1989).

Many early childhood educators assume that this is how all preschools should be, but such beliefs, like the schools themselves, are based on the values and assumptions of American culture—individuality and autonomy, for example. Elsewhere, though, where the values are different, so are the preschools (Figure 11-7).

At a preschool in Kyoto, Japan, 28 4-year-olds do a workbook project for about 30 minutes. "Throughout this session there is much laughing, talking, and even a bit of playful fighting among tablemates. [The teacher] makes no attempt to stop them but forges ahead with the task at hand." Later in the morning, after plenty of active, noisy free play, the children sit down for lunch. In unison, they sing a thank-you song to their mothers, then begin eating, as noisily as they please, and at their own pace. During outdoor playtime, Midori complains to the teacher about Hiroki, who has been especially noisy and unruly for most of the day. With a pat on the back, the teacher encourages Midori to go back out and deal with the problem herself.

The teacher being observed did not refrain from disciplining or quieting the children out of inexperience or timidity. Instead, her approach reflects how strongly the Japanese value group membership. Teachers prefer to remain in the background, refusing to single out or isolate a disruptive child from the group, maintaining order by encouraging children to deal with their classmates' misbehavior themselves.

The Chinese also value group membership, but obedience to authority comes first. These values, too, are reflected in its preschools. A group of children in the Dong-feng (East Wind) kindergarten in southwest China are eating their lunch, silently. "Finish every bite," instructs their teacher. "Concentrate on your eating as much as you do on your studying. That's the correct way to eat." Later, another teacher praises a child for her serious expression and for sitting with her hands behind her back. Instilling order, controlling and regimenting, is the essence of the Chinese preschool teacher's role, a role described by the word *guan*, "to govern." Here, the teacher is a strong authority figure, and children are expected to obey.

For Chinese parents and educators, the role of the preschool is to instill respect for the "values of self-control, discipline, social harmony, and responsibility." And indeed, teachers tell children to work silently, to play group games, and to cheer for their team. Encouraging creativity is a low priority. Handing

FOCUS ON

(continued)

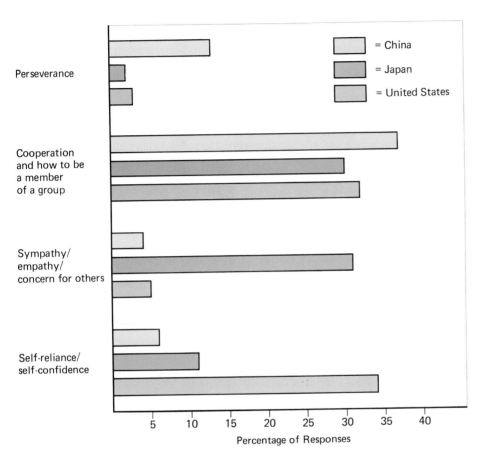

FIGURE 11-7
WHAT ARE THE MOST IMPORTANT THINGS FOR CHILDREN TO LEARN IN PRESCHOOL?
This question was asked of 300 Japanese, 240 Chinese, and 210 American preschool teachers, administrators, parents, and child-development specialists. Here are some of their first choices. (*Source:* Adapted from Joseph J. Tobin, David Y. H. Wu, and Dana H. Davidson, *Preschool in three cultures.* Reprinted by permission of Yale University Press.)

out wooden parquetry blocks, a teacher commands, ". . . [P]ay attention to the picture of the building and build it. . . . Begin. Do your best. Build according to order."

Regimentation extends even to physical needs. Explaining why preschoolers always go to the bathroom with their entire class of 26, one Chinese adult remarked, "Of course, if a child cannot wait, he is allowed to go to the bathroom when he needs to. But, as a matter of routine, it's good for children to learn to regulate their bodies and attune their rhythms to those of their classmates." Chinese preschoolers also learn to attune their rhythms to their teachers' plans. In a day that lasts from 8 A.M. until 6 P.M., the American observers noticed plenty of time for structured group activities and almost no time for free play and individuality. Despite these differences though, preschools in each of these cultures teach children how to get along in a group and encourage them to identify with "something larger than themselves and their families."

Television and Development

A 5-year-old and his father were watching a television show about labor unrest. "He was absolutely fascinated," reported the father. "I said to him, 'Would you like me to explain this to you?' and he said, 'No, Daddy, I'm just watching'" (Winn, 1985, p. 43). And just watching is what American 2- to 5-year-olds do for an average of 30 to 54 hours of every week (Winn, 1985). In fact, TV watching increases dramatically over the first 5 years of life, leveling off during the school-age years (Anderson et al., 1986). What are preschoolers getting from their viewing time, and what are they not getting because of it?

In the following pages we consider the many claims made for and against television's influence on young children. Does television violence cause aggression in preschoolers? Can television teach positive social skills? Does *Sesame Street* enhance the cognitive skills of disadvantaged preschoolers? Research has given us some unexpected answers to these questions.

TELEVISION AND SOCIAL EXPERIENCE

When television was introduced in the late 1940s, many thought it would bring families together. But the kind of togetherness families share while watching television is not always the kind that enhances development. As one observer noted 20 years ago:

> The primary danger of the television screen lies not so much in the behavior it produces—although there is danger there—as in the behavior it prevents: the talks, the games, the family festivities and arguments through which much of the child's learning takes place and through which his character is formed. Turning on the television set can turn off the process that transforms children into people. (Bronfenbrenner, 1970)

When families watch, they talk less and they play less. What they do more is argue—over what to watch, when to eat, when to go to bed (Maccoby, 1951; Robinson, 1971). In short, television seems to reduce the potential for positive communication while it increases tension in family life.

While parents rate babysitting high on the list of television's advantages (Steiner, 1963), "the tube" doesn't strike developmentalists as a good companion for young children. The issue is one of judgment and balance. A parent alone with several preschoolers can get some needed relief by turning on *Mister Rogers' Neighborhood* or *Sesame Street* in the late afternoon, and no child is going to be harmed by watching these shows after a day of playing. The trouble is that many young children are parked in front of the television for hours at a time, day after day. To develop socially and emotionally, children need to participate with others instead of just watching them. Shy children may even use television to avoid playing with others.

As a group, heavy television watchers tend to be passive, bashful, and more distractible (Murray, 1971). But which came first? Did television cause these behaviors? Probably not. Among the children in Murray's study, these traits appeared as early as age 3, suggesting that television viewing is a symptom rather than a cause of poor social adjustment. But such children can often benefit from other activities that will enhance their self-esteem and help to develop their social skills.

The other side of the issue is what children are *getting from* television. Specifically, how are preschoolers affected by television violence? Can television do anything positive for children? Do shows such as *Mister Rogers' Neighborhood* and *Sesame Street* enhance social, emotional, and cognitive growth, or do they promise more than they can deliver?

TELEVISION AND COGNITIVE DEVELOPMENT

Researcher Aletha Huston asked a 4-year-old to explain what a commercial was. The child looked at her and said, "Huh?" "Did you ever see Tony the Tiger?" continued Huston. "Oh, yes, I like him. He wants me to eat Frosted Flakes." "Is Tony real?" asked Huston. "Yes," said the child (Huston, 1983). Because the line between fantasy and reality is still so blurred, preschoolers are apt to believe whatever they see, real or not. And even when what they see is real, most young children understand and remember very little (Calvert & Watkins, 1979). In one study, preschoolers watched an informational program directed to their age group and were tested on the material both halfway through and at the end. In both cases, the majority of children understood only half of the tested information (Friedlander et al., 1974). In another study, after watching a 20-minute fairy tale on television, only 20 percent of 4-year-olds understood the story line (Leiter et al., 1978). One reason for this low rate of comprehension has to do with the cognitive abilities of preschoolers. As we saw in Chapter 9, young children can understand and remember typical

Even Big Bird needs a helping hand. Children get the most out of watching *Sesame Street* when an adult watches with them, reinforcing concepts presented on the show. *(Tony Freeman/ PhotoEdit)*

scripts and simple sequences, but complex sequences are mentally taxing. Young children tend to see the actions in a TV show as a series of separate unrelated events, not as connected parts of a story (Collins & Duncan, 1984). Generally, children cannot really follow a story line until they reach 8 or 9 (Collins & Duncan, 1984).

But what about *Sesame Street*, a show specifically designed by educators and psychologists? Early research studies claimed great cognitive gains for the preschoolers who watched the program (Ball & Bogatz, 1970, 1971), but a follow-up study found that the success had more to do with the design of the study than with the content of the show. The children who scored the greatest gains had been part of an experimental group that received special materials and special attention. People involved with the study visited these children in their homes, and parents in this group knew about the study and often watched with their children.

Another group in the original study received no special attention or materials. And in this group, those children who watched *Sesame Street* the *most* gained *less* in cognitive skills than lighter viewers. The only significant difference between the groups was adult participation. That, and not the show itself, seems to make the difference.

Children benefit cognitively from *Sesame Street*, then, when adults watch with them, reinforcing the concepts presented. (See "Issues & Options" on living with television.) Discussing things seen on the show can extend the child's knowledge, reinforce what is learned, and enhance rapport between parent and child.

TELEVISION AND AGGRESSION

Four-year-old Mary's parents are tiring of her newest game. Leaping from behind a door or chair, with a cry of "Ay ya!" she karate-chops their nearest body part. "That's how they do it on TV!" she explains. The link between television and aggression has been so thoroughly studied that few would dispute its strength (Parke & Slaby, 1983). Nearly two decades ago, the Surgeon General concluded that a causal link exists between television violence and aggressive behavior. And the shows with the highest levels of violence of *any category* of television programming are cartoons and weekend programs for children (Gerbner et al., 1979, 1980; Huston, 1983). On these shows, characters often achieve their goals through violent means (Larsen, Gray, & Fortis, 1968; Parke & Slaby, 1983). When TV violence meets preschool viewers, the results can be both subtle and explosive.

Not only do children who watch television violence become more aggressive, they also show a passive acceptance of other people's aggression (Parke & Slaby, 1983). This is exactly opposite to the message that preschoolers need to receive as they struggle to control their own aggression. Compounding this problem, boys watch more television violence than girls, and lower-class boys watch more than middle-class boys (Lyle & Hoffman, 1972; Stein & Friedrich, 1972 in Parke & Slaby, 1983). In short, children who may have the most trouble expressing their aggression nonviolently are watching the most television violence.

But even children *without* histories of highly aggressive behavior can become more aggressive after watching television violence (Huesmann, Lager-

Issues & OPTIONS

Living with Television

The issue is not really TV or not TV. Television's presence in the U.S. home is a given, but its negative influences need not be. Parents can monitor *what*, *when*, and *how much* TV their children watch. Early morning cartoons, for example, are not going to help a child make a calm transition to nursery school or day care. And when children watch TV before bedtime, they often want to stay up for more. It's likely, too, that action shows will keep their spirits high instead of calming them down. Reading aloud, singing, playing a soothing record or a quiet game in bed are usually preferable preludes to sleep. Parents can make occasional exceptions for special shows, but many battles can be avoided when parents decide in advance, not day by day, how much and what kind of TV programming children can watch.

Probably the best way to use TV with young children is as a catalyst—for humor, for sharing, for learning. When *Sesame Street* is "brought to you by the letter B," children can be B-detectives, searching for B-things and -pictures. When Mr. Rogers discusses sensitive topics such as the birth of a sibling, starting school, or the death of a relative, parents can then continue the discussion. By watching together, parents can help children distinguish between "TV reality" and the real world: between cartoon violence and human cruelty, between TV stereotypes and real people, between the lure of commercials and the necessity for limits.

Perhaps nowhere is the struggle between parents, children, and commercials clearer than in the cereal aisle of any supermarket. The child lights on Cocoa Crispies or Froot Loops or Count Chocula, resisting the less sweet Cheerios favored by her parent. The parent either buys peace with a box of Froot Loops, resists and endures a tantrum, or tosses boxes of Frosted Flakes and Cheerios into the cart and moves on.

While Madison Avenue gloats, many parents feel angry and manipulated. Almost 75 percent of the mothers of preschoolers interviewed in one study reported that their children were singing commercial jingles by 3 years of age (Levin, Petros, & Petrella, 1982), understandable when the average television-viewing child sees over 20,000 commercials each year (Adler, 1978). And the food advertised most frequently on commercials aimed at preschoolers is cereal. Unless they are told, preschoolers usually don't know that Tony the Tiger and Captain Crunch are there to sell. Adults can enlighten children by asking them what the cartoons are promoting. Even 3-year-olds can easily perceive commercial purposes when questioned in this way.

To study the effects of commercials, researchers observed preschoolers and their mothers in the supermarket. The children tried to influence their mothers' choices about once every 2 minutes, most frequently requesting cereals (Barcus, 1978). To learn more about the cause and effect between TV commercial viewing and behavior one researcher showed cartoons to 3- to 6-year-olds over a 4-week period (Galst, 1980). Between cartoons, commercials advertised sugary foods (including sweetened cereals, candy, cookies, fruit drinks, and soda) or foods without added sugar (apples, oranges, milk). In addition, child-oriented, public service announcements promoted fresh fruits and vegetables, dairy products, and other healthful foods, while discouraging a sugar-rich diet. An adult sitting with the children either remained silent after the commercial or commented on the advertised foods. Remarks stressed the poor nutritional value of sugared foods and their link to tooth decay and the healthfulness of nonsugared foods. After watching television each day, the children were allowed to choose a snack. Children who routinely wanted the least-sugared foods were those who saw the commercial with good food *and who also heard the adult praise the merits of the food*. The lesson for parents is clear: Praising healthful foods is more effective than criticizing the sugary kind.

Viewing violence leads to aggression, and aggressive children watch more television violence. Even a nonviolent scene can elicit violent fantasies in preschoolers who identify with aggressive characters. *(Rick Kopstein/Monkmeyer Press)*

spetz, & Eron, 1984). Nor does it matter whether they are watching at home or in a lab, cartoon violence or realistically portrayed violence (Bandura, 1965; Hartmann, 1969; Parke et al., 1977; Steuer et al., 1971). We know too that the relationship between aggression and television works two ways: viewing violence causes aggression, and aggressive children watch more television violence. And the more the child viewer believes that TV portrays life just like it is, identifies strongly with the aggressive characters in the show, and frequently has aggressive fantasies, the more this is true (Huesmann et al., 1984).

Given the weight of this evidence, and the major campaign against television violence that was mounted in the mid-1970s by both parent and professional groups, it is discouraging to report that "the amount of violence has changed little since 1967" (Huston, 1985). In part, this is because there has been no consensus on what exactly is to be regulated. Even commercials can spark aggression. Preschoolers behave more aggressively after watching highly charged commercials—with lots of action, quick pacing and changing images—than after seeing slower-paced ads (Greer, Pott, Wright, & Huston, 1982). Children are also more likely to *watch* fast-paced commercials, so there is no incentive for advertisers to slow them down. Imposing restrictions on producers or advertisers crosses the line from advocacy into censorship, raising serious First Amendment questions about free speech.

Nevertheless, some television executives have voluntarily reduced the violence on children's shows. Among preschoolers, one of the most popular cartoon characters is He-Man, a superhero who rescues the needy through a mixture of strength, cunning, and moral righteousness. In one episode, He-Man defended a deaf-mute man who was being persecuted because he seemed strange. Do messages about respect for individual differences and other prosocial themes influence young children? Can children learn cooperation, sensitivity, persistence from television?

TELEVISION AND PROSOCIAL BEHAVIOR

Aletha Huston, long involved in this area of research, described her study of *Mister Rodgers' Neighborhood*, a show aimed at furthering the social and emotional development of young children. "It stresses helping, sharing, sympathy, understanding feelings, persistence and the worth of each individual" (Huston, 1985, p. 4). Nursery school children who viewed episodes of the show subsequently did show greater cooperation, helpfulness, and willingness to work longer at a difficult task. But how long-lasting are these effects, and do they show up under some conditions more than others? Interestingly, the effects of watching prosocial programs are greatest in children from lower socioeconomic families, but they were not matched by a drop in aggressive behavior (Friedrich & Stein, 1973). Children in Head Start benefited the most when other aspects of the environment supported prosocial behaviors. The most prosocial interaction occurred when the class had play materials related to the show and when they acted out the program's themes with a teacher. So even the context within which children watch prosocial shows makes a difference. As to the duration of positive effects, neither dramatic nor lasting effects have been demonstrated.

Ultimately, to make a difference, quantity may count as much as quality. Television has the power to influence the social behavior of viewers in the direction of the content of the programs. If, on the one hand, prosocial helping and kindness appear frequently on television, children will think of this conduct as appropriate, normative behavior. But if antisocial behaviors and uncontrolled aggression are shown frequently, viewers will then consider this kind of action as the norm. This statement should not be surprising. Television networks earn billions of dollars each year because advertisers know that even 30-second exposures of their product, if seen enough times, will significantly influence viewers' behavior toward these products. The message is clear: Viewers learn from watching television and what they learn depends on what they watch (Rushton, 1979).

Summary

1. How families influence children depends on several interlocking factors, including parenting styles. Developmentalists define parenting styles via two continuums, or pairs of opposite traits: accepting/rejecting and demanding/lenient. Based on these two dimensions, Baumrind has identified three main types of parenting styles: authoritative, authoritarian, and permissive.

2. Authoritarian parents value unquestioned obedience and rarely discuss the reasons for their demands. They anger easily and discipline through punishment. Children of authoritarian parents tend to be moody, fearful, and withdrawn. As they grow older, they often have low self-esteem.

3. Permissive parents are noncontrolling and nonthreatening, making few demands and imposing little discipline. Children make their own decisions with little guidance and may feel that their parents don't care what they do. Preschoolers usually do not do well with so much freedom and may become impulsive and aggressive.

4. Authoritative parents set clear standards and explain the reasons for their requests. They listen to their child's opinions and are often willing to negotiate. Reasoning is their main tool for disciplining: They try to make the child understand *why* one kind of behavior is preferable to another. Preschoolers with authoritative parents approach new situations with curiosity. They are self-reliant and cheerful; as older children, they have high self-esteem.

5. Parenting styles are determined by a pattern of forces, including parents' personalities and their satisfaction with marriage and work; each child's own temperament and behavior; and the social forces of class and culture.

6. Child abuse, whether physical or emotional, compromises children's feelings about their own worth and their ability to trust others. Abused children are often overly aggressive and impulsive and have low self-esteem.

7. About one-third of abusing parents were abused as children. Generally, child abusers have not learned how to form warm, secure relationships. They may become abusive when their children do not meet their expectations. Premature, ill, or difficult children are at risk for abuse with vulnerable parents.

8. Social factors, such as poverty and the conditions associated with it, add considerable stress to potential abusers' lives, making them more likely to strike out. Social isolation is an added risk factor, as is U.S. culture itself, with its violence and reverence for privacy. Traits of the parent, the child, and society set the stage for abuse.

9. Successful prevention programs for poor, single teenage mothers teach them about infant development, help them form stronger ties to friends and offer links to social service agencies.

10. How siblings feel about each other has a lot to do with how the older child has been prepared for the younger one's birth and how she or he is treated afterward. If an older child feels ignored, misbehavior often follows.

11. Preschoolers often blame themselves when their parents divorce. Boys may act out their anger, becoming impulsive and demanding. Then, alternatively, they may become overly dependent and less masculine, especially if they are under 5 when their fathers leave. Girls seem to adjust more quickly but may develop problems during adolescence.

12. After divorce, parenting is affected by anger, depression, guilt, and a sense of being overwhelmed. Financial security and emotional support from family and friends can help relieve the pressures divorced parents feel.

13. Family day care, offered in a private home or apartment, offers flexibility but is often an unstable arrangement. Center-based day care programs are licensed and regulated by local governments in some way. Nursery schools offer more structured cognitive and social experiences, usually to middle- or upper-income children. Compensatory education programs serve the intellectual, emotional, and nutritional needs of children from poor families. One such program, Head Start, was very successful initially, when teachers were well-trained and well-paid. Today, because of budget limitations, the program reaches less than one-quarter of all eligible children.

14. Early childhood programs seem to enhance social development. That may reflect on the teachers and other adults in such programs, who tend to be more authoritative than parents of preschoolers or home caregivers. There is little cognitive difference between children with and without day care experience.

15. Both group size and child:caregiver ratio help to assure quality care. These things matter more than where children are cared for.

16. Television watching reduces the potential for positive communication while it increases tension in family life. Heavy viewing deprives preschoolers of experiences that could enhance their social and emotional growth. Educational shows such as *Sesame Street* stimulate cognitive development when adults watch with children and reinforce the concepts presented.

17. Children who watch television violence become more aggressive and show a passive acceptance of other people's aggression as well. The effects of watching prosocial behavior on television are greatest for children from low socioeconomic households, but they are not matched by a drop in aggression. Ultimately, seeing more prosocial behaviors on television may help children to think that kindness is more acceptable than uncontrolled aggression.

Key Terms

authoritarian parents
authoritative parents
center-based day care
compensatory education programs
custody
family day care

Head Start
induction
joint custody
nursery schools
permissive parents

Suggested Readings

Cherlin, A. (Ed.). (1988). *The changing American family and public policy.* Washington, DC: The Urban Institute Press. Demographers, sociologists, and economists examine changes that have occurred in the structure of the American family over the past several decades, evaluate the effectiveness of public policies to promote family well-being, and make suggestions with regard to unmet needs.

Cicchetti, D., and Carlson, V. (Eds.). (1989). *Child maltreatment: Theory and research on the causes and consequences of child abuse and neglect.* New York: Cambridge University Press. This handbook of research and theory on child maltreatment provides a state-of-the-art evaluation of what is known about the causes and consequences of child abuse and neglect. It also provides reports on interventions designed to prevent maltreatment before it occurs and to remediate its disastrous consequences once they have emerged.

Emery, R. (1989). *Marriage, divorce, and children's adjustment.* Beverly Hills, CA: Sage. A clinical psychologist with expertise in research on family conflict and law related to child custody critically examines what we know about the effects of divorce and marital conflict on children's psychological and behavioral development.

Phillips, D. (Ed.). (1987). *Quality in child care: What does research tell us?* Washington, DC: National Association for the Education of Young Children. In a series of original reports, state-of-the-art research on the conditions that foster positive child development during the preschool years is shared. Useful introductory and concluding chapters tie all the material together.

July 13

Dear Mom, Dad, Kenny, and Sammy,

I'm having a super time here. I learned how to snorkel today in one period. I like it a lot. The waterfront here is great. I even took a kayak out halfway across the lake!! I also went on a canoe and a catamaran. I've had 3 inter-camp games—2 soccer and 1 baseball. We lost 2 and won 1. Guess what? Last night we had camper talent night and Burke, Howe, and I won! We got a bannana [sic] split each! The kids are nice except for Chris, who I told you about in my last letter. He has an earring, he spits on people, he smokes, and he punches people when he gets bored. Please send more envelopes soon. All mine are stuck together. I miss you. Write soon! Give Sammy a hug, a kiss, rub the fur above his nose, and give him a piggy-back ride for me.

Love,
Eric [age 10]

FOUR

Middle Childhood

Physical and Cognitive Development in Middle Childhood

The elementary school years are a time of preparation, practice, and learning, as children hone skills they will use throughout life. Things as ordinary as driving a car, balancing a checkbook, or baking a cake are grounded in the physical and cognitive skills mastered during middle childhood. As strength and coordination rapidly mature, the 6-year-old who runs, skips, and throws can become a 10-year-old who cracks a bat, shoots a basketball, kicks a soccer ball, or cuts a figure eight. Maturing too on the playing fields are social skills and morality, as children learn that games have rules for taking turns, for competing, and for sharing. From children's play, social understanding and moral development grow.

Paralleling physical and social growth are major advances in thinking. The kindergarteners who can recognize a few words, count to 30, and write their names will read novels and write creative stories by age 8, and by age 11, some will even be solving for *x* in math lessons. The pace of these developing skills is astounding. In this chapter we consider first some aspects of physical growth and then examine cognitive changes, schooling, intelligence tests, and social cognition.

Physical Growth and Development

Unlike the rapid and striking physical changes that mark infancy and adolescence, growth during middle childhood is more gradual, and physical changes are more subtle. On average, school-age children grow about 2 or 2½ inches and gain about 4½ to 6 pounds per year (Lowrey, 1978). Still, this steady change means that by the start of junior high school, children are about twice as heavy as they were in the preschool years. But because they are also about a foot taller, they are generally much slimmer than preschoolers.

There is a true physical equality between the sexes during this period. Boys and girls weigh about the same and stand about as tall, and most school-age girls can run as fast, jump as high, and hit a ball as well as most school-age boys. Modern American society is slowly recognizing this equality by allowing both sexes to play together in sports such as soccer and Little League baseball, sports long reserved for boys only.

Like other aspects of development, physical growth in middle childhood reflects both biological and environmental differences. Some children are genetically destined to be bigger and stronger than others and to develop faster, but environmental factors, such as diet, hygiene, medical care, and opportunities to participate in sports can strongly influence physical development as well. In general, children who grow up in advantaged environments—children who get plenty of nourishing food, who are taken to the doctor when they are sick, who are encouraged to exercise and participate in sports—are likely to grow taller and stronger than children without these advantages.

Children like these first- and fifth-graders who grow up eating healthful foods are likely to grow taller and stronger than those whose diets are inadequate. *(Blair Seitz/Photo Researchers)*

EXERCISE AND DIET

On Saturday mornings, no matter what the weather outdoors, millions of school-age children sit indoors watching TV cartoons. In the days before television arrived, Saturday morning meant outdoor play. Without knowing it, children of this age were exercising. All in all, elementary school children report spending 16 hours a week watching television and only 5 hours a week on sports or other outdoor activities (Collins, 1984).

Besides influencing how much children move, television also affects what they eat. Commercials present a powerful message, and it isn't "eat your vegetables." Perhaps encouraged by commercials, many children eat diets high in fat, salt, and sugar. One study found that, typically, about one-third of a school-age child's diet consists of foods high in fat, salt, and sugar, and the children themselves often have high blood serum lipid levels, a condition related to the development of coronary artery disease later in life (Shonkoff, 1984).

Although schools can help children get the physical exercise they need, too often they don't. Only one out of every three school-age children participates in a daily program of physical exercise, and for adolescents, the number is sharply lower. Critics accuse school physical education programs of overemphasizing competitive sports, rewarding the star athletes while discouraging children with average abilities from participating in sports just for the fun of it. (See "Issues & Options.")

One reason to be concerned about the eating and exercise patterns of schoolchildren is that these patterns often persist into adulthood, sometimes with serious consequences. Sedentary adults with poor eating habits have much higher rates of obesity, heart disease, and related ailments than do those who exercise and eat a healthy diet. To help their children avoid future health

Issues & OPTIONS

Building Healthy Attitudes toward Athletics

Playing "pick-up" softball with their friends, a group of 10-year-olds isn't too fussy. Everyone plays. Rules are bent, clothes are casual, and adults are absent. Everyone seems to have a good time. Three strikes still make an out and three outs a half-inning, but the number of innings and the score are relatively unimportant. Often such games go on until parents call the players in for dinner or bed.

In contrast, an authorized Little League game looks very much like professional baseball in miniature. Dressed in uniforms, children concentrate fiercely as they seek the pitch or hit that will propel their team to glory. Adult coaches plot their strategy, sending the best hitters up in key situ-

Having fun often gets lost amid the pressure to do well in organized sports. Children do their best when coaches encourage more and criticize less. *(Susan Lapides/Design Conceptions)*

ations and leaving others on the bench. Parents look on, shouting encouragement for their team and sometimes contempt for the other guys. An official scoreboard keeps meticulous track of hits, runs, and errors. Everyone is aware of the score.

Certainly, some competitiveness is natural and healthy, and even sand-lot teams recognize that some children are more skilled than others. But organized sports for children accentuate the competitive element, often making less "naturally" athletic children feel that there is no point in playing. Even in gym classes, where everyone gets to play, the emphasis on winning may teach children who cannot win that playing is no fun and even that these children are

problems, parents need to take a firm but realistic approach. It is nearly impossible to prevent children from eating all junk food, but by selecting the snacks that are available at home, serving nutritious meals, limiting their own television viewing, and exercising themselves, parents can strongly influence their children's behavior.

For children from poor families, nutritional problems are caused as much by money as by motivation. Milk, meat, fresh fruits, and vegetables are expensive and therefore scarce in poor children's diets. In contrast, sources of carbohydrates (such as breads and rice) and fats (such as salt pork and other non-lean meat) are relatively inexpensive and are served frequently. The resulting diet—low in protein, vitamins, and minerals (particularly iron)—can have serious physical and mental consequences. Children who do not get enough milk are far more likely to have severe dental problems than those who get

Issues & OPTIONS

"born losers." Besides damaging self-esteem, this lesson also bodes ill for the adult health of these children, since exercise patterns from childhood seem to carry over into adulthood.

What can adults do to engage *all* youngsters—not just the obvious "stars"—in athletics? Most important, adults need to stress the fun of games and sports and play down the competitive element. A child should not have to tell his gleeful parent after the other team lost badly, "It's only a game, Mom." Downplaying competition means allowing all children to play organized games on an equal basis. "Benching" less competent players is counterproductive.

Second, in organizing children's athletics, adults must be aware of physical differences among children. Some children are naturally faster, taller, heavier,

or stronger than others the same age. Children who get a chance to compete in football or basketball against others of roughly the same size—regardless of age—are more likely to do well, take pleasure in playing, and continue in the sport.

Third, parents and children need to recognize that just as children have different intellectual and academic talents, they have different physical talents as well. Each child needs to find some physical activities at which he or she can succeed. A tall, thin child may get clobbered at football but do very well at basketball or track. A child with poor vision may have trouble hitting a tennis ball but enjoy swimming and diving. Boys and girls who are teased for being "runts" can put their size to work for them in gymnastics. This is not to say that children should only participate in sports in which

they are guaranteed success. Professional sports provide many examples of individuals "too short," "too light," or "too slow" to succeed who became stars. But unless children develop some feeling of physical competence, they are unlikely to stay involved in athletic activities at all, especially as adults.

Adults need to restore elementary school physical activity to its original purposes: to help children learn physical skills and improve coordination, develop leisure interests, increase their physical health, and learn to feel comfortable about their bodies. To achieve this goal, we must keep in mind the interaction between individual and environmental factors and treat children of modest athletic ability with just as much concern as we do their very athletically skilled peers.

---

sufficient calcium. Poor nutrition may also contribute to a variety of psychosocial and learning problems. Studies have found that severely malnourished children do not perform as well on intelligence tests as do children with adequate nutrition (Levitsky, 1979).

Poor nutrition may also mean low energy for learning. A child's brain needs two to three times more energy than an adult's brain (Smith, 1976). Recognizing this need, for many years U.S. schools have offered a nutritionally balanced hot lunch at minimal or no cost. In some areas, schools also offer breakfasts. Children who have a long history of severe malnutrition usually are behind their peers in academic achievement and score lower on IQ tests. These children may also have lower motivation for school tasks, however. It is very difficult to distinguish the physiological effects of malnutrition on school achievement from social and genetic factors (Pollitt, Garza, & Leibel, 1984).

CHILDHOOD OBESITY

obese
refers to those individuals whose weight is at least 20 percent more than normal for their age, height, and sex

Obesity is the most common single health problem among elementary schoolchildren, and it has increased sharply during the past 20 years. At least 5 percent of all schoolchildren are **obese**, meaning that they weigh at least 20 percent more than normal for their age, height, and sex. Because almost 50 percent of all obese adults were obese children, and because of the link between obesity and diabetes, hypertension, and heart disease in adulthood, health professionals are highly concerned about childhood obesity. In addition to future health problems, fat children face peer rejection. Frequently they are teased, passed over for team sports, and excluded from parties.

Many factors cause childhood obesity, including inheritance, lack of physical activity, and cultural eating patterns. Members of some ethnic groups, for example, admire plumpness in children and promote excessive eating by constantly offering food, but whatever is behind it, the major cause of obesity in both children and adults is overeating. A diet laden with junk foods coupled with inactivity is most likely to lead to obesity (Kolata, 1986).

Except in very rare cases involving medical disorders, childhood obesity can be treated by a program of healthful eating and increased exercise. But perhaps as important as changing obese children's diet and exercise habits is improving the way obese children feel about themselves. Controlling their own behavior, the key to successful weight reduction, is not easy. Neither is participating in sports when children see themselves as athletically inept. Parents and teachers need to help obese children feel competent (whether or not they lose weight), to praise weight-loss efforts, and to find substitutes for food as a reward.

Cognitive Development: Revolutionary Changes

It is no accident that universally children start school between ages 5 and 7—a time of remarkable changes in their abilities to think and learn. Indeed, the pace of these changes is so quick that some call it a "cognitive revolution."

What revolutionary changes occur? First, children are no longer fooled by appearances. If Daddy dresses up like Santa Claus, they know he is still Daddy. And if a row of cookies is spread out, children know the number hasn't changed. By age 7, children understand enduring identities. They have grasped *conservation* (discussed in Chapter 9). Now they can judge number, amount, mass, and other physical dimensions based on actual quantitative changes in the objects. Superficial changes in the way things look no longer fool them.

Second, children reason better about causation. They realize that just because two things happen at about the same time one does not necessarily cause the other. They can understand, for example, that rain does not cause thunder. But logical thinking is still limited. Children don't yet reason clearly about hypothetical situations, which is why Piaget called their thinking "concrete." Third, school-age children can classify objects based on several characteristics. They can understand how classes of things are related to each other, in the phylogenetic scale, for example. Preschoolers may not understand that insects and people are both animals or that plants and animals are both part of the larger set of living things. School-age children can reason about natural classes as well as arbitrary classes of shapes or different colors, for example. Fourth, the intellectual revolution is stimulated by children's increasing ability to manipulate symbols. Now children easily grasp the relationship between letters and sounds, an ability that helps them learn to read. By 6 or 7, most children can add and subtract small numbers without using their fingers or counting the actual objects. Mental arithmetic and emerging abilities to read and write open the doors to academic learning.

There is no simple explanation for the cognitive revolution, because for most 5- to 7-year-olds many factors are changing at once. As they spend more time at school and with peers, children are influenced by other people and challenged by new tasks to master.

In school—both in the classroom and on the playground—children learn to pay attention, to avoid distractions, to control their emotions, and to plan. When they tackle a math problem they are more likely to *think* about it before trying a solution. They can list the materials they'll need before beginning an art project. They know if they'll need more red paint or glue even before they start. As they practice their new skills, children begin to perform them automatically (Case, 1985). Where the 5-year-old had to sound out each letter of a word, the 7-year-old automatically recognizes it. Seven-year-olds can resist temptations and control their emotions without talking aloud to themselves; they can memorize a list of words without too much repetition; they can recall arithmetic facts without calculating each problem from scratch.

Social experiences promote cognitive changes as well. For example, 7-year-olds are more independent in many ways than 5-year-olds are. They ride the bus, go to the store, stay over with friends, join teams and clubs, and meet new peers at school. As they share ideas and play together they solve problems, and problem solving, in turn, fosters cognitive development (Flavell, 1985).

Like physical changes, cognitive changes occur gradually throughout middle childhood, and in each child they occur at a slightly different rate. Thus the term **5-to-7 transition** refers to the age at which those changes usually *start*, even though many children do not complete this stage until the end of elementary school.

During the elementary school years, children improve old skills and develop new ones in many areas. By the age of 10 or so, most have the cognitive abilities to cope with many of the ordinary things of life—choosing clothes, repairing a leaky faucet, deciding how to spend free time. Underlying all these advances are the hallmarks of this cognitive stage—the major advances in logic and strategy. **Logic** refers to general principles about the relations among objects and people, and **strategy** is the ability to use those principles to solve problems. The first to identify and describe these milestones was Piaget.

5-to-7 transition
period in which children begin to develop a sense of logic and strategy as part of their cognitive skills

logic
general principles about the relations among objects and people

strategy
the ability to use logical principles to solve problems

PIAGET'S PERSPECTIVE: CONCRETE OPERATIONS

If you show a preschool child two balls of clay and then roll one into a long rope, she'll tell you that the rope has more clay than the ball. As Piaget observed, preschoolers pay attention to the way things *seem* rather than the way they *are* (Chapter 9). By 7, reality takes hold. Now, when you roll out a ball of clay and ask, "Are they the same amount now or does one have more?" the concrete operational child (1) understands the trade-off between the length and thickness of the clay ball, (2) infers that the rope could be rolled back into a ball like the other piece of clay, and (3) is not fooled by the different appearances of the two pieces of clay. This new awareness, said Piaget, comes from a new cognitive ability. Children can now perform mental operations—they can mentally represent or think about an action and they know that it is reversible. Without rolling the clay back into a ball children now grasp the principles involved: Physically rearranging things doesn't change their identity. What is arranged one way can be rearranged and then reversed. Moving beyond preoperational thinking (Chapter 9), now children know that lengthening a row of cookies won't yield more cookies. This operation conforms to the rule of arithmetic that states that if nothing has been added or subtracted, then identity (or numerosity) remains the same. Piaget called this period the stage of **concrete operations** because children's cognitive "actions" are applied to con-

concrete operations
according to Piaget, the stage of development between ages 6 and 12 when children acquire the mental schemes of seriation, classification, and conservation that allow them to think logically about "concrete" objects

By fourth grade, children's ability to perform concrete operations enables them to use computers for problem solving and for fun. *(Bob Daemmrich/Stock, Boston)*

crete objects or events. An operation is an action that is represented mentally, preserves an unchangeable relation, is reversible, and is part of a system of rules.

Now children begin to pay attention to and can remember several features of an object. They can infer changes in objects even if they don't see these changes; children can now use maps or other representations to guide them and are not easily fooled by physical appearances. School-age children can begin to reason quantitatively about number, distance, velocity, and time. They can reason about spatial relationships such as area and horizontality. Children think logically about observable, concrete objects or events but will have difficulty reasoning about hypothetical situations until they reach early adolescence and the stage of formal operations.

Piaget observed concrete operations in the rules children invent for playing games and in the judgments they make about moral issues. Foremost, though, he identified concrete operations in children's logical and mathematical thinking, as we'll see in the following three examples.

Classification

Benjamin, age 5, has a set of baseball cards that he likes to sort by team (Yankees, Phillies, Cubs, etc.). If you ask him to sort them by playing position (catcher, pitcher, outfielder, etc.), he can do this too. But if you ask him to sort them by playing position *within* a team (Yankees' catchers, Phillies' pitchers, Cubs' outfielders, etc.), it is too taxing for him. He understands the instruction, but he seems able to focus on only one sort at a time. Piaget would not have been surprised. Until they reach the period of concrete operations, he claimed, children could not classify objects by two criteria simultaneously. Younger children are often confused by the idea that an object can be two "things" at once, that categories overlap.

Now, in middle childhood, children have developed a **classification** scheme. They can now recognize relations between sets and subsets, between the whole and parts within the whole. For example, if you show children ten flowers—three roses and seven daisies—and ask whether there are more daisies or more flowers, preoperational children say daisies, the larger subset, because they implicitly compare the roses and daisies. Children who have reached the concrete operational period can compare the whole set, flowers, to each of its subsets and correctly answer "more flowers." Because they understand hierarchical set relations, children at the operational stage delight in telling you that they live in Ottumwa, Iowa, U.S.A., in North America, on the planet Earth, in the Milky Way Galaxy.

Like many of Piaget's claims, his views about children's classification abilities have sparked controversy. Newer research shows that when the objects are part of a naturally occurring collection, such as a bunch of grapes or an army of toy soldiers, children are often able to compare the subsets with the total set (Markman, 1984). Nevertheless, Piaget correctly perceived that children progress during middle childhood in their ability to classify objects and to recognize relations between sets and subsets.

classification
the cognitive ability to understand how things fit into categories and how these categories can be arranged relative to each other

Team, position, league. Classifying baseball cards into several categories at once is easy for children in the period of concrete operations. Now they understand the relationships between sets and subsets. *(Richard Hutchings/Info Edit)*

Seriation and transitivity

seriation

the ability to rank objects in a meaningful order

Seriation is the ordering of objects according to a dimension such as size. In one of his experiments, Piaget arranged a series of sticks from smallest to largest and asked children to do the same with their sticks. Preoperational children usually lined them up randomly or made groups of "big" and "little" sticks. By age 6, children can copy a seriated order with some difficulty. Even children who have not quite reached the concrete operational stage can order a series of coins and dolls from smallest to largest. But Piaget claimed that only children in the concrete operational stage could understand seriated orders. Part of the problem, he believed, is that children must first understand dimensions, such as size, and the rules of progressive change. Objects in the middle of the series are both smaller than some objects and larger than others. This *dual role* of each object confuses young children. Before they can create a seriated array, they need both decentration and reversibility. Because seriation preserves an invariant relation and is part of a system of rules, it is a good example of a concrete operation.

transitivity

concrete operation acquired between ages 6 and 12 that rests on understanding of relationships between objects

Another concrete operation that children acquire between the ages of 7 and 11 is **transitivity**. Now they will know that if we ordered sticks A, B, and C from largest to smallest so that A is greater than B and B is greater than C, then A must be greater than C. This is a logical conclusion based on the transitive relation. When Piaget asked children questions such as, "If Lilly is fairer than Edith and Edith is fairer than Suzanne, then who is the fairest?," concrete operational children knew it was Lilly.

Conservation

Long after you have forgotten most of the information in this book, you will probably still remember *conservation,* the trademark of the concrete operational period. In his now classic experiment, Piaget showed children two identical glasses holding equal amounts of water (Figure 12-1). Then, with the children watching, he poured the water from one glass into a tall, skinny glass. "Now," he asked, "does one glass have more water or do they both have the same amount?" Preoperational children, younger than 7, focus on the greater height in the tall, skinny glass and claim that it now has more water. Not until age 10 or 11, when they are well into the concrete operational stage, do children know that the amount of water remains constant. If you perform this experiment with children over age 10, they'll probably say, "It's the same. You could just pour it back and it would have the same amount."

Children who fully understand conservation can reason about the weight, length, mass, or volume of objects without being fooled by changes in their external appearances as we saw earlier in the ball of clay experiment. Children learn conservation of number first, perhaps because they have more clues to help them reason about discrete quantities like coins (Siegler, 1981). Even young children can line up coins, count them, notice their correspondence, or move them around. These manipulations are not always possible for the other types of conservation, which may explain why conservation of liquid and mass usually follows conservation of number. Not until age 9 or 10 do children understand that weight can be conserved, and only by 10 or 11 do they understand conservation of volume.

Critics of Piaget's conservation studies claim that telling children to watch the experimenter may encourage them to think that something has been changed (Donaldson, 1979). Sometimes, too, the experimenter's words influence children's choices (Rose & Blank, 1974), and many experimenters believe that children know more about conservation than Piaget's experiments revealed (Siegler, 1986). But no one denies that children acquire a systematic set of rules or operations for reasoning from ages 7 to 11: (1) They pay attention to many characteristics of an object; (2) they can classify objects by several traits at the same time; (3) they understand that changing the way something looks doesn't change its amount; (4) they can reason about ordered series of objects; and (5) they can reverse actions mentally. These skills strengthen during middle childhood and underlie cognitive achievements during the school years.

THE INFORMATION-PROCESSING PERSPECTIVE

Recall Benjamin and his baseball cards. At age 5, he couldn't classify them into two categories at the same time. Piaget believed preoperational children lacked a classification scheme that would permit double sorting, but information-processing theorists offer a different reason. Whereas Piaget explained cognitive changes in terms of schemes and operations, information-processing theorists look to storage space and strategies, positing that new cognitive skills emerge from children's expanding memories; these theorists focus on the way we perceive, store, and understand information. Generally, the theories sug-

CONSERVATION SKILL	BASIC PRINCIPLE	TEST FOR CONSERVATION SKILLS	
		Step 1	Step 2
Number (Ages 5 to 7)	The number of units in a collection remains unchanged even though they are rearranged in space.	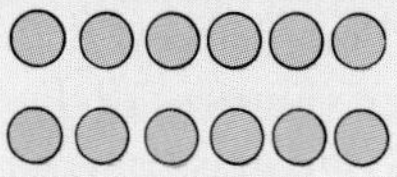 Two rows of pennies arranged in one-to-one correspondence	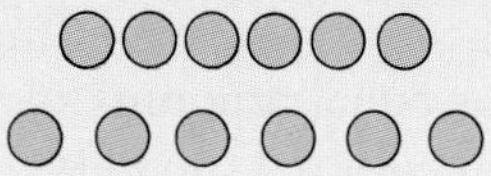 One of the rows elongated or contracted
Substance (Ages 7 to 8)	The amount of a malleable, plastic-like material remains unchanged regardless of the shape it assumes.	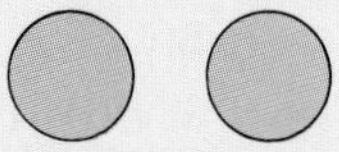 Modeling clay in two balls of the same size	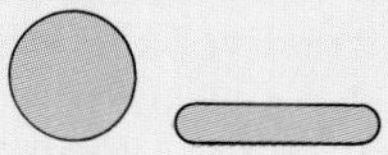 One of the balls rolled into a long, narrow shape
Length (Ages 7 to 8)	The length of a line or object from one end to the other end remains unchanged regardless of how it is rearranged in space or changed in shape.	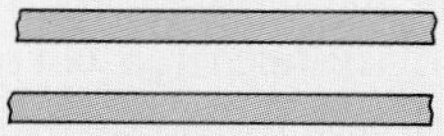 Strips of cloth placed in a straight line	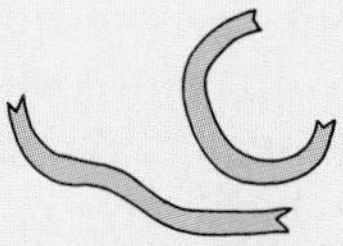 Strips of cloth placed in altered shapes
Area (Ages 8 to 9)	The total amount of surface covered by a set of plane figures remains unchanged regardless of the position of the figures.	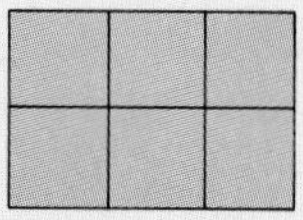 Square units arranged in a rectangle	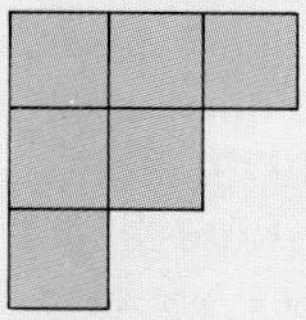 Square units rearranged
Weight (Ages 9 to 10)	The heaviness of an object remains unchanged regardless of the shape that it assumes.	 Units placed on top of each other	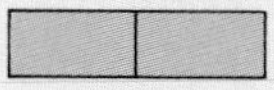 Units placed side by side
Volume (Ages 12 to 14)	The space occupied by an object remains unchanged regardless of a change in its shape.	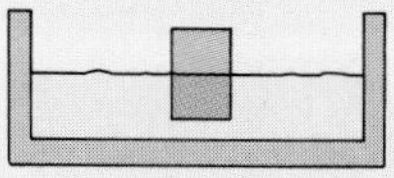 Displacement of water by object placed vertically in the water	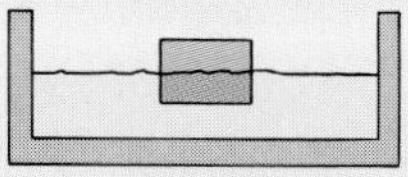 Displacement of water by object placed horizontally in the water

FIGURE 12-1
SEQUENTIAL ACQUISITION OF CONSERVATION SKILLS
During the period of concrete operations, Piaget says, children develop conservation skills in a fixed sequence. They acquire the concept of conservation of number first, then that of substance, and so on. (*Source*: J. Vander Zanden. [1989]. *Human development*, 4th ed. Reprinted with permission of McGraw-Hill, Inc.)

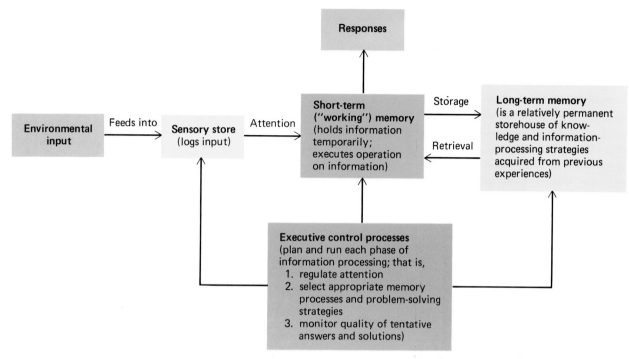

FIGURE 12-2
A schematic model of human information processing. (From R. C. Atkinson and R. M. Shiffrin (1968). Human memory: A proposed system and its control processes. In K. W. Spence and J. T. Spence (Eds.), *The psychology of learning and motivation: Advances in research and theory,* vol. 2. Reprinted by permission of Academic Press.)

gest that information from the environment enters the brain's "sensory register," where it is first perceived; it is then transferred to short-term memory. Information stays in short-term or working memory for fewer than 30 seconds (see Figure 12-2). During this brief time, it is responded to, prepared for long-term memory (encoded), or discarded. The processes that act on information in short-term memory are critical for transferring information to and from long-term memory.

Bottlenecks, or lapses of attention, perception, and memory occur, say information-processing theorists, because we cannot operate simultaneously on all incoming stimuli. In other words, our capacity for processing information is limited. Some of the most interesting work from this perspective concerns the development of memory during middle childhood.

MEMORY DEVELOPMENT

Preschoolers have few strategies for recalling information, but between ages 5 and 11, memory improves dramatically. For example, when 10-year-olds and adults were given a list of digits to remember, the adults recalled more than the children (see Figure 12-3). But when the children—all experienced chess players—were asked to remember chess positions, they were much more successful than the adults (Chi, 1978). Why the difference? Memory is strengthened by organization, so when information can be chunked and organized meaningfully, even young children can show considerable memory prowess. The psychologist who conducted the experiment described above concluded that the children performed better because of their organized knowledge about plausible chess positions (Chi, 1978).

FIGURE 12-3

The average memory span for digits and chess arrays by chess-expert children and college-educated adults. (*Source*: Adapted from *Children's thinking* by D. J. Bjorkland. Copyright © 1989 by Wadsworth, Inc. Reprinted by permission of Brooks/Cole Publishing Co., Pacific Grove, CA 93950. And adapted from M. T. H. Chi, "Knowledge Structure and Memory Development," in R. Siegler (Ed.), *Children's thinking: What develops?* Lawrence Erlbaum Associates, Inc., 1978.)

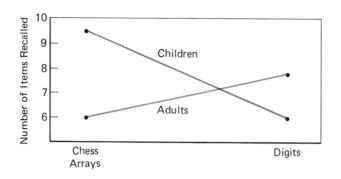

Children may not always use deliberate strategies to organize information; they just recall things better when they have a network of associations. First-, third-, and fifth-graders in one study remembered the names of their classmates with over 80 percent accuracy but couldn't describe any strategies for doing so. Most first-graders simply said, "I used my brain." The researchers concluded that the strong associative links between the names of their classmates helped to make automatic retrieval possible (Bjorklund & Zeman, 1982).

However, learning information—lists of spelling words, math facts, poetry, a part in a play—is facilitated by specific methods or strategies. The most basic is *verbal rehearsal*, simply repeating information over and over (Flavell, 1985). When studying a list, children who rehearse the most recent word along with other words in a *cumulative* way tend to recall more words later than

Memory improves dramatically in middle childhood. With enough practice, elementary school children can even learn the lines of Shakespeare. *(Suzanne De Chico/NYT Pictures)*

children who just repeat isolated words. Linking words creates a more active and larger set for memory (Ornstein, Baker-Ward, & Naus, 1975).

During the middle years, children develop many strategies that transform information, making it easier to remember. For example, they can organize information into categories such as animals, toys, and tools to facilitate recall. Although only a few 7- and 8-year-olds use categories to organize pictures or words, older children generate the associations and use them spontaneously as memory aids (Best & Ornstein, 1986; Salatas & Flavell, 1976).

Some strategies for retrieving information improve as we age. During the school years, children learn to use associations, inferences, and retrieval cues to recall information. To recall a former classmate's name, a child may try to visualize the seating arrangement in the old classroom and retrieve the name by associating the child with a specific location in the class. Children aged 10 to 12 remember what they read because they elaborate the information in the text, make it personally meaningful, summarize the main ideas, and use images and notes as memory cues. Some researchers claim that improvements in memory with age are more likely due to improvements in retrieval than to improvements in encoding.

Metacognition

Metacognition is the awareness children develop about their own knowledge and abilities. It's a way of knowing what you know and what you don't know. When children say, "I think organizing pictures in groups will help me remember," "I have trouble remembering that 7 times 8 is 56," or "I'm good at adding but have trouble with subtracting," we know that they have developed at least some metacognition.

metacognition
the ability to think about thinking, including thinking about reasoning and thinking about memory

Parents and teachers can help children improve their metacognitive skills by asking questions like "Where do you think you went wrong in doing this division problem?" Thinking about the answers helps students to examine the accuracy and efficiency of their own problem solving.

There are two general types of metacognition—self-appraisal and self-management (Paris & Winograd, 1990). *Self-appraisal* means you can evaluate your own knowledge and then choose appropriate plans and strategies for increasing it. When writing a report, for example, self-appraisal helps you to see where you need more information. Self-appraisal also helps children to distinguish what they know from what they don't know. Before self-appraisal develops, children often miss stumbling blocks to comprehension when they listen and read. For example, when nonsense words appear in a reading passage, when words are scrambled, or when obvious contradictions occur, young children tend to miss these distortions (Markman & Gorin, 1981; Paris & Meyers, 1981). Later in the chapter we'll see that metacognition is critical to children's independent learning.

Critical too is the second type of metacognition, *self-management*, the "executive management" of thinking. Self-management enables us to select appropriate strategies for solving a problem and to change those plans if they do not work. When children are able to shift gears in solving problems, they persist longer and are ultimately more successful (Brown, Bransford, Ferrara, & Campione, 1983). Self-management helps fourth-graders to know that they've multiplied when they should have divided, for example.

Metamemory

metamemory
knowledge about one's own memory

Metamemory is knowing about your own memory—what strategies work best for you. This is the cognitive skill that helps you decide *how* to remember something (Kail, 1984). To find out what children know about their memories, researchers ask them. Kindergarteners and first-, third-, and fifth-graders were asked, "Would it be easier to remember a phone number immediately after being told the number or after getting a drink of water?" Even young children knew that a delay would interfere with memory. Yet only half of the kindergarten and first-grade children understood that remembering a list of opposite word pairs would be easier than remembering pairs of arbitrary words (Kreutzer, Leonard, & Flavell, 1975). Metamemory is important because what children believe about memory strategies influences whether they use them. If young children are unaware of various strategies or believe that they are not useful or necessary, then they are unlikely to apply them.

We turn now to children's emerging cognitive skills as they are applied in the classroom.

Cognition in Elementary School

Psychologists devise experiments to test for cognitive developments, but one of the clearest settings in which to see the results of these improvements is in the classroom. Cognition in the classroom requires special strategies, metacognition, and motivation. As the "three Rs" develop, these cognitive skills advance sharply as well.

READING

Five-year-old Sandra can't read a book yet, but she knows what a stop sign says, and she can spot her own name. And like many *Sesame Street* watchers who are also read to often, she became comfortable with letters and sounds long before she began school. Like many other kindergarteners, Sandra invents spellings and pretends to read. All these reading-related activities are signs of **emergent literacy** (Teale & Sulzby, 1986).

emergent literacy
a focus on the creative uses of reading and writing by young children before they learn the formal rules and conventions of print

A key task for young readers is to break the code—to understand the relationship of sounds and symbols. For example, beginning readers need to know how to break words into phonemes, or letter combinations such as *th, br, st,* and how phonemes are related to sound combinations. Children whose phoneme skills are strong usually score high in word recognition at the end of first and second grade (Juel, Griffith, & Gough, 1986).

Young readers also have to master print conventions. They have to perceive the difference between letters and numbers; train their eyes to read from left to right, top to bottom; understand that the spaces between words and the periods between sentences are boundaries. These concepts about print and

"Who knows the contraction for 'there is'?" By first or second grade, most children can learn the simple rules of English grammar. *(Elizabeth Crews/The Image Works)*

the nature of reading and writing are part of young children's metacognition. The concepts are usually mastered by third grade, but metacognition about reading—learning the strategies that enhance comprehension—continues to develop for many years (Garner, 1987; Lomax & Mcgee, 1987). By age 10 to 11, students can use the title, headings, and pictures as clues about a topic before they begin reading; they can infer information and create images as they read, helping them to consolidate the meaning. By this age, too, after they have read a selection children can skim selectively to find information (Paris, Wasik, & Turner, in press). Spotting inconsistencies is now easier too. For example, 9- and 11-year-olds read a story in which koalas were first described as sleeping in trees and then, later, as sleeping on the ground. The 9-year-olds had trouble finding the contradiction, but the 11-year-olds found it easily (Baker, 1984).

Nevertheless, reading skills are still limited. Even seventh-graders can't always distinguish important from unimportant ideas (Baker & Brown, 1984), and many college students have difficulty highlighting important information in a text and taking notes as they read. Cognitive strategies and concepts about reading continue to develop into adulthood, enhancing comprehension and memory.

WRITING

When most of us were in the fourth grade, writing a story or a composition meant that we stared at a blank piece of paper until, finally, we thought of something to say. We wrote it down and waited for another thought. When we'd filled the page, we made a "final copy" and handed it in.

Unless taught otherwise, elementary school children still typically use two strategies when writing an essay. One, called "knowledge telling" is simply spilling everything they know in an unconnected series of sentences (Scardamalia & Bereiter, 1984). Instead of planning the composition, they focus on one aspect of the topic and simply tell what they know. Then they begin a new topic. The composition reads like a series of statements or observations instead of a coherent essay. A second common but ineffective strategy is "copy-delete." Young children use it most when they write reports from secondary sources. They read a passage in an encyclopedia and then selectively edit it by copying or paraphrasing some sentences and deleting others. The result is a series of disconnected sentences. Knowledge-telling and copy-delete are shortcuts that interfere with thoughtful writing, and educators have identified effective strategies that children can use to learn to write well.

Now, writing is taught as a *process:* Children choose from a group of topics; they "brainstorm" or jot down all their ideas about it, they write a first draft, edit it for the flow of ideas and for style, listen to a classmate's comments ("peer conferencing"), and then make final corrections. This "process writing approach" recognizes that good writing involves metacognition and strategies such as brainstorming and outlining. It can be very effective in helping children get started and in overcoming the belief that, once written, an idea is forever fixed. Thus, process writing is an approach that fosters better strategies, metacognition, and motivation for learning.

MATHEMATICS

The way children first understand arithmetic is similar to their early attempts to read. Like the alphabet, the number string has to be memorized, and as with emergent literacy skills, math skills too exist well before first grade begins.

Most kindergarteners can easily add and subtract numbers below 10, and some 4- and 5-year-olds can automatically recall simply addition facts (Siegler & Shrager, 1984). Children of this age solve harder problems, such as 8 + 3, with backup strategies, such as counting on from the larger number or counting on their fingers. With these cognitive strategies children can find an answer even when they can't immediately recall it. In fact, in one study, first-graders who excelled at addition and subtraction used strategies more often and more effectively than other students (Siegler, 1988).

As children learn basic facts about arithmetic, they begin to induce rules about the relationships among numbers (Baroody, 1985). For example, children begin to understand that when zero is added to or subtracted from a number, the number doesn't change. They realize that adding one simply ups the number to the next number in the sequence. They learn that two numbers can be added by counting on from the higher number—5 + 2 yields the sequence 5-6-7—rather than starting at the number 1 and counting all the way to 7. Children also discover regularities for subtracting, multiplying, and dividing that reflect rules and strategies. These rules are based in part on a better conceptual understanding of number that involves operations such as seriation, transitivity, and reversibility. With the realization that addition and subtraction are complementary, just as multiplication and division are, comes deeper insight into mathematics.

But children do not always learn rules easily or smoothly. Sometimes they learn shortcuts or incorrect rules. For example, 7- to 9-year-olds often have difficulty borrowing from zero when subtracting, so they devise shortcuts. Some children subtract zero from the other number, some subtract the number from 10 but forget to diminish the next column by 10, and others simply write zero whenever they see something subtracted from zero. Similarly, when subtracting 27 from 54, some children automatically subtract 4 from 7 to avoid borrowing. On the one hand, this is an extension of a successful rule in which smaller numbers are subtracted from larger ones. But on the other hand, this is the invention of an erroneous shortcut, similar to the copy-delete or knowledge-telling-strategies that children devise for writing. Parents and teachers who are aware of these incorrect, or "buggy," strategies can help children overcome them.

Many children need special help with word problems. For example, "Nancy has 6 marbles. Eve has 3 marbles. How many marbles does Nancy need to give away to have as many as Eve?" Typically, third-graders have trouble solving this problem. At age 8, they look for word clues, such as "more" and "less," and when these signals don't appear, they get confused (Morales, Shute, & Pellegrino, 1985). By 10 or 11, children begin to interpret problems conceptually instead of looking for words cues. This change may reflect better reading skills, but part of the improvement comes from increased understanding of the conceptual relations among numbers, from grasping the concrete operations that Piaget identified.

To sum up, school work and the cognitive skills of middle childhood reinforce each other. New skills enable children to do more sophisticated tasks, and the tasks exercise newly emerging skills. Many math problems are based on *conservation:* If you have five apples and give away three, you have only two, but there are still five apples. Science requires classification (Is this leaf from a maple tree, an oak, a birch?), and social studies requires *seriation* (What country in the world has the biggest area? The next biggest? The next?). Similarly, learning spelling words and math facts improves memory skills.

School is particularly helpful in fostering *metacognitive abilities.* By the middle of elementary school, children begin to understand that considering how to attack a problem *before* starting it makes it easier to solve. For instance, when asked to compare distances when some figures are in miles and others are in kilometers, children learn that they must first convert both distances to one system or the other. And as their metacognitive skills develop, children are taught that memory aids can make remembering easier. Rhymes ("Thirty days has September, April, June, and November"), "chunking" (memorizing the names of the four New England colonies, the five Southern colonies, and so on), and rehearsal strategies, such as repeating information aloud, all help children remember.

Finally, elementary school promotes **self-monitoring.** In order to complete gradually more complex tests, children learn to pace themselves, judging when they've spent too much time on one problem and moving on to the next. In a problem with several steps, they learn to check their work, and as children read more independently, they learn to monitor their comprehension, to stop and read something over again when necessary.

self-monitoring
the cognitive ability to observe one's own behavior and evaluate it

Individual Differences in Cognitive Development

If all normal children pass through the 5-to-7 transition by the middle of elementary school, then why are some in gifted classes, while others work at grade level, and still others fall behind? Any attempt to answer this question brings us back to the theme of individual differences. Differences in cognitive development include timing (at what age developmental changes occur), the speed with which the processes are used (how fast a child can retrieve information, for example), the size of a child's memory, and the amount of information to which a child has access. Some children have traveled around the country, for example, while others have never left their own neighborhood. How much environment influences intelligence is one of the most hotly debated topics in the field of child development.

INTELLIGENCE AND INTELLIGENCE TESTING

We all know what intelligence is, or at least we think we do. Smarter people do better in school, can express themselves well in words, and know how to size up a situation quickly. But what about the child who gets As in English but Cs in math? Or the 7-year-old who can explain how an engine works but has trouble remembering that "engine" ends in "e"? Clearly, intelligence is a complex ability, and most of us are smarter in some ways than in others. In many schools, particularly where children are grouped by ability, intelligence testing is done early in elementary school. But what are these tests actually measuring?

Early tests

One of the first to try measuring human intelligence was the English mathematician Francis Galton (1822–1911), who believed that most mental abilities are inherited. Galton tried to measure mental abilities with laboratory tests of hearing, vision, and reaction time (the time it takes a subject to press a key after hearing a buzzer, for example). But he found that people who did well on one kind of test often didn't do well on others, and that those who did well on all the tests didn't seem particularly gifted in school.

Another early investigator of intelligence was Alfred Binet (1857–1911), a French psychologist. In the early 1900s, Binet developed a test for the Paris school system aimed at identifying students who needed extra help with their schoolwork. Binet's test focused on mental skills that commonly increase with age, such as verbal and reasoning ability. It was divided into a series of test items linked to chronological age. For example, a series aimed at 10-year-olds consisted of questions most children that age could answer but most 9-year-olds could not. A 10-year-old who could not answer these questions would be deemed slow; a 9-year-old who could answer the 10-year-old questions would be considered gifted. Children who could answer most questions appropriate for their age but not many beyond that series would be considered average. These children were assigned a "mental age" equal to their chronological age.

In later tests, Binet used mental age to compute the number he called an **intelligence quotient**—the famous IQ score. In Binet's system, IQ is simply mental age divided by chronological age, multiplied by 100 to eliminate decimals. A child whose mental age is 10 and who is exactly 10 years old has an IQ of 100: $(10/10) \times 100 = 1 \times 100 = 100$. A child who is 8 but whose mental age is 10 has an IQ of 125: $(10/8) \times 100 = 1.25 \times 100 = 125$.

Binet believed that intelligence was complex, not a simple "thing" that people had more or less of throughout life, but many of his successors disagreed. One of them, Stanford psychologist Lewis Terman, thought that intelligence was a relatively stable quality determined mostly by inheritance. He revised Binet's test to produce the Stanford-Binet Test, which is still widely used today.

Some American psychologists, including David Wechsler, sided with Binet about the complex nature of intelligence. In the 1940s, Wechsler developed the Wechsler Intelligence Scale for Children (WISC), which was followed by the Wechsler Adult Intelligence scale (WAIS). Because Wechsler saw intelligence as a broad concept involving many different abilities, not just scholastic aptitude, both tests include performance tasks, such as assembling puzzles, as well as verbal tasks. Within each of these two major categories are several subtests. The verbal category, for instance, includes subtests in "General Information" ("What is steam made of?") and "Similarities" ("In what way are a saw and a hammer alike?"). The Wechsler tests, instead of yielding a single IQ score, give several scores—one for each subtest, an overall verbal score, an overall performance score, and a summary IQ.

intelligence quotient (IQ) a measure of intelligence computed by dividing an individual's mental age by his or her chronological age. This number is multiplied by 100, with 100 being an average score and scores above and below 100 indicating greater or lesser intelligence, respectively

How useful are intelligence tests?

One problem facing anyone seeking to test a child's intelligence is what to test. A child may be good at one kind of intellectual task and poor at another, and the kind of intelligence useful in one environment (a big city neighborhood) may be less vital in another (a primitive farming village).

The tests typically given to U.S. schoolchildren measure the sort of intelligence that it takes to succeed in Western-style educational environments— what might be called "school smarts." Although the tests do measure problem-solving skills, they also rely heavily on verbal ability. The mathematically bright child who lags behind in English skills may not do well on a conventional intelligence test.

Another drawback of intelligence tests is that, although they are useful for diagnosing learning problems and identifying students who need extra help, they are less reliable at predicting school achievement for the average child. This is because achievement is influenced by so many things besides intelligence, including motivation, opportunity, and the influence of parents and peers.

In recent years, intelligence testing has been both sharply attacked and staunchly defended. Critics have charged that most tests are biased against children from any but white, middle-class English-speaking homes. Since

Testing for an IQ score is simple; using the test well is harder. Critics charge that tests are biased toward verbally skilled white middle-class children. Defenders argue that the tests measure abilities needed for success in school. *(Dan McCoy/Rainbow)*

many tests require extensive verbal ability and familiarity with middle-class culture, these charges cannot be dismissed. Defenders of the tests argue that they are basically sound, and that, properly used, they do a good job of measuring mental ability—at least those aspects of mental ability needed to succeed in school.

INTELLIGENCE AND INHERITANCE

A persistent controversy involving intelligence concerns the extent to which it is inherited. Children's intelligence scores tend to resemble their parents' (Scarr & Weinberg, 1983), but heredity is only part of the reason. Another is environmental: Smart parents usually give their children the kinds of experiences that stimulate intellectual development.

Twenty years ago, the issue of intelligence *heritability* was hotly debated among psychologists and educators. Some scientists argued (on the basis of studies that have since been criticized) that intelligence was 80 percent genetic and only 20 percent environmental. They opposed compensatory education programs, arguing that it was a waste of money to try to stimulate intellectual development if intelligence was determined by inheritance. One proponent of this view, Arthur Jensen (1969), focused primarily on the differences in intelligence test scores between white and black children. On average, white youngsters score higher than blacks, and Jensen asserted that this difference resulted from genetic differences between the races. Jensen's position sparked a fierce debate about the heritability of intelligence, racial differences in test scores, and about the nature and fairness of IQ tests in general.

Today, most psychologists disagree with Jensen's claims. Several studies have shown that intelligence is actually quite malleable and that efforts to stimulate children's intellectual development can succeed (Ramey & Haskins, 1981). Most agree, too, that trying to quantify genetic and environmental influences is pointless. Rather, we should ask how nature and nurture *interact* in shaping a child's intellect. As one psychologist put it, the question isn't "How much?" it's "How?" (Anastasi, 1958).

Social Cognition in Middle Childhood

Much of children's thinking has nothing to do with logical problems or items that test intelligence. Things much closer to home concern them: themselves and the other people in their lives. This kind of thinking—known as **social cognition**—focuses on interpersonal relations, social rules, and roles.

social cognition
thinking about oneself and the other people in one's life, including interpersonal relations and social rules and roles

Researchers studying social cognition during middle childhood have focused on three main areas: the way children think about other people, how they view relations between people, and how they think about moral problems. In all three areas a shift in thinking occurs between ages 5 and 7—the period when children's other cognitive skills are shifting too.

NEW CONCEPTIONS ABOUT OTHER PEOPLE

Five-year-old Leslie has been working on a jigsaw puzzle for a long time when her little brother, Stevie, dashes through the room and runs over it. The puzzle breaks apart and Leslie tries to hit Stevie. Leslie has trouble distinguishing between accidental and deliberate behavior, because like most 5-year-olds, she judges actions only in terms of their consequences: good consequences, good intentions; bad consequences, bad intentions. So Leslie is as angry as if Stevie had trampled her puzzle intentionally. Within a few years she'll understand that sometimes behavior is purposeful, sometimes it's accidental, and sometimes motivation is complicated.

Middle childhood is a time when children begin to think about motivation. Besides learning to distinguish between intentional and accidental behavior, children begin to recognize that other people have feelings, needs, and reasons for acting as they do. For example, in selecting a birthday present for his father, 4-year-old Peter chose a toy truck, assuming that since he wanted one, so would his father. By age 8, he knows that people have their own interests, and he buys a Red Sox T-shirt for his baseball-loving father.

Being able to choose the right gift or to understand another's behavior rests on children's growing ability to take the perspective of another, to see things from others' points of view, and to see themselves through the eyes of others. According to a theory advanced by Robert Selman (1971), this ability unfolds in five stages (see Table 12-1).

In Selman's view, the most important shift occurs at the same time as the 5-to-7 cognitive transition, when children make the transition from level 1 to level 2 (see Table 12-1). Those who cannot see how their behavior looks to

Pleasing another. While they wouldn't want a jar of jelly for a birthday present, these boys, ages 7 and 10, can understand that their grandfather would. *(Elizabeth Crews/Stock, Boston)*

TABLE 12-1   SELMAN'S STAGES OF PERSPECTIVE TAKING

Level	Age	Characteristics	Example
0	Preschool	Blurred perspective; child attributes own point of view to others or refuses to understand another's viewpoint	"*Sesame Street* is my favorite show, and my mommy's, too."
1	4–9 years	Understands that people can have different perspectives on the same situation	"I like to swim, but my brother doesn't."
2	6–12 years	Child can put self in others' shoes and see self through the eyes of others	"Danny doesn't like me because I'm always getting him in trouble."
3	9–15 years	Understands that a third person can have an opinion about a relationship between two others	"I think you think I'm crazy to go out with Mike, Dad, but Mom likes him."
4	12+ years	Thinks of social relations as part of larger network; knows that society has viewpoints of its own	"'Jocks' just don't date 'Nerds.'"

Source: Adapted from R. L. Selman (1971). Taking another's perspective: Role-taking development in early childhood. *Child Development, 42,* 1721–1732.

others will have difficulty making and keeping friends. For example, Robert, age 6, is big for his age and overly aggressive, frequently pushing smaller children out of the way to get to the swings at playtime. When the other children refuse to play with him, he first calls them names, then forces his way into their games. Consequently, other children often leave the area when they see Robert coming.

Unable to see himself as others see him, Robert has no idea why he is so unpopular. In fact, like many children with similar problems, he tends to misinterpret other people's reactions. He may even believe that the other children are afraid to play with him because he is bigger, stronger, and better at games than they are. Teachers and parents can help children like Robert by using role-playing exercises, especially games in which the aggressor plays the victim of aggression and begins to see how that can feel. Simulation games such as "What if I didn't have any friends?" can also foster understanding of others' feelings.

NEW CONCEPTIONS ABOUT RELATIONSHIPS

As children become more sensitive to other people's motives and feelings, they also begin to think about relationships in a new way. For toddlers and pre-schoolers parents are both omniscient and omnipotent, but during the school years, children's views about relationships begin to change. For some children, elementary school offers the first real exposure to an authority other than their parents. At first, they accept their teacher's authority as they do their parents'. Holding a kind of "might makes right" point of view, children often think that teachers and parents are right because they have the power to make them behave. Once they complete the 5-to-7 transition, though, children begin to understand that authority can also derive from knowledge and experience. But realizing that parents and teachers aren't omniscient seems to be a turning point: If grownups don't know everything, perhaps they don't know anything! Because most children are relatively obedient during the early elementary school years, parents are often shocked when, around fourth grade, children begin to think of authority as something they can choose to disobey.

Children's conceptions about friendship change too as they spend less time with adults and more time with their peers. Specifically, they get better at understanding their friends' feelings. Whereas preschoolers base friendship on their own self-interest (someone to play with), the cognitive changes of the 5-to-7 transition lead children toward understanding that friendships are based on shared likes and dislikes and on caring. Relationships now tend to be more enduring than the friendships of preschoolers, partly because likes and dislikes last longer and partly because their increased understanding of how other people think and act helps children to act in friendly ways (sharing, helping, and so on) that maintain the relationship. By late elementary school, children perceive that friendship is based on understanding, intimacy, and mutuality and that it provides mutual intimacy and support. Relationships now become more permanent and much deeper, as we will discuss in more detail in the next chapter.

Advances in cognition further social relationships as well. During middle childhood, friends go from sharing toys to sharing feelings. *(Steve Takatsuno/The Picture Cube)*

MORAL DEVELOPMENT

"Where did you get that candy bar, Ricky?"

"From the store."

"Did you pay the man for it?"

"It's O.K., Mommy. They have lots of candy bars."

Like every other child, 4-year-old Ricky was not born knowing right from wrong. He is slowly learning it, as now, when he must return the candy bar and apologize to the manager.

Psychologists who have studied children's ideas about ethical behavior believe that they change as their cognitive abilities develop. In fact, the most influential thinker in this field, Laurence Kohlberg (1969) developed a theory that is related to Piaget's views about cognitive development. Kohlberg contended that children pass through distinct stages of **moral development**, that is, the way they reason about morality changes as they mature. To understand Kohlberg's theory, consider the following problem:

moral development
changes in the ability to reason about morality that occur as a child grows up

In Europe, a woman was near death from a very serious disease, a special kind of cancer. A druggist in the woman's town had recently developed a new drug that the doctors said was her only hope. The drug was expensive to make, but the druggist was charging ten times its cost—$2000 for a small dose. The sick woman's husband, Heinz, went to everyone he knew to borrow money, but he could only raise about $1000. He told the druggist that his wife was dying, and asked him to sell the drug more cheaply or let him pay later. But the druggist refused. Desperate, Heinz broke into the store one night and stole some of the drug for his wife. Was it right or wrong for Heinz to do that? (Kohlberg & Gilligan, 1972)

In Kohlberg's model, whether a child thinks Heinz should steal the drug is less significant than the reasoning behind that decision. Kohlberg suggested that there are three levels of moral reasoning—preconventional, conventional, and principled (postconventional)—which unfold in that order. Each level is composed of two stages (see Table 12-2). And as Piaget held for cognitive development, Kohlberg asserted that each level is qualitatively different from and more advanced and mature than previous ones.

During most of childhood, said Kohlberg, we reason at the preconventional level, but elementary school children are also capable of conventional moral reasoning. As Table 12-2 shows, **preconventional thinking** is not based on society's standards or conventions (hence the label *pre*conventional) but on external, physical events. When faced with a moral issue, children at this level do not ask themselves whether something is right or wrong. Instead, they focus on consequences: Will a given behavior bring rewards or punishment? One preconventional child might say that Heinz should not steal the drug because he could get caught and sent to jail. Another might say that Heinz should steal the drug because people will treat him like a hero for saving his wife. (We discuss the principled level in Chapter 15.)

The parallel between overall cognitive development and moral development shows clearly in children's transition to conventional thinking. While cognitive changes enable children to better understand society's rules and roles, **conventional thinking** enables them to consider how well people actually follow those rules, and how well they play their social roles. A child at the conventional level might say that Heinz should not steal the drug because stealing is against the law. Another might counter that Heinz should steal the drug because that is what a good husband is supposed to do.

Researchers testing Kohlberg's theory have found that moral development generally proceeds in the sequence he described (Colby et al., 1983). Studies also support Kohlberg's idea that moral thinking is stimulated when children are exposed to ethical conflicts and to people who reason at a more advanced level. For example, children whose parents encourage them to participate in family discussions show more advanced levels of moral reasoning than do children whose parents don't include them in family-related talks (Haan, Smith, & Block, 1968; Holstein, 1972).

But so far, research has not confirmed Kohlberg's contention that moral development proceeds in separate, distinct stages. Like cognitive development, reasoning about morality develops gradually. More advanced forms of reasoning do appear with age, but aspects of earlier kinds of reasoning are present in all ages, and different levels of reasoning are called into use at different times and in different situations. Although a preschooler's responses to moral dilemmas would probably be consistently preconventional, a school-

preconventional thinking according to Kohlberg, the first level of moral development, in which children make decisions about what is right and wrong based not on society's standards of conventions, but on external, physical events

conventional thinking according to Kohlberg, the second level of moral development, in which children make decisions about what is right and wrong based on how well a person follows the rules and conventions of society and keeps within the roles people are expected to play

TABLE 12-2   KOHLBERG'S SIX STAGES OF MORAL REASONING

Level One: Preconventional		Child's Response to Theft of Drug
Stage 1	*Obedience-and-punishment orientation.* The child obeys rules to avoid punishment. There is as yet no internalization of moral standards.	*Pro:* Theft is justified because the drug did not cost much to produce.
		Con: Theft is condemned because Heinz will be caught and go to jail.
Stage 2	*Naïve hedonistic and instrumental orientation.* The child's behavior is motivated by a selfish desire to obtain rewards and benefits. Although reciprocity occurs, it is self-serving, manipulative, and based on a marketplace outlook: "You can play with my blocks if you let me play with your cars."	*Pro:* Theft is justified because his wife needs the drug and Heinz needs his wife's companionship and help in life.
		Con: Theft is condemned because his wife will probably die before Heinz gets out of jail, so it will not do him much good.

Level Two: Conventional		Child's Response to Theft of Drug
Stage 3	*"Good boy"—"nice girl" morality.* The child is concerned with winning the approval of others and avoiding their disapproval. In judging the goodness or badness of behavior, consideration is given to a person's intentions. The child has a conception of a morally good person as one who possesses a set of virtues, hence the child places much emphasis upon being "nice."	*Pro:* Theft is justified because Heinz is unselfish in looking after the needs of his wife.
		Con: Theft is condemned because Heinz will feel bad thinking of how he brought dishonor on his family; his family will be ashamed of his act.
Stage 4	*"Law-and-order" orientation.* The individual blindly accepts social conventions and rules. Emphasis is on "doing one's duty," showing respect for authority, and maintaining a given social order for its own sake.	*Pro:* Theft is justified because Heinz would otherwise have been responsible for his wife's death.
		Con: Theft is condemned because Heinz is a law-breaker.

Level Three: Principled		Child's Response to Theft of Drug
Stage 5	*Social-contract orientation.* The individual believes that the purpose of the law is to preserve human rights and that unjust laws should be changed. Morality is seen as based upon an agreement among individuals to conform to laws that are necessary for the community welfare. But since it is a social contract, it can be modified so long as basic rights like *life* and *liberty* are not impaired.	*Pro:* Theft is justified because the law was not fashioned for situations in which an individual would forfeit life by obeying the rules.
		Con: Theft is condemned because others may also have great need.
Stage 6	*Universal ethical principle orientation.* Conduct is controlled by an internalized set of ideas which, if violated, results in self-condemnation and guilt. The individual follows self-chosen ethical principles based upon abstract concepts (e.g., the equality of human rights, the Golden Rule, respect for the dignity of each human being) rather than concrete rules (e.g., the Ten Commandments). Unjust laws may be broken because they conflict with broad moral principles.	*Pro:* Theft is justified because Heinz would not have lived up to the standards of his conscience if he had allowed his wife to die.
		Con: Theft is condemned because Heinz did not live up to the standards of his conscience when he engaged in stealing.

child's responses would probably have a mixture of both preconventional and conventional responses. Like all of human development, moral development is not a perfectly regular, even process.

Summary

1. Growth during middle childhood is gradual and physical changes are subtle. Even though genes strongly influence size and strength, environmental factors, such as diet, hygiene, medical care, and opportunities to participate in sports play a role as well.

2. Heavy television viewing, coupled with inactivity and a diet high in fats and sugars, can set the stage for obesity and, eventually, coronary disease.

3. If children's athletic programs downplayed the competitive aspect of sports, all children would benefit from the exercise and skills gained during athletics.

4. Obesity is the most common health problem among elementary school children. It can lead to future health problems, but can be treated by a program of healthful eating and exercise.

5. Between ages 5 and 7 a cognitive revolution carries children into the stage of concrete operations. By age 7 they understand enduring identities; they have grasped conservation and superficial changes no longer fool them. They also reason better about causation, but their thinking is still tied to the concrete.

6. For Piaget, children's new awareness stems from the ability to perform mental operations—they can mentally represent an action and they know that it is reversible. Being able to perform concrete operations expands children's logical thinking skills. Now they classify things by two criteria simultaneously. They can also perform tasks requiring seriation: They can arrange objects according to a specific dimension, such as size. Other concrete operations acquired are transitivity and conservation.

7. Information-processing theorists explain cognitive changes in terms of growing memory capacity that facilitates better strategies for organizing information.

8. Metacognition—awareness of one's knowledge and abilities—improves during middle childhood. Such self-evaluation helps children know when they need to learn more about something or if they've used the right strategies for solving problems. Schoolwork and the cognitive skills of middle childhood reinforce each other.

9. Intelligence tests measure a range of intellectual abilities, focusing on those that enable children to succeed in school. Critics charge that they are biased toward white middle-class children.

10. Research has proven intelligence to be quite malleable, rather than fixed by inheritance. Rather than ask whether nature or nurture is more important, psychologists now ask how environment and heredity interact to shape a child's intellect.

11. Much of children's thinking concerns interpersonal relations and social rules and roles—what we call social cognition. As with other cognitive skills, the way children think in these areas changes between ages 5 and 7.

12. Children begin to consider the motives that guide behavior and start seeing things from another's point of view. They also change the way they think about right and wrong, moving, according to Laurence Kohlberg, toward the conventional level of moral reasoning. Now they think about moral dilemmas in terms of social roles and rules of right and wrong.

Key Terms

classification

concrete operations

conventional thinking

emergent literacy

5-to-7 transition

intelligence quotient (IQ)

logic

metacognition

metamemory

moral development

obese

preconventional thinking

self-monitoring

seriation

social cognition

strategy

transitivity

Suggested Readings

Bjorklund, D. (1989). *Children's thinking.* Pacific Grove, CA: Brooks-Cole. An overview of children's cognitive development with especially good coverage of research and theory on individual differences in children's mental performance.

Elkind, D. (1981). *Children and adolescents: Interpretive essays on Jean Piaget* (3rd ed.). New York: Oxford University Press. A series of articles by a psychologist who demonstrates how children's behavior can be better understood through the application of Piaget's theory.

Siegler, R. (1986). *Children's thinking.* Englewood Cliffs, NJ: Prentice-Hall. This overview of cognitive development during childhood emphasizes the information-processing approach to the study of cognition.

Turiel, E. (1983). *The development of social knowledge: Morality and convention.* New York: Cambridge University Press. This book examines numerous aspects of social cognition from a cognitive-developmental point of view.

Social and Emotional Development in Middle Childhood

*I*nterested in learning about children's emotional and social growth, a researcher asked boys and girls of different ages if they would share some toys with a playmate (Damon, 1977, pp. 78, 81):*

Researcher:	Suppose you and Sammy are playing together and you have these [five] toys? Would you give him any?
James (4 yrs., 8 mos.):	I would give him these two.
Researcher:	Why those two?
James:	Because I got to keep three. These are the ones I like.
Researcher:	Suppose Sammy said, "I want to have more"?
James:	If he took one then I would take it back from him.
Researcher:	Why is that?
James:	Because I want three.
Researcher:	What will Sammy do then?
James:	He'll say that's O.K., because he likes these [the two toys originally given].

Researcher:	Would you give Kevin any of these to play with?
Mike (6 yrs., 11 mos.):	Yeah.
Researcher:	You would?
Mike:	I'd give these, so it'd be equal, so we can each have five.
Researcher:	Well, where would you put that [extra] one?
Mike:	Put it back.
Researcher:	You wouldn't use it then?
Mike:	Yeah.
Researcher:	Why is that a good thing?
Mike:	'Cause like if I have six, that wouldn't be equal, like see— and if he has six, it wouldn't be equal.
Researcher:	Why wouldn't that be a good thing?
Mike:	Because then we would start fussin'. Like, say I have four and you have seven, then we start fighting.

Moving from early childhood's me-first, me-best style of interaction toward fairness is a sign of the social growth that occurs during middle childhood. Mike, for example, is not yet 7, but he knows that sometimes equity serves his own interests best. By the end of middle childhood he will probably be more sophisticated in applying the equity rule, more flexible when considering alternatives and judging what is fair.

Elementary school children build social competence in other ways too. As their self-concept becomes more sophisticated, they can compare their own feelings and behavior to other people's. They also gain more control over their own behavior, needing fewer curbs from adults. School-age children begin forming true friendships based on mutual trust and shared interests. Many of these friendships form in school, where, for the first time, children's achievements are closely monitored. Each developmental change helps to build the social skills that we use throughout our lives.

---

*Excerpts in this chapter from W. Damon, *The social world of the child*, 1977. Reprinted by permission of Jossey-Bass, Inc., Publishers.

For the 6- to 12-year-old, the challenge of mastering new skills occurs in an arena far broader than the preschooler's, primarily because middle childhood marks the beginning of formal education. The 6-year-old enters a classroom very different from nursery school, a day care setting, or kindergarten. For the first time children have real "work" to do; academic skills must be mastered before moving up to the next grade. Outside of school too, on teams and in clubs and organizations, achievements and performance are evaluated often (merit badges are earned, players are selected or passed over). The social world of middle childhood, then, is not just broader than the preschool world, it is more demanding. Elementary school children increasingly evaluate each other's personal traits, and not measuring up to fairly strict codes of dress, speech, and behavior often means rejection.

In this chapter we will repeatedly stress two basic themes: Middle childhood is a time of developing psychological and social competence in a world that is both expanding and demanding, and middle childhood is a time when psychosocial and cognitive development strongly interact. The many accomplishments of middle childhood are made possible in part by the intellectual advances typical of this age. Mike, for example, can adopt a more adultlike approach to sharing partly because he has the cognitive capacity to take another person's perspective. He grasps that shortchanging Kevin would annoy the other boy, something that 4-year-old James does not foresee. To James, Sammy *must* want the same distribution of toys that he does. And just as cognitive advances spur social development, social development spurs cognitive growth. The ability to form a close and lasting friendship, for example, creates an arena in which the intellectual challenge of taking another's perspective can be worked on and mastered. Thus, cognitive and psychosocial development interact. This is especially apparent when you consider how the sense of self matures.

Who Am I?: The Developing Self in Middle Childhood

The toddler who tries on a new hat, then rushes to the mirror to admire himself has a rudimentary sense of himself. More advanced in her self-concept is the preschooler who proudly calls herself a "big girl" now. During the school years, a child's sense of self continues to develop into the highly personal mental image we call self-concept.

When studying the self, researchers consider three interrelated components: the cognitive, the affective, and the behavioral. The cognitive component is the way we *think* about ourselves. It is composed of the various attributes people see themselves possessing—in short, their **self-conceptions**. A child may see herself as a redhead, a gymnast, a fifth-grader in Mrs. Jones's class. The affective component is the way that we *feel* about ourselves, how we

self-conceptions
the various attributes people see themselves possessing

self-esteem
one's feelings about oneself

self-regulation
the extent to which we can monitor and control our own behavior

evaluate the traits we associate with ourselves. A 10-year-old, for instance, might be proud of her musical and writing talents but ashamed of her clumsiness in sports. In sum, such feelings about the self form a person's **self-esteem**. The third component of the self is **self-regulation**: the extent to which we can monitor and control our own behavior. The growing ability of elementary school children to plan their own schedules, comply with social rules, tolerate frustration, and work toward goals illustrates their improving capacity for self-regulation. In the following sections we will look more closely at how each of these three components of the self develops in middle childhood. We begin with the development of self-conceptions.

CHANGES IN SELF-CONCEPTION

Researcher:	(addressing a girl, age 5½) Could you become Patches (child's dog) if you wanted to?
Girl:	No.
Researcher:	Why not?
Girl:	'Cause he's brown and black and white. And he has brown eyes. And 'cause he walks like a dog.

Researcher:	(this time interviewing a girl who is almost 9) Could you become Tim (child's brother) if you wanted to?
Girl:	No. Because I'm me and he's him. I can't change in any way 'cause I've got to stay this, like myself.
Researcher:	Would you still stay the same even if your name were taken away?
Girl:	I'd still be the same person.
Researcher:	What stays the same?
Girl:	(speaking slowly and carefully to get the pronunciation right) My per-son-al-i-ty? (Adapted from Guardo & Bohan, 1971)

Both these children have a sense of self-constancy, a perception of the self as stable and enduring. Yet there is something fundamentally different about these two girls' self-conceptions. When asked why she could not become her dog, the 5-year-old notes the physical differences between them—differences in hair and eye color and in number of legs. We could imagine that if asked why she could not become her sister, she might point out that she is blonde while her sister is a redhead and that her sister is also much smaller than she. This view of the self as synonymous with the physical body is typical of preschoolers (Broughton, 1978). Children this young usually lack a sense of themselves as unique individuals with their own personality.

Based on interviews with children ages 6 to 9, psychologists Carol Guardo and Janis Bohan (1971) found that this more abstract, less physically based view of the self emerges gradually during the early elementary school years. The 8-year-old quoted above has come to realize that she has an inner personality that stays the same over time. A more articulate statement of the same idea came from a 10-year-old in another study: "I am one of a kind," the child explained. "There could be a person who looks like me or talks like me, but no one who has every single detail I have. Never a person who *thinks* exactly like me" (Broughton, 1978, p. 86). Notice how this change in self-conception parallels the change in children's understanding of others that occurs during the elementary school years. As we noted in Chapter 12, children this age are increasingly able to perceive the thoughts and feelings of other people, and to grasp that others are unique individuals with their own personality traits. The shift to a less physically based view of the self is part of this same cognitive advance.

As elementary school children become increasingly able to "see inside themselves," they develop a much fuller, more mature understanding of what the self is feeling. For instance, when psychologist Susan Harter (1982) studied children's ability to understand ambivalent feelings in themselves, she found that preschoolers deny that someone can have opposite emotions at the same time (such as simultaneously feeling happy and sad). By about the age of 8, children begin to acknowledge that opposing feelings can coexist. At this stage, however, they tend to attribute the different emotions to different events or situations. An 8-year-old might say, for example: "I was happy when I saw my granddad in the hospital, but then I got sad when he said he couldn't come home with us." Finally, around age 10, children grasp that a person can feel a positive emotion while also feeling a negative one. "I was happy to see my granddad," a 10-year-old might say, "but it also made me sad 'cause he was sick."

Notice how this ability to recognize ambivalent feelings requires that the child integrate two pieces of information (the sense of happiness and the sense of sadness). Preschoolers have difficulty with cognitive tasks such as these, since they cannot yet focus on more than one thing at a time. Overcoming this cognitive limitation is an important step toward developing a more complex view of the self.

Not only do elementary school children begin to grasp the coexistence of different feelings in themselves, they also begin to understand that the self has many different traits, abilities, and roles (Harter, 1983). A 10-year-old, for instance, might point out that she plays the piano much better than she sings, that her spelling is better than her math, and that she is both a daughter to her mother and an aunt to her oldest sister's baby. The sense of self, in short, becomes more differentiated during middle childhood, partly because of a growing cognitive ability to integrate diverse pieces of information.

Other cognitive advances of the middle childhood years make possible other developmental changes in youngsters' self-conceptions. For example, the growing ability to adopt another person's perspective, discussed in Chapter 12, is closely related to the capacity to step back and critically view the self. A well-known developmental psychologist, Arnold Gesell, studied the emergence of self-criticism in children some 40 years ago (Gesell & Ilg, 1946). He found that at age 6 children criticize others, especially their peers, but they do not yet criticize themselves. At around age 7 youngsters start to become concerned about what *others* think of them (an indirect form of self-evaluation). And finally, at about age 8 or 9, they start to compare the self to their own internalized standards. This is the beginning of true self-criticism. When this new capacity emerges, it may be "overworked" for a while. "Boy, am I *clumsy!*," a 9-year-old might often remark, or "Oh, I'm so *stupid!*" Not surprisingly, 9-year-olds tend to be easily embarrassed by their mistakes. Such embarrassment is a sign that their view of the self is becoming much more adultlike.

DEVELOPMENT AND EFFECTS OF SELF-ESTEEM

Self-esteem is not an all-or-nothing matter. People may feel very positively about some of their qualities and negatively about others. Based on many interviews with both children and adults, psychologists have concluded that people assess themselves in four basic areas (Harter, 1983). The first is competence in meeting demands for achievement, especially on cognitive or physical tasks ("Am I good at schoolwork? At sports? At fixing things?"). The second is success at influencing other people, at getting others to go along with one's wishes and views ("Do others value my opinions? Do they follow my lead?"). The third is moral worth, or adherence to ethical standards ("Am I a good person? Do I usually do what is right?"). And the fourth is social acceptance— that is, receiving attention and affection from others ("Do other people like me? Do I have many friends?"). Self-assessment in each of these four areas adds up to a person's overall level of self-esteem. Children rate themselves in both absolute terms ("I got an 'A' so I must be smart") and in relative terms ("I got a 'B' but none of my friends did any better").

Studies of fifth- and sixth-graders show that self-esteem affects children's development in several important ways (Coopersmith, 1967). Children with high self-esteem have confidence in their abilities and judgments and expect to be successful. They are also more independent and less self-conscious than their peers with low self-esteem and less likely to be preoccupied with personal problems.

You might think that this positive outlook would enable children high in self-esteem to achieve more than youngsters whose self-esteem is low, but research does not support this prediction. Increasing a child's self-esteem is not an effective way to boost achievement. In fact, academic achievement seems to *precede* the self-perception of competence. Achievement, in other words, may boost self-esteem, but not usually vice versa (Connell, 1981; Harter, 1983; Harter & Connell, 1982).

Of course, academic achievement is not a child's only source of self-esteem. Psychologists believe that another important factor is how the significant people in a child's life, especially the parents, view that particular child. In Stanley Coopersmith's study of fifth- and sixth-graders, the parents of

High achievers, at sports and at school, often have high self-esteem as well, the quality that may spur their efforts to achieve. (left, *Bob Daemmrich/ Stock, Boston;* right, *Lawrence Migdale/Stock, Boston*)

youngsters with high self-esteem tended to have several things in common. First, they were warm and accepting toward the child, both affectionate and involved. Second, they were strict in setting rules and limits, and firm and consistent in enforcing them. Third, they were willing to listen to the child's views and to take them into account when establishing rules and standards. And fourth, they used noncoercive discipline (withdrawal of privileges, for example, rather than physical punishment), and they took care to discuss with the child *why* certain behaviors are wrong. This parenting style closely matches what Diana Baumrind (1967) has called authoritative parenting (see Chapter 11).

It is easy to understand why love and acceptance from others would encourage a positive self-image. During childhood, how we see ourselves is shaped largely by how other people behave toward us. When parents show, through their words and actions, that they love their children just as they are, the children are likely to develop a favorable self-assessment. Similarly, when parents are willing to listen to their children's opinions and take the time to explain why certain behaviors are wrong, they are showing respect that is likely to encourage high self-esteem. But why parental strictness would breed positive self-regard is less clear. It may be that parental rules help to make the social environment more manageable for children, thus helping them to feel more confident and in control. It may also be that children see their parents' rules as a sign that the parents consider the children worthy of adult concern.

ADVANCES IN SELF-REGULATION

We expect very young children to have some trouble controlling their behavior, to act impulsively and to need frequent adult supervision, but by school age, most children can tolerate mild frustration. They can endure a brief delay without pushing and shoving, whining and complaining. The greatly improved capacity for self-regulation that normally develops in middle childhood shows itself in other ways as well. Elementary school children can be counted on to act the "right" way in many situations. When 3-year-olds go visiting, their parents must often remind them not to run in other people's houses or climb on their furniture. By age 7 or so, most children have internalized their parents' standards and don't need constant admonishment. School-age children are quite good, too, at balancing their own desires for pleasure against social demands. You can tell most third- or fourth-graders to be home by 6 P.M., knowing that they will try to comply.

Psychologists have tried to explain the development of this important form of social competence during the elementary school years. Most have taken one of three perspectives: psychoanalytic, social learning, or cognitive. Each offers different ideas about why youngsters become more effective self-regulators during middle childhood and what can be done to help those who have problems controlling their behavior.

The psychoanalytic perspective

Sigmund Freud described middle childhood as a *latency period*, a time when sexual impulses are pushed to the background while the child works at devel-

Following the rules with relative ease is a mark of middle childhood, a time when self-regulation has become more consistent. *(Tony Freeman/PhotoEdit)*

oping a wide range of skills. Many of these skills affect the child's ability to negotiate effectively between the needs of the pleasure-seeking id and the demands of the real world. According to Freud, improvements in self-regulation during middle childhood derive from two related developments. The first concerns the growth of the *superego*, or conscience. The latency period begins with the resolution of the Oedipal conflict and the identification of children with their parents, especially the parent of the same sex (see Chapters 1 and 10). By the age of 6, youngsters have come to realize that they cannot win in a struggle against the control that parents exert. The parents are much too powerful. So children do the next best thing: They try to become *like* the parents, including taking on the parents' role of regulating the child's behavior. At first children simply remind themselves of the parents' rules and standards, often parroting their words ("No! Don't touch that! You might break it!"), but eventually this parental role is so ingrained that it becomes an internalized part of the child's self (Breger, 1974). The superego strengthens during this stage, and the internalized standards it contains provide the basis for the development of self-control.

The second development concerns the strengthening of the ego itself. As the child struggles to keep sexual feelings unconscious, he develops ways of managing his impulses. These skills, called **ego skills**, are called on to keep all sorts of impulses in check—not only sexual impulses, but those involving anger and aggression as well. During the latency period, these ego skills become more and more effective and contribute to the development of self-regulation and self-control.

In the psychoanalytic view, then, middle childhood is a time of rapid improvement in self-control, because these are the years during which the identification process occurs.

ego skills
the abilities needed to negotiate among the demands of the id, the superego, and the real world

Psychoanalysts believe that elementary school children who have trouble managing themselves must have experienced disruption in their relationships with parents, which would have interfered with the development of the super-ego or the growth of ego skills. The children described below, for example, had parents who had either died or had stopped caring for them. And in fact, recent research confirms that parental neglect often leads to underdeveloped self-control in children.

> On our numerous station wagon trips, we had to stop and wait for traffic lights. This was intolerable to the children. Even though they knew the delay would automatically end in 30 to 45 seconds, even though they could *see* it right out there in front of their noses, still they were unable to handle their tension. Impulsive behavior would break out: throwing things, shoving and hitting each other, shouting "Hey, let's go! Why are we waitin'? Smash that other car!" (Adapted from Redl & Wineman, 1951, p. 92)

Psychoanalysts see such problems in self-control as signs of inner conflicts. Treatment encourages children to work through these conflicts and express them consciously, so that unconscious impulses to "act out" the conflict are diminished.

The social learning perspective

While acknowledging that parents influence children's self-control, social learning theorists disregard concepts like ego skills, emphasizing instead some of the major mechanisms of learning: reinforcement, punishment, and modeling. In this view, self-regulation improves greatly in middle childhood because basic learning mechanisms are becoming increasingly powerful. Now the link between behavior and its consequences is becoming clearer; now, too, children are susceptible to new rewards, such as pride in having performed a task better than peers. At the same time, elementary school children are more conscious than preschoolers of their efforts to imitate others. Consequently, they are better at modeling their own behavior after the more self-controlled style of admired adults.

Psychologists have long debated the value of punishment in fostering self-control (Parke, 1977). Most now agree that punishment is most effective when it is administered swiftly and consistently by people with whom the child has an emotional connection. The emotional connection is important because punishment by someone who is loved carries more weight, discouraging the child from repeating the misbehavior when adults are not around. Research also shows that punishment is most effective when accompanied by an explanation of why the behavior being punished was wrong. This helps children internalize the moral standards, which then aids them in regulating their behavior.

The type of punishment meted out can also make a difference. Impulsive verbal or physical punishments may backfire by providing a model of uncontrolled behavior that the child may later imitate (Gelfand et al., 1974). Consequently, social learning theorists favor punishment that involves withdrawal of some positive reinforcer, such as a favorite toy, the child's allowance, or the

time out
a disciplinary technique in which the child is briefly separated from people, toys, and enjoyable activities

pleasure of attention from others. Another effective technique is **time out**. A time out immediately follows undesired behavior and is a brief period away from other people, the child's toys, and enjoyable activities. For instance, a 6-year-old boy might be given 5 minutes of time out whenever he hits his younger brother. The boy knows in advance when this punishment will be given, and he is told that noncompliance with it will only add on extra time. Time out, when administered by someone with whom the child has a close emotional connection, and when coupled with positive reinforcement for desirable behavior, has helped to foster self-control even among children with serious problems in self-management (Patterson, 1976).

Time out works with self-control problems because it removes the child from the situation where he is having trouble and puts him in a calmer environment. It is most effective when used in the spirit of help rather than punishment. That is, the child should know that he is leaving to regain control, and he is welcome to return when he has.

The cognitive perspective

Developmental psychologists with a social learning perspective are interested in how basic principles of learning can account for gains in self-regulation. What children *think* about as they gain control over their own behavior doesn't interest them. In contrast, psychologists with a cognitive perspective disagree with this deemphasis on children's thought processes. They believe that how children learn to "talk to themselves" is fundamental to their growing ability to manage their own behavior.

The importance of "inner speech" to self-regulation has been shown in many studies. In one, researchers observed through a one-way window as children tried to wait for a more desirable reward of two large marshmallows rather than taking an immediate reward of one small pretzel (Mischel & Underwood, 1974). Those who were successful at waiting distracted themselves in several ways (talking to themselves, singing little songs, making up games) rather than just staring at the food. By interviewing their subjects, the researchers found that 4- and 5-year-olds have very little understanding of the thoughts that will help them exert self-control. They might say, for example, that thinking about how sweet the marshmallows will taste will help them endure the delay (a thought that, in fact, makes waiting unbearable); 7- to 9-year-olds, in contrast, are much more knowledgeable about how to use thoughts to control their own behavior.

The ability to use thoughts to exert self-control usually develops naturally as children mature cognitively. We saw in Chapter 12 that elementary school youngsters are increasingly able to plan and monitor their behavior and to think about their own thoughts, all of which are skills that aid them in controlling themselves. Some youngsters, however, seem to need help in learning to use inner speech as a tool for self-management. For them, psychologists have developed special programs. One involves teaching the children to identify a specific problem ("I blurt out answers in class when it is not my turn."), encouraging them to say things to themselves that counteract the problem ("Wait a minute. It's not my turn. Give someone else a chance."), and then helping them to monitor how well they do (Meichenbaum & Goodman, 1971). Another program combines this inner-speech technique with an effort to get children to think of alternative behaviors that are incompatible with the problematic one ("I will clench my teeth whenever I feel the urge to speak out of turn in class.") (Camp et al., 1977; Camp & Bash, 1981). These techniques foster the cognitive strategies that children their age normally use to aid in self-control.

Achievement in Middle Childhood

With the middle years, children enter the achievement-oriented world of the classroom. From first grade (or even kindergarten) on, they are tested, evaluated, graded, and grouped. During this time, children develop **achievement motivation**, the desire to perform well, especially on tasks involving intellectual skills, and especially in settings where accomplishments are monitored and judged. Achievement motivation differs from **mastery motivation**, the desire to master a challenge in order to acquire a new skill. The 6-month-old who struggles to crawl across the room and the 3-year-old who works at perfecting a somersault are exhibiting mastery motivation. In contrast, the third grader who strives to learn the "12 times table" in order to win a gold star and her teacher's approval is spurred on largely by achievement motivation.

For Erikson, the chief psychosocial crisis of middle childhood concerns the child's sense of accomplishment. Meeting the social and psychological

achievement motivation
the desire to perform well

mastery motivation
the desire to master a challenge in order to acquire a new skill

Meeting challenges and mastering skills boost a child's confidence, essential for developing a sense of industry. (*Bob Daemmrich/Stock, Boston*)

industry versus inferiority according to Erikson, the crisis over the sense of accomplishment, characteristic of middle childhood

challenges of this period gives children a sense of **industry**, a belief that they are competent and able to master things. Coupled with this belief is an eagerness to tackle new tasks and a willingness to persist in working toward their goals. In contrast, children who fail at or withdraw from the challenges of middle childhood develop a feeling of **inferiority**. Convinced that they are unable to master new skills, these children have little motivation to keep trying. Erikson contends that failing to resolve the challenges of middle childhood restricts a child's ability to meet the psychosocial challenges that lie ahead.

PERCEIVING ABILITY

Underlying growth in achievement motivation is a change in the way children think about ability (Frieze, Francis, & Hanusa, 1981; Heckhausen, 1981; Stipek, 1981). For preschoolers, ability means mastering specific skills, especially physical ones: shoelace tying, tree climbing, ball catching, or swing pumping. At this age, children are almost immune to failure: they keep on trying. But by age 6 or 7, children begin thinking about ability more as a global, psychological trait. "Ability is being smart and good at lots of stuff," an 8-year-old might say, implying that a person's degree of "smartness" is a relatively stable general characteristic. Along with this changed perception comes a change in *judging* ability. Preschoolers say they "did good" just because they completed a task correctly, regardless of how their performance compares with their peers. By middle childhood, though, "doing good" turns to "doing better"—or worse—than someone else. Ability is now linked to comparison with others. ("I did better than most of the kids in my class.") Finally, preschoolers assess their own ability optimistically, foreseeing little difficulty in mastering a new skill. Older children perceive challenges and their own abilities more realistically.

These developmental changes can work for or against achievement motivation. Elementary school children value achievement more strongly and often strive to excel, but their still immature understanding of ability makes them very vulnerable to the effects of failure. Children who fail repeatedly think they are "dumb." They don't think that their teacher may not be very good or that other things in their lives may be keeping them from learning. Children who keep failing often just stop trying.

INDIVIDUAL DIFFERENCES IN ACHIEVEMENT MOTIVATION

Of course, not all elementary school children find failure so discouraging. Some bounce back and keep trying even when they fail many times. What is it that makes some youngsters able to take failure in stride, while others are defeated by it?

The influence of goals

learning goals goals that place value on individual accomplishment for its own sake

One answer lies in the achievement goals that children have. Table 13-1 shows several differences between goals that are learning versus those that are performance-oriented (Dweck & Elliott, 1983). Youngsters for whom **learning goals** are most important approach new tasks with the questions: How can I

TABLE 13-1   CHILDREN'S ACHIEVEMENT GOALS

	Goals	
	Learning Goal: **Competence Increase**	**Performance Goal:** **Competence Judgment**
1. Entering question:	How can I do it? What will I learn?	Can I do it? Will I look smart?
2. Focus on:	Process	Outcome
3. Errors:	Natural, useful	Failure
4. Uncertainty:	Challenging	Threatening
5. Optimal task:	Maximizes learning (becoming smarter)	Maximizes looking smart
6. Seek:	Accurate information about ability	Flattering information
7. Standards:	Personal, long-term, flexible	Normative, immediate, rigid
8. Expectancy:	Emphasizes effort	Emphasizes present ability
9. Teacher:	Resource, guide	Judge, rewarder/punisher
10. Goal value:	"Intrinsic": value of skill, activity, progress	"Extrinsic": value of judgment

Source: From Carol S. Dweck and Elaine S. Elliot, Achievement motivation, in P. H. Mussen (Ed.), *Handbook of child psychology*, 4th Ed., vol. 4, 1983. Reprinted by permission of John Wiley & Sons, Inc.

do this and what will I learn? These children stress the process of mastering things and the intrinsic value of gaining new skills: a difficult task becomes a challenge. Such youngsters see their mistakes as a useful part of learning, since mistakes provide feedback about how to do better. In contrast, children for whom **performance goals** are most important approach new tasks with the questions: Can I be successful and will I look smart? To these children, what matters is the outcome of their efforts—whether they bring success and the esteem of others, or whether they bring failure and others' disparagement. For them, a difficult task is automatically threatening, since it poses the risk of making them seem dumb. Mistakes are threatening too, because they suggest incompetence and might bring derision from others. Such children tend to avoid tasks at which they might fail.

performance goals
goals that place value on achieving in relation to others

The influence of expectations

For children, as well as adults, expectations about success or failure can help to bring it. If children "know" they will fail at something (such as scoring high on a test), they are likely to give up trying as soon as they are stumped. But when children believe that they can do well, they are likely to persist and succeed. A critical question for psychologists, therefore, is: How do children form these expectations about success and failure?

Some insights come from the study of girls' expectations. In general, girls expect less of themselves in achievement situations than boys do, *even though*

How can I do this? Children motivated to do well in school typically set learning goals for themselves and are not afraid to make mistakes. *(Randy Matusow)*

their past performance is as good as or better than boys' (Dweck & Elliott, 1983; Dweck, Goetz, & Strauss, 1980). This tells us that low expectations of achievement are not just a matter of realistically assessing that one has done poorly in the past. Other factors must also be involved, and researchers have tried to discover what these are. One recent finding is that girls tend to focus more on negative feedback about their performance. While a boy tends to shrug off occasional errors as not indicative of his "true" ability, a girl is likely to take her errors much more to heart, sometimes as evidence of low intelligence. Girls also tend to rate tasks as being harder than boys rate them. So even if a girl thinks that she has good ability, she might still expect low achievement of herself because she sees the task as very difficult. At the same time, girls may set higher standards for themselves than boys do, which may also contribute to their lower self-expectations (Dweck & Elliott, 1983).

Children with seriously low achievement expectations usually suffer either from evaluation anxiety or from learned helplessness. A child with **evaluation anxiety** feels so anxious in situations where he is being judged that he has trouble functioning and shows chronically poor performance. **Learned helplessness** is the belief or expectation that you cannot control forces in your environment, that you cannot behave in ways that make a difference (Seligman, 1975). With regard to achievement, learned helplessness is reflected in the tendency to attribute failure to one's own lack of ability ("I'm too dumb to solve these problems," such children think to themselves). As a result, the youngsters simply give up trying as soon as they have difficulties. It is as if they believe they can't possibly succeed in such situations. Unlike the child with evaluation anxiety, whose performance is *persistently* impaired, the youngster who suffers from learned helplessness does as well as peers when achievement

evaluation anxiety
anxiety manifested in situations where a child is being judged

learned helplessness
the belief or expectation that one cannot control forces in one's environment

tasks are easy. As soon as the going gets tough, though, the child simply stops trying and performance plummets (Licht & Dweck, 1984).

We aren't sure why learned helplessness develops. Some children may be more prone to it by temperament than others. For some, it may come from having been told by their parents, implicitly or explicitly, that effort doesn't make a difference. Evaluation anxiety is likely to develop when parents set high standards for performance and then react very critically when the child performs poorly. Again, there may be an inborn component to evaluation anxiety, as some children may be more prone to anxiety than others.

Girls, as we suggested earlier, are more prone to learned helplessness than are boys. This may be partly because of the way that elementary school teachers tend to criticize them (Dweck, Davidson, Nelson, & Enna, 1978; Dweck, Goetz, & Strauss, 1980). Whereas teachers criticize boys mainly for aspects of their work *not* related to ability ("You did this sloppily." "You weren't trying very hard."), they criticize girls mainly for things that *could* arise from low intelligence ("You spelled that wrong." "You forgot to carry the two.") Consequently, girls may be more apt to conclude that they have intellectual limitations.

Children with evaluation anxiety or learned helplessness need to develop more positive expectations about themselves. Encouraging them to think that their failure is *not* due to lack of ability is very important. In fact, when children with learned helplessness are taught to attribute failure to lack of effort rather than to lack of ability, they begin persisting when obstacles arise, and their performance improves markedly (Dweck, 1975). "Issues & Options" gives some other suggestions for fostering healthy attitudes toward achievement in children.

Social Relations in Middle Childhood

Researcher:	Who's your best friend?
Matthew (5 yrs., 10 mos.):	Larry.
Researcher:	Why is Larry your best friend?
Matthew:	'Cause he plays with me a lot.
Researcher:	Are you Larry's best friend?
Matthew:	Yeah.
Researcher:	How do you know that?
Matthew:	'Cause I'm friends with lots of people but Larry and me are best friends. . . .
Researcher:	How did you get Larry to like you?
Matthew:	He came to my house and I played with him and he liked me.
Researcher:	Does everyone who goes to your house like you?
Matthew:	Sometimes when I play with them, but when I don't play with them, they don't like me.

Issues & OPTIONS

Helping Children Become Healthy Achievers

When Sharon's teacher asks a question that stumps her, Sharon blushes deeply and slouches in her chair, convinced that any error means she is less intelligent than her classmates. Overly concerned about looking smart, Sharon stresses achievement over learning, and shies away from tackling a difficult task (and perhaps mastering a new challenge) out of fear that failing will make her seem dumb. Although Sharon consistently earns good grades, she lacks confidence in her ability.

Billy sits two seats away from Sharon in the same fifth-grade class. Unlike Sharon, he thrives on challenge. Math and science are his favorite subjects, and when the teacher asks a difficult question, Billy quickly suggests a possible answer. If sometimes his answers are wrong, that's all right. For Billy, it is fun to learn, even from his own mistakes.

When parents are interested in a child's schoolwork, their children learn that knowledge is what counts. *(Elizabeth Crews/Stock, Boston)*

Researcher: How do you know who to play with?
Matthew: Like when I'm doing something and they're doing something else and I walk by, they grab me in. They just grab me by the hand and I fly in. (Damon, 1977, pp. 154–155)

Five-year-old Matthew's description of making friends is charmingly simplistic. By middle childhood, he will connect friendship to shared interests,

Issues & OPTIONS

Achievement strongly motivates each of these children, but for Sharon, fear of failure is even stronger. How did striving and learning get confused with winning and losing? As with most attitudes, feelings about achievement begin at home. The parents of healthy achievers tend to set reasonable standards for performance, standards that acknowledge the child's abilities and past performance. These parents also stress the value of learning more than the value of grades, and they praise success rather than criticize failure.

In contrast, the parents of children with achievement-related problems tend to set unreasonable or inconsistent standards; they overemphasize grades; and they punish failure instead of rewarding success (Dweck & Elliot, 1983). This last behavior may even have health-related effects. Recent studies show that repeatedly punishing children's failures can encourage them to be prone to develop a "Type A" personality—highly competitive and easily frustrated.

To foster more Billys and fewer Sharons, parents can emphasize learning and mastery rather than grades. Grades will always be a part of the educational landscape, but parents can help their children put grades in proper perspective. Being involved in a child's day-to-day schooling, not just showing an interest on the day that report cards are issued, can make a difference. In fact, suddenly showing excessive pleasure or disappointment over a report card is akin to announcing that grades are the only things that matter. But showing an interest in the child's accomplishments throughout the academic year encourages the inner pride that comes from learning. This means reading the child's assignments, asking questions about school, and discussing topics taught in the classroom.

Many parents do not behave this way, but teachers can fill in the gap by setting standards, providing structure, rewarding effort, and emphasizing learning rather than performance goals. Teachers can also help by treating children as individuals—praising them for achievement relative to past performance, not achievement as measured by some absolute standard.

But words of praise and encouragement alone may not be enough. Witnessing their parents' and teachers' pleasure in learning and mastery can strongly influence children's behavior. Parents who never read should not expect their children to turn into avid readers because they *tell* them that reading can be fun. To get the most out of school, children need a home environment that both demonstrates the rewards of learning and is conducive to it. A home dominated by television is usually not conducive to learning, because family members typically spend little time talking to each other (Maccoby, 1951).

Finally, parents and teachers can foster healthy attitudes toward learning by encouraging children to attribute successes to their ability and perseverance and failure to lack of effort. Children who feel that luck brings success and stupidity brings failure are likely to stop trying when work gets hard. To be healthy achievers, children must believe in themselves and be motivated to persist despite temporary setbacks. They must also be encouraged to set challenging but realistic goals, that, with effort, will pay off in the joy of accomplishment.

mutual assistance, loyalty, and trust. Developmental psychologists believe that interactions with peers are critical to many of the social advances that occur in middle childhood. Striving to be accepted and liked by peers, youngsters gain new insights into the meaning of friendship. Through give and take with peers, children learn the importance of sharing, reciprocity, and cooperation. By trying to get peers to understand their thoughts and feelings, they learn to communicate more effectively. Psychiatrist Harry Stack Sullivan rightly stressed the importance of childhood peers in his theory of interpersonal development (Sullivan, 1953).

SULLIVAN'S THEORY OF INTERPERSONAL DEVELOPMENT

Harry Stack Sullivan, an only child born in the 1890s, spent most of his early years on an isolated farm in central New York State. His isolation was compounded by religious and ethnic prejudice, for his Irish Catholic parents were not readily accepted by the old-line Yankee Protestants of the area. When he was 8, Sullivan made friends with a boy on a neighboring farm, a relationship that, years later, he would describe as lifesaving. He believed that without this early friendship, he would not have become a psychologically healthy adult. Its impact appears too in his theory of interpersonal development.

According to Sullivan and many other psychoanalytic thinkers who came after Freud, biological drives and sexual conflicts are not the overriding factors in human development. Equally if not more important in shaping personality are the interpersonal relationships we form. Sullivan contended that we are all innately motivated to seek *security* by forming relationships with others who make us feel happy and safe. Such relationships are the "glue" holding together a healthy sense of self. Interacting with others who think well of us fosters a positive self-identity and strong self-esteem.

Sullivan proposed a developmental sequence of needs related to security, starting with the infant's need for physical contact and tenderness from adults. Next, children need adult participation in their learning experiences (the preschool years), followed by the need for peer acceptance (early middle childhood). Intimacy with a friend of the same sex is necessary in late middle childhood, followed by a need for love and sexual contact with an opposite-sex partner (early adolescence). Finally, during late adolescence, we feel the need for integration into adult society. Like Erikson, Sullivan saw psychosocial development as cumulative. The experiences of past developmental periods affect current relationships and the developing sense of self. If, for example, a child's need for physical contact and tenderness is not met during infancy, she will be too insecure and distrustful to form cooperative relationships with adults during the preschool years. Later on, if the need for peer acceptance is satisfied early in middle childhood, confidence to form very close friendships during the later elementary school years will grow.

For Sullivan, it was through these friendships—or "chumships," as he called them—that children learn how to share their thoughts and feelings and to build a mutually caring relationship based on loyalty and trust. Sullivan believed strongly that chumships are a necessary prerequisite to forming intimate relationships in adolescence and adulthood. Chumships could even help "repair" insecurities stemming from interpersonal problems in earlier developmental periods.

CHANGING CONCEPTIONS OF FRIENDSHIP

As 5-year-old Matthew sees it, a friend is someone you play with, with whom you share toys. For most preschoolers and early elementary school children, friendships form quickly just by meeting and saying "Hi." As Matthew describes it, other children "grab me by the hand, " they begin playing, and right away they are friends

But around age 8 or 9, this simple view of friendship as a sharing of fun and toys starts maturing, first with the idea that friends help each other. As one 8-year-old girl explained when asked why Shelly was her best friend:

> Because she helps when I'm getting beaten up, she cheers me up when I'm sad, and she shares. . . . She's done the most for me. She never disagrees, she never eats in front of me, she never walks away when I'm crying, and she helps me on my schoolwork. (Damon, 1977, pp. 159–160)

Later, at about 11 or 12, children begin thinking of friends not only as those who help one another, but also as those who share secrets, who understand each others's feelings, and who can be trusted not to betray the other person's confidences. Asked when he knew that Jimmy was his friend, one boy this age responded:

> After we found out that we didn't have to worry about the other guy blabbing and spreading stuff around. . . . You need someone you can tell anything to, all kinds of things that you don't want spread around. That's why you're someone's friend. (Damon, 1977, p. 63)

This increased capacity for intimacy in the late middle childhood years

Best-friend intimacy comes with the cognitive and emotional advances of middle childhood. To feel open to another, children first have to feel secure about themselves. *(Hazel Hankin)*

reflects both cognitive advances and emotional growth (Youniss, 1980). It reflects cognitive advances in that children are able to grasp not just the tangible basis of friendship (shared objects and activities) but the intangible, psychological basis as well. It reflects emotional growth in that children have the sense of security needed to open up their innermost selves to another person. Without both these factors developing together, the close friendships of late middle childhood could never be formed.

MIDDLE CHILDHOOD PEER GROUPS

At a pizza parlor in Worcester, Massachusetts, seven boys in hockey uniforms have just been served a large pizza (quoted in Damon, 1977, pp. 59–60):

Child 1: Hey, there's eight pieces here. What about the extra piece?
Child 2: The guy who's the oldest should get it. How old are you?
Child 1: Nine.
Child 3: I'm nine and a quarter.
Child 1: My birthday's coming up this summer. I'm—I'll be ten in one, two months.
Child 2: How old are you?
Child 4: Eleven, and I'll be twelve next month.
Child 2: Well, I'm twelve so I'll get the extra piece.
Child 1: What about giving it to the one with the small piece?
Child 4: Well, who's got the smallest piece?
Child 1: I've got the smallest piece—look at it!
Child 2: C'mon, let's cut it. The oldest kid will get one piece and the kid with the smallest piece will get one piece. . . .
Child 5: Hey, can we get some water here? Who's gonna play hockey tomorrow?
Child 3: I am, I am! *[Jumps up and moves over to pizza tray with extra piece still on it. Begins picking cheese off the top. Children 1 and 2 gather around, and each takes pieces off the extra piece, with child 3 getting much more than the other two.]*
Child 6: Who's the biggest eater here—who's the piggiest?
Child 2: I can eat seven pieces of pizza, but I gotta give one to my mother.
Child 6: No, no. Who's the biggest eater of us all?
Child 4: Joey [child 3] is.
Child 1: Yeah, Joey is.
Child 3: Yeah, I can eat two whole pizzas myself.
Child 1: Two whole pizzas!
Child 6: Yeah, you're the biggest pig, all right.

This segment of real-life dialogue suggests several things about middle childhood peer groups. First, and typically, members of the peer group are all the same sex (Hartup, 1983). While it may be common to see games of chase *between* the sexes on elementary school playgrounds, boys and girls in middle childhood rarely play *together*. Elementary schoolers prefer this gender segregation and actively strive to maintain it. Boys, especially, ostracize other boys who try to join the girls in their activities (Thorne, 1986).

The scene above also suggests how important the norm of fairness is to children this age. No one simply snatches the whole slice of pizza, as a pre-

A "girls only" activity. Boys and girls usually play apart—in fact, a boy who joined this game would risk being ostracized by other boys. *(Francis M. Cox/ Stock, Boston)*

schooler might do; they discuss who deserves it most. Granted, each boy proposes a criterion that biases the choice toward himself, but the criteria are at least defensible on rational grounds (the oldest boy is probably the biggest and therefore "needs" more food; the boy with the smallest piece has been short-changed and therefore deserves extra). A preschooler would typically suggest some criterion that is totally irrelevant ("I get it because my dog eats pizza"). Such reasons decline sharply during middle childhood. Youngsters this age are also much less egocentric. They realize that fairness often entails not getting all the best things for oneself.

Elementary school children learn other norms of conduct within their peer groups. In fact, children this age are extremely norm-conscious (Hartup, 1983). Bound, in part, by the "concreteness" of concrete operations, the stage of thought characteristic of this age, they expect each other to "follow the rules," to dress, act, and talk in a certain manner. Those who do not are often ridiculed and rejected by their peers. Although elementary school children may seem too rigid in enforcing their ideas of correct behavior, the experiences they have while struggling to define proper and improper conduct will help to prepare them for the world of adolescence.

THE GROWTH OF SOCIAL SKILLS

The boys' conversation about distributing the extra pizza also shows advances in social communication. Compare this conversation with those between two preschoolers (Chapter 10), in which each child virtually ignores what the other is saying. Even if these children were strongly motivated to attend to one another (say, they wanted to build a play fort that required a cooperative effort), we suspect that they would still have trouble really listening to each other and communicating their ideas.

This was illustrated in a study in which children sat on opposite sides of a screen with identical abstract drawings in front of them (Krauss & Glucksberg, 1969). One child was to try to explain to the other which picture he or she was holding. Preschool youngsters did very poorly on this task. One might say to the other, "I've got the one with the funny shape," or even less revealing, "I've got *this* one." They lacked the communication skills needed to help each other identify the drawings. Elementary school children did much better at describing the pictures, especially 10- to 12-year-olds. And if the meaning *was* still unclear, the listener quickly requested whatever additional information was needed.

Elementary school children communicate better than preschoolers do in many other ways too. The young hockey players dividing their pizza are adept at directing visual attention to help make their points: as when child 1 points to his small slice and urges the others to "look at it!" They are also quite good at interpreting nonverbal messages, such as body posture, facial expressions, and tone of voice. Child 3, for example, knows that this is a light-hearted, playful discussion (otherwise he would never have simply jumped up and started picking at the extra piece). He knows this not so much through his friends' words as through their nonverbal signals. Elementary school children have also learned how to stick to a particular topic. Although they still introduce irrelevancies from time to time (as when child 5 abruptly changes the subject), they do so much less than preschoolers do. They are also much better at inferring motives from the statements people make. For instance, all the boys realize that child 1 and child 2 are suggesting ways of distributing the extra piece that benefits themselves.

Psychologists believe that these communication advances stem from several factors, including improved role-taking abilities. Because elementary school children can imagine themselves in other people's situations, they can better interpret what others are thinking, feeling, and saying. At the same time, elementary schoolers may be forced to be better communicators because they are spending more time with their peers. Whereas adults sometimes speak *for* children and help them interpret others, conversations among peers don't provide these communication crutches. Peers must struggle to get ideas across and to understand each other. As a result, they learn techniques for communicating more effectively.

Middle childhood also sees growth in other social skills: sharing, cooperating, and helping others all increase (Radke-Yarrow, Zahn-Waxler, & Chapman, 1983). Some children, however, lag behind their peers in acquiring these social abilities. For them, then, deficiencies may be related to growing up in harsh, autocratic households (Maccoby & Martin, 1983). Other children may simply be inexperienced in social situations or lack the models for appropriate social behavior that many children have. Special programs that actively foster prosocial behavior are particularly beneficial to those children.

Psychosocial Problems of Middle Childhood

While younger children's problems often trouble their parents, problems that surface during the middle years are often taken more seriously by other adults as well, for several reasons. First, because behavior patterns tend to stabilize with age, the problems we see in middle childhood may persist into later years, so adults become concerned about long-lasting effects. Second, the new settings that children are now in may bring out new problems. Attention deficit disorder, for example, is usually not noticed until formal schooling begins. Third, behaviors that would not have caused too much concern in younger children, when a lot of learning is still occurring, are more troubling now. We expect older children to know more social rules now, so behaviors that once seemed like socialization deficiencies (being disruptive in a line, for example) now may signal more serious problems (trouble controlling impulses).

Earlier we discussed problems with self-control, evaluation anxiety, and learned helplessness. Now we turn to two other common psychosocial problems of school-age children: intense and irrational fears (often called "phobias"), and attention-deficit hyperactivity disorder.

CHILDHOOD PHOBIAS

The problem started when Julie became upset with a teacher who took her music book away from her in class. Rather than eating lunch at school that day, she went home at noontime, but her mother was nowhere to be found. Julie called her father and learned that her mother had a doctor's appointment to get an allergy shot. The next morning Julie complained that she did not feel well, but she was sent to school anyway. At school she seemed anxious and upset for no reason. This troubled behavior continued for several days until finally Julie became so panicky in the classroom that her mother had to come and take her home. Thereafter Julie refused to go to school. Each morning when her mother tried to rouse her from her bed, she complained of a terrible stomach ache and feelings of nausea. If her mother tried to coax her to get dressed she would cry so hard she could scarcely get her breath. Impatience and annoyance on her mother's part simply caused Julie to vomit. (Based on Sperling, 1961)

Fear is a normal emotional reaction to some perceived threat, and most school-age children can manage their fears without becoming overwhelmed by them. But for some, fears become intense and unreasonable—far out of proportion to the things that trigger them. Such intense, irrational fears directed toward specific objects or situations are **phobias**. Julie has developed a school phobia, a fear of attending school, and, as is typical with phobias, her

phobias
intense, irrational fears directed toward specific objects or situations

attacks of fear are accompanied by physical symptoms. Her stomach knots, she feels nauseated, if pushed too far she vomits.

Childhood phobias typically fall into three major categories (Rutter & Garmezy, 1983). The first consists of phobias about *physical injury*, such as fear of germs, fear of choking, fear of having an operation, or fear of falling from a high place. The second consists of phobias about *natural events*, such as fear of the dark, fear of storms, fear of blood, or fear of animals (dog, snake, insect, and mice phobias are common). The third category consists of phobias about *social situations*, such as fear of crowds, fear of going to the doctor or dentist, fear of attending school, or fear of being separated from one's parents. Many experts believe that these last two social phobias are often related. Acute anxiety over being separated from one's parents often underlies a school phobia such as Julie's.

Psychologists disagree about the causes of childhood phobias. Psychoanalysts think they are symptoms of unconscious conflicts. The therapist who treated Julie, for example, suspected that the child really feared that something terrible would happen to her mother while she was away at school. This fear supposedly stemmed from the fact that Julie, in a moment of anger toward her mother, had wished that the mother was dead. Like many young children, Julie believed that "bad thoughts" can magically make things happen. When her mother suddenly had to go to the doctor, Julie was sure her horrible wish was coming true.

Psychoanalytic therapy involves helping children to understand the unconscious conflicts that are troubling them. Analysts believe that when conflicts are uncovered and discussed they lose much of their power to control the child's behavior. In Julie's case, the therapist helped her to see that a recent fainting spell her mother had suffered had started the child's secret fear, which then quickly heightened with the unexpected visit to the doctor. The therapist reassured Julie that many children sometimes feel angry toward their mothers but that thoughts and wishes can't kill. After discovering these hidden conflicts and talking about them, Julie was able to go back to school.

A therapist who subscribes to social learning theory would have explored Julie's learned experiences rather than her unconscious conflicts. These therapists view phobias as learned responses. A child might learn to fear school, for example, after an incident in which she is embarrassed when her teacher criticizes her in front of peers. Thereafter the child associates school with humiliation and refuses to go. Staying home from school is reinforcing because it lowers anxiety. Of course, not all phobias begin with some incident in which the feared object is paired with real physical or psychological harm. A boy might learn to fear dogs, for example, even though he has never been bitten by one. Social learning theorists suspect that modeling may play a role in many of these cases. If the boy sees others acting fearfully toward dogs, he may begin to imitate them.

According to social learning theory, what is learned can be *un*learned. Phobic children relearn how *not* to fear. A cognitive-behavioral therapist looks for the stimuli that are controlling the fear response. A child with school phobia, for example, is asked which aspects of school make him feel most afraid (riding the school bus? being in the school yard? meeting a certain teacher? answering questions in class?). Is the child also afraid of leaving his or her parents? Using this information, the therapist develops a program which gradually exposes the child to the school routine, starting with the least-feared aspects and working up to the most-feared ones. Throughout this process, called **desensitization**, the child is taught to remain calm, often using techniques of physical relaxation. Sometimes other children help by modeling how the behaviors can be performed without fear. When the phobic child's anxiety has lessened enough to make returning to school possible, rewards for school attendance are often offered while the inadvertent rewards for staying home (unlimited snacks and TV viewing, for instance) are withdrawn. All these methods have been successful, especially when used together.

desensitization
gradual exposure to feared aspects of the object of a phobia

ATTENTION-DEFICIT HYPERACTIVITY DISORDER

Seven-year-old Sammy was a trial to everyone who knew him. He chattered away constantly, but oddly enough he often never finished his sentences. His small, thin body was in perpetual motion—flitting here and there with jerky, bouncy movements, compulsively touching everything and everyone in sight. His mother could not remember a single meal or TV program that Sammy had managed to sit through from beginning to end. Sammy could never decide what he wanted to do. He would run outside to play, banging the door behind him and carelessly tripping over the cat, then a few minutes later he'd run back in, grab a piece of candy, and turn on the TV. After trying all the channels, he would abandon the set (which was still blaring), and run to his closet, where he'd frantically dig through the toys to find his baseball mitt. Sometimes he got so impatient unbuttoning a shirt that he would simply tear it open, letting the buttons fly. Other children refused to play with Sammy because he would never share, wait his turn, or follow the rules of a game. At school Sammy's behavior had his teacher at her wit's end. He didn't pay attention; he didn't concentrate; he didn't finish anything he started. After detailed instructions were given to the entire class, Sammy would inevitably shout out: "What are we supposed to do?" (Based on Fine, 1980)

Most elementary school children show *some* of Sammy's behaviors once in a while. But those who display them all, day after day in a variety of settings, are usually diagnosed as having **attention-deficit hyperactivity disorder** (Shaywitz & Shaywitz, 1984). "Attention deficit" describes Sammy's inability to keep his mind on anything for very long. "Hyperactivity" refers to his constant and rapid motion. In short, Sammy can't pay attention and he can't sit still. Between 2 and 5 percent of elementary school children suffer from this disorder, most of them boys (Lambert, Sandoval, & Sassone, 1978). Not all children with attention-deficit disorder are hyperactive, but many suffer from both problems.

attention-deficit hyperactivity disorder
a disorder in which children can neither pay attention nor remain still

Researchers have proposed several theories to explain this disorder. Most psychologists believe that there is at least some biological basis for the problem, resulting from prenatal or perinatal conditions, food allergies, or inherited factors (Shaywitz & Shaywitz, 1984). In fact, about 20 percent of hyperactive children do have a parent who was also hyperactive (Cantwell, 1975; Morrison & Stewart, 1971). But, say environmentalists, this doesn't prove a genetic link. Hyperactivity might run in families because young children imitate the "hyper" behavior of parents and siblings (Ross & Ross, 1982). A third theory contends that environment and heredity both play a part. If, for example, a child with a biological predisposition to hyperactivity undergoes pro-

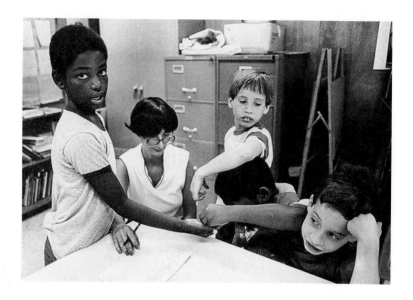

Children with attention-deficit hyperactivity disorder have great difficulty concentrating and keeping still. These boys work with their own teacher in a special class. *(David M. Grossman/Photo Researchers)*

longed excessive stress, symptoms may appear. Thereafter, stigmatizing the child with the label "hyperactive" may intensify the problem (Lambert & Hartsough, 1984).

During the 1970s, doctors often treated attention-deficit hyperactivity disorder with stimulant drugs, especially Ritalin (Whalen & Henker, 1976). Like all stimulants, Ritalin increases the ability to concentrate, and so children who take it usually perform better in school. These effects tend to last only 4 to 6 weeks though, so there seems to be little justification for keeping children on Ritalin year after year (Barkley & Cunningham, 1978).

It makes more sense to combine the short-term use of Ritalin with a program of behavior management that can effect a longer-lasting change. Such a program involves rewarding children with points, tokens, or stars whenever they behave appropriately (such as sitting still long enough to finish a meal or to do schoolwork). These intermediate rewards can then be "cashed in" for some special treat, toy, or privilege. Research shows that classroom behavior often improves with this type of treatment (O'Leary & Becker, 1967).

Reducing hyperactivity through a change in diet, especially eliminating artificial food additives, is not a solution in most cases. While there are some children whose hyperactivity is caused by an allergic reaction to certain foods, they form a small minority. Scientific studies have failed to establish a general link between food sensitivities and attention-deficit hyperactivity disorder (Goyette & Conners, 1977).

Summary

1. During the middle years, children gain increasing control over their behavior and begin forming friendships based on similarities and common interests.

Children's social worlds expand and become more competitive, as they are evaluated in school, on teams, and by their own peers.

2. The child's self-concept becomes more stable as children recognize the various attributes they possess. Self-esteem, how we feel about ourselves, has both positive and negative elements. Children with generally high self-esteem are generally more confident and independent than those with lower esteem.

3. The capacity for self-regulation is markedly stronger than it was during early childhood. Psychoanalytic theory attributes improved self-control to the development of ego skills, which help keep impulses in check. For social learning theorists, self-regulation improves because children spend more time in environments that reward self-control and punish impulsivity. As a consequence, children learn how to regulate their actions and model their behavior after the more self-controlled style of admired adults. Cognitive theorists contend that children can now use their thoughts, or inner speech, to control their actions.

4. Achievement motivation, the desire to perform well, continues to develop, and becomes especially important in settings where accomplishments are monitored and judged, such as school. For Erikson, the chief psychosocial crisis of middle childhood concerns the child's sense of accomplishment. Meeting the social and psychological challenges of this period gives children a sense of industry, a belief that they are competent and able to master things. Children who fail at or withdraw from the challenges of middle childhood develop a feeling of inferiority.

5. Underlying growth in achievement motivation is a change in the way children think about ability. Rather than being tied to specific skills, as in early childhood, older children think of it as a global, relatively stable psychological trait. Comparison with other children begins, and thinking about challenges becomes more realistic. But still, an immature understanding of ability makes children very vulnerable to the effects of failure.

6. Among the things that influence achievement motivation are the kinds of goals children have, whether they are primarily learning- or performance-oriented. Learning goals stress mastery, and mistakes are accepted as part of the process. Performance goals are more concerned with how one appears to others than with what one actually learns. Mistakes are particularly threatening since they carry the risk of appearing incompetent. Children with chronically low achievement may suffer from evaluation anxiety or from learned helplessness.

7. Peer relationships are critical to many of the social advances of middle childhood. Give and take with friends teaches children the importance of sharing, reciprocity, and cooperation. By trying to get peers to understand their thoughts and feelings, children learn to communicate more effectively.

8. The psychoanalytic theorist Harry Stack Sullivan believed that we are motivated to seek security by forming relationships with others who make us feel happy and safe. Interacting with others who think well of us fosters a positive self-identity and strong self-esteem. By age 11 or 12, children begin to appreciate the intimacy that friends can share, a capacity reflecting both cognitive and emotional growth.

9. Two common psychosocial problems of school-age children are phobias (intense, irrational fears) and attention-deficit hyperactivity disorder (difficulty sitting still and paying attention). Treatment for phobias can include psychoanalytic therapy, which seeks to help children resolve inner conflicts that may cause their fears, and cognitive-behavioral therapy, which helps children "unlearn" fears that have been acquired. Through desensitization children are exposed gradually to the things they fear and are rewarded for performing previously avoided behaviors. Attention-deficit disorder is most successfully treated with both drugs and behavior modification techniques.

Key Terms

achievement motivation

attention-deficit hyperactivity disorder

desensitization

ego skills

evaluation anxiety

industry versus inferiority

learned helplessness

learning goals

mastery motivation

performance goals

phobias

self-conceptions

self-esteem

self-regulation

time out

Suggested Readings

Eisenberg, N., and Strayer, J. (Eds.). (1987). *Empathy and its development.* New York: Cambridge University Press. A collection of articles dealing with research and theory on this aspect of prosocial development.

Hetherington, E. M., and Arasteh, J. (1988). *The effects of divorce, single parents, and stepparents on children.* Hillsdale, NJ: Erlbaum. A collection of articles based on the most recent and best research on family structure and its impact on child development.

Lamb, M. (Ed.) (1981). *The role of the father in child development* (2nd ed.). New York: Wiley. A collection of articles on fathers and the ways in which they effect their children.

Winn, M. (1984). *Children without childhood.* New York: Penguin. A journalist examines whether today's society is forcing children to grow up too fast and speculates on how children are affected by this pressure.

The Child in the Family

The Effects of Parenting Styles

Families with Working Mothers: The Importance of Attitudes

Divorce in Middle Childhood

Difference among Siblings

The Child in the Peer Group

The Structure and Functioning of Children's Groups

The Peer Group as a Context for Development

Popularity and Rejection in Peer Groups

Schools and Development

What Makes a Good School? Traditional versus Open Education

Patterns of Teacher-Student Interaction

Educating Children with Special Needs

School and Family

The Social Context of Middle Childhood

The preschool boys we discussed in Chapter 11 tested their strength, their daring, their cleverness through superhero scenarios. All foes could be vanquished, all fantasies fulfilled. If the action got rough, a teacher was there to soothe hurt feelings or redirect the game. If girls' play was gentler and more domestic, imagination still reigned, and protective adults could still be counted on. And for both sexes, parents influenced whom children played with, when they played, and even what they played.

In middle childhood, the rules of the game get more complicated. The psychological, physical, and cognitive advances of this period allow boys and girls to enter a social world where they are both more independent and less protected. The world of make-believe has given way to the real world where actions count. They are, in fact, out of the sandbox and onto the blacktop, where teachers handle first aid emergencies but generally don't smooth social interactions. Children find their own friends, play their own games, learn their own rules. Boys stop pretending to be superheroes now; in sports and with peers they really have to *be* strong. Girls stop dressing up in mommy's clothes, but they are often judged on how they look and act. For both sexes, the pressures to perform, to compete, to be popular all begin to grow. In the classroom children begin to make the choices that will shape their educations. Do you work hard or fool around, prefer reading or math, learn your spelling words or watch TV? These and many other decisions begin to have real consequences. Development is influenced too by the kind of school children attend. Is the classroom traditional or open? How well do teachers balance memorizing and creativity, rote learning and intellectual inquiry?

Still, the most important context for development is the family, and here too, children become more active shapers of their lives. Many learn to negotiate effectively for what they want while they struggle with the personal styles of their parents and siblings. In this chapter, we'll see how all the contexts of a child's life, including the values and pressures of the larger culture, shape development.

The Child in the Family

While middle-childhood boys and girls test and develop their social skills in peer groups and at school, considerable development is still going on within the family. Children at this age test their parents in many ways, a process that in turn strongly influences parenting behavior.

In this section we'll look again at the give and take of parent-child relations. We'll also examine an important contemporary issue: the possible effects of a mother's employment on children in middle childhood. Finally, we will consider why children within the same family can differ from one another so greatly.

THE EFFECTS OF PARENTING STYLES

The parenting styles we discussed in Chapter 11—authoritarian, authoritative, and permissive—continue to influence development across middle childhood. The authoritarian style, with its perfectionism, rigidity, and harsh discipline, affects children adversely, especially boys. Compared with other children, those with authoritarian parents tend to be lower in social responsibility but higher in social assertiveness and cognitive responsibility. Sons of authoritarian parents are lower than their peers in social assertiveness, cognitive ability, competence, and self-esteem (Baumrind, in preparation; Coopersmith, 1967; Loeb et al., 1980). Finally, authoritarian parenting is linked with high levels of aggressiveness in children (Yarrow et al., 1968).

Interestingly, overly permissive parents who set few limits and rarely punish have overly aggressive children as well. They may allow the child to behave aggressively for a variety of reasons: They may believe in letting a child "act out"; they may be indifferent to the child; or they may be weary of dealing with chronically aggressive behavior (Olweus, 1980; Sears et al., 1957). Children of permissive parents also tend to be more impulsive, less self-reliant, and less responsible (Baumrind, 1967, 1971).

In contrast, the children of authoritative parents are socially competent, responsible, and show high self-esteem (Baumrind, 1971; Coopersmith, 1967). Authoritative parents set clear standards and exert firm discipline, but they are warm, they listen to their children, and they respond to their children's reasonable demands.

These results raise again the question we asked in Chapter 11: To what extent does parenting create a certain kind of child, and how much does the child elicit a certain kind of parenting? The problem with studies showing the "effects" of parents' behavior on children is that they ignore the influence of the child's inborn temperament. How much of what we see is due to parenting and how much stems from a child's innate self? We also don't know whether a genetic predisposition to be passive or aggressive elicits a particular parenting style. Do responsible, competent children encourage warm, authoritative parenting, while aggressive children elicit harsh controlling parenting behavior (Lewis, 1981)? Researcher Gerald Patterson, who studied the relationship between parents' disciplining techniques and highly aggressive children, contends that such children have characteristics that make them difficult to control in the first place. Typically, they seek instant gratification, ignoring the possible consequences of their actions. And though overly aggressive, they are *under*responsive to many kinds of social stimulation, including both positive reinforcement for behaving properly and punishment for behaving badly. After observing families with overly aggressive and average boys, Patterson (1982) found that children with average amounts of aggressive behavior behaved less aggressively after being punished, but overly aggressive children were twice as likely to respond to punishment by maintaining or even *increasing* their aggressiveness. In fact, a cycle of aggression and punishment often develops in families with overly aggressive children, another instance of individual differences interacting with the environment. Breaking the cycle includes intervention: teaching parents to be more consistent in setting standards and guidelines and in providing rewards and punishments.

FAMILIES WITH WORKING MOTHERS: THE IMPORTANCE OF ATTITUDES

Not only is the number of women in the labor force steadily rising, but of all women, mothers are more likely to work than women without children. In

Between parent and child, feelings matter more than jobs. How a mother feels about working or staying home matter more to her children's well-being than the number of hours she spends each day with them. *(Nancy J. Pierce/Photo Researchers)*

1986, 63 percent of all women with children under 18 were working and among those with children aged 6 to 17 about 70 percent were employed (U.S. Bureau of the Census, 1987). The question for developmentalists used to be, how does maternal employment affect children? Now, research says a better question is, what effect does a mother's *attitude* about working have on her children's development?

When middle-class mothers routinely stayed at home in the past, those who worked felt guilty, and society's disapproval only reinforced their fears. Today, working mothers are the norm, and the woman whose self-esteem benefits from her work may even become a better parent (Hoffman, 1983). In contrast, women who stay home when they would rather be working may be less effective mothers. Several studies have found that a mother's *satisfaction* with being a homemaker *or* an out-of-home worker matters more than whether she works. Simply put, children of parents who feel good about their lives tend to be better adjusted than children of more dissatisfied parents (Hoffman, 1974; Scarr, 1984).

From about age 11 on, children of working mothers are likely to have household responsibilities as well as specific rules structuring their activities (just one television show before homework, for example) (Hoffman, 1974). Wisely administered, such rules and responsibilities can enhance a child's development, but the effects of maternal employment seem to differ for girls and boys.

Girls trained to be independent in the home tend to be positively adjusted and perform well in school (Hoffman, 1979). Daughters of employed mothers also are less likely to have sex-stereotyped attitudes about appropriate careers for men and women than do girls whose mothers do not work (Hoffman, 1983). The change in attitude that has occurred in just the last generation is startling. Many studies have found that girls with working mothers have higher self-esteem and career aspirations than do those whose mothers don't work (Bronfenbrenner & Crouter, 1982; Hoffman, 1974).

The impact of a mother's employment on boys appears to vary with the family's social class. In general, middle-class boys are more affected—*positively and negatively*—by their mother's working than are working-class boys (Hoffman, 1979; Lamb, 1982). Middle-class boys whose mothers work are less likely to develop sexist attitudes than are the sons of full-time homemakers (Hoffman, 1979). But several studies also show that middle-class sons of working mothers don't do as well in school as boys whose mothers are not employed (Bronfenbrenner & Crouter, 1982). For working-class boys, the differences between those whose mothers work and do not work are minimal. One reason for this pattern is that working-class families usually hold more traditional attitudes toward sex roles than do middle-class households, regardless of the mother's work status. Relationships and ideas are therefore less likely to change as a result of a mother being in the labor force (Hoffman, 1979).

Latchkey children

Between 2 and 10 million school-age children let themselves into empty houses after school each day (Goleman, 1988a). These **latchkey children** stay home without an adult while their parents are working.

Concern for the emotional well-being of these children has led to a number of research studies. One study compared groups of children in the fourth through seventh grades who were unsupervised at home after school with children in the same grades who were cared for by a parent or grandparent. Overall, the latchkey children and the unsupervised group were very similar on measures of emotional adjustment (Rodman et al., 1985). But not all self-care situations are alike, and it can be misleading to group all latchkey children together (Steinberg, 1986). Self-care children who go straight home after school, report in by phone to their parents, and stay at home, for example, are far less likely to succumb to peer pressure and possibly get into trouble than are children who stay unsupervised at a friend's house or just "hang out" after school. Further, children of authoritative parents are less susceptible to peer influence than are those reared permissively, regardless of their after-school situations. In short, good parent-child relations probably influence a child's behavior more strongly than any type of child-care arrangement.

Many people are concerned about the fears and anxieties children may feel when left on their own. One latchkey child confessed that several things make her feel fearful when she is home alone—including the sound of the wind and the sky getting dark fast (*The Christian Science Monitor*, November 27, 1985). Heightened fears are more common among urban than rural or suburban children who are home alone, which is hardly surprising given the higher crime rates in city neighborhoods. "Issues & Options" offers some guidance to parents who must leave their children alone.

latchkey children children who stay home without an adult while parents work

Issues & OPTIONS

Latchkey Children: Some Practical Suggestions for Parents and Educators

In the ideal world there would be no latchkey children. All working parents could find and afford loving, reliable adults to care for their children after school; all communities would offer supervised, imaginative after-school activities as an alternative. When neither of these options is available, parents can do a lot to help their children feel more secure at home alone.

1. Prepare the child for self-care before the arrangement begins. Have a regular place where the child is expected to be and a set of activities for the child to do. Give thorough instructions about how things work in the house, what to do in an emergency, what to do until parents come home, and when to expect a parent home. Make sure not to press the child into household responsibilities before he or she is ready for them.

2. Ask the child to "check in" with an adult as soon as he or she gets home. This can be a parent or a relative or neighbor.

3. Teach the child how to reach a nearby adult in case of problems. Children should be encouraged to call if they feel at all worried or concerned. Some neighborhoods identify an adult whom children on the block can call.

4. Give the child careful instructions about how to answer the phone and how to respond to visitors. Children should not tell strangers on the phone that they are home alone, nor should they let strangers into the house.

5. Parent in ways that facilitate healthy decision-making skills. Children raised authoritatively fare better on their own than other children do.

Being a latchkey child needn't be all bad. When children have guidelines to follow, they are less vulnerable to the harmful consequences of being home alone. (*John Lei/Stock, Boston*)

DIVORCE IN MIDDLE CHILDHOOD

When divorce causes families to reorganize, older elementary school children are likely to do better emotionally than younger children (Hetherington & Camara, 1984). The older elementary school child has more sophisticated coping abilities and a more extensive network of friendships and support outside the family. By middle childhood, in fact, most children whose parents divorced earlier have relatively few problems that are attributable to their parents' separation.

Some elementary school children do not respond well to their parents' divorce, however, and four factors seem to make a difference (Hetherington, 1989). First, boys have more difficulty with divorce than girls, especially if they live with their mother following the marital breakup. Following a divorce, boys and single mothers are often likely to get drawn into a coercive cycle of aggression (Hetherington & Camara, 1984). Second, children whose relationship with their father continues after the divorce do better than children who lose the father-child tie (Peterson & Zill, 1986). Third, children whose parents behave well toward each other after the divorce have fewer problems than those whose parents continue to quarrel (Hetherington & Camara, 1984). And finally, children whose financial circumstances are not dramatically harmed by the divorce do better than those whose lifestyles decline sharply (Hetherington & Camara, 1984). And as "Focus On" suggests, when overly burdened parents load adult responsibilities onto already stressed children, development suffers.

Even if older children seem less upset by their parents' divorce than younger ones, the older children are not necessarily immune to its impact. At least one recent study indicates that some of the negative consequences of divorce often emerge years later (Wallerstein & Blakeslee, 1989). In Wallerstein's study, although as children they had apparently adapted well, years later, young adults whose parents had divorced earlier felt embittered and troubled. Because this study lacked a control group (young adults whose parents did not divorce), the results should be considered inconclusive, although the study does remind us that in assessing any single life event, we need to look carefully at both long- and short-term consequences.

DIFFERENCES AMONG SIBLINGS

They share the same parents, live in the same house, and even have some matching genes, but siblings' personalities may be as different as strangers'. The reasons lie in the innate differences of temperament and in the fact that, while addresses may be shared, experiences and feelings may not be (Daniels et al., 1985).

Experiences within the family

One brother describes his family as close, while another feels it is distant. One sister finds her family life stressful, but her siblings do not. A girl recalls cooperation in her family; her brother says family members never cooperated. Such differences in experience and perception can have significant consequences for development. For example, children who say their families are

FOCUS ON   *Hurried Children, Stressed Children*

Janet is ten years old but has many adult responsibilities. In addition to taking care of her clothes and room, she must prepare breakfast for herself and her younger sister and make sure that they get off to school on time. (Her mother leaves for work an hour before Janet needs to get to school.) When she gets home, she has to do some house-cleaning, defrost some meat for dinner, and make sure her sister is all right. When her mother gets home Janet listens patiently to her mother's description of the "creeps" at work who never leave her alone and who are always making cracks or passes. After Janet helps prepare dinner, her mother says, "Honey, will you do the dishes? I'm much too tired," and Janet barely has time to do some homework. (Elkind, 1981, p. 149)

Like many children of divorce, Janet is being stressed by an overload of adult responsibilities—caring for the house, her little sister, her mother. At the same time, she is separated from one parent and living with another who is herself experiencing great stress.

But divorce alone isn't hurrying children out of their childhood and putting them under stress (Elkind, 1981). The trend toward early academics may be pushing children along too far, too fast. Even in their clothing, children are encouraged to look like mini-adults, in designer jeans, jogging suits, earrings, sheer stockings, and heels. As child psychologist David Elkind notes, "When children dress like adults, they are more likely to behave as adults do, to imitate adult actions" (1981, pp. 8–9).

Traditionally, argues Elkind, children vented their stress through physical activity—exercise, free play, and sports. But these outlets are increasingly cut off by the pressure of academics, the dominance of television (see Chapter 11), household responsibilities, and

Hurrying childhood. "When children dress like adults they are more likely to behave as adults do. . . ." Many developmentalists think children today are being pushed toward adulthood too soon. *(Bruce Forrester/Jerobaum)*

so on. Stress then dissipates itself through other body systems and can lead to hypertension, peptic ulcers, headaches, and heart disease. In fact, pediatricians find children today are suffering from a greater incidence of headaches, stomach aches, allergic reactions, and so on, than children in past generations (Elkind, 1981). Elkind urges parents and educators to respect the innocence and uniqueness of childhood. Adults who ask children to help carry their burdens only do children harm. "Children need time to grow, to learn, and to develop. To treat them differently from adults is not to discriminate against them but rather to recognize their special estate" (1981, pp. 21–22).

unfriendly are far more likely to show signs of emotional or behavioral problems than siblings who do not perceive their families this way.

To understand how siblings can experience their families so differently, recall the theme of interaction that we've been discussing throughout this book: Within every family, each child's temperament meshes differently with his or her parents' temperaments, characteristics, and life circumstances. An athletic child may be favored by an athletic parent over a less active sibling. One child may remind a parent of an ill-liked relative, while another resembles a favorite sister. Child one excels in school; child two is slower. In some families, child one is favored and child two is criticized; in others, child two gets extra help and support. One child may grow up during difficult financial times, while a later sibling is born in a more prosperous, less stressful period. A death in the family, divorce, or even a move can be very troubling to one child but may not affect an older or younger one as much. A very sensitive child could have emotional difficulties in one set of circumstances but might fare much better in less stressful times.

Birth order and family size

How many siblings you have and where you fall in the order strongly influence both your experiences and your development. New parents may lack confidence, but they may spend more time with their child. And while later-born children may feel shortchanged by their parents, they are usually more popular among their peers (Hartup, 1983). Perhaps that is because first-borns, as young children, spend more time with adults. Later-borns grow up with other children, learning social skills that help them get along with their peers. It is difficult to generalize about the effects of birth order, however, because these effects are themselves affected by spacing, gender, and family

A child's birth order in the family can have distinct advantages and disadvantages. First-born children can enjoy the fun of adult family life without competing for attention with a younger sibling. Although first-borns get more attention from parents, later-born children often have special relationships with their older siblings. (left, *Mimi Forsyth/Monkmeyer;* right, *George W. Gardner/The Image Works*)

size. Closely spaced children's experiences differ from those of children born further apart, and a first-born girl will be treated differently from a third-born girl. But what if that same girl followed two boys? Similarly, being second of two is likely to be very different from being second of five.

Sibling deidentification

Marie is the family athlete. Trophies fill her shelves, and team practices occupy her afternoons. Younger sister Kate shuns sports and spends most of her free time drawing and painting. Are these differences inborn or cultivated? Would Kate be more athletic if Mary were less so? Perhaps. Some children deliberately carve out an identity that is different from their siblings'. This phenomenon, **sibling deidentification** (Schacter, 1982), suggests again how children can actively shape their own development. By choosing to be unlike their sibling (that is, by *de*identifying with them), children participate in determining their own personality. It is likely that the effects of sibling deidentification will persist into adulthood because many personality traits are consolidated during adolescence.

sibling deidentification
one process through which children develop identities different from siblings

The Child in the Peer Group

In William Golding's novel *Lord of the Flies*, a plane carrying a load of British schoolboys, aged 6 to 12, crash-lands on an uninhabited tropical island. All the adults are killed, and the boys must fend for themselves. Some try to impose organization; others resist, intent on acting out their own fantasies and running wild. Leaders emerge, cliques form, rivalries spring up. In the end, the rational democratic group is overcome by the violent irrational group. While Golding's portrayal of the social world of a group of schoolboys is bleak, it does show how the peer group in childhood is really a little society, with ingroups and outgroups, leaders and scapegoats, cliques and status hierarchies.

The development of a peer group is one of the most important transitions of middle childhood. Children have peer relations in early childhood, but they aren't organized around a social network with norms and standards that structure behavior. Here we will consider the structure of peer groups and how they function, why some children are more popular than others, and how peer relations affect psychological development.

THE STRUCTURE AND FUNCTIONING OF CHILDREN'S GROUPS

Group characteristics

Nothing distinguishes middle childhood peer groups so much as their sameness: same age, same sex, same race. In classrooms, clubs, and teams, children are grouped by age because their interests and developmental abilities are similar. But they tend to group themselves by race, from preschool through early adolescence (McCandless and Hoyt, 1961; Schofield & Sagar, 1977; Spencer, 1981). This is likely to be related to social class and residential patterns, but it is less obvious among boys, for whom participation in sports tends to break down racial barriers.

An even stronger grouping factor than race is sex. By this age, boys and girls are becoming very sensitive to the way they think the sexes should behave. For the most part, boys and girls play separately because they play differently. Boys' play is rougher, more boisterous, more competitive and takes place in larger groups than girls' play (DiPietro, 1981; Lever, 1976). Girls tend to form more intimate, more exclusive groups than boys, and girls make a point of avoiding boys who play roughly (Haskett, 1971). Outside of school, though, at home and in their neighborhoods, boys and girls are more relaxed about joining in each others' games (Maccoby, 1988).

Among boys particularly, middle childhood peer groups tend to be activity-oriented: Children who want to play the same game or sport come together whether they are friends or not. Among girls, whom you like usually counts more than what you do, as girls' groups center more on friendships than activities.

Group functioning

In a study known as the Robbers Cave experiment, investigators brought 22 fifth-grade boys to a summer camp and divided them into two groups with separate campsites (Sherif et al., 1961). Each group lived closely together, participating in both organized games and cooperative activities. Soon, strong feelings of cohesion developed among the boys in each group. When the two groups began to meet in friendly contests, such as baseball games and tugs of war, keen competitive feelings arose. At first, the losing group began turning against itself, with bickering and dissension accompanying each defeat, but things quickly changed. Intergroup competition *increased* the sense of cohesiveness and solidarity within each group, and all aggression was directed against the "others." Finally, the competition got out of hand. One side raided the other side's campsite, and, armed with rocks, the boys whose camp was raided attempted a counterattack. Counselors intervened before any damage could be done.

Now the experimenters tried to reduce the intergroup conflict. Joint activities, such as watching a film together, didn't work, but another strategy did. The investigators created a series of problems that could only be solved by intergroup cooperation. For instance, when the water supply broke down, the boys had to conduct a lengthy search of the pipes to find the source of the trouble. Another day a food supply truck developed engine trouble just when everyone was hungry. The boys worked together to get the engine started. A common goal, just as much as a common enemy, reduced group conflict and increased cohesiveness.

What Sherif and his colleagues discovered need not be confined to Robbers Cave. A camp counselor with a bunk full of squabbling boys can encourage them to work toward a common goal by designing a bunk logo or writing a bunk skit. In classrooms, too, teachers have found that children perform better in situations where they must cooperate rather than compete. For example, cross-racial harmony can be aided by structuring cooperative interaction and activities.

Common goals foster friendship. Working together draws children closer together as well. *(Susan Johns/Rapho/Photo Researchers)*

While a group's goal affects its functioning, an adult's leadership style can be just as important. And as with parenting, authoritative adult leadership is more desirable than authoritarian or permissive leadership. The Little League coach who screams at his players on the field—"You should have caught that, Tony"—and reproaches them for losing—"You guys really blew this game"—breeds only resentment and self-doubt in his players. But the coach who treats all his players with consideration, praises them for their successes, and works with them to improve their weaknesses engenders group contentment and cohesion.

THE PEER GROUP AS A CONTEXT FOR DEVELOPMENT

Beyond the pleasures of companionship that friends offer, peers foster development in ways that adults do not. Within the peer group, children learn sex-role norms; when, where, and whether to fight; how to cooperate and share with equals; how to nurture friendships. Children who have had poor relationships during middle childhood show a wide range of behavioral and psychological problems later. In fact, one of the best childhood predictors of delinquency is not getting along with others (Hartup, 1983).

Researchers studying male delinquents and nondelinquents used school records and self-evaluations to learn about their subjects' childhood peer relations. While similar in age, social class, IQ, and ethnicity, these two groups differed in one key way: The delinquents had poor relationships with their peers; they were both more aggressive and less well-liked by other children (Conger & Miller, 1966). Often, children having trouble with peers are also having trouble at home. Both sets of problems—with family relationships and with friends—may lead a child to seek satisfaction outside of cultural norms.

Even during adulthood, psychological problems can be traced back to childhood peer relations. Eleven years after finishing third grade, subjects whose school records showed negative ratings by their peers were more than twice as likely to have been treated for mental health problems. Peer ratings, in fact, were the best predictors of mental health—more accurate than IQ, school performance, school attendance, or even teacher ratings (Cowen et al., 1973).

POPULARITY AND REJECTION IN PEER GROUPS

Popularity among school-age children comes to those who are socially skilled, have above-average intelligence and strong academic skills, and are physically attractive (Eitzen, 1975; Langlois & Stephan, 1977; Lerner & Lerner, 1977). Strong self-esteem enhances popularity (Hartup, 1983; Reese, 1961), and later-born children are often more popular than first-borns, perhaps because they have developed the social skills they needed to get along with their older siblings (Miller & Maruyama, 1976; Sells & Roff, 1964). Actually, the best predictor of healthy peer relations is a happy family life. Children who get along with their parents are likely to get along with peers, and those with serious problems at home frequently have problems in the peer group (Maccoby & Martin, 1983). Again we see how family life and development outside the family are intimately connected.

Researchers often study popularity by asking the students in a class to list the children with whom they would and wouldn't like to play. Using these techniques of **sociometry** (Figure 14-1) (measures of social relationships within a group), researchers then categorize children into four groups, or levels of popularity (Asher & Gottman, 1981; Gottman, 1977; Perry, 1979).

sociometry

measures of social relationships in a group

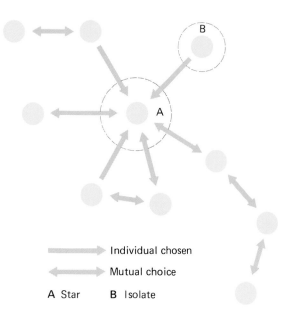

Individual chosen

Mutual choice

A Star B Isolate

**FIGURE 14-1
A SOCIOGRAM**
To construct a sociogram, researchers ask individuals to name group members with whom they would like to participate in an activity. Relationships between individuals can be seen graphically. Here, "A" is clearly a well-liked *star*, while "B" is viewed as an *isolate*. (*Source:* J. Vander Zanden. [1989]. *Human development*, 4th ed. Adapted with permission of McGraw-Hill, Inc.)

1. *Stars* are very well liked and have considerable status and influence in the peer group.
2. *Amiables* are liked by others, but they have less status and impact than the stars.
3. *Isolates* are neither liked nor disliked; these children are often simply ignored.
4. *Rejects* are actively disliked by others and have a negative impact on their peer group.

Both stars and amiables are smart and attractive, but the stars have better social skills and are more likely to act as leaders. They are the children who organize a game at recess, who plan after-school games, who initiate parties and other social events. The two lower categories, isolates and rejects, behave very differently from one another. Isolates have poor social skills, but they don't behave in the bizarre, deviant, or dishonest ways that cause rejection. Researchers watching socially isolated children discovered that these children do not know how to join in an activity or conversation of a group of peers. They hover on the fringes and then call attention to themselves in inappropriate ways—by disagreeing with group members, by asking irrelevant questions, by gratuitously stating their feelings or opinions, by telling stories involving themselves (Putallaz & Gottman, 1981). Usually, these awkward behaviors annoy the others, causing further isolation from the group. In contrast, rejects earn their rejection by being hostile and aggressive. Where isolates hover or stay away, rejects barge in and disrupt.

Intervention strategies

Social isolates can learn to stop hovering and make an early bid to enter the group. An adult can tell a child to just say "Can I play?" Learning to avoid

Social isolates have trouble joining in. They hover and often don't know what to say. *(Elizabeth Zuckerman/PhotoEdit)*

making inappropriate remarks comes next. Children can learn to fit into the group's frame of reference by asking relevant questions and sharing information. It helps, too, to avoid disagreements at the outset. These are not easy tasks, and even popular children sometimes have trouble joining a new group. Some children are helped by therapy that involves watching videotapes of themselves interacting with other children while a therapist points out better or more appropriate strategies.

Rejects need training in social skills too, but they must also learn how to control their aversive or disruptive behavior. Some theorists believe that very aggressive children have problems processing information when they meet with others (Dodge, 1986). As we noted in Chapter 10, highly aggressive children perceive hostile intentions where there are none. For example, if Maria accidentally runs into Brian in the playground, instead of shrugging it off, as most children would, Brian responds as if the accident were deliberate. He punches Maria, who then gets angry. After a number of incidents like this, Brian gets labeled as a troublemaker and is rejected by the peer group. A psychologist working with Brian might try to help him develop more accurate perceptions of his own and other's behaviors. As well, the child might be taught how to exercise leadership skills in a nonaggressive way. One popular approach has focused on helping aggressive children learn to "read" social cues more accurately in order to prevent them from misinterpreting other children's behavior (Dodge, 1986; Slaby & Guerra, 1988). (See "Focus On.")

Schools and Development

It is a rite of spring in middle-class America: the parent-principal meeting. Parents urge principals to consider their child's personality when making next year's class assignments. Some favor highly structured, strict teachers, while others prefer a more relaxed, creative style. While not every teacher is right for every child, teachers with certain traits do facilitate learning. We'll consider the way teachers affect children's emotional and cognitive development and how schools themselves influence the way children learn. Finally, we'll address the special needs of the physically, emotionally, or mentally handicapped child.

WHAT MAKES A GOOD SCHOOL?
TRADITIONAL VERSUS OPEN EDUCATION

In the Johnson School, the desks line up in neat rows. Today's math problems cover the blackboard, and pictures cut from *National Geographic* decorate the walls. Little else pulls attention away from the work at hand, a writing assignment. Grading papers at her desk is the teacher, who occasionally cautions one child or another to quiet down. Writing time over, the teacher rises and says, "Please turn to page 90 of your social studies book." The children take turns reading aloud about the Plains Indians.

FOCUS ON   *Training Programs for Aggressive Children*

When asked how he sees himself, a highly aggressive boy drew a picture of a fire-breathing dragon. Psychologists working with this child say the picture expresses the boy's wish to dominate others. Developmentalists are particularly concerned about such children because, besides causing trouble for their teachers and classmates, aggression alienates children from others, leading to isolation and rejection. And, says the newest research, aggression during childhood is the best predictor of adjustment problems later in life, including drug abuse and criminality (Goleman, 1988b).

We've seen that both innate and environmental conditions contribute to excessive aggression (Chapter 10). Some children are, by temperament, more prone to outbursts and loss of control than others, and boys are, biologically, more prone to aggression than girls. Environmentally, aggressive children are more likely than others to live in hostile families where parents have been overly punitive or aggressive themselves. Such children may model their aggressive behavior after their parents. In addition, these children may

When researchers showed this picture to overly aggressive children, interpretations differed. Some said the boy in the center was being picked on; some said the boy at left was bullying, while others said he was helping the middle child. *(Permission granted by American Guidance Service, Circle Pines, MN 55104. "Developing Understanding of Self and Others" [DUSO] by Don Dinkmeyer, Sr., and Don Dinkmeyer, Jr. Copyright 1982. All rights reserved.)*

be acting out the angry feelings induced by living with hostile parents.

Even if the causes differ, the behavior of overly aggressive children is the same: When angry they strike out,

---

traditional education
education that stresses uniformity and measures success through standardized test scores

This is the kind of classroom where most of us spent our elementary school days, getting a **traditional education**. If one word can sum up the way things are structured here, it is *uniformity*. Teachers try to bring their students to a prescribed level of achievement while following a prescribed curriculum. Children must conform to preset standards of behavior instilled through routines, rules, and the exercise of authority. Progress is measured by test scores, and achievement is encouraged through competitions, honors certificates, and other incentives. Classroom activities rarely involve teamwork.

In the Lincoln School, things look and are very different. Desks form clusters, not rows; pictures and projects cover the walls and tables; and the room is home to several hamsters, a snake, and a rabbit. On the blackboard, a list of questions asks about life among the Northwest Coast Indians. The chil-

FOCUS ON

(continued)

and they get angry too often. Where other children know how to joke back when teased, these children flare up. Where others know an accidental bump from an intentional push, these children always feel pushed.

Intervention, or training programs, have two kinds of goals. One concerns gaining control over aggressive outbursts; the second involves expressing anger or frustration in ways that will not harm others. At this age, most aggression is spontaneous, so if we can help children delay their responses, they may act less aggressively. Meeting these goals means teaching children to check both their physical sensations (Am I getting angry?) and their perceptions (*Should* I be getting angry?). If a child is being teased, for example, spotting the physical cues to his own anger, (feeling flushed or sensing his muscles tense up) can signal him to count to 10, for example. By then, the impulse to lash out may be gone. Training children to appraise their own perceptions is often done in group sessions. After looking at drawings of social interactions children explain what they think is happening. Psychologists working with them offer different interpretations,

and what at first may have seemed threatening can become less so.

Many aggressive children don't know how to behave in ways that other children like. Through *social skills training* they learn new behaviors to use in situations that tend to make them angry. In one training program, "one kid said, for example that he just stared at the kid who bumped him and told him not to do it again, then walked away. That put him in the position of exerting some control and keeping his self-esteem, without starting a fight" (John Lochman in Goleman, 1988b, p. B25). Teachers can show aggressive children how to ask for what they want ("You've been playing with that basketball for a long time. I'd like a turn."), how to behave prosocially in order to get what they want from someone ("Is it all right if I play, too?"), and how to respond when they feel aggressed against (saying "Watch where you're going" rather than hitting someone who bumped into you accidentally). Many social skills training programs are conducted in groups, so that aggressive children can learn appropriate strategies by brainstorming different situations along with their classmates.

dren are gathered in groups around the room, and can move freely among them. One group is building an Indian teepee while other children at a computer are designing decorations for it.

The teacher is showing a third group how to view a butterfly wing through a microscope, but when an unusual bird appears outside the window, she calls the class to watch it. A lively discussion follows about the possible purposes of the bird's brilliant color. Several children go off to the library corner, trying to identify the bird in a guidebook.

The activities in this classroom reflect the tenets of **open education**. Here, both teacher and children are active agents in the learning process. Teachers listen as well as talk, and children learn from each other through cooperative projects. Rules are flexible, and knowledge is more than facts; it is also what

open education
education in which both teacher and child are active agents in learning; evaluation accomplished through individual profiles

In open classrooms, activity centers foster cooperation and children learn by doing. *(Bohdan Hrynewych/Stock, Boston)*

students learn through the process of exploring (Watts, 1980). *How* a student learns matters more than *what* is taught. The curriculum springs from the interaction of teacher, student, and the environment (Noddings & Enright, 1983). Teachers encourage speculation, imaginative thinking, trial and error, and intelligent guesswork. Children are evaluated by means of individual profiles.

Which type of education is best for a child's social and emotional development? The evidence so far favors open education. Compared with children in traditional schools, children in open environments like school and their teachers better; they make more friends and are more likely to have opposite-sex as well as same-sex friends. They are more cooperative with peers, more self-reliant, and they develop fewer discipline problems (Raywid, 1983). These developmental effects of open education appear most often when the following conditions are met:

1. Children have an active role in their education; they can make choices among learning activities.
2. Evaluation is individual. Instead of receiving letter grades that compare children to each other, every child is compared to him- or herself regarding past performance and the potential for future work.
3. Materials are diverse. Reading about electricity in a textbook, for example, is enhanced by conducting experiments, watching a movie, visiting a power plant, hearing a lecture by an electrical engineer, and so on.
4. Instruction is individualized. Rather than teaching all students at the same pace or on the same level, the teacher spends some time with each child, helping to develop skills and overcome weaknesses.

Many classrooms, of course, combine elements of open and traditional education, but on balance, open environments are preferable in the elementary school years because they yield social and emotional benefits without compromising academic goals. Although achievement in reading and math is slightly higher in traditional environments, especially for students who are not self-starters (Brophy, 1979; Horowitz, 1979), traditional environments can impede social development by encouraging competition, discouraging cooperation, and stifling creativity. While learning the basics—reading, writing, and math skills—is essential, the way children are taught matters just as much. The *structure* of learning and its components are different issues, and it is still possible to learn traditional content through open means.

PATTERNS OF TEACHER-STUDENT INTERACTION

In many ways, good teachers are like good parents. They make demands, but they are also highly responsive to the children. Effective elementary school teachers set clear learning goals, communicate warmth, and provide appropriate rewards and punishments.

In short, good teachers are *authoritative*, not authoritarian or permissive (Minuchin & Shapiro, 1983; Rutter, 1983). They also respond differently to the needs of different children, offering less control to those capable of self-direction and more control to those who need more structure in learning.

But sometimes differential treatment is inappropriate or even prejudicial. After studying third-grade teachers in their classrooms, Charles Silberman identified four types of relationships that teachers have with different types of students: *attachment, concern, indifference, rejection* (Silberman, 1969, 1971). Teachers become *attached* to those children who achieve, conform, and make few demands. They are *concerned* about students who make appropriate demands in the class, but the teachers are *indifferent* to the silent and invisible child. Finally, they *reject* children whom they consider "behavior problems." (You might say teachers love the stars, like the amiables, ignore the isolates, and reject the rejects.)

Not only do teachers not spread their attention evenly over the class, students may even perform the way their teachers *expect* them to perform, making the link between school and development both subtle and powerful. In one now-famous experiment designed to test the influence of teachers' expectations on students' achievement, researchers changed the records of students' aptitude test scores. Children who were in fact low achievers now were ranked as high achievers; high achievers appeared to be low achievers. By the end of the school year a majority of the children performed the way their altered test scores—rather than their *actual* test scores—would have predicted. Researchers felt these results reflected teachers' expectations far more than students' abilities. Believing the test scores were accurate, teachers expected certain children to be slow, or average, or bright. And those expectations, said the researchers, affected achievement more than ability itself (Rosenthal & Jacobson, 1968).

A self-fulfilling prophecy—it becomes so if you think it is so—turned out to be only one of several variables at work in the classroom. Other researchers found that the effects of teacher expectations based on scores are not as strong

"I never knew that." When teachers combine high expectations with personal warmth, children thrive. *(Kathy Sloane)*

as Rosenthal and Jacobson suggested (Brophy, 1983), but the effects of another kind of prejudice—based on race and class—can be even more harmful. When asked which children they liked and disliked, teachers tended to rate blacks lower than whites and low-income children below middle-class children, *even when the lower-rated children had high IQ scores* (Leacock, 1969). In another study, one kindergarten teacher, after only 8 days in the class, sorted her students into reading groups that strongly resembled their socioeconomic status (Rist, 1970).

The effects of such prejudicial treatment can be powerful and insidious. Those students who are not expected to do well can lose confidence in their ability and gradually lose interest in school altogether. As performance falls, teachers justify their own stereotyped thinking, and other students learn to accept them as well: "What happens to one child happens to all. The classroom is a public place and when one child is treated unfairly the event is everybody's data for the construction of social reality" (Minuchin & Shapiro, 1983, p. 228). Academics, then, are only a fraction of schooling. The attitudes children absorb about themselves and others can be even more enduring, even if they are sometimes dead wrong.

The influence of sex

Joining the impact of scores, race, and social status in the classroom is sex: Teachers treat boys and girls differently. Boys get more attention than girls, but they also get more criticism (Minuchin & Shapiro, 1983). Girls perform and behave better than do boys in elementary school, so teachers are less critical of them. Yet later, in high school, boys begin to do better than girls, particularly in science and math, and they maintain their confidence and persistence in academic work, despite more critical feedback from their teachers.

One explanation for this paradox might lie in the *pattern* rather than in the *amount* of teacher feedback (Minuchin & Shapiro, 1983). One study found that teachers tend to criticize the intellectual aspects of girls' work, while boys were more often criticized for not following rules or not trying hard enough (Dweck, Davidson, Nelson, & Enna, 1978). Girls get one message (Don't bother to try harder; you just can't do the work) while boys learn another (Try a little harder; you'll get it right next time). Messages like these can reverberate in and out of the classroom, affecting both academic achievement and emotional development. Where boys learn to persevere through difficult tasks, girls often learn to feel helpless. (We'll examine this more closely in Chapter 16.) Again, teachers' responses to students can have serious enduring psychological consequences.

We turn now to schoolchildren who have special educational needs—the physically, emotionally, and mentally handicapped.

EDUCATING CHILDREN WITH SPECIAL NEEDS

May is one of the most popular children in her first-grade class. Other children seek her out, show her their latest treasures, and banter happily with her. So many children want to eat lunch with May each day that the teacher has to keep an engagement calendar. May is a quadriplegic, propped up in a wheelchair, immobile below her neck. She is also one of about 10 percent of school-age children in the United States with special educational needs stemming from a physical, emotional, or mental handicap (Lipsitz, 1977).

Among this group are the mentally retarded, with an IQ under 70; children with severe speech impediments; the emotionally disturbed; children with learning disabilities; and children with visual and hearing impairments

This girl's wheelchair makes her different at recess but not during science. For that reason, many parents and educators favor mainstreaming certain handicapped children. (*Jerry Howard/Stock, Boston*)

mainstreaming
placement of handicapped children in classrooms with nonhandicapped children

(Kakalik et al., 1973). Such a broad range of handicaps suggests an equally broad range of educational needs, and the debate persists among educators as to *where* these needs are best met: in special schools geared to special needs or by **mainstreaming** these children in classrooms with the nonhandicapped.

Until 1950, few special programs existed; all children attended regular classrooms. Gradually, the idea of separate needs took hold, and the 1960s and 1970s saw a dramatic rise in the number of special education programs. But in the late 1970s, opinion turned *against* separate classes, and federal law mandated mainstreaming wherever possible.

Mainstreaming has both benefits and costs. It allows handicapped children to interact and develop relationships with a wide range of peers and reduces the stigma associated with being segregated in a special class. Consequently, mainstreaming can aid a handicapped child's psychological development, particularly when the child develops close ties with classmates. Because differences often become more acceptable as they become more commonplace, mainstreaming also helps dispel prejudices toward the handicapped and reduces anxieties about them. It also prevents the ill effects of misdiagnosis (putting a normal child into a "slow" class by mistake, for example).

But despite its social and emotional benefits, mainstreaming may not be the best way to meet the cognitive needs of handicapped children. Teachers in regular classrooms gear their attention and lessons to a large group of students, most of whom are average. Those who fall below this range may not get the sort of instruction they need.

It may be that a compromise between mainstreaming and separate education is the best solution. Handicapped children could stay in regular classrooms most of the time, spending part of each day in resource centers receiving individualized instruction. They might also attend additional programs after school to help them keep up. Nonhandicapped students could then gain a better understanding of their handicapped peers, while the handicapped could learn both the social skills needed to interact with others and the cognitive skills to progress in schoolwork.

SCHOOL AND FAMILY

We end our discussion of middle childhood where we began, with the family. How children behave with peers and how they learn at school often reflects the quality of their lives at home.

It isn't enough for parents to simply ask "What did you learn today?" or to attend an occasional PTA meeting. Children do better in school when parents are actively interested in their homework, when they create an atmosphere conducive to studying, and when they provide sources of intellectual stimulation, whether on the bookshelf or at the dinner table.

Learning is not confined to schools; it can happen anywhere, and what is learned at home reinforces what is learned at school. In one study of elementary school children, researchers examined achievement scores in September, June, and the next September (Heyns, 1982). Most children's achievement advanced at about the same rate during the school year, but some children showed improvements between June and September, because they kept learning when school was out through stimulation provided at home.

Not only teachers teach. Parents who encourage curiosity tend to have children who value learning. *(Sybil Shackman/Monkmeyer)*

School-family influence can work the other way as well. Children whose daily lives are stressful, during a divorce, for example, can benefit from a supportive school environment. These students are generally less motivated, more disruptive, and don't do as well in schoolwork as children from stable families (Hetherington, Featherman, & Camara, 1981). These effects are particularly true of boys and show up most often during the first year or two of the crisis at home. After that, children do adjust to new family circumstances and are more able to cope (Hetherington, 1989; Wallerstein & Kelly, 1980).

Some parents, wanting to avoid labeling their child, try to conceal the divorce from the school. While family privacy is important, concealment does not help the child. Teachers need to be sensitive to the child's particular circumstances and to avoid labels that outlive the crisis. And schools need to keep *both* parents informed of the child's progress and of school activities. A nurturant school atmosphere that provides consistency, structure, warmth, and responsiveness can do a great deal to help children cope with changing life circumstances (Hetherington, Cox, & Cox, 1982).

Summary

1. During middle childhood, psychological, physical, and cognitive advances allow for greater independence. Pressures to compete increase, and children make choices that affect their own development. The most important contexts for development are the family, school, and peers.

2. As in early childhood, authoritative parenting is linked with high self-esteem, social competence, and responsibility in children. Authoritarian parenting is associated with lower self-esteem and more aggressiveness, while children of permissive parents are less responsible and more impulsive. We don't know how much a child's own personality influences the way he or she is treated, but overly aggressive children are usually difficult to control.

3. A mother's satisfaction either with working or not working affects children more than whether she works.

4. Girls whose mothers work tend to have higher career goals and self-esteem than girls whose mothers don't work. Middle-class sons of working mothers have more egalitarian attitudes about sex roles, but they may not do as well in school as boys whose mothers don't work. In working-class homes, where attitudes about sex roles are more fixed, boys seem almost unaffected by maternal employment.

5. Latchkey children, who stay home alone after school, are more affected by the relationship they have with their parents than by their after-school arrangements. Children raised by authoritative parents do best, especially when structure is provided for handling emergencies and for spending time alone.

6. Older children tend to be less harmed by divorce than younger children, especially if their financial circumstances remain fairly stable and if their parents treat each other well.

7. The markedly different personalities of siblings result from differences in temperament, treatment by parents, and circumstances within the family.

8. Birth order and the number of children in a family strongly influence development. Through sibling deidentification, too, children carve out identities sharply different from those of their brothers and sisters.

9. The peer groups that form during middle childhood, with their norms and structures, differ markedly from the friendships of early childhood. Now, groups include children of the same age, sex, and race. Working toward common goals increases cohesiveness and reduces conflict.

10. The most popular children at this age are socially and academically skilled, intelligent, and physically attractive.

11. Both social isolates and rejected children can learn the social skills they need to make friends. Training programs can help highly aggressive children to control aggressive impulses and to perceive other people's actions more accurately.

12. Traditional schools stress uniformity and individual competition. In schools favoring open education, cooperation and creativity are encouraged through more flexible curriculums and projects based on teamwork.

13. Effective teachers, like good parents, are authoritative. They set clear learning goals, communicate warmth, and provide appropriate rewards and punishments. When teachers are prejudiced, children's expectations for themselves can decline.

14. Teachers give boys both more attention and more criticism than girls, who tend to do better academically. By high school, though, boys do better than girls in math and science. Boys are encouraged to keep trying, whereas girls are led to believe that they lack the ability to improve.

15. Mainstreaming handicapped children can aid their development because it facilitates relationships with normal children, reducing the stigma of being different. Individual instruction may also be needed to meet the handicapped child's academic needs.

16. A stimulating home environment helps children achieve in school, and when problems arise at home, schools can offer children emotional support.

Key Terms

latchkey children   sibling deidentification
mainstreaming   sociometry
open education   traditional education

Suggested Readings

Dunn, J. (1984). *Sisters and brothers.* London: Fontant. One of the leading researchers on sibling relations discusses the relationships children have with their brothers and sisters and the impact of siblings on development.

Fine, G. (1988). *With the boys.* Chicago: University of Chicago Press. An ethnographic study of a Little League season and the interactions of the preadolescent boys who play on the teams.

Kidder, T. (1989). *Among schoolchildren.* Boston: Houghton-Mifflin. A journalist's moving account of his year observing in an elementary school classroom.

Liebert, R., and Sprafkin, J. (Eds.) (1988). *The early window: Effects of television on children and youth* (2nd ed.). Elmsford, NY: Pergamon. A collection of articles on television and its impact on the developing child's cognitive, social, and emotional development.

"Listen," F. Jasmine said. "What I've been trying to say is this. Doesn't it strike you as strange that I am I, and you are you? I am F. Jasmine Addams. And you are Berenice Sadie Brown. And we can look at each other, and touch each other, and stay together year in and year out in the same room. Yet always I am I, and you are you. And I can't ever be anything else but me, and you can't ever be anything else but you. Have you ever thought of that? And doesn't it seem to you strange?"

Carson McCullers, *The Member of the Wedding*

Adolescence

Physical and Cognitive Development in Adolescence

I was about six months younger than everyone else in my class, and so for about six months . . . after my friends had begun to develop (that was the word we used, develop), I was not particularly worried. I would sit in the bathtub and look at my breasts and know that any day now, any second now, they would start growing like everyone else's. They didn't. "I want to buy a bra," I said to my mother one night. "What for?" she said. My mother was really hateful about bras. . . . "I'm too old to wear an undershirt." Screaming. Weeping. Shouting. "Then don't wear an undershirt," said my mother. "But I want to buy a bra." "What for?" (Nora Ephron, *Crazy Salad*, pp. 4–6)

For every Nora Ephron bemoaning her late-arriving breasts, an early maturer is wishing hers would slow down. Being first in your Maiden-form can feel as miserable as being last in your undershirt. For both sexes, maturing bodies, whether fast-paced or slow, mark the dramatic shift from middle childhood to adolescence, a shift marked by self-consciousness and uncertainties, but also by pride, pleasure, and confidence. In this chapter, we'll discuss the physical changes of adolescence and the way teenagers feel about them. We'll discuss, too, the cognitive advances that carry a child from the limits of concrete reality to the unbounded mental world of abstract reasoning.

Parents of adolescents often say their teenagers are "going through a phase." Actually, they are going through three phases. Researchers usually distinguish among *early adolescence*, which covers the period from about age 12 through 14, *middle adolescence*, which lasts from about 15 through 18, and *late adolescence*, the years from 19 to 21 (Kagan & Coles, 1972; Keniston, 1970; Lipsitz, 1977). These divisions correspond roughly with those used by our educational system: Early adolescence spans the junior high years, middle adolescence the high school ones, and late adolescence the years at college. When you consider the great differences between a seventh-grader and a college senior, the usefulness of subdividing adolescence becomes clear.

Physical Development During Adolescence

"Now I'm opening out like the largest telescope that ever was!" "Goodbye feet!" Adolescents may not grow as quickly as Alice did in Wonderland, but many share her feeling of a body gone out of control. This rapid change is the final phase in physically becoming an adult and involves far more than simply growing taller. Adolescents develop all the physical characteristics of a mature man or woman, including the capacity to reproduce. These physical transformations are collectively called **puberty**.

puberty
physical transformation from child to adult

Not a child, not a man. Between ages 9 and 14, puberty added several inches each year to Jason's height, as his body changed from a child's to an adolescent's. (both, *Judy Gelles/Stock, Boston*)

CHANGES AT PUBERTY

The five major changes during puberty are (Marshall, 1978):

1. *Rapid growth and weight gain.*
2. *Further development of the gonads, or sex glands.* In males, the testes become able to release sperm; in females, ovaries begin releasing ova, or egg cells.
3. *Development of secondary sex characteristics.* These characteristics include changes in the genitals and breasts; the growth of pubic, facial, and body hair; a deepening of the voice in males; and further development of the sex organs.
4. *Changes in body composition.* Specific changes in the quantity and distribution of fat and muscle.
5. *Changes in the circulatory and respiratory systems.* Strength and stamina increase.

All these physical changes are triggered by **hormones**, chemical substances that act on specific organs and tissues. Most students are surprised to learn that no new hormones are produced at puberty. Instead, there is an increase in the production of certain hormones that have been present since before birth. In boys a major change is the increased production of testosterone, a male sex hormone, while girls experience increased production of the female hormone estrogen. And in both sexes, a rise in growth hormone produces the adolescent growth spurt.

hormones
chemical substances that act on specific organs and tissues

The growth spurt

In many homes, lines on a door mark the path of a child's growth. The lines move slowly upward, 1½ to 2 inches yearly. Then, soon after the eleventh line, the spaces between the lines widen, to 3, 4, even 5 inches in a single year, signaling the **adolescent growth spurt**, the pronounced increase in height and weight that marks the first half of puberty.

At the peak of the adolescent growth spurt, teenagers grow at the same rate as toddlers: for boys, a little over 4 inches per year (10.5 centimeters); for girls about 3½ inches (9.0 centimeters) (Tanner, 1972). As Figure 15-1 shows, the spurt for girls occurs about 2 years earlier than for boys, explaining why many seventh-grade girls tower over their male classmates.

Much of the height gain stems from a lengthening of the torso rather than the legs (Tanner, 1972). When young teenagers complain of feeling awkward, that some parts of their bodies are out of proportion to others, they are right. Different parts of the body tend to spurt at different times: first the hands and feet, then the arms and legs, finally the torso and shoulders. Accompanying the spurt in height is a gain in weight and in heart and lung capacity. These increases are different for boys and girls. For example, muscle tissue grows faster in boys, while fat increases more in girls. Compared with girls, boys also develop larger hearts and lungs relative to their size, which

adolescent growth spurt
pronounced increase in height and weight during first half of puberty

FIGURE 15-1
Left: Height (in centimeters) at different ages for the average male and female youngster. Right: Gain in height per year (in centimeters) for the average male and female youngster. Note the adolescent growth spurt. (*Source*: Marshall, W. [1978]. Puberty. In F. Falkner & J. Tanner (Eds.), *Human growth* [Vol. 2]. New York: Plenum Press.)

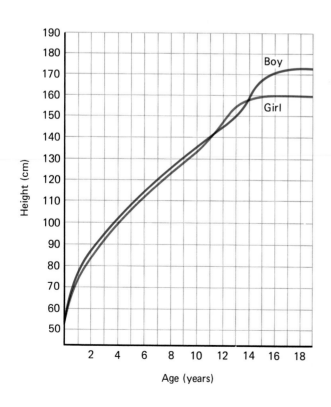

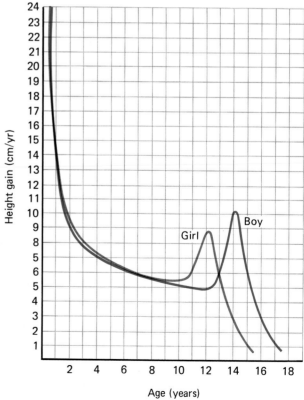

means their blood is pumped more forcefully and more oxygen is delivered to their bloodstreams. In addition, males develop a greater capacity for carrying oxygen in the blood and a greater ability to neutralize the chemical byproducts of exercise (Petersen & Taylor, 1980). These differences between the sexes help explain why, by the end of adolescence, boys on average have an advantage over girls in many sports.

Becoming a sexual being

The most dramatic physical changes of puberty involve sexuality: Internally, through the development of **primary sex characteristics**, adolescents become capable of sexual reproduction. Externally, as **secondary sex characteristics** appear, girls and boys begin to look like mature women and men. In boys primary and secondary sex characteristics usually emerge in a predictable order, with rapid growth of the testes and scrotum, accompanied by the appearance of pubic hair, coming first. About a year later, when the growth spurt begins, the penis also grows larger, and pubic hair becomes coarser, thicker, and darker. Later still comes the growth of facial and body hair, and a gradual lowering of the voice. Increased sweat gland development and a roughening of the skin are other changes of later adolescence. Around mid-adolescence internal changes begin making a boy capable of producing and ejaculating sperm. The first ejaculation of semen usually occurs about a year after the beginning of accelerated penis growth (Tanner, 1972).

primary sex characteristics developments in the structure and function of reproductive organs and systems

secondary sex characteristics visible characteristics of sexual maturity not directly related to reproduction

By late adolescence, boys generally have more muscle tissue than girls do, as well as greater heart and lung capacity. These physical differences can give boys an advantage over girls in certain sports. (*Bob Daemmrich/ Stock, Boston*)

In girls, sex characteristics develop in a less regular sequence. Usually, the first sign of puberty is a slight elevation of the breasts, known as the breast buds, but sometimes this is preceded by the appearance of pubic hair. Pubic hair changes as it does in males—from sparse and downy to denser and coarser. Concurrent with these changes is further breast development. After the "bud" stage, the nipple and area around it (the areola) become distinct from the breast and project beyond it. In the final stages, the areola recedes to the contour of the breast, and only the nipple is elevated. The female breast undergoes these changes regardless of breast size. In fact, changes in the shape and definition of the areola and nipple are far better indicators of sexual maturation than is breast size alone.

menarche
first menstrual period

In teenage girls, internal sexual changes include maturation of the uterus, vagina, and other parts of the reproductive system. **Menarche**, the first menstrual period, happens relatively late, not at the start of puberty as many people believe. Further, regular ovulation and the ability to carry a baby to full term usually follow menarche by several years (Hafetz, 1976). It is possible, however, for a girl to become pregnant at any time after her first menstruation.

Variations in timing and tempo

The timing and tempo of physical maturation vary widely. Among the Lumi people of New Guinea, the average girl doesn't begin to menstruate until she is 18 (Eveleth & Tanner, 1976). In the United States, in contrast, menarche typically occurs around age 12. And even within a single society, there are great differences. Some U.S. youngsters start puberty when they are only 8 or 9, others when they are well into their teens. The duration of puberty also varies greatly: 1½ years to 6 years in girls and 2 years to 5 years in boys (Tanner, 1972). This means that someone who begins to mature early and does so quickly can have finished puberty by age 10 or 11—*seven years* before some other adolescents are winding up the process. Of course, there is no guarantee that an early start to puberty means that it will proceed quickly. Sometimes an early starter takes longer to finish maturing than someone who starts late. There is also no relationship between the timing of puberty and height; late maturers reach the same average height as early maturers do (Marshall, 1978).

Why do some people mature early and others late? Both genetic and environmental factors play a part (Marshall, 1978). Identical twins are usually more similar in the timing and pace of puberty than other siblings are, suggesting that each of us inherits a predisposition to begin the transition to adulthood at a certain age and to have that transition unfold at a certain rate. However, the extent to which this predisposition is actually realized depends on the environment, especially on nutrition and health. Puberty usually begins earlier among youngsters who have been well nourished and free of serious illness throughout life. In fact, improvement in nutrition, sanitation, and disease control have led to earlier maturing over the last two centuries (Eveleth & Tanner, 1976). For example, the average age at menarche in Norway some 150 years ago was about 17; today it is about 13. The trend toward earlier puberty, called the **secular trend**, has occurred in other industrialized

secular trend
trend over time toward earlier puberty

Though close in age, these teenagers are far apart in size. By the end of puberty though, the shortest may now end up being the tallest. *(Alan Carey/The Image Works)*

nations and, more recently, in developing countries as well. But the declining age of puberty is leveling off in most industrialized nations. For instance, no substantial change in the average age of first menstruation has occurred in Oslo or London over the past 25 years (Eveleth & Tanner, 1976). Apparently, environmental conditions there have improved to the point where the average age at menarche is approaching its genetically determined lower limit and probably won't decline much below 12.

ADJUSTING TO PUBERTY

As writer Nora Ephron makes wonderfully clear (p. 434), when the outward signs of puberty don't arrive on time, inner turmoil often does. Looking different from peers—whether one is the last to mature or the first—can lead to unease and embarrassment. And whether these feelings are soothed or churned up often depends on how parents react. Parents can ease adjustment to puberty by responding to their children's worries with tact and understanding. In fact, physical changes can be a springboard for frank discussions about sex and pregnancy, discussions that can help parents and children feel closer to each other. Parents who have trouble adjusting to their youngster's development may feel depressed to see their child growing up or nervous at the prospect of their adolescent's sexual maturity.

Parents sharply influence their child's reactions to puberty through their own expectations and attitudes (Brooks-Gunn & Ruble, 1982). Below, two women recall their mothers' reactions to their first menstruations:

When I discovered [my period, my mother] told me to come with her, and we went into the living room to tell my father. She just looked at me and then at him and said, "Well, your little girl is a young lady now!" My dad gave me a hug and congratulated me and I felt grown up and proud that I was a lady at last. (Shipman, cited in Brooks-Gunn & Ruble, 1979)

Another woman, who started menstruating at 11, got a very different response.

> I had no information whatsoever, no hint that anything was going to happen to me. . . . I thought I was on the point of death from internal hemorrhage. . . . What did my highly educated mother do? She read me a furious lecture about what a bad, evil, immoral thing I was to start menstruating at the age of eleven! So young and so vile! Even after thirty years I can feel the shock of hearing her condemn me for "doing" something I had no idea occurred. (Weideger, cited in Brooks-Gunn & Ruble, 1979)

Pride or shame. When parents sound these messages about puberty, adolescents listen and are affected. Doubtless, the first woman quoted above had an easier time adjusting to puberty than did the second. Actually, parents' signals about physical maturation begin before puberty and have a lasting effect. When a girl's mother leads her to believe that menstruation will be unpleasant, the girl tends to experience greater menstrual discomfort than peers whose attitudes are not negatively biased. Also experiencing greater distress at puberty are girls who menstruate early or who are otherwise unprepared (Brooks-Gunn & Reiter, in press; Brooks-Gunn & Ruble, 1979, 1982). In adjusting to puberty, then, stress is minimized if adolescents know what changes to expect and have positive attitudes toward them.

Adjusting to puberty is especially difficult if the physical transformations are coupled with other major life changes. For example, girls who started to menstruate, began dating, and entered junior high school all in the same year tended to suffer a decline in self-esteem not experienced by their later-maturing peers (Simmons & Blyth, 1987). Coping with all these changes at once seemed to take its toll, making these young adolescent girls less confident about themselves. Interestingly, boys in this study did not suffer a drop in self-esteem at puberty, perhaps because they physically matured *after* the transition to junior high school was over. This suggests that puberty, by itself, need not have negative effects on a youngster's self-image (Simmons & Blyth, 1987).

Just as adolescents must adjust to the changes of puberty, so must their parents. Generally, parents and children bicker more during the teenage years than they do during childhood or late adolescence (Steinberg, 1987). This is especially true of early adolescence, before age 15 or 16. The heightened period of conflict may be due to hormonal changes or to the disruption of established family patterns caused by the transformation of a child into a near-adult. In the past this conflict may have served the useful purpose of helping to push young adolescents out of the family nest. Today, of course, when many young adolescents still have years of education before them, the value of being nudged away from the family is less obvious. Still, teenagers eventually need to separate from their parents and become autonomous. The family squabbling of early adolescence may help them to begin this process.

The disagreements between teenagers and parents may help adolescents prepare for independence. *(Spencer Grant/The Picture Cube)*

EFFECTS OF EARLY VERSUS LATE MATURATION

Rachel, age 12, looks more like the singer Madonna than a schoolgirl, while her classmate Steven can pass for her kid brother. For both sexes, differences in the timing of physical maturation affect social and emotional development.

Early-maturing boys, for example, are more likely to experience problem behaviors, such as truancy, minor delinquency, and difficulties at school (Duncan et al., 1985). For this group, physical maturity encourages them to make friends with older boys who lead them into "trouble." But early-maturing boys also tend to be more popular, to have more positive self-conceptions, and to be more self-assured than their later-maturing peers (Livson & Peskin, 1980).

These social advantages often come with a price, however. Although men who matured early tend to be more responsible, cooperative, and self-controlled, they are also more conforming, conventional, and humorless. Men who matured late, in contrast, are often more insightful, inventive, and creatively playful (Livson & Peskin, 1980). What can explain these personality differences that emerge in later life? One possibility is that, because of their more adult appearance, early-maturing boys are pushed into leadership roles sooner than their peers. But this early push into positions of responsibility may come too fast, stifling creativity and willingness to take risks. By contrast, late-maturing boys, whose physical appearance makes it harder for them to gain social status when young, may be forced to be more inventive in meeting life's challenges.

For girls, early and late maturation leads to different—often opposite—experiences. (H. Jones, 1949; Jones & Mussen, 1958). This is partly because girls, on average, mature 2 years earlier than boys, so the early-maturing girl is very far out of sync with her classmates, just as the late-maturing boy is. As a result, the early-maturing girl may feel awkward and self-conscious, even embarrassed about her body (Simmons & Blyth, 1987). This is especially true in a culture such as ours which admires women with the willowy, "leggy" look of preadolescence. Not surprisingly, the early-maturing girl is often less poised and self-assured than other girls her age (Livson & Peskin, 1980). This does not necessarily detract from her popularity, however. Frequently, she is just as popular as her later-maturing peers, sometimes even more so if the attitudes of boys are considered (Simmons, Blyth, & McKinney, 1983). But ironically, this attention from boys, particularly older ones, can cause an early-maturing girl anxiety and distress. Pressure to date or even to have sexual relations can be overwhelming when a girl is not psychologically ready. A sizable minority of early-maturing girls become drawn into deviant activities (drug use, truancy, delinquency) by older adolescents. This can have negative effects on their educational aspirations. In one study conducted in Sweden, early-maturing girls were much less likely to go beyond the compulsory level of high school than were their late-maturing peers (Magnusson et al., 1986).

But being an early-maturing girl isn't entirely a disadvantage (Peskin, 1973). Because early-maturing girls, like late-maturing boys, are forced to cope with being physically far "off-schedule," they often develop some positive traits to help them deal with being different from peers. These traits include creativity and independence, both of which can be highly beneficial throughout adult life.

Health Problems During Adolescence

"I discovered that I hated all the stupid things I was doing," explained a 15-year-old who had recently given up drugs. "I just looked deep into myself and realized what I was—and what I refused to be." This teenager's decision underscores an important truth about some of the major health problems of adolescents: Many result from *choices* and so can be minimized or completely avoided. Here we'll discuss three such problems: eating disorders, drug and alcohol abuse, and sexually transmitted diseases.

EATING DISORDERS

Teenagers and their huge appetites are legendary. Overnight pounds of cookies, entire roast chickens, and quarts of ice cream disappear from the kitchen. But eating a lot doesn't mean eating well. In fact, teenagers are one of the most poorly nourished groups in the country. Girls, in particular, have poor eating habits. They skip meals, especially breakfast, snack frequently on foods high in sugar, and are prone to fad dieting (Mounger, 1970). One survey found that 80 percent of all teenagers get inadequate iron, 61 percent inadequate protein, and over 30 percent inadequate amounts of vitamins A and C (McGanity, 1976).

By themselves, poor nutrition and lack of exercise would lead to extra pounds, but a third factor—lowered basal metabolism—makes gaining weight even more likely. **Basal metabolism** is the rate at which the resting body burns off calories. During adolescence, basal metabolism normally drops by about 15 percent, so young people who don't adjust their food intake usually put on pounds. Obesity, in fact, is about three times as common in adolescence as in childhood (Paulsen, 1972). The problem is best handled through a program of exercise combined with proper nutrition (Mayer, 1968).

basal metabolism
rate at which resting body burns calories

Between 1 and 3 percent of adolescent girls try to avoid excessive weight gain by forcing themselves to vomit after gorging on high-calorie foods. This disorder, known as *bulimia*, can cause serious problems, including digestive disorders, eroded tooth enamel, rupture of the esophagus, and depression. Small therapy groups that teach bulimics self-control skills and raise their low self-esteem have proven quite effective in treating this disorder.

More serious, even life-threatening, is **anorexia nervosa**, the "starving disease." During their early or middle adolescence, about 1 in 250 teenage girls becomes anorectic. Nearly all are white or Asian from upper- or middle-class families. Anorexia often begins with dieting to lose a few pounds, but then the "dieting" continues until weight drops drastically. Even when an anorectic becomes gaunt, she still sees herself as heavy and in need of further weight loss. While her parents argue, threaten, and beg her to eat, she refuses. If forced to eat she may force herself to vomit, as a bulimic does. The causes of anorexia are often traced to feelings about growing up and becoming independent. Dieting can make a teenager feel in control, while extreme weight loss allows her to feel like a child again: Her parents worry and fuss over her, her skinny body is childlike, she stops menstruating. Typically, anorectics resist treatment; some lose as much as half their body weight, and about 20 percent actually starve to death. In advanced cases, hospitalization and force-feeding are often required. Treatment then continues with individual counseling, behavior modification, and group or family therapy (Vigersky, 1977). The following danger signs for anorexia should alert parents to seek medical help (Steinberg & Levine, 1990).

anorexia nervosa
eating disorder in which young people may starve themselves

- Intense fear of becoming fat that does not diminish as weight is lost
- Disturbance of body image (claiming to look "just right" or to "feel fat" even when emaciated)
- Extreme, self-induced weight loss (25 percent or more of original body weight, or 25 percent below normal weight for someone her age and height)
- Denial that anything is wrong*

*Excerpt from *You and Your Adolescent* by Laurence Steinberg and Ann Levine. Copyright © 1990 by Laurence Steinberg and Ann Levine. Reprinted by permission of Harper & Row, Publishers, Inc.

DRINKING AND OTHER DRUG USE

While TV ads on Saturday morning cartoon shows urge children to "just say NO!" to drugs, afternoon football commercials tell them that saying "yes" to beer is essential to having fun. And while many celebrities speak out against cocaine and marijuana, many others admit to using and enjoying drugs.

Most teenagers are lured into drinking and drug use, at least to some extent. As Figure 15-2 shows, nearly all high school seniors have tried alcohol, and about half have tried marijuana. About 5 percent of U.S. high school seniors use marijuana daily, and many report being "stoned" in school at least once during the past 6 months (Johnson & Uppal, 1980). The percentages who have tried other drugs are much smaller, ranging from 26 percent for stimulants to 1.2 percent for heroin. By far, the most common drug tried, and abused, by U.S. teens is alcohol (Johnston, O'Malley, & Bachman, 1986).

About 5 percent of U.S. high school seniors drink alcohol daily, and over a third report having had more than five drinks in a row at least once in the past two weeks (Johnston, O'Malley, & Bachman, 1986).

Those who are optimistic about teenage alcohol and drug use note that the problem was worse during the late 1970s. But others contend that the problem is still too widespread and that adolescents are now experimenting with drugs at a younger age. Many psychologists believe that this early experi-

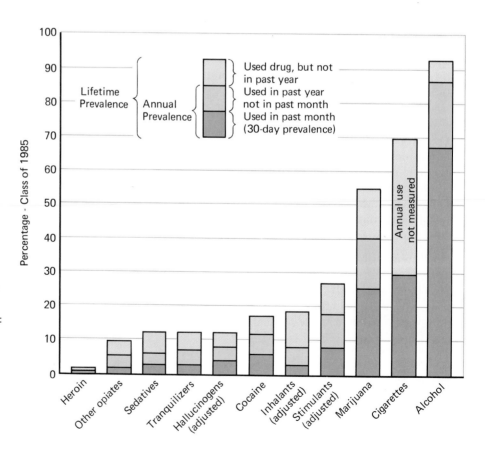

FIGURE 15-2

Prevalence of recency of use of 11 types of drugs among seniors in the class of 1985. (*Source*: Johnston, L., O'Malley, P., & Bachman, J. [1986]. *Drug use among American high school students, college students, and other young adults: National trends through 1985*. Washington, DC: National Institute on Drug Abuse.)

mentation is particularly risky, because using drugs can prevent young teenagers from successfully meeting the important social and psychological challenges of their age group (Baumrind & Moselle, 1985). And at any age, adolescents who abuse alcohol or other drugs are more likely to be depressed, to have troubles in school, to engage in unprotected sex, and to become involved in crime and delinquency (Irwin, 1986). Abusers expose themselves to serious long-term health risks, including brain damage, as well as to injury and even death from drug-related accidents, including drownings, falls, and burns. A particularly lethal combination is drinking and driving. Each year, approximately 3300 adolescents are killed in alcohol-related car accidents, and overall, 49 percent of fatal crashes involving teenagers also involve alcohol (National Highway Traffic Safety Administration, 1987).

Despite all the ad campaigns and drug abuse education programs, why do some teenagers start using alcohol or other drugs? Contrary to what many adults believe, they are not *forced* to do so by peer pressure. Instead, many adolescents reach a point in their lives when they come to feel that this "adult" behavior is desirable. If some of their friends then start using drugs, the "transition-prone" youngsters are tempted to start too (Jessor & Jessor, 1977).

Of course, not all teens who try drugs become drug abusers. Other factors, including personality characteristics and family relationships, put certain adolescents at risk. Those who develop problems with alcohol or other drugs tend to be more angry and impulsive than their peers. They also have more problems with achievement and are more inclined to be depressed. These teens are more likely to have distant, even hostile family relations and to have parents who are very permissive, uninvolved, or rejecting, or who themselves abuse drugs or alcohol (Barnes, 1984; Brook, Whiteman, Gordon, & Brook, 1984; Newcomb, Maddahian, & Bentler, 1986). All these factors together could pull an adolescent toward the psychological escape that drugs seem to offer.

Thereafter, friends play an important role in encouraging and maintaining drug abuse. Adolescents with drug or alcohol problems are more likely than other youngsters their age to have friends who also use drugs. Some of these friends probably precede the teenager's initiation into alcohol and other drugs. Most likely, their interest in drugs encourages the novice's experimentation. Then, once the novice is more experienced, he or she is drawn to new friends who are also drug users. These new friends, in turn, reinforce the established patterns of drug abuse (Kandel, 1978).

If drug abuse has so many causes, preventing the problem requires a multipronged attack. Simply encouraging adolescents to "say NO!" to drugs is not enough. Adults should identify teenagers with the personality traits of drug abusers and monitor these youngsters closely. Professional help should also be available to families in which parent-child relationships are troubled. Intervention can help adolescents develop the emotional resources they need to resist using drugs. At the same time, adults should pay careful attention to the friends an adolescent makes. When a teenager begins to run with a drug-using crowd, it is usually only a matter of time before problems arise. Finally, adults should be aware that there are periods in a young person's life when she or he is more vulnerable to experimentation with drugs. If at these times adults give the adolescent more attention, understanding, and support, preventing the onset of drug abuse may be possible (see "Focus On").

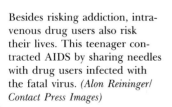

Preventing Teenage Drug Abuse

At 14, Andrea had it all. She was a cheerleader in suburban Atlanta, a member of the homecoming queen's court and an honor student who thought that taking drugs was dumb. But Andrea did an abrupt about-face when she was suspended from the cheerleading squad for putting on lipstick during class. She bleached her hair white and cut it in a Mohawk. As her mother, Jan, remembers, "She went from preppy to punk in 7 months."

No longer in the teenage social elite, Andrea sought acceptance in the school's drug culture. "I just wanted to be 'in' again, and I was, with another group," she says. Soon her grades dropped to F's, she couldn't wake up in the morning, and she had screaming fights with her divorced mother. "I was strung out on coke, acid—everything I could put in to my body," Andrea recalls. Jan suspected drugs, but when she broached the subject, Andrea ran away. Friends found her a sanctuary in a run-down Atlanta neighborhood called Cabbagetown and introduced her to free-based cocaine. Andrea called an old school friend, giving her a phone number "in case anything happens to me." The call probably saved her life.

The friend finally betrayed Andrea's secret to Andrea's frantic parents. Two juvenile officers plucked her from a seedy apartment about 4 A.M. And later that day she was committed to Charter Brook Hospital, a drug-rehabilitation center for youths. "She was screaming and carrying on," Jan says. But shortly after admission, Andrea grew determined to come clean. "I wanted help," she said. "I was about dead."*

Andrea's case is most parents' worst nightmare—a teenager who seems to be doing fine turns to drugs to cope with disappointment and spirals downward into a life that almost kills her. Adults wonder what can be done to prevent this kind of disaster. These are some steps that experts recommend:

1. Create a home environment of warmth, acceptance, and concern about a young person's problems, an environ-

*From T. Johnson with G. Carroll, Tale of three addictions: A cheerleader's fall and rise, from *Newsweek,* March 17, 1986. © 1986 by *Newsweek,* Newsweek, Inc. All rights reserved. Reprinted by permission.

Besides risking addiction, intravenous drug users also risk their lives. This teenager contracted AIDS by sharing needles with drug users infected with the fatal virus. *(Alon Reininger/ Contact Press Images)*

continued

ment in which troubles such as those Andrea first faced can be discussed before they lead to greater difficulties. Having this kind of relationship with their parents can help teenagers develop the psychological resilience needed to cope with life's inevitable setbacks without turning to drugs.

2. Know the early warning signs of teenage drug use. These include a reduced interest in schoolwork and in extracurricular activities, arriving late at school and skipping classes, and the occasional unexplained disappearance of liquor from the family liquor cabinet. As drug use increases, the signs become more obvious. The adolescent may drop old friends and start spending time with new ones who are never introduced to parents. He or she experiences rapid mood changes, argues explosively with parents, and denies the use of drugs. Frequently, drug abusers run into trouble with police for disorderly conduct, drunk driving, using a false ID, or pilfering money.

3. Seek help immediately for a drug abuser. Across the country there are hospitals, clinics, groups, and pro-grams designed to help teenagers with a drug problem. A state department of mental health, a local hospital, or a drug abuse hotline can offer valuable advice.

Of course, cases like Andrea's are so severe that the need for professional help is obvious. But often teenage drug use is more difficult to spot because it occurs only occasionally and can be hidden from parents until tragedy occurs, often behind the wheel of a car. Even "good kids" who stay out of trouble can become highway fatalities when they drink and drive. Why teenagers continue to risk their lives in this way may have to do with the adolescent egocentrism we'll discuss more fully later in this chapter. When adolescents first develop a sense of their own uniqueness, they may get the mistaken impression that they are so different from others they aren't susceptible to the same fates. Many teenagers therefore take enormous risks, convinced that nothing terrible could possibly happen to them. Disabusing young teens of this misperception may help to reduce alcohol-related deaths.

SEXUALLY TRANSMITTED DISEASES

As soon as adolescents become sexually active they face possible exposure to sexually transmitted diseases. A **sexually transmitted disease (STD)** is an infection transferred from one person to another through sexual contact. These diseases, all of them highly contagious, are more common during adolescence than at any other time of life. Approximately three-fourths of all reported cases of sexually transmitted diseases involve adolescents and young adults. One reason for this high incidence among young people is a failure to use condoms, especially when involved with more than one sexual partner. In addition, many teenagers who have contracted an STD are embarrassed to get treatment for it and are likely to infect someone else.

Two common sexually transmitted diseases among adolescents are *gonorrhea* and *chlamydia* (discussed in Chapter 3). The main symptoms of gonorrhea and chlamydia are painful urination and a cloudy discharge from the penis or

sexually transmitted disease (STD)
infection transferred through sexual contact

genital herpes
sexually transmitted disease
caused by a virus

vagina. Both are quite easily cured with the right antibiotics. If left untreated, they can damage the reproductive systems and cause sterility.

Another widespread sexually transmitted disease is **genital herpes** (caused by a virus), an infection causing tiny, itching blisters on the penis, vulva, or cervix, blisters that eventually erupt into open sores. Other symptoms include fever, headaches, and pain in the pelvic area. After these symptoms appear for the first time, they disappear for a while, in some cases only to arise again and again. An infected person is contagious just before and during an outbreak of the blister sores, but these may be so small that they go unnoticed. Although medications can help relieve the symptoms of herpes, as yet there is no cure. Genital herpes is all the more serious in women because it increases the risk of cervical cancer and can cause damage to the fetus during pregnancy and delivery.

During the 1980s, a new and deadly sexually transmitted disease began appearing in the U.S. population: *acquired immune deficiency syndrome* (see Chapter 3). AIDS, as yet incurable and always fatal, is transmitted only through intimate contact with infected semen, vaginal secretions, and blood. In the United States, it has occurred primarily among homosexual men and, increasingly, intravenous drug users who share infected needles. AIDS is caused by a virus that attacks the immune system, destroying the body's ability to defend itself against disease. The Centers for Disease Control in Atlanta estimates that 1 million to 1.5 million Americans have the AIDS virus. About 25 percent of all infected people develop symptoms within 5 years and about half of all individuals in the United States known to have AIDS have died as a result. Most researchers think that the others will eventually die as well. Of particular concern to doctors is the growing spread of AIDS among adolescents. The reasons for this alarming trend, and how to curb it, are discussed in "Issues & Options."

Cognitive Development During Adolescence

The experimenter faces her young subjects across a table strewn with poker chips of various colors. She explains that she will hold one of the chips (sometimes hidden, sometimes visible) and make statements about it. The subject is to say whether each statement is "true," "false," or "can't say." Then the experimenter, holding a green chip, says one of the following: "Either the chip in my hand is green or it isn't green." "The chip in my hand is green and it is not green."

For his answers, 8-year-old Paul relies almost completely on what he can see. When the experimenter hides the chip, he replies "can't tell" to her statements. If he can see the chip, and it is green, he replies "true" to both statements. Sharon, at 14, answers these questions with her mind, not her eyes. Logically, the first statement is always true, and the second is always false. Sharon is using advanced reasoning to perform this task. Her thinking, like her body, is growing up.

Issues & OPTIONS

AIDS and Adolescents: A Preventable Plague

In 1987 a 17-year-old boy sat in a high school classroom and listened to a doctor talk about AIDS. "I was like, 'This is real great but I don't have time for this. I have things to do. I have homework.' I thought I knew everything." Eight months later, the boy learned he had AIDS. At 15, he had had numerous unsafe sexual experiences with people in their twenties whom he did not know well (Kolata, 1989).

Among sexually active teenagers that is often the case, and that is precisely the problem. Each year, 2.5 million teenagers are infected with a sexually transmitted disease, indicating that condoms are not being used (Centers for Disease Control, 1988). Additionally, "one of every six sexually active high school girls has had at least four different partners" (Kolata, 1989). In an AIDS epidemic, too few condoms and too many partners spell disaster. Compounding the problem, many adolescents think they are invincible, immune from danger.

The data say otherwise. From 1987 to 1989, the number of reported AIDS cases among 13- to 19-year-olds increased by *40 percent*. In New York and Miami, 1 percent of 15- and 16-year-olds are infected, and among 21-year-olds, the rate is two to three times as high. Among 20- to 29-year-olds overall, reported cases have jumped from 2 percent to 20 percent of all reported cases through 1988. Given the long incubation period for AIDS (that is, the time between infection and diagnosis—about 3 to 5 years), many of the young adults who now have the disease contracted it as adolescents (Centers for Disease Control, as reported in Kolata, 1989).

The disease is not just a city problem, and it is not just homosexuals and intravenous drug users who are in danger. AIDS is spreading through heterosexual intercourse, and boys and girls are equally at risk. So are teenagers who are not "supposed" to get AIDS. In one highly publicized case, a young woman from a privileged background—a wealthy family, private schools—learned that a man she had had sex with *once*, six years earlier, when she was 16, died of AIDS. She hadn't known it then, but the man was bisexual. She now has AIDS.

So too will thousands of other adolescents and young adults who think this disease is for someone else. In Massachusetts, for example, of 860 adolescents surveyed, 70 percent said they were sexually active, but only 15 percent reported changing their sexual behavior because of concern about contracting AIDS. Of those, only 20 percent made changes that really offered protection (abstinence and using condoms) (Strunin & Hingson, 1987).

There is still no cure for this always fatal disease, so avoiding infection is the only defense. The best way for sexually active adolescents to protect themselves is to be certain of the sexual and drug use histories of their partners and to use condoms. When properly used, condoms can prevent the transfer of semen and vaginal secretions that may carry the virus. Being certain of a partner's sexual past is not always possible, and if a sexual encounter is casual, the risk is high.

NEW WAYS OF THINKING

Quite honestly, I can't imagine how anyone can say: "I'm weak," and then remain so. After all, if you know it, why not fight against it, why not try to train your character? The answer was: "Because it's so much easier not to!" This reply rather discouraged me. Easy? Does that mean that a lazy, deceitful life is an easy life? Oh, no, that can't be true, it mustn't be true, people can so easily be tempted by slackness . . . and by money.

> I thought for a long time about the best answer to give Peter, how to get him to believe in himself and, above all to try and improve himself. I don't know whether my line of thought is right though, or not.
>
> I've so often thought about how lovely it would be to have someone's complete confidence, but now, now that I'm that far, I realize how difficult it is to think what the other person is thinking and then to find the *right* answer. (Anne Frank, *The Diary of a Young Girl*, 1952/1989, p. 229)

As she wonders about her own character, about influencing another's, about the pleasures and limits of intimacy, 15-year-old Anne Frank displays the adolescent's new ability to think in complex and subtle ways. Psychologists group these advances in thinking into four categories: thinking about possibilities, thinking through hypotheses, thinking about abstractions, and thinking about thoughts (Keating, in press).

What if . . . ? Thinking about possibilities

Children's thinking is oriented toward the concrete, the here and now, things and events they can see: What is possible is what is real, but for adolescents, what is real is only one of many possibilities. Children do not wonder about who they might become; they are who they are. For adolescents, the "you" of the moment is just one version of the "you" that might be. Anne Frank, for example, wonders whether she is too independent, whether she should be a more malleable person.

This doesn't mean that children are incapable of imagination or fantasy. As you've seen, even young children have vivid and creative imaginations. Nor does it mean that children are unable to imagine things as different from the way they are. In thinking about possibilities, however, adolescents do better because they can move more easily between the concrete and the abstract; they have no trouble comparing what they see to a whole range of alternatives that *might* be.

The adolescent's ability to reason systematically about possibilities is essential for solving scientific and logical problems. Consider a high school chemistry experiment in which the object is to identify an unknown substance by performing various tests. In order to know what tests to conduct, the experimenter must first imagine the different things that the substance might be.

Adolescents use this sort of thinking often, not just in science and math classes. When Brian's parents react negatively to his plans for an after-school job, he can marshal a host of arguments to make his case. He can imagine what his parents' major objections will be and be prepared to refute them. Although many parents believe that their children become more argumentative during adolescence, what is usually happening is that their children are becoming better arguers. Adolescents like to speculate about all kinds of "what if" questions: What if we all lived to be 200? What if there were two-way television? What if there were no weapons?

If, then . . . Thinking through hypotheses

Another hallmark of adolescence is the ability to think in hypothetical terms— to consider all the logical consequences of a possible situation. Unlike a child,

What if . . . ? Adolescents think about what is and what might be. Their ability to think abstractly—to imagine possibilities, and to consider several sides of an issue—signals cognitive growth. *(Robert Frerck/The Stock Market)*

an adolescent is much more adept at reasoning: "If this is true, then X or Y must be true as well." Consider, for example, this "if, then" problem (from Shapiro & O'Brien, cited in Flavel, 1977, p. 112):

(a) If this is Room 154, then this is a class in child development. This is Room 154. Is this a class in child development?

(b) If this is Room 154, then this is not a class in child development. This is Room 154. Is this a class in child development?

(c) If this is Room 154, then this is a class in child development. This is not Room 154. Is this a class in child development?

Although most children are able to answer the first two questions correctly, they have trouble with the third. The first two propositions lead to obvious conclusions, but the third doesn't provide enough information to answer yes or no. Because adolescents are much better than children at thinking through hypotheses, they are more likely to know that the answer to the third question is: "Can't say."

The ability to think through hypotheses is a powerful tool. It allows a much deeper understanding of causes and consequences. Consider this hypothetical situation:

It takes brave pilots to fly airplanes in the Swiss Alps. One afternoon, a pilot was flying in the Alps and flew into a cable that suspended a cable car traveling between two mountain peaks. The cable snapped, and many of the passengers in the car died in the ensuing crash. Was the pilot careless? Why? (After Peel, 1971)

Children generally answer either yes or no, providing little logical support for their conclusion: "Yes, he was careless because he hit the cable." "No, he wasn't careless because careless people aren't allowed to be pilots." Adolescents are more likely to see that the answer depends on the situation, which hasn't been fully described. Suppose the pilot didn't know that a cable car had been installed there. Should he still be considered careless? Suppose the visibility was very poor that day. Should the pilot be held negligent? Adolescents' answers are often phrased in "if, then" terms: "*If* the pilot knew the cable was there, *then* he should have tried to fly above it." "*If* there was a lot of fog, *then* the pilot might not have been able to avoid the accident."

Like thinking about possibilities, hypothetical thinking enables adolescents to argue more effectively. They are able to see the consequences of different propositions, and so can modify their views to be more logical and harder to refute. Hypothetical thinking also helps teenagers plan ahead and make decisions. "If I decide to go out for the football team," an adolescent might reason, "then I'll have to drop my after-school job." Here the hypothesis of playing football leads to an awareness of time constraints and their consequences.

Thinking about abstract concepts

The poker chip experiment described earlier illustrates adolescents' ability to deal with abstract concepts—things that cannot be experienced directly through the senses. Because 8-year-old Paul fixates on whether he can see the chip's color, he responds incorrectly much of the time. Fourteen-year-old Sharon is less bound to observable events; she can understand the logic, or illogic, of the experimenter's statements. This ability to think abstractly enables high school students to handle topics beyond the grasp of most elementary schoolchildren: the conservation of energy, for example, or capitalistic versus socialistic economic principles. Adolescents, in fact, often spend hours mulling over abstract issues of personal interest to them: How do you know when you really love someone? What makes a true friend? Can you tell a lie and still be a religious person?

Thinking about thoughts

second-order thinking ability to think about thoughts

Closely related to thinking abstractly is the ability to think about thoughts—sometimes referred to as **second-order thinking**. Second-order thinking permits teenagers to think about the strategies they use to solve problems. A high school chemistry student can explain the steps she uses to identify an unknown substance. Second-order thinking also includes introspection and intellectualizing. To introspect is to think about one's own thoughts and feelings. "I wonder," wrote Anne Frank, "if it's really a good quality not to let myself be influenced. Is it really good to follow almost entirely my own conscience?" To intellectualize is to apply abstract logic to emotions. ("I got mad at Richard because I think unfairness should be punished.")

An interesting by-product of second-order thinking is the tendency for adolescents to develop a new kind of egocentrism. This is not the egocentrism of the preschooler who cannot see the perspectives of other people. Instead, it is an intense preoccupation with the self. Convinced that the self is unique, adolescents develop **personal fables**—erroneous beliefs that their thoughts, feelings, and experiences are totally different from those of other people (Elkind, 1967, 1978). A teenage boy, for example, might tell his mother that she couldn't possibly understand how he feels upon breaking up with his girlfriend, even though the mother, like most adults, has had the same experience. Many adolescents even develop the personal fable that they are so unique they are immune to ordinary dangers. Whether driving too fast or having sex without protection, "It can't happen to me," may be the thought behind these very serious risks. (In Chapter 17 we'll discuss the link between personal fables and teenage pregnancies.)

In the classic adolescent nightmare, everyone—on a bus, in a store, in a classroom, at a party—*everyone* stares at his ears, her tooth, his pimple. Acute adolescent egocentrism leads teenagers, even when awake, to believe that others are constantly watching and evaluating them, much as an audience glues its attention to an actor on a stage. Of course, this belief is again incorrect, which is why the effect is referred to as the **imaginary audience** (Elkind, 1967, 1978). This extreme self-consciousness declines with age, as young people come to realize that others are more concerned with their own thoughts.

personal fables
erroneous beliefs that one's thoughts, feelings, experiences are unique

imaginary audience
erroneous belief that one's behavior is the subject of public attention

Acutely self-conscious, adolescents worry that even a small pimple will make a big impression. *(Elizabeth Crews/Stock, Boston)*

WHY DOES THINKING ADVANCE IN ADOLESCENCE?

Why does thinking become more advanced during adolescence? Does this development mean that adolescents think in a different way than children do? Is it simply a result of having lived more years and acquired more information? Or is it something else altogether? Psychologists have proposed three different answers: the Piagetian perspective, the information-processing perspective, and the behavioristic view.

The Piagetian perspective

In Piaget's cognitive scheme, from ages 6 to 12, children's thinking is at the concrete operational level (Chapter 12), the stage when the cognitive tools develop for handling most ordinary problems. Elementary school children can judge whether statements are true or false, solve many types of logical problems, and use evidence to make decisions. Even in adulthood most everyday problems can be answered quite adequately using concrete operational reasoning, but it has its limits.

As the term suggests, concrete operational thinking is tied to observable things; it is inadequate for possibilities and hypotheticals, for abstractions and alternatives. Concrete thinking can help you calculate the flying time to Chicago or Chattanooga, but it alone could never have gotten the Wright brothers off the ground.

Piaget believed that transitions to higher stages of reasoning are more likely to occur at times when biological readiness interacts with environmental demands, creating cognitive disequilibrium. Adolescence is one such time of life. At puberty, dramatic biological changes occur simultaneously with a new, much more demanding curriculum in the classroom. Old cognitive skills are often no longer enough, so youngsters are gradually stimulated to develop a higher level of reasoning, characteristic of the **formal operational stage**. In contrast with concrete thinking, formal thinking is based on theoretical, abstract principles of logic.

formal operational stage
according to Piaget, the stage at which one's thinking is based on theoretical, abstract principles of logic

The development of formal thinking appears to take place in two steps. In the first, characteristic of early adolescence, formal thinking has a sort of "now you see it, now you don't" quality. Young adolescents may demonstrate formal thinking only at some times or on some tasks. For example, a ninth-grader may use formal thinking to solve an algebra problem but rely on concrete thinking when considering careers. Virtually all adolescents go through this period of "emergent formal operations" (Kuhn, Langer, Kohlberg, & Haan, 1977).

During middle or even late adolescence formal operational thinking advances to the second step, becoming consolidated and integrated into the general way of reasoning. Actually, the attainment of "consolidated formal operations" is not universal. Only an estimated 60 percent of college students consistently demonstrate formal thinking on tests used to measure it (Neimark, 1975). Formal operational thinking becomes consolidated only if there is enough environmental stimulation. This might take the form of courses, such as chemistry or logic, which demand hypothetical thinking. This suggests that schools can help to stimulate cognitive development by adding experiences to the curriculum which require hypothetical thinking.

The information-processing perspective

Information-processing theorists take a different view of cognitive development. They believe that as children grow older, they acquire new capacities for inputting information, mentally storing and manipulating it, and arriving at answers and solutions. Information-processing researchers, as we've said in earlier chapters, study how these cognitive capacities change with age.

Consider the differences in how children and adolescents process analogy problems like these (Sternberg, 1977; Sternberg & Nigro, 1980; Sternberg & Rifkin, 1979):

narrow:wide / question: (trial) (statement) (answer) (ask)

shoe:foot / hat: (head) (bucket) (clothes) (cap)

Eight- to twelve-year-olds tend to end their processing of such problems prematurely, before they have considered all four possible answers. For example, in the second analogy an 8-year-old might say "cap" because it is a synonym of "hat." In contrast, adolescents age 14 and older easily process every piece of information given. This difference occurs, say information-processing researchers, because adolescents can hold more data in their working memories than children can. Therefore, they do better with problems requiring repeated comparisons between new and old information. This difference in memory capacity could also explain the emergence of hypothetical thinking. If children have more limited "storage space" than adolescents, they are apt to become confused when thinking through the consequences of a complex hypothetical situation. Adolescents, in contrast, whose working memories can hold more data, are much better able to reason hypothetically.

Memory capacity is just one of many information-processing components that might account for differences between children's and adolescents' thinking. Adolescents may also have learned how to use strategies that elementary school children lack for efficiently storing and manipulating data. Such strategies include careful planning and using mnemonic (memory-aiding) devices, organizational techniques for keeping track of data, and effective rule-of-thumb approaches to solving problems. In contrast to children, adolescents are not only more skilled at using these strategies, they also are better able to judge when the strategies will be helpful (Brown, 1975). Thus, the cognitive differences between the two age groups may be due to differences both in information-processing capabilities and in the ability to control them.

The behavioristic view

A third perspective on cognitive development is that of behavioristic thinkers, who study *quantitative* changes in mental abilities, often through intelligence testing. Performance on IQ tests generally improves from childhood to adolescence, and these psychologists believe the improvements reflect gains in the kinds of abilities that IQ tests measure. In part, such gains involve simply a greater store of knowledge. For example, when given the question about the pilot who flew into the cable car, adolescents may offer more complex answers because they know more about planes, mountains, weather, and so forth. To

FOCUS ON   *Are There Sex Differences in Mental Abilities?*

During childhood, sex and intelligence seem unrelated: Boys and girls average the same scores on all parts of IQ tests. But after puberty, while on average, boys and girls still earn the same *overall* IQ scores, many girls start to outscore boys on verbal tasks while boys often do better on spatial problems and to a lesser extent on math (Maccoby & Jacklin, 1974). To explain, psychologists look to both biology and society.

One possibility is that sex hormones, which increase at puberty, affect cognitive abilities. For instance, both males and females with higher levels of male sex hormones have been found to perform somewhat better than peers on tasks involving spatial ability (Petersen, 1979), but that alone doesn't prove that hormone differences account for cognitive differences. Another biological theory involves the two sides of the brain, which in humans tend to specialize in different tasks. Some researchers propose that males develop a more strongly dominant right brain, whereas in females there is less dominance by one brain hemisphere over the other. Since spatial ability is usually controlled by the brain's right side, males would be expected to excel at it. The reason that males acquire this biological trait might be that the development of right-brain dominance largely ends at puberty (Waber, 1977). Because boys begin puberty about 2 years later than girls, boys have a longer time for right-brain dominance to emerge. Of course, if this theory were right, early-maturing boys would have poorer spatial ability than their later-maturing peers (including girls who start puberty very late). But this appears *not* to be the case. Sex differences in cognitive abilities do not seem to be related to differences in the timing of puberty (Newcombe & Dubas, 1987).

A third possibility is that cognitive differences between the sexes are socially, not biologically, based. In elementary school, boys and girls take the same courses and so develop the same abilities. But once they are able to take electives, they may be encouraged down different educational paths by guidance counselors, parents, and friends. Adolescent males, for instance, are often encouraged to pursue math and science, while females are often steered away from these subjects (Fennema & Sherman, 1977). Interestingly, individual differences in mathematical ability have been found to be more closely related to *attitudes* toward math than they are to gender (Paulsen & Johnson, 1983). In short, changing our stereotyped ideas about male and female abilities might then change the cognitive differences we see between the sexes (Hill & Lynch, 1983). Finally, although sex differences in abilities are consistent, the *magnitude* of these differences is very small (Hyde, 1981). Even now, the similarities between most males and females on tests of verbal and mathematical abilities are greater than the differences.

behavioristic thinkers, advances in cognition at adolescence reflect the gradual acquisition of information over time.

Once a person enters adolescence, her IQ score tends to remain quite stable. This does not mean that mental abilities no longer improve. They improve a great deal. People who score high on intelligence tests early in adolescence also score high when tested some years later. (Remember that IQ

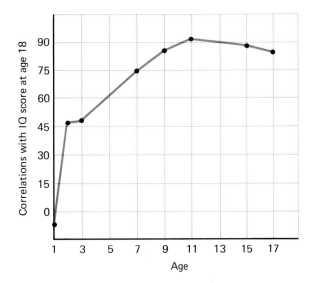

FIGURE 15-3
Average correlations between individuals' intelligence test scores at various ages from 1 to 17 and their scores at age 18. By age 11, the correlation is over .90. (*Source:* Bayley, N. [1949]. Consistency and variability in the growth of intelligence from birth to eighteen years. *Journal of Genetic Psychology, 75,* 165–196. Reprinted with permission of the Helen Dwight Reid Educational Foundation. Published by Heldref Publications, 4000 Albemarle St., N.W., Washington, DC. 20016. Copyright © 1949.)

scores are not absolute; they reflect a person's standing relative to peers.) As you can see in Figure 15-3, someone's score at ages 1 to 5 is not highly correlated with his score at age 18. The correlation increases in the age 6-to-11 period and is high from early adolescence on.

Social Cognition During Adolescence

As we noted in Chapter 12, **social cognition** refers to thinking about people, social relationships, and social institutions. Young children tend to form impressions on the basis of externals, such as how someone dresses or talks. Teenagers often look deeper, considering personality and intelligence. In at least three areas of social cognition—assessing others, thinking about social conventions, and reasoning about moral issues—teenagers are decidedly more mature than children.

social cognition
thinking about and awareness of people and social relationships

ASSESSING OTHER PEOPLE

Writer Roald Dahl in his memoir *Boy* recalls how the headmaster of his school looked to him at age 7:

> His name was Mr. Coombes and I have a picture in my mind of a giant of a man with a face like a ham and a mass of rusty-coloured hair that sprouted in a tangle all over the top of his head. All grown-ups appear as giants to small children. But Headmasters (and policemen) are the biggest giants of all and acquire a marvel-

ously exaggerated stature. It is possible that Mr. Coombes was a perfectly normal being, but in my memory he was a giant, a tweed-suited giant who always wore a black gown over his tweeds and a waist coat under his jacket. (Roald Dahl, *Boy*, 1984, pp. 40–41)

Holden Caulfield, the 17-year-old hero of J. D. Salinger's *The Catcher in the Rye*, describes another headmaster with a bit more insight:

On Sundays, . . . old Haas went around shaking hands with everybody's parents when they drove up to school. He'd be charming as hell and all. Except if some boy had little old funny-looking parents. You should've seen the way he did with my roommate's parents. I mean if a boy's mother was sort of fat or corny-looking or something, and if somebody's father was one of those guys that wear those suits with very big shoulders and corny black-and-white shoes, and old Haas would shake hands with them and give them a phony smile and then he'd go talk, for maybe a half an *hour*, with somebody else's parents. I can't stand that stuff. It drives me crazy. (J. D. Salinger, *The Catcher in the Rye*, 1951, p. 14)

impression formation
assessment of others

While a 7-year-old sees the way people seem, an adolescent sees the way they are. Holden Caulfield can spot a phony because he is old enough to do so. Assessing other people—what psychologists call **impression formation**—is a skill that broadens with age in five main ways (Hill & Palmquist, 1978). First, impressions become *more differentiated*. Instead of assessing people according to a few broad distinctions, such as sex, age, and physical traits, (a ham-faced giant in tweeds, for example), adolescents begin using narrower descriptive categories, such as interests and personality traits (is someone phony or sincere, for example). Second, adolescents form less egocentric impressions than children do. They are more aware that we judge others subjectively, that dif-

During adolescence, who you are becomes more important than how old you are. Teenagers can assess people with more insight than they could as children. *(Evelyn Scolney/Monkmeyer Press)*

ferent people can feel differently about the same person. Third, adolescents' impressions of others become more *abstract*, less rooted in physical characteristics and more tied to psychological ones. Fourth, adolescents use *more inferences* when forming impressions of others. Like Holden Caulfield sizing up Haas, they know that subtle clues can be widely revealing. Fifth, adolescents' impressions of others are *more highly organized*. Often they link personality traits to situations ("She's impatient when she works with other people.") and reconcile seemingly inconsistent information ("He's friendly toward girls but not toward boys."). For example, seeing someone become uncomfortable in a certain situation might be used to infer something about her personality. A confident person who gets nervous at a party might then be seen as being less secure, for example. Taken together, all these developments suggest that teenagers are acquiring an **implicit psychological theory** of people—a tacit understanding that people are more than what they seem on the surface (Barenboim, 1981).

implicit psychological theory
intuitive theory of human behavior

THINKING ABOUT SOCIAL CONVENTIONS

A fidgety 7-year-old standing in line to buy a movie ticket might wonder why he has to wait so long, but his mother told him he has to, so he does. In middle childhood we follow **social conventions**—the norms that guide day-to-day behavior—because we see them as "rules" set by authority figures. By early adolescence, this view changes. Young teenagers stress the arbitrariness of social conventions, seeing them as merely social expectations which don't *have* to be followed. ("Why wait in a dumb ticket line just because other people are waiting?" a 13-year-old might say. "There's no *law* that makes you wait, is there?") A few years later, adolescents are more apt to accept social conventions as deeply ingrained habits. They may be arbitrary, and sometimes even annoying, but we comply with them because we have always done things that way. In the final step in thinking about social conventions, older adolescents realize that social conventions regulate people's interactions in ways that seem appropriate and right. Waiting in line for a ticket is a way of making sure that tickets are distributed fairly. If we didn't do it, the pushiest and strongest would get more than they deserve (Turiel, 1978).

social conventions
norms that guide day-to-day behavior

In following social conventions, then, people progress from unthinking compliance to acceptance based on an understanding of abstract principles. The same pattern seems to shape the development of moral reasoning as well.

MORAL DEVELOPMENT

Recall that, in Lawrence Kohlberg's theory (Chapter 12), young children resolve moral dilemmas by asking, Is it right for *me*? At this age fear of punishment guides behavior (preconventional level). For school-age children, the question becomes, what does *society* say is right? Doing the right thing means obeying society's rules and conventions (conventional level). At adolescence, moral reasoning can shift again. For those who reach the highest level of moral reasoning, questioning, even disobeying, laws and authority, is justified when higher principles of equality, justice, and the sanctity of human life are at issue. The individual's conscience now becomes a stronger force than society's rules, and the guiding question becomes, Is it *right*? For this reason

postconventional moral reasoning
thought in which decisions of conscience are more important than society's rules

Kohlberg called this stage **postconventional moral reasoning**. People can see several sides of a dilemma, and deciding what is right can be a hard struggle. In the moral dilemma of Heinz and the drug (Chapter 12), one postconventional or principled thinker might say Heinz should not steal the drug because doing so would violate the druggist's rights, while another would argue that saving a life is more important.

Like many theories in psychology, Kohlberg's has generated much controversy. It has been criticized as biased toward Western morality, ignoring the different kinds of ethical thinking that exist in other cultures (Simpson, 1974). For example, in some cultures, preserving the sanctity of family relationships is more important than any other moral aim, but in our culture, this is not the case.

Kohlberg's theory has also been called biased toward male values (Gilligan, 1982). According to psychologist Carol Gilligan, his scheme equates higher moral reasoning with the way males typically view moral problems. Socialized to be autonomous and emotionally detached, males equate justice with fairness and equality. But females, says Gilligan, speak with a different voice, one that values caring more than strict equality. Because girls are socialized to value intimate relationships, the female moral ideal emphasizes sensitivity to the needs of others more than strict equality. For example, if asked to divide resources among members of a group, men would focus mainly on fairness—making sure everyone got an equal share. Women might focus more on maintaining good relations among groups members, even if it did not result in an absolutely even distribution. This, Gilligan argues, does not make women any "lower" in moral development than men, just different.

A third criticism of Kohlberg's theory is that it focuses too much on life-and-death moral issues, which people rarely face, at the expense of everyday ethical problems, about which we are constantly forced to make choices (Yussen, 1976). Finally, Kohlberg's theory has been criticized because it fails to consider the relationship between moral *reasoning* and moral *behavior*. Although people who have reached higher levels of moral reasoning tend to be more ethical in certain respects (Rest, 1983), moral reasoning and moral behavior don't always go together. People sometimes fail to act morally in situations that have little to do with their general way of thinking about ethical issues (Sobesky, 1983). Although most of us agree that it is immoral to break the law, many of us exceed highway speeding limits when we are in a hurry.

Though his theory isn't perfect, Kohlberg observed accurately that moral reasoning does become more principled from childhood to adolescence. And while it does seem to follow the sequence he described (Colby, Kohlberg, Gibbs, & Lieberman, 1983; Hoffman, 1980), earlier levels of moral thinking are never fully discarded. We reach new moral levels gradually and thereafter reason on different levels in different situations (Fischer, 1983). In fact, people sometimes switch from one level to another in thinking about the same moral issue (Colby, Kohlberg, Gibbs, & Lieberman, 1983; Walker, de Vries, & Trevethan, 1987). Thus, the development of moral reasoning seems more additive in nature than stagelike.

Why do some adolescents reach higher levels of moral reasoning than others do? Part of the answer has to do with parents. Those who encourage family discussions, including discussions of ethical issues, tend to raise adolescents who think more in terms of moral principles (Holstein, 1972; Haan, Smith, & Block, 1968). This finding has important implications for parents' approach to matters such as teenage drug use and sexual activity. Simply setting guidelines for their children may not be enough. If parents want their teenagers to consider these matters from a "moral" point of view, then discussing these subjects openly and fully is essential.

Summary

1. The physical changes that occur during adolescence are collectively called *puberty*. Puberty includes five major changes: (a) rapid growth and weight gain; (b) continued development of sex glands: testes become able to release sperm and ovaries begin releasing ova; (c) development of secondary sex characteristics; (d) changes in body composition, especially in the quantity and distribution of fat and muscle; (e) changes in the circulatory and respiratory systems, leading to increased strength and stamina. All the above changes are triggered by an increased production of *hormones*, in particular testosterone in males and estrogen in females.

2. The age of onset of puberty varies from culture to culture and even within the same society. American girls typically begin to menstruate at about 12. Puberty spans 1½ to 6 years in girls and 2 to 5 years in boys.

3. Parents influence their childrens' reactions to puberty through their own expectations and attitudes. Stress is minimized if adolescents know what changes to expect and have positive attitudes toward them.

4. The timing of puberty, whether early or late, affects social and emotional development for both sexes. Early-maturing boys may get into more trouble, but they are also more popular and self-assured than late-maturers. Late-maturers tend to be more insightful and creatively playful. Early-maturing girls often feel awkward and embarrassed about their bodies, but they tend to become more creative and independent than later-maturers.

5. Some of the major health problems of adolescents result from choices and so can be minimized or completely avoided. Because of poor eating habits, many teenagers are malnourished or obese. A small minority of girls try to avoid gaining weight by vomiting after gorging on high-calorie goods. This disorder, *bulimia*, can be cured through therapy that attempts to raise self-esteem. *Anorexia nervosa* is a life-threatening eating disorder afflicting about 1 in 250 teenage girls. Anorectics refuse to eat, insisting that they are fat even when they have become skeletally thin. Hospitalization and therapy are often required to prevent starvation and death.

6. Alcohol is the drug most frequently used and abused by U.S. teenagers. Alcohol use puts adolescents at risk for many health problems, accidents, and even death. Teenage drug abusers tend to be more angry and impulsive than their peers. They have more problems with achievement and are more inclined to be depressed. Their parents may be distant or hostile and often are drug abusers themselves. Intervention can help adolescents develop the emotional resources they need to resist using drugs.

7. Sexually transmitted diseases are more common during adolescence than during any other time in life. Minimizing sexual activity and using condoms are the best defenses against contracting these diseases, including AIDS.

8. Cognitive advances during adolescence include thinking about possibilities, thinking through hypotheses, thinking about abstractions, and thinking about thoughts. Three different theories have been proposed to explain these changes: Piaget's theory of developmental stages, the information-processing perspective, and the behavioristic view.

9. Adolescents mature, too, in social cognition, in their ability to assess others, to think about social conventions, and to reason about moral issues. Assessing others, or *impression formation*, broadens in five main ways, all leading toward an understanding that people are more than what they appear to be. In following social conventions, teenagers progress from unthinking compliance to acceptance based on an understanding of abstract principles. They realize that conventions help society function more smoothly. Morality becomes more principled, based less on social conventions. Not all adolescents reach this level of morality. Those who do tend to have parents who discuss ethical issues with them.

Key Terms

adolescent growth spurt	personal fables
anorexia nervosa	postconventional moral reasoning
basal metabolism	primary sex characteristics
formal operational stage	puberty
genital herpes	secondary sex characteristics
hormones	second-order thinking
imaginary audience	secular trend
implicit psychological theory	sexually transmitted disease (STD)
impression formation	social cognition
menarche	social conventions

Suggested Readings

Brooks-Gunn, J., and Petersen, A. (Eds.) (1983). *Girls at puberty.* New York: Plenum. A collection of articles on various biological and social aspects of pubertal change among female adolescents.

Gardner, H. (1983). *Frames of mind.* New York: Basic Books. A theory of intelligence that begins from the assumption that there are different types of intelligence and more to its measurement than IQ testing.

Gilligan, C. (1982). *In a different voice.* Cambridge, MA: Harvard University Press. This book on moral reasoning explores differences in the ways men and women think about moral problems.

Paige, K., and Paige, J. (1981). *The politics of reproductive rituals.* Berkeley, CA: University of California Press. These authors examine puberty rituals in other cultures and explain how the nature of these rites of passage are affected by economics and politics.

Social and Emotional Development in Adolescence

I'll never forget my twelfth birthday. My mom came into my room with this serious look on her face and started to talk about my future. "When you go to junior high school," she said, "you're probably going to go through some tough times." She wasn't very specific about what might happen, just that it was going to be a "difficult phase" with "lots of pressures." The way she talked, it would start sort of magically, as if an alarm had gone off. Well, things didn't turn out that way. I mean, life just went on with its usual ups and downs. I guess my mom was exaggerating.

The mother of this 15-year-old, anxious to prepare her child for the future, probably stirred up unnecessary worry. Like more parents, she expected adolescence to be difficult and stressful. Surely her young teenager would suffer from a storm of pressures, anxieties, and doubts that inevitably arrive with every child's twelfth birthday.

Early in this century, this "storm and stress" view of adolescence received official sanction from G. Stanley Hall, the acknowledged father of the scientific study of adolescence. Hall compared adolescence to a turbulent, transitional phase in early human history, when a new, more sophisticated social order was about to emerge. "Adolescence is a new birth," he wrote. "Development is less gradual [than during other periods], suggestive of some ancient period of storm and stress" (1904/1976, p. 6). Hall offered no scientific evidence for his view, which persisted until quite recently. Today few developmental psychologists agree with the "storm and stress" theory of adolescence. Although the biological and cognitive changes of this period make it distinctive, it is not inevitably stormy.

Adolescents do tackle important social and emotional tasks as they make the transition to adulthood. First, they are developing a sense of identity to which they will carry through their adult lives. Second, they become more responsible and independent, better able to make their own decisions. And third, they learn to form intimate, enduring social relationships that will prepare them for adult love and marriage. In this chapter we'll look at how adolescents face each of these three tasks. Then we'll examine some of the social and emotional problems that can arise during adolescence.

The Development of the Self During Adolescence

If I [think] of my life in 1942 it feels like something unreal. It was quite a different Anne who lived that life than the one who is being brought up in the "Secret Annexe." At home, on the Merry, things look so wonderful from here, lots of boy friends and girl friends, spoiled by Mummy and Daddy, lots of sweets, enough pocket money, what more could one want?

. . . Now I look back at that Anne as an amusing, but very superficial, girl who has nothing to do with the Anne of today. . . . Oh, don't worry, I haven't forgotten how to laugh or to answer back readily. I'm just as good, or better, at criticizing people and I can still flirt if . . . I wish.

. . . I don't want followers, but friends, admirers who fall not for a flattering smile but for what one does and for one's character. . . .

> Now I think seriously about life and see that one period of my life is over forever; the carefree schooldays are gone, never to return. I don't even long for them much; I have outgrown them. I can't just play the fool as my serious side is always there. (Anne Frank, *The Diary of a Young Girl*, 1952/1989, pp. 515–517)*

Though physically confined to an attic, Anne Frank explored her own self, asking the questions that have always preoccupied adolescents: Who was I? Who am I? What do people think of me? What do I think of myself? It's not that we don't ask these questions at age 10, or 30, or 50. We do. But it is during adolescence that self-scrutiny begins to preoccupy us. This newly emerging sense of self includes several connected parts: self-conceptions (the traits we see ourselves as having), self-esteem (how we feel about ourselves), and identity (knowing who we are now, and who we will be in the future).

CHANGES IN SELF-CONCEPTION: WHO AM I?

The same mental skills that help teenagers solve algebra problems, perform experiments in science, and discuss abstract concepts such as love and religion also help them to perceive the self more maturely. For instance, while elementary school children typically have very concrete self-conceptions (I am a boy, I have brown hair, I have two brothers, I play hockey), young adolescents describe themselves partly in terms of more abstract social and psychological traits. Here is one 12-year-old's self-description.

> My name is A. I'm a human being. I'm a girl. I'm a truthful person. I'm not pretty. I do so-so in my studies. I'm a very good cellist. I'm a very good pianist. I'm a bit tall for my age. I like several boys. I like several girls. I'm old-fashioned. I play tennis. I am a very good musician. I try to be helpful. I'm always ready to be friends with anybody. Mostly I'm good, but I lose my temper. I'm not well liked by some girls and boys. I don't know if boys like me or not. (Montemayor & Eisen, 1977)

Although A names several concrete traits (cellist, pianist, tennis player, tall for my age), she also cites social and psychological ones (truthful, helpful, eager for friendship, liked by some but not all classmates). This trend toward a less concrete, more abstract self-conception continues throughout adolescence. One 17-year-old ended her self-description with this highly abstract view: "I am not a classifiable person (i.e., I don't want to be)."

Adolescents' self-conceptions become more sophisticated in other ways too. They can understand that different circumstances elicit different personal qualities. "I'm shy with strangers," a teenager might say, "but very friendly with people I know." This linking of traits to situations allows for a more coherent self-description, one that reconciles seemingly contradictory characteristics (shyness and friendliness, for example). At the same time, adolescents can understand that other people may have a different view of them than they do. "Most people think that nothing bothers me," a teenager might confide, "but underneath I have a lot of worries." All these developments mean

---

*Excerpts in this chapter from *Anne Frank: The Diary of a Young Girl* by Anne Frank, copyright 1952 by Otto H. Frank. Used by permission of Doubleday, a division of Bantam, Doubleday, Dell Publishing Group, Inc.

"Most people think that nothing bothers me." Even teenagers who appear poised and self-assured worry about their appearance and their appeal to others. (*Jeff Persons/Stock, Boston*)

that adolescents are now acquiring more complex, better organized, and more finely differentiated self-conceptions (Harter, in press; Hill & Palmquist, 1978).

CHANGES IN SELF-ESTEEM: HOW WELL DO I LIKE MYSELF?

Peering into the self, teenagers ask not only what they see but also how well they like it. Conventional wisdom holds that adolescents have low self-esteem—that they are more insecure and self-critical than children or adults are. After all, the argument goes, the physical developments of adolescence are sometimes awkward and ungainly, while new cognitive abilities make teenagers more self-conscious and more worried about what others think of them.

But most research says otherwise. Although teenagers' feelings about themselves may fluctuate, especially during early adolescence, their self-esteem remains fairly stable from about age 13 on. If anything, self-esteem increases over the course of middle and late adolescence (Bachman, O'Malley, & Johnston, 1978; Harter, in press; McCarthy & Hoge, 1982).

These findings are generalizations, of course. Some adolescents do evaluate themselves more negatively than others. For instance, young adolescents (ages 12 to 14) tend to have lower self-esteem than either preadolescents (ages 8 to 11) or teenagers age 15 and older (Simmons, Rosenberg, & Rosenberg, 1973). Perhaps the dramatic physical changes of early adolescence—arriving too early, too late, growing too big or too small—are responsible. The young adolescents who feel *least* positive about themselves tend to be white females. Compared with young adolescent black girls and boys this age of either race, white girls age 12 to 14 tend to say more negative things about themselves, feel insecure about their abilities, and worry about whether others like them. Twelve-year-old A's self-description is fairly typical. She negatively evaluates her looks, her scholastic talents, and her temper. She feels she is unpopular with some of her classmates, and she questions whether boys like her. We don't know why A and many other young adolescent white girls feel so negatively about themselves, but one suspicion is that, more than any other group, they feel a conflict between doing well in school and trying to be popular.

It is also not clear if A's negative self-statements reflect temporary feelings about the self or more permanent ones. Some researchers think that self-esteem really has two aspects. One consists of moment-to-moment shifts in self-assessment, as when a student who is normally self-confident becomes embarrassed because of a teacher's criticisms. This is called **barometric self-esteem** because, like a barometer, it fluctuates—with changes in a person's situation or personal climate. In contrast, **baseline self-esteem** is a more stable, *general* feeling about oneself that endures despite temporary ups and downs. Apparently, the negative self-assessment sometimes seen in young adolescents is due to greater volatility in their barometric self-esteem, not to a more permanent drop in their baseline self-evaluation (Rosenberg, 1986). Because young adolescents are so conscious of others' reactions to them (recall our discussion in the last chapter of the "imaginary audience"), they tend to be bothered more by the occasional blows to the ego that all of us experience. Young adolescents are also just beginning to realize that what people feel may be very different from what they do. If the boy who smiled at you on Monday ignores you on Tuesday, is it because he no longer likes you, or because he *does*? Adolescents worry about how others *really* see them, uncertainty that places their self-image on shaky ground.

barometric self-esteem
moment-to-moment shifts in self-assessment

baseline self-esteem
stable, general feelings about the self

ESTABLISHING ONE'S IDENTITY

If you had to discuss your developing identity, you might say that you are beginning to clarify your long-term goals, or that you have a new understanding of yourself and where you are heading. For Erik Erikson, establishing this sense of who you really are is the major psychological task of adolescence. Before adolescence, a child's identity is like separate patches of fabric. By the end of adolescence, the patches have been sorted, and those retained have been connected into a quilt of integrated pieces. In Erikson's model, this process triggers a psychosocial crisis of **identity versus identity diffusion**. A young person can successfully resolve it only if the earlier crises involving trust, autonomy, initiative, and industry were positively resolved as well.

identity versus identity diffusion
according to Erikson, the psychosocial crisis of establishing one's identity, characteristic of adolescence

Erikson contends that each crisis builds on the previous one. "Without a healthy sense of trust, autonomy, initiative, and industry, it is difficult to establish a coherent sense of identity. Moreover, the way in which the adolescent resolves the crises of identity will have an impact on his or her struggle with the crises of adulthood" (Steinberg, 1989, p. 250). What occurs during adolescence, then, is intimately connected to the past and to the future.

Adolescents who successfully resolve the identity crisis can make a whole series of important life commitments: occupational, ideological, social, religious, ethical, and sexual (Bourne, 1978a). They enjoy a sense of well-being, a feeling of being at ease with their bodies, and an inner certainty of approval from people who matter to them. They also have a sense of continuity through time—a view that their past, present, and future are all connected.

Making choices

Writing about the adolescent's search for identity, Erikson said: "[F]rom among all possible and imaginable relations, [the young person] must make a series of ever-narrowing selections of personal, occupational, sexual, and ideological commitments" (1968, p. 245). Adolescents, in short, must *choose* who they are going to be.

Sixteen-year-old Bill, for example, has always loved hiking, camping, and fishing. He also has a keen interest in biology and excels in science courses. In high school, he begins reading about environmental issues and becomes concerned about the pollution of a local river. He joins and becomes active in an environmental group. Note that one of this young man's important *past* identifications (a love of nature) is retained and incorporated into his newly emerging sense of self. The *present* is the context in which he repudiates some of his past attitudes and behavior (a childish unconcern about littering, for example), while he holds onto others. Bill's ideas about who he might become in the *future* (an environmentalist) guide many of the choices he makes during his search for self-definition (the groups he joins, for instance, and the courses he takes in school).

Erikson contends that the key to resolving the identity crisis lies in the adolescent's interactions with others. When people who matter react positively to a young person's aspirations, he or she has an easier time making the choices involved. For instance, if the young man interested in environmental issues is encouraged by parents and teachers, and has the approval of peers, he is apt to integrate this new dimension quite smoothly into his developing sense of self.

Establishing an integrated, coherent identity can take years. The search for self may begin at puberty, but consolidating the patchwork of pieces

Belonging to a club, such as this high school dramatics group, contributes to an adolescent's sense of identity. *(Ted Streshinsky/Photo 20-20)*

doesn't start until late adolescence (Adams & Jones, 1983; Archer, 1982; Marcia, 1980). The late teens and early twenties are usually a critical time for identity to crystallize, and experimenting with possible new dimensions to the self often continues well into young adulthood and beyond. In fact, Erikson believed that the search for identity is never really over. "[A] sense of identity is never gained nor maintained once and for all," he wrote. "It is constantly lost and regained" (1959, p. 14).

Occupational identity

Ask children what they want to be when they grow up, and their answers have more to do with fantasy and familiarity than with reality: a teacher, a police officer, a baseball player, a ballet dancer, a great scientist. But with the transition from childhood to adolescence, thinking about work becomes more mature. Adolescents begin to understand where their true abilities and interest really lie, and how these mesh with possible careers (Grotevant & Cooper, 1988).

Career planning in adolescence generally occurs in two stages (Super, 1967). In the first, from ages 14 to 18, adolescents start to think seriously about broad categories of work, but they don't usually make any specific decisions. One teenager thinks that he'd like to work with computers; another is attracted to art; a third considers some kind of teaching; a fourth something in science. These years have been called a period of **crystallization** because during them, career ideas first start to coalesce (Super, 1967) as adolescents gather information about specific occupations (Osipow, 1973).

crystallization
stage of occupational development when career ideas coalesce

Then, between the ages of 18 and 21, a period of **specification** usually takes place. This is when young people narrow their focus and start considering specific careers. Someone interested in science, for example, might think about becoming a research scientist, a doctor, a science writer, or a laboratory technician. By the end of this period, an occupation has been chosen, and it becomes an important part of the young adult's identity.

specification
stage of occupational development when career choices are specified

Gender role and ethnic identity

Identity also has a sexual component, and adolescents feel increased pressure to behave in "gender-appropriate" ways (Hill & Lynch, 1983). This pressure is especially strong on girls, who are often expected to be model-pretty and cheerleader-popular. Much of the pressure to be "masculine" or "feminine" comes from peers, partly because of a growing awareness of their own sexual maturation. Pressure to conform to gender stereotypes can have negative effects. Girls may suffer a drop in academic achievement, especially in "unfeminine" subjects such as math and science. Boys, however, may squelch emotional displays for fear of being labeled unmasculine. When a 12-year-old boy cries after striking out at bat in an important baseball game, he is not usually ridiculed by peers unless he is disliked (Fine, 1981). But a 15-year-old who does the same thing is a target of derision, quickly labeled a wimp and a sissy.

Not all adolescents conform rigidly to gender-role stereotypes, however. As with other aspects of the self, a range of choices is available. Deviating

My people, myself. A strong sense of ethnic identity can enhance adolescents' feelings of self-esteem. *(Larry Kolvoord/The Image Works)*

somewhat from gender-role expectations may even be advantageous, at least for girls. Adolescent girls who adopt some of the traits generally considered "masculine" (assertiveness, independence, competitiveness) often feel better about themselves than their stereotypically "feminine" peers (Massad, 1981). Perhaps this is because our society highly values many of the "masculine" traits, so girls who possess them have reason to take pride in themselves. These traits also help people feel in control, a condition associated with good mental health.

Another important aspect of self-identity is a sense of ethnic heritage, especially for those who are not part of the white majority (Phinney & Alipuria, 1987). Among blacks, Hispanics, and other minority youth, the search for ethnic identity may follow a crisis in which the adolescent's separateness from the white majority is stressed (Cross, 1978; Kim, 1981). For a time, the young person may turn against whites and white culture, becoming immersed in her own ethnic group. Eventually, when a sense of ethnic identity is firmly established and integrated into the self, she generally possesses a new, higher level or self-esteem. Such a young person is apt to have the self-confidence needed to help other, younger minority-group teenagers engage in the same struggle.

Moratorium

psychosocial moratorium according to Erikson, a necessary "time out" for adolescents

Establishing a sense of identity is so demanding that Erikson advocates a **psychosocial moratorium** for it, a time out from excessive obligations during which an adolescent can pursue the search for "Who am I?" In the United States, we provide a moratorium by encouraging young people to stay in school, free from the need to support themselves and the obligations of raising a family. In this way, adolescents are permitted "to explore, test out, and experiment before assuming . . . adult responsibilities" (Gallatin, 1975, p. 208).

During the psychosocial moratorium, teenagers can experiment with a smorgasbord of roles and identities. Terry, once considered very preppy, has dyed her hair red and joined a rock band. Doug, once a fast-food addict and avid skateboarder, has taken up vegetarianism and yoga. Parents talk of "phases," but much of this behavior is simply experimentation. The young person embraces many possibilities in the search for a self that "fits."

Does going to college help adolescents establish their identities? Yes and no. In one study that compared college students 18 to 21 with working young people the same age who were not in school, it was the *non*students who were more apt to have established a sense of identity, especially regarding values (Munro & Adams, 1977). Apparently, being out in the working world with its responsibilities and obligations hastens the formation of a strong sense of "who I am." Attending college, because it serves as a moratorium period, tends to prolong the identity search. College youth, then, may take longer to carve out a sense of self, but they also have time to explore more possibilities before making commitments.

The Development of Autonomy

A *C* in Economics! Sheila was devastated. "My first impulse was to phone my parents for comfort. But I resisted the temptation. I was trying to establish my independence and if I kept complaining to them about every little trouble, they would hardly think of me as an adult." (Komarovsky, 1985, p. 61)

Like most adolescents, this freshman is struggling with the process of **individuation**, an urge that began many years before. It pushes the toddler toward independence and continues throughout childhood, but during adolescence individuation intensifies. Teenagers have their own ideas and want to make their own decisions. At the same time, teenagers become more willing to take responsibility for their actions. "Individuation," writes psychoanalyst Peter Blos, "implies that the growing person takes increasing responsibility for what he does and what he is, rather than depositing this responsibility on the shoulders of those under whose influence and tutelage he has grown up" (1967, p. 168). Individuation, in short, is the process of becoming a separate person who can both act independently and accept responsibility for choices (Josselson, 1980).

individuation
the process of becoming an individual, emotionally speaking

AUTONOMY AND FAMILY RELATIONSHIPS

Becoming a separate person requires, first and foremost, autonomy from parents. This autonomy has several different components. One is being able to depend on oneself for solving problems, rather than always turning to parents for help. Another is seeing oneself with one's own eyes; adolescents come to realize that parents do not know everything about their children. Third is deidealizing parents, recognizing that parents, too, can make mistakes. Figure 16-1 shows that between grades 5 and 9, youngsters develop autonomy from parents in all three of these ways (Steinberg & Silverberg, 1986). By late adolescence most have come to be quite separate individuals. Parents, for their part, may feel they have lost a child, but at the same time gained a friend. Often they find they can confide in their adolescent son or daughter, something that wasn't possible a few years ago.

How rebellious must adolescents be to become independent from parents? Writers and moviemakers have long been intrigued by the adolescent rebel. Tom Jones, Stephen Dedalus, Holden Caulfield, and the young protagonists in *Rebel without a Cause* and *A Clockwork Orange* are a few examples. It is, however, a mistake to consider rebellion an inevitable part of growing up, just as it is mistaken to think of adolescence as an inevitably stressful time of life. In most cases, individuation is gradual and undramatic. The relationship between a teenager and his or her parents progressively changes, usually without a great deal of conflict. Parents and adolescents may bicker more than they did before, but these are not intense disagreements, and they are not apt to diminish feelings of closeness (Hill & Holmbeck, 1986). In the end, parents and teens develop a different kind of relationship, a relationship more of equals. Only very rarely are family ties severed.

Rebellion, then, is not necessary to achieve a healthy sense of independence; in fact, it probably hinders it. Adolescents who feel the most autonomous, who believe they have been granted enough freedom of choice, tend to be close to their parents, not in constant conflict with them (Grotevant & Cooper, 1986). Their parents are likely to have been "authoritative," rather than "authoritarian" or "permissive" (Steinberg, in press). These teenagers enjoy doing things with their families, feel free to turn to their parents for advice, and say they would like to be like their parents (Kandel & Lesser, 1972). A strained relationship with parents, in contrast, is often related to a *lack* of autonomy. It is the immature adolescent, the still-dependent one, who is most apt to be rebellious and negative toward the family (Josselson, Greenberger, & McConochie, 1977a, 1977b). Autonomy, apparently, develops best

FIGURE 16-1
AGE DIFFERENCES IN THREE ASPECTS OF EMOTIONAL AUTONOMY
(*Source*: Adapted from Steinberg, L., & Silverberg, S. [1986]. The vicissitudes of autonomy in early adolescence. *Child Development*, 57, 841–851. © The Society for Research in Child Development, Inc.)

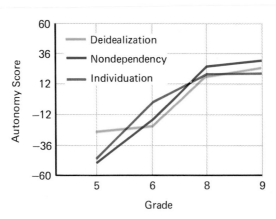

in an environment of emotional closeness, and emotional closeness is best maintained when parents and teens accept each other as individuals (Steinberg, in press.)

AUTONOMY AND DECISION MAKING

Being autonomous means being able to make your own choices, to decide on a sensible course of action by yourself. Today, many adolescents are forced to become independent decision makers at an early age (Elkind, 1982). For instance, young teenagers must often make choices about drinking, drug use, and sex, choices that many are very reluctant to discuss with their parents. Many adolescents are also expected to function without adult supervision each day until their parents get home from work. This independence requires better decision-making skills, including what to do in an emergency, whether to allow some friends to come over, how to make dinner.

The cognitive skills that youngsters acquire during adolescence help to make them better decision makers. For one thing, improved information-processing skills allow teenagers to consider different points of view, comparing the pros and cons of each. And because they can think hypothetically, they can imagine many of the consequences of any possible course of action. In addition, now that they can take another person's perspective, adolescents can detect biases and vested interests in the advice they get. In short, these cognitive advances make adolescents' decisions more thoughtful and rational than those of children.

Research confirms that decision making improves measurably during adolescence. In one study (Lewis, 1981), subjects aged 12 to 18 were asked to

Cognitive and emotional growth lead to more mature decision-making skills during adolescence. Teenagers may enjoy the opportunity to care for younger children. *(Henley & Savage/The Stock Market)*

help solve peers' personal problems. (Should I get involved in a certain risky situation? Can I still respect X after what he has done? How can I reconcile different advice from two experts? Should I have cosmetic surgery to remove an ugly bump on my cheek?) Older teens offered decision-making help that was decidedly more mature. Compared with younger teens, they were more likely to be aware of possible dangers, to consider long-term implications, to recommend independent specialists as consultants, and to warn against accepting advice from people who might be biased. Older teens, in short, tended to analyze the problems more fully than younger teens did. They made decisions by seeking reliable information and weighing all the alternatives.

AUTONOMY AND CONFORMITY

Look at a group of adolescents, and "independence" doesn't leap to mind. More likely, "conformity" does. From the cut of their hair to the color of their jeans, most adolescents want to look, think, and act like their friends. But if teenagers are conformists, how can they also become more autonomous during adolescence? Aren't the two tendencies incompatible? They aren't if we look at conformity and independence in relation to different groups of people.

From puberty onward, conformity to parents' ideas and wishes declines steadily, so in relation to parents, adolescents *are* continually becoming more autonomous. But in relation to peers, conformity *increases* during the early and middle teenage years, perhaps because at this age, adolescents don't yet have the self-assurance to stand apart from parents *and* friends (Brown, Clasen, & Eicher, 1986; Steinberg & Silverberg, 1986). In any case, during

While becoming more autonomous from their parents, adolescents become more conforming among their peers. During early and middle adolescence, dressing like your friends means you belong. *(Kate Connell)*

early and middle adolescence, youngsters are *less* independent in relation to peers than they were as children. This is especially true when the peer group is encouraging some antisocial behavior, such as cheating, trespassing, stealing, or vandalism. The trend is also stronger for boys than for girls. By later adolescence, though, the influence of peers diminishes. Teenagers are now much more apt to take a stand against the peer group when they think that it is wrong. This is the age when autonomy *overall* increases.

But even in early and middle adolescence, when peer conformity is greatest, teenagers are not slaves to the peer group. Seventh-, eighth-, and ninth-graders tend to go along with their friends on social matters and decisions that don't have long-term consequences. Clothing, music, and leisure activities are all strongly influenced by peers. But when values, religion, or ethics are involved, or when a decision has long-term consequences (careers, for example), adults (especially parents) still have the greatest influence (Wintre et al., 1988; Young & Ferguson, 1979).

Changing Social Relationships

Peter is a peace-loving person; he's tolerant and gives in very easily. He lets me say a lot of things to him that he would never accept from his mother, he tries most persistently to keep his things in order. And yet why should he keep his innermost self to himself and why am I never allowed there? By nature he is more closed-up than I am, I agree, but I know—and from my own experience—that at some time or other even the most uncommunicative people long just as much, if not more, to find someone in whom they can confide.

Both Peter and I have spent our most meditative years in the "Secret Annexe." We often discuss the future, the past, and the present, but, as I've already said, I still seem to miss the real thing and yet I know that it's there. (Anne Frank, *The Diary of a Young Girl*, 1952/1989, p. 225)

Finding "the real thing," for Anne Frank and for all adolescents, is a search for *intimacy*—a close emotional attachment based on concern, sharing, and love. Intimacy need not include sex. In fact, the nonsexual, intimate friendships of childhood are among the most important we can have. They are a prerequisite, contended Harry Stack Sullivan (1953a), for establishing deeper intimacy during adolescence and adulthood. Sullivan maintained that we must make a transition from the nonsexual, intimate same-sex friendships of childhood to the sexual, intimate, opposite-sex friendships of later adolescence (1953).

BEST-FRIEND INTIMACY

A need for intimacy with friends emerges at age 11 or 12. As children begin to share secrets with their friends, a new sense of loyalty and commitment grows, a belief that friends can trust each other. After interviewing children between

As the search for intimacy grows, adolescents share secrets and experiences with best friends. *(Bryan Peterson/The Stock Market)*

the ages of 6 and 12, one researcher identified several different bases of friendship they have (Berndt, 1981). These included *play or association* ("He calls me all the time."), *prosocial behavior* ("She helps me do things."), *intimacy and trust* ("I can tell her secrets."), and *loyal support* ("He'll stick up for me when I'm in a fight."). Children of all the ages studied mentioned association and prosocial behavior as bases of their friendships, but the youngest ones never talked about intimacy, trust, and loyal support. These more sophisticated ideas about friendship didn't appear until the later elementary school years.

During adolescence, the search for intimacy intensifies, and self-disclosure between best friends becomes an important pastime. Teenagers, especially girls, spend hours discussing their innermost thoughts and feelings, trying to understand one another. The discovery that they tend to think and feel the same as someone else becomes another important basis of friendship (Diaz & Berndt, 1982; Sharabany, Gershoni, & Hofman, 1981).

Why does this increased intimacy with friends occur during adolescence? Partly because adolescents need it and partly because they can now achieve it. In short, the biological, social, and cognitive changes of adolescence combine to make intimacy not only desirable, but possible. Along with their awakening sexuality come questions and concerns that almost demand baring one's soul: How do you act on a date? When do you kiss? How much?

In addition, intimacy grows because it *can* grow. Children have a narrow ability to see things from another person's perspective, which limits their capacity for intimacy (Selman, 1980). The cognitive changes of adolescence, though, include a growing capacity for empathy, for understanding another's feelings and needs. With such understanding comes the ability to form more mature friendships. Further, since many teenagers feel awkward discussing

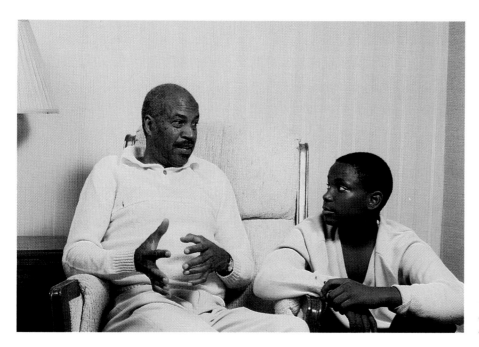

While adolescents are becoming more intimate with their friends, their parents may begin confiding in them. *(Brent Jones/ Stock, Boston)*

sex and other boy-girl matters with their parents, they naturally turn to their friends. But at the same time, many parents now view their children as near-adults, and who confides in whom sometimes takes a new twist (Youniss & Smollar, 1985).

So while adolescents are becoming closer to their friends, they aren't necessarily distancing themselves from their parents. In one study, adolescents from the age of about 12 on reported that they were closer to their best friends than to their parents. This didn't mean that their feelings toward their parents had grown cooler. It was simply that relationships between friends were becoming so much stronger (Hunter & Youniss, 1982). Leaving both family and friends to go away to college makes many first-year college students feel both lonely and adrift. "Issues & Options" offers advice to students who may be undermining their own ability to make new friends.

OPPOSITE-SEX RELATIONSHIPS

Though adolescents are often preoccupied with the opposite sex, friendship with "the other sex" is quite rare. Older elementary school children and young adolescents rarely have opposite-sex friends (Hallinan, 1981). In fact, having the same gender is the single most important determinant of friendship at this age, more important even than shared race or socioeconomic background (Schofield, 1981). The gulf between boys and girls during pre- and early adolescence has several causes. One is sex-role socialization. Despite some changes in the past 20 years, the two sexes still have different interests and pastimes, and most importantly they perceive themselves as different from each other.

Issues & OPTIONS

Loneliness and the College Student: When Intimacy Is Lacking

Late adolescence is one of the loneliest times of life. Adolescents need intimacy, but wanting independence too, many leave family and friends behind when they go off to college. One study of UCLA students found that nearly half felt extremely lonely during their first months at a large, impersonal university where they knew virtually no one. Speaking with a researcher, two students expressed their feelings this way:

> I do not feel my interests and ideals are the same as other people's. I get especially lonely when I realize that I am an isolated person, alone even in a group. It's depressing because I might always feel this way.
>
> This is a big impersonal school that treats people like

numbers rather than people. . . . Here everybody cares about just one thing—grades. I like people. I like to be around them, and it was hard for me to realize that people don't really care for one another like high school, but for themselves and grades. (Cutrona, 1982, pp. 299, 303)

All kinds of students were susceptible to these feelings of isolation—males as well as females, members of different ethnic groups, those living on campus as well as those living off.

For most UCLA students loneliness subsided by the end of the first year, but a sizable number continued to feel lonely throughout their college years (Cutrona, 1982). Why couldn't they overcome their isolation and make some close friends? Part of

the answer lies in the attitudes of these chronically lonely students. They did join clubs, strike up conversations, and go through the motions of meeting people, but they remained pessimistic about the chances of their social lives improving. Most became resigned to isolation, telling themselves that they didn't need friends or that their schoolwork was far more important. Ironically, these rationalizations probably increased their chances of staying lonely. To break out of a shell of isolation, a person apparently needs an optimistic outlook that things will get better, even in the bleakest of times.

In addition to a negative outlook, chronically lonely students may also be shyer than those who manage to make friends. Many

When asked why boys and girls sit apart in the school lunchroom, one young adolescent boy replied: "So they can talk. The boys talk about football and sports and the girls talk about whatever they talk about" (Schofield, 1981, p. 68).

Another factor is the fear of being romantically involved. As one girl remarked when asked why boys and girls rarely work together on class projects: "People like to work with their friends. . . . When you're working on a project . . . your friend has to call and come over to your house. If it's a boy, it can be complicated." Even the appearance of romantic involvement causes worries at this age. "If you talk with a boy," said one girl, "they [other girls] say that you're almost going with him" (Schofield, 1981, p. 69).

For most of us, early romance evokes a muddle of emotions, part tenderness, part passion, part terror. Some of the intense discomfort young adoles-

Issues & OPTIONS

adolescents suffer from shyness to some extent. In a study conducted at Stanford University, over 80 percent of 5000 students surveyed admitted having a problem with shyness at some point in their lives, and 42 percent said that the problem still existed. For some of these young people the shyness is so acute that the security of a lonely room seems preferable to the pain of meeting new people.

Severe shyness is often related to a negative self-image, a feeling that you are not really a very attractive, interesting, or desirable companion. The problem is that with this negative self-image you are likely to behave in ways that prompt the very social rejection you fear. "I'm so shy" said a 16-year-old girl named Tara, "that it's hard for me to look at another person, much less start up a conversation. Every time I try to talk with someone, especially if it's a guy, my hands start shaking, my mouth feels like it's full of cotton balls, and I blush like crazy" (Mackey, 1984). It is likely that Tara's awkwardness makes others feel uncomfortable around her, only adding to her negative self-image and isolation.

Psychologists offer several suggestions for overcoming shyness (Mackey, 1984):

1. Learn and *use* friendly behaviors when meeting people. Instead of avoiding eye contact, defensively folding your arms, and mumbling a brief "Hello," practice looking the person in the face, extending your hand, and offering a very cheerful "Hi." At first, these behaviors may seem artificial, but keep working on them. The friendly responses you get in return should start to convince you that it's not *you*, but your normally reserved manner that puts people off.

2. If when talking to a new person you temporarily run out of things to say, don't be embarrassed and assume that you must be boring the other person. All conversations have occasional lulls; lulls don't mean that the speakers are dull and uninteresting. Nor should you feel that filling a silence is solely your job. Your partner is probably just as eager as you are to find another topic.

3. An easy way to keep a conversation going is to be genuinely interested in the people with whom you're speaking. Ask them questions about themselves, preferably ones that require more than a simple yes or no answer. Taking an active interest in others is also an excellent way to keep from being overly conscious of your own words and actions.

4. Remember the statistics about how common a problem shyness is. If some 40 percent of Americans say they feel shy at least some of the time, the chances are good that the people with whom you strike up conversations are secretly feeling just as shy as you are.

---

cents feel is linked to fears about their emerging sexuality. Young teenagers "are aware that they are approaching the age when they may begin to become deeply involved with each other in a romantic or sexual way" (Schofield, 1981, p. 71). It is an awareness that can create extreme self-consciousness in front of members of the opposite sex. Accordingly, intimacy between males and females develops very gradually. In grades 7 through 10, half of all the boys and about a quarter of all the girls do not list even one opposite-sex peer as a significant person in their lives (Buhrmester & Furman, 1987). This pattern may be more of a loss to boys than to girls. Having a close relationship with an opposite-sex peer is more strongly related to a boy's general level of interpersonal intimacy than it is to a girl's. This is because, in our society, boys are not encouraged to be emotionally expressive toward other boys. As a result, boys who are friends only with boys often have less experience in self-disclosure

Although most teenagers begin dating by age 17, intimacy between the sexes tends to come later. *(Richard Hutchings/ PhotoEdit)*

and mutual caring than girls do. Some researchers think that girls may therefore play an important part in teaching boys how to be more open and sensitive (Simon & Gagnon, 1969).

DATING

More than half of U.S. girls begin dating between ages 13 and 14, while boys begin between 14 and 15. When dating starts depends partly on a youngster's physical maturity, but more importantly on the social norms in his or her school (Simmons & Blyth, 1987). A physically *im*mature 14-year-old attending a school where 14-year-old dating is common is more likely to date than a mature 14-year-old in a school where dating doesn't start until age 16 (Dornbusch et al., 1981). After that time more than 90 percent of all U.S. adolescents have had at least one date, and between the ages of 16 and 18 (the last 2 years of high school) over 50 percent average one or more dates a week. By the end of high school, moreover, 75 percent have been steadily involved with someone at least once (Dickenson, 1975).

Whether dating fosters the development of intimacy between the sexes is not at all clear. For many, it produces only a superficial intimacy rather than genuine closeness (Douvan & Adelson, 1966). In the United States at least, the dating game is highly ritualized, and how you look often outweighs who you are (Walster, Aronson, Abrahams, & Rottman, 1966). This is particularly true during early and mid-adolescence when young people tend to stick very closely to a stereotyped dating "script." Later dating may involve somewhat more emotional depth, but even among college juniors and seniors intimacy in dating is rare. In one study, less than a fourth of all the male college students interviewed reported genuinely intimate relationships with women (Orlofsky et al., 1973). Young women report intimacy in their dating relationships only slightly more often (Hodgson & Fischer, 1979; Kacerguis & Adams, 1980).

ADOLESCENT SEXUALITY

Like establishing an identity or becoming autonomous, social context affects how adolescents approach and experience sexuality as well. What and how adolescents learn about sexuality, is called **sexual socialization**, a process in which family and peers play key roles. Because of the risk of pregnancy, girls' sexuality is more closely monitored by parents, and family and friends give girls more encouragement to be sexually cautious. Different sexual norms also apply to girls and boys. Despite a gradual erosion of the double standard, our society is still much more disapproving of casual sex among females than males (Carns, 1973). As recently as 1980, more college students believed it was immoral for a woman to have sex with many men than believed it was immoral for a man to have sex with many women (Robinson & Jedlicka, 1982). Today, however, for both sexes, the danger of AIDS has shifted the focus from morality to mortality. But still, the influences of norms, parents, and peers make the first sexual experiences of boys and girls quite different.

sexual socialization what and how adolescents learn about sexuality

Boys' first experiences

A boy's first sexual experience typically occurs in early adolescence through masturbation (Gagnon, 1972). (Note that the subjects in the studies cited here, because they are usually college students, are typically middle class as well.) His first sexual satisfaction therefore has nothing to do with an intimate relationship. This separation between sex and intimacy also characterizes the typical boy's first sexual intercourse. Often his first partner is a "casual date" or "pickup" (Carns, 1973). About a third of boys never have intercourse with their first sexual partner again, and less than a quarter have sex with her again more than five times (Simon, Berger, & Gagnon, 1972). Apparently, a male seldom feels close to the woman with whom he lost his virginity, even though he is apt to feel love toward a woman who loses *her* virginity with him (Peplau, Rubin, & Hill, 1977).

Typically, when an adolescent boy describes his "first time" to other people (usually to his male friends soon after the event), he gets their overwhelming approval (Carns, 1973; Miller & Simon, 1980). The boy's anticipation of this positive reaction, coupled with his lack of emotional commitment to the girl, make this confiding relatively easy (Kallen & Stephenson, 1982). The anticipated approval of friends probably also enhances the boy's feelings about the experience itself. Often he describes it as "exciting" (46 percent), "satisfying" (43 percent), "exhilarating" (43 percent), and "happy" (43 percent) (Sorenson, 1973).

In short, an adolescent boy's first sexual intercourse usually has to do with achievement, or "scoring." Emotional intimacy in a sexual relationship typically comes later. Thus, a boy's task is to integrate intimacy into an already existing sense of sexual capacity.

Girls' first experiences

Most often, girls follow a different path. A girl's first sexual encounter is usually with a boy she feels close to, and her first intercourse is with a boy she is "planning to marry" or "in love with" (Carns, 1973; Kallen & Stephenson, 1982). Nearly two-thirds of all young women have sex with their first partner many times afterward (Simon et al., 1972). To them, losing their virginity is a dramatic event that helps to seal a long-term emotional commitment (Peplau et al., 1977).

A girl doesn't usually disclose her first sexual experience as quickly and easily as a boy does (Kallen & Stephenson, 1982). When she does confide in other people (usually her female friends), the news is often greeted with mixed feelings or even outright disapproval (Carns, 1973). This mixed or negative reaction, plus concern about pregnancy, helps to color a young woman's feelings. Compared with a boy, she is more likely to report feeling "afraid" (63 percent), "guilty" (36 percent), "worried" (35 percent), and "embarrassed" (31 percent) (Sorenson, 1973).

In summary, most middle-class sexually active teenage girls worry about becoming pregnant and are ambivalent about losing their virginity; they do not take initiation into sex lightly. The adolescent girl's first sexual experience is nearly always tied to feelings of love. A girl, then, must integrate sexual activity into an already existing capacity for intimacy and emotional involvement.

Attitudes toward premarital sex

Today's adolescents have been indelibly affected by the sexual revolution that began in the mid-1960s. They are far more tolerant of premarital sex than were teenagers a generation ago. For the vast majority, marriage is not a prerequisite for sexual intercourse. Most adolescents believe that "It's all right for young people to have sex before getting married if they are in love." A sizable minority also believe that "liking someone as a person" is enough justification for sex (Sorenson, 1973). These attitudes, although permissive, are far from promiscuous. Most teenagers today feel that sex should be accompanied by mutual caring and respect. The prevailing view is best described by a label coined more than 30 years ago: "permissiveness with affection" (Katchadourian, in press; Reiss, 1960). This is not to say there aren't some teenagers who think more conservatively about sexual matters. In fact, the trend toward increasingly permissive attitudes began to level off in the early 1980s and may have even reversed. Relatively more students in the 1980s believed that premarital sex is wrong than did students in the 1970s (Robinson & Jedlicka, 1982). But young people with this outlook are still a minority.

Age of sexual initiation

By late adolescence, most young Americans have become sexually active, but what is done—from petting to intercourse—depends more on sociology than sexuality. Geography, gender, and ethnic background all influence the start of sexual experiences. Values and attitudes are more conservative in the Deep

South than in New York City and California, for example. And while only 12 percent of white males have had intercourse by the age of 15, 19 percent of Hispanic males have, as have 42 percent of black males (Hayes, 1987). Compared with boys, girls are more delayed in sexual initiation, regardless of race. By age 15, only about 4 to 5 percent of white or Hispanic females and 10 percent of blacks have had intercourse (Hayes, 1987). Most 15-year-olds, however, do neck and pet, the first steps in sexual initiation. But it is not until the end of high school, by age 18 or so, that about half have had intercourse at least once. Four years later, at the age of college graduation, about 80 percent are sexually experienced (DeLamater & MacCorquodale, 1979).

These statistics make clear that premarital sex is not limited to certain subgroups of young people. Another myth is that early sexual activity suggests insecurity and emotional problems, but adolescents who become sexually active earlier than their peers usually have just as high self-esteem and life satisfaction as other teenagers (Jessor et al., 1983). How closely parents keep tabs on their adolescents or how openly they discuss sex with them is also unrelated to the age of sexual initiation (Newcomer & Udry, 1984; Moore et al., 1986). What does seem to matter is how intact a teenager's family is. For reasons that social scientists do not yet understand, adolescents whose parents are divorcing are more apt to be sexually active. Interestingly, girls who live with their mother (regardless of why the father is absent from the home) are also more prone to early sexual experimentation (Newcomer & Udry, 1987). The reason may be that the mother is likely to be dating and so provides a model of sexual activity for her daughter.

Contraception

One reason adults are so concerned about adolescent sexuality is the failure of many teenagers to use birth control. While more teenagers today use birth control than did a decade ago, the statistics are still alarming. Only about half of adolescent girls say they used contraception the first time they had intercourse. Of the half that did not, about a third continue to have unprotected sex, even though they remain sexually active. Nearly half of all sexually active teens use contraception only sporadically, and when they use it has little to do with the girl's time of peak fertility. Predictably, older adolescents use contraception more often than younger teens do, and contraception is more likely when sex is planned than when it occurs spontaneously (Hayes, 1987).

Why do so few adolescents use contraception on a regular basis? One reason is that for many teenagers contraceptives aren't readily available (or teenagers don't know that they are). About 15 percent of teenage girls and 25 percent of boys say they didn't use contraceptives when they first had sex because they couldn't get them (Hayes, 1987). This is especially a problem for younger adolescents who feel uncomfortable revealing their sexual activity to adults whose help they need to obtain birth control. Having ready access to a free, confidential family planning service that doesn't require parental consent is a strong predictor of whether adolescents use contraceptives and do so consistently (Chilman, 1980).

Another barrier to the effective use of contraception is lack of education about sex, pregnancy, and birth control. For instance, many adolescents mistakenly believe that if a girl really doesn't want to get pregnant, she won't, even if she has sex without using birth control. Many teenagers are also misinformed about how the chances of pregnancy vary over the course of the menstrual cycle. Many still believe that the risk of pregnancy is greatest *during* the menstrual flow, when in fact the risk is greatest two weeks after the menstrual flow begins. In addition, many adolescents are simply unaware of available contraceptive devices. About a third of those who didn't use birth control when they first had sex say they didn't know about contraception or didn't think of using it (Hayes, 1987). (In Chapter 17, we discuss the need for sex education programs in schools.)

Finally, there are psychological reasons for not using contraception. Many young people underestimate the seriousness of pregnancy and child-rearing (Hayes, 1987). When teenagers don't see these as disastrous to them, they are much more willing simply to take their chances with sex. This willingness to take chances is also encouraged by adolescent egocentrism and the personal fable, which we discussed in the previous chapter—the tendency to view yourself as so unique that you are not susceptible to the problems that befall other people. Young adolescents are particularly prone to this flawed thinking. They are also more likely to reject birth control because it makes sex seem too calculated (Cvetkovich et al., 1975). Going on the pill acknowledges an intention to have frequent sex, an admission many girls find difficult to make.

Homosexuality

For as long as researchers have been studying sexual preferences in America, 8 percent of the population has been found to be *non*heterosexual. Of this 8 percent, about a third are exclusively homosexual and the remaining two-thirds have both heterosexual and homosexual interests (Conger, 1977).

Why does homosexuality develop, especially when our culture is so prejudiced against it? Apparently, sexual preference is not something we can control; it seems to be shaped by a complex interaction of early biological and social forces (Green, 1980, 1987). One early biological force may be sex hormones, which appear to influence children's tendencies toward aggressive play. Boys whose biological makeup inclines them away from rough-and-tumble activities may take up pastimes generally considered more appropriate for girls. Consequently, they may be rejected by other boys and alienated from their fathers. Later, as adolescents, these ostracized youngsters may seek the male affection they missed as children by turning to homosexual relationships.

Some research findings are consistent with this general theory. For instance, young children who don't conform to expected gender roles often do grow up to be homosexual (Bell et al., 1981; Green, 1987). In addition, both male and female homosexual adults are more likely than heterosexuals to describe their same-sex parent as cold, distant, and rejecting (Bell et al., 1981). This is not to say that all homosexuals have the same developmental histories, nor that certain events in a person's life destine him or her to be homosexual. The development of a sexual preference is a complex process that undoubtedly varies from one individual to another. Still, there are patterns that may help to explain how this important part of human identity is formed.

Some Psychological and Social Problems of Adolescence

Throughout this chapter we have emphasized that adolescence is not inevitably a stormy time of life. Most people handle the physical, cognitive, and social changes of adolescence with relative ease, emerging into young adulthood with positive feelings about themselves and a good sense of where they're going. Most adolescents also learn to form close relationships with others, to make career decisions, and to work toward long-range goals—all with little turmoil and stress. For others, though, the teenage years are indeed stressful, sometimes to the point of being overwhelming. These troubled youngsters are not just having the normal self-doubts, conflicts, and setbacks that all of us face once in a while. For them, life is colored by serious psychological or social problems which often require professional help.

In Chapter 15 we discussed one of the major psychosocial problems of adolescence, drug and alcohol abuse. Here, we focus on teenage crime, delinquency, depression, and suicide. Chapter 17 examines teenage pregnancy and single parenthood and the plight of the high school dropout. Not surprisingly, many of these problems often afflict the same youngsters. The teenager with an alcohol problem may also drop out of school, get involved in delinquency, and conceive or father a child before marriage. We begin here with teenage crime and delinquency.

CRIME AND DELINQUENCY

In the spring of 1989, a group of teenaged boys brutally beat and repeatedly raped a young woman jogging in New York City's Central Park and left her near death. That the boys charged with the crime were poor and black and the woman affluent and white made as many headlines as the crime itself. A short time later, another group of teenage boys were charged with sexually assaulting a young girl. This time, the crime occurred in suburban New Jersey. The boys were white, from families with money, and the girl was mentally retarded and white.

Both of these crimes filled the media for weeks. Words such as "wolf pack" and "savages" were applied to the Central Park suspects, while they themselves described the attack as a kind of adventure, a night of "wilding." The New Jersey assault stirred up defensiveness, anger, and shame among adults in the boys' community. Both crimes left people asking whether the boys' parents should be held responsible and whether the youths should be tried as adults. But the most difficult question posed by these and by all teenage crimes is *why*. We can't answer for the boys who committed these particularly violent acts, but we can say something about the young people who, as a group, commit far more than their share of crimes.

Adolescents and young adults break the law more than any other part of the population. These violations include both *delinquency* (truancy, underage drinking, minor vandalism, and other misdemeanors typical of youth) and

Adolescents commit about half of all crimes against property. *(Tony Freeman/PhotoEdit)*

crime (robbery, arson, rape, murder, and other felonies committed against property or people). In the United States, where individuals under 18 make up only about a quarter of the population, they commit about *half of all the crimes against property*. Similarly, about *one third of all the violent crimes against people* are committed by those in the 18 to 24 age group, which makes up only about *one-tenth* of the population (U.S. Bureau of the Census, 1985).

Between 1950 and 1980, juvenile arrests of all kinds increased steadily, but the rate of arrests leveled off in the early 1980s and has even dropped slightly since then (Farrington, 1986). And as disturbing as these figures are, adolescent crime and delinquency are probably *under*reported substantially. Often authorities fail to catch youthful offenders, especially for delinquency, and many such offenders who *are* caught are "handled" outside the justice system. But when researchers ask adolescents if they have ever committed an illegal act, surprising numbers say yes. Between 60 and 80 percent admit to some kind of crime or delinquent behavior, even though most of these are fairly minor offenses (Gold & Petronio, 1980; Huizinga & Elliot, 1985).

Adolescents' own reports also call into question the accuracy of official statistics regarding ethnic groups and crime. When social class is held constant, there are very few ethnic or racial differences in the prevalence of criminal or delinquent activities. Nearly equal percentages of white, black, and Hispanic youth admit to having committed some kind of delinquent act, and roughly equal percentages also admit to having committed a serious crime (Krisberg et al., 1986).

In general, the earlier a young person's "criminal career" begins, the more likely he or she is to become a chronic offender, to commit serious and violent crimes, and to continue criminal behavior as an adult. If delinquency doesn't start until mid-adolescence, it is much more apt to be less serious, more occasional, and more short-lived. Psychologists therefore distinguish between youngsters who start having problems of conduct *before* adolescence and those who begin *during* adolescence. The first type of youngster is quite different from the second.

Typically, children who begin breaking the law before adolescence are troubled boys, often from poor families. They tend to have parents who are hostile and neglectful and who fail to instill the standards of behavior that form the foundations of conscience and self-control. These youngsters are sometimes called **unsocialized delinquents** because they have not learned the basic norms and values of their society. Because this basic learning process begins early in life, unsocialized delinquents-in-the-making are often apparent at a very early age, sometimes even during the preschool years.

unsocialized delinquents delinquents who have not learned basic social norms

In contrast are youngsters who don't engage in delinquent behavior until after they are adolescents. Many of these teenagers do not have any deep psychological problems or serious family troubles. The delinquent acts they commit are often minor crimes against property. They know what they did was wrong, and they are apt to be remorseful when their parents are called by the police. These youngsters usually don't go on to a life of crime as adults. Because such youngsters seem to have learned the norms and values of society, they are often called **socialized delinquents**.

socialized delinquents delinquents who have learned values of society

Socialized delinquents differ from their nondelinquent peers in several ways. First, they are often monitored less carefully by their parents (Dornbusch et al., 1985; Patterson & Stouthamer-Loeber, 1984). Unlike the parents of Jack, Peter, and Mike, who let their sons roam freely on a school night, the parents of teenagers who have never been delinquent tend to keep close tabs on their children. Second, socialized delinquents are more susceptible to peer pressure than nondelinquents are, and peer pressure is an important factor in less serious forms of youthful misconduct (Brown, Clasen, & Eicher, 1986). Socialized delinquents are often cajoled and dared by friends to engage in misbehavior. Because susceptibility to peer pressure tends to be greatest during mid-adolescence, this is also the age at which socialized delinquency tends to peak (Berndt, 1979).

Such different forces shape socialized and unsocialized delinquents that prevention and treatment strategies differ as well. To prevent the crimes of unsocialized delinquents we would have to stop troubled relationships from forming in their families, a very formidable task. Americans are reluctant to intervene in family life just because parents are at risk for child-rearing problems. More typically, we act after trouble has occurred in the family, but by then, intervention may do little good. If basic norms and values aren't learned during childhood they tend to stay unlearned: Attempts at rehabilitating unsocialized delinquents usually fail. Most in this group continue serious criminal behavior into adulthood.

The outlook for socialized delinquents is much better. Because they *have* internalized basic norms and values, it is easier to help them control their own behavior. Four approaches, in particular, are often successful. One is teaching socialized delinquents how to resist the peer pressure that drew them toward delinquency in the first place (Kaplan, 1983). A second is to train parents to monitor their children more closely and so minimize the chances for misbehavior (Loeber & Stouthamer-Loeber, 1986). A third is to treat acts of delinquency, even minor ones, as serious breaches of acceptable conduct that deserve punishment. When adolescents know that a behavior has negative consequences, they are not apt to repeat it in the future. And a fourth approach is to steer a young person's time and energy into more productive activities. Some gang intervention programs have successfully encouraged adolescents to abandon delinquent behavior in favor of community renovation projects.

DEPRESSION AND SUICIDE

Major depression

> Stacie was 15 years old when her family moved to Massachusetts so her father could pursue a graduate degree in engineering. She was excited about the move but sorry to leave her friends and old, familiar neighborhood.
>
> At her new school, things seemed strange and different. She didn't feel like participating in extracurricular activities.
>
> She just came home, went to her room, and slept. Sometimes right through supper. She often felt on the verge of tears for no reason at all.
>
> Her brothers and sisters teased her by calling her "one of the Seven Dwarfs"— Sleepy or Grumpy.
>
> She knew something was wrong. But there didn't seem to be anyone to turn to for help. Her parents were busy. She had some new friends. But she didn't feel she knew them well enough to discuss anything very personal.
>
> Meanwhile, things were getting worse, not better. And she didn't know what to do. . . . (Herskowitz, 1988, pp. 103–104)

Stacie was suffering from major depression. In its milder form, depression is probably the most common psychological disturbance of adolescence (Weiner, 1980). Depressive feelings are usually caused by a loss of some kind, the death of a loved one, change in an important relationship (divorcing parents, breaking up with a girlfriend or boyfriend), the end of something safe and familiar (leaving the town you grew up in), or a blow to self-esteem (failing an important test). Mild depression usually lifts in a few days or weeks.

Major depression like Stacie's is much more enduring. Week after week the person feels sad and dejected. Activities that used to give great pleasure now seem meaningless and empty. Loss of motivation and apathy are accompanied by diminished appetite, sleep difficulties, and excessive tiredness. Depressed people often feel pessimistic, viewing themselves and their situation as hopeless. And for many, this sense of hopelessness triggers thoughts of suicide.

Depression is rare during childhood, but minor bouts of depression are experienced by about 25 percent of teenagers, and about 3 percent of U.S. adolescents suffer from severe enough symptoms to be classified as having a

Minor depression, short-lived and caused by a loss of some kind, is common among adolescents. Major depression is both more enduring and more serious. *(Jim Whitmer/Stock, Boston)*

major depression (Chartier & Ranieri, 1984). One reason for the increased prevalence at adolescence could be the hormonal changes that occur at puberty. For girls, there is some evidence that fluctuations in sex hormones at puberty are related to higher rates of depression (Brooks-Gunn & Reiter, in press). The improved cognitive abilities of teenagers may also be involved. Adolescents may begin to see long-term negative implications they might never before have noticed. New social demands may also play a part. At puberty most young people go to a new school, meet new friends, and deal with their emerging sexuality. These experiences can be very stressful and if not well resolved might lead to depression. Interestingly, whereas depression is more common among boys *before* adolescence, it is much more common among girls *after* puberty. Perhaps this is because after puberty girls are under more pressure to conform to gender-role stereotypes, and the stereotypic female role is one of fragility and dependence—traits that could encourage helpless reactions and trigger depression.

The symptoms of severe depression are not always easy to spot in teenagers. Often they are masked by other behavioral problems. Because adolescents' self-esteem is often quite fragile, they may find it hard to admit self-critical thoughts to themselves or others. Some try to cover up their negative feelings through restless, unproductive activity. Others run away from home, rebel against their parents, or become involved in delinquency. Although

FOCUS ON

Preventing Teenage Suicides

The bright news about teenage suicide prevention is that treatment can be very effective, making it especially urgent to seek help for depressed or suicidal adolescents. Once treatment begins, drug therapies can correct the chemical imbalances in the brain that may trigger or accompany depression, and psychotherapy can help depressed teenagers understand the causes of their despondent feelings. Such insight helps to relieve the self-criticism that often accompanies depression. Therapy can also help to foster an active approach to solving life's problems, rather than yielding to feelings of helplessness. Many therapists try, too, to reinvolve depressed teenagers in activities that they enjoy.

Adults who counsel teenagers often tell them that people who are suicidal cannot be rational about their actions; they need to be protected from themselves. When suicide is a risk, concerns about a friend's safety have to outweigh fears about breaking a trust. Friends, parents, or adults should intervene if the following signs appear after a significant loss or family disruption:

• Direct suicide threats and comments ("I wish I were dead."; "You'd be better off without me.")
• A previous suicide attempt, no matter how minor
• Preoccupation with death in music, art, and writing
• Problems with sleeping, eating, and personal hygiene
• Problems with schoolwork; loss of interest in school or favorite hobbies
• Dramatic changes in behavior patterns (such as a shy adolescent suddenly becoming extremely outgoing)
• Prevailing sense of gloom, hopelessness, and helplessness
• Withdrawal from family members and friends; alienation of important people
• Giving away valued possessions
• A series of "accidents," increase in risk taking, or loss of interest in personal safety (Steinberg & Levine, 1990).*

*Excerpt from *You and your adolescent* by Laurence Steinberg and Ann Levine. Copyright © 1990 by Laurence Steinberg and Ann Levine. Reprinted by permission of Harper & Row, Publishers, Inc.

these behaviors are often caused by factors other than depression, they may indicate an underlying sense of hopelessness, especially when they arise suddenly and follow some kind of loss.

Teenage suicide

"I was depressed. Things were so terrible. I missed my old friends a lot! I wanted to go back, but I knew I couldn't.
I felt very alone, and I didn't know what to do." (Herskowitz, 1988, p. 104)

What Stacie (p. 490) did was to attempt suicide, as 1 out of every 1000 U.S. teenagers do each year. Luckily, Stacie failed, as do most of the teens who try to take their lives. But 5000 succeed. This figure has been fairly stable since 1980, but from 1950 until then, the rate quadrupled for 15- to 19-year-olds (National Center for Health Statistics, 1982).

To the obvious question, "Why?" there is no one answer. Perhaps society is changing in ways that make adolescence a more difficult time of life. Teenagers feel pressure to grow up quickly. Divorce is common, parents busy, and moves to new towns frequent. All these factors could contribute to more anxiety and depression, and ultimately to more suicide attempts.

A particularly tragic side effect of teenage suicides is that one often leads to others. In the mid-1980s, thinking that publicity would prevent suicides, community leaders called for heightened news coverage of these tragedies. But instead of preventing others, publicity seemed to engender more (Gould & Shaffer, 1986; Phillips & Carstensen, 1986). Helping adolescents cope with the stresses that lead to suicide—pressures, family problems, and drug abuse— is probably a far more effective route to prevention than publicity. Adolescent suicide attempts are rarely impulsive reactions to a single distressing situation. Teenagers who attempt suicide have usually appealed unsuccessfully for help and emotional support. They may even discuss death with some of their friends, but, reluctant to betray a friend's confidence, adolescents often keep silent. "Focus On" describes what teenagers and adults can do to help prevent teenage suicide.

Summary

1. Although the biological and cognitive changes of adolescence make it distinctive, it need not be a time of extreme "storm and stress."

2. Self-scrutiny preoccupies individuals for the first time in adolescence. Adolescents' developing sense of self includes self-concept (the traits we see ourselves as having), self-esteem (how we feel about ourselves), and identity (knowing who we are now and sensing who we will be in the future).

3. The self-concept shifts in adolescence from the concrete descriptions of childhood to an understanding based on more abstract social and psychological traits.

4. Self-esteem stays fairly constant from about age 13 on and tends to improve during middle and late adolescence. Among young adolescents, white females tend to have the lowest self-esteem.

5. In Erik Erikson's model, the main psychosocial crisis of adolescence is *identity versus identity diffusion*. Successfully resolving this crisis permits an adolescent to make a series of commitments. These include choosing a career and a mate and making political and ideological choices that are consistent with one's sense of self.

6. Resolving the identity crisis is easier when people who matter react positively to a young person's aspirations. Establishing an integrated identity can take many years, extending well into adulthood.

7. Identity also has sexual and ethnic components. Adolescents feel increased pressure to behave in gender-appropriate ways. Girls are especially prone to this kind of pressure, feeling they must match society's ideal of female looks and behavior. Minority teenagers may first feel estranged from the white majority while they are establishing their identity as part of an ethnic or racial minority.

8. During the psychosocial moratorium, in which adolescents are free from adult responsibilities, they can explore different possibilities before committing to the self that "fits."

9. Most adolescents are engaged in the process of individuation, becoming less emotionally dependent on their parents and more willing to take responsibility for their actions. Becoming autonomous from one's parents has three components: (a) being able to depend on oneself for solving problems; (b) seeing oneself with one's own eyes: realizing that parents do not know everything about their children; and (c) deidealizing parents: understanding that they can make mistakes.

10. The decision making that is necessary for becoming autonomous is fostered by growing cognitive skills, including gains in information-processing abilities and hypothetical thinking.

11. Adolescents become more conforming toward their peers' ideas and more independent from their parents, particularly in matters of taste and style. But when values, religion, or ethics are involved, or when a decision has long-term consequences, adults, especially parents, still have the most influence.

12. Adolescents seek intimacy, a close emotional attachment based on concern, sharing, and love. Intimacy need not include sex. Sullivan maintained that the nonsexual, intimate friendships of childhood are a prerequisite for deeper intimacy during adolescence.

13. A need for intimacy with friends emerges at age 11 or 12. As children begin to share secrets with their friends, a new sense of loyalty and commitment grows, a belief that friends can trust each other. The search for intimacy intensifies during adolescence, and self-disclosure becomes very important. Intimacy becomes possible because the cognitive changes of adolescence include a growing capacity for empathy, for understanding another's feelings and needs.

14. Even though young adolescents are often preoccupied with the opposite sex, such friendships are rare, partly because of differences in interests, and partly from fear of romance. After age 16, however, almost all U.S. teenagers have had at least one date; but even when dating begins in earnest, intimacy doesn't often follow.

15. Social context affects the way in which adolescents approach and experience sexuality. Family and peers play key roles in adolescents' sexual socialization. Boys' early sexual experiences generally lack intimacy and emotional commitment, whereas girls tend to feel emotionally close to the boys with whom they first have sex. Sexually active teenagers all too frequently fail to use contraceptives.

16. Adolescents and young adults break the law more than any other part of the population, with acts of both delinquency and crime. Nearly equal percentages of white, black, and Hispanic youths admit to having committed some kind of delinquent act, and roughly equal percentages also admit to having committed a serious crime. Children who begin breaking the law before adolescence are usually troubled boys from poor, troubled families, where parents did not instill the standards of behavior that form the foundations of conscience and self-control. Adolescents who commit delinquent acts after they become teenagers may not be especially troubled. These socialized delinquents understand that what they did was wrong.

17. Depression is the most common psychological disturbance of adolescence, usually caused by a loss or some kind of a blow to self-esteem. Mild depression is short-lived, but major depression is more enduring and more serious. Depression can be alleviated through various kinds of therapy and medications. Prompt treatment is important to restore a positive outlook on life and to prevent suicide attempts.

Key Terms

barometric self-esteem

baseline self-esteem

crystallization

identity versus identity diffusion

individuation

psychosocial moratorium

sexual socialization

socialized delinquents

specification

unsocialized delinquents

Suggested Readings

Csikszentmihalyi, M., and Larson, R. (1984). *Being adolescent.* New York: Basic Books. This study of high school students provides interesting insights into the adolescents' moods and the factors in their lives that affect them.

Douvan, E., and Adelson, J. (1966). *The adolescent experience.* New York: Wiley. Although nearly 25 years old, this study captures the psychological experience of adolescence better than any other work published to date.

Hayes, C. (Ed.) (1987). *Risking the future.* Washington, DC: National Academy Press. A collection of papers commissioned by the National Academy of Sciences on adolescent sexuality, childbearing, and contraception.

Simmons, R., and Blyth, D. (1987). *Moving into adolescence.* New York: Aldine de Gruyter. A study of the transition from childhood into adolescence, with a special emphasis on the move from elementary into middle school.

The Social Context of Adolescence

*I*n the 1950s, career day in the high school gym found the girls gathered around the teachers, secretaries, nurses, and social workers. Everyone knew that these low-paying, low-status jobs were for women only, and everyone knew, too, that for women, power and money came with their husbands, not with their work.

Throughout the culture, the message was consistent: A woman worked only if she didn't have a husband, or if her husband didn't earn much money. On television, June Cleaver and Donna Reed were professional moms, always home and always happy, while the popular women's magazines, *McCall's* and *Ladies' Home Journal,* vied for the best meat loaf recipe and the most tips for shinier floors.

During the 1970s the women's movement changed both the facts and the images of women's lives. Today, 42 percent of students enrolled in law schools, 38 percent of medical students, and 33 percent of graduate business students are female. At newsstands, *McCall's* and the *Journal* compete for space with *Ms., Working Woman,* and *Working Mother,* and on television, the women on *LA Law* are partners, not paper pushers. Women appear as doctors and police officers nightly on television programs, and female news anchors have become the rule. And unlike Edith Bunker, the working-class woman's stereotype of an earlier era, even Roseanne has a job.

These transformations in social context have affected adolescent development profoundly, touching every issue we discussed in the last chapter, for females and for males as well. Perhaps the biggest change is in the way young women view themselves. Free to imagine any career they have the talent and the resources to pursue, adolescent girls think more about their own development than their boyfriends'. In college, they are more apt to focus on choosing a career than on catching a husband. Achievement now has a broader context, a goal beyond a college degree. This fundamental shift reverberates in several ways. In their relationships with adolescent boys, for example, girls are freer to form casual friendships because they are less apt to be searching for a husband. And young men, too, are freed of the pressure to marry early.

But if the modern social context provides opportunities for growth, it also causes stresses of its own. Many young women today feel pressured to do it all, to be supermothers and successful career women as well. And unlike television's Claire Huxtable, the professional women they see around them work long hours and need housekeepers to keep things running smoothly at home. Today's young women worry about devoting time to their children, their husbands, and themselves.

A subgroup of adolescents, poor and black, has another set of concerns, and indeed, almost another social context. In inner cities, where drug sellers and abusers control the streets, to leave your home is to risk your life. Staying in school long enough to graduate, avoiding pregnancy and the lure of drugs and drug money are challenges many face with strength and grace. But for too many others, the pressures of the street are overwhelming, and the effects on development, even for those who avoid drugs, are profound and often tragic. In this chapter, we discuss the usual contexts of family, peers, and schools. We also introduce two other powerful social influences on adolescents: the workplace and the community.

Adolescents in the Changing American Family

While "family" may still conjure up the image of a mother who does not work outside the home and a breadwinner father, with both parents living with their children, for 90 percent of teenagers, reality is something else. Before reaching adulthood, 60 percent of all teenagers will have spent some time in a single-parent household; about one-quarter will spend at least some time in a stepfamily, and more than half of these will experience a second divorce. Over two-thirds of married mothers of teenagers work outside the home, and for single mothers of teenagers, the figure is 80 percent (Furstenberg, in press). While these numbers are very different from those of your parents' generation, what they actually mean for many adolescents may surprise you. So too will the latest research on the famous generation gap.

PARENT-TEENAGER RELATIONS

In the 1960s and early 1970s, adolescents and their parents were assumed to live on opposite sides of an unbridgeable generation gap in which their relationships were filled with misunderstanding and mistrust. But like adolescent storm and stress, alienation between the generations may be more imagined than real. Studies across racial, cultural, and socioeconomic groups found that most teenagers feel close to their parents, not distant. A majority of teenagers love their parents, value their judgment, and feel that their parents care about them (Offer, Ostrov, & Howard, 1981). In one survey, 19-year-old college students reported being just as close to their mothers and fathers as fourth graders did (Hunter & Youniss, 1982). Surveys also reveal mutual respect, support, and consideration between parents and teens. In one study, for example, over 75 percent of respondents in early and middle adolescence said that they could count on their parents most of the time, that their parents were usually patient with them, and that they wanted their own future family to be in some ways like the family they grew up in. Nearly 90 percent said that most of the time their parents were very satisfied with them (Offer, Ostrov, & Howard, 1981).

The feeling seems to run both ways. Basic disagreements between teenagers and parents are unusual. Further, adolescents do not usually side with their peers against their parents. Even young adolescents are not slaves to the peer group (Chapter 16). Youngsters who have healthy relationships with their parents grow up to be self-directed, autonomous, and self-assured, even in the face of strong peer pressure (Devereux, 1970). In fact, such adolescents tend to seek out friends who reaffirm their parents' attitudes and values, including those regarding the use of drugs (Hill, 1980).

Adolescents in the United States and their parents hold similar opinions about many other important issues including work, education, and admired personal qualities (Conger, 1977). As is true for adults, socioeconomic status,

Rather than living on opposite sides of a generational gulf, most adolescents and their parents feel close to one another. *(Kindra Clineff/The Picture Cube)*

not age, forms the common link where values are concerned. So teenagers, who share their parents' social and economic status, tend to share their values as well. Thus, teenagers from wealthy families in affluent suburbs are much more like their parents in attitudes, goals, and values than they are like teens living in poverty in inner cities (Conger, 1977). In this respect the diversity among adolescents is much more striking than the difference between generations.

When parents and teenagers *are* at odds, it is usually over matters of personal taste. For many parents, a son wearing an earring or a daughter dressed like Madonna can arouse passionate feelings. It is over them that much family conflict takes place (Hill, 1980; Montemayor, 1982). But scornful intolerance on the parents' part is not likely to change an adolescent's opinions. When it comes to matters of personal taste, peers generally have more influence than adults.

A NEW BALANCE OF POWER

Before their children become adolescents, parents are clearly dominant. But between early and late adolescence the balance shifts toward a relationship more nearly that among equals.

During early adolescence, when youngsters first start reaching toward greater power, parents typically resist. The old balance of power is being challenged from below, and new understandings of family relations have not yet emerged. A period of temporary disruption occurs, and tension may rise, especially between adolescents and their mothers, until a new balance of power is reached (Hill et al., 1985a, 1985b; Steinberg, 1981).

Studying this stage in family relations, researchers asked boys between ages 11 and 16 to reach a consensus with their parents on family issues such as setting the adolescent's curfew (Jacob, 1974). The 11-year-olds carried less weight in the family's decisions than did the 16-year-olds, but the younger boys were more assertive in the discussions than were the older ones. The younger boys interrupted their parents more often, tended to raise their voices, and kept trying to get their way, but the parents usually ignored or rebuffed them despite the boys' forceful efforts. Apparently, young adolescents try to play a more influential role in the family, but their parents aren't ready for the change. It is not until mid-adolescence that teenagers are treated more like adults. Now they have more of a say in family decisions, and they don't have to be so strident in expressing their views.

Parents need to adapt to their adolescent's need for greater influence within the family. Resisting this change usually makes matters worse. When parents fail to grant greater equality to their teenagers, their children are apt to respond negatively, sometimes with delinquent behavior (Alexander, 1973).

THE INFLUENCE OF PARENTING STYLES

In Chapter 11 we discussed the parenting styles outlined by psychologist Diana Baumrind (1967): *Authoritative* parents are loving but firm with their

As teenagers depend less on their parents, their parents may depend more on them. Keeping up with the latest technology, for example, is easier for adults who have teenage teachers. *(David Shafer)*

children. While they encourage independence, they set clear standards of behavior and explain why these standards must be met. *Authoritarian* parents, in contrast, value obedience for its own sake, and they discipline forcefully to obtain it. They are not very responsive to their children's wishes; children obey "or else." While loving toward their children, *permissive* parents set few rules in matters of discipline. They believe that rules tend to inhibit creativity and self-expression, so they generally let their sons and daughters do what they want.

How do these three different parenting styles affect adolescent development? As in earlier periods, the authoritative style is the most successful. Teenagers of authoritative parents tend to be confident, flexible, creative, curious, and socially skilled. Those with authoritarian parents are more dependent and passive, less socially adept, and not very intellectually curious. Permissive parents seem to produce adolescents who are immature, irresponsible, and overly conforming. These youngsters are less able than their peers to assume leadership roles.

The link between authoritative parenting and healthy adolescent development is both strong and widespread. In many different ethnic groups and socioeconomic strata its benefits are clear (Steinberg, in press): First, authoritative parenting balances freedom and restriction. An authoritative framework gives young people the opportunity to develop self-reliance within clear limits. Second, the give-and-take between authoritative parents and their children promotes intellectual development. Youngsters are encouraged to reason about matters of right and wrong and to understand why certain standards of behavior are established. Third, the warmth of authoritative parents tends to encourage their children to identify with them. As a result, the children internalize their parents' values; they make those values their own.

In addition, children's reaction to this kind of treatment reinforces the parents' behavior (Lewis, 1981). Youngsters who experience authoritative guidance become more self-directed, responsible, and confident, which in turn stimulates parental warmth, clear limits, and good communication. Positive results, in other words, help maintain effective parenting.

THE IMPACT OF MARITAL CONFLICT AND DIVORCE

The best data we have suggest that divorce affects children most adversely when it occurs earlier; there are few, if any, serious effects of divorce during adolescence (Allison & Furstenberg, 1989). Teenagers are better able to understand divorce and to cope with the stresses it brings. They also tend to have close friends in whom they can confide and perhaps to whom they can even turn for advice. If adolescents have few psychological problems before their parents divorce, and if they can avoid taking sides in any parental conflict, they usually suffer no lasting harm. This is especially true if the parents remain friendly and cooperative, if the custodial parent has adequate emotional and economic support, and if both parents remain involved with their children (Wallerstein & Kelley, 1974, 1980). As we noted in Chapter 14, however, some of the adverse consequences of divorce may not surface until later, when young adults begin thinking about their own marriage plans.

The absence of conflict between the parents is especially important. In fact, the degree of conflict between parents is a better predictor of an adoles-

Over half of all American teenagers will live in a single-parent family before they become adults. As a group, teenagers cope better with divorce than do younger children. *(Bob Daemmrich/The Image Works)*

cent's adjustment than is the parents' marital status. More than divorce, parental conflict contributes to maladjustment (Hetherington & Camara, 1984). Boys whose parents have high levels of marital conflict are more likely to show a wide range of acting-out behaviors, including aggression and delinquency, but girls are more likely to develop internal distress signs, including anxiety and depression. This means that constant conflict between parents living together may be worse for a child than a parental separation (Peterson & Zill, 1986). A youngster may be better off if divorce ends such conflict.

A child's sex affects reactions to divorce as well. Boys are more affected by divorce because the father's absence means the loss of a role model with whom they can identify on a day-to-day basis. Not surprisingly, the problems that may be related to a father's absence (difficulties in school, for instance) are more common in boys than girls. These problems can be minimized, however, when another male role model (an uncle, older brother, or stepfather, for example) is nearby (Biller, 1981). For girls, the effects of fathers' absence are different. One classic study showed that girls from divorced or widowed homes had more difficulty in their relationships with boys in early adolescence than did their peers (Hetherington, 1972).

ADOLESCENTS IN STEPFAMILIES

Although stepparents can be positive role models for children, the relationship is often stressful, especially when the stepparent comes into the young person's life during early adolescence. Young adolescents may find it hard to accommodate a new stepparent when they are struggling to establish a sense of identity that both bonds them to, and separates them from, their family. Part of the problem is adjusting to a new authority figure in the family when youngsters are trying to increase their autonomy. And if the new authority figure has different ideas about rules and discipline than the teenager's birth parent, problems intensify. Adolescents who have recently had other stresses in their lives are particularly prone to problems with a stepparent.

Such difficulties may surface in a number of ways. Compared with teenagers in intact families or even with those in single-parent homes, teenagers in stepfamilies are more likely to get involved in delinquency (Dornbusch et al., 1985; Steinberg, 1987b). And adolescents in stepfamilies may be especially susceptible to child abuse: 47 percent of the known cases of child abuse involve adolescents, even though adolescents account for only 38 percent of U.S. youth (Garbarino, Sebes, & Schellenbach, 1984). Although many adults and their teenage stepchildren get along well, the lack of a biological connection between them and the stresses of their new situation make their relationship especially vulnerable.

Adolescent Development in the Peer Group

The world over, teenagers "hang out" with teenagers. Some observers fear that spending too much time together contributes to serious problems such as delinquency, drug abuse, and teenage suicide (Coleman, 1961; Bronfenbrenner, 1974). Others, however, see this socializing time as a learning experience (e.g., Mead, 1978). They believe that as society becomes more advanced technologically, adolescents actually help prepare each other for adulthood.

According to anthropologist Margaret Mead (1978), the extent to which teenagers help one another become adults depends on how fast their society is changing. In some societies, change is so slow that what a child needs to master to function as an adult is virtually the same from one generation to the next. Mead calls these **postfigurative societies**. In them, young people can learn what they need to know from their elders. A girl might learn pottery making, for example, from her mother or her grandmother.

The past century has seen the rise of **cofigurative societies**, in which change is so rapid that parents' knowledge may be outdated by the time their children grow up. In such societies, young people learn the skills of adulthood from their peers as well as their elders. Thus, an adolescent might learn the basics about electrical equipment from his father, but a peer might be more knowledgeable about the use of computers.

Mead believed that as change accelerates even more, the result would be **prefigurative societies**, in which young people teach adults as well as one another. There are signs that we may be on the verge of entering such an era. Already, young people teach their elders about computers. Does such role reversal mean that adolescents of the future won't need close relationships

postfigurative societies societies that change so slowly that children must master the same skills for adulthood as did their parents

cofigurative societies societies in which change is so rapid that parents' knowledge may be outdated by the time their children grow up

prefigurative societies societies in which children teach adults as well as each other

with adults? No. Teenagers will always need the support, affection, and advice of people older than themselves. In a prefigurative society, however, the adolescent peer group will probably be even more important. Not only will it help to educate young people, it will also help to educate adults.

TEENAGE CLIQUES AND CROWDS

"Punks," "freaks," "jocks," "brains," "burnouts," "preppies"—teenagers have a colorful vocabulary for classifying their peers. But within these broad, descriptive categories there exist **cliques**, the basic social groups of adolescents. A clique consists of two to twelve close friends (the average is five or six), who are of the same age and who typically have similar interests and backgrounds (Berndt, 1982; Dunphy, 1975; Hollingshead, 1949/1975). Cliques play a vital role in structuring adolescent life. Members of a clique often spend hours together each day. A clique of 14-year-old boys might eat lunch together, play basketball after school, and check the answers to their homework assignments by phone in the evening.

> **cliques**
> exclusive social circles of friends

Besides providing companionship, cliques also give adolescents an important **reference group**—a group that serves as a basis for evaluating one's own experiences. Suppose, for example, that a teenage girl feels that her parents are too strict and demanding. She discusses her situation with other girls in her clique and discovers that their parents impose even more restrictions. As a result, her own parents seem more tolerable, and she stops resenting their rules so much. Making such comparisons between themselves and other clique members helps adolescents put their experiences into a broader perspective.

> **reference group**
> group that serves as basis for evaluating one's own experiences

Cliques also help to give teenagers a sense of identity—in their own eyes as well as those of peers. Adolescents judge themselves and each other partly by the company they keep. If a boy hangs out with a group of preppies, he will think of himself as a preppy, and so will others outside his clique. And if that group of preppies has high status in this youngster's school, he will see himself near the top of the social ladder and enjoy a boost to self-esteem (Brown & Lohr, 1987). Cliques, in short, provide an important way of judging one's own standing among peers. In this way they help to give adolescents a sense of who they are.

Several cliques, some of boys and some of girls, may get together for social activities, forming a larger and more loosely knit group—the adolescent **crowd**. Crowds, which usually have about 20 members, are formed chiefly on the basis of shared activities rather than close friendship. Several cliques may form a crowd to hold a large party, for example.

> **crowd**
> loosely formed group organized chiefly on the basis of shared activities

The makeup of cliques and crowds changes as adolescents grow older. Young adolescents form same-sex cliques that keep largely to themselves. Later, same-sex cliques come together to form a crowd of boys and girls. Within this crowd, those who are most actively dating begin to form mixed-sex cliques, and this pattern of mixed-sex cliques and crowds gradually becomes the dominant pattern. Finally, during late adolescence, the crowd starts to disintegrate as dating pairs split off from the larger group. Couples may go out together from time to time, but the feeling of being a crowd disappears. This pattern in which the couple is the focus of social life continues into adulthood.

For teenagers, whom you're with is who you are. "Hanging out" in a clique provides companionship and a sense of identity. *(Karen Rantzman/Photo 20-20)*

POPULARITY AND LEADERSHIP IN THE PEER GROUP

As at any age, being socially adept is tied to popularity. The best-liked adolescents are generally those who act appropriately in the eyes of other teenagers, who are good at perceiving and meeting people's needs, and who are confident without being conceited. Popular adolescents are also friendly, cheerful, good-natured, and humorous. They also tend to be more intelligent than their unpopular peers (Hollingshead, 1949/1975; Hartup, 1983). Intelligence is probably related to popularity because it helps people to figure out how they should behave to be liked by others.

Interestingly, popularity does not automatically confer leadership. That role often falls to those who can accomplish the things a group wants done. This means that as group interests change with age, new leaders may emerge. For instance, in early adolescence, when sports are very important to boys, the most athletic in an all-male clique may have leadership roles. A few years later, however, when dating is also important, those who are especially successful with girls may acquire new status.

Adolescents who are neglected by their peers, or actively rejected by them, have very different characteristics. The neglected adolescent is often timid, unenthusiastic about group activities, or generally unskilled at relating to peers. Rejected adolescents act in ways that more actively irk others. They are tactless, conceited, overly critical, or highly aggressive and bullyish (Coie &

Dodge, 1983). Rejected adolescents, by and large, are the most lonely of all teenagers, and they are the most likely to develop psychological problems. Friendless teens are also more likely than popular ones to do poorly in school, to drop out, and to become delinquent (Asher & Wheeler, 1985; Putallaz & Gottman, 1981). What is causing what here is difficult to say. We don't really know whether poor peer relations lead to poor psychosocial adjustment, or whether poorly adjusted adolescents have more trouble making friends. In all likelihood the process is circular: Psychological difficulties are probably both the cause and the result of problems with peers (Hartup, 1977).

AREAS OF PEER GROUP INFLUENCE

The peer group affects individual development in several ways. Most important, the peer group helps adolescents establish their identity (Erikson, 1968). The particular image and status of a clique gives its members a sense of who they are. The clique is also a setting where teenagers can "try on" roles and get feedback from their friends about how well the roles fit. In addition, adolescents can discuss problems with their friends, who, because of similar experiences, can offer empathy and support.

Peers also help adolescents develop autonomy. When teenagers make decisions with their friends, adults are not there to veto or direct (Hill & Steinberg, 1976). In the peer group, teens are also forced to assess their own values, to determine what they consider to be right and wrong. If adolescents were *only* in the company of adults (parents, teachers, and so forth), it is likely that these authority figures would continue to dominate their thinking, as they did in childhood (Piaget, 1932). Among peers, then, teenagers are freer to think independently, for peers by definition are equals.

The support teenagers give to and get from each other can help them through the hard times of growing up. *(Hazel Hankin)*

Peers also play a vital role in helping adolescents learn about intimacy and sexuality. These learning experiences require interaction between two people who think of each other as equals. If one person is an adolescent and the other is an adult, the equality is missing, and the learning process is severely limited.

Finally, peers can affect adolescents' achievements (Brown, in press). Teenage friends can encourage or discourage one another to excel at school, sports, hobbies, and so forth. On the one hand, for instance, peers may encourage an adolescent girl to perform academically below her potential, fearing she'll be rejected as too "brainy." On the other hand, peers might encourage a boy with athletic talent to put in the work needed to play professional sports. In the area of achievement, of course, parents, teachers, and other adults also have a major influence on teenagers, usually even greater than the one peers exert (Kandel, 1978; Simpson, 1962).

Adolescent Development in School

Whether it's an inner-city high school or an exclusive boarding school, the educational setting is a major arena for adolescent development. An immense amount of learning goes on in this setting, and much of it has nothing to do with *Hamlet* or algebraic equations. How adolescents influence each other depends in part on the structure of the schools they attend, a structure that has two key elements: the age of the students in the school and the achievement level of the students in the class.

AGE GROUPING

A perennial problem among educators is *where* to educate young adolescents. Early in this century seventh- and eighth-graders were the oldest students in elementary school or the youngest students in high school. Both these arrangements raised concerns, however. Young adolescents, some argued, had "peculiarities of disposition" which might make it better to separate them from younger and older students. So the junior high school was created for seventh-, eighth-, and ninth-graders. But still the questions about what is the best school for young adolescents persist. Specifically, should they be in their own school?

One group of researchers tried to answer this question by exploring the effects that different age groupings have on students' grades, self-esteem, participation in extracurricular activities, and feelings of anonymity (Blyth, Simmons, & Bush, 1978; Blyth, Simmons, & Carlton-Ford, 1983). They found that the transition to a new school can be hard at any age, but it is particularly so during early adolescence. This is especially true for girls, who tend to be beginning puberty at this time and may be starting to date. These changes may make them more vulnerable to the stresses a new school can bring. Although the junior high school structure has a less negative impact on young adolescent boys, remaining in a school that includes grades 1 through 8 may be better for them.

Researchers have also explored the value of variations on the junior high theme. Should grades 7 through 9 and grades 10 through 12 be in separate buildings? Should they be subdivided further into *three* secondary schools: grades 7 and 8 together, grades 9 and 10, and finally grades 11 and 12? Researchers have found that, at any age, the presence of older students has negative effects on younger ones (Blyth, Hill, & Smyth, 1981). Ninth-graders who attend school with tenth-graders often avoid both extracurricular activities and leadership roles. They are more likely to feel anonymous and to experiment with sex or drugs than are other ninth-graders who are separate from older students. Conversely though, separating ninth-graders from seventh- and eighth-grade students has positive effects on the younger group. The seventh- and eighth-graders participate more in school activities, use drugs less, feel less anonymous, and are less apt to be picked on. Given this situation, it makes more sense to stay with a 3-year junior high (grades 7 through 9), or a 3-year middle school (grades 6 through 8), if young adolescents are not grouped with elementary schoolers.

TRACKING

In many schools, students identified as especially bright are placed in more challenging classes, while slow learners are placed in remedial groups, and everyone else attends classes geared to average ability. This system, in which students are divided like trains on different lines, is called **tracking**.

Proponents of tracking say that it allows teachers to design lessons that are suited to students' abilities. Bright youngsters need not be bored in a classroom where many students need slow, step-by-step instruction. Conversely, children needing remedial help need not feel lost in a course geared to more able students. But critics argue that tracking has many hidden costs. Youngsters in the remedial track are apt to be labeled stupid by their higher-track peers and even by some of their teachers. As a result, their self-esteem suffers, they see themselves as failures, and they lower the goals they set for themselves (Rutter, 1983; Vanfossen et al., 1987). Typically, too, educators place a disproportionate number of poor and minority students in the remedial track, which, because of the labeling process, can stifle their potential (Rosenbaum, 1976). Finally, academic tracking also leads to social tracking, which can polarize students into academic groups that dislike or resent one another (Rosenbaum, 1976).

As for academic achievement, students usually do just as well in mixed-ability classes as they do in classes where youngsters are all at one level (Rutter, 1983). It is hard then to argue for tracking, with its negative social and psychological consequences for remedial students. Mixed-ability classes seem to offer advantages to these slower learners without impairing the achievement of their brighter peers.

tracking
schooling system that divides students according to academic ability

WHAT MAKES A HIGH SCHOOL GOOD FOR STUDENTS?

Good high schools share several traits that foster high achievement (Boyer, 1983; Goodlad, 1984; Lightfoot, 1983; Powell et al., 1985; Sizer, 1984). In the best high schools, administrators, teachers, parents, and students place a high value on education. Second, good high schools have teachers who are committed to their students and who are free to express that commitment in the classroom. Third, staff members at good high schools seeks ways to become even better teachers. Criticism is viewed as a means toward self-improvement. Fourth, good high schools are well integrated into the communities they serve, encouraging parents to be involved in their youngsters' education. Advanced students can take more challenging courses at local colleges or universities; links are forged with local employers to help students see the relevance of their high school education. Fifth, in good high schools students participate in the educational process. Teachers challenge them to think critically and to debate important issues rather than to passively accept other people's ideas.

In addition, good high schools feel good: The atmosphere is warm, standards are high, and limits on students' behavior are reasonable but firm. Successful schools, in short, have much in common with authoritative families. Generally, these schools have lower rates of delinquency, better attendance records, and higher scores on achievement tests (Rutter, 1983). In contrast, the high school with an authoritarian approach, which stresses obedience and control, tends to breed problems. Youngsters in such schools are often anxious, unhappy, and uninterested in their studies (Moos, 1978). Overly permissive schools breed problems, too, because students aren't sure what is expected of them.

In the best high schools, or course, the overall climate is often adjusted to suit the needs of particular students. For example, able students usually respond well to teachers who are challenging, demand effort, and are critical of inferior work, while less able students do better with teachers who are warm, supportive, and encouraging. In successful high schools, teachers usually modify their styles to bring out the best from all the students in their classrooms.

CRITICISMS OF AMERICAN HIGH SCHOOLS

Critics charge that most U.S. high schools fall very short of the best institutions. Some, they say, namely those in poor, inner-city districts, are little more than detention centers for teenagers labeled "troublesome." At the other extreme are high schools that resemble country clubs, with swimming pools and screening rooms but little intellectual stimulation. The students who suffer the most in poor-quality schools are unfortunately those with the greatest need for education. Youngsters who enter high school deficient in basic skills usually gain little from their 4 years of attendance. In the twelfth grade, most earn the same scores on achievement tests as they did in the ninth (Stipek, 1981).

Most unsuccessful high schools fall short in two key ways: They are not creating an environment conducive to cognitive growth, and they tend to ignore the psychological development that all healthy adolescents must undergo (Hill, 1980). For instance, instead of encouraging independence, responsibility, and self-reliance, poor schools tend to emphasize obedience and conformity (Friedenberg, 1967). Nor do poor schools do much to help teenagers find their own identity. Rather than fostering a sense of individuality, many high schools make adolescents feel like nameless faces in the crowd. In addition, poor schools do little to prepare youngsters for their future roles as adults, so the students see little relevance to the information they are learning. Finally, teachers in poor schools tend to have low expectations for many of their students, especially those from low-income, minority-group families. These low expectations tend to become self-fulfilling prophecies: The youngsters accept the view that they have little ability and give up trying to achieve.

Educators can work toward improving high schools in all these areas. First, teachers and curriculum planners can pay more attention to the cognitive changes of adolescents (Elkind, 1976), gearing teaching methods toward stimulating intellectual growth. For instance, experiments in science classes can stress hypothetical thinking, while computer courses can help refine logical thought. Second, teachers can help adolescents develop autonomy by giving them opportunities to make meaningful decisions and think independently. Third, schools can help prepare young people for future work and family roles by offering practical information in academic courses. Background on work and careers, for example, can be included in social studies classes, information on child development in biology courses, and information on personal finance in courses on mathematics. Fourth, teachers can raise their expectations concerning low-income, minority-group students. These higher expectations may rub off on the students themselves, encouraging them to strive for greater accomplishments.

Work and Adolescent Development

The next time you're in a fast-food restaurant during non–school hours, take a look at the staff. You'll see that almost everyone, aside from the manager, is a teenager. The same pattern can be seen in many other kinds of jobs, from clerks in drugstores to baggers in supermarkets. Like adults, adolescents work to earn money, but how they earn it and spend it has many developmentalists concerned.

RECENT TRENDS

Before 1940, U.S. teenagers either worked or went to school; they rarely did both. Today, about half of all high school sophomores and two-thirds of all seniors are in the part-time work force. By the time they graduate from high school, over 80 percent of U.S. teenagers will have worked at some time (Greenberger & Steinberg, 1986).

Not only are there more student workers than ever before, those employed also work more hours. In 1980, the average high school sophomore worked almost 15 hours a week, and the average senior 20 hours (Lewin-Epstein, 1981). These rates have remained constant, which means that high school students are typically putting in some 45 to 50 hours a week in school and work commitments combined.

The main reason for the increase in adolescent employment can be summed up in one word: money. The cost of being a teenager has risen sharply over the last few decades—20 percent alone at the end of the 1970s, when inflation was running high. Although inflation took its toll on people of all ages, it hit adolescents especially hard. The prices of things teenagers like to buy, such as clothing and movie tickets, went up faster than the rate of inflation overall. Since adolescents have traditionally relied for spending money on a fixed weekly allowance, many had to turn to the world of work for the extra cash they wanted (Rotbart, 1981).

THE TYPICAL JOB OF AN ADOLESCENT

> Melissa, a high school junior, stows her books and coat in a locker, punches the time clock, and takes her place behind the cosmetics counter. Her late afternoon shift, from 4 to 7 P.M., is one of the busiest at the drugstore because people are constantly stopping in on their way home from school and work. The three hours are tiring because she's on her feet all the time, and she hasn't had anything to eat since a candy bar at 3 P.M. Melissa earns the minimum wage and gets a small discount on merchandise.

Melissa's job is typical of those most teenagers hold (Lewin-Epstein, 1981). About 20 percent of all employed high school students work in retail stores as cashiers, sales clerks, or shelf stockers. Another 17 percent work in restaurants. They staff fast-food counters, help in kitchens, serve customers, clear tables, wash dishes, and so forth. Two other common jobs are clerical assistant in a business office (10 percent) and unskilled laborer, perhaps doing janitorial or cleaning work (another 10 percent).

Jobs usually divide by sex, with boys doing gardening, yard work, carrying trash, and so forth, and girls waiting on tables, cleaning houses, or babysitting. The average hourly wage of a teenage boy is about 15 percent higher than that of a girl (Greenberger & Steinberg, 1983). Thus, even before they become adults, young people are exposed to the gender-based inequalities of the workplace.

Like much of adolescent life, teenage employment tends to be peer-oriented. On the job, young people spend as much time interacting with other adolescents as they spend interacting with adults. In the typical fast-food restaurant, for example, not only are most of the workers in their teens, but many of the customers are too (Greenberger & Steinberg, 1986; Greenberger, Steinberg, & Ruggiero, 1982).

For most teenagers like Melissa, work is not very challenging. Adolescents in the workplace are rarely allowed to act independently or make their own decisions. Nor do they get much of a chance to use the skills they've learned in school (Greenberger & Steinberg, 1986). Teenage workers, on average, spend less than 6 percent of their time in activities such as reading, writing, and mathematics. Most jobs they hold are monotonous and intellectually dull. About one-quarter of their time is spent either cleaning or carrying things. Sometimes, too, the job environment is quite stressful—the surroundings are dirty and noisy, and the work is fast-paced (Greenberger, Steinberg, & Ruggiero, 1982; Greenberger, Steinberg, & Vaux, 1981).

THE IMPACT OF WORK ON ADOLESCENT DEVELOPMENT

Melissa's mother and father believe that working builds character and independence, helps young people prepare for adulthood, and teaches them about the "real" world. Many other parents of teenagers share their view, but their assumptions are not always right.

Teenage employment may indeed encourage maturity and independence. One classic study conducted during the Great Depression found that boys with part-time jobs tended to grow up faster (Elder, 1974). These youngsters tended to show a greater interest in adults, to spend more time with adults, and to generally be more adultlike than their nonworking peers. They were also viewed as more "industrious" and more autonomous in their social relations. Today employment still seems to have these positive effects. Most working teenagers are more self-reliant than nonworking ones, and they tend to have a more mature attitude toward working (they stick with tasks they are assigned and take pride in doing them) (Steinberg, Greenberger, Garduque, Ruggiero, & Vaux, 1982).

But work doesn't seem to strengthen ethics. In fact, teenagers with jobs seem more cynical and less principled than those who don't work. In one study, working adolescents were more likely than nonworking peers to agree with such statements as "Anyone who works harder than he or she has to is a little bit crazy" and "In my opinion it's all right for workers who are paid a low salary to take little things from their jobs to make up for it" (Ruggiero, Greenberger, & Steinberg, 1982). Why would working have this negative effect on the ethics of some teenagers? It may be that they feel exploited in dull, stressful, minimum-wage jobs and so feel justified in exploiting their employers back.

As for whether teenage employment enhances knowledge of the "real" world, the findings are mixed. Adolescents with jobs do sometimes score higher on tests that measure career-planning skills and knowledge about occupations (Owens, 1982; Steinberg, 1982). They also tend to know more about

Working teenagers earn more but study less than nonworking teens. The way they spend what they earn, and the values that seem to accompany working, have developmentalists concerned. (left, *Barbara Kirk/The Stock Market;* right, *Michal Heron/Woodfin Camp & Associates*)

consumer and financial matters—how credit cards work, how prices are determined, how to recognize good buys (Steinberg, Greenberger, Garduque, & McAuliffe, 1982). But whether such knowledge offers an advantage is unclear. Adolescents who work have a slight edge when it comes to landing jobs after graduation (Stevenson, 1978), but this advantage is short-lived. Within a short time, young people who didn't work during their school years are just as likely to be employed and to earn as much money (Freeman & Wise, 1982).

It is also unclear if working today teaches teenagers "the value of money," as their parents like to think. Very few adolescents put a sizable proportion of their earnings toward a college education or some other long-range goal, and fewer still contribute much money toward family living expenses (rent, groceries, and so forth). Most are allowed to spend their earnings simply to enjoy themselves. They buy designer clothes and expensive stereo equipment, eat out often, and go to many movies. Some also use their money to buy alcohol and other drugs (Greenberger & Steinberg, 1986). Many working teenagers are experiencing **premature affluence**. They have too much money for discretionary spending at too early an age (Bachman, 1983). Such premature affluence often breeds self-indulgence, not financial responsibility.

Furthermore, working robs time from things that are important in a teenager's life. Compared with nonworking adolescents, those who work more than 15 to 20 hours a week tend to spend less time on homework, to earn lower grades, to miss school more often, and to have less ambitious plans for their future education (Damico, 1984; Mortimer & Finch, 1986; Wirtz et al., 1987). They also participate less in extracurricular activities and in family events and outings, and they report feeling more distant from their parents and friends (Steinberg et al., 1982; Greenberger et al., 1980). In addition, those who work long hours under stressful conditions are more likely to smoke, to use marijuana or cocaine, and to abuse alcohol (Greenberger, Steinberg, & Vaux, 1981; Bachman et al., 1986). Thus, parents and counselors should be especially wary of the job that demands too much of a teenager, despite its financial appeal (see "Issues & Options"). (Note that most of the research on teenagers and work has focused on working- and middle-class youths, because getting jobs is relatively easy for them. As yet, we don't know much about the impact of employment on poor adolescents.)

premature affluence
adolescents' acquisition of too much money too early in life

Today's Teenagers: Problems and Possibilities

When the United States was young, adulthood arrived earlier than it does today. Typically, adolescents left home to live with other families in the community, where they learned a specific skill as apprentices or worked as domestic servants (Kett, 1977). This "placing out" often coincided with the onset of puberty (Katz, 1975). Today, adolescents are primarily students with few adult responsibilities. Even teenagers who hold jobs rarely support themselves, and the kind of work they do is usually different from what they will do in later life.

Issues & OPTIONS

When Teenagers Work

The lure of a paycheck brings millions of teenagers into the part-time work force each year. Most enjoy the money but are not prepared for the problems: boring jobs, less time for friends and after-school activities, falling grades. Parents, teachers, and school counselors can guide young people toward making realistic decisions about part-time jobs. Here are five important steps they can take:

1. *Help teenagers consider all the pros and cons of working.* Adults can encourage teenagers to assess employment realistically and to make decisions regarding work that matches their goals and values.

2. *Help teenagers make intelligent choices about what kind of job to take and how many hours to work.* Although adolescents usually have a limited range of employment options, they can still pick a job that complements their personal-

ity and interests. A teenager interest in computers, for instance, might find work in a store that sells them. Adults can also steer young people away from jobs that are highly stressful. Washing dishes in the hot, noisy kitchen of a fast-paced restaurant may not be worth the extra dollar an hour it pays. Finally, adults can encourage limits on the number of hours worked so that the job does not interfere too much with other aspects of the teenager's life. Fifteen hours a week for high school freshmen and sophomores and 20 hours weekly for juniors and seniors are reasonable maximums to set.

3. *Stay involved in the adolescent's work experiences.* Encourage discussions of events at work, conflicts on the job, and so forth. Such discussions can teach young people a great deal about the world of work and interpersonal relations. In courses such as social studies, economics, business, and

psychology, teachers can ask students to share with their classmates what they have learned at work.

4. *Encourage teenagers to keep records of their job experience.* An employment history, including special accomplishments and letters of recommendation, can be useful for a student who wants a better job or is looking for full-time work after graduation.

5. *Encourage regular reassessment of the job situation.* Does the job consume more time than expected? Is the young person losing interest in schoolwork or earning poorer grades? Is he or she giving up too many other activities or no longer spending much time with friends? Is the job fostering too great a concern for earning money and buying material things? If the answer to any of these questions is yes, the job may be doing more harm than good.

This makes the transition to adulthood quite *discontinuous*—it is characterized by many changes in roles and responsibilities.

In less-industrialized, agrarian societies, adolescents have fewer changes to contend with. They are not full-time students set apart from the world of adults but rather "adults-in-training," working side by side with their elders. Boys hunt with their fathers or help them tend crops and livestock. Girls assist their mothers in preparing food, managing the home, and caring for younger children. When these young people start families of their own, their work is familiar, making their transition to adulthood *continuous* and therefore easier.

In tribal rituals, like this Apache puberty rite, adolescents are welcomed into adult life. *(Bill Gillette/Stock, Boston)*

Compared with these adolescents, teenagers in industrialized societies endure a transition to adulthood that is both longer and more abrupt, a condition that often leaves a young person wondering: "When am I an adult?" Industrialized societies tend to lack clear rites of passage from adolescence to adulthood. In traditional societies, young people participate in elaborate ceremonies or rituals, after which the entire community recognizes them as adults. In the African Mandingo tribe, for example, adolescent boys have their courage tested by a "ghost" and are then circumcised in a group ceremony. Subsequently, they live together in a hut, separated from the tribe until completing their religious instruction. In contemporary societies, rites of passage are both less dramatic and less clear. Are you an adult when you finish high school? When you are old enough to vote? When you graduate from college? When you land your first full-time job? When you marry or become a parent?

For adolescents living in poverty, the transition to adulthood is harsh, often disastrous. The two conditions that traditionally push adolescents into adulthood prematurely—dropping out of high school and teenage pregnancy—are highest among the poor. And because minority teenagers are more likely than others to grow up in poverty, they are also more prone to experience these problems. Today, the most powerful and dangerous influence on the lives of many inner-city youths comes from drugs. We look first at teenage pregnancy and parenthood.

TEENAGE PREGNANCY AND PARENTHOOD

Every year, over a million U.S. teenage girls become pregnant. Eighty percent of them are unmarried; fewer than half choose to have an abortion, and most do not elect to put the child up for adoption. The most common decision is to keep the baby and raise it as a single parent (Hayes, 1987). That decision, *not* an increase in the rate of teenage pregnancies, explains why the number of unmarried teenage mothers has risen so steeply. In 1955, for example, babies born outside of marriage accounted for only about 14 percent of all births to young women, but by 1984, this figure exceeded 55 percent (Furstenberg et al., 1987), and the vast majority were born into poverty. Adding to the financial difficulties of unwed teenagers are the stresses that go along with minority status. White and middle-class women are more likely to abort their pregnancies than are nonwhite and poor women, hence the problem of teenage child-bearing is densely concentrated among economically disadvantaged black and Hispanic youth. Among white young women, 41 percent of all births occur outside of marriage; among black women of the same age, the figure is nearly 90 percent (Furstenberg et al., 1987). For many in this group, with its high rate of school failure and drug abuse, child-rearing occurs in the context of limited social and economic resources (Steinberg, 1989). Studies suggest that these young women perceive themselves as having few career options and so feel they have little to lose by having a child at an early age (Hayes, 1987). If so, their decision to bear and raise an infant is partly a product of the social environment in which they live, an environment that has a profound impact on both the mother and her child.

Effects on life chances

Before I got pregnant and had Robbie I always thought that having a baby would be like you see in those magazine pictures. The mother's there in this beautiful nursery smiling and playing with the baby, and the kid is laughing and gurgling and having a blast. Well, it's not like that at all. I found that out quickly. At least most of the time it's not. Robbie was pretty little when he was born—just over 6 pounds—and he cried *all* the time. I mean, from morning to night that kid was either screaming, or spitting up, or messing his diaper, or something, 'til I thought I would go crazy. And my mom would just say: "He's *your* responsibility, Justine. You decided to have this baby. You should have thought about all the work he'd be 9 months ago." Some help, huh? I mean, 9 months ago what did I know about kids or anything.

Bearing and raising a child outside of marriage is much less stigmatized than it used to be. Celebrities such as Mia Farrow and Jessica Lange have even made it seem glamorous. But the reality for most young, unwed mothers is far from glamorous. For them, life is filled with stress, uncertainty, and lack of assistance from others. Unmarried teenage mothers are much more likely than their peers to drop out of high school, to go on welfare, and to have trouble finding and keeping a job. They are also more likely to fall into a vicious cycle of poverty and dependence on public assistance. If they drop out of school their occupational opportunities are so limited that they may never find a job that pays enough to cover both child care and running a household.

Although many people think that getting married is the solution to these girls' problems, this is not necessarily true. The sexual partners of adolescent girls are frequently young adult males who have had problems at school, at work, and with the law, often related to alcohol or drug abuse (Elster et al.,

Preventing Pregnancy: Sex Education That's More than Biology

"Sex," announces the teacher to a class of teenagers—"What do you think of when you hear that word?" Students call out the usual body parts. "Love" is heard. The teacher adds "commitment," "relationships," "contraceptives," "babies," "sexually transmitted diseases," "AIDS." In the modern approach to sex education, the emotional and physical consequences of sex receive at least as much attention as the mechanics. The new curriculum marks a shift away from programs that emphasized biology over behavior, where many students were relearning what they already knew. With the steep rise in the number of teenage mothers and the spread of sexually transmitted diseases (Chapter 15), adolescents need information that will change their patterns of sexual activity. Specifically, the National Academy of Sciences favors early education in "sex, contraception and pregnancy, combined with courses designed to teach decision-making skills and interpersonal assertiveness. [Courses] should teach adolescents the skills they need to resist peer pressure to become sexually active" (Steinberg, 1989).

Indeed, it is peers, not parents or teachers, who teach adolescents the most about sex. And much of what teenagers teach each other is biased, half true, or simply wrong. To counter both misinformation and peer pressure, sex education programs now emphasize personal responsibility—to one's partner and to oneself. Topics such as pressuring a date for sex, resisting such pressures (from peers and from dates), the emotional consequences of sexual relationships (for men and for women), preventing sexually transmitted diseases, and preventing pregnancy are central to the new courses. To be most effective, courses should inform students how to use, and where to get, contraceptives. In fact, a combination of sex education and school-based clinics where teenagers can learn about and get contraceptives can more effectively deter teenage pregnancies than can education alone (Zabin, Hirsch, Smith, Streett, & Hardy, 1986).

While granting that sex education can prevent pregnancies, many adults think it will increase sexual activity among teenagers. That is false (Furstenberg, Moore, & Peterson, 1985; Hanson, Myers, & Ginsburg, 1987). In Europe, where sex is discussed far more openly than in this country and contraceptives are much easier for young people to get, the rates of sexual activity are the same as for U.S. adolescents (Jones et al., 1985). What U.S. teenagers *do* have is a higher rate of pregnancy.

1987). Marrying this type of man tends to add to rather than diminish a young mother's problems. Such marriages often end in divorce, creating still more stress for the adolescent mother and her child. And if she's had another baby during the marriage, the mother's financial and emotional burdens increase even more.

Not only does early childbearing diminish a young woman's chances in life, it may also put her baby at a higher than normal risk for certain develop-

Unmarried teenage mothers tend to drop out of high school, limiting their chances for financial independence and increasing their child's risk for developmental problems. *(Katherine McGlynn/The Image Works)*

mental problems, including low birth weight (a serious threat to health and even survival), hyperactivity, misbehavior sometimes leading to juvenile delinquency, and poor achievement in school. Recent studies suggest that these problems aren't caused directly by the mother's young age but by the economically deprived environments in which teenage mothers are often forced to raise their children (Furstenberg et al., 1987).

Prevention, intervention, and support

The best approach to teenage parenthood is, of course, prevention, and in fact, this is a major goal of the most effective sex education courses (see "Focus On"). For those girls who *do* become pregnant, programs offering financial aid and emotional support can help these young mothers improve their lives. For instance, some high schools offer flexible schedules and child-care centers to help teenage mothers attend classes and graduate. Government could also expand subsidized day care so that teenage mothers who are out of school could afford to work. In addition, more family planning services could be offered to adolescent mothers so they could avoid getting pregnant again. These, and other similar programs, have been shown to help teenage mothers remain in school and prepare for the labor force (Hayes, 1982). The families of teenage mothers, of course, can help as well. Adolescent girls with babies who live with their parents, at least for a while, are more likely to finish school and find a job than are those who live alone. Their children also tend to fare better because the mother is relieved from the burden and stress of caring for an infant completely on her own. With a caring and supportive environment, then, teenage mothers can go on to accomplish the same things as other girls their age (Furstenberg et al., 1987).

DRUGS AND INNER-CITY ADOLESCENTS

When middle-class or affluent teenagers use drugs, their parents have the means to use the system. Those who wish to can find therapists and rehabilitation programs. Often, too, teenagers' own peers encourage them to give up drugs. Not all adolescents are so lucky.

Perhaps nowhere are the pressures of social context so powerful and so destructive as they are in poor city neighborhoods. In inner cities, teenagers encounter drug sellers and threats of physical violence just getting to and from school. In such neighborhoods, identity too often means choosing between dealing drugs or refusing and being victimized by those who do. For many inner-city teenagers, the lure of earning big money by selling drugs creates an intense pressure. For those who succumb—as well as for those who don't—the consequences for development are profound.

Traditionally, the balance of power between teenagers and their parents was controlled in part by money. Adults, with more of it, could use it to reward and punish behavior. This difference in power helped adults to socialize adolescents toward their own values concerning school, morality, and family life. But drug dealing has turned the balance upside down.

Distributors higher up in the drug trade like to hire adolescents because they are often willing to take risks. And with the risks can come hundreds of dollars a day (Kolata, 1989b). (Others earn far less but are lured by expectations.) When children earn more money than their parents do, the balance of power in their families and in all their relationships with adults shifts dramatically. Parents, profiting from their adolescents' success as drug sellers, often using the money to support their own drug addiction, are reluctant to stop them. In such families, the children have the power to reward and punish their parents by withholding money. Some even sell drugs to their own teach-

Inner-city teenagers who say no to drugs face severe pressures. "If you go outside people will jump you," said this 14-year-old Chicago boy who refused to sell drugs. *(New York Times Photo by Jonathan Kirn)*

ers. Such extreme shifts in power and roles carry dire consequences for development. With fewer adults in positions of authority, many adolescents in inner-city neighborhoods are "running wild." Family ties are broken, roles are reversed, and teenagers are accountable only to each other. When a teenager's parents use drugs, the "child-as-parent" syndrome makes things even worse. "On the surface," said psychologist Peter Pinto, "the child has an exhilarating feeling of power. But inside, the little adult is an angry, deprived, lonely child who is hungry for parental nurturance" (quoted in Kolata, 1989b, p. A13).

When teenagers refuse to sell drugs, their family structure remains intact, but their relationships with peers are often destroyed. On Chicago's South Side, teenagers who won't sell have been threatened, beaten, and isolated by gangs who attempt to recruit them as drug dealers. One 14-year-old boy who refused when a friend proposed drug selling lost the friend. Others have rejected him too, and the boy now stays at home all the time. "If you go outside people will jump you," he told a reporter (Johnson, 1990, p. A20). And even though he knows drugs "mess up your body," he is lonely and frightened. "I get real tempted to join a gang and sell drugs," he said. "Then I wouldn't have to worry about getting beaten up" (quoted in Johnson, 1990, p. A20).

Indeed, peer pressure to use drugs in this community is so strong that in school, students won't raise their hands when asked who *doesn't* use drugs. Those who do resist credit their families with helping them to withstand the pressure. One girl who was beaten several times for avoiding drugs praised her mother for "giving her the strength and the values to resist drugs and gangs" (1990, p. A20). Such encouragement also ups the odds that this girl will not become a high school dropout.

DROPPING OUT OF HIGH SCHOOL

Because educational attainment so accurately predicts success in life, high school dropouts quickly find that their futures are shut down. The 25 percent of adolescents who don't graduate are more likely than their peers from similar backgrounds to continue being poor, unemployed, and dependent on welfare or crime for a living. The dropout rate is even higher if we include youths who quit before they even reach high school as well as those who are still officially students but are chronically absent.

As a group, high school dropouts have a history of academic failure and poor performance on achievement and IQ tests. Typically, they come from large, lower-class families, often headed by a single parent, and often living in a poor neighborhood (Bachman, Green, & Wirtanen, 1972). And when those neighborhoods are in inner cities, the added effects of crack and cocaine on teenagers and their families push the dropout rate still higher. Among ethnic groups, Hispanics are the most likely to leave school early. While both black teenagers and white teenagers have dropout rates close to the national average (the black rate is only slightly higher than the white), the dropout rate for Hispanic youth is 40 percent. Many Hispanic adolescents, not proficient in English and overwhelmed by the struggles of inner-city life, opt to drop out (Steinberg, 1982).

Because high school dropouts tend to be similar in so many ways, psychol-

High school dropouts have plenty of time for sitting around, as quitting school is linked to chronic unemployment. (*Joel Gordon*)

ogists can accurately predict who will not finish school. Based on a young person's socioeconomic background, age, and grade level (an indicator of how many grades have been repeated), and scores on achievement and IQ tests, we can identify with 75 percent accuracy which *third-graders* will later drop out of high school (Lloyd, 1978). By the time students enter the ninth grade, these predictions can be over 90 percent correct (Walters & Kranzler, 1970). Dropping out of high school, then, is not so much a decision made in middle or later adolescence. Instead, it is the end of a long history that sets the stage for academic failure and lack of interest in education. Parents, teachers, and counselors need to intervene early if they hope to lower the rate at which teenagers abandon their schooling.

Intervention

In 1981, Eugene Lang, a wealthy New York City businessman, promised a group of 61 sixth-graders graduating from an East Harlem public school that he would pay their college tuition if they stayed in school long enough to need it (Berger, 1989). To see his students through, Lang gave far more than money. Like a loving parent, he offered advice, assistance, and comfort through hard times. Acknowledging the importance of his "good parent" role, he explained, "You have to keep reinvigorating them, rekindling their ambition, helping them overcome immediate problems—which may be emotional, economic, sociological. . . ." For the majority of Lang's sixth-graders, his philosophy proved true. Over half went on to college, at least part-time, and nine more graduated from high school or earned equivalency diplomas.

Following Lang's lead, most intervention programs stress the need for a personal bond between the student and at least one adult at school who cares about that student. Successful programs attempt to overcome the impersonal nature of most big-city schools in other ways as well. For example, attempting to create a more personalized, smaller, more protected environment for students, many school districts are now forming "schools within schools." In the end, Eugene Lang's advice is probably the best there is for helping adolescents do well in school and in life: "You don't just put the child on the track and assume that the child will not be derailed. The chances are that the child *will* be derailed, and you have to be there and be sensitive and reach out and try to bring the child back on track" (Berger, 1989, p. 28).

Summary

1. Rather than being separated by a generation gap, most adolescents and their parents feel quite close to each other and hold similar opinions about work, education, and admired personal qualities. Social class and values coincide, so teenagers, whose social and economic status matches their parents', generally share their values as well. They still may differ on matters of personal taste.

2. Between early and late adolescence the balance of power between parents and children shifts toward a relationship more nearly that of equals.

3. As in other stages of development, parenting styles influence children's feelings toward themselves and the way they function in the world. Again, authoritative parenting is the most successful. Teenagers who experience such parenting tend to be confident, flexible, creative, curious, and socially skilled.

4. Adolescents show far fewer problems after a divorce than do younger children. Teenagers can understand the reasons for divorce and cope better with the stresses it brings. Far worse for adolescents than divorce is parental conflict. If a father doesn't see his teenage sons regularly, a close adult male friend or relative can minimize the problems of separation. Girls with absent fathers tend to have more problems in their relationships with boys in early adolescence than do their peers.

5. Relationships with stepparents can be especially stressful for young adolescents, particularly because they are trying to increase their autonomy while adjusting to a new authority figure. Such teenagers are more apt to get involved with delinquency than are those in intact families or in single-parent homes.

6. Cliques are the basic social groups of adolescents. They consist of two to twelve close friends who typically have similar interests and backgrounds. Members of a clique may spend several hours together each day. Cliques provide companionship as well as an important reference group for evaluating personal experiences. They may also give teenagers a sense of identity.

7. Social adeptness is tied to popularity. The best-liked adolescents are those who act appropriately in the eyes of other teenagers, who are good at perceiving and meeting people's needs, and who are confident without being conceited. Popular teenagers also tend to be outgoing and intelligent.

8. Neglected adolescents are often timid, unenthusiastic about group activities, or generally unskilled at relating to peers. Rejected adolescents act in ways that more actively irk others. They are tactless, conceited, too critical, or highly aggressive and bullyish. These are the loneliest teenagers, and they tend to develop psychological problems, to do poorly in school, to drop out, and to become delinquent.

9. Besides gaining a sense of identity in cliques, teenagers can discuss problems with their friends, who can offer empathy and support. Peers also help adolescents develop autonomy. When teenagers make decisions with their friends, adults are not there to veto them, so independent thinking is fostered. Peers also teach each other about intimacy and sexuality and can influence both achievement and the pursuit of interests and hobbies.

10. How adolescents influence each other in school depends partly on the age of the students in the school and the achievement level of the students in the class. Keeping young adolescents in a school with younger children may be better for them than switching them to a junior high school, where the presence of ninth-graders can feel intimidating to younger teenagers.

11. When schools track students according to academic achievement or ability, social tracking often results as well, dividing students into academic groups that dislike or resent one another. Academically, students usually do just as well in mixed-ability classes as they do in uniform groups.

12. Good high schools share several traits that encourage high achievement from their students. Administration, teachers, parents, and students place a high value on education. Teachers are committed to their students and express that commitment in the classroom. Staff members seek ways to improve their performance; good high schools are well integrated into their communities. Students participate in the educational process as teachers challenge them to think critically. The atmosphere is warm, and respect for students is high.

13. Most high schools fall short in two key ways: They are not creating an environment conducive to cognitive growth, and they tend to ignore the psychological development that all healthy adolescents must undergo. They stress obedience and conformity instead of autonomy and responsibility.

14. High school students typically work 15 to 20 hours each week in jobs that are dull but afford them considerable amounts of spending money each week. Working teenagers tend to be more self-reliant, but work does not strengthen ethics or enhance knowledge of the "real" world or of the value of money. Few who work save or contribute to family expenses. Further, the more time teenagers spend working, the less they have for studying or for extracurricular activities.

15. In less-industrialized, agrarian societies children grow up practicing adult skills with their parents, making the transition to adulthood easier and continuous. In industrialized societies the transition to adulthood is both longer and more abrupt.

16. For teenagers who come from poor families, the high dropout rate and a high rate of teen pregnancies make the transition to adulthood particularly hard. Sex education courses aim to prevent early pregnancy, and intervention with inner-city youngsters can also encourage them to stay in school. In inner cities, crack and other drugs are destroying the structure of families and subjecting teenagers to strong and often brutal peer pressure.

Key Terms

cliques   prefigurative societies
cofigurative societies   premature affluence
crowd   reference group
postfigurative societies   tracking

Suggested Readings

Furstenberg, F., Jr., Brooks-Gunn, J., and Morgan, S. (1987). *Adolescent mothers in later life.* New York: Cambridge University Press. A landmark long-term follow-up of a sample of teenage mothers and their children that explores the impact of early childbearing on the psychological and social well-being of youth and their infants.

Greenberger, E., and Steinberg, L. (1986). *When teenagers work: The psychological and social costs of adolescent employment.* New York: Basic Books. This book examines the costs and benefits, for both teenagers and society, of part-time employment during the school year.

Ogbu, J. (1974). *The next generation: An ethnography of education in an urban neighborhood.* New York: Academic Press. An anthropologist examines the problems of inner-city minority youth through an intensive ethnographic study.

Powell, A., Farrar, E., and Cohen, D. (1985). *The shopping mall high school.* Boston: Houghton Mifflin. A devastating look at the problems of contemporary high schools, with some recommendations about what can be done to improve them.

Working with Infants, Children, & Adolescents

T here are more options today for those interested in working with youngsters than ever before. An increase in two-income and single-parent families has accelerated the demand for qualified child-care providers, and the current political emphasis on the improvement of education is opening new career paths for teachers.

Opportunities exist in a variety of settings, such as schools, hospitals, libraries, day care centers, social service agencies, and museums, and it is possible to choose to work with a particular age group—infants, preschoolers, elementary school children, or high school students. Most positions require at least an undergraduate degree and some require masters' degrees, but many require only short training programs and perhaps licensing.

Following are brief descriptions of some of the many career options available as well as information about the training and education required for each position.

Adoption Agency Official

The job of an adoption agency official usually starts several months prior to the birth of an infant and ends with the placement of that infant in an adoptive home.

Most agencies divide their social workers into two groups. One group works exclusively with expectant mothers who plan to give their infants up for adoption. Their task is to provide both emotional support and counseling and to assist in finding financial support, housing, and medical care for the woman during the last stages of her pregnancy, if she needs such assistance. These social workers are also responsible for exploring options other than adoption with the expectant mother. The second group of social workers is charged with the responsibility of evaluating the adoptive parents, both psychologically and financially. This work always involves a "home study," consisting of interviews with the prospective parents and a visit to their home. During the home study, while evaluating the home environment, the social worker helps potential parents explore their feelings about adoption. The study may last weeks or months and ends with the preparation of a written report by the social worker outlining the reasons for acceptance or rejection.

Training in social work is generally needed to become an adoption agency official. Many colleges offer undergraduate degrees in social work, but a master's degree is often required in this field.

Child Life Specialist

Child life specialists work in a hospital setting with infants, children, and adolescents before and after hospital admission.

These workers help children overcome their fear of a hospital experience by orienting them to the hospital and explaining any medical procedure they may have to undergo. In their work, child life specialists need to be very sensitive to the child's developmental level and needs. When explaining a medical procedure, for example, they may encourage very young children to play "doctor" for a doll, using toy medical instruments. They also conduct tours of the hospital and tell children what to bring with them for their stay and what the hospital routine will be.

After admission, child life specialists provide daily activities for the patients. They supervise playrooms in which group activities—such as watching films, cooking, and arts and crafts—are stressed. They may also help the children keep up with their schoolwork.

Although children are the primary concern of child life workers, people in this career often serve as parent advocates, ensuring that parents' questions and concerns are addressed. The child life specialist may schedule meetings with parents and hospital staff to discuss a child's progress. In planning a child's daily activities, workers must also keep in close touch with nurses in order to review the child's medical condition and emotional state so that activities can be individualized according to the child's condition, age, and experience. Child life workers also sometimes supervise and train volunteers or students to work in the hospital's child life department.

Most child life workers are accredited teachers trained in child development, early childhood education, or elementary education. Intensive, short-term training programs (10 weeks) are offered by some hospitals for students who have coursework in child growth and development and experience in working with children. The training in a child life program includes direct supervised work with children and the medical staff on hospital units, as well as seminars on relevant topics (parent education and developmental assessment, for example). Trainees are exposed to work with all age groups but can select one in which they would like to specialize.

Child Protective Service Worker (Child Welfare Worker)

Child welfare workers are employed by the Child Protective Services unit of the state's social service system to protect children and to ensure that their rights are not violated. These workers investigate reports from lay or professional people who suspect that a child is being abused, neglected, or exploited by visiting the child's home and interviewing those who have contact with the child. Following this visit, the child welfare worker prepares a comprehensive written report, including the names and address of the child's custodians, any evidence of abuse or neglect they find, and other information that can help to establish the cause of any abuse or neglect found. If the child welfare worker finds that the child is being abused but feels that treating the family will successfully end the abuse, social services and programs may be provided to stabilize and maintain the family. This may include instruction about child care and rearing. The child and the family in such a case will be monitored by the child welfare worker by means of both scheduled and unscheduled visits. If the worker feels that the family will not respond to treatment, the abused or neglected children will be taken into custody by the state and temporary foster care will be provided.

Child welfare workers must have a bachelor's degree in human services, social work, or one of the social sciences. A master's degree in any of these fields or completion of a certificate or associate degree program is usually necessary for advancement.

Childbirth Instructor

A childbirth instructor plans, prepares, and conducts courses for pregnant women and their "support persons," or "coaches" (usually the expectant fathers). Some childbirth instructors begin by introducing expectant mothers to the choices they will have to make during labor and delivery and then go on to teach general relaxation, breathing, and coping techniques. They also instruct the support person in coaching and massage techniques. Other instructors take a specific approach to labor and delivery, such as the Lamaze method. Typically, a childbirth course lasts 5 to 8 weeks and ends as closely as possible to the expectant mother's due date.

Some training centers offer workshops and courses of instruction for those who want to become childbirth educators. To enroll in these courses, one needs a background in labor and delivery, health education, nursing, midwifery, or, at the very least, one must have experienced labor and delivery herself. These courses, which can be as short as 4 days of intensive training plus 6 months of independent readings and tests, always include some teacher training as well as training in labor and delivery.

Some childbirth instructors are independent contractors working out of their homes or offices; others work for organizations, private doctors, or hospitals. The requirements to become a childbirth educator vary according to the work setting. Some settings require certification from the International Childbirth Education Association (ICEA) or a local chapter of this organization; others require a nursing degree only.

Children's Librarian

A children's librarian manages a library's program for children, organizing the children's section and deciding what books and other materials the library should acquire.

These librarians also acquaint children with the library and its resources, help them select books, and, in consultation with community educators and parent groups, organize special programs to encourage children to read. These programs may include storytelling sessions, puppet shows, and films.

Children's librarians usually have undergraduate degrees in fields such as education, library science, or child development and may have master's degrees in library science with a specialty in working with children.

Children's Publishing

The field of children's book publishing offers a variety of opportunities for those interested in editing, sales, marketing, advertising, art, or writing.

Entry-level positions in a publishing company usually require an undergraduate degree. Experience in business is helpful to sales and marketing work, training in literature or journalism is helpful to editing and advertising, a background in education may lead to a position in a school book department, and experience in design is required for work in an art department.

Authors and illustrators of children's books usually do not work in a company but submit their manuscripts for consideration. Many successful children's book authors have had no specialized training but have a feeling for children's interests and reading levels.

Children's Television

Positions in children's educational television fall into three general categories: content, production, and research.

Those involved in the content area develop educational goals and curricula for specific age groups. Entry-level positions generally require undergraduate degrees in psychology, education, communications, or child development. Most supervisors in the content area have doctoral degrees in at least one of these areas.

The production of children's television programs may involve organizing production schedules, arranging for guest stars and actors to be available for filming, and budgeting production costs.

Researchers test the ideas, characters, and skits developed by workers in the content domain to ensure that the concepts are entertaining and understandable. This may involve piloting completed television programs in school settings. Researchers generally have masters' degrees in education.

Clinical Psychologist

A clinical psychologist evaluates, diagnoses, and treats persons with emotional disorders. An evaluation is made on the basis of information gathered through personal observation and the interpretation of cognitive, emotional, personality, or other psychological tests.

Once an evaluation is made, a treatment program is chosen to meet the specific needs of the individual. Such a program may include techniques such as psychodrama or role playing. If a psychologist chooses to work with children, a technique often used is play therapy. Children may have difficulty expressing their feelings verbally, and so they are encouraged to express them indirectly by playing with dolls or other toys.

A psychologist may also choose to work as a consultant to other health professionals, to administer tests, to design or conduct research in the area of personality development and emotional functioning, or to teach at the graduate or undergraduate level.

A doctoral degree is usually required to practice clinical psychology, and most states have licensing requirements that may include one or two years of experience working in a supervised internship program.

Day Care Supervisor

Day care supervisors are the directors of the programs in preschool or day care centers. They oversee the operation of the program and the curriculum administered by workers in the center. Supervisors may also sometimes work directly with the children, interact with the parents, or serve as liaisons between the community and the center. Some supervisors organize and run informational and educational workshops for parents or for workers in the center.

Every state has different requirements for day care supervisors. Qualifications for the position also vary according to the type of preschool or day care center. Some centers are maintained and monitored by a central company; some are individual, freestanding centers; and some are casually organized centers operated from the supervisor's home. In many states, the Department of Public Welfare publishes a book specifying the qualifications necessary for day care supervisors.

Early Childhood Educator

Early childhood educators train people for a career in day care. Most often, this instruction is given in a community college that offers an associate or bachelor's degree in early childhood education with a specialty in day care. Some states, however, have special schools devoted to training workers in the field of day care.

Early childhood educators affiliated with colleges typically have at least a master's degree in early childhood education or a related subject area. As part of their training for that degree, they have some field experience (work experience in a day care or early childhood education setting).

Elementary Classroom Teacher

In the typical elementary school, each teacher is assigned to one particular grade, instructing students in that grade in all academic subjects.

Besides their regular classroom teaching, elementary school teachers are generally required to prepare the curriculum (which may involve field trips); assign and correct homework; administer and correct tests; and maintain careful records of each student's attendance, performance, and progress in order to give grades at the end of the year and to spot any academic or behavioral problems early enough to provide some remedial action.

In the course of their work, the teachers must interact not only with the children but with the parents, other teachers and school administrators, and the school board. This may involve attending lectures or workshops on curriculum planning or getting involved in special projects. Teachers almost always meet at least twice a year with parents to discuss their children's progress.

Elementary school teachers in a public school system must have at least an undergraduate degree, with a major or concentration in education. Most states require that teachers be licensed, which involves passing a standardized test. For advancement in the field, a master's degree is usually required.

Guidance Counselor

The primary responsibility of high school guidance counselors is to help students form their educational and career goals and to help them meet these goals. In order to do this, they must maintain files on students, including their academic records and extracurricular activities, and meet with them to appraise their interests and abilities. They may also conduct programs in career and educational options. A guidance counselor may work closely with students who are experiencing social and emotional problems, if necessary referring them to other support systems, such as the school psychologist or a community agency.

In addition to working with students, a guidance counselor interacts with school personnel, recruitment personnel at educational institutions, and career placement agencies.

Guidance counselors usually have at least undergraduate degrees in education. In some states, they need additional course work or training and teacher certification.

Health Educator

In a school setting, a health educator will plan and organize health education programs for the educational level and developing needs of the students. Programs of instruction may include sex education (accurate information concerning safe sex, contraceptive use, and other, related issues) or drug and alcohol awareness (information about substance use, abuse, and treatment, for example). Health educators may also give instruction in personal hygiene and healthy eating habits.

In addition to working with students, health educators interact with school personnel to make them more aware of any behavior in their students that might suggest a problem with drugs or other health issues. They also need to maintain contact with community agencies that can provide counseling or other intervention if needed. Health educators attend educational and health conferences to keep them abreast of new developments in the field.

They must have at least an undergraduate degree, often in education or a scientific or health-related field. They may also have more advanced training in the health field, such as nursing course work or experience or work experience in a medical setting.

Infant Day Care Provider

An infant day care provider cares for infants and toddlers while their parents are at work. The amount of time that a provider spends with the infant may vary from a whole day to part of a day, from 1 to 5 days a week.

Infant day care providers work in many different settings. They may provide their services in the infant's home, in their own homes, or in a day care center. If they work from their own homes or in a center, they may care for one or more infants at a time. Many states specify the maximum number of infants that can be supervised by a single provider.

The training and requirements needed to become an infant day care provider vary from state to state. Some states require licensing and certification, with guidelines indicating the minimal education necessary to be a provider. Many colleges offer courses in early childhood education that will help an infant day care provider, and some high schools and community colleges offer programs to become a certified baby-sitter. Parents will likely want to know about a provider's previous work experience.

Juvenile ("Family") Court Judge

Juvenile or "family" court judges preside over legal cases involving youth under the age of 18. In most cities, they work in divisions of the court system specifically established for juvenile work. Often a child or adolescent is brought before the judge by a social worker, caseworker, or police officer, who will present the youth's case. Most hearings are informal, with the judge speaking directly with the persons involved, including the youth and his or her parents. These judges hear cases involving minor delinquency, lawbreaking, severe home disciplinary problems, and child abuse or neglect and then recommend appropriate action (such as sending a child to a foster home, referring a child for treatment or rehabilitation, or removing the child legally from the parents' custody).

In addition to having knowledge about the law, particularly as it applies to juveniles, most states require that a juvenile court judge hold a law degree and be licensed to practice law by the state bar association. Usually, lawyers must practice several years before becoming judges and acquire specific work experience with children's social service agencies before being elected or appointed to a position in juvenile court. This background helps the judge become familiar with the services available to children and adolescents.

Midwife

Midwives assist women during labor and delivery and also sometimes provide support and care before and after they give birth. Traditionally, midwives worked exclusively in the patients' homes, but recently they have been able to provide their services in some hospitals and clinics specializing in midwife-assisted births. Midwives are trained to recognize the complications that can arise during a home delivery; if such difficulties do arise, they contact a physician and the pregnant woman is transferred to a hospital.

There are two types of midwives. A nurse-midwife is a registered nurse who has completed a one- or two-year midwife training program and has been certified by the American College of Nurse-Midwives. A lay-midwife has received no formal training in this profession. Midwives may be licensed by the state, but not all states require licenses for the practice of midwifery.

Museum Educator

Museum educators are employed by museums to educate the public (primarily children) about topics related to the museum's various scientific, historical, cultural, or art exhibits. Instruction may involve designing and teaching classes for preschool or elementary school children within the museum or organizing and conducting weekend and overnight programs combining educational with recreational activities.

Museum educators may also work with teachers by showing them how to use the museum's displays to enrich and enhance their school's curriculum or by directing their classes' field trips through the museum.

Museum educators usually have at least undergraduate degrees in the museum's specialty—science, history, or art, for example—and frequently hold masters' degrees in these subjects. They often have taken course work in education as well.

Neonatal Intensive-Care-Unit Clinician

Neonatal clinicians are professional or technical nurses with specialized training in the care of newborns. They are trained to manage the daily care of neonates, monitoring their physical condition and their medicinal and nutritional needs. They also oversee and manage the life-support systems of infants born prematurely or with physical abnormalities. Although neonatal clinicians interact primarily with infants, they must also work with the hospital staff to ensure that the babies' needs are being met. They may also interact with new parents, offering them any necessary emotional support and guidance.

Training programs for professional and technical nurses range from 2 to 5 years and include course work in the biological sciences and nursing care and supervised clinical experience in a medical setting. To become a neonatal clinician, one must take additional course work and acquire additional clinical experience in newborn care. This additional training usually leads to a master's degree.

New-Parent Educator

A new-parent educator helps the parents of newborns (most often the mothers) develop parenting skills and "styles." In some settings, these educators may act as facilitators, helping the mother recognize her ability to nurture her own newborn and helping her adjust to her own postpartum emotional needs. In other settings, new-parent education may consist of instruction in basic skills, such as how to bathe and breast- or bottle-feed infants, for example.

Most new-parent educators are registered nurses who work on hospital maternity wards. Some childbirth-education organizations have begun to offer courses to train educators to work with parents for the first 6 months after their baby's birth. These educators will focus on the new parents' emotional needs and also provide basic skills training.

Occupational Therapist

Occupational therapists work in hospital or community settings to promote the rehabilitation or improve the functioning of physically, mentally, or emotionally handicapped persons. They organize and conduct individualized treatment programs to help restore normal physical and mental functioning or to help patients adapt and adjust to their permanent handicaps. The treatment program might consist of recreational activities or craftwork designed to improve the patient's sensorimotor skills or vocational, homemaking, and personal hygiene tasks designed to improve the skills necessary for daily living.

Occupational therapists often work one-on-one with their patients, conferring with medical professionals and other members of the rehabilitation team as needed to meet the patient's emotional and physical needs. They may also conduct training programs for nursing and medical students and may be involved in the design and development of orthotic devices.

Occupational therapists generally have undergraduate degrees and specialized training in occupational therapy. They need licensing to become certified.

Physical Therapist

Physical therapists work in hospitals, rehabilitation centers, health agencies, or private practice to increase the mobility, alleviate the pain, or prevent the permanent disability of those whose functioning has been affected by disease or injury. Many therapists limit their practice to a specific disability or to a specific group of patients. Those who work only with children are called pediatric physical therapists.

The treatment plan for a particular patient is determined only after consultation with both the patient and the patient's physician.

Physical therapists generally have undergraduate degrees in either physical health or the biological sciences and further specialized training in physical therapy. States offer licensing exams for physical therapists.

Preschool Worker/Teacher

Preschool teachers work with prekindergarten-age children, organizing and leading activities designed to promote the children's interpersonal, physical, and intellectual development. They attempt to create a stimulating environment for the children by leading them in games that encourage cooperation and consideration, by reading books to them, by leading them in song, and by providing them with opportunities to develop their creative and visual-motor skills through painting, drawing, and other craftwork. A preschool teacher also helps children develop self-care habits by teaching them to perform simple tasks such as hanging up their coats and putting away their toys and books when they are finished with them.

The amount of time a preschool teacher spends with the children may vary from a half day to a full day, from 1 to 5 days a week, often depending upon the work schedule of the children's parents. In addition to working with children, preschool teachers often interact with other child care professionals to exchange ideas for activities. They also work with parents, informing them of their child's progress and letting them know about any special needs the child may have.

A preschool teacher often has an undergraduate degree, with a major or concentration of classes in early childhood development. Because the children in a preschool may be at different developmental levels, the preschool teacher must be aware of and sensitive to the needs and abilities of each child and plan activities accordingly. Some states require that preschool teachers be certified and some that they have not been convicted or tried on charges of child abuse or neglect.

Probation Officer

A probation officer who works with juvenile offenders has the responsibility of making recommendations before a court hearing and maintaining contact with the offender after a court decision has been made.

In order to make recommendations to the court, the officer must interview the child or adolescent, the family, and others in the community. On the basis of these interviews, the officer will recommend that the case be heard either by the court or by some other agency, such as a mental-health agency. If the case is to be heard by the court, the probation officer will recommend that the offender be held in a detention facility or released to parental custody. After a court decision has been handed down, it is the probation officer's responsibility to see that the court's recommendations are followed and to assist the offender in following these recommendations.

A probation officer is usually required to have knowledge and skills in casework management; such instruction can be acquired through college or graduate programs offering social work training.

Psychology Professor

A psychology professor teaches undergraduate and/or graduate courses in specific areas of psychology, such as developmental psychology (concerned with the growth and development of emotional, physical, and interpersonal functioning across the life span), experimental psychology (concerned with perceptual, memory, cognitive, and learning processes), and social psychology (concerned with the understanding of human social relationships). In addition to teaching, psychology professors design and conduct research to further understanding within their field and present and publish their research findings.

Psychology professors are generally required to have doctorate degrees in their area of specialization.

Recreation/Art Therapist

A recreation therapist works with children who are experiencing emotional distress, helping them develop skills in nonacademic areas and providing an outlet for them to express their feelings. Arts and crafts, sports, games, music, play, and puppet shows are some of the activities that a recreation/art therapist organizes and develops. Often this kind of therapist works in a psychiatric hospital and meets with groups of children and adolescents one or more times a week.

Recreation/art therapists usually have undergraduate degrees in the social sciences with additional course work in recreation therapy.

Remedial Subject Instructor

These instructors evaluate and teach students who are not performing up to their grade levels in specific subjects—most often reading and math. They also may work with children with limited attention spans.

In order to evaluate a particular student, the instructor will administer and interpret achievement tests designed to identify the specific area of dysfunction. If these tests are inconclusive, the instructor may attempt to find out what is disturbing the learning process by conferring with other school personnel or even requesting additional testing by outside agencies.

Once the problem is isolated, the instructor can design lessons that will meet the needs of the specific student. The instructor will also keep in close touch with the parents to encourage their cooperation.

Remedial subject instructors have undergraduate degrees in education with a specialty in remedial or special education. Most states require that they be licensed, and in certain states a master's degree or passing a standardized exam is necessary for this license.

Research Assistant

A psychology research assistant compiles and analyzes data from an experiment so that it can be presented to professionals in the field or published, according to specific guidelines, in specialty journals. In developmental psychology, this work may involve studies with children of different ages. A research assistant may also conduct searches of the published literature in libraries to find references and help formulate questions that could be answered with an experiment.

Research assistants work with the subjects of an experiment (human or animal) and consult with the professor or other investigator who designed the experiment about difficulties, potential problems, and the status of data collection.

Research assistants generally have a college degree with a major in an area related to their research position. Frequently, research-assistant work is used to provide experience for individuals who anticipate graduate work in their field of interest.

School Psychologist

School psychologists evaluate and treat gifted, average, and emotionally or physically handicapped children referred to them by schools. To make their evaluations, they administer tests, observe the child in the classroom, and consult with parents, the child, and school personnel.

Once an evaluation is made, the psychologist administers a program designed to meet the student's special limitations or potential. This program may include individual counseling or group counseling, using techniques such as psychodrama or play therapy.

In addition to working with students, school psychologists may teach or advise other school personnel about methods for providing an enriching and motivating environment in the school. They also have contacts with community agencies to meet the potential medical, vocational, or social service needs of children and their families. A school psychologist may also serve as a consultant to the school board or to a parent-teacher association.

School psychologists have either a master's or a doctorate degree in school psychology and are licensed to practice in a particular state.

Secondary School Teacher

Teachers in secondary schools instruct students in one or more academic subjects, preparing a curriculum that consists of lessons, lectures, and demonstrations. They also assign and correct homework and administer and correct tests. If a student exhibits academic, adjustment, or behavior problems, they may confer with the student's other teachers, the student, the parents, and other school personnel to decide on appropriate remedial action.

Secondary school teachers interact with other professionals at faculty meetings and in teacher-training workshops and conferences to exchange ideas for providing enrichment and motivation in the classroom. In some secondary school systems, they may also direct extracurricular programs and serve as student advisers.

Secondary school teachers must have at least undergraduate degrees, with a major in education or in the subject or subjects they teach. Most states also require teachers to be licensed, which involves passing a standardized exam. In some states, a master's degree is also necessary for this license.

Psychiatric Social Worker

Psychiatric social workers provide services for mentally and emotionally disturbed individuals and their families in hospitals and community mental health agencies. They collaborate with psychologists, psychiatrists, and other members of the mental-health treatment team in obtaining enough social and background information on the client to arrive at a diagnosis and to plan a treatment program. Such a program may involve individual counseling, family counseling, or group counseling by the social worker or by other agencies. Social workers also help support patients in making a transition from hospital to community living.

Psychiatric social workers need an undergraduate or master's degree in social work. There are also state licensing exams for social workers.

Special-Education Teacher

Special-education teachers work at the elementary and secondary school level, instructing students who are educationally handicapped because of some physical, emotional, or neurological disability. They design curricula in specific subject areas to meet each student's special physical, emotional, or educational need. In addition to providing academic training, special-education teachers may counsel their students to help them adjust and modulate their behavioral and emotional outbursts. Special-education teachers may also work with the children's parents so that the progress made in the school setting can be transferred to the home and other social settings. They also confer with other school personnel to design and implement programs to fill the educational, physical, and emotional needs of children with different types of handicaps.

Special-education teachers have undergraduate degrees in general education with a concentration in special education. Most states require that special-education teachers be licensed, and in some states a master's degree or passing a standardized exam is necessary for this license.

Speech Therapist

Speech therapists evaluate, diagnose, and treat the speech and language problems of both children and adults. They plan and conduct specialized treatment programs to create or restore effective communication skills. A speech therapist will often serve as a consultant to professionals in educational or medical settings to help determine appropriate treatment strategies.

Training in speech therapy is usually acquired through an undergraduate degree in education with a specialization in speech therapy. Some states require speech therapists to pass a licensing exam.

Youth Worker

A youth worker provides services to troubled teens in residential treatment settings (often called "group homes"). They lead informal and formal therapeutic group activities, helping the youths to develop new skills and interests. They may counsel individual clients, helping them to increase healthy attitudes and patterns of behavior by developing a better understanding of themselves and their problems and the cycle of behavior creating them.

A youth worker usually has an undergraduate degree in one of the social sciences, with skills or training in social work or psychology. They are employed through a social service agency and, in most states and settings, are supervised by licensed psychologists or social workers.

Credits

PART OPENER TEXT CREDITS

Part One, page 34: Lauren Green Shafer

Part Two, page 130: Reprinted with permission of Charles Scribner's Sons, an imprint of Macmillan Publishing Company, from *The Magic Years* by Selma Fraiberg. Copyright © 1959 Selma H. Fraiberg; copyright renewed.

Part Three, page 240: Vivian G. Paley, *Mollie Is Three* (Chicago: Univ. of Chicago Press, 1988). Reprinted with permission.

Part Four, page 340: Eric Meyer

Part Five, page 430: Carson McCullers, *The Member of the Wedding* (New York: Bantam, 1974; orig. pub. 1946). Reprinted with permission.

PART AND CHAPTER OPENER PHOTO CREDITS

CO1A	Robert Brenner/*PhotoEdit*
CO1b	Michal Heron/*Woodfin Camp & Associates*
1-0	Barbara Rios/*Photo Researchers*
PO1a	Dan McCoy/*Rainbow*
PO1b	Petit Format/Nestle/*Photo Researchers*
PO1c	Milton Feinberg/*The Picture Cube*
CO2a	CNRI/Science Photo Library/*Photo Researchers*
CO2b	W. Rosin Malecki/*PhotoEdit*
CO3a	Petit Fromat/Nestle/*Photo Researchers*
CO3b	Kathy Sloane
CO4a	Mimi Forsyth/*Monkmeyer*
CO4b	Petit Format/J. da Cunha/*Photo Researchers*
PO2a	Alan Carey/*The Image Works*
PO2b	George Bellerose/*Stock, Boston*
PO2c	Bill Aron/*PhotoEdit*
PO2d	Robert Brenner/*PhotoEdit*
CO5a	Hella Hammid/*Photo Researchers*
CO5b	Robert Brenner/*PhotoEdit*
CO6a	Elizabeth Crews/*Stock, Boston*
CO6b	Peter Menzel/*Stock, Boston*
CO7a	Barbara Alper
CO7b	Andrew Brilliant/*The Picture Cube*
CO8a	Judy Gelles/*Stock, Boston*
CO8b	Chester Higgins, Jr./*Photo Researchers*
PO3a	Jacques Chenet/*Woodfin Camp & Associates*
PO3b	Randy Matusow
PO3c	Myrleen Ferguson/*PhotoEdit*
CO9a	Coco McCoy/*Rainbow*
CO9b	Susan Lapides/*Design Conceptions*
CO10a	Carol Lee/*The Picture Cube*
CO10b	Elizabeth Crews/*The Image Works*
CO11a	Dada Lynn/*Photo 20-20*
CO11b	Joseph Schuyler/*Stock, Boston*
PO4a	Michael Weisbrot/*Stock, Boston*
PO4b	Myrleen Ferguson/*PhotoEdit*
PO4c	K. Rantzman/*Photo 20-20*
CO12a	Bob Daemmrich/*Stock, Boston*
CO12b	Susan Lapides/*Design Conceptions*
CO13a	Randy Matusow
CO13b	Frances M. Cox/*Stock, Boston*
CO14a	Nancy J. Pierce/*Photo Researchers*
CO14b	George W. Gardner/*The Image Works*
PO5a	Elizabeth Crews/*The Image Works*
PO5b	Christopher Brown/*Stock, Boston*
PO5c	Joel Gordon
co15a	Bob Daemmrich/*Stock, Boston*
co15b	Spencer Grant/*The Picture Cube*
co16a	Kate Connell
co16b	Richard Hutchings/*PhotoEdit*
co17a	Kindra Clineff/*The Picture Cube*
co17b	Karen Rantzman/*Photo 20-20*

Bibliography

Aber, J. L., & Allen, J. P. (1987). Effects of maltreatment on young children's socioemotional development: An attachment theory perspective. *Developmental Psychology, 23*(3), 406–414.

Abramovitch, R., & Grusec, J. E. (1978). Peer imitation in a natural setting. *Child Development, 49,* 60–65.

Acheson, R. M. (1960). Effects of nutrition and disease on human growth. In J. M. Tanner (Ed.), *Human growth* (pp. 73–92). New York: Pergamon Press.

Adams, G., & Crane, P. (1980). An assessment of parents' and teachers' expectations of preschool children's social preference for attractive or unattractive children and adults. *Child Development, 51,* 224–231.

Adams, G., & Jones, R. (1983). Female adolescents' identity development: Age comparisons and perceived child-rearing experience. *Developmental Psychology, 19,* 249–256.

Adams, R. (1987). An evaluation of color preference in early infancy. *Infancy Behavior and Development, 10,* 143–150.

Adler, R. (1978). *Research on the effects of television advertising on children.* Washington, DC: National Science Foundation.

Ainsworth, M. D. S. (1973). The development of infant-mother attachment. In B. M. Caldwell & H. N. Ricciuti (Eds.), *Review of child development research* (Vol. 3). Chicago: University of Chicago Press.

Ainsworth, M. D. S. (1979). Attachment as related to mother-infant interaction. In R. Hinde & J. Rosenblatt (Eds.), *Advances in the study of behavior.* New York: Academic Press.

Ainsworth, M. D. S., Bell, S. M., & Stayton, D. J. (1972). Individual differences in the development of some attachment behaviors. *Merrill-Palmer Quarterly, 18,* 123–143.

Ainsworth, M. D. S., Blehar, M., Walters, E., & Wall, S. (1978). *Patterns of attachment.* Hillsdale, NJ: Erlbaum.

Ainsworth, M. D. S., & Wittig, B. (1969). Attachment and exploratory behavior of one-year-olds in a strange situation. In B. M. Foss (Ed.), *Determinants of infant behavior* (Vol. 4). New York: Wiley.

Alexander, J. (1973). Defensive and supportive communications in normal and deviant families. *Journal of Consulting and Clinical Psychology, 40,* 223–231.

Allison, P., & Furstenberg, F., Jr. (1989). How marital dissolution affects children: Variations by age and sex. *Developmental Psychology, 25,* 540–549.

Ambron, S. (1980). Causal models in early education research. In S. Kilmer (Ed.), *Advances in early education and day care* (Vol. 2). Greenwich, CT: JAI Press.

Ambrose, J. (1961). The development of the smiling response in early infancy. In B. M. Foss (Ed.), *Determinants of infant behavior* (Vol. 1). London: Methuen.

American Academy of Pediatrics (1985). *Pediatrics Nutrition Handbook* (2nd ed.). Elk Grove, IL: Author.

Anastasi, A. (1958). Heredity, environment, and the question "How?" *Psychological Review, 65,* 197–208.

Anderson, D. et al., (1986). Television viewing at home: Age trends in visual attention and time with TV. *Child Development, 57,* 1024–1033.

Andrews, L. B. (1982, November) Genetic counselors: How they can help and how they can't. *Parents,* 92–184.

Antonov, A. (1947). Children born during the siege of Leningrad in 1942. *Journal of Pediatrics, 30,* 250–259.

Apgar, V. (1953). A proposal for a new method of evaluation of the newborn infant. *Current Research in Anesthesia and Analgesia, 104,* 419–428.

Apgar, V., & Beck, J. (1973). *Is my baby all right?* New York: Trident Books.

Archer, S. (1982). The lower age boundaries of identity development. *Child Development, 53,* 1551–1556.

Arend, R., Gove, F., & Sroufe, L. (1979). Continuity of individual adaptation from infancy to kindergarten: A predictive study of ego-resiliency and curiosity in preschoolers. *Child Development, 50,* 950–959.

Arkrum, C., Clavadetscher, J., & Teller, D. (1986). Chromatic discrimination and brightness matches in infants. *Investigative Ophthalmology and Visual Science, 27* (Suppl. 264).

Aronfreed, J. (1968). *Conduct and conscience: The socialization of internal controls over behavior.* New York: Academic Press.

Asher, S. R., & Gottman, J. M. (1981). *The development of children's friendships.* New York: Cambridge University Press.

Asher, S., and Wheeler, V. (1985). Children's loneliness: A comparison of rejected and neglected peer status. *Journal of Consulting and Clinical Psychology, 53,* 500–505.

Aslin, R. (1981). The development of

smooth pursuit in human infants. In D. Fisher, R. Monty, & J. Senders (Eds.), *Eye movements: Cognition and visual perception.* Hillsdale, NJ: Erlbaum.

Aslin, R., Pisoni, D., & Jusczyk, P. (1983). Auditory development and speech perception in infancy. In J. Campos & M. Haith (Eds.), *Handbook of child psychobiology; Vol. 2. Infancy and developmental psychobiology.* New York: Wiley.

Assor, A. (1988). *Representation of mother and dependency in kindergarten children.* Unpublished manuscript. Ben-Gurion University, Israel.

Bachman, J. (1983). Premature affluence: Do high school students earn too much? *Economic Outlook USA, Summer,* 64–67.

Bachman, J., Bare, D., and Frankie, E. (1986). *Correlates of employment among high school seniors.* Unpublished manuscript. Institute for Social Research, University of Michigan, Ann Arbor.

Bachman, J., Green, S., and Wirtanen, I. (1972). *Youth in transition: Vol. 3. Dropping out—problem or symptom?* Ann Arbor: Institute for Social Research, University of Michigan.

Bahrick, L. E. (1983). Infants' perception of substance and temporal synchrony. *Infant Behavior & Development, 6,* 429–450.

Bakeman, R., & Brown, J. (1980). Analyzing behavioral sequences: Differences between preterm and full-term infant-mother dyads during the first months of life. In D. Sawin, R. C. Hawkins, II, L. O. Walker, & J. H. Pentieuff (Eds.), *Exceptional infant: Vol. 4. Psychosocial risks in infant-environment transactions.* New York: Brunner-Mazel.

Baker, L. (1984). Spontaneous versus instructed use of multiple standards for evaluating comprehension: Effects of age, reading proficiency, and type of standard. *Journal of Experimental Child Psychology, 38,* 289–311.

Baker, L., & Brown, A. L. (1984). Metacognitive skills and reading. In P. D. Pearson, M. Kamil, R. Barr, & P. Mosenthal (Eds.), *Handbook of reading research* (pp. 353–394). New York: Longman.

Ball, S., & Bogatz, G. A. (1970). *The first year of* Sesame Street*: An evaluation.* Princeton, NJ: Educational Testing Service.

Ball, S., & Bogatz, G. A. (1971). *The second year of* Sesame Street*: A continuing evaluation.* Princeton, NJ: Educational Testing Service.

Ball, S., & Bogatz, G. A. (1972). Summative research of *Sesame Street:* Implications for the study of preschool children. In A. D. Pick (Ed.), *Minnesota Symposia on Child Psychology* (Vol. 6. pp. 3–17). Minneapolis: University of Minnesota Press.

Bandura, A. (1965). Influence of models' reinforcement contingencies on the acquisition of imitative responses. *Journal of Personality and Social Psychology, 1,* 589–595.

Bandura, A. (1977). *Social learning theory.* Englewood Cliffs, NJ: Prentice-Hall.

Bandura, A., Ross, D., and Ross, S. (1961). Transmission of aggression through imitation of aggressive models. *Journal of Abnormal and Social Psychology, 63,* 575–582.

Bane, M. J. (1976). Marital disruption and the lives of children. *Journal of Social Issues, 32,* 103–117.

Barber, B. (1987). Marital quality, parental behavior and adolescent self-esteem. *Family Perspective, 21,* 244–368.

Barcus, F. (1978). *Commercial children's television on weekends and weekday afternoons.* Newtonville, MA: Action for Children's Television.

Barenboim, C. (1981). The development of person perception in childhood and adolescence: From behavioral comparisons to psychological constructs to psychological comparisons. *Child Development, 52,* 129–144.

Barglow, P. (1985, April). *Other-than-mother in-home care and the quality of the mother-child relationship.* Paper presented at the biennial meetings of the Society for Research in Child Development, Toronto.

Barglow, P., Vaughn, B., & Molitor, N. (1987). Effects of maternal absence due to employment on the quality of infant-mother attachment in a low-risk sample. *Child Development.*

Barkley, R., and Cunningham, C. (1978). Do stimulant drugs improve the academic performance of hyperkinetic children? A review of

outcome research. *Clinical Pediatrics, 17,* 85–93.

Barnes, G. (1984). Adolescent alcohol abuse and other problem behaviors: Their relationship and common parental influences. *Journal of Youth and Adolescence, 13,* 329–348.

Barnes, K. E. (1971). Preschool play norms: A replication. *Developmental Psychology, 5,* 99–103.

Barnett, R. C. (1979, March). *Parent child-rearing attitudes: Today and yesterday.* Paper presented at the meeting of the Society for Research in Child Development, San Francisco.

Baroody, A. J. (1985). Mastery of basic number combinations. *Journal for Research in Mathematics Education, 16,* 83–98.

Barrett, D. E., Radke-Yarrow, M., & Klein, R. E. (1982). Chronic malnutrition and child behavior: Effects of early caloric supplementation on social and emotional functioning at school age. *Developmental Psychology, 18,* 541–556.

Bar-Tal, D., Raviv, A., & Goldberg, M. (1982). Helping behavior among preschool children: An observational study. *Child Development, 53,* 396–402.

Bar-Tal, D., Raviv, A., & Leiser, T. (1980). The development of altruistic behavior: Empirical evidence. *Developmental Psychology, 16,* 516–524.

Barton, M., & Schwarz, J. (1981, August). *Day care in the middle class: Effects in elementary school.* Paper presented at the annual convention of the American Psychological Association, Los Angeles.

Bates, E., Camaioni, L., & Volterra, V. (1975). The acquisition of performatives prior to speech. *Merrill-Palmer Quarterly, 21,* 205–226.

Baumrind, D. (1967). Child care practices anteceding three patterns of preschool behavior. *Genetic Psychology Monographs, 75,* 43–88.

Baumrind, D. (1971). Current patterns of parental authority. *Developmental Psychology Monograph, 4*(1, Pt.2).

Baumrind, D. (1972). An exploratory study of socialization effects on black children: Some black-white comparisons. *Child Development, 43,* 261–267.

Baumrind, D. (1977, March). *Socialization determinants of personal agency.*

Paper presented at the biennial meeting of the Society for Research in Child Development, New Orleans.

Baumrind, D. (1978). Parental disciplinary patterns and social competence in children. *Youth and Society, 9,* 239–276.

Baumrind, D. (1980). New directions in socialization research. *Psychological Bulletin, 35,* 639–652.

Baumrind, D., & Black, A. E. (1967). Socialization practices associated with dimensions of competence in preschool boys and girls. *Child Development, 38,* 291–327.

Baumrind, D., and Moselle, K. (1985). A developmental perspective on adolescent drug abuse. *Advances in Alcohol and Substance Abuse, 4,* 41–67.

Bayley, N. (1949). Consistency and variability in the growth of intelligence from birth to eighteen years. *Journal of Genetic Psychology, 75,* 165–196.

Beckwith, L. (1971). Relationships between attributes of mothers and their infants' IQ scores. *Child Development, 42,* 1083–1097.

Beere, C. A. (1979). *Women and women's issues. A handbook of tests and measures.* San Francisco: Jossey-Bass.

Bell, A., Weinberg, M., and Hammersmith, S. (1981). *Sexual preference: Its development in men and women.* Bloomington, IN: Indiana University Press.

Bell, R. (1971). Stimulus control of parent or caretaker behavior by offspring. *Developmental Psychology, 4,* 63–72.

Bellinger, D., Leviton, A., Waternaux, C., Needleman, H., & Rabinowitz, M. (1987). Longitudinal analyses of prenatal and postnatal lead exposure and early cognitive development. *New England Journal of Medicine, 316,* 1037–1043.

Belsky, J. (1979). The interrelation of parental and spousal behavior during infancy in traditional nuclear families: An exploratory analysis. *Journal of Marriage and the Family, 41,* 749–755.

Belsky, J. (1980a). Child maltreatment: An ecological integration. *American Psychologist, 35,* 320–335.

Belsky, J. (1980b). A family analysis of parental influence on infant explor-

atory competence. In F. Pederson (Ed.), *Observational studies of the father-infant relationship.* New York: Praeger.

Belsky, J. (1981). Early human experience: A family perspective. *Developmental Psychology, 17,* 3–23.

Belsky, J. (1984). The determinants of parenting: A process model. *Child Development, 55,* 83–96.

Belsky, J. (1988). The "effects" of infant day care reconsidered. *Early Childhood Research Quarterly, 3,* 235–272.

Belsky, J., & Benn, J. (1982). Beyond bonding: A family-centered approach to enhancing parent-infant relations in the newborn period. In L. Bond & J. Joffee (Eds.), *Facilitating infant and early childhood development: Sixth Vermont conference on the primary prevention of psychopathology* (pp. 281–308). Hanover, NH: University Press of New England.

Belsky, J., Garduque, L., & Hrncir, E. (1984). Assessing performance, competence, and executive capacity in infant play: Relations to home environment and security of attachment. *Developmental Psychology, 20,* 406–417.

Belsky, J., Gilstrap, B., & Rovine, M. (1984). The Pennsylvania Infant and Family Development Project: 1. Stability and change in mother-infant and father-infant interaction in a family setting at one, three, and nine months. *Child Development, 55,* 692–705.

Belsky, J., Lang, M., & Huston, T. (1986). Sex typing and division of labor as determinants of marital change across the transition to parenthood. *Journal of Personality and Social Psychology, 50,* 517–522.

Belsky, J., Lang, M., & Rovine, M. (1985). Stability and change across the transition to parenthood: A second study. *Journal of Marriage and the Family, 47,* 855–866.

Belsky, J., & Nezworski, T. (1988). Clinical implications of attachment: An introduction. In J. Belsky & T. Nezworski (Eds.), *Clinical implications of attachment.* Hillsdale, NJ: Erlbaum.

Belsky, J. Robins, E., & Gamble, W. (1984). The determinants of parenting: Toward a contextual theory. In M. Lewis & L. Rosenblum (Eds.), *Beyond the dyad: Social connections.* New York: Plenum.

Belsky, J., & Rovine, M. (1987). Temperament and attachment security in the strange situation: An empirical rapproachment. *Child Development, 58,* 787–795.

Belsky, J., & Rovine, M. (1988). Nonmaternal care in the first year of life and the security of infant-parent attachment. *Child Development, 59,* 157–167.

Belsky, J. Rovine, M., & Taylor, D. G. (1984). The Pennsylvania Infant and Family Development Project: 3. The origins of individual differences in infant-mother attachment: Maternal and infant contributions. *Child Development, 55,* 706–717.

Belsky, J., Spanier, J. B., & Rovine, M. (1983). Stability and change in marriage across the transition to parenthood. *Journal of Marriage and the Family, 45,* 553–556.

Belsky. J., & Steinberg, L. (1978). The effects of day care: A critical review. *Child Development, 49,* 929–949.

Belsky, J., Steinberg, L., & Walker, A. (1982). The ecology of day care. In M. E. Lamb (Ed.), *Nontraditional families* (pp. 71–116). Hillsdale, NJ: Erlbaum.

Belsky, J., & Tolan, W. (1981). Infants as producers of their own development: An ecological analysis. In R. Lerner and N. Busch-Rossnagle (Eds.), *Individuals as producers of their own development: A lifespan perspective* (pp. 87–116). New York: Academic Press.

Belsky, J., & Volling, B. (1989). Mothering, fathering, and marital interaction in the family triad during infancy: Exploring family system's processes. In P. Berman & F. Pedersen (Eds.), *Men's transition to parenthood: Longitudinal studies of early family experience.* Hillsdale, NJ: Erlbaum.

Belsky, J., Ward, M., & Rovine, M. (1986). Prenatal expectations, postnatal experiences, and the transition to parenthood. In R. Ashmore & D. Brodzinsky (Eds.), *Thinking about the family.* Hillsdale, NJ: Erlbaum.

Belson, W. A. (1959). *Television and the family.* London: British Broadcasting Corporation.

Benedict, Helen. (1976). *Language comprehension in 9 15-month-old infants.* University of Stirling Lecture.

Benson, J. B., & Užgiris, I. Č. (1985). Effect of self-initiated locomotion on infant search activity. *Developmental Psychology, 21,* 923–931.

Berger, J. (1989, August 27). East Harlem students clutch a college dream. *The New York Times,* pp. 1, 28.

Beck, L. E. (1986). Relationship of elementary schoolchildren's private speech to behavioral accompaniment to task, attention, and task performance. *Developmental Psychology, 22,* 671–680.

Berk, L. E., and Garvin, R. A. (1984). Development of private speech among low-income Appalachian children. *Developmental Psychology, 20,* 271–286.

Berndt, T. (1979). Developmental changes in conformity to peers and parents. *Developmental Psychology, 15,* 608–616.

Berndt, T. (1981). Relations between social cognition, nonsocial cognition, and social behavior: The case of friendship. In J. Flavell and L. Ross (Eds.), *Social cognitive development: Frontiers and possible futures.* Cambridge: Cambridge University Press.

Berndt, T. (1982). The features and effects of friendship in early adolescence. *Child Development, 53,* 1447–1460.

Bertenthal, B. I., Campos, J. J., & Barnett, K. C. (1984). Self-produced locomotion: An organizer of emotional, cognitive, and social development in infancy. In R. N. Emde & R. J. Harman (Eds.), *Continuities and discontinuities in development* (pp. 175–210). New York: Plenum.

Best, D. L. & Ornstein, P. A. (1986). Children's generation and communication of mnemonic organizational strategies. *Developmental Psychology, 22,* 845–853.

Best, D. L., Williams, J. E., Cloud, J. M., Davis, S. W., Robertson, L. S., Edwards, J. R., Giles, H., & Fowles, J. (1977). Development of sex-trait stereotypes among young children in the United States, England, and Ireland. *Child Development, 48,* 1375–1384.

Bever, T. G. (1970). The cognitive basis for linguistic structures. In J. R. Hayes (Ed.), *Cognition and the development of language.* New York: Wiley.

Bierman, K., Miller, C., & Stabb, S. (1987). Improving the social behavior and peer acceptance of rejected boys. *Journal of Consulting and Clinical Psychology, 55,* 194–200.

Biller, H. (1981). Father absence, divorce, and personality development. In M. Lamb (Ed.), *The role of the father in child development* (2nd ed.). New York: Wiley.

Biller, H. B. (1970). Father absence and the personality development of the male child. *Developmental Psychology, 2,* 181–201.

Biller, H. B., & Bahm, R. M. (1971). Father absence, perceived maternal behavior, and masculinity of self-concept among junior high school boys. *Developmental Psychology, 4,* 178–181.

Biller, H. B., & Borstelmann, L. J. (1967). Masculine development: An integrative review. *Merrill-Palmer Quarterly, 13,* 253–294.

Birch, H., & Gussow, D. (1970). *Disadvantaged children: Health, nutrition, and school failure.* New York: Harcourt, Brace & World.

Birrell, R., & Birrell, J. (1969). The maltreatment syndrome in children: A hospital survey. *Medical Journal of Australia, 2,* 1023.

Bjorklund, D. F. (1989). *Children's thinking: Developmental function and individual differences.* Pacific Grove, CA: Brooks/Cole.

Bjorklund, D. F., & Zeman, B. R. (1982). Children's organization and metamemory awareness in their recall of familiar information. *Child Development, 53,* 799–810.

Black, L., Hersher, L., & Steinschneider, A. (1978). Impact of the apnea monitor on family life. *Pediatrics, 62,* 681–685.

Blakeslee, S. (1987, April 21). Genetic discoveries raise painful questions. *The New York Times,* pp. 19, 23.

Blass, E., Ganchrow, J., & Steiner, J. (1984). Classical conditioning in newborn humans 2–48 hours of age. *Infant Behavior and Development, 7,* 223–235.

Block, J. H. (1979, September). *Personality development in males and females: The influence of differential socialization.* Paper presented as part of the Master Lecture Series at the meeting of the American Psychological Association, New York.

Block, J. H. (1983). Differential premises arising from differential socialization of the sexes: Some conjectures. *Child Development, 54,* 1335–1354.

Block, J. H. (1987, April). *Longitudinal antecedents of ego-control and ego-resiliency in late adolescence.* Paper presented at the biennial meeting of the Society for Research in Child Development, Baltimore.

Bloom, L. (1973). *One word at a time.* The Hague, Netherlands: Mouton.

Bloom, L., & Lahey, M. (1978). *Language development and language disorders.* New York: Wiley.

Bloom, L., Lightbown, P., & Hood, L. (1975). Structures and variation in child language. *Monographs of the Society for Research in Child Development, 40* (2, Serial No. 160).

Bloom, L., Merkin, S., and Wootten, J. (1982). Wh-Questions: Linguistic factors that contribute to the sequence of acquisition. *Child Development, 53,* 1084–1092.

Blos, P. (1967). The second individuation process of adolescence. In R. S. Eissler et al. (Eds.), *Psychoanalytic study of the child* (Vol. 15). New York: International Universities Press.

Blyth, D., Hill, J., and Smyth, C. (1981). The influence of older adolescents on younger adolescents: Do grade-level arrangements make a difference in behaviors, attitudes, and experiences? *Journal of Early Adolescence, 1,* 85–110.

Blyth, D., Simmons, R., & Bush, D. (1978). The transition into early adolescence: A longitudinal comparison of youth in two educational contexts. *Sociology of Education, 51,* 149–162.

Blyth, D., Simmons, R., & Carlton-Ford, S. (1983). The adjustment of early adolescents to school transitions. *Journal of Early Adolescence. III,* 105–120.

Boccia, M., & Campos, J. (1983, April). *Maternal emotional signaling: Its effect on infants' reaction to strangers.* Paper presented at the meeting of the Society for Research in Child Development, Detroit.

Borjeson, M. (1979). The aetiology of obesity in children. *Acta Pediatrica Scandinavia, 65,* 279–287.

Borke, H. (1971). Interpersonal perception of young children: Egocentrism or empathy? *Developmental Psychology, 5,* 263–269.

Borke, H. (1975). Piaget's mountains revisted: Changes in the egocentric landscape. *Developmental Psychology, 11,* 240–243.

Bornstein, M. (1981). Two kinds of perceptual organization near the beginning of life. In W. A. Collins (Ed.), *Aspects of the development of competence.* Hillsdale, NJ: Erlbaum.

Bornstein, M., & Sigman, M. (1986). Continuity in mental development from infancy. *Child Development, 57,* 251–274.

Boston Women's Health Book Collective. (1976). *Our bodies ourselves: A book by and for women.* New York: Simon & Schuster.

Boston Women's Health Book Collective. (1978). *Ourselves and our children.* New York: Random House.

Bourne, E. (1978a). The state of research on ego identity: A review and appraisal. Part 1. *Journal of Youth and Adolescence, 7,* 223–251.

Bowerman, M. (1976). Semantic factors in the acquisition of rules for word use and sentence construction. In D. M. Morehead and A. E. Morehead (Eds.), *Normal and deficient child language.* Baltimore: University Park Press.

Bowlby, J. (1969–1980). *Attachment and loss (Vols. 1–3).* London: Hogarth.

Boyer, E. (1983). *High school.* New York: Harper & Row.

Brackbill, Y. (1958). Extinction of the smiling response in infants as a function of reinforcement. *Child Development, 29,* 115–124.

Brackbill, Y. (1979). Obstetrical medication and infant behavior. In J. Osofsky (Ed.), *Handbook of infant development* (pp. 76–125). New York: Wiley.

Bradley, R., & Caldwell, B. (1976). The relation of infants' home environments to mental test performance at fifty-four months: A follow-up study. *Child Development, 47,* 1172–1174.

Bradley, R., & Caldwell, B. (1984). 174 children: A study of the relationship between home environment and cognitive development during the first 5 years. In A. Gottfried (Ed.), *Home environment and early cognitive development: Longitudinal research* (pp. 5–57). New York: Academic Press.

Brazelton, T. (1973). Neonatal behavioral assessment scale. *Clinics in Developmental Medicine* (No. 50). London: Heinemann.

Brazelton, T. (1978). Introduction. In A. Sameroff (Ed.), Organization and stability of newborn behavior. *Monographs of the Society for Research in Child Development, 43* (Serial No. 77).

Brazelton, T., Tronick, E., Lechtig, A., Lasky, R. E., & Klein, R. E. (1977). The behavior of nutritionally deprived Guatemalan infants. *Developmental Medicine and Child Neurology, 19,* 364–372.

Breger, Louis (1974). *From Instinct to Identity,* Englewood Cliffs, NJ: Prentice-Hall.

Bretherton, I. (1978). Making friends with one-year-olds: An experimental study of infant-stranger interaction. *Merrill-Palmer Quarterly, 24,* 29–51.

Bretherton, I., Stolberg, U., & Kreye, M. (1981). Engaging strangers in proximal interaction: Infants' social initiative. *Developmental Psychology, 17,* 746–755.

Bridges, K. (1932). Emotional development in early infancy. *Child Development, 3,* 324–334.

Bristol, M., Gallagher, J., & Schopler, E. (1988). Mothers and fathers of young developmentally disabled and nondisabled boys: Adaptation and spousal support. *Developmental Psychology, 24,* 441–451.

Brody, G., Pillegrini, A., & Sigel, I. (1986). Marital quality and mother-child and father-child interactions with school-aged children. *Developmental Psychology, 22,* 291–296.

Brodzinsky, D., & Huffman, L. (1988). Transition to adoptive parenthood. *Marriage and Family Review, 12,* 267–286.

Bronfenbrenner, U. (1970). *Who cares for America's children?* Paper presented at the Conference of the National Association for the Education of Young Children.

Bronfenbrenner, U. (1974). The origins of alienation. *Scientific American, 231,* 53–61.

Bronfenbrenner, U., and Crouter, A. (1982). Work and family through time and space. In S. Kammerman & C. Hayes (Eds.), *Families that work: Children in a changing world.* Washington, DC: National Academy Press.

Bronson, W. C. (1986). *The development of basic auditory abilities.* Paper presented at the International Conference on Infant Studies.

Brook, J., Whiteman, M., Gordon, A., and Brook, D. (1984). Paternal determinants of female adolescents' marijuana use. *Developmental Psychology, 20,* 1032–1043.

Brooks, J., & Lewis, M. (1976). Infants' responses to strangers: Midget, adult, and child. *Child Development, 47,* 323–332.

Brooks-Gunn, J., & Lewis, M. (1982). Affective exchanges between normal and handicapped infants and their mothers. In T. Field & A. Fogel (Eds.), *Emotion and early interaction.* Hillsdale, NJ: Erlbaum.

Brooks-Gunn, J., & Reiter, E. (in press). Pubertal development. In S. Feldman and G. Elliot (Eds.), *At the threshold: The developing adolescent.* Cambridge: Harvard University Press.

Brooks-Gunn, J., and Ruble, D. (1979). *The social and psychological meaning of menarche.* Paper presented at the biennial meeting of the Society for Research in Child Development, San Francisco.

Brooks-Gunn, J., and Ruble, D. (1982). The development of menstrual-related beliefs and behaviors during early adolescence. *Child Development, 53,* 1567–1577.

Brophy, J. E. (1979). Teacher behavior and its effects. *Journal of Educational Psychology, 71,* 733–750.

Brophy, J. E. (1983). Research on the self-fulfilling prophecy and teacher expectations. *Journal of Educational Psychology, 75,* 631–661.

Broughton, J. (1978). Development of concepts of self, mind, reality, and knowledge. *New Directions for Child Development, 1,* 75–100.

Brown, A. L. (1975). The development of memory: Knowing, knowing about knowing, and knowing how to know. In H. Reese (Ed.), *Advances in child development and behavior* (Vol. 10). New York: Academic Press.

Brown, A. L., Bransford, J. D., Ferrara, R. A., & Campione, J. C. (1983). Learning, remembering, and understanding. In J. H. Flavell & E. M. Markman (Eds.), *Handbook of child psychology: Vol. 3. Cognitive development*. New York: Wiley.

Brown, A. L., & Campione, J. C. (1972). Recognition memory for perceptually similar pictures in preschool children. *Journal of Experimental Psychology, 95*, 55–62.

Brown, B., Clasen, D., & Eicher, S. (1986). Perceptions of peer pressure, peer conformity dispositions, and self-reported behavior among adolescents. *Developmental Psychology, 22*, 521–530.

Brown, B, & Lohr, M. (1987). Peer-group affiliation and adolescent self-esteem: An integration of ego-identity and symbolic-interaction theories. *Journal of Personality and Social Psychology, 52*, 47–55.

Brown, J., & Daniels, R. (1968). Some observations on abusive parents. *Child Welfare, 47*, 89–94.

Brown, J. V., & Bakeman, R. (1979). Relationships of human mothers with their infants during the first year of life. In R. W. Bell & W. P. Smotherman (Eds.), *Maternal influences and early behavior*. New York: Spectrum.

Brown, J. V., Bakeman, R., Snyder, P. A., Frederickson, W. T., Morgan, S. T., & Hepler, R. (1975). Interactions of black inner-city mothers with their newborn infants. *Child Development, 46*, 677–686.

Brown, P., & Elliot, R. (1965). Control of aggression in a nursery school class. *Journal of Experimental Child Psychology, 2*, 103–107.

Brown, R. (1966). Organ weight in malnutrition with special reference to brain weight. *Developmental Medicine and Child Neurology, 8*, 512–522.

Brown, R. (1968). The development of *wh* questions in child speech. *Journal of Verbal Learning and Verbal Behavior, 7*, 279–290.

Brown, R. M. (1977). An examination of visual and verbal coding proces-

sors in preschool children. *Child Development, 48*, 38–45.

Brown, R. M. (1973). *A first language.* Cambridge, MA: Harvard University Press.

Brownell, C. (1986). Convergent developments: Cognitive-developmental correlates of growth in infant/toddler peers skills. *Child Development, 57*, 275–286.

Bruner, J. S. (1970). The growth and structure of skill. In K. J. Connolly (Ed.), *Mechanisms of motor skill development*. New York: Academic Press.

Bruner, J. S. (1973). *Beyond the information given: Studies in the psychology of knowing.* New York: Norton.

Bruner, J. S. (1973). Organization of early skilled action. *Child Development, 44*, 1–11.

Bruner, J. S. (1975). The ontogenesis of speech acts. *Journal of Child Language, 2*, 1–19.

Buhrmester, D., & Furman, W. (1987). The development of companionship and intimacy. *Child Development, 58*, 1101–1113.

Buisseret, P., Gary-Bubo, E., & Imbert, M. (1978). Ocular motility and recovery of orientational properties of visual cortex neurons in dark-reared kittens. *Nature, 272*, 816–817.

Burke, B., Beal, V., Kirkwood, S., & Stuart, H. (1943). Nutrition studies during pregnancy. *American Journal of Obstetrics and Gynecology, 46*, 38–52.

Burnside, L. H. (1927). Coordination in the locomotion of infants. *Genetic Psychology Monographs, 2*, 281–372.

Buss, A. H., & Plomin, R. (1984). *Temperament.* Hillsdale, NJ: Erlbaum.

Butler, J. A., Starfield, V., and Stenmark, S. (1984). Child health policy. In H. W. Stevenson and A. W. Siegel (Eds.), *Child development research in social policy* (Vol. 1, pp. 110–188). Chicago: University of Chicago Press.

Butler, N. R., & Goldstein, H. (1973). Smoking in pregnancy and subsequent child development. *British Medical Journal, 4*, 573–575.

Calvert, S. L., and Huston, A. (1987). Television and children's gender

schema. In L. Liben & M. Signorella (Eds.), Children's gender schemata. *New Directors for Child Development* (No. 38). San Francisco: Jossey-Bass.

Calvert, S. L., & Watkins, B. A. (1979). Recall of television content as a function of content type and level of production feature use. Paper presented at the meeting of the Society for Research in Child Development, San Francisco.

Camp, B. W., & Bash, M. A. (1981). *Think aloud: Increasing social and cognitive skills—a problem-solving program for children*. Champaign, IL: Research Press.

Camp, B. W., Blom, G. E., Herbert, F., & van Doorninck, W. J. (1977). "Think aloud": A program for developing self-control in young aggressive boys. *Journal of Abnormal Child Psychology, 5*(2), 157–169.

Campbell, S. (1979). Mother-infant interactions as a function of maternal ratings of temperament. *Child Psychiatry and Human Development, 10*, 67–76.

Campos, J., Barrett, K., Lamb, M., Goldsmith, H., & Stenberg, C. (1983). Socioemotional development. In J. Campos & M. Haith (Eds.), *Handbook of child psychobiology: Vol. 2: Infancy and psychobiology*. New York: Wiley.

Campos, J., & Bertenthal, B. I. (1984). The importance of self-produced locomotion in infancy. *Infant Mental Health Journal, 5*, 160–171.

Campos, J., & Stenberg, C. (1981). Perception, appraisal, and emotion: The onset of social referencing. In M. E. Lamb & L. R. Sherrod (Eds.), *Infant social cognition*. Hillsdale, NJ: Erlbaum.

Campos, J., Svejda, M. J., Campos, R. G., & Bertenthal, B. I. (1972). The emergence of self-produced locomotion: Its importance for psychological development in infancy. In D. Brinker (Ed.), *Intervention for at-risk and handicapped infants* (pp. 195–216). Baltimore, MD: University Park Press.

Cantor, D. S., Fischel, J. E., & Kaye, H. (1983). Neonatal conditionability: A new paradigm for exploring the use of interceptive cues. *Infant Behavior and Development, 6*, 403–413.

Cantwell, D. P. (1975). Genetic studies of hyperactive children. In R. Fieve, D. Rosenthal, and H. Brill, (Eds.), *Genetic research in psychiatry*, Baltimore: Johns Hopkins University Press.

Caplan, G. (1974). *Support systems and community mental health: Lectures on concept development.* New York: Behavioral Publications.

Caputo, D., & Mandell, W. (1970). Consequence of low birth weight. *Developmental Psychology, 3,* 363–383.

Carew, J. V. (1979, April). *Observation study of caregivers and children in day-care homes: Preliminary results from home observations.* Paper presented at the Biennial Meeting of the Society for Research in Child Development, San Fransciso.

Carew, J. V. (1980). Experience and the development of intelligence in young children at home and in day care. *Monographs of the Society for Research in Child Development, 45* (6–7, Serial No. 187).

Carey, S. (1978). The child as word learner. In M. Halle, J. Bresnan, & G. A. Miller (Eds.), *Linguistic theory and psychological reality.* Cambridge, MA: Massachusetts Institute of Technology Press.

Carlson, D., & Labarba, R. (1979). Maternal emotionality during pregnancy and reproductive outcome: A review of the literature. *International Journal of Behavioral Development, 2,* 343–376.

Carns, D. (1973). Talking about sex: Notes on first coitus and the double sexual standard. *Journal of Marriage and the Family, 35,* 677–688.

Carpenter, T. P., & Moser, J. M. (1982). The development of addition and subtraction problem-solving skills. In T. Carpenter, J. Moser, & T. Romberg (Eds.), *Addition and subtraction* (pp. 9–24). Hillsdale, NJ: Erlbaum.

Carr, D. (1970). Chromosome studies in selected spontaneous abortions: 1. Conception after oral contraception. *Canadian Medical Association Journal, 103,* 343–348.

Case, R. (1985). *Intellectual development: Birth to adulthood.* New York: Academic Press.

Caudill, W., & Weinstein, H. (1969). Maternal care and infant behavior in Japan and America. *Psychiatry, 32,* 12–43.

Caudill, W., & Frost, L. (1972). A comparison of maternal care and infant behaviour in Japanese-American, American, and Japanese families. In U. Bronfenbrenner (Ed.), *Influences on human development* (pp. 329–342). Hinsdale, IL: Dryden.

Cazden, C. (1968). The acquisition of noun and verb inflections. *Child Development, 39,* 433–448.

Cernoch, J., & Porter, R. (1985). Recognition of maternal axillary odors by infants. *Child Development, 56,* 1593–1599.

Chambers, C. D., & Griffey, M. S. (1975). Use of legal substance within the general population: The sex and age variables. *Addictive Diseases, 2,* 7–20.

Chance, N. (1984). Growing up in a Chinese village. *Natural History, 93,* 72–81.

Chapman, M. (1977). Father absence, stepfathers, and the cognitive performance of college students. *Child Development, 48,* 1152–1154.

Chartier, G., & Ranieri, D. (1984). Adolescent depression: Concepts, treatments, prevention. In P. Karoly and J. Steffen (Eds.), *Adolescent behavior disorders: Foundations and contemporary concerns.* Lexington, MA: Lexington.

Chase-Lansdale, P., & Owen, M. (1987). Maternal employment in a family context: Effect on infant-mother and infant-father attachment. *Child Development, 58,* 1505–1512.

Chasnoff, I. J., Burns, W. J., Schnoll, S. H., & Burns, K. A. (1985). Cocaine use in pregnancy. *New England Journal of Medicine, 313,* 666–669.

Chi, M. T. H. (1978). Knowledge structure and memory development. In R. Siegler (Ed.), *Children's thinking: What develops?* Hillsdale, NJ: Erlbaum.

Chibucos, T., & Kail, P. (1981). Longitudinal examination of father-infant interaction and infant-father attachment. *Merrill-Palmer Quarterly, 27,* 81–96.

Children's Defense Fund (1987). *A children's defense budget, FY 1988: An analysis of our nation's investment in children.* Washington, DC: Author.

Chilman, C. (1980). Social and psychological research concerning adolescent childbearing: 1970–1980. *Journal of Marriage and the Family, 42,* 793–805.

Chodorow, N. (1978). *The reproduction of mothering: Psychoanalysis and the sociology of gender.* Berkeley: University of California Press.

Chukovsky, K. (1968). *From two to five* (rev. ed.). Berkeley: University of California Press.

Chun, R., Pawsat, R., & Forster, F. (1960). Social localization in infancy. *Journal of Nervous and Mental Diseases, 130,* 472–476.

Cicchetti, D., & Sroufe, L. (1976). The relationship between affective and cognitive development in Down's syndrome infants. *Child Development, 46,* 920–929.

Cicchetti, D., & Sroufe, L. (1978). An organizational view of affect: Illustration from the study of Down's syndrome infants. In M. Lewis & L. Rosenblum (Eds.), *The development of affect.* New York: Plenum.

Clark, E. V., Gellman, S. A., & Lane, N. M. (1985). Compound nouns and category structure in young children. *Child Development, 56,* 84–94.

Clarke-Stewart, K. A. (1973). Interactions between mothers and their young children: Characteristics and consequences. *Monographs of the Society for Research in Child Development, 38,* 6–7.

Clarke-Stewart, K. A. (1977). A review of research and some propositions for policy. *Child care in the family.* New York: Academic Press.

Clarke-Stewart, K. A. (1978). And daddy makes three: The father's impact on mother and young child. *Child Development, 44,* 466–478.

Clarke-Stewart, K. A. (1980). Observation and experiment: Complementary strategies for studying day care and social development. In S. Kilmer (Ed.), *Advances in early education and day care.* Greenwich, CT: JAI Press.

Clarke-Stewart, K. A. (1980). The father's contribution to children's cognitive and social development in early childhood. In F. Pederson (Ed.), *The father-infant relationship.* New York: Praeger.

Clarke-Stewart, K. A., & Fein, G. G. (1983). Early childhood programs. In J. Campos & M. Haith (Eds.), *Handbook of child psychology: Vol. 2. Infancy and developmental psychobiology* (pp. 917–999). New York: Wiley.

Cochran, M., & Henderson, C. (1985). *Family matters: Evaluation of the parental improvement program. Final report to the National Institute of Education* (Contract No. 400-76-0150). Washington, DC: National Institute of Education.

Cochran, M. M., & Brassard, J. A. (1979). Child development and personal social networks. *Child Development, 50,* 601–616.

Cohen, D., Stern, V., & Balaban, N. (1983). *Observing and recording the behavior of young children* (3rd ed.). New York: Teachers College Press.

Cohen, L. B. (1972). Attention-getting and attention-holding processes of infant visual preferences. *Child Development, 43,* 869–879.

Cohen, L. B., DeLoache, J. S., & Strauss, M. S. (1979). Infant perceptual development. In J. D. Osofsky (Ed.), *Handbook of infant development.* New York: Wiley.

Cohen, R., Stevenson, D., et al. (1982). Favorable results of neonatal intensive care for very low birthweight infants. *Pediatrics, 69,* 621–625.

Coie, J., & Dodge, K. (1983). Continuities and changes in children's social status: A five-year longitudinal study. *Merrill-Palmer Quarterly, 29,* 261–281.

Coie, J., Dodge, K., & Kupersmidt, J. (1989). Peer group behavior and social status. In S. Asher & J. Coie (Eds.), *Peer rejection in childhood.* New York: Cambridge University Press.

Colby, A., Kohlberg, L., Gibbs, J., & Lieberman, M. (1983). A longitudinal study of moral judgment. *Monographs of the Society for Research in Child Development, 48* (Serial No. 200).

Coleman, J. (1961). *The adolescent society.* Glencoe, IL: Free Press.

Colletta, N. D. (1983). At risk for depression: A study of young mothers. *Journal of Genetic Psychology.*

Collins, W. (1984). Introduction. In W. A. Collins (Ed.), *Development during middle childhood.* Washington, DC: National Academy Press.

Collins, W., & Duncan, S. (1983). *Out-of-school educational influences in middle childhood.* Unpublished manuscript. Institute of Child Development, University of Minnesota, Minneapolis.

Condon, W., & Sanders, L. (1974). Synchrony demonstrated between movements of the neonate and adult speech. *Child Development, 45,* 456–462.

Conger, J. J. (1977). *Adolescence and youth* (2nd ed.). New York: Harper & Row.

Conger, J. J., & Miller, W. C. (1966). *Personality, social class and delinquency.* New York: Wiley.

Conger, R., McCarty, J., Yang, R., Lahey, B., & Kropp, J. (1984). Perception of child, childrearing values, and emotional distress as mediating links between environmental stressors and observed maternal behavior. *Child Development, 55,* 2234–2247.

Connell, J. (1981). *A model of the relationships among children's self-related cognitions, affects, and academic achievement.* Unpublished doctoral dissertation, University of Denver.

Connor, J. M., & Serbin, L. A. (1977). Behaviorally based masculine- and feminine-activity-preference scales for preschoolers: Correlates with other classroom behaviors and cognitive tests. *Child Development, 48,* 1411–1416.

Connor, J. M., & Serbin, L. A. (1978). Children's responses to stories with male and female characters. *Sex Roles, 4,* 637–646.

Conway, E., & Brackbill, Y. (1970). Delivery medication and infant outcome: An empirical study. In W. A. Bowes, Jr., Y. Brackbill, E. Conway, & A. Steinschneider, The effects of obstetrical medication on fetus and infant. *Monographs of the Society for Research in Child Development, 35* (Serial No. 137, pp. 24–34).

Coopersmith, S. (1967). *The antecedents of self-esteem.* San Francisco: Freeman.

Corby, D. G. (1978). Aspirin in pregnancy: Maternal and fetal effects. *Pediatrics, 62*(Suppl.), 930–937.

Cornell, E. H., & Gottfried, A. W.

(1976). Intervention with premature human infants. *Child Development, 47,* 32–39.

Corno, L. (1986). The metacognitive control components of self-regulated learning. *Contemporary Educational Psychology, 11,* 333–346.

Cotterell, J. (1986). Work and community influences on the quality of childrearing. *Child Development, 57,* 362–374.

Cowan, C. (1983, August). *A preventive clinical intervention aimed at marriages of new parents.* Paper presented at the annual meeting of the American Psychological Association, Anaheim, CA.

Cowan, P. A., & Cowan, C. P. (1983, April). *Quality of couple relationships and parenting stress in beginning families.* Paper presented at the biennial meeting of the Society for Research in Child Development, Detroit.

Cowen, E. L., Pederson, A., Babijian, H., Izzo, L. D., & Trost, M. A. (1973). Long-term follow-up of early detected vulnerable children. *Journal of Consulting and Clinical Psychology, 41,* 438–446.

Cravioto, J., & DeLicardie, E. (1970). Mental performance in school aged children. *American Journal of Diseases of Children, 120,* 404.

Cravioto, J., & DeLicardie, E. (1976). Microenvironmental factors in severe protein-energy malnutrition. In N. Scrimshaw & M. Behar (Eds.), *Nutrition and agricultural development: Significance and potential for the tropics* (pp. 25–35). New York: Plenum.

Crawley, S., & Spiker, D. (1983). Mother-child interactions involving 2-year-olds with Downs syndrome: A look at individual differences. *Child Development, 54,* 1312–1323.

Crittenden, P. M. (1988). Relationships at risk. In J. Belsky & T. Nezworski (Eds.), *Clinical implications of attachment* (pp. 136–174). Hillsdale, NJ: Erlbaum.

Crnic, K. A., Greenberg, M. T., Ragozin, A. S., Robinson, N. M., & Basham, R. (1983). Effects of stress and social support on mothers of premature and full-term infants. *Child Development, 54,* 1199–1210.

Crockenberg, S. (1987). Predictors and correlates of anger toward and punitive control of toddlers by adolescent mother. *Child Development, 58,* 964–975.

Cross, W. (1978). The Thomas and Cook models of psychological nigrescence: A literature review. *Journal of Black Psychology, 4,* 13–31.

Cummings, E. M., Iannotti, R., & Zahn-Waxler, C. (1985). Influence of conflict between adults on the emotions and aggression of young children. *Developmental Psychology, 21,* 495–507.

Cutrona, C. (1982a). Nonpsychotic postpartum depression review of recent research. *Clinical Psychology Review, 2,* 487–503.

Cutrona, C. (1982b). Transition to college: Loneliness and the process of social adjustment. In L. Peplau and D. Perlman (Eds.), *Loneliness: A sourcebook of current theory, research, and therapy.* New York: Wiley.

Cvetkovich, G., Grote, B., Bjorseth, A., & Sarkissian, J. (1975). On the psychology of adolescents' use of contraceptives. *Journal of Sex Research, 11,* 256–270.

Dale, N. (1983). *Early pretend play in the family.* Unpublished doctoral thesis, University of Cambridge, England.

Damico, R. (1984). Does working in high school impair academic progress? *Sociology of Education, 57,* 157–164.

Damon, William (1977). *The social world of the child.* San Francisco: Josey-Bass.

Daniels, D., Dunn, J., Furstenberg, F., Jr., & Plomin, R. (1985). Environmental differences within the family and adjustment differences within pairs of adolescent siblings. *Child Development, 56,* 764–774.

Daniels, D., & Plomin, R. (1985). Origins of individual differences in infant shyness. *Developmental Psychology, 21,* 118–121.

Davie, R., Butler, N., & Goldstein, H. (1972). *From birth to seven: The second report of the child development study (1958 cohort).* London: Longman & National Children's Bureau.

Davison, A., & Dobbing, J. (1966). Myelination as a vulnerable period in brain development. *British Medical Bulletin, 22,* 40–44.

DeCasper, A., & Fifer, W. (1980). Of human bonding: Newborns prefer their mothers' voices. *Science, 208,* 1174–1176.

DeLamater, J., & MacCorquodale, P. (1979). *Premarital sexuality: Attitudes, relationships, behavior.* Madison: University of Wisconsin Press.

Dennis, W. (1940). Infant reactions to restraint. *Transactions of the New York Academy of Science, 2,* 202–217.

Dennis, W. (1960). Causes of retardation among institutional children: Iran. *Journal of Genetic Psychology, 96,* 46–60.

Dennis, W., & Dennis, M. (1940). The effect of cradling practices upon the onset of walking in Hopi children. *Journal of Genetic Psychology, 56,* 77–86.

Dennis, W., & Najarian, P. (1957). Infant development under environmental handicap. *Psychological Monographs, 17*(7, Whole No. 436).

Desor, J. A., Maller, O., & Greene, L. S. (1977). Preference for sweet in humans: Infants, children and adults. In J. M. Weiffenbach (Ed.), *Task and development: The genesis of sweet preference.* Bethesda, MD: National Institute of Dental Research.

Devereux, E. (1970). The role of peer group experience in moral development. In J. Hill (Ed.), *Minnesota Symposium on Child Psychology* (Vol. 4). Minneapolis: University of Minnesota Press.

DeVries, R. (1969). Constancy of gender identity in the years three to six. *Society for Research in Child Development Monographs, 34*(3, Serial No. 127).

Diaz, R. (1985). Bilingual cognitive development. *Child Development, 56,* 1376–1388.

Diaz, R., & Berndt, T. (1982). Children's knowledge of a best friend: Fact or fancy? *Developmental Psychology, 18,* 787–794.

Dickenson, G. (1975). Dating behavior of black and white adolescents before and after desegregation. *Journal of Marriage and the Family, 37,* 602–608.

DiPietro, J. A. (1981). Rough and tumble play: A function of gender. *Developmental Psychology, 17,* 50–58.

Dittrichova, J. (1969). Development of sleep in infancy. In R. J. Robinson (Ed.), *Brain and Early Behavior,* New

York: Academic Press.

DiVitto, B., & Goldberg, S. (1983). The development of early parent-infant interaction as a function of newborn medical status. In T. Field, A. Sostek, S. Goldberg, & H. H. Shuman, (Eds.), *Infants born at risk.* New York: Spectrum.

Dix, T., & Grusec, J. (1983). Parent attribution processes in child socialization. In I. Siegal (Ed.), *Parental belief systems* (pp. 201–233). Hillsdale, NJ: Erlbaum.

Dobbing, J. (1964). The influence of early malnutrition on the development of myelination of the brain. *Proceedings of the Royal Society of London,* Series B., *159,* 503–509.

Dodge, K. (1982). Social information processing variables in the development of aggression and altruism in children. In C. Zahn-Waxler, M. Cummings, & M. Radke-Yarrow (Eds.), *The development of altruism and aggression: Social and sociobiological origins.* New York: Cambridge University Press.

Dodge, K. (1986). A social information-processing model of social competence in children. In M. Perlmutter (Ed.), *Minnesota symposium on child psychology* (Vol. 18, pp. 77–125). Hillsdale, NJ: Erlbaum.

Dodge, K., Pettit, G., McClaskey, C., & Brown, M. (1986). Social competence in children. *Monographs of the Society for Research in Child Development, 51*(2, Serial No. 213).

Donald, M. (1979). *Children's minds.* New York: Norton.

Donovan, J. (1977). Randomised controlled trial of antismoking advice in pregnancy. *British Journal of the Society for Preventive Medicine, 31,* 6–12.

Dornbusch, S., Carlsmith, J., Bushwall, S., Ritter, P., Leiderman, P., Hastorf, A., & Gross, R. (1985). Single parents, extended households, and the control of adolescents. *Child Development, 56,* 326–341.

Dornbusch, S., Carlsmith, J., Gross, R., Martin, J., Jennings, D., Rosenberg, A., & Duke, P. (1981). Sexual development, age, and dating: A comparison of biological and social influences upon one set of behaviors. *Child Development, 52,* 179–185.

Dornbusch, S., Ritter, P., Liederman, P.,

Roberts, D., & Fraleigh, M. (1987). The relation of parenting style to adolescent school performance. *Child Development, 58,* 1244–1257.

Douglass, R. (1982). Youth, alcohol, and traffic accidents. In *Alcohol and health: Monograph No. 4.* Washington, DC: National Clearinghouse for Alcohol Information.

Douvan, E., & Adelson, J. (1966). *The adolescent experience.* New York: Wiley.

Drake, C. T., & McDougall, D. (1977). Effects of the absence of a father and other male models on the development of boys' sex roles. *Developmental Psychology, 13,* 537–538.

Drillien, C. (1964). *The growth and development of the prematurely born infant.* Baltimore, MD: Williams & Wilkins.

Duncan, P., Ritter, P., Dornbusch, S., Gross, R., & Carlsmith, J. (1985). The effects of pubertal timing on body image, school behavior, and deviance. *Journal of Youth and Adolescence, 14,* 227–236.

Dunn, J. (1983). Sibling relationships in early childhood. *Child Development, 54,* 787–811.

Dunn, J. (1985). *Sisters and brothers.* Cambridge, MA: Harvard University Press.

Dunn, J., & Kendrick, C. (1980). The arrival of a sibling: Changes in patterns of interaction between mother and firstborn child. *Journal of Child Psychology and Psychiatry, 21,* 119–132.

Dunn, J., & Kendrick, C. (1981). Interaction between young siblings: Association with the interaction between mother and firstborn child. *Developmental Psychology, 17,* 336–343.

Dunn, J., & Kendrick, C. (1981). Social behavior of young siblings in the family context: Differences between same-sex and different-sex dyads. *Child Development, 52,* 1265–1273.

Dunn, J., & Kendrick, C. (1982). *Siblings: Love, envy, and understanding.* Cambridge, MA: Harvard University Press.

Dunphy, D. (1975). The social structure of urban adolescent peer groups. In R. Grinder (Ed.), *Studies in adolescence* (3rd ed.). New York: Macmillan. (Reprinted from *Sociometry,* 1963, *26,* 230–246)

Durfee, J. T., & Lee, L. C. (1973). Infant-infant interaction in a daycare setting. *Proceedings of the 81st Annual Convention of the American Psychological Association, Montreal, Canada, 8,* 63–64.

Dweck, C. S. (1975). The role of expectations and attributions in the alleviation of learned helplessness. *Journal of Personality and Social Psychology, 31,* 674–685.

Dweck, C. S., Davidson, W., Nelson, S., & Enna, B. (1978). Sex differences in learned helplessness: II. The contingencies of evaluative feedback in the classroom; and III. An experimental analysis. *Developmental Psychology, 14,* 268–276.

Dweck, C. S., & Elliott, E. S. (1983). Achievement motivation. In E. M. Hetherington, (Ed.), *Handbook of Child Psychobiology: Vol. 4. Socialization, personality, and social development.* New York: Wiley.

Dweck, C. S., Goetz, T. E., & Strauss, N. (1980). Sex differences in learned helplessness: IV. An experimental and naturalistic study of failure generalization and its mediators. *Journal of Personality and Social Psychology, 38,* 441–452.

Dyer, E. (1963). Parenthood as crisis: A restudy. *Marriage and Family Living, 25,* 488–496.

Dyson, S. E., & Jones, D. G. (1976). Undernutrition and the developing nervous system. *Progress in Neurobiology, 7,* 171–196.

Easterbrooks, M.A., & Goldberg, W. A. (1984). Toddler development in the family: Impact of father involvement and parenting characteristics. *Child Development, 55,* 740–752.

Easterbrooks, M. A., & Lamb, M. E. (1979). The relationship between quality of infant-mother attachment and infant competence in initial encounters with peer. *Child Development, 50,* 380–387.

Eckerman, C. O., & Whatley, J. L. (1975). Infants' reactions to unfamiliar adults varying in novelty. *Developmental Psychology, 11,* 562–567.

Eckerman, C. O., Whatley, J. L., & Kutz, S. (1975). Growth of social play with peers during the second year of life. *Developmental Psychology, 11,* 42–49.

Edelman, B., & Maller, O. (1982). Facts and fictions about infantile obesity. *International Journal of Obesity, 6,* 69–81.

Edwards, C., & Whiting, B. (1988). *Children of different worlds.* Cambridge, MA: Harvard University Press.

Eisenberg, R. (1970). The organization of auditory behavior. *Journal of Speech and Hearing, 13,* 454–471.

Eisenberg, R. (1976). *Auditory competence in early life: The roots of communicative behavior.* Baltimore, MD: University Park Press.

Eisenberg-Berg, N., & Neal, C. (1979). Children's moral reasoning about their own spontaneous presocial behavior. *Developmental Psychology, 15,* 228–229.

Eitzen, D. S. (1975). Athletics in the status system of male adolescents: A replication of Coleman's *The adolescent society. Adolescence, 10,* 267–276.

Ekman, P. (1972). Universals in cultural differences in facial expressions of emotion. In J. K. Cole (Ed.), *Nebraska symposium on motivation* (Vol. 19). Lincoln: University of Nebraska Press.

Ekman, P., & Friesen, W. (1972). Constants across cultures in the face and emotion. *Journal of Personality and Social Psychology, 17,* 124–129.

Elder, G., Jr. (1974). *Children of the Great Depression.* Chicago: University of Chicago Press.

Elkind, D. (1967). Egocentrism in adolescence. *Child Development, 38,* 1025–1034.

Elkind, D. (1978). Understanding the young adolescent. *Adolescence, 13,* 127–134.

Elkind, D. (1981). *The hurried child.* New York: Addison-Wesley.

Elmen, J., DeFrain, J., & Fricke, J. (1987). *A nationwide comparison of divorced parents with sole vs. joint custody.* Paper presented at biennial meeting of the Society for Research in Child Development, Baltimore.

Elster, A., Lamb, M., Peters, L., Kahn, J., & Tavare, J. (1987). Judicial involvement and conduct problems of fathers of infants born to adolescent mothers. *Pediatrics, 79,* 230–234.

Emde, R., Gaensbauer, T., & Harmon, R. (1976). Emotional expression in infancy: A biobehavioral study. *Psychological Issues, 10*(37).

Engel, M., & Keane, W. (1975). *Black mothers and their infant sons: Antecedents, correlates, and predictors of cognitive development in the second and sixth year of life.* Paper presented at the biennial meeting of the Society for Research in Child Development, Denver.

Engfer, A. (1988). The interrelatedness of marriage and the mother-child relationship. In R. Hinde & J. Stevenson-Hinde (Eds.), *Relationships within families: Mutual influences.* Oxford: Clarendon Press.

Engfer, A., & Schneewind, K. (1982). Causes and consequences of harsh parental punishment. *Child Abuse and Neglect, 6,* 129–139.

Epstein, H. T. (1980). EEG developmental stages. *Developmental Psychobiology, 13,* 629–630.

Erickson, M., Egeland, B., & Sroufe, L. (1985). The relationship between quality of attachment and behavior problems in a high-risk sample. In I. Bretherton & E. Waters (Eds.), Growing point in attachment theory and research. *Monographs of the Society for Research in Child Development, 50*(1–2, Serial No. 209).

Erikson, E. (1959/1980). *Identity and the life cycle.* New York: Norton.

Erikson, E. (1963). *Childhood and society* (2nd ed.). New York: Norton.

Erikson, E. (1968). *Identity: Youth and crisis.* New York: Norton.

Erikson, E. Interview by E. Hall. (1987). The father of the identity crisis. In E. Hall, *Growing and changing* (pp. 128–140). New York: Random House.

Ervin-Tripp, S. (1970). Discourse agreement: How children answer questions. In J. R. Hayes (Ed.), *Cognition and the development of language.* New York: Wiley.

Ervin-Tripp, S. (1971). An overview of theories and grammatical development. In D. Slobin (Ed.), *The ontogenesis of grammar.* New York: Academic Press.

Eveleth, P., & Tanner, J. (1976). *Worldwide variation in human growth.* New York: Cambridge University Press.

Fagan, J. F. (1976). Infants' recognition of invariant features of faces. *Child Development, 47,* 627–638.

Fagan, J. F. (1984, April). *Infants' attention to visual novelty and the prediction of later intellectual deficit.* Paper presented at the International Conference on Infant Studies, New York.

Fagan, J. F., & McGrath, S. (1981). Infant recognition memory and later intelligence. *Intelligence, 5,* 121–130.

Fagot, B. (1977). Consequences of moderate cross-gender behavior in preschool children. *Child Development, 48,* 902–907.

Fagot, B., Leinbach, M., & Hagan, R. (1986). Gender labelling and the adoption of sex-typed behavior. *Developmental Psychology, 22,* 440–443.

Fantz, R. L. (1963). Pattern vision in newborn infants. *Science, 140,* 296–297.

Fantz, R. L. (1965). Visual perception from birth as shown by pattern selectivity. *Annals of the New York Academy of Sciences, 118,* 793–814.

Farran, D. C., & Ramey, C. T. (1980). Social class differences in dyadic involvement during infancy. *Child Development, 51,* 254–257.

Farrington, D. (1986). Parenting and delinquency: Parent training and delinquency prevention. *Today's Delinquent, 5,* 51–66.

Feil, R. N., Larsey, G. P., & Miller, M. (1984). Attitudes toward abortion as a means of sex selection. *Journal of Psychology, 116,* 269–272.

Fein, G. G. (1979). Play and the acquisition of symbols. In L. Katz (Ed.), *Current topics in early childhood education.* Norwood, NJ: Ablex.

Feiring, C., & Lewis, M. (1981). Middle-class difference in cognitive development. In T. Field et al. (Eds.), *Culture and early interactions.* Hillsdale, NJ: Erlbaum.

Feldman, H. (1971). Changes in marriage and parenthood: A methodological design. In A. Michel (Ed.), *Family issues of employed women in Europe and America.* Lieden, The Netherlands: Brill.

Feldman, S. S., Nash, S. C., & Aschenbrenner, B. (1985). Antecedents of fathering. *Child Development, 54,* 1628–1636.

Fennema, E., & Sherman, J. (1977). Sex-related differences in mathematics achievement, spatial visualization, and affective factors. *American Educational Research Journal, 14,* 51–71.

Fernald, A. (1985). Four-month-old infants prefer to listen to motherese. *Infant Behavior and Development, 8,* 181–195.

Fernald, A. & Simon, T. (1984). Expanded intonation contours in mothers' speech to newborns. *Developmental Psychology, 20,* 104–113.

Field, D. (1987). A review of preschool conservation training: An analysis of analyses. *Developmental Review, 7,* 210–251.

Field, T. (1978). Interaction patterns of primary vs. secondary caretaker fathers. *Developmental Psychology, 14,* 183–184.

Field, T. (1980). Supplemental stimulation of preterm neonates. *Early Human Development, 3,* 301–314.

Field, T. (1981). *Five year follow-up of preterm respiratory and postterm postmaturity syndrome infants.* Paper presented at the American Psychological Association Meetings, Los Angeles.

Field, T. (1982). Affective displays of high-risk infants during early interactions. In T. Field & A. Fogel (Eds.), *Emotion and interactions.* Hillsdale, NJ: Erlbaum.

Field, T. (1982). Infants born at risk: Early compensatory experiences. In L. Bond & J. Joffee (Eds.), *Facilitating infant and early childhood development.* Vermont: University of Vermont Press.

Field, T. (1984). Separation stress of young children transferring to new schools. *Developmental Psychology, 20,* 786–792.

Field, T., Dempsey, J., Hallock, N., & Shuman, H. (1978). Mothers' assessments of the behavior of their infants. *Infant Behavior and Development, 1,* 156–167.

Field, T., & Roopnarine, J. L. (1982). Infant peer interactions. In T. Field, A. Houston, H. Quay, L. Troll, & G. Finley (Eds.), *Review of human development.* New York: Wiley.

Field, T., Woodson, R., Greenberg, R., & Cohen, D. (1982). Discrimination and imitation of facial expressions by neonates. *Science, 218,* 179–181.

Field, T., Widmayer, S. M., Stringer, S., & Ignatoff, E. (1980). Teenage, lower-class, black mothers and their preterm infants: An intervention and developmental follow-up. *Child Development, 51,* 426–436.

Fine, G. (1981). Friends, impression management, and preadolescent behavior. In S. Asher and J. Gottman (Eds.), *The development of children's friendships.* Cambridge: Cambridge University Press.

Fine, M. (Ed.). (1980). *Intervention with hyperactive children.* New York: SP Medical and Scientific Books.

Fischer, K. (1983). Illuminating the processes of moral development. In A. Colby, L. Kohlberg, J. Gibbs, and M. Lieberman (Eds.), A longitudinal study of moral judgment. *Monographs of the Society for Research in Child Development, 48* (Serial No. 200).

Fischer, K. (1984). *Human Development.* New York: Freeman.

Fischer, K. (1987). Relations between brain and cognitive development. *Child Development, 58,* 623–632.

Fischer, K., & Silvern, L. (1985). Stages and individual differences in cognitive development. *Annual Review of Psychology, 36,* 613–648.

Flavell, J. H. (1985). *Cognitive development* (2nd ed.). Englewood Cliffs, NJ: Prentice-Hall.

Flavell, J. H. (1988). The development of children's knowledge about the mind: From cognitive connections to mental representations. In J. W. Astington, P. L. Harris, and D. R. Olson (Eds.), *Developing theories of mind* (pp. 244–267). Cambridge, MA: Cambridge University Press.

Flavell, J. H., Beach, D., & Chinsky, J. (1966). Spontaneous verbal rehearsal in a memory task as a function of age. *Child Development, 37,* 283–299.

Flavell, J. H., Green, F., & Flavell, E. (1986). Development of knowledge about the appearance reality distinction. *Monographs of the Society for Research in Child Development,* Serial No. 212, Vol. 51, No. 1.

Fogel, A. (1979). Peer versus mother-directed behavior in one- to three-month-old infants. *Infant Behavior and Development, 2,* 215–226.

Fraiberg, S. (1959). *The magic years.* New York: Scribner.

Fraiberg, S. (1977). *Every child's birthright.* New York: Basic Books.

Fraiberg, S. (1977). *Insights from the blind.* New York: Basic Books.

Frauenglass, M., & Diaz, R. (1985). Self-regulatory functions of children's private speech, *Developmental Psychology, 21,* 357–364.

Freeman, R., & Wise, D. (Eds.). (1982). *The youth labor market problem: Its nature, causes, and consequences.* Chicago: University of Chicago Press.

French, L. A. (1989). Young children's responses to "when" questions: Issues of directionality. *Child Development, 60,* 225–236.

Freud, S. (1938). *An outline of psychoanalysis.* London: Hogarth Press.

Freud, S. (1953). *A general introduction to psychoanalysis* (J. Rivière, Trans.). New York: Permabooks.

Frias, P. (1975). Prenatal diagnosis of genetic abnormalities. *Clinical Obstetrics and Gynecology, 18,* 221–236.

Fricker, H., & Segal, S. (1978). Narcotic addiction, pregnancy and the newborn. *American Journal of the Diseases of Children, 132,* 360–366.

Friedenberg, E. (1967). *Coming of age in America.* New York: Vintage Books.

Friedlander, B. Z., Wetstone, H. S., & Scott, C. S. (1974). Suburban preschool children's comprehension of an age-appropriate informational television program. *Child Development, 45,* 561–565.

Friedman, S., Jacobs, B., & Wertmann, M. (1981). Sensory processing in pre- and full-term infants in the neonatal period. In S. Friedman and M. Sigman (Eds.), *Preterm birth and psychological development.* New York: Academic.

Friedman, S., Jacobs, B., & Werthmann, M. (1982). Preterms of low medical risk: Spontaneous behaviors and soothability at expected date of birth. *Infant Behavior and Development, 5,* 3–10.

Friedman, S., Zahn-Waxler, C., & Radke-Yarrow, M. (1982). Perceptions of cries of full-term and preterm infants. *Infant Behavior and Development, 5,* 161–173.

Friedrich, L. K., & Stein, A. H. (1973). Aggressive and prosocial television programs and the natural behavior of preschool children. *Monographs of the Society for Research in Child Development, 38* (Serial No. 151).

Frieze, I., Francis, W., & Hanusa, B. (1981). Defining success in class-room settings. In J. Levine and M. Wang (Eds.), *Teacher and student perceptions: Implications for learning.* Hillsdale, NJ: Erlbaum.

Frisch, H. L. (1977). Sex stereotypes in adult-infant play. *Child Development, 48,* 1671–1675.

Frodi, A., Lamb, M., Leavitt, L., Donovan, W., Neff, C., & Sherry, D. (1978). Fathers' and mothers' responses to the faces and cries of normal and premature infants. *Developmental Psychology, 14,* 490–498.

Furstenberg, F., Jr. (in press). Coming of age in a changing family system. In S. Feldman and G. Elliot (Eds.), *At the threshold: The developing adolescent.* Cambridge, MA: Harvard University Press.

Furstenberg, F., Jr., Brooks-Gunn, J., & Morgan, S. (1987). *Adolescent mothers in later life.* New York: Cambridge University Press.

Furstenberg, F., Jr., Moore, K., & Peterson, J. (1985). Sex education and sexual experience among adolescents. *American Journal of Public Health, 75,* 1331–1332.

Furth, H. G. (1971). Linguistic deficiency and thinking: Research with deaf subjects 1964–1969. *Psychological Bulletin, 76,* 58–72.

Gagnon, J. (1972). The creation of the sexual in early adolescence. In J. Kagan and R. Coles (Eds.), *Twelve to sixteen: Early adolescence.* New York: Norton.

Gallagher, R., Jens, K., & O'Donnell, K. (1983). The effect of physical status on the affective expression of handicapped infants. *Infant Behavior and Development, 6,* 73–77.

Gallatin, J. (1975). *Adolescence and individuality.* New York: Harper & Row.

Galler, J. (1984). Behavioral consequences of malnutrition in early life. In J. Galler (Ed.), *Nutrition and behavior* (pp. 63–117). New York: Plenum.

Galler, J., Ramsey, F., & Solimanon, G. (1984). The influence of early malnutrition on subsequent behavioral development: 3. Learning disabilities as a sequel to malnutrition. *Pediatric Research.*

Galler, J., Ricciuti, H., Crawford, M., & Kucharski, L. (1984). The role of mother-infant interaction in nutritional disorders. In J. Galler (Ed.), *Nutrition and behavior* (pp. 269–304). New York: Plenum.

Galst, J. (1980). Television food commercials and pro-nutritional public service announcements as determinants of young children's snack choices. *Child Development, 51,* 935–938.

Garai, J. E., & Scheinfeld, A. (1968). Sex differences in mental and behavioral traits. *Genetic Psychology Monographs, 77,* 169–299.

Garbarino, J., Sebes, J., & Schellenbach, C. (1984). Families at risk for destructive parent-child relations in adolescence. *Child Development, 55,* 174–183.

Garbarino, J., & Sherman, D. (1980). High-risk neighborhoods and high-risk families. *Child Development, 51,* 188–198.

Garcia, E. (1983). Becoming bilingual during early childhood. *International Journal of Behavioral Development, 6,* 375–404.

Garcia, E., Maez, L., & Gonzalez, G. (1981). *A national study of Spanish/English bilingualism in young Hispanic children of the United States* (Bilingual Education Paper Series 4, No. 12). Los Angeles, CA: National Dissertation and Assessment Center, California State University.

Gardner, H. (1980). *Artful scribbles: The significance of children's drawings.* New York: Basic Books.

Gardner, H. (1982). *Art, mind, and brain: A cognitive approach to creativity.* New York: Basic Books.

Garner, R. (1987). *Metacognition and reading comprehension.* Norwood, NJ: Ablex.

Garrett, E. (1983, August). *Women's experiences of early parenthood: Expectations versus reality.* Paper presented at the annual meetings of the American Psychological Association, Anaheim, CA.

Garvey, C., & Hogan, R. (1973). Social speech and social interaction: Egocentrism revisited. *Child Development, 44,* 562–568.

Gath, A. (1978). *Down's syndrome and the family.* London: Academic Press.

Gelfand, D. F., & Hartmann, D. P., Lamb, A. K., Smith, C. L. Mahan, M. A., & Paul, S. C. (1974). The effects of adult models and de-

scribed alternatives on children's choice of behavior management techniques. *Child Development, 45,* 585–593.

Gelles, R., Straus, M., & Harrop, J. (1988). Has family violence decreased? *Journal of Marriage and the Family, 50,* 286–291.

Gellman, S. A., & Markman, E. M. (1985). Implicit contrast in adjectives vs. nouns. *Journal of Child Language, 12,* 125–143.

Gelman, R. (1972). Logical capacity of very young children: Number invariance rules. *Child Development, 43,* 75–90.

Gelman, R. (1979). Preschool thought. *American Psychologist, 34,* 900–905.

Gelman, R. (1982). Accessing one-to-one correspondence: Still another paper on conservation. *British Journal of Psychology, 73,* 209–220.

Gelman, R., & Baillargeon, R. (1983). A review of some Piagetian concepts. In J. Flavell & E. Murkman (Eds.), *Handbook of child psychobiology:* Vol. 3. *Cognitive development* (pp. 167–230). New York: Wiley.

Gelman, R., Bullock, M., & Meck, E. (1980). Preschoolers' understanding of simple object transformations. *Child Development, 51,* 691–699.

Gelman, R., & Gallistel, C. R. (1978). *The child's understanding of number.* Cambridge, MA: Harvard University Press.

General Accounting Office (1984). *WIC evaluations provide some favorable but no conclusive evidence on the effects expected for the special supplemental program for women, infants, and children* (PEMD-84-4). Washington, DC: U.S. Government Printing Office.

Gerbner, G., Gross, L., Signorielli, N., Morgan, M., & Jackson-Beeck, M. (1979). The demonstration of power: Violence profile no. 10. *Journal of Communication, 29,* 117–196.

Gesell, A., & Ames, L. B. (1937). Early evidence of individuality in the human infant. *Scientific Monthly, 45,* 217–255.

Gesell, A., & Ilg, F. (1946). *The Child from five to ten.* New York: Harper & Row.

Gewirtz, J. (1979, March). Maternal "attachment" outcomes. Paper presented to the Society for Research in Child

Development, San Francisco.

Gewirtz, J., & Gewirtz, H. (1965). Caretaking settings, background events, and behavior differences in four Israeli child rearing environments: Some preliminary trends. In B. M. Foss (Ed.), *Determinants of infant behavior* (Vol. 4). London: Methuen.

Gibson, E. J. (1969). *Principles of perceptual learning and development.* New York: Appleton-Century-Crofts.

Gibson, E. J., & Walker, A. S. (1984). Development of knowledge of visual-tactual affordances of substance. *Child Development, 55,* 453–460.

Gilligan, C. (1982). *In a different voice.* Cambridge, MA: Harvard University Press.

Glenn, N. D., & McLanahan, S. (1981). Children and marital happiness: A further specification of the relationship. *Journal of Marriage and the Family, 44,* 63–72.

Globus, M., Loushman, W., Epstein, C., Halbasch, G., Stephens, J., & Hall, B. (1979). Prenatal genetic diagnosis in 3000 aminocenteses. *New England Journal of Medicine, 300,* 157–163.

Gold, M., & Petronio, R. (1980). Delinquent behavior in adolescence. In J. Adelson (Ed.), *Handbook of adolescent psychology.* New York: Wiley.

Goldberg, S. (1978). Prematurity: Effects on parent-infant interaction. *Journal of Pediatric Psychology, 3,* 137–144.

Golden, M., & Birns, B. (1976). Social class and infant intelligence. In M. Lewis (Ed.), *Origins of Intelligence.* New York: Plenum.

Goldman-Rakic, P. (1987). Development of cortical circuitry and cognitive function. *Child Development, 58,* 601–622.

Goldsmith, H. H. (1978). *Behavior-genetic analyses of early personality (temperament): Developmental perspectives from the longitudinal study of twins during infancy and early childhood.* Unpublished doctoral dissertation, University of Minnesota.

Goldsmith, H. H., & Campos, J. J. (1982). Toward a theory of infant temperament. In R. N. Emde and R. J. Harman (Eds.), *The development of attachment and affiliative sys-*

tems: Psychological aspects. New York: Plenum.

Goldsmith, H. H., & Gottesman, I. I. (1981). Origins of variation in behavioral style: A longitudinal study of temperament in young twins. *Child Development, 52,* 91–103.

Goleman, D. (1986, October 21). Child development theory stresses small moments. *The New York Times,* p. C1, C3.

Goleman, D. (1986a, September 22). Studies play down dangers to latch key children. *The New York Times,* p. B12.

Goleman, D. (1986b, October 6). Aggression in children can mean problems later. *The New York Times,* p. B25.

Goodall, M. M. (1980). Left-handedness as an educational handicap. In R. S. Laura (Ed.), *Problems of handicap.* Melbourne: Macmillan.

Goodlad, J. (1984). *A place called school.* New York: McGraw-Hill.

Gottfried, A. W., & Bathhurst, K. (1983). Hand preference across time is related to intelligence in young girls, not boys. *Science, 22,* 1074–1076.

Gottfried, A. W., Rose, S. A., & Bridger, W. H. (1977). Cross-model transfer in human infants. *Child Development, 48,* 118–123.

Gottman, J. M. (1977). Toward a definition of social isolation in children. *Child Development, 48,* 513–517.

Gould, M., & Shaffer, D. (1986). The impact of suicide in television movies. *New England Journal of Medicine, 351,* 690–694.

Gould, S. J. (1976). Human babies as embryos. *Natural History, 85,* 22–26.

Goyette, C. H., & Conners, C. K. (1977). *Food additives and hyperkinesis.* Paper presented at the 85th annual convention of the American Psychological Association.

Grant, E. (1985). *The bitter pill: How safe is the 'perfect contraceptive'?* London: Elm Tree Books.

Green, D., Potts, R., Wright, J., & Huston, A. (1982). The effects of television commercial form and commercial placement on children's social behavior and attention. *Child Development, 53,* 611–619.

Green, R. (1980). Homosexuality. In H. Kaplan, A. Freedman, & B. Sadock

(Eds.), *Comprehensive textbook of psychiatry* (Vol. 2.) (3rd ed.). Baltimore, MD: Williams & Wilkins.

Green, R. (1987). *The 'Sissy Boy' syndrome and the development of homosexuality.* New Haven, CT: Yale University Press.

Greenbaum, C. W., & Landau, R. (1982). The infant's exposure to talk by familiar people: Mothers, fathers, and siblings in different environments. In M. Lewis & L. Rosenblum (Eds.), *The social network of the developing child.* New York: Plenum.

Greenberg, D. (1971). Accelerating visual complexity levels in the human infant. *Child Development, 42,* 905–918.

Greenberg, D., Hillman, D., & Grice, D. (1973). Infant and stranger variables related to stranger anxiety in the first year of life. *Developmental Psychology, 9,* 207–212.

Greenberg, M., & Marvin, R. S. (1982). Reactions of preschool children to an adult stranger: A behavioral systems approach. *Child Development, 53,* 481–490.

Greenberg, M., & Morris, N. (1974). Engrossment: The newborn's impact upon the father. *American Journal of Orthopsychiatry, 44,* 520–531.

Greenberger, E., & Steinberg, L. (1981). The workplace as a context for the socialization of youth. *Journal of Youth and Adolescence, 10,* 185–210.

Greenberger, E., & Steinberg, L. (1983). Sex differences in early work experience: Harbinger of things to come? *Social Forces, 62,* 467–486.

Greenberger, E., & Steinberg, L. (1986). *When teenagers work: The psychologicial and social costs of adolescent employment.* New York: Basic Books.

Greenberger, E., Steinberg, L., & Ruggiero, M. (1982). A job is a job is a job . . . Or is it? Behavioral observations in the adolescent workplace. *Work and Occupations, 9,* 79–96.

Greenberger, E., Steinberg, L., & Vaux, A. (1981). Adolescents who work: Health and behavioral consequences of job stress. *Developmental psychology, 17,* 691–703.

Greenberger, E., Steinberg, L., Vaux, A., & McAuliffe, S. (1980). Adolescents who work: Effects of part-time employment on family and

peer relations. *Journal of Youth and Adolescence, 9,* 189–202.

Greenough, W., Black, J., & Wallace, C. (1987). Experience and brain development. *Child Development, 58,* 539–559.

Greer, D., Potts, R., Wright, J., & Huston, A. (1982). *Child Development, 53,* 611–619.

Grieser, T., & Kuhl, P. (1988). Maternal speech to infants in atonal language: Support for universal prosodic features in motherese. *Developmental Psychology, 24,* 14–20.

Grossman, K., & Grossman, K. E. (1982, March). *Maternal sensitivity to infants' signals during the first year as related to the year olds' behavior in Ainsworth's strange situation in a sample of Northern German families.* Paper presented at the International Conference on Infant Studies, Austin, TX.

Grossman, K., Grossman, K. E., Huber, F., & Wartner, U. (1981). German children's behavior towards their mothers at 12 months and their fathers at 18 months in Ainsworth's strange situation. *International Journal of Behavioral Development, 4,* 157–182.

Grossman, K., Grossman, K. E., Spangler, G., Suess, G., & Unzner, L. (1983). *Maternal sensitivity and newborns' responses as related to quality of attachment in Northern Germany.* Unpublished manuscript.

Grossman, K., Thane, K., & Grossman, K. E. (1981). Maternal tactual contact of the newborn after various postpartum conditions of mother-infant contact. *Developmental Psychology, 17,* 159–169.

Grotevant, H., and Cooper, C. (1986). Individuation in family relationships: A perspective on individual differences in the development of identity and role-taking skill in adolescence. *Human Development, 29,* 82–100.

Grotevant, H., & Cooper, C. (1988). The role of family experience in career exploration during adolescence. In P. Baltes, D. Featherman, & R. Lerner (Eds.), *Life-span development and behavior* (Vol. 8). Hillsdale, NJ: Erlbaum.

Grusec, J., & Kuczynski, L. (1980). Direction of effect in socialization: A comparison of the parent vs. the child's behavior as determinants of disciplinary techniques. *Developmental Psychology, 16,* 1–9.

Grusec, J., & Lytton, H. (1968). *Social development: History, theory and research.* New York: Springer-Verlag.

Grusec, J., & Lytton, H. (1988). *Social development.* New York: Springer-Verlag.

Guardo, C. J., & Bohan, J. B. (1971). Development of a sense of self in children. *Child Development, 42,* 1909–1921.

Guralnick, M. J., & Paul-Brown, D. (1977). The nature of verbal interactions among handicapped and non-handicapped preschool children. *Child Development, 48,* 254–260.

Gutmann, D. (1975). Parenthood: A key to the comparative study of the life cycle. In N. Datan & L. Ginsberg (Eds.), *Life-span developmental psychology: Normative life crisis.* New York: Academic Press.

Haan, N., Smith, M., & Block, J. (1968). Moral reasoning of young adults: Political-social behavior, family background, and personality correlates. *Journal of Personality of Social Psychology, 10,* 183–201.

Habicht, J., Yarbrough, C., Lectis, A., & Klein, R. (1974). Relation of maternal supplementary feeding during pregnancy to birth weight and other sociobiological factors. In M. Winick (Ed.), *Nutrition and fetal development* (pp. 127–145). New York: Wiley.

Hafetz, E. (1976). Parameters of sexual maturity in man. In E. Hafetz (Ed.), *Perspectives in human reproduction: Vol. 3. Sexual maturity: Physiological and clinical parameters.* Ann Arbor, MI: Ann Arbor Science Publishers.

Haith, M. (1978). Visual competence in early infancy. In R. Held, H. Leibowitz, & H. Teuber (Eds.), *Handbook of sensory physiology* (Vol. 8, pp. 311–356). New York: Springer-Verlag.

Haith, M., Bergman, T., & Moore, M. (1977). Eye contact and face scanning in early infancy. *Science, 198,* 853–855.

Haith, M., & Campos, J. (1977). Human infancy. In M. Rosenzweig & L.

Porter (Eds.), *Annual Review of Psychology, 28,* 251–293.

Hall, J. A., & Halberstadt, A. G. (1980). Masculinity and femininity in children: Development of the Children's Personal Attitude Questionnaire. *Developmental Psychology, 16,* 270–280.

Halliday, M. A. K. (1975). *Learning how to mean—Explorations in the development of language.* London: Edward Arnold.

Hallinan, M. (1981). Recent advances in sociometry. In S. Asher and J. Gottman (Eds.), *The development of children's friendships.* New York: Cambridge University Press.

Hanson, S., Myers, D., & Ginsburg, A. (1987). The role of responsibility and knowledge in reducing teenage out-of-wedlock childbearing. *Journal of Marriage and the Family, 49,* 241–256.

Hardy-Brown, K., Plomin, R., & DeFries, J. (1981). Genetic and environmental influences on the rate of communicative development in the first year of life. *Developmental Psychology, 17,* 704–717.

Harkness, D. (1987). *The infertility book.* San Francisco: Volcano Press.

Harlap, S., Shiono, P. H., & Ramcharan, S. (1979). Alcohol and spontaneous abortions. *American Journal of Epidemiology, 110,* 372.

Harlow, H. F., & Zimmermann, R. (1959). Affectional responses in the infant monkey. *Science, 130,* 421–432.

Harris, P. (1983). Infant cognition. In M. Harth & J. Campos (Eds.), *Handbook of child psychology: Vol. 2. Infancy and developmental psychology* (pp. 689–782).

Harter, S. (1982). Children's understanding of multiple emotions: A cognitive-developmental approach. In W. Overton (Ed.), *The relationship between social and cognitive development.* Hillsdale, NJ: Erlbaum.

Harter, S. (1983). Developmental perspectives on the self system. In E. M. Hetherington, (Ed.), *Handbook of child psychology: Vol. 4. Socialization, personality, and social development.* New York: Wiley.

Harter, S., & Connell, J. (1982). A comparison of alternative models of the relationships between academic

achievement and children's perceptions of competence, control, and motivational orientation. In J. Nicholls (Ed.), *The development of achievement-related cognitions and behaviors.* Greenwich, CT: JAI Press.

Hartmann, D. P. (1969). Influence of symbolically modelled instrumental aggression and pain cues on aggressive behavior. *Journal of Personality and Social Psychology, 11,* 280–288.

Hartup, W. (1977). Adolescent peer relations: A look to the future. In J. Hill & F. Monks (Eds.), *Adolescence and youth in prospect.* Guildford, England: IPC Press.

Hartup, W. (1983). Peer relations. In E. M. Hetherington (Ed.), *Handbook of child psychology: Vol. 4. Socialization, personality, and social development.* New York: Wiley.

Hartup, W., Moore, S. G., & Sager, G. (1963). Avoidance of inappropriate sex-typing by young children. *Journal of Consulting Psychology, 27,* 467–473.

Haskett, G. J. (1971). Modifications of peer preferences of first-grade children. *Developmental Psychology, 4,* 429–433.

Haskins, R. (1965). Public school agression among children with varying day-care experience. *Child Development, 56,* 689–703.

Haskins, R., & Kotch, J. (1986). Day care and illness: Evidence, costs, and public policy. *Pediatrics, 77,* 951–982.

Hay, D. F., & Rheingold, H. L. (1979). *The early appearance of some valued social behaviors.* Unpublished manuscript, State University of New York at Stony Brook.

Hayes, C. (Ed.). (1987). *Risking the future: Adolescent sexuality, pregnancy, and childbearing* (Vol. 1). Washington, DC: National Academy Press.

Hayes, D. S. (1978). Cognitive bases for liking and disliking among preschool children. *Child Development, 49,* 906–909.

Heckhausen, H. (1981). The development of achievement motivation. In W. Hartup (Ed.), *Review of child development research* (Vol. 6). Chicago: University of Chicago Press.

Herrenkohl, E. C., & Herrenkohl, R. C. (1981). Some antecedents and developmental consequences of child maltreatment. *New Directions for Child Development, 11,* 57–76.

Herskowitz, J. (1988). *Is your child depressed?* New York: Pharos Books.

Hess, R. D., & Camera, K. A. (1979). Post-divorce family relationships as mediating factors in the consequences of divorce for children. *Journal of Social Issues, 35,* 79–96.

Hess, R. D., Price, G. G., Dickson, W. P., & Conroy, M. (1981). Different roles for mothers and teachers: Contrasting styles of child care. In S. Kilmer (Ed.), *Advances in early education and day care.* Greenwich, CT: JAI Press.

Hetherington, E. M. (1967). Effects of paternal absence on sex-typed behavior in Negro and white preadolescent males. *Journal of Personality and Social Psychology, 4,* 87–91.

Hetherington, E. M. (1972). Effects of father absence on personality development in adolescent daughters. *Developmental Psychology, 7,* 313–326.

Hetherington, E. M. (1981). Children and divorce. In R. Henderson (Ed.), *Parent-child interaction: Theory, research, and prospects.* New York: Academic Press.

Hetherington, E. M. (1979). Divorce: A child's perspective. *American Psychologist, 34,* 851.

Hetherington, E. M. (1989). Coping with family transitions: Winners, losers, and survivors. *Child Development, 60,* 1–14.

Hetherington, E. M., & Camara, K. (1984). Families in transition: The processes of dissolution and reconstitution. In R. Parke (Ed.), *Review of child development research* (Vol. 7). Chicago: University of Chicago Press.

Hetherington, E. M., Cox, M., & Cox, R. (1978a). The aftermath of divorce. In J. H. Stevens, Jr., & M. Matthew (Eds.), *Mother-child, father-child relations.* Washington, DC: National Association for the Education of Young Children.

Hetherington, E. M., Cox, M., & Cox, R. (1978b, May). *Family interaction and social, emotional and cognitive development of children following divorce.* Paper presented at the Symposium on the Family: Setting Priorities, sponsored by the Institute for Pedi-

atric Service of the Johnson & Johnson Baby Company, Washington, DC.

Hetherington, E. M., Cox, M., & Cox, R. (1979). Play and social interaction in children following divorce. *Journal of Social Issues, 35,* 26–49.

Hetherington, E. M., Cox, M., & Cox, R. (1982). Effects of divorce on parents and children. In M. Lamb (Ed.), *Nontraditional families.* Hillsdale, NJ: Erlbaum.

Hetherington, E. M., & Parke, R. (1978). *Child psychology* (2nd ed.). New York: McGraw-Hill.

Heyns, B. (1982). *Summer learning and the effects of schooling.* New York: Academic Press.

Hill, J. (1980). The family. In M. Johnson (Ed.), *Toward adolescence: The middle school years.* Chicago: University of Chicago Press.

Hill, J., & Holmbeck, G. (1986). Attachment and autonomy during adolescence. In G. Whitehurst (Ed.), *Annals of child development.* Greenwich, CT: JAI Press.

Hill, J., Holmbeck, G., Marlow, L., Green, T., & Lynch, M. (1985a). Pubertal status and parent-child relations in families of seventh-grade boys. *Journal of Early Adolescence, 5,* 31–44.

Hill, J., Holmbeck, G., Marlow, L., Green, T., & Lynch, M. (1985b). Menarcheal status and parent-child relations in families of seventh-grade boys. *Journal of Youth and Adolescence, 14,* 301–316.

Hill, J., & Lynch, M. (1983). The intensification of gender-related role expectations during early adolescence. In J. Brooks-Gunn & A. Petersen (Eds.), *Female puberty.* New York: Plenum.

Hill, J., & Palmquist, W. (1978). Social cognition and social relations in early adolescence. *International Journal of Behavioral Development, 1,* 1–36.

Hill, J., & Steinberg, L. (1976). *The development of autonomy during adolescence.* Paper presented at the Symposium on Research on Youth Problems Today, Fundacion Faustino Orbegoza Eizaguirre, Madrid.

Hillard, P. (1983). Nutrition and pregnancy. *Parents,* 92–94.

Hirsch, H., & Spinelli, D. (1970). Visual

experience modifies distribution of horizontally and vertically oriented receptive field in cats. *Science, 168,* 869–871.

Hobbs, D. (1965). Parenthood as crisis: A third study. *Journal of Marriage and the Family, 27,* 677–689.

Hobbs, D., Wimbish, J. (1977). Transition to parenthood by black couples. *Journal of Marriage and the Family, 39,* 677–689.

Hodgson, J., & Fischer, J. (1979). Sex differences in identity and intimacy development in college youth. *Journal of Youth and Adolescence, 8,* 37–50.

Hofer, M. (1981). *The roots of human behavior.* San Francisco: Freeman.

Hofferth, S., & Phillips, D. (1987). Child care in the United States, 1970–1995. *Journal of Marriage and the Family, 49,* 559–571.

Hoffman, L. W. (1963). Mother's enjoyment of work and effects on the child. In F. I. Nye and L. W. Hoffman (Eds.), *The employed mother in America.* Chicago: Rand McNally.

Hoffman, L. W. (1974). Effects of maternal employment on the child: A review of the research. *Developmental Psychology, 10,* 204–228.

Hoffman, L. W. (1977). Changes in family roles, socialization, and sex differences. *American Psychologist, 32,* 644–657.

Hoffman, L. W. (1979). Maternal employment. *American Psychologist, 34,* 859–865.

Hoffman, L. W. (1983). Work, family, and the socialization of the child. In R. Parke (Ed.), *Review of child development research: Vol. 7. The family.* Chicago: University of Chicago Press.

Hoffman, M. L. (1970). Moral development. In P. H. Mussen (Ed.), *Carmichael's manual of child psychology* (Vol. 2). New York: Wiley.

Hoffman, M. L. (1980). Moral development in adolescence. In J. Adelson (Ed.), *Handbook of adolescent psychology.* New York: Wiley.

Hoffman-Plotkin, D., & Twentyman, C. T. (1984). A multimodal assessment of behavioral and cognitive deficits in abused and neglected preschoolers. *Child Development, 55,* 794–802.

Hollingshead, A. (1975). *Elmtown's youth*

and *Elmtown revisited.* New York: Wiley. (Original work published 1949.)

Holstein, C. (1972). The relation of children's moral judgment level to that of their parents and to communication patterns in the family. In R. Smart and M. Smart (Eds.), *Readings in child development and relationships.* New York: Macmillan.

Hook, E., & Lindsjo, A. (1978). Down syndrome in live births by single-year maternal age interval in a Swedish study. *American Journal of Human Genetics, 30,* 19.

Hoopes, J. (1982). *Prediction in child development: A longitudinal study of adoptive and nonadoptive families.* New York: Child Welfare League of America.

Hopkins, J., Marcus, M., & Campbell, S. (1984). Postpartum depression: A critical review. *Psychological Bulletin, 45,* 498–515.

Horwitz, R. A. (1979). Psychological effects of the "open classroom." *Review of Educational Research, 49,* 71–86.

Howard, J. (1978). The influence of children's developmental dysfunctions on marital quality and family interaction. In R. Lerner & G. Spanier (Eds.), *Child influence on marital and family interaction.* New York: Academic Press.

Howe, M. L., Brainerd, C. J., & Kingma, J. (1985). Development of organization in recall: A stages-of-learning analysis. *Journal of Experimental Child Psychology, 39,* 230–251.

Howes, C. (1987). Social competence with peers in young children: Developmental sequences. *Developmental Review, 7,* 252–272.

Huesmann, L. R., Lagerspetz, K., & Eron, L. D. (1984). Intervening variables in the TV violence-aggression relation: Evidence from two countries. *Developmental Psychology, 20,* 746–775.

Huizinga, D., & Elliot, D. (1985). *Juvenile offenders prevalence, offender incidence, and arrest rates by race.* Boulder, CO: Institute of Behavioral Science.

Humphrey, M., & Kirkwood, R. (1982). Marital relationship among adopters. *Adoption and Fostering, 6,* 44–48.

Hunt, J. M. (1970). Attentional preference and experience: 1. Introduction. *Journal of Genetic Psychology, 117,* 99–107.

Hunter, F., & Youniss, J. (1982). Changes in functions of three relations during adolescence. *Developmental Psychology, 18,* 806–811.

Huston, A. (1983). Sex typing. In E. M. Hetherington (Ed.), *Handbook of child psychology: Vol. 4. Socialization, personality, and social development* (pp. 387–467). New York: Wiley.

Huston, A. (1985). *Television and human behavior.* Paper presented at Science and Social Policy Seminar, Federation of Behavioral, Psychological and Cognitive Sciences, Washington, DC.

Hyde, J. (1981). How large are cognitive gender differences? *American Psychologist, 36,* 892–901.

Irwin, C. (1986). Biopsychosocial correlates of risk-taking behaviors during adolescence: Can the physician intervene? *Journal of Adolescent Health Care, 7,* 82–96.

Irwin, O. (1947). Infant speech: Consonant sounds according to the manner of articulation. *Journal of Speech Disorders, 12,* 397–401.

Isabella, C., Belsky, J., & von Eye, A. (1989). The origins of infant-mother attachment: An examination of interactional synchrony during the infant's first year. *Developmental Psychology, 25,* 12–21.

Isabella, R., & Belsky, J. (1985). Marital change during the transition to parenthood and the security of infant-parent attachment. *Journal of Family Issues, 6,* 505–522.

Izard, C. E. (1971). *The face of emotion.* New York: Appleton-Century-Crofts.

Izard, C. E. (1978). On the ontogenesis of emotions and emotion-cognition relationships in infancy. In M. Lewis & L. Rosenblum (Eds.), *The development of affect.* New York: Plenum.

Izard, C. E., Hembree, E., Dougherty, L., & Coss, C. (1983). Changes in two- to nineteen-month-old infants' facial expressions following acute pain. *Developmental Psychology, 19,* 418–426.

Jacob, T. (1974). Patterns of family conflict and dominance as a function of child age and social class. *Developmental Psychology, 10,* 1–12.

Jacobsen, J., & Willie, D. (1984). Influence of attachment and separation experience on separation distress at 18 months. *Developmental Psychology, 20,* 477–484.

Jacobson, J. L., Boersman, D., Fields, R., and Olson, K. (1983). Paralinguistic features of adult speech to infants and small children. *Child Development, 54,* 436–442.

Jacobson, J. L., Jacobson, S. W., Fein, G. G., & Schwartz, P. M. (1984). Factors and clusters for the Brazelton Scale: An investigation of the dimensions of neonatal behavior. *Developmental Psychology, 20,* 339–353.

Jacobson, S. (1983, April). *Maternal caffeine consumption prior to pregnancy.* Paper presented at the biennial meetings of the Society for Research in Child Development, Detroit, MI.

Jensen, A. R. (1969). How much can we boost IQ and scholastic achievement? *Harvard Educational Review, 39,* 1–123.

Jessor, R., & Jessor, S. (1977). *Problem behavior and psychosocial development: A longitudinal study of youth.* New York: Academic Press.

Jessor, R., Costa, F., Jessor, L., & Donovan, J. (1983). Time of first intercourse: A prospective study. *Journal of Personality and Social Psychology, 44,* 608–626.

Johns, J. (1984). Student's perceptions of reading: Insights from research and pedagogical implications. In J. Downing & R. Valtin (Eds.), *Language awareness and learning to read* (pp. 57–77). New York: Springer-Verlag.

Johnson, B., & Morse, H. A. (1968). Injured children and their parents. *Children, 15,* 147–152.

Johnson, B., & Uppal, G. (1980). Marihuana and youth: A generation gone to pot. In F. Scarpitti and S. Datesman (Eds.), *Drugs and the youth culture.* Beverly Hills, CA: Sage.

Johnson, D. (1990, January 4). Teenagers who won't join when drug dealers recruit. *The New York Times,* pp. A1, A20.

Johnson, D. L., & Breckenridge, J. N. (1982). The Houston Parent-Child

Development Center and the primary prevention of behavior problems in young children. *American Journal of Community Psychology, 10,* 305–316.

Johnson, D. L., & McGowan, R. J. (1984). Comparison of three intelligence tests as predictors of academic achievement and classroom behaviors of Mexican-Indian children. *Journal of Psychoeducational Assessment, 2,* 345–352.

Johnson, D. L., & Walker, T. (1987). Primary prevention of behavior problems in Mexican-American children. *American Journal of Community Psychology, 15,* 375–385.

Johnson, J. (1989, July 19). Bush administration seeks policy that will reduce infant deaths. *The New York Times,* p. D24.

Johnson, W., Emde, R. N., Pannabecker, B., Stenberg, C., & Davis, M. (1982). Maternal perception of infant emotion from birth through 18 months. *Infant Behavior and Development, 5,* 313–322.

Johnston, L., O'Malley, P., and Bachman, J. (1986). *Drug use among American high school students, college students, and other young adults: National trends through 1985.* Washington, DC: National Institute on Drug Abuse.

Jones, E. (1963). *The life and work of Sigmund Freud.* New York: Anchor Books.

Jones, E., Forrest, J., Goldman, N., Henshaw, S., Lincoln, R., Rosoff, J., Westhoff, C., & Wulf, D. (1985). Teenage pregnancy in developed countries; Determinants and policy implications. *Family Planning Perspectives, 17,* 53–63.

Jones, H. (1949). Adolescence in our society. In *The Family in a democratic society* (Anniversary papers of the Community Service Society of New York). New York: Columbia University Press.

Jones, M. C. (1957). The later careers of boys who were early- or late-maturing. *Child Development, 28,* 113–128.

Jones, M. C. (1965). Psychological correlates of somatic development. *Child Development, 36,* 899–911.

Jones, M. C., & Bayley, N. (1950). Physical maturing among boys as related to behavior. *Journal of Educational Psychology, 41,* 129–148.

Jones, M. C., & Mussen, P. (1958). Self-conceptions, motivations, and interpersonal attitudes of early- and late-maturing girls. *Child Development, 29,* 491–501.

Josselson, R. (1980). Ego development in adolescence. In J. Adelson (Ed.), *Handbook of adolescent psychology.* New York: Wiley.

Juel, C., Griffith, P., & Gough, P. (1986). The acquisition of literacy: A longitudinal study of children in first and second grades. *Journal of Educational Psychology, 78,* 243–255.

Julien, R. (1981). *A primer of drug action* (3rd ed.). San Francisco: Freeman.

Kacerguis, M., & Adams, G. (1980). Erikson's stage resolution: The relationship between identity and intimacy. *Journal of Youth and Adolescence, 9,* 117–126.

Kach, J., & McGhee, P. (1982). Adjustment to early parenthood: The role of accuracy of preparenthood expectations. *Journal of Family Issues, 3,* 361–374.

Kagan, J. (1967). The growth of the "face" schema: Theoretical significance and methodological issues. In J. Hellmuth (Ed.), *The exceptional infant: Vol. 1. The normal infant.* New York: Bruner/Mazel.

Kagan, J. (1976). Emergent themes in human development. *American Scientist, 64,* 186–196.

Kagan, J. (1978). On emotion and its development: A working paper. In M. Lewis & L. Rosenblum (Eds.), *The development of affect.* New York: Plenum.

Kagan, J. (1982). *Psychological research on the human infant: An evaluative summary.* NY 4: Grant Foundation.

Kagan, J., & Coles, R. (Eds.). (1972). *Twelve to sixteen: Early adolescence.* New York: Norton.

Kagan, J., Kearsley, R., & Zelazo, P. R. (1978). *Infancy: Its place in human development.* Cambridge, MA: Harvard University Press.

Kail, R. V., Jr. (1984). *The development of memory in children* (2nd ed.). San Francisco: Freeman.

Kallen, D., & Stephenson, J. (1982). Talking about sex revisited. *Journal of Youth and Adolescence, 11,* 11–24.

Kamerman, Sheila B. (1980). *Maternity and parental benefits and leaves: An international review.* New York: Center for Social Sciences, Columbia University.

Kaminski, M., Rumeau, C., & Schwartz, D. (1978). Alcohol consumption in pregnant women and the outcome of pregnancy. *Alcoholism: Clinical and Experimental Research, 2,* 155–163.

Kandel, D. (1978). Homophily, selection, and socialization in adolescent friendships. *American Journal of Sociology, 84,* 427–436.

Kandel, D., & Lesser, G. (1972). *Youth in two worlds.* San Francisco: Jossey-Bass.

Kaplan, L. (1983). *Coping with peer pressure.* New York: Rosen.

Karzon, R. (1985). Discrimination of polysyllabic sequences by 1- to 4-month-old infants. *Journal of Experimental Child Psychology, 39,* 326–342.

Katchadourian, H. (in press). Sexuality. In S. Feldman and G. Elliott (Eds.), *At the threshold: The developing adolescent.* Cambridge, MA: Harvard University Press.

Katz, M. (1975). *The people of Hamilton, Canada West: Family and class in a mid-nineteenth century city.* Cambridge, MA: Harvard University Press.

Katz, P. (1987). Variations in family constellation: Effects of gender schemata. In L. Liben & M. Signorella (Eds.), *Children's gender schemata: New directions in child development research* (No. 38). San Francisco: Jossey-Bass.

Katz, V. (1971). Auditory stimulation and developmental behavior of the premature infant. *Nursing Research, 20,* 196–201.

Kaufman, J., & Cicchetti, D. (1989). The effects of maltreatment on school-age children's socioemotional development. *Developmental Psychology.*

Kaufman, J., & Zigler, E. (1987). Do abused children become abusive parents? *American Journal of Orthopsychiatry, 57,* 186–197.

Keating, D. (1980). Thinking processes in adolescence. In J. Adelson (Ed.), *Handbook of adolescent psychology.* New York: Wiley.

Keating, D. (in press). Cognitive development. In S. Feldman and G. Elliott (Eds.), *At the threshold: The developing adolescent.* Cambridge, MA: Harvard University Press.

Kellogg, R. (1970). *Analyzing children's art.* Mountain View, CA: Mayfield.

Kemper, T., & Reichler, M. (1976). Fathers' work integration and frequencies of rewards and punishments administered by fathers and mothers to adolescent sons and daughters. *Journal of Genetic Psychology, 129,* 207–219.

Keniston, K. (1970). Youth: A "new" stage of life. *American Scholar, 39,* 631–641.

Kennedy, W. (1971). *Child psychology.* Englewood Cliffs, NJ: Prentice-Hall.

Kennell, J., Jerauld, L., Wolf, P., Chesler, R., Kreger, N., McAlpine, W., Steffa, M., & Kennell, J. (1974). Maternal behavior one year after early and extended post-partum contact. *Developmental Medicine and Child Neurology, 16,* 172.

Kennell, J., & Klaus, M. H. (1976). Caring for parents of a premature or sick infant. In M. H. Klaus & J. H. Kennell (Eds.), *Maternal-infant bonding.* St. Louis: Mosby.

Kerr, M., Begues, J., & Kerr, D. (1978). Psychosocial functioning of mothers of malnourished children. *Pediatrics, 62,* 778–784.

Kessen, W. (1979). The American child and other cultural inventions. *American Psychologist, 34,* 815–820.

Kett, J. (1977). *Rites of passage: Adolescence in America, 1790 to the present.* New York: Basic Books.

Kilbride, J. E. (1977). Mother-infant interaction and infant sensorimotor development among the Baganda of Uganda. *Dissertation Abstracts International, 37,* (10-B), 5326–5327.

Kirchner, G., & Knopf, I. (1974). Differences in the vigilance performance of second-grade children as related to sex and achievement. *Child Development, 45,* 490–495.

Kitzinger, S. (1972). *The experience of childbirth.* London: Victor Gollancz.

Kitzinger, S. (1985). *The complete book of pregnancy and childbirth.* New York: Knopf.

Klaus, M., Jerauld, R., Kreger, N., McAlpine, W., Steffa, M., & Kennell, J. (1972). Maternal attachment: Importance of the first postpartum days. *New England Journal of Medicine, 286,* 460–463.

Kohlberg, L. (1966). A cognitive-developmental analysis of children's sex-role concepts and attitudes. In E. E. Maccoby (Ed.), *The development of sex differences* (pp. 82–172). Stanford, CA: Stanford University Press.

Kohlberg, L. (1969). Stage and sequence: The cognitive-developmental approach to socialization. In D. Goslin (Ed.), *Handbook of socialization theory and research.* Chicago: Rand McNally.

Kohlberg, L., & Gilligan, C. (1972). The adolescent as philosopher: The discovery of the self in a postconventional world. In J. Kagan and R. Coles (Eds.), *Twelve to sixteen: Early adolescence.* New York: Norton.

Kohn, M. (1977). Social competence, symptoms and underachievement in childhood: A longitudinal perspective. Washington, DC: Winston.

Kolata, G. (1986). Obese children. *Science, 232,* 20–21.

Kolata, G. (1989a, October 8). AIDS is spreading in teen-agers, a new trend alarming to experts. *The New York Times,* pp. 1, 30.

Kolata, G. (1989b, August 11). In cities, poor families are dying of crack. *The New York Times,* pp. A1, A13.

Koop, C. E. (1984). Keynote address. I. *Report of the Surgeon General's Workshop on Breastfeeding and Human Lactation.* Washington, DC. Dept. of Health & Human Services, pp. 3–5.

Korner, A. (1974). The effect of infant's state, level of arousal, sex, and autogenic stage on the caretakers. In M. Lewis & L. Rosenblum (Eds.), *Effect of the infant on the caregiver.* New York: Wiley.

Korner, A., & Grobstein, R. (1967). Individual differences at birth: Implications for mother-infant relationship and development. *Journal of the American Academy of Child Psychiatry, 6,* 676–690.

Korner, A., Kaemer, H., Hoffner, M., & Thoman, E. (1974). Characteristics of crying and noncrying activity in full-term neonates. *Child Development, 45,* 953–958.

Korner, A., & Thoman, E. (1972). The relative efficacy of contact and vestibular-proprioceptive stimulation in soothing neonates. *Child Development, 43,* 443–453.

Korner, A., Zeanah, C., Lindin, J., Berkowitz, R., Krapmen, H., & Agras, W. (1985). The relation between neonatal and later activity and temperament. *Child Development, 56,* 38–42.

Kotelchuck, M. (1975, September). *Father caretaking characteristics and their influence on infant-father interaction.* Paper presented to the American Psychological Association, Chicago.

Kotelchuck, M., Schwartz, J., Anderka, M., & Finison, K. (1984). WIC participation and pregnancy outcomes: Massachusetts Statewide Evaluation Project. *American Journal of Public Health, 74,* 10–14.

Kramer, M., Barr, R., Leduc, M., Boisjoly, C., McVey-White, L., & Pless, I. (1985). Determinants of weight and adiposity in the first year of life. *Journal of Pediatrics, 106,* 10–14.

Krauss, R., & Glucksberg, S. (1969). The development of communication: Competence as a function of age. *Child Development, 40,* 255–266.

Krauss, R., & Glucksberg, S. (1977). Social and nonsocial speech. *Scientific American, 236,* 100–105.

Kreppner, K., Paulsen, S., & Schuetze, Y. (1981). *Infant and family development: From triads to tetrads.* Paper presented at the International Society for the Study of Behavioral Development, Toronto.

Kreutzer, M. A., Leonard, C., & Flavell, J. H. (1975). An interview study of children's knowledge about memory. *Monographs of the Society for Research in Child Development, 40* (Serial No. 159).

Krisberg, B., Schwartz, I., Fishman, G., Eisikovits, Z., & Guttman, E. (1986). *The incarceration of minority youth.* Minneapolis: Hubert H. Humphrey Institute of Public Affairs, National Council on Crime and Delinquency.

Kuczja, S. A. (1978). Children's judgments of grammatical and ungrammatical irregular past-time verbs. *Child Development, 49,* 319–326.

Kuczynski, L. (1984). Socialization goals and mother-child interaction: Strategies for long-term and short-term compliance. *Developmental Psychology, 20,* 1061–1073.

Kuhn, D., Langer, J., Kohlberg, L., & Haan, N. (1977). The development of formal operations in logical and moral judgment. *Genetic Psychology Monographs, 95,* 97–188.

Ladd, G., & Asher, S. (1985). Social skill training and children's peer relations. In L. L'Abate & M. Milan (Eds.), *Handbook of social skill training* (pp. 219–244). New York: Wiley.

LaFreniere, P., Strayer, F., & Gauthier, R. (1984). The emergence of same-sex preferences among preschool peers. *Child Development, 55,* 1958–1965.

Lamb, M. E. (1976). The role of the father: An overview. In M. E. Lamb (Ed.), *The role of the father in child development.* New York: Wiley.

Lamb, M. E. (1977). Father-infant and mother-infant interaction in the first year of life. *Child Development, 48,* 167–181.

Lamb, M. E. (1977). The development of mother-infant and father-infant attachments in the second year of life. *Developmental Psychology, 13,* 631–648.

Lamb, M. E. (1977). The development of parental preferences in the first two years of life. *Sex Roles, 3,* 495–497.

Lamb, M. E. (1978a). Influence of the child on marital quality and family interaction during the parental, perinatal, and infancy periods. In R. Lerner & G. Spanier (Eds.), *Child influences on marital and family interaction: A life-span perspective.* New York: Academic Press.

Lamb, M. E. (1978b). The development of sibling relationships in infancy: A short-term longitudinal study. *Child Development, 49,* 1189–1197.

Lamb, M. E. (1981). The development of father-infant relationships. In M. E. Lamb (Ed.), *The role of the father in child development.* New York: Wiley.

Lamb, M. E., & Bornstein, M. H. (1987). *Development in infancy: An introduction* (2nd ed.). New York: Random House.

Lamb, M. E., & Easterbrooks, M. (1980). Individual differences in parental sensitivity. In M. E. Lamb & L. Sherrod (Eds.), *Infant social cognition.* Hillsdale, NJ: Erlbaum.

Lamb, M. E., Frodi, A., Frodi, M., & Hwang, C. (1982). Characteristics of maternal and paternal behavior in traditional and nontraditional Swedish families. *International Journal of Behavioral Development, 5,* 131–141.

Lamb, M. E., Frodi, A., Hwang, C., Frodi, M., & Steinberg, J. (1982a). Mother- and father-infant interaction involving play and holding in traditional and nontraditional Swedish families. *Developmental Psychology, 18,* 215–221.

Lamb, M. E., Frodi, A., Hwang, C., Frodi, M., & Steinberg, J. (1982b). The effects of gender and caretaking role on parent-infant interaction. In R. Emde & R. Harmon (Eds.), *Development of attachment and affiliative systems.* New York: Plenum.

Lamb, M. E., & Hwang, C. (1982). Maternal attachment and mother neonate bonding: A critical review. In M. E. Lamb & A. Brown (Eds.), *Advances in developmental psychology* (Vol. 2). Hillsdale, NJ: Erlbaum.

Lamb, M. E., Hwang, C., Frodi, A., & Frodi, M. (1982). Security of mother- and father-infant attachment and its relation to sociability with strangers in traditional and nontraditional Swedish families. *Infant Behavior and Development, 5,* 355–367.

Lambert, N., & Hartsough, C. (1984). Contribution of predispositional factors to the diagnosis of hyperactivity. *American Journal of Orthopsychiatry, 54,* 97–109.

Lambert, N., Sandoval, J., & Sassone, D. (1978). Prevalence of hyperactivity in elementary school children as a function of social system definers. *American Journal of Orthopsychiatry, 48,* 446–463.

Landesman-Dwyer, S. (1981). Drinking during pregnancy: Effects on human development. *Alcohol and health* (Vol. 4 Monograph Series).

Landesman-Dwyer, S., & Emmanuel, I. (1979). Smoking during pregnancy. *Teratology,* 119–126.

Landesman-Dwyer, S., Keller, L. S., & Steissguth, A. P. (1978). Naturalistic observations of newborns: Effects of maternal alcohol intake. *Alcoholism: Clinical and Experimental Research, 2,* 171–177.

Landesman-Dwyer, S., Ragozin, A. S., & Little, R. E. (1982). Behavioral correlates of prenatal alcohol exposure: A four-year follow-up study. *Neurobehavioral Toxicology and Teratology, 46,* 24–38.

Langlois, H. H., & Stephan, C. (1977). The effects of physical attractiveness and ethnicity on children's behavioral attributions and peer preferences. *Child Development, 48,* 1694–1698.

Langlois, J., & Downs, A. (1980). Mothers, fathers, and peers as socialization agents of sex-typed play behaviors in young children. *Child Development, 51,* 1237–1247.

Langlois, J., Rossman, L., Casey, R., Ritter, J., Reiser-Danner, L., & Jenkins, V. (1987). Infant preference for attractive faces: Rudiments of a stereotype. *Developmental Psychology, 23,* 363–369.

Larsen, O. N., Gray, L. N., & Fortis, J. G. (1968). Achieving goals through violence on television. In O. N. Larsen (Ed.), *Violence and the mass media.* New York: Harper & Row.

Latkin, M. (1957). Personality factors in mothers of excessively crying (colicky) infants. *Monographs for the Society for Research in Child Development, 22,* No. 64.

Lazar, I., & Darlington, R. (1982). Lasting effects of early education: A report from the Consortium of Longitudinal Studies. *Monographs of the Society for Research in Child Development, 47* (2–3, Serial No. 195).

Leach, P. (1980). *Your baby and child from birth to age five.* New York: Alfred Knopf.

Leacock, E. B. (1969). *Teaching and learning in city schools.* New York: Basic.

LeBoyer, F. (1975). *Birth without violence.* New York: Random House.

Lebra, T. S. (1976). *Japanese patterns of behaviour.* Honolulu: University of Hawaii Press.

Lee, K., Paneth, N., Gartner, L., Pearlman, M., & Gruss, L. (1980). Neonatal mortality: An analysis of recent improvements in the United States. *American Journal of Public Health, 70,* 15–21.

Lee, R. V. (1973, September 16). What about the right to say "no"? *The New York Times Magazine.*

Lee, V., Brooks-Gunn, J., & Schnur, E. (1988). Does Head Start Work? A

1-year follow-up comparison of disadvantaged children attending Head Start, no preschool, and other preschool programs. *Developmental Psychology, 24,* 210–222.

Leifer, Collins, Gross, Taylor, Andrews, and Blackmer (1970). Developmental aspects of variables relevant to observational learning. *Child Development.*

Lempers, J. D., Flavell, E. R., & Flavell, J. H. (1977). The development in very young children of tacit knowledge concerning visual perceptions. *Genetic Psychology Monographs, 95,* 3–53.

Lenneberg, E. H. (1967). *Biological foundations of language.* New York: Wiley.

Lenssen, B. G. (1973). Infants' reactions to peer strangers. *Dissertation Abstracts International, 33,* 6062.

Lerner, R. (1986). *On the nature of human plasticity.* New York: Cambridge University Press.

Lerner, R. M., & Lerner, J. V. (1977). Effects of age, sex, and physical attractiveness on child-peer relations, academic performance, and elementary school adjustment. *Developmental Psychology, 13,* 585–590.

Lester, B. M. (1975). Cardiac habituation of the orienting response in infants of varying nutritional status. *Developmental Psychology, 11,* 432–442.

Lester, B. M. (1979). A synergistic process approach to the study of prenatal malnutrition. *International Journal of Behavioral Development, 2,* 377–394.

Lester, B. M., Kotelchuck, M., Spelke, E., Sellers, M. J., & Klein, R. E. (1974). Separation protest in Guatemalan infants: Cross-cultural and cognitive findings. *Developmental Psychology, 10,* 79–85.

Lester, B. M., & Zeskind, P. (1982). A biobehavioral perspective on crying in early infancy. In H. Fitzgerald, B. Lester, & M. Yogman (Eds.), *Theory and research in behavioral pediatrics* (Vol. 1). New York: Plenum.

Lever, J. (1976). Sex differences in the games children play. *Social Problems, 23,* 479–487.

Levin, S., Petros, T., & Petralla, F. (1982). Preschoolers' awareness of television advertising. *Child Development, 53,* 933–937.

Levine, J., Fishman, C., & Kagan, J. (1967). Social class and sex as determinants of maternal behavior. *American Journal of Orthopsychiatry, 37,* 397–406.

Levine, L. E. (1983). Mine: Self-definition in 2-year-old boys. *Developmental Psychology, 19,* 544–549.

Levitsky, D. A. (1979). *Malnutrition, environment, and behavior.* Ithaca, NY: Cornell University Press.

Lewak, N., Zebal, B. H., & Friedman, S. B. (1984). Management of infants with apnea and potential apnea: A survey of pediatric opinion. Special Issue: Pulmonary disease. *Clinical Pediatrics, 23,* 369–373.

Lewin-Epstein, N. (1981). *Youth employment during high school.* Washington, DC: National Center for Education Statistics.

Lewis, C. C. (1981). The effects of parental firm control: A reinterpretation of findings. *Psychological Bulletin, 90,* 547–563.

Lewis, M., & Brooks, J. (1974). Self, other, and fear: Infants' reactions to people. In M. Lewis & L. A. Rosenblum (Eds.), *The origins of fear.* New York: Wiley.

Lewis, M., & Brooks, J. (1978). Self-knowledge and emotional development. In M. Lamb & L. A. Rosenblum (Eds.), *The development of affect.* New York: Plenum.

Lewis, M., & Feiring, C. (1978). The child's social world. In R. Lerner & G. Spanier (Eds.), *Child influences on marital and family interaction.* New York: Academic Press.

Lewis, M., Feiring, C., McGuffog, C., & Jaskir, J. (1984). Predicting psychopathology in six-year-olds from early social relations. *Child Development, 55,* 123–136.

Lewis, M., & Goldberg, W. (1969). Perceptual-cognitive development in infancy: A generalized expectancy model as a function of the mother-infant relationship. *Merrill-Palmer Quarterly, 15,* 81–100.

Lewis, M., & Michalson, L. (1983). *Children's emotions and moods.* New York: Plenum.

Lewis, M., & Schaeffer, S. (1979). Peer behavior and mother-infant interaction in maltreated children. In M. Lewis & L. A. Rosenblum (Eds.), *The uncommon child.* New York: Penguin.

Lewis, M., & Weinraub, M. (1976). The father's role in the child's social network. In M. Lamb (Ed.), *The role of the father in child development.* New York: Wiley.

Lewis, M., & Wilson, C. D. (1972). Infant development in lower-class American families. *Human Development, 15,* 112–127.

Lewis, M., Young, G., Brooks, J., & Michalson, L. (1975). The beginning of friendship. In M. Lewis & L. A. Rosenblum (Eds.), *Friendship and peer relations.* New York: Wiley.

Liben, L., & Bigler, R. (1987). Reformulating children's gender schemata. In L. Liben & M. Signorella (Eds.), *Children's gender schemata. New Directions in Child Development* (No. 38). San Francisco: Jossey-Bass.

Licht, B. G., & Dweck, C. S. (1984). Determinants of academic achievement: The interaction of children's achievement orientations with skill area. *Developmental Psychology, 20*(4), 628–636.

Lieberman, A. F. (1977). Preschoolers' competence with a peer: Relations with attachment and peer experience. *Child Development, 48,* 1277–1287.

Light, H., & Fenster, C. (1974). Maternal concerns during pregnancy. *American Journal of Obstetrics and Gynecology, 118,* 46–50.

Light, R. (1973). Abuse and neglected children in America: A study of alternative policies. *Harvard Educational Review, 43,* 556–598.

Lightfoot, S. (1983). *The good high school.* New York: Basic Books.

Lipsitt, L. B. (1979). Infants at risk: Perinatal & neonatal factors. *International Journal of Behavioral Development, 2,* 23–42.

Lipsitz, J. (1977). *Growing up forgotten.* Lexington, MA: Lexington Books.

Littenberg, R., Tulkin, S., & Kagan, J. (1971). Cognitive components of separation anxiety. *Developmental Psychology, 4,* 387–388.

Livesley, W., and Bromley, D. (1973). *Person perception in childhood and adolescence.* New York: Wiley.

Livson, N., & Peskin, H. (1980). Perspectives on adolescence from longitudinal research. In J. Adelson (Ed.), *Handbook of adolescent psychology.* New York: Wiley.

Lloyd, D. (1978). Prediction of school failure from third-grade data. *Educational and Psychological Measurement, 38*, 1193–1200.

Loeber, R., & Stouthamer-Loeber, M. (1986). Family factors as correlates and predictors of juvenile conduct problems and delinquency. In M. Tonry & N. Morris (Eds.), *Crime and justice* (Vol. 7). Chicago: University of Chicago Press.

Loeb, R. C., Horst, L., & Horton, P. J. (1980). Family interaction patterns associated with self-esteem in preadolescent girls and boys. *Merrill-Palmer Quarterly, 26*, 203–217.

Lomax, R. G., & McGee, L. M. (1987). Young children's concept about print and reading: Toward a model of word reading acquisition. *Reading Research Quarterly, 22*, 237–256.

Londerville, S., & Main, M. (1981). Security of attachment, compliance, and maternal training methods. *Developmental Psychology, 17*, 289–299.

Long, N., & Forehand, R. (1987). The effects of parental divorce and parental conflict on children: An overview. *Developmental and Behavioral Pediatrics, 8*, 292–297.

Lowrey, G. H. (1978). *Growth and development of children* (7th ed.). Chicago: Medical Year Book.

Luria, A. R. (1961). *The role of speech in the regulation of normal and abnormal behaviour*. New York: Pergamon.

Luster, T., Rhoades, K., & Haas, B. (1989). The relation between parental values and parenting behavior. *Journal of Marriage and the Family, 51*, 139–147.

Lyle, J., & Hoffman, H. (1972). Explorations in patterns of television viewing by preschool-age children. In E. Rubinstein, G. Comstock, & J. Murray (Eds.), *Television and social behavior. Vol. 4. Television in day-to-day life: Patterns of use*. Washington, DC: U.S. Government Printing Office.

Lyons-Ruth, K., Connell, D. B., Zoll, D., & Stahl, J. (1987). Infants at social risk: Relations among infant maltreatment, maternal behavior, and infant attachment behavior. *Developmental Psychology, 23(2)*, 223–232.

Maccoby, E. (1951). Television: Its impact on school children. *Public Opinion Quarterly, 15*, 421–444.

Maccoby, E. (1988). Gender as a social category. *Developmental Psychology, 24*, 755–775.

Maccoby, E., Doering, C. H., Jacklin, C., & Kraemer, H. (1979). Concentrations of sex hormones in umbilical-cord blood. Their relation to sex and birth order of infants. *Child Development, 50*, 632–642.

Maccoby, E., & Jacklin, C. (1974). *The psychology of sex differences*. Stanford, CA: Stanford University Press.

Maccoby, E., & Jacklin, C. (1980). Sex differences in aggression: A rejoinder and reprise. *Child Development, 51*, 964–980.

Maccoby, E., & Jacklin, C. (1987). Gender segregation in childhood. In H. Reese (Ed.), *Advances in child development and behavior* (Vol. 20, pp. 239–287). New York: Academic Press.

Maccoby, E., & Martin, J. (1983). Socialization in the context of the family: Parent-child interaction. In E. M. Hetherington (Ed.), *Handbook of child psychology. Vol. 4. Socialization, personality, and social development*. New York: Wiley.

Maccoby, E., Snow, M., & Jacklin, C. (1984). Children's dispositions and mother-child interaction at 12 and 18 months: A short-term longitudinal study. *Developmental Psychology, 20*, 459–472.

MacDonald, K. (1987). Parent-child physical play with rejected, neglected and popular boys. *Developmental Psychology, 23*, 705–711.

MacDonald, K., & Parke, R. (1984). Bridging the gap: Parent-child play interaction and peer interactive competence. *Child Development, 55*, 1265–1277.

MacFarlane, A. (1977). *The psychology of childbirth*. Cambridge, MA: Harvard University Press.

MacFarlane, J. A. (1975). Olfaction in the development of social preferences in the human neonate. *Parent-infant interaction. Ciba Foundation Symposium, 33* (New Series). Amsterdam: Elsevier.

Magnusson, D., Stattin, H., & Allen, V. (1986). Differential maturation among girls and its relation to social adjustment in a longitudinal perspective. In P. Baltes, D. Featherman, & R. Lerner (Eds.), *Life span development and behavior*

(Vol. 7). Hillsdale, NJ: Erlbaum.

Mahler, M. S., Pine, F., & Bergman, A. (1970). The mother's reaction to her toddler's drive for individuation. In E. J. Anthony & T. Benedek (Eds.), *Parenthood: Its psychology and psychopathology*. Boston: Little, Brown & Co.

Mahler, M. S., Pine, F., & Bergman, A. (1975). *The psychological birth of the human infant*. New York: Basic Books.

Main, M. (1973). *Exploration, play, and cognitive functioning as related to mother-child attachment*. Unpublished doctoral dissertation, Johns Hopkins University, Baltimore.

Main, M., & Weston, D. R. (1981). The quality of the toddler's relationship to mother and to father: Related to conflict behavior and the readiness to establish new relationships. *Child Development, 52*, 932–940.

Malatesta, C., & Haviland, J. (1982). Learning display rules: The socialization of emotional expression in infancy. *Child Development, 53*, 991–1003.

Marcia, J. (1980). Identity in adolescence. In J. Adelson (Ed.), *Handbook of adolescent psychology*. New York: Wiley.

Marcus, D. E., & Overton, W. F. (1978). The development of cognitive gender constancy and sex role preferences. *Child Development, 49*, 434–444.

Marcus, R. F., Telleen, S., & Roke, E. J. (1979). Relation between cooperation and empathy in young children. *Developmental Psychology, 15*, 346–347.

Markman, E. M. (1977). Realizing that you don't understand: A preliminary investigation. *Child Development, 48*, 986–992.

Markman, E. M. (1984). The acquisition and hierarchical organization of categories by children. In C. Sophian (Ed.), *Origins of cognitive skills*. Hillsdale, NJ: Erlbaum.

Markman, E. M., & Gorin, L. (1981). Children's ability to adjust their standards for evaluation comprehension. *Journal of Educational Psychology, 73*, 320–325.

Marshall, W. (1978). Puberty. In F. Falkner & J. Tanner (Eds.), *Human growth* (Vol. 2). New York: Plenum.

Martin, B. (1981). *Abnormal psychology:*

Clinical and scientific perspectives. New York: Holt, Rinehart, & Winston.

Martin, C. L., & Halverson, C. F., Jr. (1981). A schematic processing model of sex typing and stereotyping in children. *Child Development, 52,* 1119–1134.

Martin, H., Beezley, P., Conway, E., & Kempe, H. (1974). The development of abused children: A review of the literature. *Advances in Pediatrics, 21,* 119–143.

Martinez, G. (1984). Trends in breast feeding in the United States. In *Report of the Surgeon-General's Workshop on Breastfeeding and Human Lactation* (pp. 19–23). Washington, DC: Department of Health and Human Services.

Marzollo, J. (1976). *9 months, 1 day, 1 year: A guide to pregnancy, birth, and baby care.* New York: Harper & Row.

Massad, C. (1981). Sex role identity and adjustment during adolescence. *Child Development, 52,* 1290–1298.

Matas, L., Arend, R. A., & Sroufe, L. A. (1978). Continuity of adaptation in the second year: The relationship between quality of attachment and later competence. *Child Development, 49,* 547–556.

Matheny, A. P. (1980). Bayley's infant behavior record: Behavioral components and twin analyses. *Child Development, 51,* 1157–1161.

Matheny, A. P., Dolan, A., & Wilson, R. S. (1974). Bayley's infant behavior record: Relations between behaviors and mental test scores. *Developmental Psychology, 10,* 696–702.

Matheny, A. P., Wilson, R. S., & Nuss, S. (1984). Toddler temperament: Stability across settings and over ages. *Child Development, 55,* 1200–1211.

Matthews, W. S. (March, 1978). *Interruptions of fantasy play: A matter of breaking frame.* Paper presented at the meeting of the Eastern Psychological Association, Washington, DC.

Maurer, D., & Salapatek, P. (1976). Developmental changes in the scanning of faces by young infants. *Child Development, 47,* 523–527.

Mayer, J. (1968). *Overweight: Causes, cost, and control.* Englewood Cliffs, NJ: Prentice-Hall.

McCall, R. B. (1974). Exploratory manipulation and play in the human infant. *Monographs of the Society for Research in Child Development, 39,* (2, Serial No. 155).

McCall, R. B. (1979). The development of intellectual functioning in infancy and the prediction of later IQ. In J. Osofsky (Ed.), *Handbook of infant development.* New York: Wiley.

McCall, R. B., Eichorn, D. H., & Hogarty, P. S. (1977). Transitions in early mental development. *Monographs of the Society for Research in Child Development, 42,* (2, Serial No. 171).

McCandless, B. R., & Hoyt, J. M. (1961). Sex, ethnicity and play preferences of preschool children. *Journal of Abnormal and Social Psychology, 62,* 683–685.

McDavid, J. W., & Harari, H. (1966). Stereotyping of names of popularity in grade-school children. *Child Development, 37,* 453–459.

McDonald, R., Gynther, M., & Christakos, A. (1963). Relations between maternal anxiety and obstetric complication. *Psychosomatic Medicine, 25,* 357–363.

McDonald, R., & Parham, K. (1964). Relation of emotional changes during pregnancy to obstetrical complications. *American Journal of Obstetrics and Gynecology, 90,* 196.

McGanity, W. (1976). Problems of nutritional evaluation of the adolescent. In J. McKigney & H. Munro (Eds.), *Nutrient requirements in adolescence.* Cambridge, MA: MIT Press.

McKey, R., Condelli, L., Granson, H., Barrett, B., McConkey, C., & Plantz, M. (1985). The impact of Head Start on children, families and communities. *Final report of the Head Start evaluation, synthesis and utilization project.* Washington, DC: CSR, Inc.

McKinley, D. (1964). *Social class and family life.* New York: Free Press.

McLaughlin, B. (1984). *Second language acquisition in children: Preschool children.* Hillsdale, NJ: Erlbaum.

Mead, M. (1978). *Culture and commitment.* Garden City, NY: Anchor.

Meichenbaum, D., & Goodman, J. (1971). Training impulsive children to talk to themselves: A means of developing self-control. *Journal of Abnormal Psychology, 77,* 115–126.

Meltzoff, A., & Borton, R. W. (1979). Intermodal matching by human neonates. *Nature, 282,* 403–404.

Meltzoff, A., & Moore, M. (1977). Imitation of facial and manual gestures by human neonates. *Science, 198,* 75–78.

Meltzoff, A., & Moore, M. (1983). Newborn infants imitate adult facial gestures. *Child Development, 54,* 702–709.

Menyuk, P. (1977). *Language and maturation.* Cambridge, MA: MIT Press.

Menyuk, P. (1985). Early communication and language behavior. In J. Rosenblith and J. Simms-Knight (Eds.), *In the beginning: Development during the first two years of life.* Monterey, CA: Brooks/Cole.

Meredith, H. V. (1984). Body size of infants and children around the world in relation to socio-economic status. In H. W. Reese (Ed.), *Advances in child development and behavior* (Vol. 18, pp. 81–145). Orlando, FL: Academic Press.

Merritt, T. A. et al. (1986). Prophylactic treatment of very premature infants with human surfactant. *New England Journal of Medicine, 315,* 785–790.

Meyer, H. (1988). Marital and mother-child relationships: Developmental history, parent personality and child difficultness. In R. Hinde & J. Stevenson-Hinde (Eds.), *Relationships within families: Mutual influences.* Oxford: Clarendon Press.

Milewski, A. (1976). Infants' discrimination of internal and external pattern elements. *Journal of Experimental Child Psychology, 22,* 229–246.

Miller, B., & Sollie, P. (1980). Normal stresses during the transition to parenthood. *Family Relations, 29,* 459–465.

Miller, L. C., Barrett, C. L., & Hampe, E. (1974). Phobias of childhood in a prescientific era. In A. Davids (Ed.), *Child personality and psychopathology: Current topics* (Vol. 1, pp. 89–134). New York: Wiley.

Miller, N., & Maruyama, G. (1976). Ordinal position and peer popularity. *Journal of Personality and Social Psychology, 33,* 123–131.

Miller, P., & Simon, W. (1980). The development of sexuality in adolescence. In J. Adelson (Ed.), *Handbook of adolescent psychology.* New York: Wiley.

Milliones, J. (1978). Relationship between perceived child temperament and maternal behavior. *Child Development, 49,* 1255–1257.

Milowe, I., & Lourie, R. (1964). The child's role in the battered child syndrome. *Society for Pediatric Research, 65,* 1079.

Milunsky, A. (1977). *Know your genes.* Boston: Houghton Mifflin.

Minde, K., Shosenberg, N., Marton, P., Thompson, J., Ripley, J., & Burns, S. (1980). Self-help groups in a premature nursery—a controlled evaluation. *The Journal of Pediatrics, 96,* 933–940.

Minturn, L., & Hitchcock, J. (1963). The Kajputs of Khalapur, India. In B. Whiting (Ed.), *Six cultures studies of child rearing.* New York: Wiley.

Minturn, L., & Lambert, W. W. (1964). *Mothers of six cultures: Antecedents of childrearing.* New York: Wiley.

Minuchin, P., and Shapiro, E. (1983). The school as a context for social development. In E. M. Hetherington (Ed.), *Handbook of child psychology. Vol. 4. Socialization, personality, and social development.* New York: Wiley.

Mischel, W., & Underwood, B. (1974). Instrumental ideation in delay of gratification. *Child Development, 45,* 1083–1088.

Miyake, K., Chen, S., & Campos, J. J. (1985). Infant temperament, mother's mode of interaction, and attachment in Japan: An interim report. *Monographs of the Society for Research in Child Development, 50,* 276–297.

Moely, B. E., Skarin, K., & Weil, S. (1979). Sex differences in competition-cooperation behavior of children at two age levels. *Sex Roles, 5,* 329–342.

Money, J., & Ehrhardt, A. A. (1972). *Man & woman. Boy & girl.* Baltimore: Johns Hopkins University Press.

Montemayor, R. (1982). The relationship between parent-adolescent conflict and the amount of time adolescents spend alone and with parents and peers. *Child Development, 53,* 1512–1519.

Montemayor, R. (1984). Maternal employment and adolescents' relations with parents, siblings, and peers. *Journal of Youth and Adolescence, 13,* 543–557.

Montemayor, R., & Eisen, M. (1977).

The development of self-conceptions from childhood to adolescence. *Developmental Psychology, 13,* 314–319.

Moore, K., Peterson, J., & Furstenberg, F., Jr. (1986). Parental attitudes and the occurrence of early sexual activity. *Journal of Marriage and the Family, 48,* 777–782.

Moos, R. (1978). A typology of junior high and high school classrooms. *American Educational Research Journal, 15,* 53–66.

Mora, J. O., et al. (1979). Nutritional supplementation, early stimulation, and child development. In J. Brozek (Ed.), *Behavioral effects of energy and protein deficits.* Bethesda, MD: Department of Health, Education, and Welfare.

Morales, R. V., Shute, V. J., & Pellegrino, J. W. (1985). Developmental differences in understanding and solving simple word problems. *Cognition and Instruction, 2,* 41–57.

Morgan, G. A., & Ricciuti, H. N. (1969). Infants' responses to strangers during the first year. In B. M. Foss (Ed.), *Determinants of infant behavior* (Vol. 4). New York: Wiley.

Morrell, P., & Norton, W. (1980). Mylew. *Scientific American, 242,* 99–119.

Morris, M., & Weinstein, L. (1981). Caffeine and the fetus: Is trouble brewing? *American Journal of Obstetrics and Gynecology, 140,* 607–610.

Morrison, J. R., & Stewart, M. A. (1971). A family study of the hyperactive child syndrome. *Biological Psychiatry, 3,* 189–195.

Mortimer, J., & Finch, M. (1986). The effects of part-time work on adolescent self-concept and achievement. In P. Borman and J. Reisman (Eds.), *Becoming a worker.* Norwood, NJ: Ablex.

Mounger, J. (1970). Nutrition. In W. Daniel, Jr. (Ed.), *The adolescent patient.* Saint Louis, MO: Mosby.

Mueller, E., & Vandell, D. (1979). Infant-infant interactions. In J. Osofsky (Ed.), *Handbook of infant development* (pp. 591–622). New York: Wiley.

Muir, D., Abraham, W., Forbes, B., & Harris, L. (1979). The ontogenesis of an auditory localization response from birth to four months of age. *Canadian Journal of Psychology, 33,*

320–334.

Munro, G., & Adams, G. (1977). Ego-identity formation in college students and working youth. *Developmental Psychology, 13,* 523–524.

Murphy, L. B. (1937). *Social behavior and child personality.* New York: Columbia University Press.

Murray, J. P. (1971). Television in inner-city homes: Viewing behavior of young boys. In E. Rubinstein, G. Comstock, & J. Murray (Eds.), *Television and social behavior* (Vol. 4). Washington, DC: U.S. Government Printing Office.

Mussen, P. H. (1969). Early sex-role development. In D. A. Goslin (Ed.), *Handbook of socialization theory and research* (pp. 707–732). Chicago: Rand McNally.

Mussen, P. H., & Eisenberg-Berg, N. (1977). *Caring, sharing and helping.* San Francisco: Freeman.

Mussen, P. H., & Jones, M. C. (1957). Self-conceptions, motivations, and interpersonal attitudes of late- and early-maturing boys. *Child Development, 28,* 243–256.

Mussen, P. H., & Jones, M. C. (1958). The behavior-inferred motivations of late- and early-maturing boys. *Child Development, 29,* 61–67.

Myers, N. A., & Perlmutter, M. (1978). Memory in the years from two to five. In P. A. Ornstein (Ed.), *Memory development in children* (pp. 191–218). Hillsdale, NJ: Erlbaum.

Naerye, R., Diener, M., & Dellinger, W. (1969). Urban poverty: Effects of prenatal nutrition. *Science, 166,* 1206–1209.

Nahmias, A., et al. (1975). Herpes simplex virus infection of the fetus and newborn. In A. Gershan & S. Krugman (Eds.), *Infection of the fetus and newborn.* New York: Ciss.

National Center for Clinical Infant Programs. (1987). *Infants can't wait: The numbers.* Washington, DC: Author.

National Center for Health Statistics. (1982). *Vital statistics of the United States.* Washington, DC: U.S. Government Printing Office.

National Centers for Disease Control. (1988, January 29). Guidelines for effective school health education to prevent the spread of AIDS. *Morbidity and mortality weekly report.* Washington, DC: U.S. Department of Health and Human Services.

National Highway Traffic Safety Administration. (1987). *Fatal accident reporting system.* Washington, DC: U.S. Department of Transportation.

National Public Radio. (1989). *Health of America's children.* Washington, D.C.: National Public Radio Cassettes.

Neal, J. (1983, March). Children's understanding of their parents' divorce. In L. Kurdek (Ed.), Children and divorce. *New Directions for Child Development* (No. 19). San Francisco: Jossey-Bass.

Neimark, E. (1975). Intellectual development during adolescence. In F. Horowitz (Ed.), *Review of child development research* (Vol. 4). Chicago: University of Chicago Press.

Nelson, K. (1971). Accommodation of visual tracking patterns in human infants to object movement patterns. *Journal of Experimental Child Psychology, 12,* 182–196.

Nelson, K. (1973). Structure and strategy in learning to talk. *Monographs of the Society for Research in Child Development, 38.*

Nelson, K. (1974). Concept, word and sentence: Interrelations in acquisition and development, *Psychological Bulletin, 81,* 267–285.

Nelson, K. (1977). First steps in language acquisition. *Journal of the American Academy of Child Psychiatry, 16,* 563–583.

Nelson, K. (1981). Individual differences in language development: Implications for development and language. *Developmental Psychology, 2,* 170–187.

Nelson, K. (1981). Social cognition in a script framework. In H. H. Flavell & L. Ross (Eds.), *Social cognitive development: Frontiers and possible futures.* New York: Cambridge University Press.

Nelson, K., & Gruendel, J. (1981). Generalized event representations: Basic building blocks of cognitive development. In M. E. Lamb & A. L. Brown (Eds.), *Advances in developmental psychology* (Vol. 1, pp. 131–158). Hillsdale, NJ: Erlbaum.

Nelson, K., & Hudson, J. (1988). Scripts and memory: Functional relationships in development. In F. Weinert & M. Perlmutter (Eds.), *Memory development: Universal changes and individual differences* (pp. 147–168).

Hillsdale, NJ: Erlbaum.

Nelson, N., Enkin, M., Saigel, S., Bennett, K., Milner, R., & Sackett, D. (1980). A randomized clinical trial of the Leboyer approach to childbirth. *New England Journal of Medicine, 302,* 655–660.

Newcomb, M., Maddahain, E., & Bentler, P. (1986). Risk factors for drug use among adolescents: Concurrent and longitudinal analyses. *American Journal of Public Health, 76,* 525–531.

Newcombe, N., & Dubas, J. (1987). Individual differences in cognitive ability: Are they related to timing of puberty? In R. Lerner & T. Roch (Eds.), *Biological-psychosocial interactions in early adolescence* (pp. 249–302). Hillsdale, NJ: Erlbaum.

Newcomer, S., & Udry, J. (1987). Parental marital status effects on adolescent sexual behavior. *Journal of Marriage and the Family, 49,* 235–240.

Newport, E. (1976). Motherese: The speech of mothers to young children. In N. Costellan, D. Pisoni, & G. Potts (Eds.), *Cognitive Theory* (Vol. 2). Hillsdale, NJ: Erlbaum.

Newport, E., Gileitman, H., & Bleitman, L. (1979). Mother, I'd rather do it myself: Some effects and non-effects on maternal speech style. In C. Snow & C. Ferguson (Eds.), *Talking to children* (pp. 109–149). Cambridge, England: Cambridge University Press.

Nichols, P. L. (1977). *Minimal brain dysfunction: Associations with perinatal complications.* Paper presented at the Society for Research in Child Development, New Orleans.

O'Connor, M., Cohen, S., & Parmelee, A. (1984). Infant auditory discrimination in preterm and full-term infants as a predictor of five-year intelligence. *Developmental Psychology, 20,* 159–165.

Oates, R., Forrest, D., & Peacock, A. (1985). Self-esteem of abused children. *Child Abuse and Neglect, 9,* 159–163.

Offer, D., Ostrov, E., & Howard, K. (1981). *The adolescent: A psychological self-portrait.* New York: Basic Books.

Olds, D. (1988). The prenatal/early infancy project. In R. Price, E. Cowen, R. Lorian, & J. Ramos-

McKay (Eds.), *14 Ounces of Prevention.* Washington, DC: American Psychological Association.

O'Leary, K. D., & Becker, W. (1967). Behavior modification of an adjustment class: A token reinforcement program. *Exceptional Children, 33,* 637–642.

Olweus, D. (1979). Stability and aggressive reaction patterns in males: A review. *Psychological Bulletin, 86,* 852–875.

Olweus, D. (1980). Familial and temperamental determinants of aggressive behavior in adolescent boys: A causal analysis. *Developmental Psychology, 16,* 644–660.

Olweus, D. (1982a). Continuity in aggressive and inhibited, withdrawn behavior patterns. *Psychiatry and Social Science.*

Olweus, D. (1982b). Development of stable aggressive reaction patterns in males. In R. Blanchard & C. Blanchard (Eds.), *Advances in the study of aggression* (Vol. 1). New York: Academic Press.

Opinion Research Corporation. (1979). *Public Perceptions of Alcohol Consumption and Pregnancy.* Report of a survey conducted for the Bureau of Alcohol, Tobacco and Firearms, 1979.

Orlofsky, J., Marcia, J., & Lesser, I. (1973). Ego identity status and the intimacy versus isolation crisis of young adulthood. *Journal of Personality and Social Psychology, 27,* 211–219.

Ornstein, P. A., Baker-Ward, L., & Naus, M. J. (1988). The development of mnemonic skill. In F. Weinert & M. Perlmutter (Eds.), *Memory development: Universal changes and individual differences* (pp. 31–50). Hillsdale, NJ: Erlbaum.

Ornstein, P. A., Naus, M. J., & Liberty, C. (1975). Rehearsal and organizational processes in children's memory. *Child Development, 46,* 818–830.

Osipow, S. (1973). *Theories of career development* (2nd ed.). New York: Appleton-Century-Crofts.

Osofsky, J. D. (1987). *Handbook of infant development.* New York: Wiley.

Ostrea, E., & Chavez, C. (1979). Perinatal problems in maternal drug addiction: A study of 830 cases. *Journal of Pediatrics, 94,* 292–295.

Otake, M., & Schull, W. (1984). In vitro

exposure to A-bomb radiation and mental retardation: A reassessment. *British Journal of Radiology, 57,* 409–414.

Ottinger, D., & Simmons, J. (1966). Behavior of human neonatal and perinatal maternal emotions. *Psychological Reports, 14,* 391–394.

Owens, T. (1982). Experience-based career education: Summary and implications of research and evaluation findings. *Child and Youth Services Journal, 4,* 77–91.

Oyellette, E. M., Rosett, H. L., Rosman, N. P., & Weiner, L. (1977). Adverse effects on offspring of maternal alcohol abuse during pregnancy. *New England Journal of Medicine, 297,* 528–530.

Packer, O., Hartman, E., & Teller, D. (1984). Infant color vision: The effect of test field size on infants' Rayleigh discrimination. *Vision Research, 24,* 1247–1256.

Paley, V. G. (1984). *Boys and girls: Superheroes in the doll corner.* Chicago: University of Chicago Press.

Paley, V. G. (1986). *Mollie is three: Growing up in school.* Chicago: University of Chicago Press.

Paris, S. G., & Myers, M. (1981). Comprehension monitoring, memory, and study strategies of good and poor readers. *Journal of Reading Behavior, 13,* 5–22.

Paris, S. G., Wasik, B. A., & Turner, J. C. (in press). The development of strategic readers. In P. D. Pearson (Ed.), *Handbook of research* (2nd ed.). New York: Longman.

Paris, S. G., & Winograd, P. (1990). How metacognition can promote children's academic learning. In B. Jones and L. Idol (Eds.), *Dimensions of thinking.* Hillsdale, NJ: Erlbaum.

Parke, R. (1977a). Punishment in children: Effects, side effects, and alternative strategies. In H. L. Horn and P. L. Robinson (Eds.), *Psychological processes in early childhood.* New York: Academic Press.

Parke, R. (1977b). Some effects of punishment on children's behavior—revisited. In P. Cantor (Ed.), *Understanding a child's world.* New York: McGraw-Hill.

Parke, R. (1978). Perspectives in father-infant interaction. In J. Osofsky (Ed.), *Handbook of infancy.* New York: Wiley.

Parke, R., & Beitel, A. (1988). Disappointment: When things go wrong in the transition to parenthood. *Marriage and Family Review, 12,* 221–265.

Parke, R., MacDonald, K., Beitel, A., & Bhavnagri, N. (1988). The role of the family in the development of peer relationships. In R. DeV. Peters & R. MacMahon (Eds.), *Marriage and families: Behavioral treatments and processes* (pp. 17–44). New York: Brunner-Mazel.

Parke, R., O'Leary, S. E., & West, W. (1972). Mother-father-newborn interaction: Effects of maternal medication, labor, and sex of infant. *Proceedings of the American Psychological Association,* 85–86.

Parke, R., & Sawin, D. (1975, April). *Infant characteristics and behavior as elicitors of maternal and paternal responsivity in the newborn period.* Paper presented at the biennial meeting of the Society for Research in Child Development, Denver.

Parke, R., & Slaby, R. (1983). The development of aggression. In E. M. Hetherington (Ed.), *Handbook of child psychology: Vol 4. Socialization, personality, and social development* (pp. 547–642). New York: Wiley.

Parke, R., & Suomi, S. J. (1980). Adult male-infant relationships: Human and nonhuman primate evidence. In K. Immelman, G. Burlow, M. Main, & L. Petrinovich (Eds.), *Early development in animals and man.* Cambridge, England: Cambridge University Press.

Parker, F., Piotrkowski, D., & Peay, L. (1987). Head Start as a social support for mothers: The psychological benefits of involvement. *American Journal of Orthopsychiatry, 57,* 220–233.

Parmalee, A. H., & Sigman, M. D. (1983). Perinatal brain development and behavior. In J. Campos & M. Haith (Eds.), *Handbook of child psychology: Vol. 2. Infancy and child psychobiology* (pp. 96–155). New York: Wiley.

Parten, M. (1932). Social participation among preschool children. *Journal of Abnormal Psychology, 27,* 243–269.

Pascoe, J. M., Loda, F. A., Jeffries, V., & Earp, J. A. (1981). The association between mother's social support and provision of stimulation to their children. *Developmental and Behavioral Pediatrics, 2,* 15–19.

Patterson, G. R. (1976). *Families: Applications of social learning to family life.* Champaign, IL: Research Press.

Patterson, G. R. (1982). *Coercive family process.* Eugene, OR: Castalia Press.

Patterson, G. R., & Stouthamer-Loeber, M. (1984). The correlation of family management practices and delinquency. *Child Development, 55,* 1299–1307.

Paulsen, E. (1972). Obesity in children and adolescents. In H. Barnett & A. Einhorn (Eds.), *Pediatrics.* New York: Appleton-Century-Crofts.

Paulsen, K., & Johnson, M. (1983). Sex role attitudes and mathematical ability in 4th-, 8th-, and 11th-grade students from a high socioeconomic area. *Developmental Psychology, 19,* 210–214.

Peacock, J., & Sorubbi, R. (1983). Disseminated herpes simplex virus infection during pregnancy. *Obstetrics and Gynecology, 61,* 135–168.

Pease, D., & Gleason, J. B. (1985). Gaining meaning: Semantic development. In J. B. Gleason (Ed.), *The development of language.* Columbus, OH: Merrill.

Pedersen, F. A., Anderson, B., & Cain, R. (1979, March). *Parent-infant interaction observed in a family setting at age 5 months.* Paper presented at the biennial meeting of the Society for Research in Child Development, San Francisco.

Pedersen, F. A., & Robson, K. (1969). Father participation in infancy. *American Journal of Orthopsychiatry, 39,* 466–474.

Pedersen, F. A., Rubenstein, J., & Yarrow, L. (1979). Infant development in father-absent families. *Journal of Genetic Psychology, 125,* 51–61.

Pedersen, F. A., Yarrow, L., Anderson, B., & Cain, R. (1978). Conceptualization of father influences in the infancy period. In M. Lewis and L. Rosenblum (Eds.), *The social network of the developing infant.* New York: Plenum.

Peel, E. (1971). *The nature of adolescent judgment.* London: Staples Press.

Peery, J. C. (1979). Popular, amiable,

isolated, rejected: A reconceptualization of sociometric status in preschool children. *Child Development, 50,* 1231–1234.

Peplau, L., Rubin, Z., & Hill, C. (1977). Sexual intimacy in dating relationships. *Journal of Social Issues, 33,* 86–109.

Pepler, D. J., Abramovitch, R., & Corter, C. (1978). Sibling interaction in the home: A longitudinal study. *Child Development, 49,* 590–597.

Peskin, H. (1973). Influence of the developmental schedule of puberty on learning and ego functioning. *Journal of Youth and Adolescence, 2,* 273–290.

Peters, A. M. Language learning strategies. Does the whole equal the sum of the parts? *Language, 53,* 560–573.

Petersen, A. (1979). Differential cognitive development in adolescent girls. In M. Sugar (Ed.), *Female adolescent development.* New York: Brunner/Mazel.

Petersen, A. (1985). Pubertal development as a cause of disturbance: Myths, realities, and unanswered questions. *Genetic, Social, and General Psychology Monographs, 111,* 205–232.

Petersen, A., & Taylor, B. (1980). The biological approach to adolescence: Biological change and psychological adaptation. In J. Adelson (Ed.), *Handbook of adolescent psychology.* New York: Wiley.

Peterson, J., & Zill, N. (1986). Marital disruption, parent-child relationships, and behavior problems in children. *Journal of Marriage and the Family, 48,* 295–307.

Pettit, G., Dodge, K., & Brown, M. (1988). Early family experience, social problem solving patterns, and children's social competence. *Child Development, 59,* 107–120.

Phillips, D., & Carstensen, L. (1986). Clustering of teenage suicides after television news stories about suicide. *New England Journal of Medicine, 315,* 685–689.

Phillips, D., & Howes, C. (1987). Indicators of quality child care: Review of research. In D. Phillips (Ed.), *Quality in child care.* Washington, DC: National Association for the Education of Young Children.

Phillips, D., McCartney, K., & Scarr, S. (1987). The effect of quality of day care environment upon children's social and emotional development. *Developmental Psychology, 23,* 537–543.

Phinney, J., & Alipuria, L. (1987). *Ethnic identity in older adolescents from four ethnic groups.* Paper presented at the biennial meetings of the Society for Research in Child Development, Baltimore.

Piaget, J. (1926). *The language and thought of the child.* New York: Harcourt, Brace.

Piaget, J. (1932). *The moral judgment of the child.* New York: Harcourt.

Piaget, J. (1952). *The origins of intelligence in children.* New York: Norton.

Piaget, J. (1959). *The language and thought of the child* (3rd ed.). London: Routledge & Kegan Paul.

Piaget, J., & Inhelder, B. (1956). *The child's conception of space.* London: Routledge & Kegan Paul.

Pinto, D., Moriarty, M., Hackenson, M., & Ricks, M. (1988, August). *Thirty-six years of maternal sex typing: Sears, Maccoby & Levin's study revisited.* Poster presented at the annual convention of the American Psychological Association, Atlanta, GA.

Plomin, R. & DeFries, J. C. (1983). The Colorado Adoption Project. *Child Development, 54,* 276–289.

Plomin, R., DeFries, J. C., & Loehlin, J. C. (1977). Genotype-phenotype interaction and correlation in the analysis of human behavior. *Psychological Bulletin, 84,* 309–322.

Plomin, R., & Rowe, D. (1977). A twin study of temperament in young children. *Journal of Psychology, 97,* 107–113.

Pollitt, E., Garza, C., & Leibel, R. L. (1984). Nutrition and public policy. In H. W. Stevenson & A. E. Siegel (Eds.), *Child Development Research and Social Policy* (Vol. 1, pp. 421–470). Chicago: University of Chicago Press.

Powell, A., Farrar, E., & Cohen, D. (1985). *The shopping mall high school.* Boston: Houghton Mifflin.

Powell, D. (1979). Family-environment relations and early childrearing: The role of social networks and neighborhoods. *Journal of Research and Development in Education, 13,* 1–11.

Powell, D. (1980). Towards a socioecological perspective of relations between parents and child care programs. In S. Kilmer (Ed.), *Advances in early education and day care* (Vol. 1). Greenwich, CT: JAI Press.

Powell, L. F. (1974). The effect of extra stimulation and maternal involvement on the development of low birthweight infants and on maternal behavior. *Child Development, 45,* 106–113.

Power, T. G., & Parke, R. D. (1979, March). *Toward a taxonomy of father-infant and mother-infant play patterns.* Paper presented at the Society for Research in Child Development, San Francisco.

Power, T. G., & Parke, R. D. (1983). Patterns of mother and father play with their 8-month-old infant: A multiple analyses approach. *Infant Behavior and Development, 6,* 453–459.

Pressley, M. (1982). Elaboration and memory development. *Child Development, 53,* 296–309.

Price, G. (1977, March). *Factors influencing reciprocity in early mother-infant interaction.* Paper presented at the biennial meeting of the Society for Research in Child Development, New Orleans.

Putallaz, M., & Gottman, J. (1981). Social skills and group acceptance. In S. Asher & J. Gottman (Eds.), *The development of children's friendships.* New York: Cambridge University Press.

Radke-Yarrow, M., Zahn-Waxler, C., & Chapman, M. (1983). Children's prosocial dispositions and behavior. In E. M. Hetherington, (Ed.), *Handbook of child psychology: Vol. 4. Socialization, personality, and social development* (pp. 469–545). New York: Wiley.

Ramey, C., & Haskins, R. (1981). The modification of intelligence through early experience. *Intelligence, 5,* 5–19.

Ramey, C. T., Mills, P., Campbell, F. A., & O'Brien, C. (1975). Infants' home environments: A comparison of high-risk families and families from the general population. *American*

Journal of Mental Deficiency, 80, 40–42.

Ramsay, D. S., & Weber, S. L. (1986). Infant's hand preference in a task involving complementary roles for the two hands. *Child Development, 57,* 300–307.

Read, M., Habich, J. P., Lechtis, A., & Klein, R. (1973, May 21–25). *Maternal malnutrition, birth-weight and child development.* Paper presented before the International Symposium on Nutrition, Growth, and Development, Valencia, Spain.

Redl, F., & Wineman, D. (1951). *Children who hate.* Glencoe, IL: Free Press.

Reese, H. W. (1961). Relationship between self-acceptance and sociometric choice. *Journal of Abnormal and Social Psychology, 62,* 472–474.

Reidy, T. J. (1977). The aggressive characteristics of abused and neglected children. *Journal of Clinical Psychology, 33,* 1140–1145.

Reinisch, J. M. (1981). Prenatal exposure to synthetic progestins increases potential for aggression in humans. *Science, 211,* 1171–1173.

Reinisch, J. M., & Karow, W. G. (1977). Prenatal exposure to synthetic progestins and estrogens: Effects on human development. *Archives of Sexual Behavior, 6,* 257–288.

Reiss, I. (1960). *Permarital sexual standards in America.* New York: Free Press.

Rescorla, L., Provence, S., & Naylor, A. (1982). The Yale Child Welfare Research Program description and results. In E. Zigler & E. Gordon (Eds.), *Day care: Scientific and social policy issues* (pp. 163–199). Boston: Auborn House.

Rest, J. (1983). Morality. In J. Flavell and E. Markman (Eds.), *Handbook of child psychology. Volume 3. Cognitive development.* New York: Wiley.

Rheingold, H. L. (1979, March). *Helping by two-year-old children.* Paper presented at the meeting of the Society for Research in Child Development, San Francisco.

Rheingold, H. L. (1982). Little children's participation in the work of adults, a nascent prosocial behavior, *Child Development, 53,* 114–125.

Rheingold, H. L., & Cook, K. V. (1975). The content of boys' and girls'

rooms as an index of parents' behavior. *Child Development, 46,* 459–463.

Richards, M. P. M., & Bernal, J. F. (1972). An observational study of mother-infant interaction. In N. B. Jones (Ed.), *Ethological studies of child behaviour* (pp. 175–197). Cambridge, England: Cambridge University Press.

Ricks, M. (1985). The social transmission of parental behavior. In I. Bretherton and E. Waters (Eds.), Growing points in attachment research. *Monographs for the Society for Research in Child Development, 50,* (Serial No. 209), pp. 211–230.

Rist, R. C. (1970). Student social class and teacher expectations: The self-fulfilling prophecy in ghetto education. *Harvard Educational Review, 40,* 411–451.

Roberts, R. J., Jr., & C. Patterson (1983). Perspective taking and referential communication: The question of correspondence reconsidered. *Child Development, 54,* 1005–1014.

Robinson, I., & Jedlicka, D. (1982). Change in sexual attitudes and behavior of college students from 1965 to 1980: A research note. *Journal of Marriage and the Family, 44,* 237–240.

Robinson, J. P. (1971). Television's impact on everyday life: Some cross-national evidence. In *Television and social behavior* (Vol. 4, pp. 410–432). Washington, DC: U.S. Government Printing Office.

Rodman, H., Pratto, D., & Nelson, R. (1985). Child care arrangements and children's functioning: A comparison of self-care and adult-care children. *Developmental Psychology, 21,* 413–418.

Ronjat, J. (1913). *Le development de language observé chez un enfant bilingue.* Paris: Champion.

Roopnarine, J. (1984). Sex-typed socialization in mixed-age preschool classrooms. *Child Development, 55,* 1078–1084.

Roopnarine, J., & Johnson, J. E. (1984). Socialization in a mixed-age experimental program. *Developmental Psychology, 20,* 828–832.

Rose, S., & Blank, M. (1974). The potency of context in children's cogni-

tion. *Child Development, 45,* 499–502.

Rose, S., Gottfried, A., & Bridger, W. (1981a). Cross-modal transfer and information processing by the sense of touch in infancy. *Developmental Psychology, 17,* 90–98.

Rose, S., Gottfried, A., & Bridger, W. (1981b). Cross-modal transfer in 6-month-old infants. *Developmental Psychology, 17,* 661–669.

Rose, S., & Ruff, H. (1987). Cross-modal abilities in human infants. In J. Osofsky (Ed.), *Handbook of infant development* (pp. 318–362). New York: Wiley.

Rose, S., Schmidt, K., & Bridger, W. (1976). Cardiac and behavioral responsivity to tactile stimulation in premature and full-term infants. *Developmental Psychology, 12,* 311–320.

Rosenbaum, J. (1976). *Making inequality: The hidden curriculum of high school tracking.* New York: Wiley.

Rosenberg, M. (1986). Self-concept from middle childhood through adolescence. In J. Suls and A. Greenwald (Eds.), *Psychological perspectives on the self* (Vol. 3). Hillsdale, NJ: Erlbaum.

Rosenblith, J. F., & Sims-Knight, J. E. (1985). *In the beginning: Development in the first two years.* Monterey, CA: Brooks/Cole.

Rosenfeld, A. (1974, September 7). If Oedipus' parents had only known. *Saturday Review,* pp. 49–53.

Rosenthal, R., & Jacobson, L. (1968). *Pygmalion in the classroom: Teacher expectation and pupils' intellectual development.* New York: Holt, Rinehart, & Winston.

Ross, D. M., & Ross, S. A. (1982). *Hyperactivity: Research, theory, and action* (2nd ed.). New York: Wiley.

Ross, G., Kagan, J., Zelazo, P., & Kotelchuck, M. (1975). Separation protest in infants and home and laboratory. *Developmental Psychology, 11,* 256–257.

Rossetti-Ferreira, M. C. (1978). Malnutrition and mother-infant asynchrony: Slow mental development. *International Journal of Behavioral Development, 1,* 207–219.

Rossi, A. (1978). A biosocial perspective on parenting. In A. Rossi, J. Kagan, & T. Harevan (Eds.), *The Family.* New York: Norton.

Rotbart, D. (1981, March 2). Allowances stay flat, candy rises—And kids lose their innocence. *The Wall Street Journal*, pp. 1 and ff.

Rothbart, M. K., & Derryberry, D. (1982). Development of individual differences in temperament. In M. E. Lamb & A. L. Brown (Eds.), *Advances in developmental psychology* (Vol. 1). Hillsdale, NJ: Erlbaum.

Rothbart, M. K., & Rothbart, M. (1976). Birth order, sex of child, and maternal helpgiving. *Sex Roles, 2,* 39–46.

Rovee, C., Cohen, R., & Schlapack, W. (1975). Life-span stability in olfactory sensitivity. *Developmental Psychology, 11,* 311–318.

Rubenstein, J. (1967). Maternal attentiveness and subsequent exploratory behavior. *Child Development, 38,* 1089–1100.

Rubenstein, J., & Howes, C. (1981). Adaptation to toddler day care. In S. Kilmer (Ed.), *Advances in early education and day care.* Greenwich, CT: JAI Press.

Rubin, J. Z., Provenzano, F. J., & Luria, Z. (1974). The eye of the beholder: Parents' views on sex of newborns. *American Journal of Orthopsychiatry, 44,* 512–519.

Rubin, K. H., Fein, G., & Vandenberg, B. (1983). Play. In E. M. Hetherington (Ed.), *Handbook of child psychology Vol. 4. Socialization, personality and social development* (pp. 693–774). New York: Wiley.

Rubin, K. H., Watson, K., & Jambor, T. (1978). Free play behaviors in preschool and kindergarten children. *Child Development, 49,* 534–536.

Rubin, Z. (1980). *Children's friendships.* Cambridge, MA: Harvard University Press.

Ruggiero, M., Greenberger, E., & Steinberg, L. (1982). Occupational deviance among first-time workers. *Youth and Society, 13,* 423–448.

Rushton, J. P. (1979). Effects of prosocial television and film material on the behavior of viewers. In L. Berkowitz (Ed.), *Advances in experimental social psychology* (Vol. 12). New York: Academic Press.

Russell, C. (1974). Transition to parenthood: Problems and gratifications. *Journal of Marriage and the Family, 36,* 294–301.

Rutter, M. (1983). School effects on pupil progress. Research findings and policy implications. *Child Development, 54,* 1–29.

Rutter, M., & Garmezy, N. (1983). Developmental psychopathology. In E. M. Hetherington (Ed.), *Handbook of child psychology: Vol. 4. Socialization, personality, and social development.* New York: Wiley, 1983.

Rutter, M., & Quinton, D. (1984). Long-term follow-up of women institutionalized as children: Factors promoting good functioning in adult life. *British Journal of Development and Psychology, 2,* 191–204.

Sagi, A., & Hoffman, M. L. (1976). Empathic distress in the newborn. *Developmental Psychology, 12,* 175–176.

Sagi, A., Lamb, M., Shoham, R., Dvir, R., & Lewkowicz, K. (1985). Parent-infant interaction in families on Israeli kibbutzim. *International Journal of Behavioral Development, 8,* 273–284.

Salapatek, P. (1977). Stimulus determinants of attention in infants. In B.B. Wolman (Ed.), *International encyclopedia of psychiatry, psychology, psychoanalysis, and neurology* (Vol. X). New York: Aeaculapius.

Salatas, H., & Flavell, J. H. (1976). Behavioral and metamnemonic indicators of strategic behavior under remember instructions in first grade. *Child Development, 47,* 81–89.

Sameroff, A., & Cavanaugh, P. (1979). Learning in infancy: A developmental perspective. In J. Osofsky (Ed.), *Handbook of infant development.* New York: Wiley.

Sameroff, A. & Chandler, M. (1975). Reproductive risk and the continuum of caretaking casualty. In F. D. Horowitz (Ed.), *Review of child development research.* Chicago: University of Chicago Press.

Sandberg, E., Riffle, N., Higdon, J., & Getman, C. (1981). Pregnancy outcome in women exposed to diethylstilbestrol in utero. *American Journal of Obstetrics and Gynecology, 140,* 194–205.

Santrock, J. W., Warchak, R. A., & Elliott, G. L. (1982). Social development and parent-child interaction in father-custody and stepmother

families. In M. E. Lamb (Ed.), *Nontraditional families: Parenting and child development.* Hillsdale, NJ: Erlbaum.

Savin-Williams, R. (1976). An ethological study of dominance formation and maintenance in a group of human adolescents. *Child Development, 47,* 972–979.

Scardamalia, M., & Bereiter, C. (1984). Written composition. In M. Wittrock (Ed.), *Handbook of research on teaching* (pp. 778–803).

Scarr, S. (1984). *Mother care, other care.* New York: Basic Books.

Scarr, S., & McCartney, K. (1983). How people make their own environments: A theory of genotype-environment effects. *Child Development, 54,* 424–435.

Scarr, S., & Weinberg, R. A. (1983). The Minnesota adoption studies: Malleability and genetic differences. *Child Development, 34,* 260–267.

Schachter, F. (1982). Sibling deidentification and split-parent identification: a family tetrad. In M. Lamb and B. Sutton-Smith (Eds.), *Sibling relationships: Their nature and significance across the lifespan* (pp. 123–197). Hillsdale, NJ: Erlbaum.

Schaffer, H. (1977). *Mothering.* Cambridge, MA: Harvard University Press.

Schaffer, H. R. (1979). Acquiring the concept of dialogue. In M. H. Bornstein and W. Kessen (Eds.), *Psychological development from infancy.* Hillsdale, NJ: Erlbaum.

Schaffer, H., & Emerson, P. E. (1964a). The development of social attachments in infancy. *Monographs of the Society for Research in Child Development, 29* (Whole No. 94).

Schaffer, H., & Emerson, P. (1964b). Patterns of response to physical comfort in early human development. *Journal of Child Psychology and Psychiatry, 5,* 1–13.

Schardein, J. (1976). *Drugs as teratogens.* Cleveland: CRC Press.

Schaw, J., Wheeler, P., & Morgan, M. (1970). Emotions during pregnancy. *Journal of the American Academy of Child Psychiatry, 9,* 428.

Schmidt, C. R., & Paris, S. G. (1984). The development of verbal communicative skills in children. In H. W. Reese (Ed.), *Advances in child devel-*

opment and behavior (Vol. 18, pp. 1–47). New York: Academic Press.

Schneider, B. A. (1986, April). *The development of basic auditory abilities.* Paper presented at the International Conference on Infant Studies, Los Angeles.

Schofield, J. W. (1981). Complementary and conflicting identities: Images and interaction in an interracial school. In S. Asher and J. Gottman (Eds.), *The development of children's friendships.* Cambridge, England: Cambridge University Press.

Schofield, J. W., & Sagar, H. A. (1977). Peer interaction patterns in an integrated middle school. *Sociometry, 40,* 130–138.

Schuster, C. S., & Ashburn, S. S. (1986). *The process of human development* (2nd. ed.). Boston: Little, Brown.

Schwartz, P. (1983). Length of day-care attendance and attachment behavior in eighteen-month-old infants. *Child Development, 54,* 1073–1078.

Schwartzman, H. B. (1976). Children's play: A sideways glance at make believe. In D. F. Lancy & B. A. Tindall (Eds.), *The anthropological study of play: Problems and prospects.* Cornwall, NY: Leisure Press.

Schwarz, J. C. (1983, April). *Effects of group day care in the first two years.* Paper presented at the biennial meetings of the Society for Research in Child Development, Detroit.

Schwarz, J. C., Strickland, R. G., & Krolick, G. (1974). Infant day care: Behavioral effects at preschool age. *Developmental Psychology, 10,* 502–506.

Schweinhart, L. J., & Weikart, D. P. (1980). Young children grow up: The effects of the Perry Preschool Program on youths through age 15. *Monographs of the High/Scope Educational Research Foundation,* (No. 7).

Sears, R. R., Maccoby, E. E., & Levin, H. (1957). *Patterns of child rearing.* New York: Harper & Row.

Sedlack, A. (1989, April). *National incidence of child abuse and neglect.* Paper presented at the biennial meeting of the Society for Research in Child Development, Kansas City.

Seegmiller, B., & King, W. (1975). Relations between behavioral characteristics of infants, their mothers' be-

haviors, and performance on the Bayley mental and motor scales. *Journal of Psychology, 90,* 99–111.

Segall, M. (1972). Cardiac responsivity to auditory stimulation on low birthweight infants. *Nursing Research, 21,* 15–19.

Seitz, V., Rosenbaum, L., & Apfel, N. (1985). Effects of family support intervention: A ten-year follow-up. *Child Development, 56,* 376–391.

Self, P. A., Horowitz, F. D., & Paden, L. Y. (1972). Olfaction in newborn infants. *Developmental Psychology, 7,* 249–363.

Seligman, M. (1975). *Helplessness.* San Francisco: Freeman.

Sells, B., & Roff, M. (1964). Peer acceptance—rejection and birth order. *Psychology in the Schools, 1,* 156–162.

Selman, R. (1971). Taking another's perspective: Role-taking development in early childhood. *Child Development, 42,* 1721–1734.

Selman, R. (1980). *The growth of interpersonal understanding: Developmental and clinical analyses.* New York: Academic Press.

Serbin, L. A., Tonick, I. J., & Sternglanz, S. H. (1977). Shaping cooperative cross-sex play. *Child Development, 48,* 924–929.

Shannon, J. (1987, October). Crisis in health care. *Health.*

Shantz, C. (1983). Social cognition. In J. H. Flavell & E. M. Markman (Eds.), *Handbook of child psychology: (Vol. 3.) Cognitive development* (pp. 495–555). New York: Wiley.

Shapiro, C. (1982, September). The impact of infertility on the marital relationship. *Social Casework,* 387–393.

Sharabany, R., Gershoni, R., and Hofman, J. (1981). Girlfriend, boyfriend: Age and sex differences in intimate friendship. *Developmental Psychology, 17,* 800–808.

Shatz, M. (1983). Communication. In J. H. Flavell & E. M. Markman (Eds.), *Handbook of child psychology: Cognitive development* Vol. 3. (pp. 841–889). New York: Wiley.

Shatz, M., & Gelman, R. (1973). The development of communication skills: Modifications in the speech of young children as a function of listener. *Monographs of the Society for*

Research in Child Development, 38 (2, Serial No. 152).

Shaywitz, S., & Shaywitz, B. (1984). Evaluation and treatment of children with attention deficit disorders. *Pediatrics in Review, 6,* 99–109.

Sherif, M., Harvey, O. J., White, B. J., Hood, W. R., & Sherif, C. W. (1961). *Inter-group conflict and cooperation: The Robbers Cave experiment.* Norman: University of Oklahoma Press.

Sherrod, K. B., O'Connor, S., Vietze, P. M., & Altemeier, W. A., III. (1984). Child health and maltreatment. *Child Development, 55,* 1174–1183.

Shinn, M. (1978). Father absence and children's cognitive development. *Psychological Bulletin, 85,* 295–324.

Shipman, G. (1971). The psychodynamics of sex education. In R. E. Mutter (Ed.), *Adolescent behavior and society.* New York: Random House.

Shonkoff, J. (1984). The biological substrate and physical health in middle childhood. In W. A. Collins (Ed.), *Development during middle childhood.* Washington, DC: National Academy Press.

Shotwell, J. M., Wolf, D., & Gardner, H. (1979). Exploring early symbolization: Styles of achievement. In B. Sutton-Smith (Ed.), *Play and learning.* New York: Gardner Press.

Shrier, D. (1984). Children and stress: Sources, reactions, and interventions. *Day Care and Early Education, 11* (4), 10–13.

Siegel, L. (1982). Reproductive, perinatal and environmental factors as predictors of the cognitive and language development of preterm and full-term infants. *Child Development, 53,* 963–973.

Siegel, P. M. (1988, January/February). The guns of childhood. *Parenting,* pp. 100–104.

Siegler, R. S. (1981). Developmental sequences within and between concepts. *Monographs of the Society for Research in Child Development, 46* (Serial No. 189).

Siegler, R. S. (1986). *Children's thinking.* Englewood Cliffs, NJ: Prentice-Hall.

Siegler, R. S. (1988). Individual differences in strategy choices: Good students, not-so-good students, and perfectionists. *Child Development, 59,* 833–851.

Siegler, R. S., & Robinson, M. (1982). The development of numerical understandings. In H. W. Reese & L. P. Lipsitt (Eds.), *Advances in child development and behavior* (Vol. 14). New York: Academic Press.

Siegler, R. S., & Shrager, J. (1984). Strategy choices in addition and subtraction: How do children know what to do? In C. Sophian (Ed.), *Origins of cognitive skills.* Hillsdale, NJ: Erlbaum.

Silberman, M. (1969). Behavioral expression of teachers' attitudes toward elementary school students. *Journal of Educational Psychology, 60,* 402–407.

Silberman, M. (1971). Teachers' attitudes and actions toward their students. In M. Silberman (Ed.), *The experience of schooling.* New York: Holt, Rinehart & Winston.

Simmons, R., & Blyth, D. (1987). *Moving into adolescence.* New York: Aldine de Gruyter.

Simmons, R., Blyth, D., & McKinney, K. (1983). The social and psychological effects of puberty on white females. In J. Brooks-Gunn and A. Petersen (Eds.), *Girls at puberty.* New York: Plenum.

Simmons, R., Blyth, D., Van Cleave, E., & Bush, D. (1979). Entry into early adolescence: The impact of school structure, puberty, and early dating on self-esteem. *American Sociological Review, 44,* 948–967.

Simmons, R., Rosenberg, F., & Rosenberg, M. (1973). Disturbance in the self-image at adolescence. *American Sociological Review, 38,* 553–568.

Simner, M. L. (1971). Newborn's response to the cry of another infant. *Developmental Psychology, 5,* 136–150.

Simon, W., Berger, A., & Gagnon, J. (1972). Beyond anxiety and fantasy: The coital experience of college youth. *Journal of Youth and Adolescence, 1,* 203–222.

Simon, W., & Gagnon, J. (1969). On psychosexual development. In D. Goslin (Ed.), *Handbook of socialization theory and research.* Chicago: Rand McNally.

Simpson, E. (1974). Moral development research: A case of scientific cultural bias. *Human Development, 17,* 81–106.

Simpson, R. (1962). Parental influence, anticipatory socialization, and social mobility. *American Sociological Review, 27,* 517–522.

Sinclair, D. (1913). *Human growth after birth.* London: Oxford University Press.

Singer, J. L., & Singer, D. G. (1976). Imaginative play and pretending in early childhood. In A. Davids (Ed.), *Child personality and psychopathology.* New York: Wiley.

Singer, J. L., Singer, D. G., & Sherrod, L. R. (1980). A factor analytic study of preschooler's play behavior. *American Psychology Bulletin, 2,* 143–156.

Singer, L., Brodzinsky, D., Ramsay, D., Steir, M., & Waters, E. (1985). Mother-infant attachment in adoptive families. *Child Development, 56,* 1543–1551.

Siqueland, E. R. (1968). Reinforcement patterns and extinction in human newborns. *Journal of Experimental Child Psychology, 6,* 431–442.

Sirigano, S., & Lachman, M. (1985). Personality change during the transition to parenthood: The role of perceived infant temperament. *Developmental Psychology, 21,* 558–567.

Sizer, T. (1984). *Horace's compromise.* Boston: Houghton Mifflin.

Slaby, R., & Frey, K. S. (1975). Development of gender constancy and selective attention to same-sex models. *Child Development, 46,* 849–856.

Slaby, R., & Guerra, N. (1988). Cognitive mediators of aggression in adolescent offenders: 1. Assessment. *Developmental Psychology, 24,* 580–588.

Slobin, D. (1970). Universals of grammatical development in children. In G. Flores D'Arcais & W. Levelt (Eds.), *Advances in psycholoquistics* (pp. 174–184). New York: American Elsevier.

Skinner, B. F. (1938). *The behavior of organisms: An experimental approach.* New York: Appleton-Century.

Smith, C., & Lloyd, B. (1978). Maternal behavior and perceived sex of infant: Revisited. *Child Development, 49,* 1263–1266.

Smith, L. H. (1976). *Improving your child's behavior chemistry.* Englewood Cliffs, NJ: Prentice-Hall.

Smith, P. K. (1978). A longitudinal study of social participation in preschool children: Solitary and parallel play reexamined. *Developmental Psychology, 14,* 517–523.

Snow, C. E. (1977a). The development of conversation between mothers and babies. *Journal of Child Language, 4,* 1–22.

Snow, C. E. (1977b). Mother's speech research: From input to interaction. In C. E. Snow & C. A. Ferguson (Eds.), *Talking to children: Language input and acquisition.* London: Cambridge University Press.

Sobesky, W. (1983). The effects of situational factors on moral judgments. *Child Development, 54,* 575–584.

Sollie, D., & Miller, B. (1980). The transition to parenthood as a critical time for building family strengths. In N. Stinnet & P. Knaub (Eds.), *Family strengths: Positive models of family life.* Lincoln: University of Nebraska Press.

Somerville, S. C., Wellman, H. M., & Cultice, J. C. (1983). Young children's deliberate reminding. *Journal of Genetic Psychology, 143,* 87–96.

Sontag, L. (1941). The significance of fetal environmental differences. *American Journal of Obstetrics and Gynecology, 42,* 996–1003.

Sontag, L. (1966). Implications of fetal behavior and environment for adult personality. *Annals of the New York Academy of Science, 34,* 782–786.

Sophian, D. (1988). Early developments in children's understanding of number: Inferences about numerosity and one-to-one correspondence. *Child Development, 59,* 1397–1414.

Sorensen, R. (1973). *Adolescent sexuality in contemporary society.* New York: World Book.

Sostek, A., Quinn, P., & Davitt, M. (1979). Behavior, development and neurologic status of premature and full-term infants with varying medical complications. In T. Field, A. Sostek, S. Goldberg, & H. Shuman (Eds.), *Infants born at risk.* New York: Spectrum.

Spanier, G. B., & Glick, P. C. (1981). Marital instability in the United States: Some correlates and recent changes. *Family Relations, 31,* 329–338.

Spelke, E. S. (1984). The development of intermodal perception. In L. B. Cohen & P. Salapatek (Eds.), *Handbook of infant perception.* New York: Academic.

Spencer, M. B. (1981). *Personal-social adjustment of minority children. Final report,* (Project No. 5-R01-MH 31106). Atlanta, GA: Emory University.

Sperling, M. (1961). Analytic first aid in school phobias. *Psychoanalytic Quarterly, 30,* 504–518.

Spinetta, J. J., & Rigler, D. (1972). The child-abusing parent: A psychological review. *Psychological Bulletin, 77,* 296–304.

Spock, B. M., & Rothenberg, M. B. *Dr. Spock's Baby and Child Care* (rev. ed.). New York: Pocket Books.

Sroufe, L. A. (1977). Wariness of strangers and the study of infant development. *Child Development, 48,* 1184–1199.

Sroufe, L. A. (1979). The coherence of individual development: Early care, attachment, and subsequent developmental issues. *American Psychologist, 34,* 834–842.

Sroufe, L. A. (1983). Infant-caregiving attachment and patterns of adaptation and competence. In M. Perlmutter (Ed.), *Minnesota Symposia in Child Psychology* (Vol. 16). Hillsdale, N.J.: Erlbaum.

Sroufe, L. A., & Cooper, R. G. (1988). *Child development: Its nature and course.* New York: Knopf.

Sroufe, L. A., Waters, E., & Matas, L. (1974). Contextual determinants of infant affective response. In M. Lewis & L. Rosenblum (Eds.), *The origins of behavior.* New York: Wiley.

Stack, C. (1974). *All our kin.* New York: Harper & Row.

Standley, K., Soule, A. B. III, Copans, S. A., & Duchowny, M. S. (1974). Local-regional anesthesia during childbirth: Effect on newborn behaviors. *Science, 186,* 534–535.

Stangor, C., & Ruble, D. (1987). Development of gender role knowledge and gender constancy. In L. Liben and M. Signorella (Eds.), Children's gender schemata. *New Directions in Child Development* (No. 38). San Francisco: Jossey-Bass.

Stanjek, K. (1978). Das Uberreichen von Gaben: Funktion und Entwicklung in den ersten Lebensjahren. *Zeitschrift für Entwicklungspsychologie und Pedagogische Psychologie, 10,* 103–113.

Stebbins, G. L. (1982). *Darwin to DNA, molecules to humanity.* San Francisco: Freeman.

Steele, B. F., & Pollock, C. B. (1968). A psychiatric study of parents who abuse infants and small children. In R. Helfer & C. H. Kempe (Eds.), *The battered child* (pp. 103–147). Chicago: University of Chicago Press.

Steinberg, L. (1981). Transformations in family relations at puberty. *Developmental Psychology, 17,* 833–840.

Steinberg, L. (1982). Jumping off the work experience bandwagon. *Journal of Youth and Adolescence, 11,* 183–205.

Steinberg, L. (1986). Latchkey children and susceptibility to peer pressure: An ecological analysis. *Developmental Psychology, 22,* 433–439.

Steinberg, L. (1987a). The impact of puberty on family relations: Effects of pubertal status and pubertal timing. *Developmental Psychology, 23,* 451–460.

Steinberg, L. (1987b). Single parents, stepparents, and the susceptibility of adolescents to antisocial peer pressure. *Child Development, 58,* 269–275.

Steinberg, L. (1989). *Adolescence* (2nd ed.). New York: Knopf.

Steinberg, L., Catalano, R., & Dooley, D. (1981). Economic antecedents of child abuse, *Child Development, 52,* 975–985.

Steinberg, L., Greenberger, E., Garduque, L., & McAuliffe, S. (1982). Adolescents in the labor force: Some costs and benefits to schooling and learning. *Educational Evaluation and Policy Analysis, 4,* 363–372.

Steinberg, L., Greenberger, E., Garduque, L., Ruggiero, M., & Vaux, A. (1982). Effects of working on adolescent development. *Developmental Psychology, 18,* 385–395.

Steinberg, L., & Levine, A. (1990). *You and your adolescent: A parent's guide to development from 10 to 20.* New York: Harper & Row.

Steinberg, L., & Silverberg, S. (1986). The vicissitudes of autonomy in early adolescence. *Child Development,* 57, 841–851.

Steiner, G. (1963). *The people look at television.* New York: Knopf.

Steiner, J. (1977). Facial expressions of the neonate infant in indicating the hedonics of food-related chemical stimuli. In J. Werffenbach (Ed.), *Taste and development.* Washington, DC: Department of Health, Education, and Welfare.

Steiner, J. (1979). Human facial expressions in response to taste and smell stimulation. In H. Reese & L. Lipsitt (Eds.), *Advances in child development and behavior* (Vol. 13). New York: Academic Press.

Stenberg, C., Campos, J., & Emde, R. (1983). The facial expression of anger in seven-month-old infants. *Child Development, 54,* 178–184.

Stern, D. (1974). Mother and infant at play: The dyadic interaction involving facial, vocal, and gaze behaviors. In M. Lewis & L. Rosenblum (Eds.), *The effect of the infant on its caregiver.* New York: Wiley.

Stern, D. (1985). *Interpersonal world of the infant.* New York: Basic Books.

Sternberg, R. (1977). *Intelligence, information, processing, and reasoning: The componential analysis of human abilities.* Hillsdale, NJ: Erlbaum.

Sternberg, R. (1985). *Beyond IQ: A triarchic theory of human intelligence.* Cambridge, England: Cambridge University Press.

Sternberg, R., & Nigro, G. (1980). Developmental patterns in the solution of verbal analogies. *Child Development, 51,* 27–38.

Sternberg, R., & Rifkin, B. (1979). The development of analogical reasoning processes. *Journal of Experimental Child Psychology, 27,* 195–232.

Sterns, D. (1985). *The interpersonal world of the infant.* New York: Basic Books.

Steuer, F. B., Applefield, J. M., & Smith, R. (1971). Televised aggression and the interpersonal aggression of preschool children. *Journal of Experimental Child Psychology, 11,* 442–447.

Stevens, J. (1988). Social support, locus of control and parenting in three low-income groups of mother. *Child Development, 59,* 635–642.

Stevenson, W. (1978). The relationship between early work experience and future employability. In A. Adams and G. Mangum (Eds.), *The lingering crisis of youth unemployment.* Kalamazoo, MI: Upjohn Institute for Employment Research.

Stewart, A., Reynolds, E., & Lipcomb, A. (1981). Outcome for infants of very low birthweight: Survey of the world literature. *Lancet,* May, 1038–1041.

Stewart, A., Weiland, I., Leider, A., Mangham, C., Jolmes, T., & Ripley, H. (1954). Excessive infant crying (colic) in relation to parent behavior. *American Journal of Psychiatry, 110,* 687–694.

Stewart, R. (1983). Sibling attachment relationships: Child-infant interactions in the strange situation. *Developmental Psychology, 19,* 192–199.

Stilwell, R. (1983). *Social relationships in primary school children as seen by children, mothers, and teachers.* Unpublished doctoral thesis, University of Cambridge.

Stillwell, R., & Dunn, J. (1985). Continuities in sibling relationships: Patterns of aggression and friendliness. *Journal of Child Psychology and Psychiatry, 26,* (4). 627–637.

Stipek, D. (1981). Adolescents—Too young to earn, too old to learn? Compulsory school attendance and intellectual development. *Journal of Youth and Adolescence, 10,* 113–139.

Stockbauer, J. (1986). Evaluation of the Missouri WIC program: Prenatal components. *Journal of the American Dietetic Association, 1,* 61–67.

Stone, L. J., & Church, J. (1969). *Childhood and adolescence* (4th ed.). New York: Random House.

Stone, L. J., Smith, H., & Murphy, L. (Eds.). (1973). *The competent infant.* New York: Basic Books.

Strauss, M., & Gelles, R. (1986). Societal change and change in family violence from 1975 to 1985 as revealed by two national surveys. *Journal of Marriage and the Family, 48,* 465–479.

Strauss, M., Lessen-Firestone, J., Starr, R., & Ostrea, E. (1975). Behavior of narcotics-addicted newborns. *Child Development, 46,* 887–897.

Streissguth, A. P., Barr, H. M., Martin, D. C., & Herman, C. S. (1980). Effects of maternal alcohol, nicotine and caffeine used during pregnancy on infant mental and motor development at 8 months. *Alcoholism: Clinical and Experimental Research, 4,* 152–154.

Streissguth, A. P., Barr, H. M., Sampson, P. D., Parrish-Johnson, J., Kirchner, G., & Martin, D. C. (1986). Attention, distraction, and reaction time at age 7 years and prenatal alcohol exposure. *Neurobehavioral Toxicology and Teratology, 8,* 717–725.

Streissguth, A. P., Landesman-Dwyer, S., Martin, D. C., & Smith, D. W. (1980). Teratogenic effects of alcohol in humans and laboratory animals. *Science, 209,* 353–361.

Streissguth, A. P., Martin, D. C., Barr, H. M., Sandman, B., Kirchner, G., & Darby, B. (1984). Intrauterine alcohol and nicotine exposure: Attention and reaction time in 4-year-old children. *Developmental Psychology, 20,* 533–541.

Streissguth, A. P., Treder, R. P., Barr, H. M., Shepard, T. H., Bleyer, W. A., Sampson, P. D., & Martin, D. C. (1987). Aspirin and acetaminophen use by pregnant women and subsequent child IQ and attention decrements. *Teratology, 35,* 211–219.

Strunin, L., & Hingson, R. (1987). Acquired immunodeficiency syndrome and adolescents: Knowledge, beliefs, attitudes, and behaviors. *Pediatrics, 79,* 825–828.

Stuckey, M., McGhee, P., & Bell, N. (1982). Parent-child interaction: The influence of maternal employment. *Developmental Psychology, 18,* 635–644.

Sullivan, H. S. (1953a). *The interpersonal theory of psychiatry.* New York: Norton.

Sullivan, H. S. (1953b). *Conceptions of modern psychiatry.* New York: Norton.

Super, C. M. (1981). Cross-cultural studies of infancy. *Handbook of Cross-cultural Psychology.* New York: Wiley.

Super, D. (1967). *The psychology of careers.* New York: Harper & Row.

Susman, E., Inoff-Germain, G., Nottleman, E., Loriaux, D., Cutler, G., & Chrouses, G. (1987). Hormones, emotional dispositions and aggressive attitudes in young adolescents. *Child Development, 58,* 1114–1134.

Sussman, L., et al. (1987). Hormones, emotional dispositions, and aggressive attributes in young adolescents. *Child Development, 58,* 1114–1134.

Svejda, M., Campos, J., & Emde, R. N. (1980). Mother-infant "bonding": Failure to generalize. *Child Development, 51,* 775–779.

Tan, L. E. (1985). Laterality and motor skills in 4-year-olds. *Child Development, 56,* 119–124.

Tanner, D. (1972). *Secondary education.* New York: Macmillan.

Tanner, J. (1970). Physical growth. In P. H. Mussen (Ed.) *Charmichael's manual of child psychology* (Vol. 1). New York: Wiley.

Tanner, J. (1978). *Foetus into man: physical growth from conception to maturity.* London: Open Books.

Teale, W. H., & Sulzby, E. (1986). *Emergent literacy: Writing and reading.* Norwood, NJ: Ablex.

Thelen, E. (1979). Rhythmical stereotypes in normal human infants. *Animal Behavior, 27,* 699–715.

Thelen, E. (1981). Rhythmical behaviors in infancy: An ethological perspective. *Developmental Psychology, 17,* 237–257.

Thelen, E. (1984). Learning to walk: Ecological demands and phylogenetic constraints. *Advances in Infancy Research, 3,* 213–250.

Thelen, E., Skala, K. D., & Kelso, J. S. (1987). The dynamic nature of early coordination: Evidence from bilateral leg movements in young infants. *Developmental Psychology, 23,* 179–186.

Thomas, A., & Chess, S. (1977). *Temperament and development.* New York: Brunner/Mazel.

Thomas, A., & Chess, S. (1980). *The dynamics of psychological development.* New York: Brunner/Mazel.

Thomas, A., Chess, S., & Birch, H. (1968). *Temperament and behavior disorders in children.* New York: New York University Press.

Thomas, H. (1973). Unfolding the baby's mind: The infant's selection of visual stimuli. *Psychological Review, 80,* 468–488.

Thorne, Barry, (1986). Boys and girls together . . . but mostly apart. Gender arrangements in elementary schools. In W. Hartup & Z. Rubin (Eds.), *Relationships and development*. Hillsdale, NJ: Erlbaum.

Tobin, J. J., Wu, D. Y. H., & Davidson, D. H. (1989, April). How three key countries shape their children. *World Monitor*, pp. 36–45.

Tooke, S. (1974). *Adjustment to parenthood among a select group of disadvantaged parents*. Unpublished master's thesis, Montana State University.

Travers, J., & Ruopp, R. (1978). *National day care study: Preliminary findings and their implications: 31 January, 1978*. Cambridge, MA: Alot Associates.

Tulkin, S., & Covitz, F. (1975, April). *Mother-infant interaction and intellectual functioning at age six*. Paper presented at the biennial meeting of the Society for Research in Child Development, Denver.

Tulkin, S., & Kagan, J. (1972). Mother-child interaction in the first year of life. *Child Development, 43*, 31–41.

Turiel, E. (1978). The development of concepts of social structure: Social convention. In J. Glick and K. A. Clark-Stewart (Eds.), *The development of social understanding*. New York: Gardner.

Turner, G., & Collins, E. (1975). Fetal effects of regular salicylate ingestion in pregnancy, *Lancet, 2*, 338–339.

U.S. Bureau of the Census. (1980). *Statistical abstract of the United States*. Washington, DC: U.S. Government Printing Office.

U.S. Bureau of the Census. (1981). *Statistical abstract of the United States*. Washington, DC: U.S. Government Printing Office.

U.S. Bureau of the Census. (1985). *Statistical abstract of the United States*. Washington, DC: U.S. Government Printing Office.

U.S. Bureau of the Census. (1987). Who's Minding the Kids? Childcare arrangements: 1984–85. *Current population reports*. (Series P-70, No. 9). Washington, DC: U.S. Government Printing Office, 5.

U.S. Bureau of the Census. (1987). *Statistical abstract of the United States*. Washington, DC: U.S. Government Printing Office.

U.S. Bureau of the Census. (1982, June). *Marital status and living arrangements: March 1981*. Washing-

ton, DC: U.S. Department of Commerce.

U.S. Bureau of the Census. (1980, May). *American families and living arrangements, 1978*. Washington, DC: U.S. Department of Commerce.

Vandell, D. (1980). Sociability with peers and mothers in the first year. *Developmental Psychology, 16*, 355–361.

Vandell, D., Henderson, V. K., & Wilson, K. (1988). A longitudinal study of children with day-care experiences of varying quality. *Child Development, 59*, 1286–1292.

Vandell, D., & Powers, C. (1983). Day care quality and children's free play activities. *American Journal of Orthopsychiatry, 53*, 493–500.

Vanfossen, B., Jones, J., & Spade, J. (1987). Curriculum tracking and status maintenance. *Sociology of Education, 60*, 104–122.

Vaughn, B., Crichton, L., & Egeland, B. (1982). Individual differences in qualities of caregiving during the first six months of life: Antecedents in maternal and infant behavior during the newborn period. *Infant Behavior and Development, 5*, pp. 77–96.

Vaughn, B., Gove, F. L., & Egeland, B. (1980). The relationship between out-of-home care and the quality of infant-mother attachment in an economically disadvantaged population. *Child Development, 51*, 971–975.

Vaughn, B., & Langlois, J. H. (1983). Physical attractiveness as a correlate of peer status and social competence in preschool children. *Developmental Psychology, 19*, 561–567.

Vaughn, V. C. III, McKay, J. R., & Nelson, W. E. (Eds.). (1975). *Nelson textbook of pediatrics*. Philadelphia: Saunders.

Vigersky, R. (Ed.). (1977). *Anorexia nervosa*. New York: Raven Press.

Vincze, M. (1971). [Examinations on the social contacts between infants and young children reared together.] *Magyar Pszichologiai Szemle, 28*, 58–61.

Vogel, E. (1963). *Japan's new middle class*. Berkeley: University of California Press.

Vosniadou, S., Pearson, P. D., & Rogers, T. (1988). What causes children's failures to detect inconsistencies in

text? Representation versus comparison difficulties. *Journal of Educational Psychology, 80*, 27–39.

Vuori, L., Christiansen, N., Clement, J., Mora, J., Wagner, M., & Herrera, M. (1979). Nutritional supplementation and the outcome of pregnancy. II. Visual habituation at 15 days. *Journal of Clinical Nutrition, 32*, 463–469.

Vygotsky, L. S. (1962). *Thought and language*. Boston: MIT Press.

Waber, C. (1977). Sex differences in mental abilities, hemispheric lateralization, and rate of physical growth at adolescence. *Developmental Psychology, 13*, 29–38.

Wachs, T. D., Uzgiris, I. C., & Hunt, J. McV. (1971). Cognitive development in infants of different age levels and from different environmental backgrounds: An explanatory investigation. *Merrill-Palmer Quarterly, 17*, 283–317.

Waddington, C. H. (1966). *Principles of development and differentiation*. New York: Macmillan.

Walker, L., de Vries, B., & Trevethan, S. (1987). Moral stages and moral orientations in real-life and hypothetical dilemmas. *Child Development, 58*, 842–858.

Walker-Andrews, A. S., & Gibson, E. J. (1987). What develops in bimodal perception? In L. P. Lipsitt & C. K. Rovee-Collire (Eds.), *Advance in infancy research* (Vol. 4). Norwood, NJ: Ablex.

Walker-Andrews, A. S., & Lennon, E. M. (1985). Auditory-visual perception of changing distance by human infants. *Child Development, 56*, 544–548.

Wallach, L., & Sprott, R. L., (1964). Inducing number conservation in children. *Child Development, 35*, 1057–1071.

Wallerstein, J. (1989). *Second chances: Men, women and children a decade after divorce*. New York: Ticknor & Fields.

Wallerstein, J., & Kelley, J. (1974). The effects of parental divorce: The adolescent experience. In E. Anthony & A. Koupernik (Eds.), *The child in his family: Children as a psychiatric risk* (Vol. 3). New York: Wiley.

Wallerstein, J., & Kelley, J. (1980). *Sur-

viving the breakup: How children and parents cope with divorce. New York: Basic Books.

Wallis, C. (1985, February 4). Chlamydia: The silent epidemic. *Time,* p. 67.

Walster, E., Aronson, V., Abrahams, D., & Rottman, L. (1966). Importance of physical attractiveness in dating behavior. *Journal of Personality and Social Psychology, 4,* 508–516.

Walters, H., & Kranzler, G. (1970). Early identification of the school dropout. *School Counselor, 18,* 97–104.

Warburton, P., Susser, M., Stein, Z., & Kline, J. (1979). Genetic and epidemiologic investigation of spontaneous abortion: Relevance to clinical practice. *Birth Defects: Original Articles Series, 115 (15),* 127–136.

Warshak, J., & Santrock, J. (1983, March). The impact of divorce in father-custody and mother-custody homes: The child's perspective. In L. Kurdek (Ed.), *Children and divorce.* New Directions for Child Development, No. 19. San Francisco: Jossey-Bass.

Wasz-Hockert, O., Lind, J., Vuorenkoski, V., Partanen, T., & Valanne, E. (1968). *The infant cry: Clinics in developmental medicine,* No. 29. London: Heinemann.

Waters, E., Vaughn, B. E., & Egeland, B. R. (1980). Individual differences in infant-mother attachment relationships at age one: Antecedents in neonatal behavior in an urban, economically disadvantaged sample. *Child Development, 51,* 208–216.

Waters, E., Wippman, J., & Sroufe, L. A. (1979). Attachment, positive affects, and competence in the peer group: Two studies in construct validation. *Child Development, 50,* 821–829.

Webster, R., Steinhardt, M., & Senter, M. (1972). Changes in infant's vocalizations as a function of differential acoustic stimulation. *Developmental Psychology, 7,* 39–43.

Weideger, P. (1976). *Menstruation and menopause.* New York: Knopf.

Weiner, I. (1980). Psychopathology in adolescence. In J. Adelson (Ed.), *Handbook of adolescent psychology.* New York: Wiley.

Weinraub, M., & Lewis, M. (1977). The determinants of children's responses to separation. *Monographs of the Society for Research in Child Development, 48,* (1240–1249).

Weinraub, M., & Putney, E. (1978). The effects of height on infant's social responses to unfamiliar persons. *Child Development, 49,* 598–603.

Weir, C. (1979). Auditory frequency sensitivity of human newborns: Some data with improved acoustic and behavioral controls. *Perception and Psychophysics, 26,* 287–294.

Weissberg, J. A., & Paris, S. G. (1986). Young children's remembering in different contexts. *Child Development, 57,* 1123–1129.

Weizmann, F., Cohen, L. B., & Pratt, R. J. (1971). Novelty, familiarity, and the development of infant attention. *Development Psychology, 4,* 149–154.

Wellman, H. M. (1988). First steps in the child's theorizing about the mind. In J. W. Astington, P. L. Harris, & D. R. Olson (Eds.), *Developing theories of mind* (pp. 64–92). Cambridge, England: Cambridge University Press.

Wellman, H. M., & Estes, D. (1986). Early understanding of mental entities: A reexamination of childhood realism. *Child Development, 57,* 910–923.

Wellman, H. M., Ritter, K., & Flavell, J. H. (1975). Deliberate memory behavior in the delayed reactions of very young children. *Developmental Psychology, 11,* 780–787.

Wellman, H. M., & Somerville, S. C. (1980). The development of human search ability. In M. E. Lamb & A. L. Brown (Eds.), *Advances in developmental psychology* (Vol. 2). Hillsdale, NJ: Erlbaum.

Werner, E., & Smith, R. (1982). *Vulnerable but invincible: A study of resilient children.* New York: McGraw-Hill.

Whalen, C., & Henker, B. (1976). Psychostimulants and children: A review and analysis. *Psychological Bulletin, 83,* 1113–1130.

White, B. L. (1967). An experimental approach to the effects of the environment on early human behavior. In J. P. Hill (Ed.), *Minnesota symposium on child psychology* (Vol. 1). Minneapolis: University of Minnesota Press.

White, B., & Held, R. (1966). Plasticity of sensorimotor development. In J. Rosenblith & W. Alinsmith (Eds.), *The causes of behavior.* Boston: Allyn & Bacon.

White, S. H. (1965). Evidence for a hierarchical arrangement of learning processes. In L. P. Lipsitt & C. C. Spiker (Eds.), *Advances in child development and behavior* (Vol. 2). New York: Academic Press.

Whitehurst, G. J., & Sonnenschein, S. (1981). The development of informative messages in referential communication: Knowing when vs. knowing how. In W. P. Dickson (Ed.), *Children's oral communication skills.* New York: Academic Press.

Whiting, J. (1964). Effects of climate on certain cultural practices. In W. Goodenough (Ed.), *Explorations in cultural anthropology: Essays in honor of George Peter Murdock.* New York: McGraw-Hill.

Wideman, M. V., & Singer, J. F. (1984). The role of psychological mechanisms in preparation for childbirth. *American Psychologist, 34,* 1357–1371.

Wilkerson, I. (1987, June 26). Infant mortality: Frightful odds in the inner cities. *The New York Times,* A1, A20.

Will, J., Self, P., & Datan, N. (1976). Maternal behavior and perceived sex of infant. *American Journal of Orthopsychiatry, 46,* 135–139.

Wilson, G., McCreary, R., Kean, J., & Borka, J. (1979). The development of preschool children of heroin-addicted mothers: A controlled study. *Pediatrics, 63,* 135–141.

Winick, M. (1970). Nutrition and nerve cell growth. *Federation Proceedings, 29,* 1510–1515.

Winick, M. (1976). *Malnutrition and brain development.* New York: Oxford University Press.

Winick, M., Meyers, K., & Harris, R. (1975). Malnutrition and environmental enrichment by early adoption. *Science, 190,* 1173–1175.

Winick, M., & Rosso, P. (1969). Head circumference and cellular growth of the brain in normal and marasmic children. *Journal of Pediatrics, 74,* 774–778.

Winn, M. (1985). *The Plug-in drug.* New York: Penguin.

Winnicott, D. (1971). *Playing and reality.* New York: Basic Books.

Wintre, M., Hicks, R., McVey, G., & Fox, J. (1988). Age and sex differences in choice of consultant for various types of problems. *Child Development.*

Wirtz, P., Rohrbeck, C., Charner, I., & Fraser, B. (1987). *Intense employment while in high school: Are teachers, guidance counselors, and parents misguiding academically-oriented adolescents?* Unpublished manuscript. Graduate Institute for Policy Education and Research, George Washington University, Washington, DC.

Wolf, D., & Grollman, S. H. (1982). Ways of playing: Individual differences in imaginative style. In D. J. Pepler & K. H. Rubin (Eds.), *The play of children: Current theory and research.* Basel, Switzerland: Karger AG.

Wolff, P. (1966). The causes, controls, and organization of behavior in the neonate. *Psychological Issues, 5*(1, Whole No. 17). New York: International University Press.

Wolff, P. (1969). The natural history of crying and other vocalizations in early infancy. In B. M. Foss (Ed.), *Determinants of infant behavior* (Vol. 4). London: Methuen.

Wolman, P. (1984). Feeding practices in infancy and prevalence of obesity in preschool children. *Journal of the American Dietetic Association, 84,* 436–438.

Woodhead, M. (1988). When psychology informs public policy: The case of early childhood intervention. *American Psychologist, 43,* 443–455.

Yarrow, L. (1961). Maternal deprivation: Toward an empirical and conceptual re-evaluation. *Psychological Bulletin, 58,* 459–490.

Yarrow, L. (1984). *Parents' book of pregnancy and birth.* New York: Ballantine.

Yarrow, L., Goodwin, M., Manheimer, H., & Milowe, I. (1973). Infancy experiences and cognitive and personality development at 10 years. In L. Stone, H. Smith, & L. Murphy (Eds.), *The competent infant* (pp. 1274–1281). New York: Basic Books.

Yarrow, M. R., Campbell, J. D., & Burton, R. (1968). *Child rearing, an inquiry into research and methods.* San Francisco: Jossey-Bass.

Yarrow, M. R., Scott, P. M., & Waxler, C. Z. (1973). Learning concern for others. *Developmental Psychology, 8,* 240–260.

Yogman, M. W., Dixon, S., & Tronick, E. (1977). *The goals and structure of face-to-face interaction between infants and fathers.* Paper presented at the biennial meeting of the Society for Research in Child Development, New Orleans.

Young, H., & Ferguson, L. (1979). Developmental changes through adolescence in the spontaneous nomination of reference groups as a function of decision context. *Journal of Youth and Adolescence, 8,* 239–252.

Youngblade, L., & Belsky, J. (1984). The social and emotional consequences of child maltreatment. In R. Ammerman and M. Hersen (Eds.), *Children at risk.* New York: Plenum.

Youniss, J., (1980). *Parents and peers in social development: A Sullivan-Piaget perspective.* Chicago: University of Chicago Press.

Youniss, J., & Smollar, J. (1985). *Adolescent relations with mothers, fathers, and friends.* Chicago: University of Chicago Press.

Yussen, S. (1976). Moral reasoning from the perspective of others. *Child Development, 47,* 551–555.

Zabin, L., Hirsch, M., Smith, E., Streett, R., & Hardy, J. (1986). Evaluation of a pregnancy prevention program for urban teenagers. *Family Planning Perspectives, 16,* 119–126.

Zahn-Waxler, C., & Radke-Yarrow, M. (1982). The development of altruism: Alternative research strategies. In N. Eisenberg-Berg (Ed.), *The development of prosocial behavior.* New York: Academic Press.

Zajonc, R. B., & Markus, G. B. (1975). Birth order and intellectual development. *Psychological Review, 82*(1), 74–88.

Zarin-Ackerman, J., Lewis, M., & Driscoll, J., Jr. (1977). Language development in 2-year-old normal and risk infants. *Pediatrics, 59,* 982–986.

Zelazo, P., Zelazo, N., & Kolb, S. (1972). "Walking" in the newborn. *Science, 176,* 14–15.

Zelnick, M., & Kantner, J. (1973). Sex and contraception among unmarried teenagers. In C. Westoff et al. (Eds.), *Toward the end of growth: Population in America.* Englewood Cliffs, NJ: Prentice-Hall.

Zeskind, P. (1983). Cross-cultural differences in maternal perceptions of cries of low- and high-risk infants. *Child Development, 54,* 1119–1128.

Zeskind, P., & Lester, B. (1978). Acoustic features and auditory perceptions of the cries of newborns with parental and perinatal complications. *Child Development, 49,* 580–589.

Zigler, E. (1987). Formal schooling for four-year olds? No. *American Psychologist, 42,* 254–260.

Zigler, E., & Berman, W. (1983). Discerning the future of early childhood intervention. *American Psychologist, 38,* 894–906.

Glossary

5-to-7 transition A period in which children begin to develop a sense of logic and strategy as part of their cognitive skills.

accommodation According to Piaget, the process by which people alter their existing schemes to adapt to new information that doesn't "fit" an existing scheme.

achievement motivation The desire to perform well.

acquired immune deficiency syndrome (AIDS) A deadly viral disease, transmitted through body fluids, that attacks the immune system.

adolescent growth spurt The pronounced increase in height and weight during the first half of puberty.

agency Active, assertive, and self-confident behavior.

alleles Alternative genes for the same trait.

altricial Describes the pattern of prenatal development marked by a long gestation and a small number of well-developed young.

amniocentesis A medical technique for diagnosing genetic abnormalities *in utero* by analysis of the amniotic fluid.

amniotic sac The protective, fluid-filled membrane surrounding the embryo and fetus.

androgens The class of hormones, including testosterone, that occur in higher levels in males.

animism Crediting nonliving things with human qualities.

anorexia nervosa An eating disorder in which young people may starve themselves.

anoxia Lack of oxygen in the fetus.

anxious-avoidant attachment An insecure attachment in which an infant shows indifference to its mother or father and avoids interaction with her or him.

anxious-resistant attachment An insecure attachment in which an infant shows much distress at separation from and anger at reunion with its mother or father.

Apgar test A test that measures a baby's heart rate, breathing, muscle tone, reflexes, and color immediately after birth.

arborization The proliferation of connections among neurons by branching.

artificial insemination Fertilization by placement of the husband's or a donor's sperm directly into the cervix.

assimilation According to Piaget, the process by which people incorporate new information into their existing schemes.

associative play Play that includes sharing of materials but not extensive interaction.

attachment The close, significant emotional bond between the mother (or father) and the infant.

attention-deficit hyperactivity disorder A disorder in which children can neither pay attention nor remain still.

authoritarian parents Parents who have an absolute set of standards and expect unquestioning obedience.

authoritative parents Parents who set clear standards but legitimate their authority through warmth and explanation.

autonomy versus shame and doubt According to Erikson, the toddler's major "crisis"—the conflict between the desire for independence and the desire for security—as the sense of self emerges.

babbling An infant's repetitive sound combinations, before first words are spoken.

barometric self-esteem Moment-to-moment shifts in self-assessment.

basal metabolism The rate at which the resting body burns calories.

baseline self-esteem Stable, general feelings about the self.

basic trust An infant's strong sense that its needs will be met and the world is not a threatening place; according to Erikson, the estab-

579

lishment of trust is the major task of infancy.

Bayley Scales Tests for assessing an infant's mental and motor skills by comparison with age-related norms.

behaviorism A learning theory that looks at how concrete stimuli can, through reinforcement and punishment, produce observable changes in people's behavior.

binocular convergence The ability to focus both eyes on the same object.

blastula The hollow-ball form the new organism takes from about 4 days to 2 weeks following conception.

bloody show The blood-tinged mucus in a pregnant woman's urine or discharge, which is a sign of impending labor.

Brazelton Newborn Behavioral Assessment Scale A test evaluating a newborn's state of control, sensory capacities, reflexes, and motor abilities.

breech birth A birth in which the baby emerges feet or buttocks first.

Caesarean section Surgery in which the uterus is opened and the baby is lifted out.

canalization The extent to which a trait is susceptible to modification by the environment or by experience.

case study A study that amasses detailed information about one or, at most, a few people.

castration anxiety Freud's label for a little boy's fear that he will be punished for being his father's rival.

center-based day care Child care licensed and regulated by a local authority and located in a central facility.

centration Focusing on only one aspect of a stimulus.

cephalocaudal development The pattern of growth proceeding from the head downward.

cerebral cortex The wrinkled outer layer of the brain, which is the most highly evolved part of the brain, responsible for perception, muscle control, thought, and memory.

cerebral lateralization The process by which certain brain functions are located in one hemisphere.

cervix The narrow passage connecting the uterus and the vagina.

chlamydia A bacterial sexually transmitted disease that can harm the fetus during birth.

chorionic villus biopsy (CVB) A prenatal diagnostic technique that analyzes cells taken from hairlike villi on the embryonic sac for genetic problems.

chromosomes Twisted strands of DNA that carry genetic instructions from generation to generation.

classical conditioning Learning through the repeated pairing of a stimulus and a response.

classification The cognitive ability to understand how things fit into categories and how these categories can be arranged relative to each other.

cliques Exclusive social circles of friends.

cofigurative societies Societies in which change is so rapid that parents' knowledge may be outdated by the time their children grow up.

collective monologue A discussion between children who take turns talking but whose topics may be unrelated.

communion Supportive, helpful, and empathic behavior.

compensatory education programs Community-based programs designed to meet the needs of children at high risk of school failure.

complexity The number and intricacy of traits like color or pattern in a stimulus.

compressed sentences Phrases made up of several words slurred into one long sound.

concrete operations According to Piaget, the stage of development between ages 6 and 12 when children acquire the mental schemes of seriation, classification, and conservation that allow them to think logically about "concrete" objects.

conservation The knowledge that basic physical dimensions remain the same despite superficial changes in appearance.

constructive play Play that involves manipulating objects to construct or create.

contractions Movements of the muscular walls of the uterus that push the baby out of the mother's body.

conventional thinking According to Kohlberg, the second level of moral development, in which children make decisions about what is right and wrong based on how well a person follows the rules and conventions of society and keeps within the roles people are expected to play.

correlational studies An assessment of the extent to which two or more factors tend to be related.

critical periods Periods during gestation during which particular developing organs and structures are most vulnerable to environmental influences.

crossing-over The exchange of chromosomal segments during meiosis.

cross-modal abilities Abilities that cut across sensory modes; abilities to transfer data from one sensory system to another.

cross-sectional study A study using subjects of different ages and assessing them simultaneously.

cross-sequential study A study using subjects of different ages studied over a period of time.

crowd A loosely formed group organized chiefly on the basis of shared activities rather than close friendship.

crystallization The stage of occupational development when career ideas coalesce.

custody The legal care or guardianship of children.

decentration Focusing on more than the self; the extension of activity and awareness beyond one's own physical boundaries.

defense mechanisms Mechanisms used by the ego to repress the id.

deferred imitation Duplication of behavior seen or experienced earlier.

deoxyribonucleic acid (DNA) A chemical substance that is the carrier of genetic information in chromosomes.

desensitization Gradual exposure to the feared aspects of the object of a phobia.

developmental quotient (DQ) A score on the Bayley Scales based on agemates' scores.

diethylstilbestrol (DES) A synthetic hormone given in the late 1940s and early 1950s to prevent miscarriages that was found to affect the daughters of women who took it.

differentiation (1) The process by which groups of cells descended from the same zygote become specialized for the various tissues and organs. (2) The ability to make specific, goal-directed movements.

difficult child A baby with high negative emotionality and an undependable schedule.

dishabituation The reaction to (recovery of interest in) a novel stimulus.

dominant gene A gene that is expressed whether paired with an identical or a recessive allele.

Down syndrome A hereditary disorder caused by an extra twenty-first chromosome.

dramatic or pretense play Play in which children act out roles.

easy child An adaptable, calm baby with a predictable schedule.

ectoderm The outer layer of the embryo, which will eventually become the skin and nervous system.

ego According to Freud, the part of the personality that regulates emotion, thought, and behavior.

egocentrism The inability to consider others' perspectives.

ego skills The abilities needed to negotiate among the demands of the id, the superego, and the real world and to keep impulses in check.

Electra complex According to Freud, a psychological conflict for girls, arising from their sexual feelings toward their fathers.

embryonic disk The cells on the outer edge of the blastula, which will develop into the embryo.

embryonic period The second stage of prenatal development, from 2 to 8 weeks after conception.

emergent literacy A focus on the creative uses of reading and writing by young children before they learn the formal rules and conventions of print.

empathize To know what another person is feeling.

endoderm The innermost layer of the embryo, which will become the internal organs.

engagement (lightening) The movement of the fetus into position for birth.

engrossment Parental absorption, preoccupation, and interest in the infant.

epididymis The coiled tubes in the testes in which sperm are stored until ejaculation.

episiotomy An incision made below the vaginal opening during childbirth.

equilibration The process through which balance is restored to the cognitive structure.

equivalence The recognition that similar stimuli, or the same stimuli under changed conditions, belong to the same basic category.

ethological theory An analysis of human and animal behavior patterns in evolutionary terms.

evaluation anxiety Anxiety manifested in situations where a child is being judged.

experiment A scientific tool designed to investigate causes.

fallopian tubes The tubes that transport mature ova to the uterus and in which fertilization occurs.

family day care Child care provided in a private home.

fetal alcohol syndrome (FAS) A group of symptoms, including cognitive, motor, and growth retardation, suffered by some children of alcoholic mothers.

fetal monitor An electronic device that keeps track of the fetal heartbeat and uterine pressure during childbirth.

fetal period The third and final stage of prenatal development, from 8 weeks to birth.

fine motor skills Physical abilities involving the small-muscle groups.

formal operational stage According to Piaget, the stage at which one's thinking is based on theoretical, abstract principles of logic.

fraternal twins Twins born from two different ova fertilized at the same time by two different sperm.

functional play Play that involves simple, repetitive muscular activities.

gender constancy The understanding that one's sex will never change.

gender identity The knowledge that one is female or male.

genes The basic units of heredity, each gene consisting of a segment of a chromosome that controls some aspect of development.

genital herpes A sexually transmitted viral disease that can cause damage to the fetus during pregnancy and delivery.

genotype An individual's genetic makeup, consisting of all inherited genes.

germinal period The first 2 weeks of prenatal development.

Gesell Developmental Schedules One of the first sets of tests for assessing children 1 month to 6 years old on physical, cognitive, language, and social skills according to average developmental rates.

gestation The period of prenatal development.

gonorrhea A sexually transmitted disease caused by a bacterium.

goodness of fit The way the personalities and expectations of the parents mesh with their child's temperament.

gross motor skills Physical abilities involving the large-muscle groups.

group or cooperative play Play among children who are working together and sharing a theme or topic in conversation.

growth hormone deficiency An endocrine disorder causing short stature.

habituation The adaptation to (loss of interest in) an unchanging stimulus.

hand dominance A strong preference for using the left or right hand.

Head Start A federal program combining educational and social opportunities for 3- and 4-year-olds with social services for their low-income families.

hemophilia A sex-linked heredi-tary disorder in which production of a necessary blood-clotting substance is blocked.

heterozygous Inheriting different alleles for a given trait from each parent.

high-risk infants Infants whose physical and psychological well-being may be in jeopardy due to premature birth and/or low birth weight.

holophrases Single words that stand for whole thoughts.

homozygous Inheriting the same alleles for a given trait from both parents.

hormones Chemical substances that act on specific organs and tissues.

hostile aggression Physical and/or verbal aggression that is deliberately harmful.

human development The process through which people grow, mature, and change over time.

hypothesis An educated proposition about how factors being studied relate to each other.

id According to Freud, the part of the personality that includes all inborn human drives.

identical twins Twins born from a single fertilized ovum that divides in two.

identification A process in which children adopt the same-sex parent's attitudes, behaviors, and values.

identity versus identity diffusion According to Erikson, the psychosocial crisis of establishing one's identity, characteristic of adolescence.

imaginary audience The erronious belief that one's appearance and behavior are the subject of public attention.

implantation The process by which the blastula attaches to the uterus.

implicit psychological theory An intuitive theory of human behavior.

impression formation Assessment of others.

incubator (isolette) A glass or Plexiglas life-support box with controlled temperature and airflow for high-risk infants.

individuation The process of becoming a separate person who can both act independently and accept responsibility for choices.

individuation and separation According to Mahler, the striving toward independence and a sense of separate self during infancy and toddlerhood.

induction Discipline involving the use of reasoning to explain the expectations of the parent.

industry versus inferiority According to Erikson, the crisis over the sense of accomplishment, characteristic of middle childhood.

initiative versus guilt In Erikson's theory, the conflict for preschoolers between the wish to do and prohibitions against doing.

inner speech Verbal self-communication.

insecure attachment A relation of an infant to its mother (or father) based on lack of trust.

instrumental aggression Aggression arising out of conflicts over ownership, territory, and perceived rights.

intelligence quotient (IQ) A measure of intelligence computed by dividing an individual's mental age by his or her chronological age. This number is multiplied by 100, with 100 being an average score and scores above and below 100 indicating greater or lesser intelligence, respectively.

intentional behavior Goal-directed activity, which begins to appear from 8 to 12 months.

intentionality The purposeful coordination of activity toward a goal.

interactive imagery (elaboration) A strategy for recall.

interview   A research technique in which researchers personally question people.

joint custody   Custody in which both parents share legal guardianship of their children equally.

karyotype   A profile of an individual's chromosomes created from a tissue sample.

Klinefelter's syndrome   A hereditary disorder caused by an extra X chromosome in males.

kwashiorkor   A disease affecting children ages 2 to 3, caused by a severe protein deficiency, usually after weaning.

Lamaze method   Natural or prepared childbirth.

latchkey children   Children who stay home without an adult while their parents work.

learned helplessness   The belief or expectation that one cannot control forces in one's environment.

learning   A more or less permanent change in behavior that occurs as a consequence of experience.

learning goals   Goals that place value on individual accomplishment for its own sake.

libido   According to Freud, a finite amount of psychic energy that fuels all thought and behavior.

locus   The specific location of a gene on a chromosome.

logic   General principles about the relations among objects and people.

longitudinal study   A study following the same group of people over an extended period of time.

low birth weight   A weight of less than 5½ pounds at birth.

mainstreaming   The placement of handicapped children in classrooms with nonhandicapped children.

marasmus   A disease affecting infants under 1 year, caused by an insufficient and often contaminated food supply.

mass-to-specific development   The pattern of growth from large to small muscles.

mastery motivation   The desire to master a challenge in order to acquire a new skill.

meiosis   The multistage production of sperm and ova, which contain only half of the number of chromosomes in all other cells.

memory strategies   Plans that aid recall.

menarche   The first menstrual period.

menstruation   The third phase of the female reproductive cycle, in which the uterine lining is discharged.

mental combinations   Mental coordinations of several actions in sequence.

mesoderm   The middle layer of the embryo, which will become the skeleton and muscles.

metacognition   The understanding and control of one's own thinking skills; the ability to think about thinking, including thinking about reasoning and thinking about memory.

metamemory   Knowledge about one's own memory.

mitosis   The process of cell duplication in which chromosomes make exact copies of themselves.

modeling   A component of social learning that involves imitation.

moral development   The changes in the ability to reason about morality that occur as a child grows up.

motherese   A form of slow, high-pitched, simplified, well-enunciated language used by mothers and others in speaking to infants.

motor development   The increasing ability to control the body in purposeful motion.

mutations   Alterations in genes, which are the cause of many birth defects.

myelin   An insulating fatty sheath on nerve fibers.

myelinization   The process by which nerves become insulated with myelin, which forms a fatty sheath.

natural experiment   An experiment that takes advantage of a naturally occurring event.

naturalistic observations   Observations of people in their own environments.

negative reinforcement   Reinforcement through the removal of unpleasant stimuli.

neonatology   The branch of medicine focusing on newborns.

neurons   Nerve cells; the primary functional units of the nervous system.

New York Longitudinal Study (NYLS)   A pioneering study of infant temperament.

nursery schools   Child care that offers planned social and cognitive experiences.

obese   Refers to those individuals whose weight is at least 20 percent more than normal for their age, height, and sex.

object permanence   The slowly developing understanding that objects exist separate from one's perception of them.

observational learning   Learning through observation and imitation of others' behavior.

Oedipus complex   According to Freud, a psychological conflict for boys, arising from their sexual feelings toward their mothers.

open education   Education in which both teacher and child are active agents in learning and in which evaluation is accomplished through individual profiles.

ovaries   The pair of almond-shaped female organs that store ova.

overextension   Using words too broadly; using the same word to stand for a number of similar things.

overregularization Applying gram.natical rules too stringently.

ovulation The release of a mature ovum from one of the ovaries into one of the fallopian tubes.

oxytocin A hormone given to induce or strengthen contractions.

parallel play Play in which children are apparently playing together but are actually focused on their own activities.

perceive To interpret sensations.

performance goals Goals that place value on achieving in relation to others.

permissive parents Parents who are generally noncontrolling and nonthreatening, allowing children to regulate their own behavior.

personal fables Erroneous beliefs that one's thoughts, feelings, and experiences are unique.

personality Behaviors and response patterns developed through experience.

phenotype An individual's observable physical and behavioral traits, the result of the interaction of genetic potential and environment.

phenylketonuria (PKU) A hereditary metabolic disorder caused by a double dose of a recessive gene that blocks amino acid breakdown.

phobias Intense, irrational fears directed toward specific objects or situations.

placenta The organ along the uterine wall where nutrients and oxygen from the mother and wastes from the baby are exchanged.

plasticity Flexibility.

polygenic Caused by the interaction of a number of genes.

positive reinforcement Reinforcement through the addition of pleasant stimuli.

postconventional moral reasoning According to Kohlberg, the level of moral development in which decisions of conscience are more important than society's rules.

postfigurative societies Societies that change so slowly that children must master the same skills for adulthood as did their parents.

precocial Describes the pattern of prenatal development marked by a brief gestation and a large litter of helpless young.

preconventional thinking According to Kohlberg, the first level of moral development, in which children make decisions about what is right and wrong based not on society's standards of conventions, but on external, physical events.

prefigurative societies Societies in which change is accelerating with the result that young people teach adults as well as each other.

prelinguistic communication Literally, before-language communication; communication between parents and infants through games, gestures, sounds, facial expressions, and imitation.

premature affluence Adolescents' acquisition of too much money too early in life.

premature (preterm) baby A baby born before 35 weeks of gestation.

preoperational period According to Piaget, the period of transition from sensorimotor intelligence to rule-governed thought.

preparation The first phase of the female reproductive cycle.

prepared (natural) childbirth Childbirth without medication or anesthetics, based on relaxation techniques and psychological and physical preparation.

primary circular reaction An infant's repetition of a chance action involving a part of the infant's body.

primary sex characteristics Developments in the structure and function of the reproductive organs and systems.

proportional phenomenon The characteristic of an infant's growth in which different parts of the infant's body grow at different rates, resulting in alterations in their relative proportions.

prosocial behavior Positive, helping acts.

prostate gland The male organ that produces semen, a substance released with sperm.

proximodistal development The pattern of growth from the center of the body outward.

psychosocial moratorium According to Erikson, a necessary "time out" from excessive obligations for adolescents.

puberty The physical transformation from child to adult.

pulmonary surfactant An essential lubricating substance in the lungs.

punishment An aversive consequence that decreases the frequency of a behavior.

questionnaire A written set of carefully prepared questions given to subjects to answer.

reaction range The genetically established upper and lower limits to development of a given trait; a trait's potential for expression.

recall memory Memory based on information retrieved without strong clues.

recessive gene A gene that is not expressed if paired with its dominant allele.

reciprocal feedback A pattern of mutual, interdependent influences in which each member of a system affects and is affected by the others.

recognition memory Memory based on recognition of a previously seen object.

reference group A group that

serves as a basis for evaluating one's own experiences.

referential communication Communication that refers to something specific.

reflex A motor behavior not under conscious control.

rehearsal The labeling and repeating of names or other information to aid memory.

reinforcement A consequence that produces repetition of behavior.

representational thinking Thinking that involves manipulation of mental images (symbols).

respiratory distress syndrome (RDS) A breathing disorder in premature babies, caused by immaturity of the lungs and lack of pulmonary surfactant.

reversibility The concept representing that an action can be done and undone.

Rh factor A protein found on red blood cells.

rhythmical stereotypies Apparently reflexive, repeated rhythmic movements that serve as transition from random to controlled movement.

rubella German measles.

schemes According to Piaget, mental representations and patterns of action that structure a person's knowledge.

scientific method A procedure to collect reliable, objective information that can be used to support or refute a theory.

scripts Sequences of day-to-day activities.

secondary circular reactions Repetitions of actions that trigger responses in the external environment (for example, squeeze a toy—it squeaks).

secondary reinforcer Anything (or anyone) associated with the satisfaction of a need, so chances of a given response recurring are increased by the presence of the reinforcer.

secondary sex characteristics The visible characteristics of sexual maturity not directly related to reproduction.

second-order thinking The ability to think about thoughts.

secular trend The trend over time toward earlier puberty.

secure attachment A positive, healthy relationship of an infant to its mother (or father), based on the infant's trust in the parent's love and availability.

secure base An attachment object (usually the mother) who provides a foundation for curious exploration.

self-conceptions The various attributes people see themselves possessing.

self-esteem One's feelings about oneself.

self-monitoring The cognitive ability to observe one's own behavior and evaluate it.

self-regulation The extent to which people can monitor and control their own behavior.

sensorimotor Describes Piaget's first stage of cognitive development, in which infants explore their world with their senses and motor actions.

separation protest An infant's reaction, based on fear, to separation from its mother or other caregiver.

seriation The ability to rank objects in a meaningful order.

sex chromosomes The twenty-third pair of chromosomes, which determine the sex of the child; there are two types, X-shaped and Y-shaped.

sex-linked traits Traits determined by genes on the X chromosome.

sex-role development How children learn to behave in the ways we call feminine and masculine.

sex roles The tasks and traits that society assigns to females and males.

sex stereotypes Social expectations about how males and females behave.

sexual socialization What and how adolescents learn about sexuality.

sexually transmitted disease (STD) An infection transferred through sexual contact.

sibling deidentification One process through which children develop identities different from their siblings'.

sickle-cell anemia A hereditary disorder that affects the ability of the red blood cells to carry oxygen.

slow-to-warm-up child A child characterized by mild emotions and an initial fear of new experiences.

social class A measure of an individual's or family's standing in society, based primarily on income, education, and occupation.

social cognition Thinking about oneself and the other people in one's life, including awareness of interpersonal relations and social rules and roles.

social context All the elements in one's immediate and distant environment.

social conventions The norms that guide day-to-day behavior.

socialized delinquents Delinquents who have learned the norms and values of society.

social learning theorists Psychologists who study how people learn from one another.

social learning theory A learning theory that looks at the way social rewards and punishments influence behavior and expectations.

social referencing Looking to someone else for guidance in emotional response to new stimuli or situations.

social smile An infant's smile for pleasure in response to familiar people.

sociometry   Measures of social relationships in a group.

sound localization   The ability to locate the source of a sound.

specification   The stage of occupational development when career choices are specified.

standardized test   A carefully developed test that allows individual scores to be compared with previously established norms.

state control   The ability of newborns to shift from one state of arousal to another in response to either internal or external stimulation.

states and transformations   The concepts involved in understanding that objects and states can be transformed and rearranged.

states of arousal   Varying levels of energy, attention, and activity.

stranger wariness   The fear of unfamiliar people, which sets in at about the age of 6 to 8 months.

strange situation   An experimental procedure for observing attachment patterns.

strategy   The ability to use logical principles to solve problems.

structured observations   Observations of people in controlled environments.

sudden infant death syndrome (SIDS)   Death in early infancy for no apparent reason.

superego   According to Freud, the part of the personality that serves as a conscience.

symbiosis   The merging of self with another, as an infant with its mother.

symbolic system   A system, like language, that represents and labels elements of the world and their interrelations.

symbolic thought   Mental representation of the world.

syphilis   A bacterial sexually transmitted disease that can cross the placenta.

system   An organized, interacting, interdependent group, functioning as a whole.

Tay-Sachs disease   A hereditary disorder that destroys nerve cells, leading to mental retardation, loss of muscle control, and death.

temperament   The unique, inborn pattern of responsiveness and mood.

teratogen   Any substance, influence, or agent that causes birth defects.

testes   The male sperm-producing organ.

thalidomide   A drug given to pregnant women in the late 1950s and early 1960s that caused serious birth defects.

thyroxine deficiency   A thyroid disorder that may cause short stature, stunted growth, and mental retardation.

time out   A disciplinary technique in which the child is briefly separated from people, toys, and enjoyable activities.

toxemia   An illness affecting pregnant women, causing water retention, high blood pressure, and, if untreated, death.

tracking   A schooling system that divides students according to academic ability.

traditional education   Education that stresses uniformity and measures success through standardized test scores.

transduction   Reasoning that connects isolated events as if there were a cause-effect relationship.

transition   The end of the first stage of labor, with the cervix fully dilated.

transitional object   An object, like a blanket or teddy, to which an infant transfers attachment feeling as he or she moves toward independence.

transitivity   The concrete operation acquired between ages 6 and 12 that rests on the understanding of relationships among objects.

transverse presentation   A condition in which the fetus lies horizontally in the uterus.

Turner's syndrome   A hereditary disorder caused by a missing X chromosome in females.

turn-taking   Conversational give and take.

ultrasonography   A technique that produces a picture from sound waves bounced off the fetus; used for diagnosing developmental problems *in utero*.

umbilical cord   The lifeline attaching the embryo (and fetus) to the placenta; it transports maternal nutrients from, and wastes to, the placenta.

underextension   Using words too restrictively.

unsocialized delinquents   Delinquents who have not learned basic social norms and values.

uterus   The female organ in which the fetus grows.

vernix   A slippery substance that coats the newborn.

villi   Hairlike projections from the blastula that burrow into the uterine lining.

visual acuity   Clarity of vision.

visual recognition memory   Memory for stimuli seen before.

zygote   The fertilized cell resulting from the fusion of the ovum and sperm.

Indexes

Name Index

Subject Index